KEVIN J. MIDDLEBROOK

THE PARADOX
OF REVOLUTION

LABOR, THE STATE,
AND AUTHORITARIANISM
IN MEXICO

The Johns Hopkins University Press
Baltimore & London

To My Parents
and the Memory of My Grandparents

© 1995 The Johns Hopkins University Press
All rights reserved. Published 1995
Printed in the United States of America on acid-free paper
03 02 01 00 99 98 97 96 95   5 4 3 2 1

The Johns Hopkins University Press
2715 North Charles Street
Baltimore, Maryland 21218-4319
The Johns Hopkins Press Ltd., London

Library of Congress Cataloging-in-Publication Data will be found at the end of
this book.
A catalog record for this book is available from the British Library.
ISBN 0-8018-4922-5
ISBN 0-8018-5148-3 (pbk.)

CONTENTS

TABLES AND FIGURES

ACKNOWLEDGMENTS

In the time between the inception and the completion of this book, I benefited significantly from the encouragement, support, and example of many friends and colleagues. Research and writing can at times be solitary endeavors. Yet the questions one poses and the answers one formulates are immeasurably improved by constructive interaction with individuals sharing parallel interests. I had that good fortune.

At an early stage, the intellectual stimulation and good judgment of Jorge I. Domínguez and Samuel P. Huntington helped me sharpen the focus of my inquiry. Their insistence on clear thinking and clear writing set standards worthy of emulation. I remain grateful for their advice and support.

Several institutions contributed materially to the completion of this book. I am very pleased to acknowledge financial support for field research in Mexico from the Social Science Research Council, the Fulbright-Hays Commission, the President's Council on International Programs at Indiana University, and the Howard Heinz Endowment. During 1983–84 and 1991, my work on state-labor relations in Mexico was supported by Visiting Research Fellowships at the Center for U.S.-Mexican Studies at the University of California–San Diego.

This book could not have been completed without the cooperation and good will of numerous Mexican labor leaders, trade union members, government officials, political party activists, labor lawyers, entrepreneurs, and journalists. They freely offered me their time and hospitality, doing all they could to help an insatiably curious foreigner understand the complexities of labor politics in Mexico. Many of these individuals agreed to share their special insights with me on condition of anonymity. For this reason, some of the interview materials cited in the body of this work identify individuals by occupation or position rather than by name.

I also benefited greatly from interactions with Mexican friends and colleagues. I was privileged to know the late Mario de la Cueva, the late Eduardo Murguía, and the late Miguel Ángel Velasco. Extended conversations with them significantly increased my understanding of Mexican labor institutions, union politics, and labor history. J. Fernando Franco González Salas has for many years arranged crucial research contacts, shared with me his impressive knowledge of Mexican labor law, and graciously welcomed me into his home. Not least among his many important contributions to my work, he facilitated access to archival records at the Federal Conciliation and Arbitration Board and the Ministry of Labor and Social Welfare, materials that were essential to completing major portions of this book. During my early fieldwork in Mexico, Alejandro Álvarez Béjar provided invaluable assistance by introducing me to a number of union and political party activists. His friendship and generosity have been tremendously important to me over the years, and I have learned much from our lively discussions of Mexican politics. Víctor Manuel Durand Ponte generously shared with me his research materials on labor politics in the 1940s and 1950s and helped me understand the importance of key events during this period. I am grateful for his friendship and support.

At different times during my work on this project, I was affiliated with the Instituto de Investigaciones Sociales at the Universidad Nacional Autónoma de México and the Centro de Estudios Sociológicos at El Colegio de México. Academic colleagues at these and other institutions provided valuable advice and assistance. I especially wish to thank Jorge Basurto, Enrique de la Garza Toledo, Julio Labastida Martín del Campo, Juan Molinar Horcasitas, José Luis Reyna, and Francisco Zapata.

Yeon-Seob Ha, Chi Huang, and Jeanne Schaaf helped prepare for statistical analysis the data on union registration examined in chapter 5, and Noel Maurer ably completed the regression analysis of strike data. Christopher Wilkens prepared the graphs of strikes, strike petitions, and railroad worker grievances included in this chapter. Russell L. Hanson, a true friend and unselfish colleague, has my very special thanks for his patient counsel interpreting the statistical results reported in chapter 5. He contributed significantly to the completion of this part of the project.

As the manuscript took final form, colleagues in several different academic disciplines generously took the time to read and critique one or more draft chapters. I especially wish to thank Barry Carr, Kenneth M. Coleman, David Collier, Lisa L. Condit, Charles L. Davis, Alfred Diamant, Kenneth P. Erickson, Jonathan Fox, Gary Gereffi, C. R. D. Halisi, Russell L. Hanson, Jonathan Hartlyn, Evelyne Huber, John Lear, Cynthia McClintock, Juan Molinar Horcasitas, Geraldo Munck, Robert Packenham, Richard Stahler-Sholk, J. Samuel Valenzuela, Van R. Whiting, Jr., and Francisco Zapata for their valuable contributions. Maria Lorena Cook made very insightful comments on several chapters, and I benefited immensely from our many stimulating discussions of contemporary Mexican labor politics. Her encouragement and support were very important to me during the final stages of this project. I am especially indebted to John Womack, Jr., the reviewer for the Johns Hopkins University Press, for reading and commenting on the entire manuscript. His judicious remarks concerning labor politics, state power, and regime consolidation in postrevolutionary Mexico led me to rethink important questions.

This book was completed while I was a Senior Research Fellow at the Center for U.S.-Mexican Studies. I offer my sincere thanks to Wayne A. Cornelius, the center's founding director, for providing a supportive environment and an intellectually exciting interdisciplinary forum for research on Mexico.

With all this help, the remaining errors and omissions must surely be my own responsibility.

I wish to thank Henry Tom, executive editor of the Johns Hopkins University Press, for his patient assistance in bringing a long book manuscript to completion. Grace Buonocore did superb work copyediting the manuscript, and Barbara Lamb, Lee Campbell Sioles, Miriam Kleiger, and Stephen Siegforth ably supervised production of the book.

Finally, I am very grateful to Adolfo Mexiac and the Sociedad Mexicana de Artes Plásticas for permission to reproduce Maestro Mexiac's engraving "El primer desfile del 1° de mayo" on the dust jacket of this book. Maestro Mexiac is a well-known Mexican painter and graphic artist with a longstanding interest in Mexico's political and social problems. His woodcut commemorates the first official May Day parade held in Mexico City, an event organized by the Casa del Obrero Mundial on May 1, 1913. It was originally published in Rosendo Salazar, *La Casa del Obrero Mundial* (Mexico City: Costa-Amic, 1962).

I acknowledge publishers' permission to draw material from the following articles: "Union Democratization in the Mexican Automobile Industry: A Reappraisal," *Latin American Research Review* 24, no. 2 (1989): 69–93; "The Sounds of Silence: Organised Labour's Response to Economic Crisis in Mexico," *Journal of Latin American Studies* 21, no. 2 (1989): 195–220; "The Politics of Industrial Restructuring: Transnational Firms' Search for Flexible Production in the Mexican Automobile Industry," *Comparative Politics* 23, no. 3 (April 1991): 275–97; "State Structures and the Politics of Union Registration in Postrevolutionary Mexico," *Comparative Politics* 23, no. 4 (July 1991): 459–78.

All translations of material originally written in Spanish are by the author. Monetary values given in both Mexican pesos and U.S. dollars were converted at the contemporaneous exchange rate.

This book is dedicated to my parents, Harlan and Wilda Middlebrook, and to the memory of my grandparents, Roy and Della Middlebrook and Ben and Selma Jacobson. They taught me both to value learning and to appreciate those things that cannot be found in books.

PRINCIPAL ACRONYMS

BUO: Worker Unity Bloc
CGOCM: General Confederation of Mexican Workers and Peasants
CGT: General Confederation of Workers
CNC: National Peasants' Confederation
CNDP: National Committee for Proletarian Defense
CNIT: National Chamber of Manufacturing Industries
CNT: National Chamber of Labor
COCM: Confederation of Mexican Workers and Peasants
COM: House of the World Worker
CON: National Worker Council
COOC: Coalition of Worker and Peasant Organizations
COR: Revolutionary Labor Confederation
CPN: National Proletarian Confederation
CROC: Revolutionary Confederation of Workers and Peasants
CROM: Mexican Regional Labor Confederation
CRT: Revolutionary Workers' Confederation
CSFRM: Confederation of Mexican Railroad Societies
CSUM: Unitary Mexican Union Confederation
CT: Labor Congress
CTAL: Latin American Workers' Confederation
CTC: Confederation of Transport and Communications Workers
CTM: Confederation of Mexican Workers
CUT: Unitary Workers' Confederation
DINA: National Diesel
FAT: Authentic Labor Front
FESEBES: Federation of Goods and Services Unions
FNM: Mexican National Railroads
FSTDF: Federation of Federal District Workers' Unions
FSTSE: Federation of Public Service Workers' Unions
FTDF: Federal District Workers' Federation
IMF: International Metalworkers' Federation
IMSS: Mexican Social Security Institute
INFONAVIT: National Worker Housing Institute
JFCA: Federal Conciliation and Arbitration Board
MSF: Railroad Workers' Union Movement
PAN: National Action Party
PCM: Mexican Communist Party
PLM: Mexican Labor Party
PNA: National Agrarian Party
PNR: Revolutionary National Party

PRD: Party of the Democratic Revolution
PRI: Institutional Revolutionary Party
PRM: Party of the Mexican Revolution
SITMMSRM: Mexican Mining and Metalworkers' Union
SME: Mexican Electricians' Union
SNTE: National Education Workers' Union
STERM: Mexican Electrical Workers' Union
STFRM: Mexican Railroad Workers' Union
STPRM: Mexican Petroleum Workers' Union
STPS: Ministry of Labor and Social Welfare
STRM: Mexican Telephone Workers' Union
SUTERM: General Union of Mexican Electrical Workers
SUTIN: Nuclear Industry Workers' Union
TD: Democratic Tendency
UGOCM: General Union of Mexican Workers and Peasants
UOI: Independent Worker Unit
VAM: Mexican Automotive Vehicles

THE PARADOX

OF REVOLUTION

CHAPTER ONE

Introduction: Mass Politics and Regime Formation in Postrevolutionary Mexico

The entry of previously excluded mass actors into national politics is a critical moment in a country's history. The expansion of political participation redefines the character of elite-mass interactions by creating new bases of power and by offering both incumbent elites and their challengers additional opportunities for the competitive mobilization of support. Moreover, the presence of workers, peasants, and other lower-class groups in the national arena redraws the boundaries of the political process by multiplying the demands that decision makers must address. The political mobilization of such groups is often accompanied by violence and instability, yet the successful institutionalization of mass support greatly expands reformist elites' capacity to promote social and economic change.[1] Thus the terms under which mass actors enter the political arena are of crucial, long-term importance.

The challenge of mass political participation is particularly acute in social revolutionary situations. Social revolutions are "rapid, basic transformations of a society's state and class structures . . . accompanied and in part carried through by class-based revolts from below."[2] They are distinguished from other processes of sociopolitical change by the speed with which these transformations occur and by the extent to which changes in political organization, social structure, and dominant ideology coincide. Specific cases of revolution differ in the sequencing of the overthrow of the old regime and the competitive mobilization of such mass actors as workers and peasants by rival political factions. However, the expansion of political consciousness and the entry of previously excluded social forces into politics are central characteristics of all social revolutions.[3]

The paradox of social revolution is that popular mobilization and socioeconomic transformation most commonly eventuate in a new form of authoritarian rule. Historical examples of revolution—ranging from France in the eighteenth century to Mexico, Russia, China, Bolivia, Cuba,

Vietnam, Ethiopia, Cambodia, Iran, and Nicaragua in the twentieth century—differ considerably in such key aspects as their social origins, the characteristics of the revolutionary leadership, the impact of international alliances on the course of revolutionary struggle, the importance of ideology, the principal forms of political organization, and their long-term socioeconomic consequences. Yet in all these cases, revolutionary mobilization brought to the fore an elite bent on the expansion and centralization of political power. Revolutionary elites' drive for political control was motivated by—and usually legitimated by distinctive ideologies or ideas associated with the revolutionary experience which emphasized—their commitment to far-ranging socioeconomic change and the defense of the revolution against domestic and foreign threats. The remarkable resilience of many of these regimes in the aftermath of social revolution was due in large measure to the successful consolidation of a governing coalition in which mass actors such as peasants and workers played a central, though subordinate, part.

This book seeks to unravel the paradox of social revolution in the Mexican case by analyzing organized labor's participation in politics and economic development from the 1920s through the early 1990s. Organized labor's entry into national politics was among the most significant long-term consequences of the Mexican revolution. Despite considerable variation in organizational strength and economic bargaining leverage among different sectors and regions, the labor movement emerged from the 1910–20 revolutionary struggle as the most easily mobilized mass actor in Mexican politics. Because of workers' importance, the revolutionary leaders striving to consolidate their political control and implement the revolution's agenda were compelled to adopt innovative strategies both to mediate labor participation in national affairs and to regulate the social relations of production. In the decades after the revolution, organized labor's support helped preserve a stable governing coalition and permitted Mexico's ruling elite to resolve successfully diverse political and economic crises. Thus a focus on labor politics is an especially advantageous angle of vision from which to examine how the process of revolutionary mass mobilization and structural transformation gave rise to a regime in which the governing elite maintained a strong base of mass support while simultaneously imposing significant constraints on independent political mobilization, the autonomous representation of group interests, and the articulation of political and economic demands.[4]

Mexico's durable authoritarian regime has been difficult to understand in comparative terms because many analysts fail to give sufficient weight to the character and consequences of the most important event in the country's modern history: the 1910–20 social revolution. Portrayals of Mexico in the 1950s as an emerging two-party democracy,[5] and debate in the 1960s regarding whether to classify Mexico as "democratic" or "authoritarian,"[6] gave way in the 1970s to a scholarly consensus that Mexico could best be understood as an authoritarian regime. In adopting this perspective, different analysts highlighted what they considered at the time to be key aspects of Mexican politics: low levels of mass mobilization except during elections or as part of other officially sanctioned processes; the limited autonomy of interest groups and restrictions on political contestation; multiple controls on popular demands and highly centralized decision-making processes unresponsive to popular interests; intermittent repression; a predominantly patrimonial or clientelist style of rulership; and a nonegalitarian value structure.[7]

Yet previous attempts to situate the Mexican case comparatively have proved unsatisfactory because they applied to Mexico analytic categories developed on the basis of substantially different forms of authoritarianism.[8] This study begins with a discussion of those elements that identify postrevolutionary authoritarian regimes as a distinctive form of authoritarian rule because the features that long defined the character of Mexico's authoritarian regime—the significance of mass actors in the governing coalition, the legitimating role of political ideas associated with the revolutionary experience, and the dual importance of a hegemonic party and an interventionist state—can best be understood when compared with attributes of other postrevolutionary regimes forged in diverse geographical, cultural, and temporal settings.

Although the Mexican regime shares common traits with other instances of postrevolutionary authoritarian rule, it remains an analytically challenging case. The continuing fascination that the Mexican regime holds for students of comparative politics is due largely to its exceptional resilience despite pressures for political change. A predominantly urban, middle-class, civilian political elite long enforced strong controls on independent political mobilization and autonomous sociopolitical organization (especially among lower-class groups) without resort to extensive repression. The formal guarantee of liberal political rights (such as a relatively free national press) and the presence of legally recognized opposition political parties contribute to the comparative openness of the regime, yet for decades the "official" party's close ties to the state effectively insulated it from electoral competition. And perhaps most remarkably, key mass constituencies such as organized labor remained loyal to the established regime despite significant constraints on their ability to articulate social and economic demands and different presidential administrations' support for economic development policies that, over time, produced greater income inequality. Examining mass politics is thus especially important to understanding sources of both stability and change in Mexico.

The first part of this chapter introduces the concept of postrevolutionary authoritarian rule and develops an analytic framework for studying mass politics in postrevolutionary authoritarian regimes. The purpose of this discussion is to place the Mexican case in comparative context and identify the most important dimensions of elite control over mass political participation in these regimes. The second section establishes the historical baseline for examining Mexican organized labor's participation in national politics and economic development in the decades after the 1910–20 revolution. It does so by outlining the most significant political aspects of the revolutionary experience: mass political mobilization, the development of revolutionary political ideas, and the formation of a strong, interventionist state and a hegemonic party.

The final section summarizes the main thesis advanced in this book and details the content of subsequent chapters. In brief, this book argues that both state-centered and society-centered analytic approaches are necessary to explain the bases of elite control over labor participation and the character of state-labor relations in postrevolutionary Mexico. A strong, interventionist state was a central feature of the regime that took shape in the decades after the 1910–20 revolution. Postrevolutionary governments expanded state administrative capacity in the labor sector as part of their struggle to address the crisis of participation that accompanied urban and industrial workers' entrance into the political arena. The governing elite's effective control over the means of coercion and the institutionalized capacity to regulate worker-employer relations and enforce legal restrictions on union formation, internal union activities, and strikes contributed greatly to policymakers' relative decision-making autonomy. Attention to the institutional and legal framework in which state-labor interactions occur is therefore essential to understanding how political controls on labor have operated in the postrevolutionary period.

Yet the consolidation of Mexico's durable postrevolutionary authoritarian regime also depended crucially on the alliance that the national political elite forged with major elements of the emerging organized labor movement in the 1920s and 1930s. The alliance originated in political and military leaders' urgent need to expand their base of mass support, a crucial test of the legitimacy of a regime born of social revolution. Circumstances thus compelled them to accept labor as a legitimate political force and to make policy concessions on issues of great importance to workers. For many decades, the alliance with labor was significantly reinforced by the governing elite's endorsement of revolutionary nationalist ideas advocating state action to promote economic redistribution and social justice. Formal ties between working-class organizations and Mexico's hegemonic "party of the revolution" symbolized labor's inclusion in the postrevolutionary governing coalition, and party membership offered labor leaders a share (however modest) of national political power.

Over the long term, however, the survival of this alliance depended heavily on the governing elite's willingness to provide legal, financial, and political support to "official" (state-subsidized) labor organizations. Understanding the character of this alliance—especially the underlying imbalance of power between the contracting parties and many labor organizations' dependence on state subsidies—requires attention to those society-centered factors that conditioned labor's relationship with the postrevolutionary political leadership. These elements include the characteristics of the Mexican economy that influence patterns of unionization and workers' bargaining leverage, the organizational form of the labor movement, and the political ideas that shape labor leaders' responses to political and economic challenges. The highly unequal terms of organized labor's alliance with the governing elite and major labor organizations' heavy dependence on state subsidies often transformed unions into important instruments of political control over rank-and-file workers. The emergence of a state-subsidized labor movement in the 1920s and 1930s helps explain, then, how the mobilization of mass actors during the Mexican revolution gave rise to a highly resilient postrevolutionary authoritarian regime.

The Concept of Postrevolutionary Authoritarian Rule and a Framework for Political Analysis

Postrevolutionary authoritarian regimes have been few in number because social revolutions are rare historical events. However, with the exception of France after the formation of the Third Republic in 1876–77, the successful consolidation of revolutionary power produced—for shorter or longer periods of time—elite-dominated regimes that enforced strong controls on independent political mobilization and sociopolitical organization.[9] "Regime" refers here to the formal and informal principles, norms, rules, and procedures regarding participation, representation, decision making, and the use of force in a political community, including forms of leadership recruitment and the division of authority among different institutions and political entities.[10] It is important to analyze postrevolutionary politics at the regime level because the specific means by which governing elites control mass participation vary widely in different contexts.

On the Concept of Postrevolutionary Authoritarian Rule

Three characteristics identify postrevolutionary authoritarian regimes as a distinctive form of authoritarianism.[11] First, the prominence of mass actors in the governing coalition sets these regimes apart from many other forms of authoritarian rule.[12] Whatever the composition of the *ancien régime,* the class-based revolts that are central to social revolutions produce an upsurge in political participation and greatly increase the social complexity of politically relevant groups. Revolutionary elites' ability to effect structural transformation and consolidate their position against domestic and foreign opponents depends crucially on their success at mobilizing and organizing durable bases of mass support. In different historical contexts, urban and industrial workers, peasants, or various combinations of these and other groups have constituted the principal lower-class base for revolutionary rule. Different revolutionary experiences have also produced diverse organizational forms for the mobilization of mass support, including soviets, committees for the defense of the revolution, and the vanguard or hegemonic party.

The frequency and political prominence of mass mobilization generally decline with the consolidation of revolutionary rule. The social base of a postrevolutionary authoritarian regime may also change over time as the result of industrialization and urbanization, processes that reduce the relative importance of the peasantry and heighten the significance of urban and industrial labor. Similarly, the political role of different mass actors may vary depending upon their organizational resources, economic bargaining leverage, leadership strategies, and the social composition of the ruling elite. Yet mass actors generally retain vital importance in the governing coalition, however subordinate they may be to elite control. It is this mass social base that gives many of these regimes their remarkable strength in the face of internal and external challenges.

Second, postrevolutionary elites seek to legitimate their rule in part through reference to distinctive ideologies or political ideas associated with the revolutionary experience. The most notable instances of this phenomenon are those revolutionary situations in which Marxism and successor ideologies such as Leninism and Maoism serve as the political leadership's guiding philosophy. These ideologies are coherent, fully articulated bodies of thought that identify workers and peasants as the central actors in the revolutionary transformation and the vanguard party as the privileged agent of political mobilization. However, even in revolutions that either occurred before the Bolsheviks' triumph in 1917 (Mexico) or in which Marxism-Leninism or Maoism did not significantly shape the actions of revolutionary elites (Bolivia and Iran), revolutionary mobilization gives rise to distinctive political beliefs that link nationalism and a commitment to far-reaching social and economic change. Although they lack the internal consistency of such ideologies as Marxism-Leninism, these beliefs are often more coherent and more durable than the loosely formulated elite mentalities generally associated with other forms of authoritarian rule.[13] Revolutionary ideals often define which groups have a legitimate place in politics, establish preferred forms of political organization, and provide an important focus for mass mobilization.

Revolutionary political beliefs typically are programmatic in content. They advocate citizen participation, economic redistribution, social justice, moral fulfillment, and other, similarly general goals that reflect the heterogeneous composition of the social forces promoting change. Nationalism is a central element in such political beliefs because the revolutionary struggle is often directed against a colonial presence or an *ancien régime* closely associated with foreign political or economic interests.[14] The intensity of political and social conflict establishes "the revolution" as the founding myth of the postrevolutionary order, generates new national heroes and symbols, and enshrines revolutionary ideals as the unifying element in subsequent political discourse. The fusion of nationalism and a commitment to socioeconomic transformation as "revolutionary nationalism" provides a particularly compelling focus for popular identification with the postrevolutionary regime.

Political beliefs of this kind play a crucial legitimating role in postrevolutionary authoritarian regimes. The claim that political elites make to the legitimate exercise of authority in these regimes is both procedural and substantive in nature. Elections, referenda, or other procedural means of demonstrating public support are important methods of regime legitimation because they ratify the importance of mass actors in the political process. However, the legitimacy of postrevolutionary rule additionally depends on such real or promised substantive achievements as the restoration of stability following a period of prolonged, frequently violent political conflict, the promotion of national autonomy, and the progressive achievement of economic development and social equality. Revolutionary ideals are important in this regard because they establish the overall public policy agenda for decision makers and set broad standards of regime performance, thereby defining the basis on which governing elites attempt to win public support and the criteria by which citizens evaluate their conduct. The beliefs associated with revolutionary transformation (especially revolutionary nationalist ideals) also create a sense of common national purpose in an elite-dominated regime, making it possible for political elites both to unify a heterogeneous governing coalition and to attract and preserve mass support.

The cogency of these beliefs may decline over time as the founding experience of social revolution recedes in memory, but they frequently remain an integral part of the political vocabulary in postrevolutionary contexts. Moreover, the programmatic content of such beliefs may prove particularly important for long-term coalition maintenance. For example, an ideological commitment to economic redistribution and national autonomy may justify increased state intervention in socioeconomic affairs, including the nationalization of foreign-controlled economic resources. Different mass actors may lay claim to this rationale as they seek to advance their own interests, and elite commitment to continued state activism may thus prove to be an especially important political basis for maintaining mass actors' loyalty to the established regime.

Third, postrevolutionary regimes represent a distinctive form of authoritarian rule because of the dual, though not necessarily equal, importance of a hegemonic or single political party and an interventionist state. The restricted role (or absence) of parties in many authoritarian contexts is a direct consequence of ruling elites' preference for public apathy or, in most cases, their active attempts to demobilize the population.[15] In postrevolutionary situations, however, the prominence of mass actors in national politics requires institutionalized arrangements for mobilizing support and channeling citizen participation toward approved ends. Thus political parties play a significant—and in some instances, leading—role in postrevolutionary authoritarian regimes.

The importance of a hegemonic or single party in these contexts, and the diverse tasks for which such parties are often responsible, reflect postrevolutionary elites' desire to centralize power and effect broad economic and social change. At different times, for example, the party may serve as an institutional framework for recruiting and socializing new members of the ruling elite, mediating intra-elite conflict, and aggregating interests in the policymaking process.[16] Moreover, the "party of the revolution" embodies the key political ideas associated with the revolutionary experience, especially such ideals as citizen participation and popular sovereignty. A hegemonic or single party also typically serves as a principal means of regime legitimation by organizing participation in elections—although electoral contests in these regimes are generally structured in such a way that the outcome is never seriously in doubt.

Despite these common features, the organizational characteristics of the governing party, its relative importance vis-à-vis other institutions, and its specific responsibilities all vary widely in different historical contexts. Where the party was organized as a vanguard institution before or during the revolution and served as a principal vehicle for political mobilization, where it embodies a systematic ideology such as Marxism-Leninism or

Maoism, and where postrevolutionary elites are committed to maintaining comparatively high levels of mass mobilization in order to effect a broad transformation of social and economic structures, political practices, and cultural norms, the party may well play the leading role in policy formulation and implementation. (Indeed, in the Soviet Union under Joseph Stalin and in China during Mao Zedong's Great Cultural Revolution, a vanguard party's intrusive control over affiliated social organizations and intense, ideologically driven political mobilization designed to transform society produced periods of totalitarian rule.)[17] But in Mexico, where the party was organized in the aftermath of the revolution as a broadly inclusive organization, where dominant political beliefs are more loosely structured, and where extensive political mobilization has been confined to specific periods and comparatively narrow goals, the "party of the revolution" plays a more limited—though still important—role in national affairs. Among other things, Mexico's "official" party has made valuable contributions to coalition maintenance and elite political control by providing the leaders of affiliated mass organizations access to elected office and the symbolic and material rewards that these positions confer.

State structures are crucially important in postrevolutionary authoritarian regimes.[18] The state—the complex of administrative, extractive, and coercive organizations coordinated by an executive authority that claims compliance from the population within a delimited territory and supports this claim with superior control over the means of force, as well as those individuals who at any given time exercise formal control over this apparatus[19]—constitutes the essential basis for constructing and preserving an elite-dominated regime. As in the case of a single or hegemonic party, the content of political ideas and the nature of elite goals (for example, whether or not political decision makers are committed to organizing a command economy) strongly influence the size and organizational form of the state apparatus. The characteristics of prerevolutionary bureaucratic structures and a country's level of economic development are also important factors in this regard.

Although the form and function of governing parties vary considerably in different historical contexts, postrevolutionary elites everywhere increase the size and complexity of the state apparatus in order to centralize political power and achieve the revolution's redistributive agenda. In doing so, they respond to the political and programmatic imperatives posed by revolutionary mass mobilization. Such measures as land reform, the nationalization of foreign-owned enterprises, or the socialization of production all require a powerful, interventionist state. Indeed, especially in regimes in which elite goals and official ideology do not clearly define the party's leading role in national affairs, the state apparatus operates as the most important institutional basis for elite control even though the party may remain valuable for mobilizing popular support and preserving the overall stability of authoritarian rule.

An Analytic Framework for Studying Mass Politics in Postrevolutionary Authoritarian Regimes

The central question in the study of postrevolutionary authoritarian regimes is how governing elites maintain control over mass participation. The stability of authoritarian rule generally depends on political elites' ability to restrict mass mobilization or channel collective actions toward politically acceptable ends, control access to organization as a political resource by limiting the independent formation of sociopolitical groups, and constrain the articulation of political and economic demands by organizations or individual citizens. The forms that these controls on mass participation take differ considerably from one historical context to another. Moreover, political elites may place greater emphasis on controlling some types of mass participation than others. Authoritarian elites are likely to impose the strictest limitations on mass mobilization because uncontrolled mobilization poses the greatest risk to their position. Yet the mix of political controls may also change over time, either as a result of shifts in the composition of the governing coalition itself or in response to economic or political challenges. Finally, the effectiveness of different elite controls on participation may vary according to the socioeconomic characteristics of mass actors themselves and the institutional linkages established between them and the state administrative apparatus and the ruling party.

This section outlines a systematic way of analyzing elite control over mass participation in postrevolutionary authoritarian regimes. The categories established here—limitations on mobilization, sociopolitical pluralism, and demand articulation—are relevant to the study of mass politics in authoritarian regimes in general. However, because the crisis of participation is particularly sharp in postrevolutionary contexts, the strategies that revolutionary leaders adopt in response to this challenge often differ in important ways from the approaches that elites in other authoritarian regimes pursue to control mass participation.

Limitations on Mass Mobilization

Governing elites in authoritarian regimes in general impose both formal (legal) and informal restrictions on mass political mobilization.[20] They seek to constrain the frequency and duration of mass mobilization, direct it through approved organizational channels, and limit mobilization activities to elite-defined political or economic objectives. The form these controls take and the degree to which they are enforced depend in large part on the historical context in which the regime appears and the level of sociopolitical mobilization accompanying its consolidation. Where over-all levels of mobilization are low, ruling political elites may retain power by relying mainly on widespread political apathy or, if necessary, repression. But in postrevolutionary authoritarian regimes such as Mexico that have experienced periods of intense mobilization, the stability of elite rule depends in large part on institutionalized arrangements for limiting and controlling mass political mobilization. Even in these contexts, however, the form and extent of controls on mobilization may vary over time or among different social actors.

Restrictions on sociopolitical organizations' ability to mobilize their constituencies behind their demands may seriously limit the scope and impact of mass participation. Controls on mobilization activities substantially constrain mass actors' opportunities to form cross-class alliances and acquire broad support for their actions. Such controls may limit the focus of their demands to relatively narrow, group-specific concerns. In addition, constraints on mobilization reduce mass actors' ability to influence policy formulation and implementation, placing them in an essentially reactive position vis-à-vis national decision makers.

In some postrevolutionary authoritarian regimes, governing elites rely on an official political party to control and channel mass participation.[21] For it to perform these tasks successfully, the party must develop a complex organizational structure capable of both maintaining the party's institutional autonomy vis-à-vis other sociopolitical groups and enforcing the party's will. The availability of a coherent ideology such as Marxism-Leninism or Maoism to legitimate its actions may increase the party's capacity to direct mass mobilization. Even then, however, the party may prove more effective at periodically mobilizing public support in elections or for other specific ends than controlling the activities of such mass actors as organized labor, whose economic importance may increase its relative autonomy vis-à-vis the party bureaucracy. Elite capacity to block independent mass mobilization depends ultimately on secure control over the means of coercion.

In cases such as postrevolutionary Mexico in which the governing political elite is guided by a shared but heterogeneous set of beliefs rather than a coherent ideology, in which the inclusive representation of diverse constituencies prevents the "party of the revolution" from functioning as a vanguard organization, and in which the centralization of political power in the state apparatus overshadows the importance of other political institutions, the "official" party may find its activities significantly circumscribed. The party's lack of organizational autonomy in these circumstances may mean that, if it plays any significant role at all in limiting mass mobilization, control over mobilization activities depends more on the actions of the party's constituent sociopolitical organizations than on those of the central party bureaucracy. The contributions of party-affiliated organizations in this area depend on the socioeconomic characteristics of the organizations themselves, the strategies their leaders adopt, and their relationship to the state.

Limitations on Sociopolitical Pluralism

The restrictions that governing elites in authoritarian regimes impose on the organized expression of interests vary considerably in their form and consequences. In regimes in which low levels of social mobilization reduce the number and significance of politically relevant groups, measures such as bribery, co-optation, the manipulation of patron-client ties, and repression may suffice to limit the formation of new sociopolitical organizations. In more complex postrevolutionary contexts, however, stable authoritarian rule generally rests on a combination of informal interest-limitation strategies (including leadership co-optation) and legal restrictions on association. These restrictions typically specify conditions for group membership and delineate the jurisdictional spheres within which recognized organizations can operate. Contextual factors such as economic conditions and regional or sectoral variations in levels and rates of social mobilization may influence the actual impact of these controls on mass participation. But even when they are relatively loosely enforced, controls of this kind constitute broad limits on sociopolitical pluralism.

The constraints that postrevolutionary governing elites impose on association can have differential consequences. Restrictions on interest representation may apply only to those sectors whose size and strategic position make them politically relevant. In many cases, lower-class groups are subject to more extensive or more uniformly enforced controls on their organization and activities than are upper-class groups. By restricting lower-class actors' access to the organizational resources important to overcoming participatory disadvantages resulting from lower socioeconomic status, limitations on sociopolitical pluralism can further bias the political process in authoritarian regimes against the participation of mass actors.[22]

Restrictions on interest representation also increase the relative importance of organization as a political resource. Where sociopolitical groups cannot form without formal review by state administrative authorities, officially sanctioned organizations enjoy a privileged position as the legitimate channels for the articulation of politically relevant demands. At least in principle, these organizations can use their favored position to advance their own membership size, material advantage, and political power. They may also resist further sociopolitical organization as a challenge to their own position. This is especially likely if the formation of new associations directly undermines recognized organizations' constituencies or their claim to the monopoly representation of certain sectors. Thus the internal political dynamics of established postrevolutionary regimes may reinforce formal limitations on sociopolitical pluralism.

In addition, restrictions on interest representation often have important implications for relations between leaders and members of officially sanctioned organizations. Where the regulation of sociopolitical pluralism involves significant controls on the leadership of mass organizations, the principal criterion for leadership selection is often loyalty or acceptability to governing political elites rather than accountability to members. Constraints on leadership selection range from ruling elites' open imposition of leadership in mass organizations to more informal efforts to influence this process, including bribes and intimidation. Some mass organizations may resist such efforts more successfully than others. However, attempts to shape leadership selection in mass organizations, and the more general tendency of governing elites in authoritarian regimes to engage in a constant process of leadership co-optation by allowing individuals from diverse sectors to join a heterogeneous elite, often weaken ties between the leaders of mass organizations and their members. Disjunctions of this kind may undermine organizations' mobilizational capacity and reduce their ability to influence an elite-dominated policymaking process.

Limitations on Demand Articulation

Restrictions on political mobilization and sociopolitical pluralism constitute mutually reinforcing controls on mass participation in postrevolutionary authoritarian regimes. Together they have important consequences for both mass organizations' and individuals' capacity to express their economic and political demands. Restrictions on the ability to form organizations to articulate economic demands and political preferences may reduce the range of interests represented in the policymaking process. Similarly, formal and informal limitations on mass organizations' ability to mobilize their memberships behind economic and political objectives may significantly constrain their effectiveness in advancing their goals.

Restrictions on sociopolitical organization and mobilization can significantly shape the pattern of demand articulation by mass actors, compelling them to negotiate, compromise, and modify their goals. These controls also contribute to governing elites' relative decision-making autonomy. More generally, institutionalized limitations on political mobilization and group formation provide ruling elites with the capacity to influence the scope, frequency, and timing of popular demands, whether expressed collectively or individually.

Regime Formation in Postrevolutionary Mexico

In the years after 1910 Mexico experienced the twentieth century's first social revolution. The overthrow of Porfirio Díaz's personalistic authoritarian regime (the Porfiriato, 1876–1911) by liberal reformers initiated a protracted, violent struggle for political power among rival factions with different capabilities and disparate, often conflicting goals. The contending forces included provincial merchants and landowners from northwestern and northeastern states; unemployed miners, railroad workers, peasants, sharecroppers, and bandits in northern Mexico; and peasants displaced by the rapid expansion of commercial agriculture in the state of Morelos.[23] Some elements sought only a limited political reform of the old order (including, for example, openly contested elections and increased access to government office for upper- and middle-class groups marginalized under Díaz's rule), whereas others pursued a broad transformation of social structures and class relations.

Military confrontation and serious factional rivalry persisted until the late 1920s. However, the last successful military revolt occurred in 1920 and brought to the fore a "northwestern coalition" led by Álvaro Obregón, a principal military leader of the "Constitutionalist" forces after 1913 and the dominant figure in national politics between his election as president in 1920 and his assassination in 1928. The length of the armed struggle was the result of fluid factional alignments, the uncertainties of war, and the U.S. government's and European powers' shifting military and diplomatic support for different revolutionary leaders as they maneuvered sharply to protect strategic interests and foreign investments in Mexico. The stakes for all participants were high—ranging from opportunities for individual political mobility and material gain to the principles and rules that would govern such diverse matters as the terms for foreign investment and the social relations of production in the workplace.

The political and military struggle that raged between 1910 and 1920 did not seriously challenge capitalist production, leading some historians of the Mexican revolution to question whether it was truly a "social" revolution.[24] Certainly the most immediate consequence of the revolutionary struggle was the creation of a new political regime. However, the revolution also produced significant changes in Mexico's social structure and in the distribution of economic power by undercutting the political position of the landowning class (thereby seriously undermining hacienda production)[25] and by eroding foreign control over natural resource industries. Explicit recognition of unions as legitimate bargaining agents in the workplace, constitutional protection of the right to strike, and the creation of state administrative agencies to mediate conflicts also reshaped worker-employer relations. These changes occurred because of the rapid expansion of political consciousness among peasants and workers and their mobilization behind a popular reform program. The actual extent of socioeconomic reform varied greatly from one region or sector to another, and many of the most important transformations resulting from the revolution occurred only after 1920. Nevertheless, this "bourgeois" revolution effected a significant degree of structural economic and social change.

The entry of peasants and workers into national politics was a major departure in Mexican history. By creating new opportunities for the competitive mobilization of support, it redefined the character of elite-mass interactions. At the same time, mass actors' presence in the national arena contributed to, and was legitimated by, the emergence of a distinctive body of political ideas. These ideas, the "ideology of the Mexican revolution," emphasized nationalism, participation, economic redistribution, and social justice. They influenced both the policy agenda for postrevolutionary decision makers and the form of major political institutions. Although government actions were often at odds with the substantive and procedural content of revolutionary ideals, the ideas associated with the 1910–20 revolution had enduring importance for Mexican politics.

The mobilization of mass social forces posed a significant challenge for revolutionary leaders, and the search for mass allies began even while the military struggle still raged. The new political leadership's principal strategy for achieving national control was to increase state capacity. In a period of institutional innovation lasting from the 1920s through the early 1940s, the postrevolutionary political elite developed the coercive, administrative, and extractive capabilities that made the state apparatus both the central pillar of national political power and the engine for socioeconomic change. Direct linkages between an expanded state administrative apparatus and mass organizations were crucial to creating a reliable base of support for the regime. At the same time, however, regime consolidation also required other responses to widely expressed demands for regularized opportunities for political participation. The formation of an "official" party in 1929 established a new institution through which postrevolutionary leaders could regularly mobilize support for the regime. The party's subsequent electoral dominance depended on both its close identification with revolutionary ideals and the governing elite's firm control over the means of coercion.

Mass Political Mobilization after 1910

The forces engaged in armed struggle between 1910 and 1920 included elements from virtually every segment of Mexican society. Opposition to Díaz initially centered on Francisco I. Madero's 1910 presidential candidacy. Madero, a member of a wealthy family in the northern state of Coahuila which controlled extensive agricultural and mining properties, drew considerable support from rural and urban middle-class groups in northern and central Mexico which had been denied access to public office and economic opportunities during the Porfiriato.[26] Many of these groups resented the Díaz government's close alliance with foreign interests, increased Mexican economic dependence on the United States, and foreign investors' dominance in the most dynamic sectors of the economy (including mining, petroleum production, railroads, banking, commercial agriculture, and the textile industry). The anti-Díaz forces also included such diverse elements as the anarchosyndicalist-oriented Partido Liberal Mexicano (Mexican Liberal Party) and its supporters among the urban middle class and industrial workers. Artisans and workers in industries with a history of labor conflict (including printers and mine, textile, railroad, and electrical power workers) found Madero's promises of free elections and the protection of individual rights attractive in part because these groups perceived a relationship between political reform and opportunities for economic improvement.[27]

The simultaneous military and political mobilization of peasants and workers transformed a limited conflict between conservative supporters of the old order and liberal reformers into a protracted struggle involving conflict among rival social forces. Madero's successful ouster of Díaz in 1911 and the breakdown of national government following Madero's assassination in 1913 created the political opening necessary for widespread peasant revolt. Mexico had experienced repeated episodes of serious rural unrest since the late seventeenth century as the commercialization of agricultural production eroded the traditional peasant economy. The rapid influx of foreign investment and the accelerated capitalization of sugar and sisal production during the Porfiriato were particularly disruptive because they led to the expropriation of free-village lands in central and southern Mexico, displacing peasants as (often absentee) landlords tightened their control over land and water. This process produced widespread rural discontent, giving rise to peasant-based armies that served as the motive force for revolution.[28] The armed peasantry's capacity to block the restoration of national political control compelled less radical elements such as Venustiano Carranza's Constitutionalist coalition to embrace land reform as a main tenet of the revolution's social agenda.

Urban and industrial workers played a less central but nonetheless significant role in the revolutionary struggle.[29] Their involvement in revolutionary politics followed a slow process of working-class organization dating from the late nineteenth century. Mexico experienced protests by urban workers and miners as early as the 1620s over such issues as wages, food prices, and working conditions.[30] Artisans, who opposed the importation of cheap manufactured goods, were politically active in debates over tariff policy throughout the nineteenth century.[31] However, labor attained political significance only after the 1860s when the growth of the textile industry and other manufacturing activities produced important concentrations of workers.[32] Many early working-class organizations, especially "mutualist societies" (asociaciones de ayuda mutua) and "resistance societies," were founded by artisans facing economic competition from factory production. A number of the organizations formed in the 1860s and 1870s were influenced by utopian socialist and anarchist beliefs. Mexican anarchism, or "libertarian socialism," was a powerful ideological influence during this period because it stressed the importance of collective organization at a time when few labor groups existed. It was also influential because its emphasis on autonomous, defensive labor action and its rejection of ties between workers and either the state or political parties were appealing to displaced artisans.[33]

With the assistance of a vigorous press, several of these working-class groups succeeded in organizing affiliates throughout the country.[34] For example, between 1870 and 1875 the anarchist Gran Círculo de Obreros de México (Great Circle of Mexican Workers) organized 28 affiliates grouping some 8,000 members in the Federal District and ten states, with many concentrated in the textile industry.[35] In the early 1880s the mutualist Congreso Obrero (Workers' Congress, founded in 1879) claimed more than 50,000 members among textile workers, miners, and other workers organized in approximately 100 affiliates.[36] The Convención Radical Obrera (Workers' Radical Convention, founded in 1886) had 22 affiliates representing some 15,000 Mexico City artisans and workers. Throughout the late nineteenth century, various political leaders (including Díaz's allies) sought to win the support of labor organizations and maintain peace among an increasingly important working-class population.[37]

In the late 1880s and 1890s, labor organizations declined significantly in number and size as the Díaz government strongly discouraged (and frequently repressed) strikes.[38] However, railroad workers took advantage of their strategic economic importance to form several major unions in the last years of the Porfiriato. The most prominent of these organizations included the Unión Mexicana de Mecánicos (Mexican Union of Machinists, 1900), the Gran Liga Mexicana de Empleados de Ferrocarril (Great Mexican League of Railroad Employees, 1905), the powerful Confederación de Ferrocarrileros Mexicanos (Confederation of Mexican Railroad Workers, 1910), and the Unión de Conductores, Maquinistas, Garroteros y Fogoneros (Union of Conductors, Engineers, Brakemen, and Firemen, 1911).[39] Similarly, textile workers organized the Gran Círculo de Obreros Libres (Great Circle of Free Workers) in 1906. Major strikes by Cananea (Sonora) copper miners in 1906, Río Blanco (Veracruz) textile workers in 1906–7, and railroad workers in 1906 and 1908 contributed significantly to social discontent in the period immediately preceding the outbreak of revolution. In addition, a serious recession in 1907–8 produced a decline in real wages, increased unemployment, and greater pressures on employers to rationalize production, further intensifying labor unrest and creating fertile ground for Díaz's opponents.[40]

Rivalry among contending elite factions and the consequent erosion of state authority in the early years of the revolution permitted workers to mobilize in support of higher wages, improved working conditions, and greater political influence.[41] In a bid for labor support, Madero permitted workers enhanced opportunities to unionize and to strike, and despite continued opposition from employers and conservative political and military elements,[42] labor protests occurred throughout Mexico in 1911–13 as miners, printers, and railroad, port, textile, and commercial workers organized unions. Coahuila coal miners formed the Unión Minera Mexicana (Mexican Mining Union) in 1911. Railroad and port workers were particularly effective at using their economic leverage to strike for higher wages, shorter hours, and better working conditions and to resist government influence in their affairs; in 1913 they united to form the nationally important Confederación de Gremios Mexicanos (Confederation of Mexican Unions).[43] The Casa del Obrero Mundial (House of the World Worker, COM), the most important labor organization to appear during the early revolutionary period, formed in May 1913 under strong anarchosyndicalist influence.[44] By late 1914 the COM grouped a diverse membership of some 52,000 workers in a national network of self-governing *sindicatos,* a number of which (including those in Morelia and Monterrey) formed militias. Strikes in Mexico City in 1914–15 against railroad, electrical power, telephone, tramway, telegraph, printing, and textile companies demonstrated organized labor's growing power.[45]

Several factors—workers' new (though still limited) organizational strength, the military importance of railroad, port, and petroleum workers, labor's general political significance in urban areas, and the continuing threat of working-class violence (as evidenced by riots led by unemployed workers and displaced artisans in several cities)[46]—spurred revolutionary leaders to seek alliances with labor. Labor support was especially important to Carranza in 1914–15 because the Constitutionalist forces under his direction were then on the defensive. In 1915 the COM organized 7,000–10,000 workers from the Mexico City area to fight with Carranza's army as six "Red Battalions."[47] It exploited its alliance with Carranza to stimulate union formation in different parts of the country, including in the Veracruz textile industry. Nevertheless, Carranza simultaneously tightened government control over labor organizations in an effort to prevent political radicalization and promote economic stability. COM organizational activities encountered growing government hostility in 1915–16, and the Red Battalions were disbanded.[48] Carranza declared martial law to crush a general strike in Mexico City in late July and early August 1916, a movement spearheaded by the Sindicato Mexicano de Electricistas (Mexican Electricians' Union, formed in 1914) in support of workers' demands for payment in specie and wage increases.[49]

The armed peasantry proved more important than urban and industrial workers both politically and militarily in the first years of the revolution, but organized labor posed the more enduring challenge for Mexico's new political elite. Although peasant mobilization continued in some regions into the early 1930s, the assassination of Emiliano Zapata (the revolution's most prominent peasant leader and commander of the "Liberating Army of the South" centered in the state of Morelos) in 1919 symbolically marked the apogee of peasant participation in revolutionary politics. President Lázaro Cárdenas's (1934–40) extensive land reform program in the 1930s generated among peasants widespread, lasting support for the regime, while postrevolutionary governments systematically undermined peasants' autonomous capacity for collective action and established effective political control in the countryside. Beginning in the late 1940s and early 1950s, migration to urban areas offered a nonviolent alternative for rural populations that found deteriorating economic and social conditions intolerable. Government co-optation of peasant leaders, the debilitating effect of widespread seasonal unemployment on peasant organizational efforts, and the often arbitrary use of force by landowners' private security forces and police and army units together preserved a sullen peace in the Mexican countryside. Peasant-supported guerrilla insurgencies erupted in some areas in the 1960s and early 1970s, and in January 1994 a peasant-based guerrilla uprising in the state of Chiapas gave new impetus to popular demands for open elections and dramatically focused public attention on the social and economic inequalities endured by indigenous peoples in Mexico. For the most part, however, rural political protests in postrevolutionary Mexico provoked sporadic violence at the local level but did not seriously challenge the established political order.

In contrast, labor's political strength increased in the last years of the revolution despite the generalized rigors of inflation, unemployment, persistent organizational weaknesses, and the Carranza administration's hostility toward many strikes and militant unions. Miners and railroad workers reorganized unions, and petroleum and textile workers led impressive strikes in early 1917 in support of their demands for increased wages and official recognition of their unions. In October 1917 delegates representing twenty-nine organizations in the Federal District and eleven states reorganized the Confederación de Trabajadores de la Región Mexicana (Confederation of Workers from the Mexican Region, founded in 1916) as the Confederación General Obrera (General Labor Confederation). Carranza sought to co-opt the emerging national labor movement, but his efforts suffered a sharp reverse when delegates representing 115 working-class organizations in the Federal District and sixteen states convened in Saltillo (Coahuila) on May 1, 1918, to form the Confederación Regional Obrera Mexicana (Mexican Regional Labor Confederation, CROM). The CROM was the first labor organization in Mexico that grouped both artisans and industrial workers; it was to dominate national labor politics for the next decade.[50]

The Content of Revolutionary Political Ideas

The political ideas associated with the Mexican revolution combine liberal conceptions of individual rights and constitutional rule, nationalism, and a broad programmatic commitment to economic redistribution and social justice. Liberal ideas of constitutionalism, federalism and municipal autonomy (municipio libre), and private property particularly informed debate about political and socioeconomic reform during the early phases of the revolutionary struggle.[51] Reformers such as President Madero (1911–13) advocated the restoration of the 1857 federal constitution and its guarantees of liberal political rights, including the freedoms of expression, association, and religious practice and the popular election of government officials. Madero, whose chief slogan was "Effective suffrage and no re-election," defined his political position in opposition to the governing practices of the Porfiriato and its underlying positivist conception of change, especially its advocacy of "order and progress" and its social Darwinist assumptions concerning the appropriate ordering of economic and political life.[52]

Liberal values remained central to conceptions of political legitimacy in Mexico both during and after the revolution. However, the mobilization of mass social forces after 1910 reshaped dominant political beliefs.[53] The rapid increase in political awareness among peasants and urban workers throughout the country significantly altered the terms of debate concerning the content of citizenship rights. At the same time, the entrance of previously excluded mass actors into national politics encouraged different elite factions to propose reform programs that would attract their support.[54]

The *zapatista* movement in particular forced a radical shift in the social and political program of the revolution.[55] The *zapatistas'* "Plan de Ayala" (1911) called for the large-scale redistribution of land to village communities and small property holders, challenging the essence of the economic and social transformations that had accompanied the rapid concentration of land ownership (and, in some areas, the capitalization of agricultural production) during the Porfiriato. Similarly, the presence of worker-formed Red Battalions in Carranza's Constitutionalist forces, as well as the growing political and economic importance of organized labor in urban areas such as Mexico City, placed workers' grievances squarely on the political agenda. As a result, a commitment to far-reaching socioeconomic reforms became an essential element in revolutionary political discourse. The 1917 federal constitution, for example, included separate articles providing for land reform (Article 27) and workers' legal and social protection (Article 123). These articles were especially significant because they emphasized the *collective* character of new social and political rights for peasants and workers, not just opportunities for individual advancement. Moreover, the 1917 constitution endorsed active state intervention in socioeconomic affairs to achieve the revolution's redistributive goals. The central role of mass social forces in the revolutionary struggle and the presence of worker and peasant delegates at the 1916–17 Constitutional Convention in Querétaro were crucial to winning a place for socioeconomic reforms among formal constitutional guarantees.

The mobilization of mass actors during the revolution was also fueled by, and contributed significantly to the growth of, nationalist sentiment. The Díaz government's ties to foreign economic interests, as well as U.S. and European investors' dominance in the mining and petroleum industries, commercial agriculture, and finance, at times made foreign-owned properties the object of popular violence.[56] During the revolution there were also physical attacks on foreigners (especially Chinese immigrants, but also Spaniards).[57] The revolutionary leadership did not necessarily share this popular xenophobia (Obregón, for instance, has been described as an "americanophile").[58] Nevertheless, postrevolutionary governments were deeply committed to the renegotiation of Mexico's economic dependence on the United States.[59] The revolution also produced a pantheon of popular heroes (Zapata, Francisco "Pancho" Villa, Madero) whose fame was based in large measure on their opposition to foreign influence and their identification with patriotic themes. The appeal of "revolutionary nationalism" was particularly strong among groups such as railroad, mine, and petroleum workers whose sense of class and nationalism was fused by their experiences in foreign-owned enterprises. Railroad and mine workers had, for example, been involved in early efforts to "Mexicanize" their industries—that is, to secure equal working conditions and access to skilled jobs for Mexican citizens (and on the railroads, the use of Spanish in written and verbal workplace communications).[60]

Prolonged armed struggle between 1910 and 1920 fortified traditional regional identifications, and local myths and millenarian appeals were often more important than nationalism as catalysts for popular mobilization outside urban areas.[61] However, repeated U.S. and European military and diplomatic intervention to shape the outcome of the revolution underlined the importance of national unity as a safeguard to sovereignty.[62] Thus the revolutionary experience spurred the development of national consciousness. The greater sense of national identity forged during this period, as well as the widely shared perception that the construction of a national identity and a just society were fused in the revolutionary transformation, became important elements in the inclusionary appeal of postrevolutionary political institutions. In short, many Mexicans came to equate nationalism with support for the state and the postrevolutionary political order more generally.

The ideas associated with the 1910–20 revolution long defined the essential terms of political legitimacy in Mexico. The continuing importance of liberal political values is reflected in the formal guarantee of individual political rights in a civilian-ruled regime, the centrality of constitutional norms, and the presence of legally recognized opposition parties. Regular elections play a significant legitimating role both by validating popular consent and by periodically mobilizing public support for government activities and the party system. Electoral campaigns also offer opportunities for individual citizens to present their demands to future officeholders. The constitutional prohibition against presidential reelection represents an elite commitment to regular leadership succession, and a reliable system of office rotation creates opportunities for the expression of a comparatively broad range of sociopolitical tendencies.

There has, however, been a persistent tension between such liberal values as electoral accountability and the rule of law and the revolution's programmatic goals—a tension between formulas of procedural and substantive legitimacy which has grown more intense in recent decades as the historical memory of revolutionary accomplishments fades. Because the Mexican regime originated in revolutionary transformation rather than in an inclusive and widely accepted electoral process, public perceptions of regime legitimacy for many years depended more on overall evaluations of government performance and the fulfillment of a comprehensive revolutionary program than on government adherence to particular procedural requirements. The consecration of social reforms as constitutional guarantees permitted postrevolutionary governments to subordinate procedural requirements and individual rights to their programmatic agenda on the assumption that they acted in the general interest.[63] Thus postrevolutionary governments justified undermining such constitutional provisions as the separation of powers among the executive, legislative, and judicial branches and between federal and state governments on the grounds that effective promotion of economic growth and social reform required concentrating political power in the hands of the president. Although some government decision makers continue to invoke this rationale, prolonged economic crisis in the 1980s and opposition parties' success at translating social discontent into electoral support further eroded performance-based regime legitimacy and significantly strengthened popular commitment to elections.

The redistributive focus of postrevolutionary political ideas has, nevertheless, remained especially important to the preservation of a broad-based governing coalition in Mexico. Groups such as organized labor remain committed to constitutionalism and the rule of law because the effective protection of the right to strike and freedom of association depends on them. However, different presidential administrations' support for economic redistribution and social justice—even if, at times, more rhetorical than real—has been particularly significant because it symbolically represents the inclusion of worker and peasant demands in the revolutionary project. From the perspective of mass actors, extensive state intervention in socioeconomic affairs has been the most reliable means through which to realize these goals.

State and Party in Postrevolutionary Mexico

Presidents Álvaro Obregón (1920–24) and Plutarco Elías Calles (1924–28) sought first and foremost to build a stronger state. In particular, the "Sonoran dynasty" confronted two pressing challenges: establishing military and political control over regional bosses (caciques) whose power and autonomy had grown significantly during a decade of armed conflict, and restoring political stability and economic growth so as to increase national sovereignty vis-à-vis the United States. The northwesterners who came to power under Obregón's leadership envisioned a political economy in which a vigorous domestic private sector would contribute actively to the development of national resources and industry, thus reducing the influence of foreign (especially U.S.) capital. However, because of the manifest weakness of the national private sector, the absence of domestic financial institutions or a capital market, and the lack of adequate infrastructure, they understood that the state would necessarily play a leading role in economic reconstruction and development.[64]

Obregón and Calles acted decisively to consolidate control over the principal instruments of coercion. The appointment during the revolution of eleven divisional generals with considerable operational autonomy had badly fragmented national political power. Obregón and Calles understood that establishing unified command over the army was the essential prerequisite to achieving their long-term goals because national stability could not be guaranteed so long as rival elite factions could employ force to defend their interests.

Following the defeat of Adolfo de la Huerta's military insurrection in 1923–24 (which was initially supported by two-thirds of the army), Obregón ordered the execution of all the rebel leaders and began the long task of subordinating the armed forces to civilian authority.[65] Obregón and Calles succeeded in using their own military prestige to reduce the military's size and budgetary resources and to channel the ambitions of revolutionary generals into private enterprise and political positions such as state governorships. Building in part on Obregón's efforts as minister of war in 1916–17, they also initiated programs to professionalize the Mexican armed forces. In time, a strong national consensus formed in favor of civilian control over the military. Since the 1940s the armed forces have been employed by different presidential administrations to achieve a variety of domestic political goals, including breaking labor strikes, suppressing major political protests, repressing rural and urban guerrilla movements, and fighting drug traffickers.[66] However, military affairs have been shrouded in secrecy so as to preclude speculation about the possible politicization of the military.

At the same time, the postrevolutionary leadership laid the administrative foundations for active state economic intervention. Government involvement in economic affairs was a practical political and military necessity during the revolution, and in 1917 Carranza established the Secretaría de Industria, Comercio y Trabajo (Ministry of Industry, Commerce, and Labor). However, in the early 1920s the Obregón administration significantly expanded state economic development authority by creating the Comisión Nacional de Caminos (National Highway Commission), the Comisión Nacional de Irrigación (National Irrigation Commission), and the Comisión Nacional de Fuerza Motriz (National Power Commission). The adoption of an income tax in 1923 and the expansion of the Secretaría de Hacienda y Crédito Público's (Ministry of Finance) decision-making authority in 1925 substantially augmented the federal government's capacity to raise revenue. In 1925 Calles founded the Comisión Nacional Bancaria (National Banking Commission) and a central bank, the Banco de México. The government also created a Banco Nacional de Crédito Agrícola (National Agricultural Credit Bank) in 1925, although plans for several other development banks were suspended because of deepening economic recession.[67] Mexico regained access to external financial credit following the 1923 Bucareli Conference on foreign debt and foreign losses incurred during the revolution (the Bucareli settlement led to U.S. recognition of Obregón's government) and negotiations in 1925–27 between Minister of Finance Alberto Pani and the International Committee of Bankers on Mexico.[68] Moreover, the federal government undertook extensive infrastructure projects such as the expansion of road networks and the construction of dam and irrigation systems in the north and northwest. Even though the Mexican regime remained vulnerable during the 1920s to military revolts and pressures by foreign economic interests, these actions established the bases for subsequent agricultural modernization and industrial development.

Conceptions of what constituted appropriate state action were strongly influenced by the programmatic content of revolutionary ideas. The revolution produced a new conception of the state: as the presumed representative of all groups and classes, the postrevolutionary state was responsible for moderating and conciliating conflicting interests. The 1917 federal constitution's guarantee of substantive rights for workers and peasants and postrevolutionary governments' commitment to reform required a state capable of intervening extensively in economic and social affairs. The constitution represented

> a will that the people transmitted directly to the state, authorizing its intervention in social life as it was considered necessary, on the supposition that the state fulfilled a program that society had entrusted to it; any act of power was automatically justified. The popular will had been fixed in the Constitution and had then been passed to the state in such a manner that the will of the state was at the same time the will of the people.[69]

The consecration of socioeconomic reforms as constitutional guarantees legitimated state intervention to ensure their implementation. This view, although not without its opponents, was shared by a broad range of political actors.

The Obregón administration also initiated a broad program of public education designed to forge a cohesive sense of national identity and cement popular support for the new regime. Under the direction of José Vasconcelos, rector of the national university and minister of education between 1920 and 1924, the government devoted considerable financial resources to school construction, literacy and vocational education campaigns, the publication of books and newspapers, and the development of public arts (including the Mexican school of mural painting). Vasconcelos sought to use the educational process to build cultural nationalism, an effort that contributed significantly to popular identification with postrevolutionary institutions.

Despite the creation of administrative foundations for a strong, interventionist postrevolutionary state, the federal government's authority expanded slowly and unevenly. The process was constrained both by the power of regional political bosses and state governors and by constitutional norms safeguarding the rights of states and municipalities.[70] However, the trend toward the centralization of national political power accelerated with the creation of an "official" governing party in 1929. A number of small, often regionally based political parties formed during and after the revolution. The Partido Socialista de Yucatán (Socialist Party of Yucatán, 1917, which in 1921 became the Partido Socialista del Sureste [Socialist Party of the Southeast]), the Partido Liberal Constitucionalista (Constitutional Liberal Party, PLC, formed in 1917 by a group of military leaders that included Obregón), the Partido Nacional Cooperatista (National Cooperative Party, PNC, 1917), the Partido Laborista Mexicano (Mexican Labor Party, PLM, 1919), the Partido Comunista Mexicano (Mexican Communist Party, PCM, 1919), and the Partido Nacional Agrarista (National Agrarian Party, PNA, 1920) all played active roles in regional and national politics in the 1920s. For example, the PLC, PNC, PLM, and PNA held important blocks of seats in the federal Chamber of Deputies during this period. Although they espoused reform programs favoring workers and peasants and were united by anticlerical sentiments, even these parties were often dominated by revolutionary generals and their allies. Dozens of other parties were little more than electoral fronts or political machines supported by local and regional bosses.

Competition among parties with narrow social bases contributed to the factional rivalries that culminated in Obregón's assassination in July 1928 shortly after he won reelection to the presidency. The death of the early postrevolutionary period's most important political figure threatened to throw the country into chaos over the question of presidential succession. (Obregón's support for constitutional reforms permitting presidential reelection to a six-year term had provoked a brief military revolt in October 1927.) Calles addressed this problem in September 1928 by renouncing any intention to seek a second presidential term, and in March 1929 he organized the Partido Nacional Revolucionario (Revolutionary National Party, PNR) to contain factional rivalries. He perceived the creation of a national "party of the revolution" to be the essential basis on which to build a strong state, place both military and civilian elements of the "revolutionary family" under centralized civilian control, and thus ensure the political stability necessary for economic modernization. The PNR's motto was "Institutions and Social Reform." [71]

The formation of the PNR was a significant step in the institutionalization of postrevolutionary Mexican politics. The PNR and its successors, the Partido de la Revolución Mexicana (Party of the Mexican Revolution, PRM, 1938) and the Partido Revolucionario Institucional (Institutional Revolutionary Party, PRI, 1946), established an organizational framework within which to reconcile the interests of competing elite factions and local and regional parties. [72] The death or political marginalization of many prominent revolutionary figures in the 1920s following unsuccessful military revolts and armed confrontation between the federal government and the Catholic Church (the Cristero war, 1926–29) certainly facilitated the task of consolidating political control through the party. Calles's success in this regard was nevertheless a monumental achievement because the restoration of political stability in postrevolutionary Mexico required a negotiated consensus among the leaders of rival social forces. In subsequent decades the "party of the revolution" grouped a heterogeneous collection of actors and interests that, despite considerable internal competition and frequent conflict over policy goals, was linked by an overarching consensus on broad norms of political action and the general goals of economic development. The very heterogeneity of this governing "revolutionary coalition" symbolized the established regime's commitment to the political representation of diverse elements.

Equally important, the governing party served as a major vehicle for regime legitimation through its domination of the electoral process. The postrevolutionary political elite's control of the state apparatus gradually permitted the "official" party to establish its electoral hegemony, though resistance from regional and local political bosses made this a slow and uneven process in which PNR and PRM leaders were sometimes compelled to make substantial concessions to provincial interests in order to win their cooperation. [73] Calles evidently did not intend for the PNR to function as an official party in the strict sense, but from the beginning it was openly financed by federal and state governments. [74] Where ample access to government personnel and financial resources proved insufficient to gain victory for the "official" party, fraudulent electoral practices were often authorized or tolerated by government officials to secure the desired result. Indeed, from 1929 until 1988, the "official" party's candidates never lost an election for the presidency, the federal Senate, or state governorships. Its control over elected government positions contributed significantly to the emergence of a comparatively cohesive *clase política* drawn predominantly from the urban middle class, socialized by shared educational experiences, frequently linked by kinship ties, and distinct in background and experience from the national bourgeoisie.[75]

The party was able to fulfill such diverse functions because, at least until the late 1980s, it was closely identified with revolutionary nationalism—the political ideals and social program of the Mexican revolution. (Its colors are those of the Mexican flag: red, white, and green.) The "party of the revolution" occupied the broad center of national political life, defining the essential dichotomy of postrevolutionary politics: its supporters were those committed to the realization of the revolution's diverse objectives, whereas those who opposed it were necessarily "counterrevolutionary."[76]

The party's identification with revolutionary nationalist ideals and its strong control over the electoral process helped sustain affiliated mass organizations' loyalty to the established regime. The party has been the principal channel through which the leaders of lower-class organizations achieve upward political mobility. In the case of the labor movement, union leaders' presence in important elective positions gave organized labor a share (however modest) of political power, opening opportunities to translate its importance in national politics into influence over government decisions on matters affecting workers and to defend past policy gains. More generally, working-class organizations' affiliation with the governing party symbolized labor's inclusion in the postrevolutionary governing coalition. This is why the organized labor movement vigorously resisted attempts by different presidential administrations to reduce the formal role of mass organizations in party affairs.

Although the "official" party has played a key part in sustaining mass support for the established regime, the party itself lacks the organizational autonomy or institutional capacity to block independent political mobilization or otherwise exercise direct control over mass social forces. The party was formed "from above" after the northwestern coalition came to power, and since the mid-1930s the federal executive has exercised firm control over party activities.[77] Unlike ideological vanguard parties formed in other revolutionary contexts, Mexico's governing party was not born to rule.[78] Instead, it was designed as a broadly inclusive organization capable of linking as diverse an array of groups and interests as possible (a task facilitated by the diffuseness of postrevolutionary political ideas) and occupying political space, thus limiting potential opponents' ability to mobilize mass support. As a result, the party never developed an institutional structure independent of the state apparatus that was capable of disciplining affiliated organizations. Thus groups such as organized labor, which had significant economic bargaining leverage and some independent capacity for collective mobilization, traditionally enjoyed considerable autonomy within the party framework.

Elite control over lower-class actors in postrevolutionary Mexico has ultimately rested, then, on state power.[79] Control over the means of coercion allowed the ruling political elite to repress serious challenges to the regime from both elite factions and popular forces. The construction of a state administrative apparatus with the institutional capacity to mediate mass participation also permitted successive presidential administrations to establish the de jure and de facto parameters of sociopolitical organization and mobilization. Moreover, the Mexican state's far-reaching intervention in socioeconomic affairs provided government decision makers the means to formulate development policies that helped build and sustain a diverse governing coalition that included major labor, peasant, and business organizations. With effective control over the means of coercion, channels of political mobility, and the distribution of economic benefits, postrevolutionary governments successfully enforced a series of bargains among major socioeconomic and political actors. These bargains covered such crucial issues as political contenders' regularized access to administrative and elective office, the respective roles of the public and private sectors in economic development, and lower-class groups' opportunities for social and economic advancement.[80]

Explaining Labor Participation in Postrevolutionary Mexico

The central argument advanced in this book is that both state-centered and society-centered approaches are essential to understanding the bases of elite political control and the character of mass politics in Mexico's postrevolutionary authoritarian regime. Most examinations of organized labor's role in Mexican politics and economic development have emphasized the importance of state controls on worker participation, selective repression of labor opposition movements, and co-optation of labor leaders as explanations of labor's generally subordinate position in decision making on issues that directly affect workers.[81] State administrative capacity to control different forms of labor participation and regulate worker-employer relations did, of course, contribute greatly to the governing elite's power and relative decision-making autonomy. Moreover, effective control over the means of coercion permitted postrevolutionary governments to repress major labor opposition movements, limit the autonomy of working-class organizations, and establish de jure and de facto the permissible limits of labor action. Yet state-centered analysis alone is not sufficient to explain either the character of state-labor relations or patterns of political conflict and change in the postrevolutionary period.[82]

The stability of authoritarian rule in Mexico has also depended crucially on the alliance forged in the 1920s and 1930s between the national political elite[83] and major elements of the emerging organized labor movement, the country's most important mass political force. Two issues are particularly important to understanding the nature of this alliance and its evolution over time. First, for much of the postrevolutionary period, Mexico's governing elite shared a broad consensus on the value of a strategic alliance with organized labor. In response to varying political and economic conditions, different presidential administrations pursued sharply divergent labor policies, with important consequences for workers' welfare and for different forms of labor participation. An examination of specific political or economic crises or the formulation and implementation of particular labor policies would, moreover, show that different state officials often developed highly personalistic, sometimes contradictory alliances with individual labor organizations.

Yet at the level of regime analysis, postrevolutionary political leaders were long united in their view that preserving an alliance with leading elements of the labor movement was crucial for regime legitimation, for maintaining conditions conducive to private-sector investment and economic growth, and for political and economic crisis management. In political terms, backing from organized labor in the first decades after the 1910–20 revolution aided the governing elite in its efforts to consolidate national political control. In later years, reliable mass support from disciplined "official" labor organizations was especially important in the all-important moment of presidential succession, when the incumbent president's transfer of concentrated authority to his self-designated successor in a closed, undemocratic process—the linchpin of Mexican authoritarianism—was particularly vulnerable to disruption.

Second, understanding the origins and evolution of this alliance requires special attention to those society-centered factors that conditioned labor's relationship with the postrevolutionary leadership, especially the labor movement's dependence on a broad range of state-provided legal, financial, and political subsidies. These elements include: (1) characteristics of the Mexican economy that influence patterns of unionization and workers' bargaining leverage (the size and sectoral distribution of the economically active population at the regional or national level, the relative economic importance of different industries, the geographical or workplace concentration or dispersion of the labor force, the extent of unemployment, and so forth), as well as such considerations as the size and ownership characteristics of firms and the nature of different production processes; (2) the organizational form of the labor movement; and (3) political ideas that influence both labor leaders' policy preferences and the specific strategies they adopt in response to political and economic challenges. Attention to these factors helps explain why major segments of the labor movement have been heavily dependent on state subsidies and thus why organized labor has remained a loyal member of Mexico's governing coalition despite significant constraints on working-class organizations' ability to advance their economic and political demands.

There is a basic reason why an examination of society-centered variables is necessary in any study of labor politics: the labor movement—in Mexico or elsewhere—is never a homogeneous whole. Many analysts distinguish at least implicitly between formal and informal economic sectors, or between organized and unorganized segments of the working class. Yet in Latin America and elsewhere there is great diversity even within the organized labor movement representing workers in the formal sector, the focus of this study. The impact of specific state controls on different forms of labor participation, the basis and character of alliances that political elites and labor organizations form, the influence and operational autonomy that unions enjoy, and the depth of worker commitment to different ideological appeals are all likely to vary depending upon sociological and economic differences within the labor movement as a social formation. Labor leaders negotiate for legislation and contract terms that seek to homogenize both the labor movement and working conditions,[84] but in practice politically significant socioeconomic differences continue to exist. An analysis of labor politics that takes seriously workers and working-class organizations as sociopolitical actors must therefore be sensitive to the factors that produce heterogeneity within the organized labor movement.

Understanding workers and labor organizations as sociopolitical actors also requires attention to labor's place in the production process. This book addresses this dimension by linking an examination of national labor politics to developments in the workplace. Specifically, it focuses on union politics in railroad transportation in the 1930s and 1940s and in automobile manufacturing from the 1960s through the 1980s to illustrate the ways in which changes in workplace industrial relations influenced workers' and unions' political activities. This analysis is necessarily interdisciplinary in character, drawing on a broad range of research materials to illuminate the intersection between such political issues as the distribution of power, forms of representation, and the use of coercive force in Mexico's authoritarian regime and economic issues such as shifts in economic development strategy, changes in production processes and workplace organization, and their consequences for workers' economic welfare.

Part I of this book (chapters 2, 3, and 4) analyzes both the development of state administrative capacity to control labor participation and the formation and consolidation of the postrevolutionary alliance between organized labor and the governing political elite. Chapter 2 examines the creation of state administrative capacity in the labor sector after 1910 and the legal restrictions that government officials exercise over different forms of labor participation, the most important of which concern union formation, internal union activities, and strikes. In response to the challenge of labor mobilization, and as part of a sustained effort to centralize political power and expand the state's transformative capacity, Mexico's new political leadership established specialized administrative structures to mediate labor participation. Agencies such as the Ministry of Labor and Social Welfare and tripartite conciliation and arbitration boards offered workers new channels through which to press their demands concerning economic issues and workplace conditions. At the same time, however, expanded administrative capacity gave government decision makers institutionalized means of regulating diverse aspects of worker-employer relations and influencing the development of the organized labor movement. This chapter places the state-building process in historical context by considering how revolutionary political ideas and labor organizations themselves influenced the development of state administrative capacity. This analysis lays the basis for a subsequent examination of how linkages between the state and different labor organizations influence patterns of political change in the labor sector.

The potential power of a politically independent labor movement constituted a major challenge for the postrevolutionary leadership. In addition to creating state administrative structures to regulate worker-employer relations and control the most important forms of labor participation, Mexico's new political and military leaders responded to the crisis of mass participation by forging an alliance with key elements of the organized working class. Chapter 3 examines the origins, characteristics, and consequences of this alliance, emphasizing the ways in which economic factors and the organizational characteristics of the labor force conditioned the labor movement's early relationship with postrevolutionary political leaders. This chapter focuses in detail on the formation and evolution of the Mexican Regional Labor Confederation (CROM) and the Confederación de Trabajadores de México (Confederation of Mexican Workers, CTM), the two labor organizations most important to the political consolidation of the Mexican regime and the principal basis for the postrevolutionary alliance between the national political leadership and organized labor. It discusses the broad range of state-provided legal, financial, and political subsidies that sustained this alliance, and it shows that the highly unequal terms of the "official" labor movement's relationship with the governing elite transformed major labor organizations into important mechanisms of political control over rank-and-file workers. Thus this analysis of the emergence of a state-subsidized labor movement and the importance of "official" labor organizations as instruments of political control helps explain how the mobilization of mass actors during the Mexican revolution gave way to a resilient, comparatively open authoritarian regime.

The CTM's position in the labor movement—as well as the character of the political alliance between the governing elite and labor—was challenged in both the late 1930s and the late 1940s by secessionist movements led by powerful national industrial unions representing workers in strategically important industries. The influence that these unions derived from their economic leverage and national organizational presence made them less dependent on state subsidies and more committed to political autonomy than many other CTM affiliates. In the late 1940s, these dissident unions formed the Coalición de Organizaciones Obreras y Campesinas (Coalition of Worker and Peasant Organizations, COOC) to oppose both close ties between the CTM and the dominant "party of the revolution" and conservative government labor policies adopted during and after World War II. The opposition labor coalition questioned key elements of postwar economic policy, and it seriously threatened elite control over the labor movement. State labor officials' manipulation of the legal requirement that a union leadership be registered by labor authorities, their ability to exploit internal divisions in COOC affiliates, and selective repression ended this challenge. Government intervention against the COOC thus helped consolidate the broad pattern of state-labor relations that would prevail from the early 1950s into the 1990s.

Chapter 4 examines the political and economic origins of the 1947–51 labor crisis, the means through which the federal government demobilized the labor opposition movement that emerged during this period (and thereby ensured CTM political dominance in national labor affairs), and the long-term consequences of these events for state-labor relations. It focuses particularly on the role played by the national railroad workers' union, the main leader of the labor opposition and Mexico's single most powerful union during the 1930s and 1940s. The railroad workers' union is an especially appropriate subject for detailed study because the methods the government used to establish political control over it were subsequently employed against other national industrial unions. Moreover, by showing that the challenges railroad workers confronted as a result of government attempts in the 1940s to restructure railroad labor-management relations contributed directly to their leading role in the national labor opposition movement, chapter 4 demonstrates the value of an industry-level analysis that links a major union's political activities to developments in the workplace.

Part II (chapters 5, 6, and 7) evaluates the extent of state control over different forms of labor participation, the interplay between state-labor relations and post-1940 import-substituting industrialization, and the impact of industrial change on patterns of labor control. Chapter 5 tests the limits of a state-centered approach to labor politics in postrevolutionary Mexico by systematically analyzing how and to what extent government officials have in practice employed state administrative structures and legal requirements to limit labor strikes, union formation, and individual worker demands. It specifically examines the extent to which state control over labor participation in these areas varied with shifts in presidential policy and national economic and political conditions from the 1930s through the early 1990s. This analysis demonstrates that there were important differences in the extent of political control over labor during this period depending upon the form of labor participation involved, and it shows that in some areas the degree of political control also varied significantly among different presidential administrations. The chapter concludes that understanding political control over labor strikes, union formation, and worker demand articulation also requires attention to such society-centered factors as the organizational characteristics of labor unions and labor leaders' political beliefs.

Chapter 6 analyzes the relationship between political control over labor participation and import-substituting industrialization in Mexico. The consolidated alliance between the governing elite and leading elements of the organized labor movement created political conditions favorable to rapid economic growth from the 1940s through the 1970s. Labor organizations' dependence on state subsidies, government officials' selective distribution of economic and social benefits, and state administrative controls on strikes all limited labor's capacity to formulate a unified negotiating position and mobilize worker discontent in support of redistributive policies. Nevertheless, the political importance of organized labor did influence economic policymakers' actions at key moments in development policy formulation, such as the adoption of low-inflation, "stabilizing development" policies in the mid-1950s. More generally, the strategy of state-led, highly protected national industrialization that successive presidential administrations pursued through the 1970s established economic conditions that helped preserve organized labor's position within the postrevolutionary governing coalition.

Chapter 6 also explores the impact of industrial change during this period on the ability of state-subsidized labor organizations to control rank-and-file worker participation. This analysis focuses particularly on union democratization in the automobile manufacturing industry in the 1960s and 1970s. Although the alliance between organized labor and Mexico's governing elite contributed to rapid economic growth, "official" labor confederations' dependence on state subsidies and their consequent organizational weakness in the workplace made some political controls over labor vulnerable to rank-and-file opposition movements. In the automobile industry, these movements overthrew entrenched union leaders and instituted democratic forms of union governance that significantly increased rank-and-file participation in union affairs and heightened worker control over different aspects of the production process. Government support for some opposition labor groups during this period helped consolidate democratic unionism in several automobile firms. However, the most important source of demands for union democratization was the transformation of workplace relations that accompanied the automobile industry's rapid expansion after the early 1960s (resulting, for example, in increased worker concentrations per firm and more conflictive workplace relations) and eroded traditional mechanisms of workplace political control. This chapter concludes by examining the impact of union democratization on variations over time in leadership turnover in elections, worker participation in union affairs, contract terms governing worker influence over the production process, and strikes and interunion alliance formation.

Chapter 7 analyzes the dual crisis that confronted Mexican workers in the 1980s: prolonged economic stagnation after 1982, and industrial restructuring in major public- and private-sector firms. It examines both the consequences of economic crisis for workers' welfare and the factors that shaped leading labor organizations' response to this challenge, including state administrative control over worker mobilization, labor organizations' continued dependence on state subsidies, weaknesses within the labor movement itself, and union leaders' political beliefs. This chapter also returns to the case of the automobile manufacturing industry in order to evaluate the impact of industrial restructuring in the 1980s on union organizations, workers' economic welfare, and opportunities for workplace participation. This discussion shows that the shift from import-substituting to export-oriented industrial production led transnational firms (with strong government support) to redefine the terms of worker-employer relations in the industry, placing enterprise- and plant-based democratic unionism on the defensive. The Confederation of Mexican Workers reemerged during this period as a key actor in controlling automobile workers' economic demands. Thus this analysis demonstrates that, even as developments during the 1980s weakened many labor organizations and seriously eroded the bases for the social pact that had existed since the 1950s, there remained strong reasons for the governing elite to preserve a political alliance with organized labor.

The concluding chapter in this book (chapter 8) examines the evolving character of the alliance between organized labor and the governing political elite in the late 1980s and early 1990s, focusing particularly on the relationship between labor politics and the prospects for democratic regime change in Mexico. During these years the "official" labor movement continued to support Mexico's authoritarian regime despite sustained efforts by the administration of Carlos Salinas de Gortari (1988–94) to limit labor's national influence. Rather than pushing for a democratic opening that might have increased labor's ability to resist more effectively unfavorable government economic policies, the Confederation of Mexican Workers and other labor groups opposed electoral and party reforms. Following an examination of the most important developments affecting organized labor during the Salinas administration, this chapter examines three sets of questions concerning labor politics and regime change in Mexico. First, to what extent did the character of Mexico's postrevolutionary authoritarian regime change during the 1980s and early 1990s? By focusing on changes in the configuration of Mexico's governing coalition, Salinas's effort to reformulate inherited political beliefs, and the roles of the "official" party and the state in a neoliberal era, this discussion shows that the legacies of postrevolutionary authoritarianism remained strong in Mexico in the early 1990s.

Second, what is the broader relationship between labor politics and democratic regime change in postrevolutionary contexts? The state-subsidized labor movement's opposition to political liberalization was a particularly distinctive aspect of the Mexican experience in the 1980s and early 1990s. Part of this concluding chapter examines the Mexican case in the context of recent scholarship on labor's role in democratic political transitions, showing that there are strong reasons why organized labor in postrevolutionary authoritarian regimes might resist some aspects of regime change. A brief overview of developments in Nicaragua and Russia in the late 1980s and early 1990s supports the view that, because of organized labor's distinctive position in postrevolutionary authoritarian regimes, the labor movement's role in the transition process is significantly different in these contexts than in other instances of democratic regime change.

Third, viewed from the vantage point of the early 1990s, how likely is it that the labor movement will emerge as an active proponent of democratization in Mexico? An analysis of the most important economic changes shaping the future strength of the labor movement (especially those affecting its size, composition, organizational strength, and bargaining effectiveness) and an assessment of labor's ties to opposition political parties offer little reason for optimism concerning organized labor's independent capability to promote regime democratization in Mexico. The greatest obstacle, however, lies in political restrictions on worker participation and strong state administrative control over worker-employer relations. The prospects for successful regime change would be considerably enhanced if the removal of state controls on labor participation occurred in conjunction with the democratization of the labor movement.

I CONSTRUCTING

THE POSTREVOLUTIONARY

MEXICAN REGIME

CHAPTER TWO

State Structures and Political Control: The Development of State Administrative Capacity in the Labor Sector

Centralized political power and active state intervention in socioeconomic affairs became hallmarks of the regime that took shape in the decades after Mexico's 1910–20 social revolution. The legal foundation for post-revolutionary governments' power and relative decision-making autonomy was the distribution of political authority in the 1917 federal constitution, which placed preeminent authority in the presidency and limited the powers of the legislative and judicial branches.[1] The governing elite justified this distribution of constitutional authority by asserting that strong executive leadership was necessary to guarantee the implementation of social reforms won during the revolution and to ensure the political stability required for national economic development.[2] The formation of an "official" party in 1929 further promoted centralized political control by containing intra-elite factionalism. Moreover, the "official" party's close ties to the federal executive after the mid-1930s, and its dominance in national electoral politics during subsequent decades, strengthened presidential control over the federal legislature and state governments.

The postrevolutionary state's involvement in socioeconomic affairs featured substantial capital investment in infrastructure projects, tariff and exchange rate policies designed to promote industrialization, and, especially after the 1930s, public ownership of several basic industries. Equally important, the state intervened directly to regulate the social relations of production. The 1917 federal constitution formally redefined the relationship between labor and capital by recognizing a wide range of political and social rights for workers, including the rights to form unions and to strike. But over time, postrevolutionary governments also developed the administrative capacity to regulate diverse aspects of worker-employer relations and to control different forms of labor participation. The gradual centralization of political control during and after the 1920s permitted the governing elite to extend state regulatory authority in the labor sector; in turn, more fully institutionalized state administrative capacity to mediate worker-employer interactions and control labor participation contributed significantly to the power and relative decision-making autonomy of the ruling political elite.

Institutionalized state regulation of the social relations of production was a departure from Porfirian principle and practice. Mexico's 1857 federal constitution formally offered workers the rights to strike and unionize by guaranteeing individuals the liberal freedoms to negotiate (Article 4) and withdraw from (Article 5) labor contracts and to form associations (Article 9). In practice, however, the Díaz regime's heavy reliance on foreign and domestic private investment to stimulate economic growth led it to discourage (and often repress) unions and strikes.[3] Although the Díaz government actively sought to win the support of important labor organizations, until 1906 it maintained an essentially laissez-faire position on the operation of labor markets and sought to avoid involvement in worker-employer disputes except to preserve public order.[4] Díaz broke precedent by arbitrating the disruptive and controversial Río Blanco textile strikes in 1906–7, and in the wake of the Cananea and Río Blanco confrontations, the government tolerated peaceful strikes and adopted a more conciliatory policy on labor matters in general.[5] This policy shift, however, did not lead to national legislation to address labor problems.[6] Thus the inclusion of Article 123 in the 1917 federal constitution, creating broad social rights for workers and legitimating active state intervention in labor affairs, marked a turning point in state-labor relations.

A state-centered analytic approach offers an important perspective from which to examine elite political control in postrevolutionary authoritarian regimes because it focuses attention on the form and function of state administrative structures, especially the extent to which public bureaucracies and legal requirements shape opportunities for mass participation. Governing elites' ability to employ the administrative apparatus and legal procedures to regulate different forms of mass participation ultimately rests on their superior control over the means of coercion, but successful mediation of mass demands through these channels makes resort to repression less necessary. State-centered analysis is especially useful in explaining the character of mass politics in postrevolutionary Mexico because state building and the growth of a national organized labor movement were interactive processes. On the one hand, expanded state administrative capacity gradually increased governing elites' ability to control developments in the labor sector.[7] On the other hand, legal recognition of basic labor rights and inclusion of worker representatives in some administrative structures strengthened organized labor by providing important symbolic and material benefits to both unions and individual workers.

In Mexico as elsewhere in Latin America, political elites sought to expand state administrative capacity in the labor sector as part of their struggle to address the crisis of participation that accompanied urban and industrial workers' entrance into the political arena during the first decades of the twentieth century. Yet the actual process of state building in response to these popular mobilization crises has been largely ignored.[8] Too often discussions of state capacity to regulate societal actors either *assume* that such capacity exists, or end with a brief account of administrative agencies' organizational evolution over time and a summary of the legal bases for government officials' authority over labor affairs. These elements are undoubtedly important. However, the study of state formation must also address the political process that gave particular shape to the administrative apparatus. It is especially important in this regard to focus on the struggles that occurred among different political forces over the state's organizational form and the ideas or philosophical conceptions that influenced and legitimated different political positions. Moreover, it is essential to consider the role that societal actors themselves played in the development of state administrative capacity, an issue not examined in the more general literature on state formation in Latin America.[9] Groups such as organized labor rarely (if ever) controlled this process, but at times they significantly influenced the outcome.

In postrevolutionary Mexico, the question of state regulatory authority over labor affairs became embroiled in political conflict and philosophical debate. Local political authorities, particularly state governors, opposed legislative initiatives to expand the federal government's legal jurisdiction at the expense of state and municipal rights because such legislation threatened to erode their own influence over labor and business matters. Similarly, employers strenuously objected to increased state involvement in worker-employer relations. These political struggles were embedded in longstanding philosophical controversies over the practical meaning of Mexican federalism and the extent to which government authorities should intervene to resolve social problems. Both the content of labor law and the organizational evolution over time of state administrative arrangements in the labor sector clearly reflected these tensions.

A significant portion of the organized labor movement viewed favorably the expansion of state administrative authority over labor affairs, although there were substantial differences of opinion among worker organizations concerning the precise form that state intervention should take. From the late nineteenth century onward, workers frequently appealed to government officials to mediate major worker-employer conflicts and to pressure employers to recognize unions, negotiate collective contracts, and ameliorate the broad range of economic and social problems confronting workers.[10] Labor's political and social agenda reflected the problems arising from industrialization and the formation of an urban-industrial working class, especially conflicts produced by employers' often coercive efforts to impose new work practices ("factory discipline") on a rural and artisan labor force.[11] The adoption of Article 123 in 1917 reinforced many workers' positive views concerning the efficacy of state action, although anarchosyndicalist groups continued into the 1920s to oppose this course. Most labor organizations, however, considered state involvement essential to implementing constitutionally mandated reforms at a time when their own overall negotiating weakness in the workplace left in doubt the realization of new social rights.[12]

It is important to emphasize that labor support for state activism was selective. Worker organizations frequently sought government action to force employers to recognize unions, sign collective contracts, and improve wages and working conditions, yet they opposed state regulation of union formation, union activities, and strikes. Organized labor lacked sufficient political influence to prevail in many of the debates that occurred during the 1920s and early 1930s over the appropriate scope of state action. Nevertheless, widespread labor support for increased state intervention in socioeconomic affairs was an important stimulus to the postrevolutionary expansion of state administrative capacity.

Some elements in the labor movement saw the expansion of state regulatory authority over worker-employer relations as an opportunity to maximize their own political advantage. For example, worker representation on conciliation and arbitration boards and minimum-wage commissions offered different labor organizations the institutionalized opportunity to participate directly in administering labor law and setting minimum wages. Labor unions considered such positions important for both symbolic and substantive reasons, and they competed vigorously with one another for influence in this arena. Thus the expansion and exercise of state capacity in the labor sector shaped the development of the labor movement itself in two ways: the postrevolutionary governing elite relied upon legal controls to regulate labor participation, and different worker organizations used their ties to the state administrative apparatus as a basis on which to expand their own influence within the labor movement.

This chapter analyzes state building in the labor sector after 1910, examining the political process through which the revolutionary commitment to social reform was translated into increased state administrative capacity and legal authority over labor affairs. Different presidential administrations established a variety of institutions to deal with such specific labor-related measures as minimum wages, health care, profit sharing, housing, and credit. The main focus here, however, is on the creation of those federal government agencies principally responsible for formulating and implementing labor policy (leading up to a separate Ministry of Labor and Social Welfare in 1940) and on *juntas de conciliación y arbitraje* (conciliation and arbitration boards). The organizational evolution of these administrative structures reflected the Mexican state's progressively more interventionist role in labor affairs as the organized labor movement gained greater national political importance. The second part of this chapter examines the origins and political significance of the legal controls that state officials exercise over different forms of labor participation (particularly union formation, union activities, and strikes), giving special attention to the influence that worker organizations had on the definition of state authority in these areas.

State Building in the Labor Sector

Two main trends characterized the postrevolutionary growth of state administrative capacity in the labor sector. First, administrative agencies' legal jurisdiction expanded over time as an increasingly broad array of labor-related activities came under their control. This reflected the federal government's response to a progressively more complex national economy and the growing power of the national organized labor movement, as well as the maturation of political beliefs advocating widespread state intervention in socioeconomic affairs as the hallmark of the modern state. Second, the administration of labor affairs became more centralized over time as the federal government extended its legal authority at the expense of state and municipal officials.

From the Department of Labor to the Ministry of Labor and Social Welfare

The early history of administrative agencies specifically concerned with labor affairs reflected considerable uncertainty regarding the appropriate nature and extent of state involvement in this area. During the early years of the revolution, most of the decrees and laws addressing labor problems were enacted at the local (that is, state) level. They included health and safety measures; regulations concerning work contracts, minimum wages, the formation of unions and other worker associations, and strikes; measures regulating working hours, workplace conditions, and worker housing; and provisions for the creation of specialized departments to administer labor matters at the municipal or state level.[13] The first federal legislation on industrywide wages and working hours, occupational health and safety standards, and government recognition of labor unions appeared in the form of a July 1912 decree regulating spinning and weaving mills.

Revolutionary governments adopted measures such as these in response to labor's increasing agitation for social reforms and national political leaders' recognition that state action was necessary to address the severe socioeconomic problems confronting rural and urban workers. However, the labor movement's overall organizational and political weakness at the time, and the consequent lack of concerted pressures for additional government policies to benefit workers, meant that the scope of legislative action was limited. As late as 1914–16, Venustiano Carranza had made only a very general commitment to introduce "legislation to improve the conditions of rural workers, employees, miners, and all proletarian classes." [14] The measures adopted usually addressed very specific problems (for example, regulations regarding a Sunday rest period in Mexico City and the payment of all wages in hard currency).

The first national offices specifically charged with overseeing labor activities were the Departamento del Trabajo (Department of Labor, created in December 1911 under the jurisdiction of the Ministry of Development, Colonization, and Industry) [15] and the Bolsa del Trabajo (Labor Exchange), a job-placement agency established under the jurisdiction of the Department of Labor in September 1914. The Department of Labor was principally concerned with collecting and publishing data concerning labor issues, an activity that itself signaled the growing political relevance of the urban working class. It was also legally empowered to mediate worker-employer conflicts and facilitate worker hiring, but in both instances the department could act only at the request of the workers and employers involved. Although its restricted legal authority and small support staff limited its impact, the department did become involved in a number of labor conflicts, often supporting labor organizations it considered moderate. In January–August 1912, for example, department officials mediated worker-employer negotiations to establish uniform wage rates and work rules in the cotton textile industry. The resulting agreement did not fully satisfy workers' demands (for example, it did not formally recognize workers' right to strike). However, it did raise wages, shorten working hours, and regulate working conditions and disciplinary procedures. [16]

The adoption of Article 123 at the 1916–17 Constitutional Convention marked a turning point regarding the scope of Mexican labor legislation and the role played by state administrative institutions responsible for overseeing labor affairs. Although the proposal that Carranza (in his capacity as leader of the Constitutionalist forces) submitted to the convention made labor legislation subject to federal jurisdiction, in substance it differed little from the brief provisions included in the reformed 1857 constitution in its simple reaffirmation of liberal guarantees of workers' individual contractual rights.[17] The proposal's supporters maintained that although specific measures regarding labor issues needed to be addressed in subsequent legislation, they should not be included as formal constitutional guarantees.[18]

More radical convention delegates rejected this position, arguing that in the past a similar approach to labor problems had produced no real improvement in workers' conditions. They favored a separate constitutional article that enumerated in detail measures to improve working conditions and safeguard workers' rights. The delegations from Veracruz and Yucatán were among the most vigorous supporters of special protection for workers' rights; these states' pre-1917 labor legislation was comparatively extensive, and their experiences in large part served as the model for Article 123.[19] With revolutionary political mobilization (including general strikes in Mexico City in May and July–August 1916) as a backdrop, convention delegates—only a few of whom were themselves workers or labor organizers[20]—approved a final text that addressed the principal issues on organized labor's political and socioeconomic agenda. These included working hours and workplace conditions, occupational health and safety, minimum wages and overtime pay, educational facilities for workers, labor unions and the right to strike, work contracts, labor conciliation and arbitration boards, and consumer cooperatives. Moreover, Article 123 authorized federal and state legislatures to enact labor laws "based on the needs of each region," in accordance with the general requirements it established.[21]

By defining a tutelary role for the state in labor affairs, Article 123 prompted further institutional innovation. In December 1917 a government decree established a separate Secretaría de Industria, Comercio y Trabajo (Ministry of Industry, Commerce, and Labor), and in January 1918 a Dirección de Trabajo (Labor Office) was organized under its jurisdiction. The ministry had responsibility for regulating worker and employer organizations, insurance companies, and strikes; overseeing industrial and commercial education; maintaining industrial statistics; and resolving problems arising in industry.[22]

Although Article 123 raised social reforms to the level of constitutional guarantees, the Constitutional Convention specifically rejected a proposal for exclusive federal jurisdiction over labor matters. Opponents of the proposal argued that state- and municipal-level authorities, operating within the general framework established by Article 123, were most capable of tailoring labor legislation to fit local conditions.[23] Delegates' caution in this regard certainly reflected their respect for the principle of federalism and the rights of states and municipalities, but it was also due to the power exercised by state governors and regional political bosses (many of whom were generals). Article 123's definition of social reforms as constitutional guarantees and its implied commitment to government action to ensure their implementation stood in philosophical contradiction with the preservation of states' rights, and over time the federal government greatly expanded its authority over labor affairs. But the distinction between federal and local (state-level) administrative jurisdiction remains a centerpiece of Mexican labor law.

In the short term, however, the Constitutional Convention's refusal to permit exclusive federal jurisdiction over labor matters produced serious political problems. Individual states enacted some ninety different laws and decrees between 1918 and 1928 to codify the provisions of Article 123.[24] Legal standards and institutional arrangements varied confusingly from state to state, and conflicts arose between federal and local authorities over who had responsibility for mediating particular strikes or contract negotiations. There were especially severe difficulties in economic activities (particularly railroad transportation) whose characteristics and geographical scope required the uniform application of legal norms. Moreover, employers in states such as Puebla and Veracruz often refused to abide by local labor laws, and some state governors resisted recognizing constitutionally guaranteed labor rights. These diverse problems encouraged labor organizations to press for unified federal labor legislation, but even with some employers supporting this position, the formal jurisdiction of the Ministry of Industry, Commerce, and Labor remained restricted to the Federal District and federal territories.[25]

In 1921 and again in 1922, federal legislators sympathetic to the labor movement introduced proposals to grant Congress the authority to enact a national labor code. These initiatives enjoyed the support of the increasingly influential Confederación Regional Obrera Mexicana (Mexican Regional Labor Confederation, CROM), but the Chamber of Deputies failed to approve them.[26] In late 1927 the CROM-affiliated legislators of the "Bloque Laborista" attempted, without success, to enact constitutional reforms placing labor matters under federal jurisdiction and to create a separate ministry of labor. The main stumbling block was Senate opposition.[27]

Although the CROM's legislative initiatives were hindered by conflict with the *agrarista* movement over CROM organizing activities in the countryside,[28] the principal obstacles to enacting a national labor law during these years were employers' opposition to more extensive state involvement in labor affairs and state governors' resistance to the expansion of federal administrative authority at their expense. Some employers recognized the advantages of a uniform labor code that would have regularized workplace relations, clarified jurisdictional issues, and reduced extreme regional variations in labor policies and wage rates. However, they resisted legislation that would have facilitated unionization and strengthened workers' collective rights. They were also bitterly opposed to state regulation of collective contracts and worker-employer bargaining.[29]

The power that the CROM wielded during the Obregón (1920–24) and Calles (1924–28) presidencies was a particular source of concern to both employers and local political authorities.[30] Luis N. Morones, the CROM's secretary-general, served as minister of industry, commerce, and labor between 1924 and 1928, a position he exploited to increase the CROM's membership and expand its influence in national labor affairs. Because of the CROM's alliance with Obregón and Calles and its political dominance within the organized labor movement, the ministry's actual impact on labor issues during this period considerably exceeded its formal authority. The enactment of a federal labor law at this time would in all likelihood have substantially increased the CROM's power. Because of the CROM's noted hostility toward rival worker organizations, concerns about its expanded influence may have tempered even some labor unions' support for a national labor code.

It is significant, then, that constitutional reforms permitting the federal legislature to pass laws based on Article 123 were not enacted until September 1929, at a time when the CROM's influence was in sharp decline.[31] The action came during the presidency of Emilio Portes Gil (1928–30), who as governor of Tamaulipas between 1925 and 1928 had vigorously resisted the expansion of CROM influence.[32] The 1929 reforms laid the constitutional basis for a federal labor code.

Nevertheless, the proposal for a federal labor law which the Portes Gil administration sent to the Chamber of Deputies in July 1929 went unapproved because it encountered stiff resistance from various labor and business organizations.[33] An earlier draft of what was known as the "Proyecto Portes Gil" (prepared in 1928 when Portes Gil was minister of the interior and president-elect) had been extensively debated at a special Worker-Employer Convention held in Mexico City between November 15 and December 8, 1928, a conference attended by all major labor organizations except the anarchosyndicalist Confederación General de Trabajadores (General Confederation of Workers). Yet despite some significant modifications in the proposed legislation as a result of convention debates, many labor organizations remained strongly opposed to the 1929 *proyecto*'s procedural restrictions on the right to strike and its prohibition against union involvement in political affairs.[34] Provisions such as these may have originated in the widespread perception that the CROM had abused its privileged position during the 1920s. Indeed, the ban on union political action may have been directed specifically against the CROM,[35] though it also reflected Portes Gil's more general conviction that union activities should be restricted to economic and social welfare issues.

The Mexican private sector, U.S. business interests in Mexico, and the U.S. government also vigorously opposed key elements in the Portes Gil initiative.[36] Mexican business interests opposed provisions compelling employers to negotiate collective contracts at the request of workers; the measure's recognition of a single union as the legal bargaining agent in a given workplace, creating a de facto closed or union shop; state regulation of contract terms; tripartite conciliation and arbitration boards' broad authority over worker-employer relations; provisions for government labor inspectors; the concept of industrywide collective bargaining agreements (the *contrato-ley*); and procedural safeguards for workers' right to strike. Employers were particularly opposed to provisions that limited their flexibility during a period of deepening economic recession and widespread plant closings. In general terms, they sought to maximize restrictions on union formation and the right to strike while minimizing union involvement in managerial decisions concerning the organization of production.

Despite its eventual defeat, the 1929 Portes Gil *proyecto* defined the major contours of the first federal labor law. The Ministry of Industry, Commerce, and Labor subsequently prepared a modified version of the code, and President Pascual Ortiz Rubio (1930–32) formally submitted it to the Chamber of Deputies on July 1, 1931. Labor groups—led by the Alianza de Agrupaciones Obreras y Campesinas de la República (Alliance of Mexican Worker and Peasant Organizations), formed by the most important national labor organizations to voice their concerns regarding the initiative—protested that some of the legislation's provisions were less favorable than those in either the 1929 Portes Gil *proyecto* or several state-level labor codes.[37] The CROM leadership, which apparently had told Ortiz Rubio that it would back the legislation, withdrew its support because its declining political position prevented its Partido Laborista Mexicano (Mexican Labor Party, PLM) deputies from controlling the outcome of the legislative debate. Labor organizations' overall lack of enthusiasm for the legislation (the first draft had been prepared under the direction of Aarón Sáenz, minister of industry, commerce, and labor and a prominent ally of Monterrey business interests) led the government to make some significant last-minute concessions to labor. One of the most important changes was the addition of a provision specifically legalizing "separation exclusion clauses" in collective contracts, which require an employer to dismiss any worker who loses his or her union membership.[38] These modifications intensified business opposition to the legislation.[39]

After brief (though at times spirited) debate, Congress enacted the proposed legislation on August 17, and it went into effect on August 28,

1931, as the Ley Federal del Trabajo. Since then, labor matters in Mexico have been regulated by a single federal law, although its application is the responsibility of both federal and local (state-level) administrators.[40]

The speed with which Congress acted on the measure in part reflected legislators' concern with containing the social conflict that Mexico experienced as a consequence of international economic depression.[41] An even more important factor, however, was former president Calles's vigorous support for the measure and his determination to win its approval despite business and labor opposition. Calles considered the legislation a key part of his efforts to expand labor support for the recently established Partido Nacional Revolucionario (Revolutionary National Party, PNR).[42] The political marginalization of the CROM left the government without a strong labor ally capable of mediating rank-and-file discontent, and the potential danger of radical labor mobilization made imperative policy measures designed to preserve workers' loyalty to the new political order while simultaneously institutionalizing state authorities' capacity to regulate worker-employer relations. From the perspective of the governing political elite, then, social legislation was a basis on which to mobilize mass support for the postrevolutionary regime, although the extent of labor opposition to the 1931 law limited the effectiveness of this strategy.

The enactment of a federal labor code was a milestone in the expansion of state administrative authority over labor affairs. It symbolized the maturation of postrevolutionary political beliefs advocating active state intervention in socioeconomic affairs. This philosophical view, already explicit in the 1917 constitution, rejected a traditional liberal, limited conception of the state's role and justified legislation designed to conciliate labor-capital interests. While recognizing the legitimate interests of business, it advocated state promotion of workers' welfare at a time when labor organizations themselves were too weak to guarantee the implementation of socioeconomic reforms.[43] The preamble to the Ortiz Rubio administration's 1931 legislative proposal articulated this position clearly:

> [L]abor legislation of a decidedly protectionist character is one of the essential elements of the spirit of our time. The individualist conception that bases labor relations in the free contract, in reality legitimating servitude under the appearance of equality between the contracting parties, has been replaced by a position that refuses to view labor relations as a simple exchange of two goods, labor and wages. On the contrary, [this new position] attributes primary importance to the human rights of the worker.[44]

Advocates of this view argued that the defining characteristics of the modern state were a coordinating role in labor affairs and the active mediation of social conflicts:

The modern state has been obliged . . . to expand the limits of its activities and to intervene in numerous different questions that were unknown at the beginning of the century. Among such issues one must include all those matters which concern labor, a virgin territory that is rife with the concerns and efforts of wage earners to improve their living conditions gradually and continually. As a result of a social dynamic based in an egoistic aversion to change, capitalists have ignored the proletarian elements of the world. With the appearance of sharp, dangerous conflicts produced by both of these social forces, governments had to intervene and assume postures that are at times conciliatory, at times frankly plutocratic, at times—as with us—openly pro-labor.[45]

Realizing this political and philosophical position depended upon expanding state administrative capacity in the labor sector. In particular, the growth of industry, the emergence of a national organized labor movement, and union tactics such as sympathy strikes called for state structures capable of dealing with labor problems that often involved large geographical regions or vital economic activities.[46] Although Calles had reorganized the Labor Office to increase its operational efficiency and expand its jurisdiction over conflicts affecting workers in the railroad, mining, petroleum, textile, and electrical power generation industries, it was incapable of handling the additional administrative responsibilities arising from the new federal labor law. Thus in December 1932 the government created a separate Departamento Autónomo del Trabajo (Autonomous Department of Labor) directly responsible to the federal executive. Its principal functions were to seek solutions to labor conflicts, oversee the enforcement of the new labor code, register labor and employer organizations, regulate and inspect work contracts, and develop a social welfare policy in the labor sector.[47]

The creation of the Secretaría del Trabajo y Previsión Social (Ministry of Labor and Social Welfare, STPS) in December 1940 elevated this office to cabinet rank. The legislative proposal submitted to Congress by President Manuel Ávila Camacho (1940–46) referred to the additional administrative demands resulting from the growth of labor unions and the state's need to address the responsibilities it had acquired because of its active role in promoting industrialization.[48] The key development in this regard was the unification of most major labor organizations in the Confederación de Trabajadores de México (Confederation of Mexican Workers, CTM) in 1936.

The Ministry of Labor and Social Welfare plays a key role in mediating worker-employer conflicts. Its responsibilities in this area are not as clearly articulated in statutory terms as in the case of tripartite labor conciliation and arbitration boards, but the ministry's position as the principal agency charged with implementing government labor policy logically makes it the focal point of negotiations in contract disputes and strikes. The ministry is expressly authorized to "coordinate workers' and employers' actions in order to prevent conflicts that could arise between both parties and, when such conflicts develop, to use its familiarity with them as the basis for proposing conciliatory solutions."[49] In 1957 the ministry established a special conciliation department and a series of regional labor offices to increase its effectiveness in handling federal-jurisdiction labor problems.[50] However, the STPS's participation in resolving labor disputes extends considerably beyond its role as "friendly conciliator." Top ministry officials are normally involved in resolving important conflicts, often with presidential supervision or participation. The STPS's role in this area not only exemplifies the Mexican state's active involvement in socioeconomic affairs, but the pattern of conflict resolution also reflects the considerable degree of administrative and political centralization that has characterized the postrevolutionary Mexican regime.

The STPS's responsibility for a broad range of social welfare activities evidences the postrevolutionary state's protectionist role in labor affairs. The social welfare provisions included in the original 1931 federal labor law were essentially an elaboration of the basic provisions of Article 123. In addition to regulating labor relations and contract conditions in general, the 1931 law established requirements for working hours, rest periods, and vacations; workplace conditions; minimum wages; work by women and minors; and occupational illnesses and accidents. Over time, the ministry expanded its social welfare functions on a number of fronts. In addition to its regular inspection and enforcement activities, the STPS administers programs concerning worker medical care and hygiene, consumer cooperatives, occupational health and safety measures, working conditions for women and minors, worker housing, and free legal defense for workers in labor-employer disputes. The size of the STPS bureaucracy grew as these social welfare activities expanded. Many social welfare programs do not involve large budgetary expenditures on the part of the STPS, but they require an active regulatory involvement in a variety of different activities.[51]

Specialized state administrative capacity grew with the expansion of federal jurisdictional authority over labor affairs.[52] Table 2.1 lists the increasingly wide range of economic activities that came under federal jurisdiction between 1929 and 1990. The complete listing is an impressive statement of the postrevolutionary Mexican state's interventionist role in socioeconomic affairs and the federal government's regulatory control over those industrial activities crucial to national economic development.[53]

TABLE 2.1   The Expansion of Federal Labor Jurisdiction, 1929–1990

1929[a]	1933	1940	1942	1962	1975	1978	1990
Railroads							
Federal-concession transportation							
Mining							
Hydrocarbons							
Marine and maritime zone activities							
	Textiles						
		Electrical power generation					
			Cinematographic industry				
			Rubber industry				
			Sugar industry				
			Companies or institutions operating under federal concession or contract, or operated directly or in decentralized form by federal government				

Petrochemicals	Automobile manufacturing	Glass industry	
Steel and metalworking[b]	Pharmaceutical industry	Tobacco processing	
Cement	Pulp and paper industry	Lime production	
	Vegetable oils, food processing industry	Wood processing	
	Bottling industry		Banking

Sources: For 1929–42, Remolina Roqueñi, *Evolución de las instituciones y del derecho del trabajo en México* (1976), 71; for 1962–90, *Diario Oficial de la Federación*, 21 Nov. 1962, 7 Feb. 1975, 9 Feb. 1978, 27 June 1990.

Note: The list of activities under federal labor jurisdiction is cumulative over the 1929–90 period.

[a] The federal government claimed jurisdiction over conflicts in the railroad, mining, petroleum, textile, and electrical power generation industries before 1929, encouraging state governments to forward such cases to the Secretaría de Industria, Comercio y Trabajo's Dirección de Trabajo for resolution. However, these activities did not formally come under federal labor jurisdiction until the dates shown.

[b] Metalworking includes the processing of ores, foundry activities, and the production of basic metal products.

Labor Conciliation and Arbitration Boards

The creation of conciliation and arbitration boards *(juntas de conciliación y arbitraje)* during and after the Mexican revolution was a significant political victory for labor. Their tripartite composition (labor, business, and government representatives) gives workers sectoral representation in the administration of labor justice, providing them with an important channel for the resolution of disputes outside the workplace. Moreover, by removing worker-employer conflicts from the judicial system and giving government officials a deciding role in their resolution, the organization of conciliation and arbitration boards increased the labor movement's ability to translate its growing political importance into workplace gains. Indeed, the boards' creation demonstrated how organized labor's entry into national politics, and the consequent shift in the terms of political legitimacy, caused the governing elite to reconfigure the administrative apparatus so as to create new institutional linkages between labor and the state. Both political struggles over the shape of the postrevolutionary state apparatus (including, for example, an intense debate over federal versus local jurisdiction over labor affairs) and the growing prominence of new conceptions of social justice were important in shaping the evolution of the boards' organizational structure and their role in mediating worker-employer conflicts.

Mexico's first conciliation and arbitration boards were established after the outbreak of revolution in 1910 as part of early labor legislation enacted at the local level. This legislation varied considerably with regard to the agencies charged with administering it, ranging from political bodies to civil courts to specially created administrative-judicial organizations. Four states—Coahuila, Jalisco, Veracruz, and Yucatán—set particularly important precedents by creating specialized administrative agencies outside the boundaries of the regular judicial system. These bodies included worker and employer representatives in their membership, and they had special jurisdiction over the implementation of labor legislation and the resolution of labor conflicts.[54] However, Yucatán's Consejo de Conciliación (Conciliation Council) and Comité de Arbitraje (Arbitration Committee) were probably the most direct antecedents to the boards adopted at the 1916–17 Constitutional Convention.[55] Not only did they provide workers and employers with direct representation in a tripartite conciliation and arbitration system, but they also had broad authority to enforce labor legislation. The Yucatán labor code specifically recognized the need to resolve labor conflicts "without resorting to the strike, which is always injurious to everyone's interests."[56]

Delegates to the Constitutional Convention adopted conciliation and arbitration boards in order to introduce social justice criteria into the administration of labor legislation and to moderate increasingly disruptive conflicts between workers and employers. Advocates of the system argued that labor issues had to be removed from the jurisdiction of conservative civil courts and that the dictates of practical knowledge should be applied in such matters.[57] José N. Macías, a delegate from Yucatán, forcefully stated this position:

> But in this discussion of the conciliation and arbitration boards' functions, it must be said—before going on—that in order to be effective these boards cannot be civil courts. If the boards do not resolve these extremely grave problems in the terms under discussion, they must judge according to the law, deciding according to the agreement made between the contracting parties. Because judges cannot depart from the law, they would find against the workers. In this way law courts instead of conciliation and arbitration boards would be essentially prejudicial to the laborer because they would never seek to conciliate the interests of labor and capital.[58]

The boards were to play an active conciliatory role in each case that came before them, proposing possible compromise solutions and working to avoid disruptive worker-employer conflicts rather than simply providing a legal resolution of the dispute.

Constitutional Convention delegates were much less precise, however, regarding the organizational form and jurisdiction that these boards would have.[59] The principle of state mediation of labor conflicts was clearly established when an early proposal for the boards' joint worker-employer composition was rejected in favor of tripartite representation. The boards had authority over municipal-level minimum-wage and profit-sharing commissions, a supervisory role in strikes and lockouts, and a conciliatory role in worker-employer conflicts.[60] But such issues as whether the boards would operate on a permanent or ad hoc basis, and whether their decisions were legally binding, were not resolved. The decision not to legislate on these matters reflected convention delegates' commitment to preserving the autonomy of individual states to formulate labor legislation, as well as their intention to make the junta system as responsive as possible to local conditions.[61]

However worthy their intentions, convention delegates' failure to resolve questions regarding the jurisdiction and authority of conciliation and arbitration boards produced a long series of legal battles. In the absence of a federal labor law codifying Article 123, a number of states created local boards in accordance with the article's clause 20. In most cases the boards functioned as the court of last resort in conflicts over which they had jurisdiction, and they heard both individual and collective labor disputes.[62]

The Supreme Court, however, ruled that clauses 20 and 21 of Article

123 only provided for nonbinding conciliation and arbitration by tripartite boards. Although clause 20 stipulated that worker-employer conflicts must be submitted to such boards, clause 21 listed the penalties incurred if either workers or employers failed to submit their differences to arbitration or refused to accept the boards' decisions—implying that workers or employers could, in fact, fail to honor the specific terms of these decisions.[63] Nor would the Supreme Court allow the boards to handle individual worker grievances; it limited their jurisdiction to collective conflicts ("conflicts between capital and labor"). Between 1918 and 1924 the court handed down a number of decisions that restricted the jurisdiction and authority of local-level boards, arguing that the conflicts involved could only be definitively resolved by the appropriate civil courts because the conciliation and arbitration boards themselves had no binding authority.[64]

In 1924 the Supreme Court reversed its previous findings and declared that decisions by conciliation and arbitration boards were binding if the corresponding local legislation so provided.[65] The court's ruling acknowledged the resistance of local-level boards (especially in Puebla, Querétaro, and Veracruz) to its earlier efforts to limit their power.[66] However, the court's reversal also reflected pressures from labor organizations. Despite stiff opposition from employers, unions lobbied vigorously in the years after 1917 for the creation of conciliation and arbitration boards throughout the country.[67] Indeed, the Supreme Court's decision may have been Obregón's reward to the CROM for its invaluable support during Adolfo de la Huerta's armed revolt in 1923–24.[68]

The Supreme Court's action laid the basis for a significant expansion of federal authority over labor affairs in key industries. In September 1927 Calles established by decree a Junta Federal de Conciliación y Arbitraje (Federal Conciliation and Arbitration Board, JFCA) and subsidiary Juntas Regionales de Conciliación (Regional Conciliation Boards) under the jurisdiction of the Ministry of Industry, Commerce, and Labor.[69] A legislative proposal to establish federal jurisdiction over labor conflicts in federal zones, industries operating under federal concession (railroad transportation, mining, and petroleum production), and labor disputes involving two or more states had been under discussion since October 1926, but the Senate refused to approve the initiative. Calles was prompted to act by the 1927 strike by the Confederación de Transportes y Comunicaciones (Confederation of Transport and Communications Workers, the dominant and strongly anti-CROM railroad worker organization) against Ferrocarriles Nacionales de México, the country's most important railroad company. When the Supreme Court ruled that the Ministry of Industry, Commerce, and Labor (headed by Luis N. Morones, whose efforts to expand CROM influence among railroad workers had met with stiff resistance throughout the 1920s) lacked authority to declare the strike illegal, Calles created the JFCA to resolve the conflict. The Federal Conciliation and Arbitration Board's first action was to declare the strike illegal.[70]

Calles's action, probably taken in response to CROM demands, remained of questionable legality until the passage of the necessary constitutional reforms in 1929. Nevertheless, his initiative effectively resolved the question of federal jurisdiction over labor matters and helped open the way for subsequent enactment of a federal labor law. The Ministry of the Interior's 1928 labor code proposal, which included a fully elaborated junta system, was the first attempt to unify the diverse organizational forms and procedural criteria that characterized different conciliation and arbitration boards established by state legislatures after 1917. Although the system outlined in the 1928 *proyecto* later underwent some modifications,[71] the proposal defined the basic structure of a national conciliation and arbitration board system.

Despite the expansion of federal government authority over labor matters in these years, initial legislative proposals for a national conciliation and arbitration board system continued to safeguard state and municipal prerogatives in the administration of labor justice. For example, Portes Gil's 1929 labor code *proyecto* established under the jurisdiction of the Ministry of Industry, Commerce, and Labor an elaborate, multitiered junta system that carefully balanced local and federal jurisdictional control. At the workplace level, the project provided for the voluntary formation of worker-employer commissions *(comisiones mixtas de empresa)* to study new production methods, oversee the implementation of occupational health and safety measures, and maintain general order and discipline.[72] At the municipal level, the proposal called for the ad hoc creation of tripartite conciliation boards in both local- and federal-jurisdiction industries as labor conflicts arose. They came under the direct control of municipal *(municipio)* authorities, with the municipal president or his representative presiding over the board. At the top of the system, the *proyecto* established a tripartite National Labor Council (composed of labor and business representatives and several cabinet ministers) to examine and issue recommendations on such subjects as occupational training, minimum wages, and industrywide collective contracts.[73]

Subsequent legislative proposals both simplified the junta system and considerably reduced the importance of municipal and state-level authorities in the administration of labor justice. The March 1931 proposal prepared by the Ministry of Industry, Commerce, and Labor, as well as the federal labor law enacted later that year, eliminated the National Labor Council. Workers and employers could still organize enterprise-level mixed commissions, but these bodies played a less important role in the conciliation and arbitration system as a whole. A representative appointed by local civil authorities headed each municipal conciliation board, but in contrast to the 1929 Portes Gil proposal, this individual could no longer be the municipal president. Nor could the board president any longer name the other board representatives if workers and employers failed to do so. Federal conciliation authorities received exclusive jurisdiction over disputes arising in federal-jurisdiction industries.

Thus after 1931 the conciliation and arbitration system consisted of municipal conciliation boards in local-jurisdiction economic activities, operating under the supervision of Juntas Centrales de Conciliación y Arbitraje in state capitals; federal-jurisdiction conciliation boards; and a national Federal Conciliation and Arbitration Board with special divisions (*juntas especiales*) for different federal-jurisdiction industries.[74] The revised federal labor law adopted in 1970 left this structure unchanged, although the Juntas Municipales de Conciliación and the Juntas Centrales de Conciliación y Arbitraje were renamed, respectively, Juntas Locales de Conciliación and Juntas Locales de Conciliación y Arbitraje.[75] In 1978 the government established Juntas Federales Especiales in each state capital to decentralize the JFCA's work. In the early 1990s there were sixteen *juntas especiales* (some with a separate branch to accommodate a particularly large volume of cases) operating in Mexico City with authority over different federal-jurisdiction economic activities, as well as Juntas Federales Especiales in state capitals.[76]

One of the most noteworthy features of the Mexican conciliation and arbitration system is that, despite greater centralization of political and administrative decision making in Mexico since the 1920s, it preserves the distinction between federal and local jurisdictions. Labor organizations such as the Confederation of Mexican Workers have long criticized this arrangement, arguing that local-level juntas are subject to political manipulation by governors and regional business elites.[77] Because the principal source of the CTM's influence has been its alliance with the national political elite, and because its organizational strength varies considerably from one state to another, the "federalization" of the labor justice system would benefit the CTM and other national labor confederations. However, placing labor matters under the exclusive jurisdiction of the federal government would significantly curtail state governors' administrative authority and political power, further eroding Mexican federalism.[78] In December 1981, President José López Portillo (1976–82) submitted to Congress a reform of Article 123 which would have given the federal government exclusive authority to administer labor law. Congress approved the measure, but not surprisingly, it failed to win ratification by the required number of state legislatures.[79]

Tripartite conciliation and arbitration boards represent the postrevolutionary Mexican state's formal, routinized intervention in labor-capital relations. They are responsible for legally registering labor unions organized in local-jurisdiction economic activities (the Ministry of Labor and Social Welfare registers unions in federal-jurisdiction activities), and in both local- and federal-jurisdiction industries, collective labor agreements have legal standing only after they are deposited with conciliation and arbitration boards. Juntas also enforce a variety of specific legal requirements regarding collective labor contracts, workplace conditions, minimum wages, and so forth. Moreover, they have responsibility for investigating and approving a firm's request for contract modifications, wage cuts, or personnel reductions when economic conditions threaten the viability of the enterprise. This authority has at times placed conciliation and arbitration boards at the center of major political conflicts, including the worker-employer disputes leading up to state expropriation of the petroleum industry in 1938 and the government's economic reorganization of Ferrocarriles Nacionales de México in 1948–49.[80]

One of the junta system's most important functions is to resolve individual and collective labor disputes.[81] Whether the boards constitute a compulsory arbitration system remains a matter of legal interpretation. Parties in dispute can seek a solution under the auspices of a privately chosen arbiter,[82] but Article 123 and federal labor law interpret the employer's or the worker's failure to appear before a junta when cited in a grievance (or to be bound by its decision) as equivalent to an admission of guilt.[83] In practice, the boards are the principal mechanism for the resolution of individual worker grievances not settled privately by the parties in dispute. In the case of strikes, the boards are charged with seeing that strike petitions satisfy both the substantive and procedural requirements listed by federal labor law.

Because of their broad legal authority and the opportunity that their tripartite structure offers worker representatives to participate in the administration of labor law, labor organizations have historically attached great importance to the operation of conciliation and arbitration boards. Control over worker representation on the boards permits major labor organizations an opportunity to influence the union registration process in local-jurisdiction economic activities and to shape the boards' evolving interpretation of labor law. Such control is particularly important where the industry jurisdiction of a particular junta (that is, the industry or industries over which it has authority) permits an individual industrial union or a particular labor confederation to choose the labor representative, thus increasing the odds that the junta's decisions will reflect the union's interests even in such matters as individual worker grievances.

For these reasons, elections to select worker representatives to serve on local- and federal-jurisdiction juntas are often hotly contested by rival unions or by competing groups within the same union.[84] At times unions have selected as their candidates individuals of considerable political and administrative experience. In 1950, for example, railroad workers' elected representatives to the JFCA included David Vargas Bravo (a key figure in the formation of the Mexican Railroad Workers' Union, former secretary-general of the union's powerful Section 16 in Mexico City, and later secretary-general of the national union and a federal senator for the governing Institutional Revolutionary Party) and José Luis Vergara (a member of the union's national executive committee and director of the union newspaper, *Unificación Ferroviaria*).[85]

Control over the labor positions on conciliation and arbitration boards has at times been of great political significance. For example, the CROM's control over juntas in the Federal District (Morones's position as minister of industry, commerce, and labor permitted the CROM to control the designation of both government *and* labor representatives) and several key states during the mid-1920s was an important basis for increasing its organizational strength.[86] When the CROM fell from official favor after 1928, the Portes Gil administration removed the confederation's representatives from the Federal Conciliation and Arbitration Board[87] and used conciliation and arbitration boards' regulatory powers to attack it. During this same period, Fidel Velázquez (later the longtime secretary-general of the Confederation of Mexican Workers) and his allies used control over labor representation on state-level conciliation and arbitration boards (and thus the authority to determine which unions would receive official recognition and which strikes would be declared legal) to expand their organizational base within the labor movement. For example, Velázquez and his closest collaborators (including Fernando Amilpa, Alfonso Sánchez Madariaga, Luis Quintero, and Jesús Yurén) maintained direct control over key positions on conciliation and arbitration boards in the Federal District.[88] In subsequent years the CTM sought to coordinate actions by its junta representatives so as to maximize the confederation's administrative influence.[89]

Legal Restrictions on Labor Participation

In addition to creating specialized state institutions in the labor sector, postrevolutionary governments responded to the challenge of labor mobilization by enacting a complex body of labor law addressing both substantive and procedural matters. Labor law guarantees many political and social rights for workers, but it prohibits unions from engaging in some activities (including, for example, participating in religious affairs and owning profit-making enterprises).[90] More generally, juridical norms articulated by labor law establish the parameters for state-labor-business interactions in such areas as the negotiation of work contracts, worker participation in enterprise profits, the regulation of workplace health and safety, the setting of minimum wages and some fringe benefits, and the resolution of different kinds of labor conflicts. The terms of labor law also shape the structure of different worker organizations and their relationship with the state.

The federal labor code, enacted in 1931 and substantially revised in 1970, is the most important legislation of its kind. It defines in considerable detail the character of individual and collective labor contracts, including the legal obligations of workers and employers; requirements for working hours and working conditions, wages, and enterprise-level employee profit sharing; compensation for different kinds of work-related injuries and health problems; and the responsibilities of state labor authorities and the operation of specialized administrative agencies in the labor sector. The labor code also contains separate legal regulations for different categories of workers, including public service employees in federal zones, high-level administrative employees *(empleados de confianza),* railroad and other transportation workers, ship and airplane crew members, hotel and restaurant employees, medical students in specialized residence training, employees of universities and other legally autonomous institutions of higher education, professional athletes, actors and musicians, domestic servants, and so forth. The tradition of special legislation applying to different categories of workers dates from the 1900–1916 period of individual state labor codes, but in some cases separate legal regulations were adopted to resolve particular political problems.[91]

The most important example of this phenomenon is special legal regulations for government employees. Since the adoption of the 1917 constitution, workers employed by government agencies have come under the jurisdiction of a separate body of administrative law.[92] Early proposals for a federal labor law placed government employees (other than elected public officials) under its jurisdiction, but the final legislation adopted in 1931 excluded them. Special statutes governed public employees between 1938 and December 1960, when Article 123 was amended to include a special section (Apartado "B") regulating federal government employees and Department of the Federal District workers.[93] The provisions of this section substantially restrict government employees' rights to form unions and to strike. Moreover, military and public security personnel, foreign service employees, high-level administrative personnel, and bank employees were excluded from the normal provisions of Article 123 (Apartado "A").[94]

The political control that the postrevolutionary governing elite has exercised over the organized labor movement does not depend exclusively on the provisions of federal labor law. Nevertheless, by structuring the rules of

state-labor interaction, the labor code does establish the legal authority and
the institutional parameters that permit state officials to exercise political
control over different forms of labor participation. This section examines
the origin and political significance of legal restrictions on three broad categories of labor participation: union formation, internal union activities,
and strikes.

Restrictions on Union Formation

Mexican labor law imposes a number of restrictions on the formation of
unions. They may be formed without prior authorization, and membership
is formally voluntary. However, a union has no legal right to represent
workers, negotiate a collective contract with an employer, or engage in
other activities such as strikes until it is officially registered. Unions in
local-jurisdiction economic activities must be officially recognized by Juntas Locales de Conciliación y Arbitraje; the Ministry of Labor and Social
Welfare's Registro de Asociaciones (Associational Registry) has the authority to register unions in federal-jurisdiction industries, as well as all
labor federations and confederations.[95] Registration procedures are in principle relatively straightforward, but in practice they are subject to political
influence and purposeful delay.

The criteria for union registration, originally set in the 1931 federal
labor code, have not significantly changed: unions must have a minimum of
twenty members (a significant membership threshold given the very small
average number of employees per workplace at the time the first federal
labor law was enacted), all of whom must be at least fourteen years of age,
and the union must submit to the appropriate authorities notarized copies
of the minutes from its organizational assembly and the meeting at which
the union leadership was elected, a list of members' names and addresses
(as well as the name and address of the employer), and the union's statutes.
Registration petitions may be rejected if any of these requirements is not
met, and the registering agency may cancel a union's registration at any
time it ceases to fulfill these various conditions. (Similar requirements govern the registration of labor federations and confederations.) Labor law
also defines the purposes for which unions may be formed ("the study,
improvement, and defense of members' interests"), their legal obligations,
the minimum content of union statutes, and the specific kinds of unions
that may be organized.[96]

As with many other provisions of the 1931 federal labor law, the mandatory union registration requirement originated in a state labor code promulgated during the revolutionary period.[97] The 1918 Veracruz labor law
required unions to submit their statutes and other documentation as a

condition for their "inscription" by municipal authorities,[98] and a similar provision appeared in all drafts of a federal labor code after 1928. The main issue in debates preceding the passage of the 1931 law was how to reconcile this requirement with the broad freedom of association guaranteed in the 1917 constitution. The argument that eventually prevailed was that, because a union's right to negotiate a contract with an employer and engage in other activities might potentially affect the welfare of other individuals, the state has authority to establish minimum conditions for its formation and to regulate its legal status.[99]

The mandatory registration requirement drew only limited protest from labor organizations themselves. At the 1928 Worker-Employer Convention convened to debate an early draft of the federal labor law, CROM and railroad worker delegates criticized the state's involvement in union affairs. They argued that it was appropriate for public authorities to record basic information about unions, but that it was unacceptable for the state either to require official recognition *(reconocimiento)* as a precondition to a union's legal existence or to permit the cancellation of a union's registration.[100] The CROM's negotiating leverage was weaker in late 1928 than in previous years because of its declining national political fortunes, yet labor representatives in the Chamber of Deputies raised no objection to this provision in the debates preceding final approval of the 1931 federal labor law.

Rather, labor representatives' principal concern was to secure provisions that would strengthen nascent labor organizations vis-à-vis employers. Recognition by the state would enhance unions' bargaining leverage. The enactment of a federal labor law also served organized labor's broad interests by placing many issues under federal jurisdiction, thus eliminating often contradictory state-level labor codes and the obstacles they had posed to the formation of national unions. More specifically, there appears to have been an implicit quid pro quo between labor's willingness to accept state regulation of union formation and the adoption of provisions such as that requiring employers to give priority in hiring to unionized workers.[101]

State regulation of union formation has a double significance in Mexican politics. On the one hand, legal recognition of unions as legitimate social actors strengthens workers' position vis-à-vis both employers and politicians. Yet the institutionalized capacity to regulate association also enhances state control over labor. Even though legislation enacted during and after the revolution required entrepreneurs to join national business associations,[102] postrevolutionary governments' commitment to active private-sector participation in a mixed economy has meant that these rules have rarely been applied as restrictively as those concerning union formation. Moreover, because organization is a more important source of workplace bargaining leverage for workers than for employers, state controls on association are in practice a more significant restraint on labor's ability to influence political and economic decision making than they are for business. The state's authority to deny (or reward) registration to an affiliated union thus constitutes an important potential constraint on the activities of major labor confederations.

Restrictions on Internal Union Activities

Although most labor organizations accepted state regulation of union formation without evident protest, much greater controversy surrounded early legislative proposals for state monitoring of union activities. Labor delegates to the 1928 Worker-Employer Convention vigorously opposed state intervention in unions' internal affairs. In the words of a CROM representative, "[State] intervention in internal union affairs is equivalent to [state] intervention in the private life of the family. . . . [W]e can neither desire nor accept that the state preside at our table, in our home, nor that it preside over our union assemblies or usurp the right of union members to call to account the authorities they have designated."[103] Although several labor organizations accepted the need to provide some public accounting of their activities, they were especially concerned about provisions in the 1928 Ministry of the Interior *proyecto* that narrowly defined appropriate union goals, banned union involvement in political activities, and required unions to provide regular reports to government labor authorities on the use of members' dues.[104] Organized labor was initially unsuccessful in opposing the ban on union involvement in political activities (Article 249 (i) was finally removed from the federal labor code at the behest of President Lázaro Cárdenas in November 1940), but labor protests did lead to the elimination of a specific financial reporting requirement for unions. Instead, the 1929 Portes Gil *proyecto* and the 1931 federal labor code (Article 250) required union officials to report publicly to their members on the use of union funds at least once every six months.

The federal labor code contains a number of other provisions designed to ensure orderly conduct in internal union affairs and the accountability of union leaders to their members.[105] Unions prepare their own statutes and internal regulations, freely elect their officers, and formulate their plans of action. However, the labor code stipulates the minimum content of union statutes (they must, for example, specify the organization's overall goals, conditions for admitting new members, and the rights and obligations of members), and it requires that a union's statutes indicate how general assemblies are convened and what proportion of the total membership constitutes a quorum. Federal labor law devotes particular attention to provisions in union statutes concerning the expulsion of union members, requiring that a union general assembly be convened for this purpose, that the individual facing expulsion have an opportunity to present his or her defense, and that the basis for expulsion be specified in the union's statutes.

Despite the labor code's formal support for representative union democracy, several provisions grant union leaders substantial authority vis-à-vis rank-and-file members. For example, federal law does not require that union elections or internal decisions be taken by secret ballot.[106] Union statutes stipulating that elections be held in an open general assembly (thereby making political dissidence more visible, and perhaps more risky), or those that centralize union governance and erect significant obstacles to rank-and-file challenges, have the force of law once they are approved by federal labor authorities or local conciliation and arbitration boards. Similarly, federal labor law permits one-third of a union's members to convene a general assembly if, ten days following their request, the union's leadership fails to do so. However, the legal quorum for an assembly convened under these circumstances is two-thirds of the total membership.[107] This higher quorum requirement (it is normally 51 percent) constitutes a significant obstacle to the mobilization of internal opposition against an entrenched union leadership.

At the same time, some provisions of the federal labor code invite state intervention in internal union affairs. Unions are required to provide state labor authorities with reports on their activities upon request, "so long as [such requests] refer exclusively to their actions as unions" (Article 377 [I]). Specifically, unions must report within ten days to the appropriate state labor authority any change in their leadership or statutes, and they must report changes in union membership every three months (Article 377). Unions do not always fulfill these obligations, but their failure to do so may provide state authorities with the grounds on which to undertake investigations or disciplinary actions against dissident labor organizations.[108] Moreover, government officials may charge irregularities in union elections in order to create a pretext for failing to acknowledge a duly elected union leadership, particularly when opposition groups have successfully challenged progovernment union officials. This is but one of many ways in which state labor authorities can, depending upon the circumstances, manipulate legal requirements to achieve their political goals.

Restrictions on Labor Strikes

Legal restrictions on strikes are the most important formal controls that Mexican state authorities maintain on labor participation. Workers' political demands before the revolution often centered on the right to strike, and labor organizations considered legal recognition of this right in the 1917 constitution to be a crucial achievement. Yet in Mexico as elsewhere, employees' right to suspend work in support of economic or political goals has always been legally constrained. For example, the Federal District's 1871 penal code established the death penalty for workers participating in strikes that damaged property or caused physical injuries or death.[109] Article 123 (clause 18) of the 1917 constitution specified the purposes for which workers could strike ("to achieve equilibrium among the diverse factors of production, harmonizing the rights of labor with those of capital"), required that public service employees give ten days' notice to the appropriate conciliation and arbitration board before suspending work, and prohibited strikes when the majority of workers involved engage in violent acts against persons or property.[110] As indicated by Calles's creation of the Federal Conciliation and Arbitration Board to settle a railroad strike in 1927, the postrevolutionary governing elite's drive to develop state administrative capacity in the labor sector was closely linked to the political and economic challenges posed by major strikes.

In the debates preceding enactment of a federal labor law, no issue provoked greater controversy among worker and employer organizations than the appropriate scope of restrictions on workers' constitutionally guaranteed right to strike. Although the 1928 Ministry of the Interior *proyecto* protected worker interests by preventing employers from hiring replacement workers while a legal strike was in progress,[111] it placed very tight procedural controls on strikes. For example, a legal strike required the support of two-thirds of the employees in a given workplace and could only begin twenty-four hours after all conciliation efforts had concluded. If a junta's arbitration decision favored the employer, the existing labor contract was automatically suspended—a very significant disincentive to strike.[112] Despite strong support from employers for such restrictions, outraged protests by the CROM and other major labor organizations at the 1928 Worker-Employer Convention caused the Portes Gil administration to alter substantially these provisions. The 1929 Portes Gil *proyecto* (as well as the 1931 labor code draft) permitted strikes when supported by a majority of employees, declared that conciliation efforts would not postpone the scheduled start of a strike, and eliminated earlier provisions granting juntas broad authority to modify contract terms.[113] Yet despite these more favorable terms, labor organizations continued to oppose anything but minimal procedural limitations on the right to suspend work in support of their demands. For their part, the government officials responsible for negotiating the 1931 federal labor code considered restrictions on strikes to be their greatest success in limiting the labor movement's power.[114]

The federal labor code does, in fact, significantly restrict the type, frequency, and duration of strikes. These restrictions are principally of two kinds. First, labor law limits the nature and objectives of legal *(existente)* strikes to the suspension of work to achieve specified objectives.[115] Permissible objectives include securing an "equilibrium" between labor and capital; signing or revising a collective labor contract or an industrywide labor agreement; enforcing the terms of an existing collective contract, industrywide labor agreement, or profit-sharing legislation; and renegotiating contractually specified wages. An officially recognized union (but not an informal coalition of workers) may also suspend work in support of another legally approved strike, although this has rarely occurred in Mexico.[116]

Second, strikes are officially recognized as legal only if they fulfill various procedural requirements. The strike must be supported by the majority of workers employed in a given company or work center, and workers must present to the employer and the appropriate conciliation and arbitration board six days (ten days in the case of public service employees)[117] before suspending work a formal petition *(emplazamiento)* that specifies the goals and time of the strike action. The junta may not act on the petition if it fails to fulfill stipulated substantive and procedural requirements or if it is presented by a union that does not hold legal title to the collective contract or industrywide labor agreement in an enterprise or economic activity in which one already exists. Parties to the conflict must accept conciliation efforts by the appropriate junta, and within seventy-two hours after the suspension of work, the parties involved or an interested third party may request that the conciliation and arbitration board declare the strike nonexistent *(inexistente)*.[118] Should the board rule the strike nonexistent, striking employees are required to return to work within twenty-four hours; if they fail to do so, the employer is legally permitted to hire replacement workers. Should the board declare a strike illegal *(ilícita)* in cases in which the majority of strikers are engaged in violent acts, employees involved in such acts automatically lose their jobs.

These requirements offer both employers and state labor officials opportunities to block strikes. For example, by alleging that a majority of employees do not support a strike, an employer may win junta approval for a recount. The delay involved may permit the employer to undermine worker support for the strike action. Similarly, government officials may find various technical pretexts for a conciliation and arbitration board to declare a strike nonexistent. This is a common occurrence in politically sensitive or economically disruptive strikes.

Organized labor has long protested legal restrictions on the right to strike. For example, the Confederation of Mexican Workers' 1936 statutes specifically committed the organization to fighting for the unrestricted right to strike. In order to defend this principle, the CTM supported a strike by railroad workers in 1936 that had been declared *inexistente* by the Federal Conciliation and Arbitration Board.[119] Yet labor opposition of this kind did not achieve its purpose. Indeed, during World War II the government significantly tightened procedural requirements on strike petitions, imposed fines on individuals engaging in unauthorized work stoppages *(paros),* and set severe penalties (large fines and prison sentences of up to two years) for workers engaging in acts of "moral or physical violence or coercion" during strikes.[120]

Conclusion

State building and labor mobilization during and after the Mexican revolution were interactive historical processes. The creation of new institutions to mediate labor-capital relations was an important element in the construction of the postrevolutionary state. Because of labor's growing importance as an ally and the influence of revolutionary ideas advocating economic redistribution and social justice, key national political leaders strived to develop the administrative capacity to effect significant socioeconomic reforms at a time when most workers' organizational weakness in the workplace limited their negotiating leverage vis-à-vis employers. Local and regional political interests and most employers vigorously opposed the expansion of federal legal jurisdiction and state administrative capacity, a struggle whose consequences are still evident in the form of divided federal and state-level authority over the administration of labor law. Yet by the early 1940s, state intervention in labor-capital relations was fully institutionalized.

The gradual centralization of political power during and after the 1920s permitted Mexico's governing elite to extend state regulatory authority in the labor sector. At the same time, increased state administrative capacity to regulate worker-employer conflicts and the social relations of production significantly strengthened the position of national decision makers by expanding their opportunities to control different forms of labor participation. Legal restrictions on union formation, some union activities, and strikes are only the most prominent examples of the ways in which postrevolutionary governments have employed juridical norms to shape the structure of different labor organizations, their relationship with the state, and the permissible boundaries of labor action. Restrictions such as these have proved particularly significant during political and economic crises when the governing political elite has sought to redefine the terms of its alliance with organized labor.

Although organized labor lacked sufficient influence to prevail in many of the struggles that occurred during and after the revolution over the appropriate extent of state involvement in labor-capital relations, labor support was a crucial stimulus for expanded state intervention in this area. Moreover, even at a time of considerable labor movement fragmentation, worker organizations won important concessions in federal labor code provisions concerning strikes and the supervision of union finances. The enactment of legal controls on such forms of labor participation as union formation, union activities, and strikes certainly proved to be a major restraint on labor's political autonomy. Nevertheless, workers benefited substantially from many other aspects of federal labor legislation and from such institutional innovations as tripartite conciliation and arbitration boards. Most significant, labor's success in winning recognition of basic social rights and an institutionalized presence within the state apparatus established the organized labor movement as a key force in Mexico's postrevolutionary governing coalition.

Understanding the institutional and legal framework for state-labor interaction in Mexico is essential for analyzing the character of political controls on labor in the postrevolutionary period. Yet an examination of the development of state administrative capacity in the labor sector and legal restrictions on key aspects of labor participation is in itself insufficient. Chapter 3, therefore, focuses on the ways in which the governing elite has employed state capacity to structure the legal bases of union control in the workplace and to direct financial and political rewards to favored labor organizations. This discussion emphasizes the ways in which legal provisions and institutional arrangements strengthened the political position of progovernment labor leaders, thereby helping to transform major labor organizations into important mechanisms of political control over rank-and-file workers. Chapter 5 evaluates the actual impact over time of political control exercised through state administrative structures on labor strikes, union formation, and individual worker demands.

CHAPTER THREE

The Challenge of Mass Participation and the Origins of Mexico's State-Subsidized Labor Movement

Organized labor's entry into national politics was among the most significant consequences of Mexico's 1910–20 social revolution.[1] Worker participation in the revolutionary struggle legitimated new roles for labor. Although urban and industrial workers contributed politically and militarily to the Constitutionalists' eventual victory, the emerging labor movement proved even more vital to postrevolutionary governments' efforts to expand their base of mass support—a crucial test of the legitimacy of a regime born of revolution. In the early 1920s unionized workers still represented a very small proportion of the economically active population. But at a time when military force was the principal currency of national politics and other social forces remained largely unorganized, unionized workers' capacity either to mobilize support for the new regime or to oppose it by disrupting key economic activities gave the labor movement political importance disproportionate to its size.

The potential power of a politically independent labor movement constituted a major challenge for the postrevolutionary leadership. In addition to expanding the state's administrative capacity to regulate worker-employer relations and control the most important forms of labor participation, Mexico's political and military leaders responded to the challenge of mass participation by forging an alliance with major labor organizations. Circumstances compelled the governing elite to accept labor as a legitimate political force entitled to play a significant role in national affairs, as well as to make concessions on issues of vital importance to labor. Over the long term, the survival of this alliance depended upon postrevolutionary governments' provision of legal, financial, and political support to an "official" (state-subsidized) labor movement.

An alliance with the governing elite held ambiguous promise for labor. Emerging worker organizations sought first and foremost to preserve their operational autonomy vis-à-vis the state and political parties, a goal whose perceived importance was reinforced both by memory of the ways in which the Díaz regime had used financial assistance and selective political alliances to divide early labor groups and by the influence of anarchosyndicalist beliefs. Yet labor's capacity for autonomous action was constrained by the limited size of the urban and industrial work force, organizational weaknesses, and persistent government hostility to labor radicalism. Together these factors encouraged the rise to prominence of a pragmatic labor leadership committed to a nonconfrontational relationship with the country's new rulers. For these labor leaders, the possibility of an alliance with state authorities offered historic opportunities to organize workers rapidly and to secure real economic and political advantages for them. On the basis of this alliance and their privileged access to state resources, two labor organizations at different times—the Confederación Regional Obrera Mexicana (Mexican Regional Labor Confederation, CROM) from its founding in 1918 through the 1920s, and the Confederación de Trabajadores de México (Confederation of Mexican Workers, CTM) in the period after its formation in 1936—consolidated a politically dominant position in the labor movement.

This chapter examines the origins, characteristics, and consequences of the alliance forged in the 1920s and 1930s between the postrevolutionary governing elite and major elements of the organized labor movement. The discussion begins by examining the work force and organizational characteristics of the Mexican labor movement that conditioned its early relationship with the postrevolutionary leadership, as well as the ways in which different leadership factions maneuvered to isolate anarchist and anarchosyndicalist organizations and support groups committed to active collaboration with them. These factors are crucial to understanding why certain elements of the labor movement were more committed than others to a close political alliance with the postrevolutionary elite, as well as where divisions within the labor movement subsequently arose over the nature of this alliance.

The first section focuses in detail on the formation and evolution of the CROM and the CTM, the two labor confederations most important to the political consolidation of the postrevolutionary regime. The case of the CROM receives more attention here than in many analyses of Mexican labor politics because it was centrally important to the long-term evolution of a postrevolutionary alliance between the governing elite and segments of the organized working class. The CTM represented a more inclusive labor alliance based in part on the ideological appeal to workers of revolutionary nationalism and Lázaro Cárdenas's broad socioeconomic reform program, and its political dominance within the labor movement proved far more durable than that of the CROM. Moreover, from the 1930s onward the CTM became a key source of mass political support for the postrevolutionary regime in its capacity as an official sector organization in the Partido de la Revolución Mexicana (Party of the Mexican Revolution, PRM, 1938), reorganized in 1946 as the Partido Revolucionario Institucional (Institutional Revolutionary Party, PRI). Yet many of the elements that subsequently defined the CTM's relationship with the governing elite—especially its heavy reliance on political and financial subsidies to maintain control over a heterogeneous national membership, and the implications of this dependence for its autonomy—also characterized in an earlier period the CROM's ties with state authorities.

The second part of this chapter examines the range of legal, financial, and political subsidies that the governing elite has provided the "official" labor movement. The capacity of state authorities to structure the legal bases of union control in the workplace and to direct financial and political rewards to favored labor organizations reflected their increasingly concentrated power. In turn, the labor movement's dependence on these subsidies aggravated organizational weaknesses that placed labor in a generally subordinate position vis-à-vis the state. Although "official" labor organizations such as the CTM have traditionally enjoyed considerable autonomy in the conduct of their internal affairs, the highly unequal terms of the labor movement's alliance with the governing elite have in many instances transformed unions into important mechanisms of political control over rank-and-file workers. Thus this discussion of the emergence of a state-subsidized labor movement in the 1920s and 1930s helps explain how the mobilization of mass actors during the Mexican revolution gave way to a highly institutionalized and stable authoritarian regime.

The Origins of an "Official" Labor Movement

The relationship between working-class organizations and political authorities was a crucially important issue both during and after the Mexican revolution. Anarchist and anarchosyndicalist traditions influenced many labor groups' initial perspectives on cooperation with the victorious political and military coalition headed by Venustiano Carranza. From the 1860s onward, Mexican anarchists had stressed autonomous working-class action and rejected ties between workers and either the state or political parties.[2] This position reflected anarchists' philosophical preferences for direct action *(acción directa)* to achieve working-class emancipation, as well as their conclusion that ties to political authorities in practice had primarily negative consequences for labor. (The Díaz regime, for example, had successfully used government financial support to co-opt early working-class organizations and moderate their demands.)[3]

During the early revolutionary period anarchist groups vigorously rejected electoral involvement and stressed the futility of workers relying on government assistance to resolve their disputes with employers. The Casa del Obrero Mundial (House of the World Worker, COM) organized unions (anarchosyndicalists employed the word *sindicato* to imply that members denied the legitimacy of the state and rejected political involvement) that were, with COM coordination, to conduct industrywide general strikes to achieve their socioeconomic goals.[4] The impact of anarchism on working-class political views is still disputed,[5] but anarchists' and anarchosyndicalists' preoccupation with labor autonomy and political independence was widely shared by urban and industrial workers. Nevertheless, the temptation to form alliances with state authorities had since the 1870s been a persistent source of division even among anarchists and anarchosyndicalists.[6] This temptation became much stronger after more radical political leaders such as Álvaro Obregón came to the fore and offered the labor movement opportunities to play a new role in national politics.

Two factors undermined the viability of the anarchosyndicalist project and limited the autonomy of the labor movement during the late revolutionary period and the early 1920s. First, work force characteristics and labor's organizational weaknesses significantly constrained most unions' capacity for autonomous action. Mexican society during and after the revolution was predominantly rural. Indeed, primary economic activities (crop and livestock production, forestry, fishing, and hunting) accounted for 71.4 percent of the economically active population in 1921 and 70.2 percent in 1930. The share of the economically active population engaged in manufacturing, petroleum production, mining and other extractive activities, the generation and distribution of electrical power, and construction was only 11.5 percent in 1921 (561,318 workers) and 14.4 percent in 1930 (743,407 workers).[7] The industrial activities with the largest total employment in 1930 were cotton textile manufacturing, sugar and alcohol production, machine building and repair *(talleres mecánicos)*, and shoe manufacturing.[8]

In addition to its limited size, the dispersion of the urban and industrial work force among a large number of small- and medium-sized enterprises in diverse economic activities made the formation of large, politically and economically influential unions extremely difficult. These labor force characteristics reflected uneven industrialization in Mexico in the late nineteenth and early twentieth centuries, with considerable variation in the size and concentration of the work force among different regions and economic activities. As late as 1930, for example, the 313,153 workers in manufacturing activities and petroleum production were distributed among 48,573 different establishments, for an average of 6.4 employees per workplace.[9] An analysis of the 1930 industrial census found only 323 manufacturing enterprises in the country employing more than 100 workers and only 13 firms employing more than 1,000 workers.[10] The prevalence of paternalistic worker-employer relations in smaller workplaces further complicated organizational efforts in many economic activities.

The majority of unions formed in the organizational upsurge during and after the revolution were therefore small entities with limited resources and reduced bargaining power. Tramway employees and workers employed in the textile, electrical power generation, and typesetting industries gained additional political and economic leverage from their location in or near major urban areas, especially Mexico City. But even railroad and petroleum workers, whose strategic economic position placed them in a comparatively strong negotiating position vis-à-vis private employers and government officials, remained organizationally divided throughout the 1920s. As late as the early 1930s, railroad workers were grouped in 18 different craft organizations, and petroleum workers were organized in 21 different unions. These conditions meant that, in practice, the ability of workers to unionize and bargain successfully with employers often depended on the strength of their ties to military and political leaders.

Second, the Constitutionalist forces actively cultivated an alliance with moderate elements in the emerging organized labor movement, while at the same time forcefully opposing labor radicals.[11] The social reformist and nationalist content of revolutionary political ideas and the willingness of the predominantly middle-class Sonoran group to make specific policy concessions to labor were both crucial to the Constitutionalists' ability to forge a working political alliance with urban and industrial workers in areas such as Mexico City. For example, whereas Victoriano Huerta had suppressed the COM in May 1914, Álvaro Obregón permitted it to resume activities later in the year (even giving the COM a headquarters building in Mexico City). Obregón also won labor support by backing the strike led by the Sindicato Mexicano de Electricistas (Mexican Electricians' Union, SME) against a foreign-owned electrical power company in Mexico City in February 1915.[12] Carranza, as part of his pact with the COM in February 1915, provided material support for its organizational activities in different areas of the country. The alliance between the Constitutionalists and urban labor leaders was reinforced by their shared anticlericalism and their concern about the Catholic Church's presumed influence over the *zapatistas*.[13] At the same time, Carranza vigorously opposed labor radicalism, using army troops to break a general strike in Mexico City in late July and early August 1916. The Carranza administration continued to harass radical labor groups in the aftermath of the failed 1916 general strikes, and government authorities blocked anarchosyndicalists' efforts to reorganize in a national confederation.[14]

The combination of workers' still limited organizational and mobilizational capacity and state authorities' hostility to radical labor tactics such as the general strike encouraged the emergence of a more pragmatic, accommodationist labor leadership committed to a nonconfrontational working relationship with the political elite. The crushing defeat of general strikes in Mexico City in May and July–August 1916 starkly revealed the risks that frontal confrontation with the state posed to newly created labor organizations. Rather than rejecting political involvement, more pragmatic labor elements sought to expand their influence through an alliance with political and military authorities. They argued that this approach offered real economic and political opportunities for the labor movement, a perception strengthened by the inclusion of Article 123 and its broad guarantees of labor rights in the 1917 federal constitution. Many labor conflicts during and after the revolution focused on employer opposition to workers' demands to form unions and negotiate collective contracts, struggles in which support from national and local government officials often proved decisive. Labor, both then and later, was generally the subordinate partner in this alliance. Yet the inclusion of urban and industrial workers in Mexico's new governing coalition was a crucial departure.

The Rise and Decline of the Mexican Regional Labor Confederation

Under the leadership of Luis N. Morones (1890–1964), the Mexican Regional Labor Confederation emerged as the principal advocate of labor's new relationship with the governing elite.[15] Morones, a mechanic employed by the Mexican Light and Power Company and a founding member of the SME, played a key role in marginalizing anarchosyndicalist elements at a national workers' convention in 1917 that preceded the formation of the CROM. He held that labor organizations should reject the ideological rigidity associated with the anarchist and anarchosyndicalist traditions and embrace tactical flexibility (acción multiple). Morones recognized the labor movement's numerical and organizational weaknesses, and in his view workers needed to build political alliances with elite groups in order to achieve their basic goals—in other words, labor needed "fewer ideals and more organization."[16] The CROM's August 1919 secret pact with Obregón—in which the CROM promised to mobilize support for Obregón in the 1920 presidential election in exchange for privileged political access, creation of (and CROM influence over) a separate labor ministry, and presidential support for labor legislation codifying the provisions of Article 123—and its formation of the Partido Laborista Mexicano (Mexican Labor Party, PLM) in December 1919 signaled its definitive entrance into national politics.[17] This action contributed to the further alienation of anarchosyndicalist groups that had joined in the creation of the CROM, leading them to form a separate national organization in February 1921 committed to "nonpolitical" labor action, the Confederación General de Trabajadores (General Confederation of Workers, CGT).[18]

From the perspective of the governing elite, the CROM and the PLM were crucially important sources of mass support for a still fragile regime. Indeed, because the federal government's legal jurisdiction over labor matters was at the time limited to the Federal District and federal territories, an alliance with the CROM permitted federal authorities to exercise greater influence over labor matters in different areas of the country than they otherwise would have had. The CROM and the PLM were, moreover, the only civilian organizations able to serve as political counterbalances to the military at a time when political parties were generally weak and limited in influence to particular states or regions.[19] Armed labor and peasant support provided the vital margin that allowed Obregón and Calles to defeat Adolfo de la Huerta's military rebellion in 1923–24.[20] Calles's election in 1924 was especially dependent upon CROM support; his military prestige and ties to the army had never been as strong as Obregón's, and two-thirds of the federal army had initially joined the de la Huerta revolt to block his presidential candidacy. The CROM's willingness to limit strikes (in February 1925 the national leadership informed its affiliates that they could strike only with the permission of the central committee) and its strong endorsement of economic reconstruction (including support for direct foreign investment) within the "revolutionary community" were also important to Calles's development program. In addition, the CROM's anticlerical and anticommunist stance made it a compatible political ally of the Obregón and Calles administrations.[21]

The CROM's political ties permitted it to grow rapidly.[22] At its founding, the confederation's largest affiliate was the Coahuila-based Mexican Mining Union. The 15,000-member Federación de Sindicatos Obreros del Distrito Federal (Federation of Federal District Labor Unions)—the largest labor organization in Mexico City—joined in June 1919. By late that year the CROM had also developed a strong presence among textile workers in the region around Orizaba, Veracruz. As early as 1920 the CROM reported some 50,000 members, but it mushroomed in size during the Obregón (1920–24) and Calles (1924–28) administrations. Even if the confederation's inflated membership totals are steeply discounted (it claimed 1.5 million members in 1925 and 2 million members in 1928, as many as two-thirds of whom were peasants and rural workers),[23] by the late 1920s it clearly was the largest and most politically influential labor organization in Mexico.[24] The CROM made particularly significant contributions to labor's subsequent political and economic influence by winning the support of the Calles administration for the principle that contract terms negotiated by the union representing the largest number of employees at a work site should apply to all workers there, and by creating national federations in industries in which none had previously existed (including those representing teachers, printers, and textile, sugar, and port workers).[25] These activities also contributed to efforts by Obregón and Calles to assert control over political developments throughout the country.

The confederation's success was primarily due to its ability to exploit its political influence and control over key government positions (and resources) to launch unionization drives and undermine rival organizations such as the CGT. In many areas of the country, the CROM signed pacts with prominent political leaders in which it offered to mobilize support in gubernatorial elections in exchange for official approval for its organizational activities and access to government positions once the candidate took office. Not all of these pacts produced the results the CROM anticipated, in part because state governors sometimes gave preferential backing to rival labor organizations in order to build a loyal local base of mass support and block further expansion of CROM influence.[26] Yet the CROM's growing membership in such key economic activities as the textile industry also reflected successful plant-level organizing, in some cases despite persistent, violent employer resistance and opposition from state and local government officials. Competition from the CGT among textile workers may have compelled the CROM to devote greater energy to workplace organization in this industry, and the larger average concentration of industrial workers per plant in the industry (the 211 establishments with more than 100 workers apiece together represented 91.3 percent of total employment in the industry in 1930) presumably facilitated unionization.[27] The economic nationalist content of the CROM's program also increased its appeal to workers.[28] Moreover, in some regions the CROM's efforts to establish unions may have benefited from the previous absence of labor organizations and union organizers' consequent ability to capitalize on tensions between workers and employers.[29]

The CROM's presence in local and national government reflected its political importance in the 1920s, and control over government positions facilitated its further organizational expansion.[30] At different times during this period, CROM leaders occupied the governorship in four states and the Federal District, and they controlled such important national offices as the Departamento de Establecimientos Fabriles y Aprovisimientos Militares (Department of Industrial Enterprises and Military Supply, the agency responsible for producing arms and ammunition), the federal Labor Office, and Talleres Gráficos de la Nación (National Printing Office). CROM members also held the labor attaché positions the government created in Mexican embassies in Berlin, Buenos Aires, Rome, and Washington, D.C. Between 1924 and 1928 Morones served as minister of industry, commerce, and labor and was among the most powerful of Calles's cabinet officers. In addition, in 1926 CROM members held 11 of 58 positions in the federal Senate and 40 of 272 seats in the federal Chamber of Deputies.[31] The confederation used its government positions to enforce dues deductions from public employees' salaries, which were both a major source of financial support and a direct precedent for a similar policy adopted by the Revolutionary National Party after its formation in 1929. These positions, as well as the CROM's control over many labor conciliation and arbitration boards, were also the base from which it compelled employers to recognize its union affiliates and undermined its labor rivals.

However, despite the great organizational advantages that it derived from state patronage, the CROM never succeeded in establishing a strong presence in such strategically important activities as the railroad, electrical power generation, or petroleum industries.[32] Workers in these activities had a relatively strong labor market position that gave them considerable bargaining leverage vis-à-vis private-sector employers. In some cases their political attitudes had also been shaped by radical ideologies such as communism and anarchosyndicalism. For example, petroleum workers had been influenced by Industrial Workers of the World (IWW) and Mexican anarchist organizing drives in the area around Tampico, Tamaulipas. The Mexican Electricians' Union, influenced in part by anarchism, also had a strong reputation for democratic governance and political independence.

As a consequence, workers in these industries were both less dependent on state support for their organizational activities and more concerned about their potential loss of political independence than employees in many other sectors. This was perhaps especially the case in unions that had suffered repression as national political leaders sought to block strikes. In 1925 the CROM finally succeeded in using its political influence to force the Mexican Tramway Company in Mexico City to recognize a CROM-affiliated union. In the late 1920s railroad and electrical workers were also the object of serious government harassment during Morones's term as minister of industry, commerce, and labor. For example, in 1926 Morones ruled that the strike called by the Unión Mexicana de Mecánicos (Mexican Union of Machinists) was illegal, and CROM members served as replacements for dismissed railroad workers.[33] For the most part, however, the CROM failed to make significant organizational inroads in some of the country's most important economic activities.

Although the CROM exercised dominant influence in many parts of the labor movement throughout most of the 1920s, its political decline beginning in late 1928 revealed starkly the vulnerabilities inherent in heavy labor dependence on state support.[34] The CROM's relations with Obregón had soured after late 1924 over rival PLM and National Agrarian Party (the party that increasingly became Obregón's base of mass support) efforts to organize peasants and rural workers. Tensions between them increased sharply in 1926–28 over Obregón's bid—in violation of the central political tenet of the revolutionary creed—to win reelection to the presidency. Although the federal constitution was amended in 1927 to permit reelection for nonconsecutive terms, Morones, his inner circle of collaborators (known as the Grupo Acción, or "Action Group"), and CROM members in several states strongly opposed Obregón's return to office. Morones himself harbored presidential ambitions. But in addition, CROM leaders feared that Obregón's reelection would undermine their privileged political position (in May 1928, during his presidential campaign, Obregón had declared that *laboristas* would not hold public office in his second administration) and endanger the CROM's rural unionization drive.[35]

Because of these antecedents, Morones and the CROM were charged with direct or indirect involvement in the assassination of Obregón shortly after his reelection in July 1928. Morones and other top CROM leaders were immediately forced to resign their positions in the Calles administration. The crisis in the confederation's relationship with the government worsened when in December 1928 a longtime CROM opponent, Emilio Portes Gil, was elected provisional president for the period from 1928 to 1930. Morones complicated matters still further by openly criticizing Portes Gil's policies toward labor in a highly provocative speech in early December 1928. Moreover, Morones refused to cooperate with Calles's efforts to organize the Revolutionary National Party in the wake of the Obregón assassination, preferring instead to preserve the PLM.

These actions provoked Portes Gil to work systematically to undermine the CROM. He did so by replacing pro-CROM personnel in the federal Labor Office with individuals who favored unions opposing the CROM; eliminating the automatic deduction of CROM dues from public employees' salaries; displacing CROM representatives on conciliation and arbitration boards; depriving CROM affiliates of control over labor contracts in key sectors; and using army troops against CROM unions in worker-employer conflicts. The Portes Gil administration also provided financial support for anti-Morones factions within the CROM.[36] As a consequence, by late December 1928 nearly half of the CROM's affiliates had seceded in order to distance themselves from Morones's politically untenable position. The CROM retained important regional bases in Puebla, Tlaxcala, and Veracruz, and it succeeded in organizing new affiliates in some industries. Moreover, it remained among the largest national confederations (and perhaps *the* largest) until the formation of the Confederation of Mexican Workers in 1936.[37] Nonetheless, neither the CROM nor any other labor organization ever again attained the political power it had held between 1924 and 1928.

The CROM's rapid rise and eventual decline in the 1920s held important lessons for both the governing elite and the organized labor movement. For political and military leaders, the CROM experience underscored the immense value of organized mass support in elections and intra-elite confrontations. The importance of securing a reliable political base among urban and industrial workers lay not only in the obvious advantages it offered candidates at the polls but also in the governing elite's resulting ability to deny potential regime opponents widespread popular support. Yet at the same time, the great influence that the CROM wielded during the Calles administration highlighted the potential risks that a powerful national labor confederation posed to the decision-making autonomy of postrevolutionary governments. As part of his campaign to undercut the CROM, Portes Gil offered support even to the Mexican Communist Party (PCM), leading the PCM to organize the Confederación Sindical Unitaria de México (Unitary Mexican Union Confederation, CSUM) in December 1928.[38] Later presidential administrations sought even more vigorously to create and sustain rival labor organizations in order to prevent a single confederation from becoming the unified representative of unionized workers.

For the labor movement, too, the CROM experience held both positive and negative lessons. Despite the general distaste with which most labor organizations regarded the CROM's antidemocratic, often violent tactics and its widespread reputation for corruption, the CROM demonstrated the significant advantages that an alliance with the governing elite offered labor groups in terms of access to financial resources, support for unionization, and political and economic influence. The attractions of state support were particularly great for unions outside strategically important or easily organized economic activities. At the same time, the CROM symbolized the costs of too heavy a dependence on state subsidies or political connections. Most important, the fate that befell the CROM after 1928 clearly indicated the mortal risks involved in frontal confrontations with state power.

More generally, developments within the labor movement during the 1920s highlighted two issues that would remain of long-term importance to the character of state-labor relations in postrevolutionary Mexico. First, because the structural characteristics of the Mexican economy (a large rural sector and a still limited manufacturing base, as well as the unevenness of industrialization among different sectors and regions) made unionization difficult, the labor movement was extremely heterogeneous in composition and many worker organizations found state subsidies attractive. Both the rapidity of the CROM's organizational expansion and the top-down, preemptive character of many of its unionization efforts reflected its dependence on the Obregón and Calles administrations' political and financial support. Workers in strategic economic activities such as railroads and the petroleum industry made important, largely autonomous organizational advances during these years, although the first national industrial unions did not appear until the early 1930s. The strong rivalries that emerged between labor organizations in these activities and the CROM foreshadowed the tensions that would later develop between powerful national industrial unions and broad national confederations, whose strength derived primarily from political alliances with the governing elite and whose dependence on such support compromised their policy independence.

Second, although the influence of anarchosyndicalism declined sharply in the 1920s under the combined weight of government hostility and CROM aggression, debate did not end over the appropriate relationship between worker organizations and either political parties or the state. As the Mexican Communist Party expanded its influence among some urban and rural labor groups, Marxism-Leninism (and later Trotskyism and Maoism as well) emerged as the principal focus of ideologically motivated labor action. Some labor activists advocated an ideological position of rigorous union autonomy, while other labor leaders (in practice, if not in rhetoric) embraced the CROM's strategy of forging pragmatic, collaborative alliances with progressive elements among the governing political elite. The evolution of this political and ideological struggle was not dependent solely upon the organizational skills of rival groups operating autonomously in different sectors and regions; in practice, it was heavily influenced by state action as postrevolutionary governments both repressed nonaccommodationist tendencies and promulgated revolutionary nationalist ideas as a quasi-official "ideology of the Mexican revolution."

The Formation of the Confederation of Mexican Workers

Elite interest in preserving a dominant national labor organization waned in the period immediately following Obregón's assassination. Portes Gil's hostility toward Morones and his vigorous efforts to undermine the CROM were key factors in this regard. Even though the CROM leadership hastily disassociated itself from Gonzalo Escobar's military revolt in March 1929, the fact that some labor groups supported the uprising and the memory of armed worker contingents' participation in past military struggles led Portes Gil to view organized labor as a potential threat to political order. Equally important, Calles—the dominant figure in Mexican politics between 1928 and 1934 (the period is conventionally referred to as the *maximato* in reference to Calles's position as the "jefe máximo de la revolución")—distanced himself from Morones and the CROM to avoid alienating Obregón loyalists as he sought to organize the Revolutionary National Party.[39] Governments during this period formally supported unionization. Yet in the absence of a strong elite commitment to a political alliance with labor and active state support for it, labor organization was constrained by high levels of unemployment resulting from economic depression in the early 1930s.[40]

Despite these political and economic obstacles, three important focal points for labor movement unification emerged after the CROM's political eclipse. First, the Mexican Communist Party promoted working-class unity.[41] During much of the 1920s the party advocated the combined organization of workers and peasants and the formation of industrywide national unions. As the national political crisis deepened in 1927–28, the PCM proposed a broad labor alliance (it would have included the CGT and even the CROM, whose antidemocratic methods the party had condemned) to protect workers' interests, and the CSUM briefly united a number of labor and peasant organizations. However, the PCM's ultraleftist orientation between late 1928 and 1933 and harsh government repression in 1929–30 prevented it from advancing in these areas. Even though the party lacked legal recognition during the period between 1929 and early 1935, in 1933 it founded the Comité Pro-Unidad Obrera y Campesina (Committee for Worker and Peasant Unity) as part of its organizational efforts among peasants, railroad workers, miners, petroleum workers, and other groups. These efforts, and especially the party's shift away from sectarian positions and toward a strategy of broad alliances with progressive forces after 1934, were important contributions to labor movement unification.

Second, powerful national industrial unions organized among railroad workers, petroleum workers, and miners and metalworkers in the early 1930s played a leading role in labor movement unification. The first and most influential of these unions was the Sindicato de Trabajadores Ferrocarrileros de la República Mexicana (Mexican Railroad Workers' Union, STFRM), formed in January 1933. Railroad workers had been organized in eighteen smaller associations formed along craft lines. Enduring loyalties to these entities, workers' concerns about maintaining the autonomy of workplace-level union sections in a more centralized organization, and some groups' efforts to preserve existing differences in wages and working conditions among different employment categories all constituted major obstacles to the creation of a single railroad workers' union. However, a long history of problems associated with coordinating strikes among workers employed by different railroad companies (especially the failure of railroad strikes in 1926–27 as a result of a divided union structure, divisions that were exploited by the CROM-controlled Ministry of Industry, Commerce, and Labor) and existing organizations' inability to prevent large-scale layoffs helped workers overcome many of these reservations.[42] The formation of the STFRM demonstrated the viability—and the greatly enhanced political and economic leverage—of a union organized along national industrial lines. The STFRM, the PCM, and the CSUM subsequently collaborated to support the formation of a national union among miners and metalworkers in April 1934. Petroleum workers (also with STFRM assistance) finally succeeded in forming a national union in August 1935.[43] The STFRM also joined with the Mexican Electricians' Union, the CSUM, and other groups in proposing the creation of a national labor front to replace the CROM.[44]

The creation of these nationally organized unions introduced an important new dynamic into labor politics. Although the CROM had organized several national federations, Morones's commitment to retaining tight political control over their activities often limited the degree of support they received from rank-and-file workers. The national industrial unions formed in the early 1930s, in contrast, were primarily the product of organizing efforts by workers employed in key industries. These initiatives prospered in part because the 1931 federal labor code gave legal recognition to unions operating at the national level,[45] as well as because the CROM could no longer successfully block them. At the same time, past CROM intervention in these industries redoubled the new unions' commitment to organizational autonomy vis-à-vis political parties and the state. Their support for revolutionary nationalist economic policies and a united but politically independent national confederation would in the late 1930s, and especially in the late 1940s, place them at the center of struggles over the direction of the organized labor movement.

Third, Vicente Lombardo Toledano succeeded in bringing together diverse labor and peasant organizations to form the Confederación General de Obreros y Campesinos de México (General Confederation of Mexican Workers and Peasants, CGOCM) in October 1933. By the early 1930s, Lombardo Toledano (a member of the CROM's national executive committee between 1923 and 1932, as well as its first secretary of education and secretary-general of the National Teachers' Federation) had a national reputation as a Marxist intellectual and labor leader.[46] He emerged as Morones's principal rival within the CROM in the late 1920s and early 1930s, and he expanded his organizational activities soon after leaving the CROM in September 1932. The CGOCM was important because it linked both the Federación Sindical de Trabajadores del Distrito Federal (Federation of Federal District Workers' Unions, FSTDF, formed in February 1929 by increasingly prominent Mexico City labor leaders such as Fidel Velázquez following their secession from the CROM) and the organizations composing the "CROM *depurada*" (formed by anti-Morones dissidents, including Lombardo Toledano, in March 1933).[47] In reaction to the CROM experience, the new confederation proclaimed its independence from the government and all political groups, advocated internal union democracy, and urged attention to specific, pragmatic economic demands. The CGOCM's efforts to coordinate labor strikes and expand its membership quickly made it among the largest labor confederations in Mexico.[48] Although it did not rival the CROM's former political influence, the CGOCM constituted the most important step toward labor movement unification prior to the formation of the CTM.

These three groups shared the common goal of labor movement unification, an objective whose importance was underlined by the harsh impact of the Great Depression on the Mexican working class and the increased need for effective labor action. Yet several crucial questions remained unresolved in different proposals for a single national confederation. What was the appropriate relationship between working-class organizations and political parties? Should labor unions adopt a policy of strict political and organizational autonomy vis-à-vis the state, or should they seek to collaborate with progressive elements within the governing political elite? How was the labor movement to expand—through grassroots organizational efforts alone, or with the assistance of national and local political alliances? The answers that different elements offered to these questions were later to divide the labor movement.

Progress toward labor movement unification also reflected an important shift in elite attitudes. By the early 1930s the labor movement was badly fragmented. Some 17 different confederations, 57 federations, and 2,781 individual unions existed in late 1933.[49] Continuing clashes among rival organizations fueled political tensions arising from economic depression. Although state labor authorities held strikes to a minimum, the total number of individual grievances filed before conciliation and arbitration boards rose rapidly (from 8,529 in 1928, to 20,702 in 1930, to 36,781 in 1932),[50] indicating growing labor unrest.

National political leaders' capacity to influence developments in the labor movement was significantly reduced by its fragmentation. The formation of the PNR in 1929 helped resolve the political crisis that erupted in the wake of Obregón's assassination. Its primary function was to avoid a violent struggle for power among regional military and political strongmen by expanding the regime's base of support after the loss of the Sonoran group's dominant member. The PNR was, moreover, the first political organization to claim monopoly representation of the revolutionary tradition.

It became the means by which Calles united the very large number of l
and regional parties that had emerged during and after the revolution, th
further centralizing national political power.

Nevertheless, despite Calles's efforts to build support for the party
among popular groups (including, for example, his advocacy of the 1931
federal labor code), the PNR remained principally a vehicle for formally
uniting regional political bosses while permitting them great autonomy
in their respective spheres of influence.[51] Government efforts to build up
the Cámara del Trabajo del Distrito Federal (Federal District Chamber of
Labor, a body grouping former CROM affiliates and other labor organizations) led to the creation of a Cámara Nacional del Trabajo (National
Chamber of Labor, CNT) in 1932 and a network of state-level *cámaras*
throughout the country. These organizations constituted the PNR's principal claim to a labor base. The STFRM, representing more than thirty-five
thousand railroad workers, was briefly affiliated with the National Chamber of Labor in 1934–35, temporarily making the CNT the country's largest
national confederation.[52] Yet the *cámaras'* close identification with the government generally prevented them from developing strong support among
workers.[53]

The nomination of Lázaro Cárdenas as the PNR's presidential candidate in December 1933 marked the beginning of new efforts to organize
mass support for the postrevolutionary regime. Cárdenas sought to organize a mass social base that would permit his administration (1934–40)
to increase its political power and undertake a broad program of socioeconomic reform.[54] He judged that expanded unionization was crucial if
workers were to defend their interests in conflicts with employers. Cárdenas had first experimented with worker and peasant organization in the
context of reform implementation while he was governor of Michoacán
between 1928 and 1932; indeed, his actions there included the organization
of workers and peasants in a single entity, the Confederación Revolucionaria Michoacana del Trabajo (Michoacán Revolutionary Confederation
of Labor).[55] It was this perspective that he brought to the presidency. Accu-
mulating sociopolitical tensions as a result of economic depression during
the early 1930s persuaded Cárdenas that a similar initiative was imperative
on a national scale.[56]

On several occasions Cárdenas publicly advocated labor movement
unification to increase both workers' influence in government decision
making and their bargaining leverage with employers. For example, in his
November 30, 1934, inaugural address to Congress, Cárdenas referred to
the labor movement's lack of centralized organization as one of its principal problems.[57] His generally pro-labor stance encouraged unionization
and workers' economic demands, and a series of strikes by tramway, petro-

leum, and telephone workers broke out in the first months after he took office.[58] These strikes did not constitute a nationwide labor mobilization. Nevertheless, they occurred in important economic activities frequently controlled by foreign-owned firms. The broad popular support won by striking workers—and the growing possibility of sympathy strikes affecting other industries—raised serious concerns among business groups and conservative political elements.

The actual reorganization and consolidation of the labor movement with Cárdenas's support occurred in the context of his political confrontation with Calles. On June 12, 1935, major Mexico City newspapers published comments by General Calles condemning the wave of strikes as "treason" because they further undermined the country's fragile economic position.[59] Because Calles had dominated national politics in the years following Obregón's assassination, his declaration was widely interpreted as an attempt to reassert his personal power and prevent Cárdenas from pursuing more radical social and economic policies.[60] Cárdenas therefore immediately began to organize the mass political support necessary to prevail in this crisis. Labor groups such as the CGOCM, concerned about ties between labor and the state in the wake of the CROM experience, had initially taken a neutral stance toward the Cárdenas presidency while continuing their independent efforts to unify the labor movement. But Calles's attack on Cárdenas's pro-labor policies led many worker organizations to reconsider their position.

On June 14, 1935, Cárdenas responded publicly to Calles's statement by reaffirming both his commitment to the reformist policies outlined in the PNR's Six-Year Plan and his confidence in "the good will and patriotism" of labor and peasant organizations. The Mexican Electricians' Union, probably acting at Cárdenas's request or with his encouragement, called upon all major labor organizations to attend an emergency solidarity meeting scheduled the next day to examine the implications of Calles's declaration. The meeting brought together most of the politically important labor organizations, including the CGOCM, the CSUM, and unions representing railroad workers, miners and metalworkers, tramway workers, and typesetters. (Only the pro-Calles CROM and the CGT failed to attend.)[61] It led to the formation of the Comité Nacional de Defensa Proletaria (National Committee for Proletarian Defense, CNDP). The rapid mobilization of mass support allowed Cárdenas to consolidate his political position and replace Calles's supporters in the federal government and in the PNR. On June 19 Calles was forced to leave Mexico for exile in the United States.[62]

The Cárdenas administration became even more active in its support for labor following the clash with Calles. It promoted unionization, sought to block the creation of employer-controlled labor organizations (sindi-

catos blancos), and rapidly increased resources for government labor inspectors, who were responsible for ensuring that federal labor law and contract provisions were implemented in the workplace.[63] These policies contributed to a sharp increase in the unionized work force; 2,873 (56.9 percent) of the 5,053 federal- and local-jurisdiction unions that existed in 1940 were organized after 1935.[64] In federal-jurisdiction economic activities, the number of unions grew by 36.2 percent (from a total of 825 to 1,124) and the number of unionized wórkers increased by 45.5 percent (from a total of 233,483 to 339,604) over the 1935–40 period. The change in local-jurisdiction industries was even more dramatic. State-level conciliation and arbitration boards registered 5,005 unions representing 325,878 workers between 1935 and 1938 alone, though the fact that several hundred fewer unions existed in 1940 (5,053) than in 1939 (5,888) suggests that many of these labor organizations were short-lived.[65]

Moreover, Cárdenas's support for labor movement unification became increasingly emphatic. Facing the threat of resurgent *callista* influence after December 1935 and a major confrontation with Monterrey industrialists over workers' rights to strike and form their own unions, on February 11, 1936, Cárdenas issued his famous "Fourteen Points" synthesizing his administration's labor policy. He stressed that it was "in the national interest to provide the support necessary to create a single organization of industrial workers [Central Única de los Trabajadores Industriales] that would end the inter-union strife that [was] equally pernicious to the interests of workers, employers, and the government." Cárdenas saw the formation of a unified labor confederation and the elimination of jurisdictional disputes and factional rivalries among labor groups as important means of strengthening the regime's position by promoting social peace and expanding its political base. The organization of mass social actors would, in his view, facilitate the task of governing. At the same time, he reassured labor leaders that his administration would not favor any particular worker organization; instead, it would support the labor movement "as a whole," organized in the new national confederation he envisioned.[66] Shortly thereafter, the National Committee for Proletarian Defense convened a "national unification congress" in Mexico City for the purpose of forming a national labor front. This meeting, held between February 21 and 25, 1936, resulted in the creation of the Confederation of Mexican Workers.[67] It advocated labor movement autonomy vis-à-vis the state and policy initiatives that would over the long term result in the "total abolition of the capitalist regime."[68]

The formation of the Confederation of Mexican Workers, the product of both workers' longstanding unification efforts and the Cárdenas administration's pro-labor policies, was a turning point in Mexican labor history. Its membership in 1936 included Lombardo Toledano's CGOCM;

the Mexican Communist Party–affiliated CSUM; the government-inspired National Chamber of Labor (CNT); national industrial unions representing railroad, mining and metalworking, electrical power generation, telephone, petroleum, tramway, sugar, textile, and printing workers; and a large number of other federations and unions organized at the state and regional level. (The CGOCM, CSUM, and CNT all formally dissolved when they joined the CTM.) Only the CROM (still aligned with pro-Calles political factions, though its membership had declined significantly) and the CGT (whose leadership had clashed with the CGOCM in the early 1930s) failed to join the new national confederation.

The CTM's original national leadership represented the four principal elements in its membership: groups led by Lombardo Toledano; organizations allied with Velázquez and his allies; unions influenced by or linked to the Mexican Communist Party; and powerful national industrial unions.[69] Lombardo Toledano, the CTM's first secretary-general, was the crucial mediating link among these different elements. His background in the CROM and his pragmatism regarding government-CTM ties won him the support of the Velázquez group, while his reputation as a socialist and shared ideological perspectives reassured many leftist activists. Nevertheless, ideological differences, policy disputes, and factional rivalries plagued the CTM from the moment of its founding. For example, the Sindicato Industrial de Trabajadores Mineros, Metalúrgicos y Similares de la República Mexicana (Mexican Mining and Metalworkers' Union, SITMMSRM) withdrew from the CTM in June 1936 in a fight over the openness of internal procedures. The PCM's supporters vigorously opposed efforts by Lombardo Toledano and Velázquez to draw the CTM into electoral politics in support of the "official" party.

Tensions peaked in April 1937 when the PCM, the Mexican Railroad Workers' Union, the Mexican Electricians' Union, and other influential affiliates withdrew in a struggle over confederation governance.[70] At issue were the PCM's influence in confederation decision making, the organization of CTM-affiliated state federations, labor's role in the electoral process, and major national industrial unions' desire for operational autonomy and political independence in a national confederation. Lombardo Toledano maintained that the dissidents only accounted for 18.5 percent of the CTM's membership, but the PCM claimed that they represented as many as 55.7 percent of CTM members.[71] The conflict ended in June 1937 when the PCM's Central Committee voted to resume active cooperation with the CTM. Shortly thereafter most of the seceding unions rejoined the confederation, though the SME and the SITMMSRM delayed doing so for differing periods of time and factional conflict remained severe in some state and regional federations. Most important, the settlement reached in June

1937 did not resolve the underlying division between powerful national industrial unions (nearly half of whose members had joined the secession movement)[72] and the smaller, more numerous, but less influential enterprise unions grouped in heterogeneous state federations which came to constitute the principal political base for the Velázquez group. This essential cleavage within the CTM's membership would produce an even more serious crisis in the late 1940s.

With its internal divisions temporarily controlled, in February 1938 the CTM claimed a membership of some 3,594 affiliated organizations and 945,913 individual members, including government employees.[73] Because this would have represented 74.4 percent of existing urban and industrial worker organizations in both federal- and local-jurisdiction economic activities, one must conclude that these data were somewhat inflated. Moreover, at least 40 percent of the CTM's total membership may have been peasants who had received land through the government's agrarian reform program.[74] Nevertheless, the CTM certainly grouped a majority of unionized urban and industrial workers.

Cárdenas had played a central part in uniting the labor movement under CTM auspices, and his government encouraged worker mobilization to implement wage and social welfare policies that benefited workers. Yet at the same time, Cárdenas took other steps to limit the CTM's political power. For example, he backed the formation of the Federación de Sindicatos de Trabajadores al Servicio del Estado (Federation of Public Service Workers' Unions, FSTSE) in October 1938 in order to ensure that federal government employees would be represented by a union separate from the CTM.[75] Even more significant, Cárdenas opposed the CTM's efforts to organize urban and industrial workers in the same unions and federations as rural wage earners and peasants. Labor activists' goal of creating a unified national labor movement had long focused on such cross-sectoral organizational initiatives; indeed, the CROM, the Mexican Communist Party, and the CGOCM had all promoted worker and peasant unionization in a single national confederation. Representatives from peasant organizations attended the CTM's founding congress, and as noted above, peasants constituted a substantial proportion of the CTM's initial membership. The first CTM national executive committee also included the position of secretary for peasant action (held by Pedro Morales, a PCM peasant organizer), a position preserved on the national executive committee at least through the mid-1940s. Because of the obvious importance of the peasantry in a society whose economically active population was still predominantly rural, programmatic appeals to peasants were an important part of the CTM's early unionization strategy.[76]

The Cárdenas administration, however, vigorously attempted to exclude peasant groups from CTM membership.[77] As early as July 1935 Cárdenas took steps to organize peasant support under the auspices of the Revolutionary National Party in conjunction with, and to facilitate, his agrarian reform program. As a consequence, the CTM's efforts to unionize rural wage laborers and peasants were a source of early tension between Cárdenas and the confederation. Cárdenas's strong, public opposition prevented the CTM from convening a peasant unity congress,[78] and its organizing drives among peasants gradually ended because of its dependence on presidential support for other activities. After the formation of the PRM-affiliated Confederación Nacional Campesina (National Peasants' Confederation, CNC) in August 1938, the government successfully encouraged existing peasant leagues and newly created peasant organizations to establish direct affiliations with the CNC.[79]

Linking Organized Labor to the Governing Party

The formation of the CTM and the CNC created the basis for restructuring the governing party. As early as September 1935 Cárdenas had argued that the PNR should be reorganized to incorporate workers, peasants, and soldiers, and despite continuing resistance from conservative elements within it, the PNR adopted an "open door" policy in 1936–37 to encourage worker and peasant participation in internal party elections.[80] Cárdenas announced formal plans for a new party in December 1937. However, the Party of the Mexican Revolution (PRM) was not actually formed until March 30, 1938 (twelve days after the nationalization of foreign-owned petroleum companies), at a time when Cárdenas sought to mobilize mass support against external political and economic pressure.[81]

Until then, most important labor organizations had resisted ties to the governing party. Unions seceding from the CROM demanded political independence, and their skepticism regarding the PNR was reinforced by generally conservative government labor policies during the late 1920s and early 1930s. Many labor activists viewed Calles's "official" PNR as a threat to autonomous organization. As a result, most unionization in the early 1930s occurred independently of the party.[82] Cárdenas, president of the PNR during a ten-month period in 1930, made initial but ultimately unsuccessful efforts to expand its worker and peasant base. (One measure of his failure was that a labor coalition called the Nationalist Revolutionary Alliance actually opposed the PNR during the 1930 congressional elections.) The task of building party support among labor organizations in the early 1930s was further complicated by continuing distrust between Calles and the CROM, which remained a very important labor confederation.[83]

However, the political and programmatic alliance forged between organized labor and the government during and after the Calles-Cárdenas clash created considerable momentum for CTM membership in the newly established PRM. The fact that Cárdenas was willing to modify the ruling party's structure to permit a more active voice for popular groups, the PRM's embodiment of revolutionary nationalist beliefs and its role as the principal vehicle for legitimating the postrevolutionary regime during the late 1930s,[84] and the Mexican Communist Party's support for a "popular front" strategy all facilitated the task of defining links between the labor movement and the Party of the Mexican Revolution. Yet for many major unions, it was the substance of Cárdenas's nationalistic economic reform program which proved crucial to overcoming in part (at least temporarily) their concerns about formal ties to the ruling party. They perceived state ownership or extensive state regulation of major economic activities to be an important means through which to realize their socioeconomic demands.[85] Thus the Cárdenas administration's commitment to active state involvement in economic development and its willingness to expropriate foreign-owned properties in basic industries such as petroleum production coincided closely with major unions' nationalist economic and political demands. Government actions such as the creation of the 1938–40 Worker Administration to operate Ferrocarriles Nacionales de México, the country's largest railroad company, further cemented broad labor loyalty to the Cárdenas project.

The organization of the PRM in sectors was a symbolic commitment to the political inclusion of mass actors in the postrevolutionary regime. Whereas the PNR's internal structure had closely reflected the geographically centered influence of regional political bosses, the new party was organized in four functionally defined categories: the labor sector (dominated and represented officially by the CTM, although it also included the CROM, the CGT, and individual unions not then linked to a confederation); the peasant sector (represented by the CNC, although other small peasant organizations were also present); the "popular" sector (owners of small and medium-sized businesses, small landowners, teachers, middle-class professionals, employees of the federal government organized in the FSTSE, women's associations, and so forth); and the military sector (the armed forces).[86] Only the clergy and business interests were formally excluded from the party, although business groups had their own national bodies for the public representation of their policy positions. The PRM's sectoral organization represented the unofficial consolidation of the "popular front" strategy advocated by the PNR, CTM, Mexican Communist Party, and the Confederación Campesina Mexicana (Mexican Peasants' Confederation) in 1935–37.[87] A system of indirect membership, in which party ties were based on membership in an affiliated mass organization, permitted the party to claim a staggering (and undoubtedly exaggerated) 4 million members in the late 1930s: 1.25 million workers, 2.5 million peasants, 500,000 "popular" elements, and 55,000 soldiers.[88]

The creation of the PRM marked the high point of mobilized mass support for the postrevolutionary regime, and organized labor emerged as the central force within the party in the late 1930s and early 1940s. The CTM's expressed preference for "functional democracy"[89] found form in the party's sectoral structure and system of indirect membership. This arrangement permitted the confederation to claim a significant share of political rewards based on the assumption that all unionized affiliates were PRM members, even though there was little regular worker participation in party affairs outside of elections. However, the ruling party's new structure also had other, less advantageous consequences for organized labor. Even though the CTM exercised far greater mobilizational capacity and organizational autonomy vis-à-vis the state than did the CNC or other affiliated groups, the PRM's four sectors were forced to compete against one another on formally equal terms for control over candidate nominations and other party resources. The creation of the large, diverse Confederación Nacional de Organizaciones Populares (National Confederation of Popular Organizations, CNOP) in 1943 was particularly important in constraining the CTM's bargaining leverage within the party over matters such as the selection of congressional candidates.[90]

The 1939–40 presidential succession offered the first crucial test of organized labor's new ties to the "official" party.[91] Business, middle-class, and military opposition to *cardenista* radicalism grew significantly in the late 1930s, especially following the expropriation of foreign-owned petroleum companies in March 1938. Cárdenas increasingly leaned toward a more moderate successor, General Manuel Ávila Camacho, in order to avoid extreme political polarization and ensure an orderly transfer of power. Most CTM affiliates, however, were inclined to support the presidential candidacy of Francisco J. Mújica. Mújica was closely identified with Cárdenas's progressive agenda, and he was the candidate most likely to pursue pro-labor policies after Cárdenas left office. But CTM secretary-general Lombardo Toledano took the president's position, arguing that a Mújica candidacy would unite the conservative opposition, endanger the policy gains made under Cárdenas, and risk civil war. This was perhaps not an implausible danger in the context of Saturnino Cedillo's 1938 military revolt, the rise of fascist organizations in Mexico, and the looming threat of war in Europe.

In February 1939 Lombardo Toledano convinced the CTM national council to endorse Ávila Camacho's presidential candidacy. This decision generated considerable opposition within the confederation, both because most labor leaders had little enthusiasm for Ávila Camacho and because Cárdenas had imposed him as the PRM's candidate in violation of the party's statutory requirement that the four sectors reach consensus after open, democratic consultation with their members. In disgust, the influential Mexican Electricians' Union again left the CTM in November 1939 in order to preserve its political independence. However, Lombardo Toledano and Fidel Velázquez worked successfully to discipline most CTM affiliates and mobilize them behind Ávila Camacho's candidacy in the July 1940 presidential election. Especially in major cities, CTM support was crucial to guaranteeing Ávila Camacho's victory over the strong opposition candidacy of conservative General Juan Almazán.[92] Equally important, the CTM's conduct in 1939–40 established the pattern for its participation in subsequent presidential successions.

State Subsidies to Organized Labor

CTM membership in the ruling party symbolized the postrevolutionary alliance between organized labor and Mexico's national political elite. Shared ideological perspectives and common programmatic objectives were crucial to the Cárdenas administration's successful efforts to forge this linkage. Over time, however, as subsequent presidential administrations adopted policies far less favorable to workers' interests, the preservation of an alliance with organized labor depended on the governing elite's control over the state apparatus (including an effective monopoly over the use of force) and its consequent ability to provide a range of legal, financial, and political subsidies to labor.

These subsidies have not been equally distributed. Legal provisions granting a representational monopoly in the workplace to officially recognized unions operate as a general subsidy to unionization, but financial assistance and union leaders' access to political mobility opportunities through the "official" party are normally available only to selected progovernment labor organizations. Many unions' organizational weaknesses make them highly dependent on government financial support. The fact that financial and political subsidies are *selectively* distributed makes them an important source of elite control over union activities.

Legal Subsidies

Federal labor law and standard provisions in collective work agreements provide both a general subsidy to labor organizations and the legal basis for progovernment union leaders' control over the rank and file. Despite the 1917 constitution's guarantee of the right to organize, employers vigorously resisted unionization during the late revolutionary period and the 1920s. Thus labor groups claimed a significant victory in the 1931 federal labor law's requirement (Article 43) that an employer sign a collective contract with an officially recognized union when requested to do so, even if at the time the union represents a minority of employees. The 1931 code also gave preference in hiring to unionized workers (Article 111 [I]), and it granted legal control over the contract to the union representing the largest number of workers at a work site (Article 43). These provisions—in addition to active government support for unionization during much of the 1930s and a long-term, quite consistent government policy of not recognizing more than one union in a given workplace—greatly facilitated labor organization. Because the 1931 labor law also extended a contract's terms to all employees in a particular workplace (Article 48), a union's control over the collective contract gives it an effective monopoly over the representation of rank-and-file interests.[93]

Among the most important legal subsidies to labor organization are the exclusion clauses (cláusulas de exclusión) authorized in the 1931 federal labor law and generally included in collective work agreements after the mid-1930s. The code recognized (Article 49) the legality of contract provisions requiring employers to hire only unionized workers. The entry exclusion clause (cláusula de exclusión de ingreso) in a contract thus creates either a closed or a union shop because workers are in practice compelled to become union members as a condition of employment, even though the law stated (Article 234) that no worker could be forced to join a union. Similarly, the 1931 law permitted (Article 236) a separation exclusion clause (cláusula de exclusión de separación) in contracts, requiring employers to dismiss any worker who loses his or her union membership. This provision provides incumbent union leaders with a powerful means of preserving their position against challenges by rival factions within a union: if incumbent leaders successfully employ internal union procedures to deprive their rivals of union membership, the challengers lose their jobs as well. This has historically constituted a major disincentive to internal union dissidence, especially in economic conditions in which replacement workers are readily available.

The acceptance of exclusion clauses in the 1931 labor code reflected the political influence of organized labor and state officials' conviction that unionization was a source of stability in worker-employer relations.[94] Because of the historical influence of liberalism and the 1917 constitution's commitment to the protection of individual rights, there were few legal restrictions placed on employers' hiring and dismissal practices in the period immediately following the revolution. Such restrictions were expressly forbidden by some state labor laws enacted between 1918 and 1928.[95] The

1928 "Proyecto Portes Gil" recognized the special social value of unions as means of improving workers' living standards (Article 6), but it stipulated only that under otherwise equal circumstances an employer was to give preference in hiring to unionized workers (Article 113 [iii]). It expressly prohibited labor organizations from compelling a worker to join a union or exerting pressure on an employer to fire a worker (Article 236 [iii, v]). The 1931 Ortiz Rubio *proyecto* similarly held that workers could not be forced to join a union (Article 236).

However, organized labor's growing political leverage produced several important precedents in this area. Some labor contracts negotiated in Veracruz and Tamaulipas in the early 1920s included union shop provisions, as did the 1927 nationwide worker-employer agreement regulating working conditions in the textile industry. By the mid-1920s these clauses were apparently a standard feature in the labor contracts negotiated by CROM affiliates.[96] The CROM and other labor organizations lobbied vigorously for the addition of exclusion clause provisions to the 1931 federal labor code. The Ortiz Rubio administration did so only in the final draft legislation submitted to the Chamber of Deputies for debate; it was one of the government's last-minute attempts to win labor support for the law.[97] The 1931 code did not require obligatory union membership, but it declared both entry and separation exclusion clauses legal if they were included in a collective work contract.

The legal recognition of entry and separation exclusion clauses opened new possibilities for labor organizers, and frequently thereafter unions led strikes to establish such provisions in collective work agreements. President Abelardo L. Rodríguez (1932–34) generally supported exclusion clauses after December 1933. For example, his arbitration settlement of a petroleum workers' strike in June 1934 added both entry and separation exclusion clauses to their collective contract. In the same month he supported the addition of exclusion clauses to the STFRM's contract with the Mexican National Railroads following a conflict between the new national railroad workers' union and CROM affiliates still active among railroad workers.[98] Federal labor authorities subsequently followed these precedents in other cases, and by the late 1930s virtually all major unions had secured similar contractual provisions to protect labor organizations in the workplace. Labor leaders saw such provisions as a key weapon against employers' cooptation of workers and their efforts to create captive, company-controlled unions.[99] In the case of the STFRM, for example, exclusion clauses greatly strengthened union leaders' hand in their efforts to eliminate minority, often CROM-influenced unions.[100]

In practice, however, legal measures that were initially adopted to safeguard workers' interests by promoting unionization operated to protect incumbent union leaders from rank-and-file challenges. Both progovernment and politically independent labor leaders have used separation exclusion clauses to defeat union rivals. Yet the broader political significance of contract provisions such as these and of legally recognized unions' authority over collective work agreements is that they provide labor organizations with the means to exercise tight control over rank-and-file union members.

Financial Subsidies

Progovernment labor organizations often benefit as well from state financial subsidies. These subsidies include direct monetary and material assistance to support labor unions' normal operations, in addition to more indirect forms of economic subsidy such as government officials' decision not to tax union-owned properties or union enterprises. Some analysts have identified labor leader corruption as an important reason for "official" unions' frequent failure to act assertively in support of rank-and-file demands.[101] Corruption among labor leaders certainly exists (though its extent is virtually impossible to document), and it may even have the political significance that many analysts attribute to it. Similarly, progovernment unions' favored access to publicly funded social welfare benefits (discussed in chapter 6) has also promoted their dependence on the state. However, this discussion focuses on the more general phenomenon of state economic support for the "official" labor movement and direct monetary and material assistance to selected labor organizations.

Since the late 1930s the Confederation of Mexican Workers has been the principal—but not exclusive—beneficiary of state financial support.[102] Over several decades government financial support permitted the CTM to engage in a wide variety of activities that reinforced its politically dominant position in the labor movement. State financial support has been essential to the CTM because of its longstanding inability to compel affiliated unions to make membership dues payments. Direct public economic support has also been important to the CTM's state and regional federations, but these organizations derive considerable financial benefit from the compulsory dues checkoff specified in most enterprise-level collective labor contracts. Financial subsidies have been a key source of CTM dependence on the state.

The CTM's founders, conscious of Mexican labor organizations' long history of financial weakness and their consequent vulnerability to pressure from employers and state authorities, sought to ensure the confederation's economic and political independence. The CTM's 1936 statutes called for affiliated labor organizations to contribute 0.05 pesos monthly in regular dues for each unionized worker then employed (at the time, the minimum daily wage for workers in the Federal District was 1.50 pesos). This amount was to be deducted by the employer (as specified in each workplace's collective contract) and submitted by the union to the CTM's national secretary for statistics and finances. Individual workers without a collective contract were to submit dues directly to their local CTM-affiliated union, which was to forward payments to national union headquarters in Mexico City. Affiliated organizations that failed to pay confederation dues for three consecutive months would automatically have their CTM membership privileges suspended, and the national executive council was empowered to apply additional sanctions as it considered appropriate. Special dues *(cuotas extraordinarias)* could also be levied on members by vote of either the CTM's national council or its national congress. Each affiliated union or federation was responsible for establishing its own regulations concerning the levying and collection of membership dues for its own operations.[103]

Despite these carefully worded statutory provisions, the actual collection of regular membership dues quickly became one of the CTM's most important problems. At the second national council meeting in October 1936, for example, the finance secretary reported that only 169 of approximately 3,000 affiliates (5.6 percent) had paid their regular confederation dues.[104] CTM leaders expressed serious concern that a failure to finance the confederation's operations from internal sources—and the consequent need to rely on external economic support—would compromise its policy positions. The leadership charged that "the lack of dues payments to the Confederation [was] not the result of affiliated unions' limited economic capacity; instead, it [was] due to the lack of responsibility on the part of leaders who many times either fail[ed] to collect members' dues or improperly retain[ed] them for other use." The finance secretary proposed much stricter application of statutory sanctions to correct this situation, including petitions from the national committee to the unions in question calling for the dismissal of leaders who failed to submit confederation dues.[105]

Yet the available data for the period from 1936 through 1967 indicate that the CTM never fully remedied this problem.[106] From 1936 through 1940 the confederation's average monthly income equaled average monthly expenditures during only one period (November 1938 to June 1939). Regular and special membership dues constituted from 49.2 percent (November 1938–June 1939) to 85.6 percent (February–March 1940) of average monthly income during most of the 1937–40 period, reaching 97.1 percent only in April–June 1940. Although the CTM's total income generally equaled or exceeded its expenditures during the 1950–67 period, the relative contribution made by total membership dues fell sharply over time. In 1950, for example, membership dues only accounted for between 19.2 and 27.0 percent of total confederation income.

Complaints regarding affiliates' failure to submit required confederation dues often accompanied CTM reports on its financial situation from 1936 through the mid-1960s.[107] The CTM estimated that a mere 7 to 10 percent of its members paid their regular dues between 1950 and 1965, even though dues ranged from only 1 to 4 pesos *per year* during this period (the minimum *daily* wage for workers in the Federal District ranged from 3.39 to 21.50 pesos during these years).[108] Matters improved somewhat when the national leadership imposed monthly dues quotas on state federations and affiliated national unions,[109] and in 1972 the confederation reported that "the majority of state federations and national industrial unions ha[d] been paying their Confederation dues on time." [110] However, this statement almost certainly referred only to the most prominent CTM-affiliated labor organizations. It is unlikely that the CTM's leadership had fully resolved its longstanding dues collection problem.

The CTM pursued a variety of strategies to increase its income from union members. For instance, during its early years the CTM relied upon special contributions and loans from affiliated unions to pay rent and electrical bills for its national administrative offices, to cover the expenses incurred by delegates dispatched throughout the country to establish state-level federations, and to fund special projects such as emergency aid to the Republican effort in the Spanish civil war. However, the confederation encountered little success in convincing member organizations to allow the national executive committee to have employers deduct national dues directly from workers' salaries, and as a result its outstanding debt grew rapidly. In the late 1930s the CTM relied heavily on the good will of its creditors in order to continue operations.

Financial difficulties constrained the CTM's organizational activities by limiting the number of occasions on which the confederation could dispatch representatives from national headquarters to assist affiliates in the resolution of specific problems. As a result, the confederation increasingly came to rely on government financial and material support for its operations. For example, the land on which the CTM constructed its new national headquarters in the 1940s (on Vallarta Street in Mexico City) was expropriated by the Ávila Camacho administration for that purpose when it became clear that membership dues would not suffice.[111] Similarly, beginning in September 1937, CTM financial statements recorded the first of a series of "donations" toward confederation operating expenses. In contrast to previous loans and donations from affiliated organizations, no source was listed for these monies. Nor were these amounts included among the loans to be repaid to affiliates. It is very probable that these contributions came from the federal government.

The first of these external financial subsidies accounted for 7.2 percent of average monthly income in January–September 1937 and 14.2 percent of average monthly income in July–October 1938. Despite the problems the CTM encountered in collecting membership dues, sources other than regular and special dues and loans from affiliated organizations never constituted more than 38.0 percent (in July–October 1938) of average monthly income during the 1936–40 period. But during April–December 1950—at a time when the CTM was beset by factional conflict and heavily dependent on the federal government's political support—unspecified donations averaged 62.2 percent of monthly income.[112] During the 1970s, some observers estimated that direct government financial subsidies to the CTM ranged from 500,000 to several million pesos annually. Much of this money was apparently channeled from the federal government to the CTM through the Institutional Revolutionary Party.[113]

Political Subsidies

Major progovernment labor organizations have benefited over time from two forms of political subsidy. First, state authorities have frequently intervened to defend "official" unions and their leaders against serious challenges by opposition labor or political groups. In the late 1940s and early 1950s, for example, the federal government's forceful attacks on opposition labor organizations helped preserve the CTM's political dominance in the labor movement.[114] Less dramatically, government labor authorities at the national and state levels have on numerous occasions acted to protect the incumbent leaders of progovernment unions against rank-and-file challenges.

Preferential access to elective office and government administrative positions is a second important political subsidy to the leaders of the CTM and other important "official" unions. The principal vehicle for the distribution of political rewards to progovernment labor leaders is Mexico's "party of the revolution," which from its founding in 1929 until the late 1980s enjoyed virtually unchallenged control over access to elective office. During this period, nomination by the party as a candidate for public office essentially guaranteed election to that position, and elective positions at the federal, state, and local levels were distributed as incentives and rewards to regime supporters. Constitutional reforms in 1932 that prohibited the reelection of governors and the immediate reelection of federal and state legislators and municipal officials were especially important in this regard because they created additional mobility opportunities for worker and peasant leaders during a crucial phase of regime consolidation.[115]

The election of government-allied labor leaders to public office provides a formal channel for the articulation of organized labor's demands for legislation, social programs, and so forth. Political representation at the federal, state, or local level can also increase labor organizations' bargaining leverage with government officials and private employers. However, because of the limited influence that national and state legislative bodies have traditionally had in Mexico's executive-dominated authoritarian regime, elected legislative positions are often valued primarily for the political and social prestige they confer on the labor leaders who occupy them. Elected officials may, of course, enjoy opportunities for unlawful enrichment through commissions on government contracts, and they frequently have access to considerable patronage resources. The distribution of such political and economic resources to "official" labor organizations reinforces the political alliance between labor and the governing elite. At the state and local level, control over elective offices may even reinforce labor leaders' control within worker organizations.[116] More generally, access to political office is a symbolic confirmation of labor's inclusion in Mexico's governing coalition.

The value that labor leaders attach to important elective or appointive positions in large part derives from the fact that relatively few individuals of working-class origin have held them. Although Mexico's postrevolutionary regime has been characterized by a comparatively high rate of elite rotation, political elites have come predominantly from urban middle-class backgrounds. Only 3.6 percent of all major national officeholders during the 1946–71 period came from working-class families.[117] During this same period, no more than 7.1 percent of individuals in the national political elite were themselves workers.[118]

Those labor leaders who did succeed in gaining major elective or appointive positions generally came from "official" organizations.[119] Most of the labor leaders rising to high elective office held positions in the federal Chamber of Deputies. A small number held positions in the federal Senate, but few labor leaders became governor, a major leader in the Institutional Revolutionary Party, or the director of a state-owned enterprise.[120] Even these limited opportunities for political mobility, however, represented important incentives for continued loyalty to the established regime.

Tables 3.1 and 3.2 show that, from the late 1930s through the mid-1970s, the Confederation of Mexican Workers was the principal beneficiary of national political mobility opportunities for labor leaders.[121] Its share of "labor sector" positions in the federal Chamber of Deputies and the federal Senate far exceeded the proportion of the unionized labor force which its affiliates controlled. The CTM's political advantage was most striking in the case of the federal Chamber of Deputies (see table 3.1). The confederation's share of all labor deputies ranged from 50.0 percent (1970–73) to 95.2 percent (1958–61); its average share for the 1937–73 period was

TABLE 3.1 Labor Representation in Mexican Federal Chamber of Deputies, 1937–1973
(Total Number and as Percentage of All Labor Deputies)

Organization	1937–40	1940–43	1943–46	1946–49	1949–52	1952–55
Confederation of Mexican Workers (CTM)	6 (85.7%)	7 (77.8%)	8 (80.0%)	7 (87.5%)	4 (57.1%)	7 (77.8%)
Revolutionary Confederation of Workers and Peasants (CROC)	0	0	0	0	1 (14.3%)	0
Mexican Regional Labor Confederation (CROM)	0	1 (11.1%)	0	0	0	0
General Confederation of Workers (CGT)	0	0	0	0	0	1 (11.1%)
National industrial unions [a]	0	0	1 (10.0%)	1 (12.5%)	1 (14.3%)	1 (11.1%)
Unknown affiliation [b]	1 (14.3%)	1 (11.1%)	1 (10.0%)	0	1 (14.3%)	0
Total federal deputies affiliated with labor organizations	7	9	10	8	7	9
As percentage of all federal deputies	4.1%	5.2%	6.8%	5.4%	4.8%	5.6%

Organization	1955–58	1958–61	1961–64	1964–67	1967–70	1970–73
Confederation of Mexican Workers (CTM)	11 (84.6%)	20 (95.2%)	14 (63.6%)	21 (67.7%)	24 (64.9%)	18 (50.0%)
Revolutionary Confederation of Workers and Peasants (CROC)	1 (7.7%)	0	3 (13.6%)	4 (12.9%)	6 (16.2%)	6 (16.7%)
Mexican Regional Labor Confederation (CROM)	1 (7.7%)	0	4 (18.2%)	1 (3.2%)	2 (5.4%)	3 (8.3%)
General Confederation of Workers (CGT)	0	0	0	0	0	0
National industrial unions [a]	0	1 (4.8%)	0	5 (16.1%)	5 (13.5%)	7 (19.4%)
Unknown affiliation [b]	0	0	1 (4.5%)	0	0	2 (5.6%)
Total federal deputies affiliated with labor organizations	13	21	22	31	37	36
As percentage of all federal deputies	8.0%	13.0%	12.4%	17.3%	20.9%	20.2%

Sources: For 1937–58, author's calculations based on information presented in Basurto, "La influencia de la economía y del estado en las huelgas: El caso de México" (1962), appendix, 93–102; for 1958–73, author's correspondence with Jorge Basurto, May 1978. The data for both periods may be somewhat incomplete.

Note: These data include federal deputies but not their alternates. No information on deputies' specific organizational affiliation is available after 1973.

[a] Includes Mexican Railroad Workers' Union (STFRM), Mexican Mining and Metalworkers' Union (SITMMSRM), Mexican Petroleum Workers' Union (STPRM).

[b] Deputy's organizational affiliation cannot be determined on the basis of the available information.

TABLE 3.2 Labor Representation in the Mexican Federal Senate, 1936–1976 (Total Number and as Percentage of All Labor Senators)

Organization	1936–40	1940–46	1946–52	1952–58	1958–64	1964–70	1970–76
Confederation of Mexican Workers (CTM)	1 (33.3%)	6 (85.7%)	1 (20.0%)	1 (16.7%)	5 (71.4%)	1 (16.7%)	4 (57.1%)
National industrial unions[a]	2 (66.7%)	0	3 (60.0%)	2 (33.3%)	1 (14.3%)	4 (66.7%)	3 (42.9%)
Unknown affiliation[b]	0	1 (14.3%)	1 (20.0%)	3 (50.0%)	1 (14.3%)	1 (16.7%)	0
Total federal senators affiliated with labor organizations	3	7	5	6	7	6	7
As percentage of all federal senators	5.2%	12.1%	8.6%	10.0%	11.7%	10.0%	11.7%

Sources: For 1936–58, author's calculations based on information presented in Basurto, "La influencia de la economía y del estado en las huelgas: El caso de México," appendix, 85–88; for 1958–76, author's correspondence with Jorge Basurto, May 1978. The data for both periods may be somewhat incomplete.

Note: These data include federal senators but not their alternates. No information on senators' specific organizational affiliation is available after 1976.

[a] Includes Mexican Railroad Workers' Union (STFRM), Mexican Mining and Metalworkers' Union (SITMMSRM), Mexican Petroleum Workers' Union (STPRM), Mexican Electrical Workers' Union (STERM).

[b] Senator's organizational affiliation cannot be determined on the basis of the available information.

74.3 percent. Because it is likely that some representatives whose organizational affiliation is unknown were also CTM members, these data may somewhat underestimate the CTM's control over labor representation in the Chamber of Deputies. The low point in CTM representation occurred at a time when President Luis Echeverría (1970–76) sought to replace the CTM leadership surrounding Fidel Velázquez as part of his broader program of political and socioeconomic reform.[122]

No other labor confederation or group of unions held more than 19.4 percent of the labor positions in the federal Chamber of Deputies during the 1937–73 period (the combined share attained by three national industrial unions representing railroad, mining and metalworking, and petroleum workers in 1970–73).[123] Until the late 1950s, the government awarded labor organizations other than the CTM one or two deputy positions in each legislative session in order to maintain the appearance of pluralism in the political representation of organized labor. Only very influential national industrial unions could expect to receive a position in the Chamber of Deputies with any regularity. However, as the result of a substantial increase in the labor sector's proportion of total federal deputy positions after 1958, the government increased the access of labor organizations other than the CTM to such positions in an effort to balance the interplay among government-allied unions. Only the politically marginal General Confederation of Workers (CGT) failed to benefit from this initiative.

The data concerning labor representation in the federal Senate between 1936 and 1976 are considerably less complete than those for the Chamber of Deputies. Nevertheless, it is noteworthy that *only* the CTM and major national industrial unions placed representatives in the Senate during this forty-year period (see table 3.2). It is quite likely that some senators whose organizational affiliation is unknown were also CTM members, which would increase somewhat the relative share of labor positions it held in the Senate. From 1940 to 1988, one of the two Senate seats in the Federal District was reserved for the CTM. It was held by Fidel Velázquez or one of his closest collaborators.[124]

Conclusion

In the decades following the 1910–20 revolution, Mexico's new political leadership forged an alliance with major elements of the emerging organized labor movement. This alliance was, in the first instance, based on the postrevolutionary elite's acceptance of labor as a legitimate actor entitled to play a significant role in national political and economic affairs. The 1917 federal constitution recognized important social rights for workers, and the tripartite composition of conciliation and arbitration boards and minimum-wage commissions linked labor to the postrevolutionary state's administrative apparatus. During the 1920s and 1930s, different presidential administrations actively supported unionization at a time when labor remained organizationally weak in most industries. Both then and later, provisions in federal labor law and collective work contracts that granted officially recognized unions a representational monopoly in the workplace operated as a generalized subsidy to labor by strengthening workers' bargaining leverage in wage and contract negotiations with employers. In addition, favored labor organizations received financial and political subsidies from state authorities. Linking the Confederation of Mexican Workers to a reorganized governing party symbolized the postrevolutionary alliance between organized labor and the governing political elite.

During the Cárdenas administration, shared ideological perspectives and common programmatic objectives underpinned broad labor support for the regime. Over time, however, the durability of this alliance increasingly depended upon major labor organizations' willingness to moderate their demands and control rank-and-file participation in exchange for state-provided legal, financial, and political subsidies. Labor organizations themselves became important mechanisms of political control. Their capacity to perform this function rested in part on legal measures that protected incumbent union leaders from rank-and-file challenges. Yet the effectiveness of such instruments as separation exclusion clauses depended primarily upon the political dominance within the labor movement of an accommodationist labor leadership committed to a pragmatic alliance with the governing elite. The consolidation of a postrevolutionary social pact occurred, then, not with CTM membership in the governing party but with the political triumph of progovernment labor leaders in the aftermath of a major labor crisis in the late 1940s.

CHAPTER FOUR

Turning Point: The 1947–1951 Labor Crisis and the Consolidation of a Social Pact with Organized Labor

The labor movement unity achieved by founding the Confederation of Mexican Workers was fragile indeed. Even after the 1937 secession crisis passed, the CTM was riven by ideological and policy disputes as different groups competed to impose their vision on the country's largest and most influential labor organization. The World War II policy of "national unity" adopted by the Ávila Camacho administration (1940–46), the CTM, and the Mexican Communist Party temporarily masked these divisions, but they quickly resurfaced in the postwar period. One of the key questions in Mexican politics in the late 1940s was whether the inclusive alliance forged by union activists and Cárdenas would survive the far more conservative policies of President Miguel Alemán (1946–52). Fundamental disagreements within the CTM concerning its relationship with the Institutional Revolutionary Party (PRI) were aggravated by Alemán's generally conservative labor policies, especially the government's efforts to restrict the right to strike and its pursuit of economic policies that seriously eroded workers' living standards.

A major political crisis erupted in 1947–48 when a large, influential group of dissident unions seceded from the CTM to form an opposition labor alliance. The Coalición de Organizaciones Obreras y Campesinas (Coalition of Worker and Peasant Organizations, COOC) threatened to eclipse the CTM as the country's most important labor organization and deprive the government of a reliable base of labor support. The Alemán administration responded forcefully, intervening in the leading opposition unions to eliminate a major political and economic challenge. By the early 1950s, the government had ensured both the preeminence of pragmatic leaders within the CTM and the CTM's political dominance in the labor movement, in effect consolidating a social pact between organized labor and the governing political elite which would survive relatively intact into the 1980s. Thus the 1947–51 labor crisis marked a decisive turning point in postrevolutionary Mexican politics.

The fault lines that split the CTM in the late 1940s paralleled closely those that divided the labor movement in the 1920s and 1930s. On one side, unions representing workers in strategically important activities such as the railroad, electrical power generation, petroleum, telephone, and mining and metalworking industries strove to safeguard their members' interests by defending their autonomy vis-à-vis the government and the "official" party. Workers in these industries had an important tradition of independent labor organization, and the formation of national unions substantially increased their political and economic bargaining power. Moreover, they had a long history of militancy based in their struggles against foreign employers, which both imbued them with a strong commitment to revolutionary nationalism and progressive state action and encouraged them to link workplace demands to debate about national development strategy. In the case of the largest railroad companies and the petroleum industry, these struggles had ended in nationalization of foreigners' assets. State ownership (and, at least in the case of railroad transportation, the fact that many company managers were former railroad workers) further increased railroad and petroleum workers' political leverage.

These unions were distinguished, then, by their size, national organizational structure, and financial resources and by the fact that the industries they represented were the most important sectors of the Mexican economy in the decades before widespread industrialization. In some cases internal factionalism remained a serious problem—and a weakness that government officials sought to exploit—because their members were geographically dispersed (in the case of mining and petroleum production), employed by separate companies (mining and metalworking, railroad transportation, electrical power generation), or divided among different occupational specializations (railroad transportation and petroleum production). Nevertheless, these unions constituted the backbone of the Mexican labor movement. Their forceful opposition to conservative government economic and labor policies (especially attempts to restrict the right to strike), their resistance to some CTM leaders' efforts to reduce their political autonomy vis-à-vis the "official" party, and their desire to play a leading role in national labor affairs made them the principal base for the opposition coalition formed in 1947–48. Establishing reliable control over them was among the most pressing political tasks confronting the Alemán administration because, so long as major national industrial unions remained politically autonomous, both postwar economic policy and postrevolutionary governments' strategy of exercising political control over workers through state-subsidized organizations such as the CTM were in jeopardy.

In contrast, the majority of CTM affiliates were enterprise- and plant-level unions organized in state and regional federations. Many of these unions, reflecting labor force characteristics in light manufacturing, construction, and the service sector, were small and organizationally weak. As a result, the heterogeneous federations with which they were associated remained heavily dependent on legal, financial, and political subsidies from the state. Different state governors underscored the extent of this dependence in the early 1940s when they tried to weaken the CTM by encouraging its affiliates to join the rival labor organizations they sponsored.[1] Because the majority of CTM affiliates lacked mobilizational capacity equal to that of national industrial unions, and because they had weaker ties to opposition political groups, their leaders were more committed to preserving a pragmatic alliance with the national political elite. As a result, they generally sought accommodation with the government and the "official" party. Such organizations provided the principal base of labor support for government policies during the 1940s.

This chapter examines the causes of political division in the CTM in the 1940s, the emergence and defeat of the opposition labor coalition, and the subsequent character of state-labor relations in Mexico. The centerpiece of this analysis is a case study of the Mexican Railroad Workers' Union (STFRM) in the 1940s, the leader of the opposition labor coalition and the single most important union in Mexico during this period. The STFRM was the Alemán administration's first target as it moved to demobilize the Coalition of Worker and Peasant Organizations and establish control over national industrial unions. Moreover, the tactics the Alemán administration employed against the STFRM and the specific mechanisms used to ensure its political loyalty were later exploited to defeat democratic leaders in the petroleum workers' and mining-metalworkers' unions. The STFRM case thus exemplifies the challenge posed by politically autonomous national industrial unions during the 1940s and the long-term consequences of government action against them. A close analysis of this case also illustrates how important state administrative controls (including provisions in the federal labor code and government control over conciliation and arbitration boards) are to national political leaders' ability to defeat major labor opposition movements.

The 1947–51 labor crisis merits detailed attention because it was a defining moment in the evolution of postrevolutionary state-labor relations. Although some analyses have assumed otherwise, the formation of the CTM in 1936 and its affiliation with a restructured governing party in 1938 did not resolve the question of organized labor's place in the postrevolutionary regime.[2] It is important to emphasize that the postrevolutionary alliance with the governing political elite was not consolidated at the same time among all parts of the labor movement. The CTM's political dominance from the early 1950s onward was the product of protracted political conflict in the 1940s.

Focusing on the role of the Mexican Railroad Workers' Union sheds important new light on national labor politics during the crucial decade of the 1940s. Some analyses of this period stress that Alemán's assault on the labor opposition was an instance of Cold War anticommunism, motivated in part by these unions' association with leftist parties.[3] Anticommunism was a significant element in government policy toward these unions, though perhaps not as important a consideration as the U.S. government wished. The Alemán administration was even more concerned, however, to gain reliable political control over those parts of the labor movement most capable of spearheading national opposition to government economic and labor policies, and whose political independence obstructed the consolidation of the CTM's national influence under pragmatic, accommodationist leaders.

In the specific case of the STFRM, the Alemán administration also sought to establish the labor conditions that would permit railroad modernization. Because of the railroad transportation system's crucial importance for industrialization, the burden of postwar economic restructuring fell squarely on railroad workers. The government's actions in 1948–49 culminated a decade-long campaign to restructure workplace relations and adjust employment and wage levels in order to increase railroads' operating efficiency and limit their financial losses. Similar factors played a role in the Alemán administration's intervention in the petroleum workers' union. However, the absence of detailed studies of industry-level labor politics in mining and metalworking and other key sectors makes it difficult to judge the extent to which the STFRM episode was representative of the broad challenges confronting national industrial unions in an extensive postwar process of economic restructuring.[4]

More generally, this case study demonstrates the importance of linking an analysis of national-level labor politics to developments in specific industries. A sectoral focus highlights the relationship between socioeconomic change at the workplace level and union involvement in political activities. This connection was particularly strong for STFRM members because their principal employer was the state; consequently, government decisions regarding such matters as wage increases were closely linked to questions of national economic development policy and railroad transportation subsidies for other industries. The STFRM case, then, captures the special dilemmas confronting national industrial unions in the 1940s and their central importance in the 1947–51 labor crisis.

Political Fragmentation of the Confederation of Mexican Workers

From its founding, the CTM was divided by ideological differences, policy disagreements, disputes over internal decision-making procedures, and personal rivalries. By the early 1940s, however, these divisions increasingly reflected a broader struggle between moderate and radical factions for control over the political orientation of the organized labor movement, a battle whose course was significantly affected by President Manuel Ávila Camacho's efforts to end the labor mobilizations of the 1930s and mollify conservative business and political interests after Cárdenas left office.[5] Ávila Camacho sought to ease tensions between workers and employers and muffle divisions within the labor movement by calling for "national unity" following Mexico's formal entry into World War II on the side of the Allies in May 1942. Cárdenas's presence in the cabinet as minister of national defense between 1942 and 1945, the longtime friendship between Vicente Lombardo Toledano (CTM secretary-general, 1936–41) and Ávila Camacho (they were both from the same small town in Puebla), and the Mexican Communist Party's endorsement of wartime labor-government cooperation all helped persuade more radical labor elements to moderate their demands and continue their "popular front" policy of limiting conflict with the government.

In June 1942, Mexico's most important labor organizations signed a "Pacto de Unidad Obrera" ("Labor Unity Pact") that pledged their support for the war effort. The signatories included the CTM, the Mexican Regional Labor Confederation (CROM), the General Confederation of Workers (CGT), the Confederación Proletaria Nacional (National Proletarian Confederation, CPN, a conservative labor group formed by CTM dissidents in February 1942), the Confederación de Obreros y Campesinos de México (Confederation of Mexican Workers and Peasants, COCM, organized by CROM dissidents in January 1942), and the Mexican Electricians' Union. These organizations agreed to avoid strikes, limit wage demands, and increase productivity during the wartime emergency.[6] At Ávila Camacho's suggestion, in June 1942 the CTM, CROM, and CGT also joined with the Mexican Communist Party (PCM) and several individual unions to establish the Consejo Obrero Nacional (National Worker Council, CON), whose main goal was to reduce interunion strife. The CON helped resolve some conflicts, but it met only intermittently and virtually collapsed in 1945 when more conservative labor groups united to expel the CTM.[7] It did, however, symbolize the way in which the national unity policy temporarily masked serious divisions within the CTM and the labor movement more generally.

The CTM's commitment to avoid strikes and limit wage demands also reflected an important shift in the balance of power among its constituent organizations. By the early 1940s, a group advocating pragmatic accommodation with the government and with business interests had consolidated its hold on the confederation's main leadership positions. The group's dominant figure was Fidel Velázquez Sánchez, whose rise to national power in the labor movement resulted from his successful use of his position as CTM secretary for organization between 1936 and 1941 to build a network of state and regional federations loyal to him.[8] Equally important, however, Velázquez received strong backing from both Lombardo Toledano and President Ávila Camacho. The former promoted Velázquez's election as CTM secretary-general in March 1941, and the latter intervened to keep him at the head of the country's largest labor organization until 1947, when he was succeeded by his close ally Fernando Amilpa y Rivera.[9]

Two factors shaped Velázquez's attitude toward government and the "official" party in the 1940s. First, Velázquez's political beliefs (which might be characterized as conservative nationalism) were firmly rooted in his working-class background and his early experiences as a labor activist. Born in April 1900 in a rural village in the state of México, he worked at different times as a field hand on a local hacienda, in a lumberyard, and as a milkman.[10] The tumult of the Mexican revolution was his most important formative experience (his father was killed, and he was wounded, by forces allied with Obregón during a skirmish in Puebla). Throughout his life he was both firmly committed to realizing the revolution's egalitarian goals within the established political and economic order and deeply loyal to such institutions as the "party of the revolution." Velázquez's lifelong commitment to political pragmatism also probably reflected his close observation of the fate that befell the CROM when Luis N. Morones publicly challenged the Portes Gil administration in 1928. Moreover, his struggle with PCM supporters for control over the political direction of the organized labor movement gave a strongly anticommunist cast to his views. Velázquez came into conflict with Communist labor activists as early as 1935, and as CTM secretary-general in the early 1940s he ousted radical opponents from positions of influence within the confederation.[11]

Second, the composition of the Velázquez group's original base within the CTM made it particularly dependent on state support. Velázquez and his allies drew their strongest political support from the CTM's relatively small company- and plant-level unions organized in heterogeneous state

and regional federations. His first experience as a labor activist was organizing a union of milkmen and dairy workers in the Mexico City area in
1924. Similarly, Velázquez's closest allies in the CTM (Fernando Amilpa,
Jesús Yurén Aguilar, Alfonso Sánchez Madariaga, and Luis Quintero—
who were, with Velázquez, known collectively as the "five little wolves")
all came from union backgrounds in commerce, transportation, urban services, light manufacturing industries, and construction in Mexico City.[12]
Their organizations represented a numerically large but predominantly
low-skilled labor force with limited mobilizational capacity. Thus political skills and government connections, not their unions' size or economic
bargaining leverage, permitted Velázquez and his closest supporters to rise
through the CROM in the 1920s and take control of the CTM in the early
1940s. The Ávila Camacho administration's efforts in the early 1940s to
weaken the CTM by giving legal recognition to more conservative labor
organizations such as the CPN and COCM underscored for the Velázquez
group their dependence on state subsidies.[13] Velázquez's ability to safeguard his own position within the confederation, then, depended upon a
CTM policy of pragmatic collaboration with the governing elite.

With political support from the CTM's new leadership and other labor
groups, the Ávila Camacho administration pursued policies considerably
more conservative than those adopted by Cárdenas during the popular
mobilizations of the mid-1930s. In 1941, for example, the recently inaugurated administration tightened procedural requirements for strike petitions
in order to prevent "the abuse of the right to strike" and block spontaneous
work stoppages. New legislation imposed harsh penalties (large fines and
prison sentences of up to two years) on strikers causing "moral or physical violence or coercion."[14] In addition, the government enacted special
wartime laws that limited such individual political rights as the freedom
of assembly. A modification of federal labor law in 1943 further limited
workers' right to strike.[15] More restrictive strike legislation did not prevent labor mobilization (indeed, the number of legally recognized strikes in
federal-jurisdiction industries rose sharply in 1943 and 1944; see table 5.1).
But powerful national industrial unions especially objected to restrictions
on collective actions that reduced their bargaining effectiveness with employers.

Worker resentment of these policies was fueled by wartime inflation.
The economy grew rapidly during World War II in response to government
stimulus for domestic industrialization and heightened demand for Mexican exports. Gross domestic product (GDP, measured in constant 1970
prices) increased at an average annual rate of 5.0 percent between 1941
and 1946, and real gross domestic product per capita grew by an average
annual rate of 2.3 percent over the same period.[16] However, inflation was a

serious problem throughout the war years. The annual rate of inflation (the annual increase in the cost of living for workers in Mexico City) averaged 17.8 percent per year between 1941 and 1946, reaching 24.6 percent in 1946 (see table 6.1).

The Ávila Camacho government took several steps to control inflation and to compensate workers for its impact on their living standards. For instance, the administration tried to compel private employers to meet their constitutional obligation to provide adequate housing for workers, established a system to distribute basic commodities at subsidized prices, and in January 1943 created a national health care system, the Instituto Mexicano del Seguro Social (Mexican Social Security Institute, IMSS). Moreover, the government established a regional administrative system to implement price controls. In September 1943 it also granted an emergency wage increase to lowest-paid workers.[17] Nevertheless, the coverage of both the commodity distribution system and the IMSS was initially quite limited, and the de facto wage freeze that the Ávila Camacho administration imposed in most industries between 1940 and 1945 produced a sharp decline in real wage levels. Real minimum wages fell by 28.9 percent between 1941 and 1946 (see the real-minimum-wage index for Mexico City in table 6.1).

The CTM's response to these policies was somewhat ambivalent. In April 1945 it joined with the Cámara Nacional de la Industria de Transformación (National Chamber of Manufacturing Industries, CNIT, created to represent the manufacturing firms supportive of import-substituting industrialization) in a "Pacto Obrero Industrial" ("Industrial Labor Pact") whose principal goals were to promote worker-employer peace, restrain inflation, and thereby attract foreign investment.[18] Yet in early 1946, under growing pressure from national unions representing railroad, petroleum, textile, and tramway workers and miners and metalworkers, the CTM's national leadership took a more assertive position regarding government economic policy.[19] In February 1946, for example, the CTM organized a national work stoppage to protest the negative impact of inflation on workers' wages, and in May 1946 it called upon the Ávila Camacho administration to regulate prices, control access to consumer products, ban the export of basic consumer goods, and regulate the banking system in order to prevent financial speculation. In June 1946 it also threatened a national labor mobilization, which forced Ávila Camacho to promise more effective anti-inflation measures.[20]

Slower economic growth and continued inflation after World War II aggravated longstanding tensions within the CTM, which reached crisis proportions in 1947 and 1948. Factional divisions within the confederation's diverse membership increasingly coalesced around two opposing groups: the more moderate Velázquez faction with its support in the confederation's heterogeneous state and regional federation affiliates, and more radical elements, often influenced by leftist opposition parties, based in the CTM's national industrial unions.[21] Elections to select Velázquez's successor and a new national executive committee pitted Fernando Amilpa, a prominent member of the Velázquez faction and at the time a federal senator, against José Luis Gómez Zepeda (known as Luis Gómez Z.), secretary-general of the Mexican Railroad Workers' Union and the CTM's secretary for labor and conflicts between August 1944 and June 1946.[22]

As tensions rose, Gómez Z. and his supporters boycotted a meeting of the CTM's national council in January 1947, and the STFRM seceded from the confederation in late February. Amilpa was formally declared the CTM's new secretary-general at its national congress held on March 26–28, 1947. However, the Gómez Z. coalition protested that Amilpa's supporters had manipulated the registration of delegates' credentials at the congress in order to gain control of the executive committee. Moreover, the election procedures adopted for the congress reversed the 1936 statutory requirement that affiliated unions' accredited votes equal their total membership. Instead, in 1947 each labor organization affiliated with the CTM received one vote—thus dramatically increasing the electoral importance of the small, but numerous, company- and plant-level unions that formed the Velázquez faction's base of support, while greatly diminishing the electoral strength of large national unions.

As CTM secretary-general, Amilpa further exacerbated internal divisions by allying the confederation even more closely with the government and the Institutional Revolutionary Party and by mounting attacks on leftist influence in the CTM. For example, he endorsed the increasingly conservative Alemán administration's plans for labor law reforms that would have placed even tighter restrictions on workers' right to strike.[23] Equally controversially, Amilpa proclaimed that all CTM members were *individually* obligated to become members of the newly reorganized "official" party, the PRI, or face expulsion from the confederation.[24] Some labor groups had long viewed ties to the ruling party as a form of state control, and Amilpa's action infuriated many affiliated organizations because it violated policy statements adopted at the last CTM national congress which reaffirmed the CTM's political autonomy.[25] The shift in CTM orientation was captured well by a change in its motto in March 1947, from "For a Classless Society" ("Por una sociedad sin clases") to "For the Emancipation of Mexico" ("Por la emancipación de México").

Labor organizations opposed to Amilpa's election and the policies he represented formed a "Central Committee for Orientation, Propaganda, and Labor Unity" in March 1947. This was to be the first step toward "renewing the CTM" and organizing a new labor unity confederation (*central única).* Its advocates promised that the new confederation would respect the ideals and programmatic goals espoused by the CTM at its founding,[26] especially the labor movement's political independence from the state and the ruling party.

With Gómez Z. and the STFRM taking the lead, dissident unions met in Mexico City on March 20–22, 1947, to form an alternative labor confederation. Some 2,700 delegates, claiming to represent 352,397 workers, attended.[27] The program submitted by the organizing committee for discussion at the "Labor Unity Congress" criticized the CTM for silencing internal dissent and creating "a real dictatorship" over unions in different states. It also focused on the need for national labor unity and an "independent political orientation," calling for worker actions to influence the direction of national development strategy; alternative government policies to control inflation, protect workers' purchasing power, and improve worker access to housing and other social welfare benefits; progressive labor legislation; ideological education for workers; and the resolution of rural labor problems. However, given the anticommunist tenor of the early Cold War years in Mexico (government and PRI harassment of Communists increased sharply in early 1947),[28] Gómez Z. took pains to deny that Communists had any influence over this initiative. He also denied that it challenged the fundamental authority of the Alemán government.[29]

The thirty-seven labor organizations present at the congress included nine national unions (representing railroad, telephone, electrical power generation, tramway, cement industry, aviation, and motorized transport workers, among others); six labor federations and enterprise-level unions; five CTM state federations (those representing Guanajuato, Jalisco, México, Morelos, and Nuevo León); and seventeen additional regional or local labor groups representing workers in twelve other states throughout the country. Voting rights accredited to participating organizations were proportional to their membership size, thus increasing the influence of major national industrial unions.[30] The congress ended with the formation of the Confederación Única de Trabajadores (Unitary Workers' Confederation, CUT).

In the weeks after its founding congress, the CUT called upon the government to take various steps to resolve the country's postwar economic problems. It emphasized that unemployment and inflation affected a broad range of economic activities, including construction, textiles, footwear, and other light manufacturing industries. The mining industry was hit particularly hard by the decline in export demand following the end of World War II. The CUT expressed concern that, unless the Alemán administration took corrective measures immediately, recession would soon affect commerce, finance, transportation, and other manufacturing industries.[31]

Several months later, the Mexican Railroad Workers' Union again took the initiative in forging an alliance among the three largest national industrial unions in Mexico—the STFRM, the Mexican Mining and Metalworkers' Union (SITMMSRM), and the Sindicato de Trabajadores Petroleros de la República Mexicana (Mexican Petroleum Workers' Union, STPRM).[32] The "Friendship and Solidarity Pact" they signed in January 1948 linked 185,000 workers. It called for joint meetings of the three unions' executive committees, mutual financial assistance, and coordinated strikes when necessary to support an individual union's actions. In most cases, the signatories were obligated to provide such assistance when requested by any member of the alliance, but national strike action required unanimous agreement by all three unions. The objectives of the alliance included labor movement unity, "opposing all imperialist aggressions" by means ranging from written propaganda to a general strike, and achieving a wide range of other labor demands.[33] The STFRM's Luis Gómez Z. headed the Unity Executive Committee.

These organizational initiatives, and further polarization within the CTM (which resulted in Lombardo Toledano's expulsion in January 1948),[34] set the stage for the formation of a much broader labor coalition opposing both Amilpa's leadership and the Alemán administration's labor and economic policies. By February 1948 this coalition included the CUT; national unions representing railroad, mining and metalworking, petroleum, electrical power generation, and textile industry workers; and several other labor groups. The coalition's diverse opposition activities included a February 1948 protest march against the Supreme Court's antistrike rulings which reportedly mobilized some sixty thousand workers and prompted Alemán to defend publicly existing legislation regulating strikes,[35] as well as a call in May 1948 for effective price controls, a general wage increase, and trade restrictions that would block imports of luxury goods and prevent the export of such basic commodities as sugar and rice. Its motto was "Bread, Peace, and Liberty" ("Pan, Paz y Libertad"). The coalition also publicly endorsed the leftist Confederación de Trabajadores de América Latina (Latin American Workers' Confederation, CTAL). Other unions representing teachers and IMSS employees joined the coalition in support of these demands.[36]

These opposition groups together formed the Coalition of Worker and Peasant Organizations (COOC), which by mid-1948 constituted a serious challenge to the CTM's claim to be Mexico's most important labor organization. In June 1948 the COOC listed the following affiliates and members: CUT (400,000), STFRM (90,000), SITMMSRM (85,000), STPRM (35,000), Alianza de Obreros y Campesinos de México (Alliance of Mexican Workers and Peasants, the organization that Lombardo Toledano founded in March 1948 after his expulsion from the CTM, 180,000), and Confederación Nacional de Electricistas (National Confederation of Electricians, 40,000).[37] Because the coalition sought to establish itself as the country's largest (and therefore most politically significant) labor organization, its claim to represent 830,000 workers may well have been inflated. However, a government census of all legally registered labor organizations in 1948 found that 30.4 percent of all unionized workers in federal-jurisdiction economic activities were affiliated with the COOC, whereas only 21.0 percent were affiliated with the CTM.[38] The union census underestimated the CTM's overall support, which was located in large part in local-jurisdiction economic activities. Yet these data clearly indicate the threat that opposition elements posed to the CTM's position, especially in strategically important federal-jurisdiction economic activities.[39]

The Coalition of Worker and Peasant Organizations thus constituted a serious political challenge to the Alemán administration. It opposed the administration's labor policies and called for the dismissal of some cabinet members.[40] Even though the Velázquez faction had gained control over CTM leadership positions, the COOC threatened to eclipse the CTM and other confederations (mainly the CPN and COCM) that together represented the government's principal base of labor support.[41] Equally significant, the opposition labor coalition vigorously opposed important elements of government economic policy in the difficult post–World War II adjustment period, during which the Alemán administration sought to lay the bases for sustained industrialization. National industrial unions had the organizational capacity to mobilize opposition to the government's labor and economic policies throughout the country. In November 1947, for example, the STFRM had announced plans to use its thirty-six local sections to coordinate national meetings, a consumer boycott, and possibly a general strike to protest the high cost of living.[42]

Coalition members especially criticized the July 21, 1948, devaluation of the peso.[43] By cutting the peso's value by 41.6 percent, the Alemán administration sought to offset the effects of postwar domestic price inflation, make Mexican exports more competitive abroad, and correct a deteriorating balance-of-payments situation. Government economic planners considered the devaluation a crucial component of Mexico's industrialization program. Its immediate effect, however, was to fuel inflationary pressures by raising the cost of imported consumer and intermediate goods. The adverse effect of inflation on workers' earning power had been a major focus of labor discontent throughout the 1940s,[44] and opposition to the government's wage and price policies was the principal economic issue uniting COOC members.

On August 21, 1948, the coalition organized a demonstration in

Mexico City to protest the inflationary effects of the recent devaluation, an event that drew some forty thousand workers. Similar rallies were held at the same time elsewhere in the country.[45] Teachers, petroleum workers, and railroad workers had filed strike petitions on August 1, 1948, in support of their demands for compensatory wage increases, and in September 1948 coalition members called for a one-time, nationwide wage payment of 100 pesos (at the time, the legal minimum daily wage in Mexico City was 4.50 pesos) to offset the devaluation's effects. The coalition's position on this issue was a distinct contrast to that adopted by the CTM: its policy at the time was to avoid strikes, wage demands, or other actions that would "demonstrate a lack of confidence toward the government." Fernando Amilpa declared that strikes by affiliated unions were permissible only in those firms that recorded excessive profits; strikes to redress general economic problems such as the inflationary impact of the July 1948 devaluation were not acceptable.[46]

The opposition labor challenge to government policies was especially serious because Alemán's political position was at the time challenged by conservative military and business interests. Some elements in the armed forces strongly opposed efforts by Alemán, postrevolutionary Mexico's first civilian president, to reduce the military's role in political affairs. Business opposition to inflation-control policies had recently led to the resignation of the minister of national economy.[47] Faced with a significant labor challenge to his capacity to influence developments in the labor movement and to his control over economic policy, President Alemán maneuvered sharply to disband the Coalition of Worker and Peasant Organizations. His administration's first target was the principal source of political and financial support for the coalition, the Mexican Railroad Workers' Union.

Railroad Workers, Political Opposition, and the Challenges of Economic Restructuring on the Mexican National Railroads

No union played a more central part in opposition labor politics during the 1940s than did the Mexican Railroad Workers' Union. Railroad workers' influence during this period was due to their union's size and organizational strength and the strategic importance of railroad transportation. By using its leverage to forge a broad-based opposition coalition to contest the political direction of the labor movement and the content of government economic policy in the years after World War II, the STFRM became a major obstacle to the Alemán administration's efforts to influence developments in the labor movement and its plans for national industrialization. Limiting STFRM influence was, then, both a political and economic imperative for the Alemán government and a crucial test of its ability to establish reliable control over powerful national industrial unions.

Yet STFRM involvement in labor opposition actions in the 1940s reflected more than a long history of political activism or the ideological preferences of its leaders. Rank-and-file support for these broader initiatives flowed in large part from union resistance to the Ávila Camacho and Alemán administrations' economic restructuring program for Ferrocarriles Nacionales de México (Mexican National Railroads, FNM), the country's largest railroad company. It is thus important to understand the challenges that confronted the union as the Mexican government modernized railroad transportation and restructured workplace relations at FNM during and after World War II, as well as the full range of political and economic factors that led to state intervention in the STFRM in 1948. The Alemán administration's assault on the STFRM in October 1948 ended the union's leadership of the national labor opposition coalition and initiated a sustained government campaign to establish political control over national industrial unions. In the wake of these events, railroad managers effected changes that culminated a decade-long effort to restructure contract clauses, work rules, and employment and wage levels at FNM in order to increase railroad operating efficiency.

Railroad Workers as a Political Force

Three factors made the Mexican Railroad Workers' Union a powerful force in Mexican politics.[48] First, the union's size and national organizational structure gave it broad influence. The STFRM was both the first national industrial union formed in Mexico and among the largest labor organizations in the country. It claimed 75,118 members in 1943; only the Sindicato Nacional de Trabajadores de la Educación (National Education Workers' Union, SNTE, 1943) grouped more workers in a single industry-specific union.[49] The nationwide distribution of the STFRM's thirty-six local sections (some of them located in such important urban and industrial centers as Mexico City, Monterrey, Guadalajara, Puebla, and Veracruz), the ease of movement that the railroad system offered union organizers, and the union's financial resources all gave it greater capacity for coordinating political activities during the 1940s than any other labor organization except the CTM.

Second, railroad workers' historical formation and the ideological influence that leftist political parties had among union members underpinned a strong STFRM commitment to revolutionary nationalist economic policies (including a state-led development strategy that featured public control over basic industries) and union autonomy. In the years leading up to the

Mexican revolution, railroad workers struggled with foreign railroad companies over such issues as wages, working conditions, and the negotiation of collective contracts; the recognition of labor organizations (gremios) as bargaining agents; and employment and promotion policies that favored U.S. workers over their Mexican counterparts. The fight over "Mexicanization" of the railroads (equal access for Mexican workers to such skilled positions as engineer, machinist, fireman, and conductor, and the use of Spanish in written and verbal workplace communications) produced a series of bitter strikes by U.S. employees between 1909 and 1912, heightening Mexican railroad workers' nationalist consciousness.[50] From the early 1900s onward, railroad worker organizations also lobbied hard for the continued nationalization of railroad lines constructed during the Porfiriato. Moreover, the long struggle by railroad unions in the 1920s and early 1930s to limit CROM influence and block political interference by government officials in union affairs created a strong shared commitment among railroad workers to protect union autonomy.[51] Formative experiences such as these, railroad workers' pride in their long history of unionism and their involvement in key historical events (for example, in 1910 railroad workers helped Madero escape from San Luis Potosí at the outbreak of the Mexican revolution, and a railroad worker disguised Obregón as a brakeman and thus arranged his escape from Mexico City in 1920 after Carranza ordered his arrest), and the strong sense of occupational community shared by railroad workers with highly specialized jobs and distinctive forms of dress[52] all shaped the STFRM's commitment to take part in and influence national politics.

STFRM actions in the 1940s were also shaped by leftist opposition parties' influence among railroad workers. The Mexican Communist Party's organizational presence on the railroads dated from the 1920s.[53] The party initially won sympathy for its vigorous support of the Confederación de Sociedades Ferrocarrileras de la República Mexicana's (Confederation of Mexican Railroad Societies, CSFRM, formed in December 1920) strike in February and March 1921 to win recognition as a bargaining agent, a strike opposed by Morones and the CROM. The PCM and the CROM took similarly divergent positions on the 1926–27 strikes by the Mexican Union of Machinists and the Confederation of Transport and Communications Workers (CTC, formed in November 1926) against Ferrocarriles Nacionales de México, conflicts that resulted from railroad workers' opposition to work rule changes, the threat of large-scale layoffs, and the CTC's effort to win recognition as the principal bargaining agent for FNM employees.[54] The serious political defeat that the loosely organized CTC suffered in these strikes led several key railroad labor leaders (including Elías Barrios, Valentín Campa Salazar, and Hernán Laborde) to join the Mexican Communist Party, which advocated a more central-ized form of union organization.[55] In the aftermath of this defeat, the PCM lobbied vigorously for a unified national railroad workers' union and sought to win the reinstallation of employees dismissed as a result of their involvement in the strikes. Its contributions to railroad worker organiza-tion during an extremely difficult period were the party's principal basis for recruiting members.

The PCM had a significant membership among railroad workers,[56] and a number of prominent union leaders were PCM members or sympathiz-ers. Its influence was strongest in major urban areas and railroad main-tenance centers, including Mexico City, Monterrey, Aguascalientes, and southeastern parts of the country (Jalapa and Coatzacoalcos in the state of Veracruz; Oaxaca and Matías Romero in the state of Oaxaca; Tonalá in Chiapas). The PCM had most influence among machinists (*mecánicos*) and repairmen, office employees and station personnel (*oficinistas*), and telegraph operators (*telegrafistas*). It had little support among engineers (*trenistas*) except in the southeast. PCM organizers attributed engineers' political conservatism to their comparatively privileged economic position and the historical influence of U.S. railroad brotherhoods and Masonic traditions among them.

From the STFRM's founding in 1933 until 1948, the PCM and/or leftist organizations such as Acción Socialista Unificada (Unified Socialist Action, ASU, formed in 1946 by Laborde, Miguel Ángel Velasco, and other indi-viduals expelled from the PCM between 1940 and 1943) regularly had one or two members or supporters on the union's national executive commit-tee.[57] A PCM member served as STFRM secretary-general in both 1938–40 (Elías Terán Gómez) and 1940–41 (Jesús R. Solís). Valentín Campa (who was expelled from the PCM in 1940 but remained very active on the Left) held a number of important STFRM positions in the 1940s, and he played a major role in shaping the STFRM's opposition to post–World War II gov-ernment economic policy and in organizing the CUT. Leftist party members and supporters represented, then, an important force within the union, and their alliances with other STFRM factions significantly influenced the union's commitment to interunion solidarity activities and the positions it took on national political and economic questions.

Third, and most significant, railroad workers derived great influence from their strategic military and economic importance. Control over rail-roads was of decisive import to the outcome of armed conflicts during and after the 1910–20 revolution. The sympathy that Adolfo de la Huerta en-joyed among many railroad workers (as minister of finance he encouraged railroad workers to unite in the CSFRM in 1920, and he offered valu-able support for the CSFRM's difficult strike in 1921) led many of them to back his military revolt in 1923 and greatly exacerbated the problems that Obregón and Calles faced in defeating the rebel forces.[58] Railroad workers' stronger loyalty to the government in 1929 was a major advantage in the suppression of the Escobar revolt.[59]

In economic terms, railroads remained Mexico's most important means of passenger and freight transportation. Railroads were the principal means of shipment for many agricultural commodities, fuel (coal and petroleum), industrial and agricultural chemicals, minerals (iron, copper, lead, zinc), construction materials, and a broad range of manufactured goods. Exports of such raw materials as mineral ores depended exclusively on railroad transportation. World War II heightened both the national security and economic importance of railroads. Despite government efforts during the 1930s and 1940s to expand Mexico's network of commercial roads, as late as 1950 there were more miles of railroad (15,356) than federal and state highways (13,282) in the country.[60]

Despite these considerable strengths, the STFRM continued to confront in the 1940s internal organizational problems that were to later prove the source of significant political vulnerability. Many of these difficulties were typical of the challenges that other newly formed national industrial unions faced as they consolidated their positions in the 1930s and 1940s. Because the STFRM was a large national union representing workers employed on a number of railroad lines under different wage scales and contract terms, it regularly faced a broad range of factional disputes.[61] The most severe internal divisions were linked to the STFRM's origin among a substantial number of craft organizations, several of which resisted the exercise of centralized union leadership, the loss of physical assets (including union headquarters buildings), and long-cherished craft traditions. In addition, railroad workers' political loyalties were divided among such diverse organizations as the PCM and the CROM, the last of whose affiliates among railroad workers were formally eliminated only in July 1938.[62]

Economic Restructuring on the Railroads

The greatest challenges facing the STFRM in the 1940s were the Ávila Camacho and Alemán administrations' plans to restructure work rules, redefine contract terms, and cut employment and wage levels at FNM in order to increase the company's operating efficiency and limit its financial losses. Previous attempts to resolve FNM's longstanding financial problems had produced such novel experiments as the 1938–40 Worker Administration. Railroad workers' experience with earlier, ultimately unsuccessful reform plans conditioned them to resist government appeals for contract and work rule changes in the 1940s because they understood that FNM's perennial problems could not be solved by worker sacrifices alone. Worker resistance made economic restructuring on the railroads a bitterly contested issue that underpinned the STFRM's involvement in national labor opposition activities.

Ferrocarriles Nacionales de México had been burdened by heavy debt payments to foreign bondholders from the time the Díaz government formed the company in 1908.[63] Major equipment losses and the destruction of railroad lines during the 1910–20 revolution, military revolts in the 1920s, and the Cristero war significantly worsened the firm's problems. In order to reduce its financial obligations, the government returned FNM to foreign operational control (the government retained 51 percent of its stock) in 1926. The failure of successive reorganization schemes in the late 1920s and early 1930s eventually led the Cárdenas administration to expropriate the company in June 1937, and continuing debt problems and operating losses finally convinced the government to transfer it to union administrative control on May 1, 1938.[64] Cárdenas's action conformed to his more general pro-labor policy orientation and his support in some instances for worker-owned enterprises. It also assuaged STFRM and CTM hostility toward the government following the May 1936 strike against FNM, in which the union sought implementation of a recent federal labor code revision providing full pay for employees' weekly day off from work and which the Federal Conciliation and Arbitration Board had declared illegal. Cárdenas's main goal, however, was to contain STFRM economic demands and limit government financial responsibilities by making workers themselves directly responsible for the operation of Mexico's largest railroad company.[65]

The Administración Obrera's (Worker Administration) seven-member executive board, named by the STFRM, received full administrative authority over FNM. However, the government stipulated that FNM's operating coefficient (*coeficiente de explotación,* the ratio of expenditures to income) could not exceed .85, the level achieved in 1937. FNM financial obligations were shared equally by the Worker Administration and by the federal government,[66] but the company was required to devote a fixed share of its total income to railroad repairs and improvements and to make additional payments directly to the government.

The Worker Administration experiment did not, however, resolve FNM's serious economic problems. The executive board reduced the number of technical and administrative personnel and cut their salaries, and it initially held firm against worker demands for wage and fringe benefit increases.[67] But the Worker Administration failed to meet its financial obligations to either the federal government or its foreign creditors. Nor did it make the required amount of repair expenditures. FNM's overall operating efficiency between 1938 and 1940 met or nearly met the .85 requirement (see table 4.1). Yet the number of employees jumped from an annual average of 38,895 workers in 1937 to 44,773 in 1938 and remained at nearly this level through 1940. As a result, total FNM payments for wages and fringe benefits increased by 16.3 percent between 1938 and 1939, and by a further 9.3 percent between 1939 and 1940. Wage and benefit payments as a proportion of total company income rose from 55.4 percent in 1937 to 56.6 percent in 1938, 60.8 percent in 1939, and 64.6 percent in 1940. The number of new employees hired during the Worker Administration threatened to saddle the company with higher operating costs in future years.

In the end, the Worker Administration failed to satisfy either the government or the STFRM. Its failure to make required payments to either the federal government or foreign bondholders complicated the Cárdenas administration's financial situation and its relations with international creditors in the wake of the 1938 nationalization of the petroleum industry. In May 1940 the government charged that the Worker Administration had permitted contract revisions and work agreements (convenios) that eroded labor discipline, contributed to inefficiency, and increased expenditures for overtime wages and fringe benefits (including complimentary rail passes available to workers and their family members).[68] Moreover, several sensational train collisions between 1938 and 1940 resulted in a number of passenger deaths and sparked intense criticism by conservative groups of both the Cárdenas administration and the Worker Administration. Its executive board acknowledged that some of these accidents were due to employee negligence, and it accepted the need for contract and work rule changes that would increase operating efficiency. In addition, in August 1940 it announced a far-reaching reform plan to prevent accidents and improve FNM operating efficiency by reducing the number of administrative personnel and strictly limiting payments for wages, overtime, and sick leave. The executive board also sought government approval for an increase in railroad freight rates that would help resolve the Worker Administration's continuing financial difficulties.[69]

Some of these proposals, however, provoked intense opposition within the STFRM. Union leaders chafed under their dual responsibility as worker representatives and company managers. A special STFRM congress held in July 1940 rejected wage or employment cuts (one government proposal under discussion in mid-1940 was to either reduce employment by eight thousand workers or cut wages by 20 percent)[70] to improve the company's financial circumstances. The situation remained at an impasse until the newly inaugurated Ávila Camacho administration announced in December 1940 that the Worker Administration would be dissolved and the Mexican National Railroads returned to direct government management, an

TABLE 4.1   Employment, Wages, and Operating Efficiency at Ferrocarriles Nacionales de México, 1937–1956

Year	Total Employees[a]	Total Wages and Benefits[b] (Pesos)	Real Average Wage and Benefit Index[c] (1939 = 100)	Total FNM Income[d] (Pesos)	Total FNM Expenditures[d] (Pesos)	Operating Coefficient[e]
1937	38,895	78,710,855		142,183,876	121,466,013	.85
1938	44,773	80,966,691		143,049,902	122,271,415	.86
1939	44,241	94,143,812	100.0	154,800,174	130,831,139	.85
1940	43,377	102,910,012	107.9	159,344,553	139,895,073	.88
1941	43,414	106,543,532	108.2	171,190,066	144,066,819	.84
1942	46,938	121,316,170	98.6	197,880,342	173,386,220	.88
1943	47,807	137,861,945	84.8	248,072,062	220,381,009	.89
1944	53,036	175,049,902	76.4	292,232,861	265,875,352	.91
1945	59,192	212,633,417	78.0	352,131,226	338,878,779	.96
1946	56,941	272,605,580	83.4	396,548,770	409,068,910	1.03
1947	65,536	314,579,730	74.4	409,319,372	454,053,348	1.11
1948	57,487	372,713,522	94.3	417,523,968	510,130,067	1.22
1949	66,320	363,504,285	75.8	513,597,442	502,681,584	.98
1950	83,528	395,609,837	61.8	NA	NA	
1951	76,595	434,372,088	65.6	NA	NA	
1952	62,341	465,755,482	78.5	NA	NA	
1953	65,127	513,884,278	78.6	NA	NA	
1954	67,199	553,743,375	78.1	NA	NA	
1955	66,567	596,351,735	73.3	NA	NA	
1956	60,735	582,384,126	74.8	NA	NA	

Sources: For 1937–41, Secretaría de Comunicaciones y Obras Públicas (SCOP), Departamento de Ferrocarriles en Explotación, *Estadística de los ferrocarriles y tranvías de concesión*

action that ended Mexico's single most important experiment in worker-controlled industry.[71]

In reorganizing FNM, the Ávila Camacho administration sought to ease the company's financial difficulties by eliminating its legal obligation to dedicate a fixed proportion of gross income to the government and by reducing by half (from 10.0 to 5.36 percent) the proportion of income to be used for repairs. However, because of the dramatic increase in railroad traffic resulting from wartime disruption of commercial shipping through the Panama Canal between 1942 and 1944, the Mexican government was compelled to make much more concerted efforts to upgrade railroad transportation.[72] The length of the national railroad network remained nearly constant from the late 1930s through the early 1950s, but during the early and mid-1940s the Ávila Camacho administration substantially increased expenditures for construction and maintenance (including the replacement

TABLE 4.1 continued

federal, 1941–1942, 16, 43–44, 167; for 1942–49, *1949*, 143, 171, 197–98; for 1950–56, SCOP, Dirección General de Ferrocarriles en Operación, *Estadística de ferrocarriles y tranvías de concesión federal, 1956*, 205.

   Note: NA = Not available. Wages and benefits, income, and expenditures are at nominal prices. Various smaller railroad companies were absorbed by Ferrocarriles Nacionales de México (FNM) during the period covered by this table, increasing the size of the company's labor force. The principal mergers were Ferrocarril Oriental Mexicano and Ferrocarril Mexicano del Sur (1937); Ferrocarril Mexicano and Compañía Terminal de Veracruz (1946); Ferrocarril Interoceánico (1947); Ferrocarril Noroeste de México (1952); Ferrocarril Sud-Pacífico (1952).

   [a] Average annual employment. Year-to-year fluctuations in the size of FNM's work force reflected changes in traffic volume, repair requirements, and so forth. For testimony that during the 1940s FNM management could not reliably estimate the size of the company's total work force at any given time, see Junta Federal de Conciliación y Arbitraje case no. 8.1/302 (72) "48"/797 (cited hereafter as "Conflicto económico" case), vol. 3, no. 2(A), p. 4A.

   [b] All wages and benefits, including overtime and vacation pay, health care benefits (payments for both work- and nonwork-related illness), pensions, and scholarships.

   [c] Average wages and benefits per employee, deflated by annual inflation rate (the annual increase in the cost of living for workers in Mexico City, reported in table 6.1). No cost-of-living data are available before 1939.

   [d] Secretaría de Comunicaciones y Obras Públicas data concerning total FNM income and expenditures during the 1940s differ in amount and in year-to-year variation from those reported by other government sources, but the overall trends are parallel. Alternative data appear in "Conflicto económico" case, vol. 1, no. 5, pp. 72–73, and vol. 2, no. 1(C), p. 28; no. 2 ("Estado STFRM, No. 3"); no. 2(A), p. 4. For testimony concerning the chaotic state of FNM's accounting system during this period, see ibid., vol. 1, no. 5.

   [e] Ratio of total expenditures to total income.

of railroad ties and ballast). The number of locomotives and freight cars in service on FNM also grew to meet wartime demand.

   Even though passenger and freight revenues rose rapidly, FNM's financial situation worsened during World War II. FNM was freed of direct financial obligations to the federal government after 1940.[73] However, a devaluation of the peso in 1940 raised the cost of railroad equipment and supplies purchased in the United States, and FNM met much of the wartime demand for cargo transportation by renting privately or foreign-owned freight cars.[74] The number of FNM employees also increased sharply during the war, from an average of 43,414 in 1941 to 59,192 in 1945. Wage and benefit expenditures as a proportion of total company income remained at approximately 60 percent during this period, but FNM's operating coefficient rose from .84 in 1941 to .96 in 1945 and 1.03 (that is, total expenditures exceeded gross income) in 1946 (table 4.1).[75]

   Despite FNM's worsening financial situation, railroad workers continued to lobby for increased wages and benefits and improved working

conditions. In order to avoid work stoppages and disruptions in railroad transportation during World War II, the Ávila Camacho administration granted railroad employees higher wage increases than it allowed
workers in most other industries. Thus, following a series of work stoppages (paros), the government gave railroad workers a 10.0 percent pay
increase in March 1942 despite the general wage freeze in effect at the
time.[76] Wages rose again in October 1943 under the terms of the government's emergency wage legislation.[77] Sustained STFRM lobbying secured
yet an additional forty-five pesos per month for FNM employees in September 1944 (approximately equivalent to a 25 percent wage increase),[78]
and Ávila Camacho granted FNM employees still another wage increase of
forty-five pesos per month in October 1946 just prior to leaving office. Total
wage increases for the STFRM's different occupational specialties ranged
from 62.1 percent to 187.1 percent between 1941 and 1947—a faster rate
of growth in nominal terms than for workers in any other major industry
except woolen textiles.[79] Nevertheless, because of high wartime inflation,
the real value of railroad worker wages and benefits fell by 22.9 percent
between 1941 and 1946 (table 4.1).

At the same time, the government tried hard to restructure industrial relations at FNM. Railroad managers and government officials traced
FNM's wage and employment problems to the Worker Administration,
and from 1941 onward they sought to increase managerial control over
the labor force and reduce expenditures for overtime work, sick leave, and
other fringe benefits.[80] In November 1942 the FNM's newly appointed general manager, Margarito Ramírez (the former railroad conductor who had
effected Obregón's escape from Mexico City in 1920), announced a proposal for broad changes in workplace regulations and contract terms.[81] His
proposal did not call for immediate reductions in either employment or
wages; rather, it sought to increase managerial control over disciplinary
procedures and work practices by revising contract terms adopted before
and during the Worker Administration.[82] His "Twenty-seven Points" (later
reduced to eighteen at the insistence of President Ávila Camacho) called for
the elimination of joint labor-management disciplinary committees then
operating at local and regional levels and the adoption of new disciplinary
procedures that defined infractions more clearly and permitted supervisors
to punish workers by suspending or dismissing them, rather than merely
adding demerits to their service records;[83] greatly increased managerial
flexibility in the appointment of railroad administrative personnel (empleados de confianza), who under contract terms then in effect could only
be appointed if nominated by the union and if they fulfilled a variety of
highly restrictive selection criteria;[84] enhanced managerial control over the
movement of employees among different work areas and job assignments;

limitations on overtime work, paid holidays, and hospitalization benefits or wage payments for illnesses not directly attributable to working conditions (syphilis, for example); and the gradual reduction of FNM employment by not filling vacancies when they arose.[85]

President Ávila Camacho emphasized his support for these contract and work rule modifications by criticizing the "chaotic conditions" and the "complete lack of discipline" at Mexican National Railroads.[86] At the same time, a special investigation of FNM operations by the Ministry of Labor and Social Welfare endorsed many (though not all) of Ramírez's proposed contract and work rule changes. The investigating committee specifically supported FNM plans to limit payments for overtime work and illnesses not directly attributable to working conditions, and committee members called attention to what they considered to be the exaggerated number of FNM personnel. They concluded that government financial investments in railroad modernization would be pointless unless a more effective disciplinary system was adopted.[87]

Facing a broad challenge to contract rights and union prerogatives, the STFRM promptly stated its willingness to cooperate in finding a solution to FNM's problems. It noted that wartime financial assistance from the United States constituted a unique opportunity to modernize Mexico's railroad transportation network, and it agreed to consider contract changes as part of railroad workers' contribution to the war effort ("nuestra postura antinazifascista").[88] On March 9, 1943, the union wrote President Ávila Camacho to offer compromise reforms in the three areas to which Ávila Camacho attached highest priority.[89] These involved the appointment of administrative personnel, disciplinary procedures, and health care costs. In each instance, the union proposed that established contract terms be suspended or revised for the duration of World War II but that the contract provisions in question resume force once the national security emergency had passed. For example, the union agreed to allow railroad management to appoint administrative personnel without union participation so long as they continued to fulfill contractually specified selection criteria. Similarly, the STFRM offered to eliminate temporarily local and regional labor-management disciplinary commissions and replace them with a single disciplinary appeals board located in Mexico City. The union also proposed modest, temporary cutbacks in workers' medical benefits; rather than fifteen days' full pay for illnesses not directly related to working conditions, they would receive full pay for eight days and half pay for the duration of the illness.

Although the collective contract then in effect contained many provisions very favorable to the union, the STFRM vigorously challenged the underlying assumption in Ramírez's plan that contract terms were the root of FNM's complex problems. Union leaders called for cuts in administrators' salaries and proposed "Labor-Management Cooperation Commissions" to promote operating efficiency. At the same time, STFRM leaders reiterated longstanding demands for fundamental reform in Mexico's railroad transportation system. Among other measures, they proposed that all railroad lines be nationalized. Expropriating privately operated railroad companies would have improved their financial situation by eliminating U.S. dollar–denominated debt payments, and it would have strengthened the union's bargaining position by unifying work contracts held by different private employers. Union leaders also called for coordinated construction of highways and rail lines in order to develop an integrated, efficient national transportation system.[90]

Perhaps the STFRM's most contentious proposal was its renewed call for revision of FNM freight rates. Because railroads carried 92.6 percent of all cargo traffic in Mexico in 1943, and because FNM was the principal railroad freight transporter,[91] freight rate levels were of crucial importance to the company's financial well-being. The STFRM had argued throughout the 1930s and 1940s that railroad financial and administrative reform was incomplete without a substantial increase in freight tariffs. Union leaders held that FNM managers' and government officials' attribution of the company's financial difficulties to high employment, wage, and benefit levels and inflexible contract terms was unfair so long as the rates charged for transporting many products were lower than actual transportation costs. Indeed, overall freight rates had not been raised between 1925 and 1942, and throughout this period the federal government itself received a 50 percent rate reduction on all its railroad shipping.[92]

The STFRM particularly criticized the freight rates charged for mineral ores and semirefined metals, many of which were produced by foreign-owned mining companies (especially the American Smelting and Refining Company, ASARCO) and destined for export. Freight rates for mineral ores and metals were not raised between 1925 and 1947. As a result, FNM income in the early 1940s from the transportation of these products (coke, calcium, coal, carbide, concentrated mineral ores, and semirefined metals) covered only 53.6 percent of actual costs.[93] The international competitiveness of these and other primary products depended heavily upon low railroad transportation charges, and during World War II a special agreement between the Mexican government and the U.S. Metals Reserve Company guaranteed low railroad freight rates for strategic ores and minerals.[94] Yet the mineral and metal products in question together represented 24.7 percent of all paid freight carried by FNM in 1943 (slightly more than all agricultural products combined).[95] The substantial losses incurred transporting them contributed centrally to the company's financial difficulties.[96]

Thus the issue of tariff reform posed directly the more general question of whether FNM should be operated as a profit-making enterprise or as a publicly subsidized service dedicated to advancing broader economic development goals. Sharp opposition by foreign mining companies, national business organizations, and some labor groups had blocked earlier attempts to increase railroad freight tariffs.[97] Nevertheless, the STFRM judged this issue a high priority in any proposed FNM reform program.

Despite intense pressure from FNM management, the STFRM's March 1943 compromise reforms concerning the appointment of administrative personnel, disciplinary procedures, and medical benefits were quite modest in scope. Its position reflected strong rank-and-file opposition to major contract concessions and union leaders' confidence that the strategic importance of railroad transportation during World War II placed them in a strong negotiating position.[98] Yet in reality, the STFRM's bargaining leverage was significantly weakened during this crucial period by legal restrictions on its ability to strike and by union factionalism.

Two internal conflicts were particularly important in this regard. First, rivalry among candidates to lead the union was unusually tense and divisive in 1943 and 1944.[99] The slate headed by José R. Cavazos, an engineer, had the support of both senior FNM managers and disaffected *trenistas* (engineers, conductors, brakemen, firemen, and stokers).[100] Tomás Cueva, a Monterrey office worker who had been a candidate for STFRM secretary-general in 1936 and who was a member of the incumbent national executive committee, led a slate backed by the Mexican Communist Party and other leftist activists. Yet a third slate was headed by Luis Gómez Z., an office worker employed on the Ferrocarril Mexicano who had been head of STFRM Section 17 in Mexico City (1934–35), the STFRM's secretary for education and propaganda in the early 1940s, and the CTM's secretary for conflicts (1941–42, 1944–46). The election campaign was divisive in part because Gómez Z.'s candidacy challenged the monopoly that FNM workers had held on the secretary-generalship since the union's founding.[101]

Gómez Z. claimed victory in a bitter contest in which he was accused of serious ballot fraud.[102] The outgoing secretary-general refused to surrender access to STFRM union offices, spurring Gómez Z.'s supporters to seize the headquarters building on January 31, 1944. When FNM management withheld union dues deductions from Gómez Z. (thereby preventing his executive committee from conducting union business), President Ávila Camacho intervened to settle the dispute. In February 1944, Ávila Camacho negotiated the formation of a coalition executive committee constituted by designated representatives from each of the three contending factions (its secretary-general was Ladislao Larraguível, a member of Gómez Z.'s political group and also an office worker employed on the Ferrocarril Mexicano). However, this arrangement proved untenable, in part because of persistent opposition by *trenistas*. A second coalition committee took office in May 1944; it included the leading members of all three rival groups, with Gómez Z. as secretary-general.[103] Ávila Camacho, under union pressure, removed Margarito Ramírez as FNM general manager in February 1944 because of his role in encouraging union factionalism. Yet the internal struggle among these competing groups seriously undermined the STFRM's ability to resist government plans for administrative reorganization.

Second, the formation in February 1944 of separatist organizations representing train crews *(trenistas)* and boilermakers *(caldereros)* provoked a major political struggle within the STFRM.[104] Strong loyalties to older craft traditions persisted well after the formation of a single national union in 1933. The sense of belonging to a distinctive occupational community was particularly strong among train crews, who shared special forms of dress, irregular shifts, often dangerous working conditions, and frequent isolation from other railroad workers.[105] The STFRM's organizational structure acknowledged such workplace identities in the form of recognized occupational specialties *(especialidades)*, and union governance procedures and wage levels, retirement benefits, and work rules were all defined in terms of them. Nevertheless, some groups resented their loss of operational autonomy (including legal control over collective work agreements) within a more centralized union organization and the fact that they no longer owned buildings and other real assets that had belonged to former railroad *gremios*. *Trenistas* and *caldereros*, for example, were concerned about the higher union dues required by a larger union bureaucracy, the loss of certain job prerogatives, wage and benefit differences among *especialidades*, and unequal wage increases in the 1940s.[106] No STFRM secretary-general had come from either of these large and strategically placed *especialidades*, perhaps heightening their concerns regarding union governance. In the case of *trenistas*, the January 1944 defeat of their candidate for secretary-general amid bitter accusations of electoral fraud was an important reason for the formation of a separate union.[107]

Legal registration of these separatist organizations—whose members together constituted more than 10 percent of STFRM membership and, because they held high-paid positions, provided an even larger proportion of union dues[108]—significantly undercut the union's bargaining leverage. It also encouraged secessionist aspirations among other railroad workers,[109] and it permitted FNM managers to exploit long-simmering internal union tensions for their own gain. Indeed, some senior FNM managers actively encouraged the formation of separate *trenista* and *calderero* unions; several FNM administrative employees even held office in them.[110] The Ávila Camacho administration's July 1944 agreement to permit all railroad companies to deduct automatically *trenista* and *calderero* union dues for the dissident organizations, and FNM's decision in October 1945 to permit the secessionist organizations to submit lists of prospective employees (openly challenging the STFRM's contractually guaranteed monopoly over job candidate selection), were nothing less than hostile acts.[111] Although the schism within the union produced problems for the government when *trenistas* and *caldereros* conducted work stoppages in March 1944, November 1944, July 1945, and especially December 1945,[112] its immediate consequence was to erode the bargaining leverage of STFRM leaders at the very time when railroad administrators were pressuring for further contract and work rule concessions.[113]

With the STFRM weakened, the government and FNM management successfully implemented broad administrative changes designed to improve operating efficiency and lay the basis for postwar economic expansion. On March 9, 1944, Ávila Camacho issued a presidential decree that, for the duration of World War II, gave FNM's general manager unlimited authority to select administrative personnel (none of whom could have ties to the union) and make any contract revisions necessary to improve railroad productivity.[114] At the same time, FNM managers announced Circular GG-96 (in effect after June 16, 1944), which, along with subsequent management directives, eliminated joint union-management disciplinary commissions, established detailed procedures for disciplining workers, lengthened work shifts, and gave supervisors much greater flexibility to move employees among different work areas to cover vacancies as they arose. These measures also regulated access to medical care more closely and reduced some sick leave benefits, although treatment of venereal diseases remained among the services available to workers.[115] Moreover, the new regulations substantially increased the number of workers classified as high-level administrative personnel—depriving the STFRM of direct control over as much as one-fourth of its membership.[116]

Railroad workers in Puebla and Monterrey organized work stoppages to protest these measures, and STFRM leaders lobbied hard to prevent layoffs.[117] Yet reaction was generally muted. Workers feared the consequences of highly restrictive wartime strike legislation. Moreover, both the Ávila Camacho administration and railroad managers implemented other policies to reduce labor opposition to contract and work rule modifications. For example, in addition to a wage increase in September 1944, the government increased budgetary support for such worker fringe benefits as sports facilities, education for workers' children, and workplace cafeterias. FNM expanded workers' access to credit and housing facilities.[118] Moreover, in November 1944 the government inaugurated a special system of subsidized commodity outlets for railroad workers *(tiendas ferronales)* in several major cities.[119] The Ávila Camacho administration also addressed longstanding union demands by raising most freight and passenger transportation rates (although not those for minerals and metal products) by 20 percent in January 1945 and by eliminating some inequities in FNM's rate structure. These changes modestly increased FNM income,[120] but they did not improve the company's operating coefficient.

The Allies' victory in World War II did not ease the workplace challenges confronting railroad workers. In January 1947, the newly inaugurated Alemán administration announced an extensive program of railroad reform called the "Alemán Railroad Rehabilitation Plan." [121] Railroads remained the key transportation system for the importation of capital and consumer goods and the export of primary products and many manufactured goods, and the government sought to lay the infrastructure basis for accelerated national industrialization. The government did not substantially increase the number of locomotives or freight cars in service on the Mexican National Railroads during a period in which passenger and freight volumes remained generally stable. It did, however, invest heavily in FNM equipment modernization (for example, the number of diesel-electric engines in service grew) and the repair and improvement of rail lines and facilities (the replacement of narrow-gauge track, installation of heavier rails, modernization of freight and passenger terminals and repair facilities, and improvements in communications systems).[122] As part of the modernization program, the Alemán administration enacted modest transportation rate increases in March 1947 which covered mining products.[123] With the continuing assistance of U.S. technical advisers, FNM managers also adopted administrative reforms that reduced overtime payments.[124]

Some elements of the modernization program posed novel challenges for the STFRM. For instance, the greater tractional power of diesel-electric engines permitted fewer locomotives to pull longer trains carrying more passengers and freight, a development that over time sharply reduced the number of train crews required.[125] However, with railroad workers' real income still substantially below prewar levels, union demands remained focused primarily on wages, fringe benefits, and working conditions. STFRM leaders pushed for improved benefit programs (especially expanded medical services, worker housing, and retirement benefits), a six-day workweek, and freight rate increases and administrative reforms that would improve FNM's financial condition and permit significant wage increases. The union also renewed its call for a coordinated transportation policy that would protect the railroads' freight and passenger business from competition from trucking and bus companies.[126]

The STFRM's bargaining position was at this time stronger than it had been for several years. Some of the emergency legislation limiting the right to strike and restricting individual political rights was lifted at the end of World War II, and railroad workers no longer felt bound by patriotism to limit their demands. The resolution of the *trenista* and *calderero* secession crisis also did much to restore internal unity and strengthen the leadership's position. Equally important, the STFRM's prominent role in national labor politics increased its capacity to bring pressure on the government and FNM management. Union involvement in national opposition activities received considerable support from the rank and file because the CUT's call for politically independent unionism and nationalist economic development policies coincided with STFRM demands for wage and benefit increases, the nationalization of privately owned railroad companies (especially the Ferrocarril Sud-Pacífico), and a coordinated national transportation policy.

The union did not achieve such broad goals as compelling the government to adopt a coordinated transportation policy, but it did win a sizeable wage hike of forty-five pesos per month in March 1948 that produced a 26.7 percent rise in real wages and benefits between 1947 and 1948.[127] Yet even while making a concession on wages, the Alemán administration redoubled its efforts to improve FNM's operating efficiency. The size of the company's labor force declined somewhat in the early postwar years.[128] However, wage and benefit payments as a percentage of FNM income rose sharply between 1946 and 1948 (reaching a peak of 89.3 percent in 1948).[129] This was due in part to the fact that total revenues, after several years of double-digit annual percentage increases, remained nearly constant in 1947 and 1948 because of a postwar fall in exports and the end of bracero traffic to the United States.[130] The consequence was that FNM's operating coefficient deteriorated rapidly. Indeed, expenditures exceeded total income in 1946, 1947, and 1948. The operating coefficient achieved in this last year (1.22) made it the most financially difficult in FNM history (see table 4.1). Quite apart from the STFRM's involvement in opposition politics, the company's perilous financial condition placed the union and the Alemán administration on a collision course.

The 1948 Charrazo: *Struggle for Political Control of the Railroad Workers' Union*

Alemán's was not the first administration to attempt to limit the STFRM's political influence and workplace bargaining leverage. Unlike Ávila Camacho, however, his efforts to undercut union power were not constrained by the strategic need to avoid disrupting railroad service in wartime. Indeed, the early years of the Cold War constituted a supportive ideological context for an assault on a union long known for its ties to leftist opposition parties. Thus in October 1948 the government acted decisively to break the STFRM's capacity to resist restructuring at Mexican National Railroads and spearhead a broader labor coalition opposed to government economic policies. As in 1943–44, the government's strategy revolved around its ability to foment divisions within the union, but the consequences of government actions in 1948 were far more important. The Coalition of Worker and Peasant Organizations collapsed following the Alemán administration's intervention in support of more conservative STFRM leaders, and during late 1948 and 1949 the government won changes in contract clauses, work rules, and union statutes which redefined the labor context at FNM and sharply reduced (but did not completely eliminate) opportunities for resistance by the rank and file. The blow against the STFRM was of special historical significance because it marked the beginning of a systematic government campaign to establish political control over major national industrial unions, the key to creating a durable base of labor support for the postrevolutionary regime.

The proximate cause of the struggle that erupted within the STFRM in October 1948 was a dispute over the use of union funds.[131] Jesús Díaz de León, a railroad engineer and a member of STFRM's largest local (Section 16 in Mexico City), took office as STFRM secretary-general in February 1948. He received strong backing in his election campaign from Gómez Z., Campa, and Laborde, and he initially expressed support for Gómez Z.'s role in forming the CUT.[132] But on September 23, 1948, Díaz de León filed a complaint with the Office of the Federal Attorney General against Gómez Z., Campa (president of STFRM's national oversight committee in the early 1940s, secretary for organization, propaganda, and education on the STFRM executive committee headed by Gómez Z. between 1944 and 1948, and during this period director of *Unificación Ferroviaria*, the union newspaper), and other former union officials, charging them with misuse of 206,250 pesos (U.S.$30,022) in union funds used to found the CUT.[133] Díaz de León claimed that although the STFRM had authorized the expenditure of funds to contest the political direction of the CTM and to support Gómez Z.'s campaign to become CTM secretary-general, this authorization did not extend to the use of union monies to form the CUT in March 1947. He argued that the circumstances surrounding this expenditure—the large amount involved, the fact that the expenditure was formally acknowledged just four days before the Gómez Z. executive committee left office, and the fact that Gómez Z. had become the CUT's secretary-general—all suggested that STFRM funds had been misappropriated by former union officials for their personal use.[134]

Díaz de León had introduced several internal organizational reforms in the name of combating union financial corruption,[135] but it is very unlikely that he was motivated primarily by the desire to correct what he perceived to be an actual instance of fraud. Both Gómez Z. and Campa argued that the CUT organizational monies had been duly authorized by local STFRM sections and that the formal approval of this expenditure given by the national executive and oversight committees (Accord 529/48) on January 27, 1948, was only an accounting measure for funds spent in 1946 and 1947. The Federal Superior Court, in the course of reviewing and overturning in October 1951 the prison sentence imposed on Campa, later confirmed that at least twenty-seven of the thirty-six STFRM sections had approved in October–November 1946 the expenditure of "unlimited" funds to back Gómez Z.'s electoral campaign. It also ruled that the formation of the CUT was a logical extension of the STFRM's efforts to reorient CTM policy.[136]

There is little doubt that Gómez Z. had used railroad union funds to advance his own political career. (He had, for example, assured himself a strong base for his national political activities by arranging in 1947 for a one-year extension of his executive committee's regular three-year term, an action without precedent in a union in which reelection was strictly forbidden for national union officials who had served more than eighteen months in office.) [137] Both the amount of union funds spent and the timing of Accord 529/48 were certainly politically embarrassing, but no evidence of large-scale fraud was ever uncovered. Díaz de León even acknowledged later that he himself had received part (5,500 pesos) of the money in question for expenses he incurred during organizational activities leading to the CUT's formation.[138] Nonetheless, the union fraud issue proved crucially important because it provided the legal basis for the ouster and imprisonment of those former union leaders active in opposition labor activities and the CUT during the postwar years.

A more compelling reason for Díaz de León's accusation was that he had been placed in an untenable political position by Gómez Z.'s endorsement of a far-reaching railroad reorganization plan that promised to provoke intense rank-and-file discontent. The STFRM had requested in September 1947 that President Alemán appoint a special commission to study FNM's financial problems and make appropriate recommendations. The union took this initiative in the hope that the adoption of various administrative reforms and transportation rate hikes would permit wage and benefit increases. Gómez Z. served as the union's principal representative on what was called the "Comisión Tripartita," even though his term as secretary-general expired shortly after the group began deliberations in January 1948.[139]

The commission's report, issued on August 30, 1948, called for various measures designed to improve Ferrocarriles Nacionales' financial health. These included the retirement over four years of nine thousand workers who had reached retirement age, a freeze on promotions affecting all newly hired employees, a reorganization of seniority lists (escalafones), and permission for FNM managers to move personnel among different work areas to cover vacancies as they arose.[140] Even more controversially, the Tripartite Commission concluded that FNM's operating deficit in 1947 and 1948 was due principally to unnecessarily rigid contract provisions. It criticized:

> collective contract clauses that are excessively onerous for [the company's] economic well-being and that impede its free operation because they provide insufficient control over various aspects of personnel management, encourage waste of materials and fuel and inefficiency in the use of equipment, permit excessive expenditures for medical services and other benefits, and contribute to frequent and costly accidents—all of which represent a crucial problem that must be resolved without delay because satisfactory levels of productivity cannot be achieved without establishing effective administrative control in the workplace.[141]

The STFRM had resisted pressures such as these for years, but even if FNM's financial situation in 1948 required drastic measures, the commission's report was politically explosive. Díaz de León later claimed that he first heard a summary of its contents on August 18, 1948, in the course of remarks made by Gómez Z. at CUT headquarters. He said he was shocked to learn that a railroad worker had even admitted that employment levels, fringe benefit costs, and worker discipline were problems— much less that a former union official had voluntarily joined in recommendations for far-reaching contract and work rule modifications. Díaz de León accused Gómez Z. and other worker representatives on the commission of "high treason" and "selling out workers' hard-won contract gains to the company," claiming that the proposed reorganization plan would cost one-fourth of all FNM employees their jobs. His comment that the commission's labor delegation "obviously sought to throw the blame for their actions on [him]" strongly suggests that the charges Díaz de León soon filed against Gómez Z. and other former union officials represented his attempt (leavened, no doubt, by the feeling that his former political mentor had betrayed him) to rally support under the banner of fighting union corruption at a time when rank-and-file discontent was high.[142]

It is also likely that government officials endorsed or encouraged Díaz de León's charges against Gómez Z., Campa, and other former union officials. Díaz de León seemingly was a poor candidate for the role of government stooge. During the early 1940s he had led a series of job actions protesting *trenista* working conditions which resulted in numerous FNM disciplinary actions against him (including his temporary dismissal in 1942), and he had served as president of a national STFRM convention in 1943 and as a national representative of railroad engineers in 1946–47.[143] Yet it is improbable that Díaz de León would have challenged Gómez Z. and Campa—both of whom continued to exercise great influence within the STFRM even after their terms as union officials ended—without prior assurance of government support.

The Alemán administration had at least two major reasons to support such an action. First, as railroad workers themselves clearly perceived at the time,[144] conflict within the union leadership increased the government's ability to implement the far-reaching modifications in FNM employment conditions recommended by the Tripartite Commission. Second, the STFRM was the principal source of financial support for the CUT, which in turn was the main force in the Coalition of Worker and Peasant Organizations. Railroad union funds paid for STFRM and other union delegations to attend the CUT's founding congress in Mexico City, and the STFRM continued to pay 9,000 pesos (U.S.$1,056) per month in CUT dues and the salaries of two typists. The union also provided financial assistance to other unions opposing government economic policies, spending some 100,000 pesos on interunion solidarity activities in 1947.[145] The government had, therefore, a strong incentive to undermine Gómez Z.'s and Campa's union base and thereby cut the flow of STFRM funds to opposition labor and political activities. The circumstances surrounding Díaz de León's actions—the fact that Díaz de León invoked anticommunism to justify what he did and specifically accused his opponents of dividing the CTM,[146] the government's immediate decision to investigate his allegations of union fraud, the involvement of federal secret police in the events of October 14, and vigorous government support for Díaz de León's position during the months following his ouster of union opponents—all point to government involvement in the struggle for political control of the STFRM.[147]

Díaz de León's request to the federal attorney general's office for an audit of union financial records provoked serious opposition within the STFRM. Other union officers (including the leaders of Díaz de León's own Section 16 in Mexico City) were willing to conduct a full internal review of STFRM financial matters, but the prospect of a precedent-setting government investigation into union affairs generated widespread opposition.[148] Members of the union's national executive and oversight committees sought on October 4 to block Díaz de León's request for a government investigation on the grounds that the secretary-general, acting alone, did not have statutory authority to do so.[149] When this effort failed, the national oversight committee formally charged Díaz de León with dividing the union and suspended him from office on October 14, naming his alternate, Francisco Quintana Medrano, secretary-general.[150] This action was endorsed by twenty-seven of thirty-six local union sections.

Later that same day, however, Díaz de León mobilized some six hundred railroad workers from various Mexico City work sites to evict the incumbent union leadership and occupy forcibly both STFRM national headquarters and the offices of the four union sections located in the Federal District. His action was supported by approximately one hundred members of the recently created Dirección Federal de Seguridad (Federal Security Directorate, modeled on the U.S. Federal Bureau of Investigation) dressed as railroad workers; the force was commanded by Colonel Carlos I. Serrano, a personal aide to Alemán. The ousted union leadership (led by Quintana and backed by Gómez Z. and Campa) established new headquarters elsewhere in Mexico City, but in the weeks and months after October 14 the government arrested and jailed Gómez Z., Campa, and their supporters among railroad union officials throughout the country.[151] Díaz de León created a "14 de octubre" political group to displace Gómez Z.'s "Hidalgo 96" clique, and his loyalists soon took control in a number of local STFRM sections.

The success of Díaz de León's counterattack depended upon both government backing for his actions and his ability to mobilize significant rank-and-file support. He probably found a sympathetic audience among fellow *trenistas,* and he reportedly offered a reduction in union dues to those workers who joined him in the assault on STFRM headquarters. His opposition to Communist influence within the union (especially Campa's prominent role in union affairs) also won support from workers in some local sections.[152] More important, however, Díaz de León's accusation that former union officials had illegally appropriated union funds touched a raw nerve among railroad workers. Díaz de León made much of the fact that railroad workers' hard-won resources had been expended on an organization, the CUT, which brought much fame to Gómez Z. but produced no tangible benefits for the STFRM. The fact that Gómez Z. (who as an employee of the Ferrocarril Mexicano, Díaz de León charged, had not been truly committed to protecting the interests of Ferrocarriles Nacionales workers) had also endorsed employment cuts and contract concessions, and had not given the union membership timely warning of impending changes, came as confirming evidence of his betrayal of STFRM members.[153] Díaz de León later claimed that he wrested a commitment from President Alemán not to reduce FNM employment or wage levels, thus portraying himself as the true defender of railroad worker interests.[154]

Díaz de León's actions—thereafter referred to popularly as the *charrazo,* in reference to his enthusiasm for Mexican popular rodeos and horsemanship *(charrería)* [155]—provoked widespread opposition both within the railroad workers' union and among other labor groups. Workers in twenty-four of the thirty-six local STFRM sections throughout the country protested his forcible takeover of union offices, and dissenting railroad workers held an assembly in Mexico City on October 26 attended by representatives of the CUT and the petroleum workers', telephone workers', and teachers' unions. Labor organizations representing petroleum, mining and metalworking, and electrical power generation workers joined the CUT in public statements condemning state intervention in internal union affairs. Representatives of these unions met with Manuel Ramírez Vázquez, minister of labor and social welfare, to protest the action. Nevertheless, the Ministry of Labor and Social Welfare legally recognized Díaz de León as STFRM secretary-general on October 27, 1948.[156]

Several labor organizations announced their readiness to conduct coordinated work stoppages *(paros escalonados)* in support of the rival executive committee led by Francisco Quintana, yet none of them actually mobilized their members to support protesting railroad workers. The solidarity pact negotiated by the STFRM, SITMMSRM, and STPRM required that each union's national executive committee consult with its local union sections before initiating a solidarity strike. This procedure produced delays and apparently contributed to the failure of allied unions to mobilize in support of railroad worker demands.[157] Equally important, at least some of these labor organizations failed to act because they believed that the charges against Gómez Z., Campa, and others were valid. For example, the Mexican Communist Party (which virulently opposed Gómez Z.'s and Campa's influence among railroad workers and their role in provoking the 1947 split in the CTM) supported Díaz de León's actions on the grounds that the fraud charges were true.[158]

The Aftermath: Political and Economic Consequences of the Charrazo

The *charrazo* had three important consequences for railroad workers and national labor politics more generally. First, Díaz de León and his union allies rewrote the STFRM's statutes in order to centralize executive control over union governance and erect significant institutional barriers to rank-and-file challenges. The most important change concerned union elections. STFRM statutes in effect between 1933 and 1948 guaranteed individual members the right to vote by secret ballot for local and national union officials. However, the Fourth Special National Convention that Díaz de León convened (in session, under armed guard, during February–

September 1949) established a system of more easily controlled, indirect union elections. Under the statutes adopted in 1949, union members voted directly (on ballots they were required to sign) only for their corresponding local and national *especialidad* representatives. These representatives voted for local STFRM section officers, and local section officials assembled in Mexico City to select their functional counterparts on the national executive committee (that is, local section treasurers voted for national treasurer, and so forth). The STFRM's national secretary-general was elected by local section secretaries-general and national *especialidad* representatives.[159]

The 1949 statutes also empowered the national executive committee to appoint national union representatives who had previously been elected, and they gave the national secretary-general legal authority to act formally for the union (authority Díaz de León had lacked in September–October 1948).[160] By altering union statutes in these ways and legally registering the new statutes with the Ministry of Labor and Social Welfare, Díaz de León and his supporters ensured that the new political order in the union rested on state power.

Second, the arrest of Díaz de León's opponents and the consolidation of his position within the union led to a dramatic shift in the STFRM's political alliances. Immediately after the *charrazo* the STFRM broke its ties with other national industrial unions and the CUT, actions that resulted in the de facto dissolution of the Coalition of Labor and Peasant Organizations. During the following months Díaz de León affirmed the union's support for the Alemán administration, and many of his subsequent public statements were stridently anticommunist in nature.[161] Indeed, the union's Fourth Special National Convention approved a resolution urging union members "to fight tirelessly in all areas against communist tendencies, preventing them from gaining force and constituting a national threat, and promoting free Mexican development and national independence." The convention also repealed a previous resolution that called for STFRM participation in "militant national politics," and it used the separation exclusion clause to expel Gómez Z., Campa, and other former union officials associated with this policy.[162] The union's motto changed from "For the Class Struggle" ("Por la lucha de classes") to "Always United" ("Siempre unidos").

In subsequent years, the STFRM also became a loyal supporter of the Institutional Revolutionary Party. Until the *charrazo,* no STFRM secretary-general had ever held national elective office during or after his term as union leader. However, the Fourth Special National Convention eliminated the STFRM's longstanding prohibition against union officials holding elective positions while in office,[163] and beginning in 1952, secretaries-general and other union leaders regularly served as federal deputy or senator during or after their terms as union officers.[164] Unlike some other major national unions (including those representing telephone workers, teachers, and parts of the electrical power industry) after the late 1940s and early 1950s, the STFRM never included in its statutes a provision formally affiliating itself with the PRI. Railroad union leaders did, nevertheless, mobilize the rank and file in support of the governing party and its candidates.[165]

Third, the Alemán administration seized the political opening created by the *charrazo* to push through extensive contract and work rule modifications designed to increase productivity by substantially strengthening FNM managers' control over the railroad work force. The means government officials chose to effect these changes was an economic conflict *(conflicto de orden económico)* petition to the Federal Conciliation and Arbitration Board (JFCA). Federal labor law authorizes conciliation and arbitration boards to approve an employer's request for changes in wage and employment levels, working hours, and contract terms ("las condiciones de trabajo") when altered economic conditions threaten a company's economic viability.[166] Acting on President Alemán's specific instructions, on November 15, 1948, FNM managers sought JFCA approval for far-reaching contract and work rule changes that would ease the company's financial difficulties.[167]

In essence, FNM managers sought to make permanent the contract and work rule modifications put in place on an emergency basis during World War II.[168] In its petition to the JFCA, Mexican National Railroads claimed that the company's deepening economic crisis was largely the result of insufficient managerial control ("falta de autoridad") in the workplace and excessive wage and benefit payments. The company wanted to eliminate union influence over high-level administrative personnel by simplifying selection criteria, requiring that administrators have no contact whatsoever with the union, and increasing the proportion of workers classified in this special employment category. Railroad managers also sought to reduce operating costs by simplifying disciplinary procedures (for example, by eliminating formalities and shortening notification periods during disciplinary proceedings), de-emphasizing seniority in promotion decisions, and giving supervisors greater flexibility to fill temporary vacancies and move personnel among different jobs as circumstances required.

FNM managers argued in their petition that, as a result of the wage increase that Ávila Camacho had decreed in October 1946, wage and benefit payments represented an unreasonably high proportion of total expenditures. FNM officials did not propose cuts in basic wage rates or employment, perhaps because they wished to limit union resistance to their initiative.[169] They did, however, ask that wage and benefit levels be frozen for two years and that overtime pay be strictly limited. (The dramatic drop in real average wages and benefits reported in table 4.1 for 1949–50 may reflect the combined effect on workers' income of inflation and a sharp cut in FNM payments for overtime work.) Moreover, they requested JFCA approval to eliminate contract language requiring management to seek union approval on the basis of demonstrated need for cuts in personnel or wage and benefit levels, and they proposed tighter restrictions on workers' access to complimentary travel passes and payments for occupational disabilities.

STFRM leaders protested both the substance of FNM's petition and the procedures followed by the Federal Conciliation and Arbitration Board.[170] In addition to defending the October 1946 wage increase as necessary compensation for the higher cost of living (which, the union noted, could have been absorbed by raising tariff rates just on those products transported at a loss), the union blamed FNM's economic difficulties on administrative inefficiencies and on the physical deterioration of railroad lines and equipment (due in part to increased traffic during World War II), which required a larger labor force to handle a given volume of freight and passenger traffic. STFRM representatives also emphasized what FNM managers themselves acknowledged in their petition to the JFCA: there were multiple causes of the company's dire financial condition, including tariff rates that failed to cover actual transportation costs and the rising expense of fuel, equipment, and materials.[171] STFRM representatives contended that it was therefore unreasonable for railroad managers to focus only on wage and benefit levels, contract terms, and work rules.

On procedural grounds, the union argued that the JFCA violated federal labor law by giving FNM management provisional approval (on November 16, 1948, the day after it received FNM's petition) to implement contract and work rule changes even before appointing a technical commission to evaluate the merits of FNM's case. The STFRM also protested that it did not have timely access to statistical evidence submitted by Ferrocarriles Nacionales and that the technical commission appointed by the JFCA on November 29 failed to take into account evidence submitted by union representatives.[172]

The report filed by the JFCA-appointed technical commission on January 20, 1949, offered some support for the STFRM's position. For example, commission members found that the deteriorated condition of railroad lines and equipment reduced productivity and accounted for the large number of workers employed in track repair. They concluded that recent FNM wage increases were appropriate given the higher cost of living; indeed, their calculations showed that the impact of inflation on the cost of equipment and supplies, a sharp increase in the cost of fuel oil in September 1946, and the July 1948 devaluation of the peso together represented a greater combined drain on FNM financial resources than the October 1946 wage increase granted by Avila Camacho. Commission members also offered particularly scathing criticism of FNM's accounting system, which was so inadequate that it was impossible either to value current inventory or to evaluate the company's overall financial situation.[173]

At the same time, however, the technical commission called for greater labor discipline and efficiency, sharply criticized the escalating cost of overtime and benefit payments and the importance given to seniority in promotion decisions, and argued that wage and benefit payments represented a "dangerously" high proportion of total FNM income. The commission also concluded that the contract and work rule modifications requested by FNM management would produce substantial cost reductions. It recommended that the Federal Conciliation and Arbitration Board make them permanent.[174]

Even if the STFRM found comfort in some parts of the technical commission's evaluation, internal union divisions and the Alemán administration's commitment to strengthening managerial control at Ferrocarriles Nacionales severely reduced the union's odds of prevailing in the economic conflict proceedings. The continuing political struggle between Díaz de León and his union opponents prevented the STFRM from presenting a united defense against FNM management.[175] Even more important, the politically sensitive economic conflict proceedings were chaired by the president of the Federal Conciliation and Arbitration Board, Alfonso Guzmán Neyra, a presidential appointee and a close political ally of President Alemán from the president's home state of Veracruz (where he served as Alemán's state campaign director during the 1946 presidential election).[176] The JFCA's institutional structure—an equal number of representatives from Ferrocarriles Nacionales and the STFRM, with the deciding vote held by the board president—gave Guzmán Neyra the power to determine the outcome of the proceedings. If union leaders had any doubts about their ability to prevail under such circumstances, their hopes were quickly dashed by the JFCA's resolution on November 16 to grant provisionally Ferrocarriles Nacionales' petition; the issue was decided by a 3–2 majority in which Guzmán Neyra cast the deciding vote. On November 23, the same 3–2 majority dismissed the union's charges of procedural violations.[177]

Although STFRM representatives continued throughout these proceedings to marshal evidence in support of their position,[178] the strong probability that the Federal Conciliation and Arbitration Board would eventually rule in favor of Ferrocarriles Nacionales prompted the union leadership to enter negotiations with FNM managers. Talks held nearly continuously between December 14, 1948, and February 24, 1949, produced two agreements (convenios) that modified numerous contract clauses and work rules.[179] These revisions increased sharply the proportion of jobs classified as high-level administrative positions, specified in great detail how such positions were to be filled, and prohibited administrative personnel from having any involvement in union affairs (including attending union meetings); strengthened managerial control over work rules affecting different occupational specialties such as *trenistas;* and imposed detailed restrictions on railroad workers' and their dependents' access to complimentary travel passes, although access to such passes remained generous.

The agreements also simplified the procedures to be followed in disciplinary investigations, increased work supervisors' authority (especially their ability to impose sanctions for work rule violations not immediately reported to management), and made it more difficult for workers to win reinstatement after their dismissal from Ferrocarriles Nacionales. Nevertheless, the STFRM successfully resisted a number of other changes in disciplinary procedures, and the union retained the contractual right to monitor the temporary movement of employees among different work areas. Seniority remained an important consideration in promotions. Díaz de León's ability to marshal support from the STPRM, SITMMSRM, and the Mexican Electricians' Union may have strengthened the union's bargaining position on such issues.[180]

Most significant for long-term labor relations at Ferrocarriles Nacionales, the agreements signed in January–February 1949 greatly simplified those contract provisions defining the terms under which FNM managers could reduce employment and wage levels, clauses that dated from September 1936 and April and October 1937. The agreements vested in the union's national executive committee the authority to approve FNM requests for personnel or wage cuts. However, in the event that the national executive committee objected to personnel or wage reductions and the matter could not be resolved within thirty days by a special FNM-STFRM commission, FNM's general manager and the STFRM's secretary-general were empowered to reach mutual agreement. If they, in turn, were unable to reach agreement, the proposed reductions would be implemented on a provisional basis pending final approval by FNM's Administrative Council. Thus the contract modifications made in 1949 greatly reduced the STFRM's legal capacity to block personnel and wage cuts (the union's only recourse was a formal complaint to the JFCA), even while concentrating authority over such crucial matters in the hands of the secretary-general. The FNM-STFRM agreement ending the economic conflict proceedings foreshadowed what was to come by freezing wages and benefits for two years.[181]

The *charrazo,* then, initiated a new era in STFRM internal affairs and in worker-employer relations. Díaz de León and his "14 de octubre" group continued to face rank-and-file resistance in some local sections, but government support and expanded statutory authority permitted Díaz de León to survive these challenges and complete his term as secretary-general in 1951. (When dissident railroad workers kidnapped Díaz de León in January 1951 and compelled him to resign, the Ministry of Labor and Social Welfare restored him to office.)[182] However, this same dependence on state support and the Alemán administration's commitment to stabilizing FNM's financial condition severely limited Díaz de León's bargaining leverage in wage and contract negotiations. For example, despite persistent (though quite deferential) lobbying throughout 1949 and early 1950 for a wage increase to compensate for the inflationary effects of the June 1949 devaluation, the 10.0 percent raise that FNM eventually granted its employees in August 1950 was considerably less than what the union sought— and it came with the condition that all other contract terms would be frozen through February 1953.[183] Economies such as these, combined with tariff increases for the transportation of basic foodstuffs, minerals, and mining products in 1949 and 1950, permitted FNM to reduce its financial losses in 1949 and achieve a balanced budget in 1950.[184] The company's stronger financial position, in turn, permitted increased wage and benefit payments, which in real terms rose by 6.1 percent in 1951 and 19.7 percent in 1952. Yet despite these substantial gains, FNM employees' inflation-adjusted income in 1952 was barely higher than the amount they had received in 1944–45 (see table 4.1).

The failure of STFRM leaders to prevent a decline in real wages and benefits in the mid-1950s, their inability to negotiate contract provisions that protected workers against such disruptive effects of railroad modernization as the use of diesel-electric locomotives, and the increase in union dues they enacted in 1949 all produced growing rank-and-file dissatisfaction with the *charros*, as workers called Díaz de León and his successors.[185] Several local union sections staged slowdowns *(tortuguismo)* in 1954–55 to protest these problems. Accumulated discontent erupted in a widespread railroad worker revolt in 1958–59 that succeeded in winning a significant wage increase and temporarily democratizing union governance.[186] But the political damage the *charrazo* did to the opposition labor coalition in the late 1940s was irreversible.

Labor "Unity" Restored: The Consolidation of Labor Support for the Postrevolutionary Regime

In the three years after the STFRM *charrazo*, the Alemán administration also intervened in support of government-allied factions in the Mexican Petroleum Workers' Union and the Mexican Mining and Metalworkers'

Union.[187] Although the specific circumstances surrounding the government's "purifying" campaigns differed in each case, there were several important similarities in the strategy and tactics employed. First, in each instance, state labor officials (especially Manuel Ramírez Vázquez, Alemán's minister of labor and social welfare between 1948 and 1952) played upon existing divisions within these unions to undermine more assertive, democratically elected union leaders and ensure the triumph of elements open to accommodation with the government and the "official" party. The STPRM, for example, was organized in geographically disperse local sections that reflected the union's origins among multiple, company-specific labor organizations formed in the petroleum industry from the revolutionary period through the early 1930s. Similarly, the SITMMSRM represented workers in different private and state-owned mining companies and metalworking plants throughout Mexico. As in the case of railroad workers, STPRM and SITMMSRM members grouped in local sections often represented distinct occupational specializations and had different contracts, wage and benefit levels, and working conditions. These circumstances were a propitious environment for intraunion rivalries and separatist movements, problems that were especially acute during the consolidation phase following the creation of national unions representing miners and metalworkers (1934) and petroleum workers (1935).

Second, state authorities relied heavily on the manipulation of legal restrictions on labor participation to achieve their political goals. In the STPRM and SITMMSRM cases, Ministry of Labor and Social Welfare (STPS) officials used their control over the registration of delegates at national union conventions in 1949 and 1950, respectively, to influence the selection of accommodationist leaders, who proved adept at exploiting rank-and-file discontent with the performance of more politically independent union officials. When internal struggles for control of the SITMMSRM produced two rival national executive committees, STPS officials used their legal authority to certify the election of union leaders to sustain the faction they favored, which by 1951 had consolidated its control.[188] State authorities' ability to exploit divisions within unions, and their capacity to employ established legal requirements to shape the outcome of internal union conflicts, explain in large part why the Alemán administration could achieve its objectives in these two influential national unions without recourse to extensive repression. Indeed, with the notable exception of strikes and a sensational "hunger march" to Mexico City staged by coal miners from Nueva Rosita, Palau, and Cloete in the state of Coahuila, the imposition of government-allied leaders in the STPRM and SITMMSRM occurred without much public protest from the rank and file.

Third, as in the case of the STFRM, accommodationist union leaders in

the STPRM and SITMMSRM modified union statutes in order to centralize governance procedures and erect significant obstacles to rank-and-file
challenges. Before 1949 and 1951, respectively, local sections in these unions
exercised considerable autonomy in wage and contract negotiations with
employers and in the conduct of their internal affairs. In the SITMMSRM,
for instance, the national executive committee had no authority over collective contracts negotiated at the local level, and only local sections could
declare strikes. In both cases, however, the imposition of government-allied
leaders led to statutory changes (sanctioned by state labor authorities) that
significantly reduced local section autonomy. After 1950, for example, only
the SITMMSRM's national executive committee had the legal authority to
declare a strike.[189]

The STFRM, STPRM, and SITMMSRM cases are emblematic of the
way in which the Alemán administration established political control over
powerful national industrial unions in the late 1940s and early 1950s. Redefining union governance procedures and centralizing authority in the
hands of top union leaders were instrumental in this process. The decline
in local section autonomy, as well as arrangements such as the system of
indirect elections established in the STFRM, meant that the government
could ensure reliable control over these unions' actions by influencing who
occupied key positions on the national executive committee. This system
of control ultimately rested on state officials' authority to approve union
statutes and certify union elections. Rank-and-file challenges continued to
surface in different national unions; indeed, democratization movements
by railroad workers in 1958–59, electrical workers in the early 1970s, and
teachers in the late 1970s and 1980s served as catalysts for broader labor
and popular protests. However, after the early 1950s the leaders of revolts such as these faced both the inherent difficulty of mobilizing worker
discontent against incumbent union officials, and the statutory protection
they enjoyed backed by the administrative authority and coercive power of
the state. These obstacles were not insuperable. Yet in several strategically
important industries, they gradually eroded the traditions of rank-and-file
participation and militancy which had for decades characterized union life.

The principal beneficiary of the shackles forged on national industrial
unions in the late 1940s and early 1950s was the CTM.[190] After March
1950 the confederation again came under the strong leadership of Fidel
Velázquez, now serving the first of many six-year terms.[191] With the elimination of more radical alternatives and the threat that nationally organized
industrial unions posed to the Velázquez group's control over CTM state
federations, the CTM's political dominance within the organized labor
movement went without serious challenge until the early 1970s.

Yet at the same time that they protected the CTM's position, successive presidential administrations pursued two strategies to prevent the confederation from establishing tight control over a unified labor movement and thereby increasing organized labor's bargaining power vis-à-vis government and the private sector. First, the major national industrial unions that had seceded from the CTM in the 1940s were not compelled to rejoin it, even though the STPRM and the Sindicato de Telefonistas de la República Mexicana (Mexican Telephone Workers' Union, STRM) did so in 1951 and 1954, respectively.[192] As a consequence, the CTM never recouped direct organizational control over national unions in several strategically important economic activities. In the late 1950s, for example, the CTM claimed a national membership of approximately 1.6 million workers organized in more than 4,200 unions, grouped in some 200 regional, state, and local federations. Its 21 national industrial unions primarily represented workers in light manufacturing (textiles, food processing), construction, maritime and highway freight transportation, printing and mass communications (radio and cinema), and tourism and entertainment (hotels, restaurants, professional sports, and musical entertainment). Only unions representing workers in the electrical power generation, petroleum, and telephone industries gave the CTM a strong presence in strategic economic sectors.[193]

Second, from the early 1950s onward different presidential administrations pursued a policy of controlled organizational diversity in the labor sector: while avoiding extreme fragmentation in the labor movement, they sought to enhance their leverage over the CTM by sustaining (and sometimes creating) rival national confederations. In 1952 the Alemán administration, which had defeated the CTM's most threatening rivals, facilitated the formation of the Confederación Revolucionaria de Obreros y Campesinos (Revolutionary Confederation of Workers and Peasants, CROC) to unite disparate labor groups in an organization that was simultaneously loyal to the government (it was affiliated with the PRI) and hostile to the CTM.[194] Its politically heterogeneous membership included the conservative National Proletarian Confederation (CPN) and Confederation of Mexican Workers and Peasants (COCM), as well as such former members of the Coalition of Worker and Peasant Organizations (though now much reduced in size and often under the direction of government-allied leaders) as the CUT, led by a chastened and politically disciplined Luis Gómez Z. President Adolfo López Mateos (1958–64) pursued a similar goal in 1960 with the creation of the Central Nacional de Trabajadores (National Workers' Central), which grouped more than six hundred labor organizations (including the CROC and the SME) opposed to the CTM.[195]

In order to counter rivalry from the CROC and the Confederación Revolucionaria de Trabajadores (Revolutionary Workers' Confederation, CRT, formed in 1954), the CTM engineered the creation of the Bloque de

Unidad Obrera (Worker Unity Bloc, BUO). Its formation was formally announced in January 1955 following several years of CTM efforts to establish loosely structured fora for labor movement coordination.[196] The BUO's affiliates included the CTM, CROM, CGT, FSTSE, and national industrial unions representing workers in the railroad, mining-metalworking, petroleum, electrical power generation, tramway, and textile industries.[197] From the CTM's perspective, the formation of the BUO did much to re-create the appearance of labor movement unity under the auspices of an organization in which it was the dominant actor. The BUO was not designed to function as a closely united confederation, and it had no clearly defined social or economic program.

The formation of the Congreso del Trabajo (Labor Congress, CT) in February 1966 culminated CTM and government efforts to unite the labor movement in a single organization closely identified with the Institutional Revolutionary Party.[198] The CTM, CROC, CROM, CGT, CRT, Confederación Obrera Revolucionaria (Revolutionary Labor Confederation, COR), the FSTSE, major national industrial unions, and numerous other labor organizations signed the "Pact of Definitive and Permanent Unity of the Working Class" leading to the creation of this new peak organization.

The CT served two functions. First, it became the principal vehicle for articulating the "official" labor movement's political and economic demands. After 1966, for example, the labor sector's share of PRI seats in the federal Chamber of Deputies and Senate went exclusively to CT affiliates. Second, the CT served as a loosely structured institutional framework within which affiliates could negotiate and resolve their conflicts without compromising their organizational autonomy. (The Labor Congress's resolutions became binding for its affiliates only when they were adopted unanimously.) Each member, regardless of size, had only one vote in its National Assembly. Nevertheless, the CTM's substantial membership, its alliances with other labor organizations, and its close ties with the governing political elite (reinforced by its network of state and regional federations) permitted it to retain leadership of the Labor Congress.[199] Fidel Velázquez served as the CT's first president, and even though leaders of other prominent labor unions held this position at different times, from the late 1960s through the early 1990s Velázquez always resumed leadership of the Labor Congress in the year preceding a presidential election.[200]

The Labor Congress's membership in the late 1970s embraced most of the organized labor movement; indeed, the decision of several unions formed during the "labor insurgency" of the early 1970s (including unions representing nuclear industry workers and university employees) to join the congress significantly strengthened its claim to represent a broad labor constituency.[201] In 1978 the CT grouped 33 major confederations and national

TABLE 4.2   Membership in the Labor Congress, 1978

Affiliated Organization	Number of Unions	Percentage of Total	Number of Workers	Percentage of Total	Average Number of Workers per Union
Confederation of Mexican Workers (CTM)[a]	4,987	63.9%	731,015	32.6%	147
Other national confederations[b]	2,736	35.1	313,508	14.0	115
Federation of Public Service Workers' Unions (FSTSE)[c]	68	0.9	835,534	37.3	12,287
National industrial unions[d]	10	0.1	358,230	16.0	35,823
Total	7,801	100.0	2,238,287	99.9	287

Source: Zazueta and de la Peña, La estructura del Congreso del Trabajo (1984), table 7.4.

[a] Includes Federal District Workers' Federation (FTDF).

[b] Includes Revolutionary Confederation of Workers and Peasants (CROC), Mexican Regional Labor Confederation (CROM), General Confederation of Workers (CGT), and a number of other labor confederations.

[c] Includes National Education Workers' Union (SNTE) with 544,000 members.

[d] Includes national industrial unions representing railroad (STFRM), mining-metalworking (SITMMSRM), petroleum (STPRM), electrical power generation (SME), nuclear energy, telephone, cinematographic, woolen textiles, television, and airline workers.

industrial unions that represented a total of 7,801 unions and 2,238,287 workers. The Confederation of Mexican Workers accounted for the majority of affiliated unions (4,987; 63.9 percent of the total), yet it represented only 32.6 percent of individual workers (see table 4.2). The Federation of Public Service Workers' Unions (FSTSE) grouped the largest number of individual members (37.3 percent of the total), 544,000 of which were affiliates of the National Education Workers' Union (SNTE). National industrial unions constituted an extremely small proportion of the CT's total affiliated organizations (0.1 percent), but they accounted for 16.0 percent of the workers it represented.

The creation of the Labor Congress symbolized an important shift in the character of Mexico's postrevolutionary social pact. During and immediately after the revolution, the alliance between organized labor and the governing political elite rested narrowly on links between such prominent political figures as Obregón and Calles and specific labor organizations, particularly the CROM. Cárdenas forged a far more inclusive alliance with labor, but this broad alliance was short-lived. The social pact was effectively institutionalized only after the resolution of the 1947–51 labor crisis, the elimination of more radical alternatives, and the consolidation of CTM political dominance within the labor movement. Even then, however, the labor movement remained divided among multiple rival organizations. Although the Labor Congress did not eliminate longstanding factional rivalries and jurisdictional conflicts, it masked them within a broadly inclusive labor forum.

Conclusion

The resolution of the 1947–51 labor crisis on terms favorable to the CTM, and the restoration of labor movement "unity" in the 1950s and 1960s, consolidated and gave new form to the postrevolutionary alliance between organized labor and Mexico's governing political elite. The terms of the social pact that prevailed after the 1950s were never as explicit as they were in the secret agreement negotiated in 1919 between the Mexican Regional Labor Confederation and Obregón concerning labor support for the latter's presidential bid.[202] Rather, the social pact embodied a more general set of understandings regarding the terms of state-labor collaboration. Successive presidential administrations provided a broad range of legal, financial, and political subsidies to the "official" labor movement, and when necessary, they used force to defeat opposition labor and political movements that threatened the position of favored organizations and their leaders. Moreover, labor received a wide variety of socioeconomic benefits, including government-subsidized housing, health care, basic commodities, and a legally mandated share of enterprise profits. Preferential access to these and other programs became an important basis for many labor leaders' legitimacy within their own organizations.

For its part, the state-subsidized labor movement provided crucial backing for the established regime during major political crises, and, at least until the late 1980s, "official" unions reliably mobilized their members in electoral support of the ruling party. Labor's mobilizational capacity during elections varied considerably from one organization and region to another. Yet government-allied unions generally constituted a key base of mass support for ruling party candidates in urban and industrial areas.[203] Even more important, organized labor's renowned political discipline during presidential elections was a crucial element in the survival of a closed presidential succession process. Government-allied labor leaders' willingness—and their capacity—to contain rank-and-file wage demands and block worker mobilization also permitted government policymakers to control inflation during periods of economic instability. The CTM's agreement to limit wage increases proved vital to the success of government economic stabilization programs following devaluation crises in 1954, in 1976–77, and after 1982.

Two additional points are important to understanding the dynamics of the social pact consolidated after the 1947–51 labor crisis. First, the terms of this alliance were highly unequal: the governing political elite's unchallenged control over the principal means of coercion and well-developed state administrative capacity permitted the national political leadership to define (and redefine) the terms of its alliance with labor, while organizational weaknesses and factional divisions within the labor movement generally placed labor in a subordinate role in decision making on wage levels, income policies, and economic development strategies. Organized labor was sufficiently powerful to influence decisions in these areas and, at times, to win important policy concessions. Yet overall, the underlying imbalance in the alliance (evident even as labor reaped the benefits of Cárdenas's populist reform program between 1935 and 1938) became increasingly apparent as subsequent presidential administrations pursued more conservative labor policies.

Major labor organizations such as the CTM generally enjoyed substantial autonomy vis-à-vis the state in the conduct of their internal affairs. Nevertheless, the existence of formal legal controls on union formation, internal union activities, and strikes constituted important constraints on labor participation. Heavy reliance on state-provided legal, financial, and political subsidies also had significant consequences in other areas. For example, access to these subsidies encouraged labor leaders to rely on political contacts to unionize new plants, resolve conflicts with employers over wage and contract issues, and mediate relations with union members. As a result, "official" unions often lacked a well-developed organizational presence at the workplace level—a situation that further heightened their dependence on state-provided subsidies.[204] Indeed, dependence on such support and only limited competition among different national confederations may have reduced labor leaders' incentives to expand their membership beyond those economic activities that could be most easily unionized through political contacts. Although employer resistance and labor force characteristics remained serious obstacles in many areas, the character of labor's political relationship with the governing elite may in part explain why the unionized proportion of the economically active population only grew from 9.8 percent in 1950, to 15.2 percent in 1970, to 16.3 percent in 1978.[205]

Second, state-subsidized labor organizations themselves operated as important instruments of political control. Because of the postrevolutionary regime's historical origins, Mexico's governing political elite has been particularly concerned about the threat that uncontrolled popular mobi-

lization poses to its dominance. The political litmus test for government-
allied labor leaders, therefore, has been their willingness to limit rank-
and-file demands and block strikes during periods of actual or potential
economic and political instability. Their ability to do so depends in large
part on the availability of legal sanctions such as separation exclusion
clauses. However, the fact that union officials can exploit the multiple advantages of incumbency is also important. Potential opponents face the
difficult, often insurmountable task of organizing rank-and-file opposition
movements against long odds. They must overcome incumbents' ability to
preserve their position against union rivals by calling upon the employer
or state labor officials for assistance, their control over formal avenues of
worker participation such as union general assemblies, favoritism in hiring
decisions or job assignments, or the manipulation of temporary workers'
insecure employment status.[206] The effectiveness of such tactics depends,
of course, on the abilities of individual labor leaders, and rank-and-file
challenges do succeed in some instances. But state-subsidized labor organizations constitute an extremely effective mechanism of political control
in Mexico precisely because successful challenges are generally limited to
a single workplace, region, or industry.

II ORGANIZED LABOR, THE STATE, AND ECONOMIC CHANGE

CHAPTER FIVE

State Structures, Political Control, and Labor Participation: An Assessment

By building an administrative apparatus in the labor sector and establishing various legal requirements governing workers' actions, Mexico's postrevolutionary elite increased its capacity to control worker activities in crucial areas. Yet an examination of administrative arrangements and labor law does not reveal how extensively formal restrictions on labor participation have been employed over time. This chapter tests the limits of a state-centered explanation of elite political control in Mexico by analyzing state administrative regulation of those forms of labor participation which chapter 1 identified as theoretically important in the study of postrevolutionary authoritarian regimes: labor mobilization (strikes), union formation, and individual worker demand articulation.[1]

Three questions are examined here. First, to what extent did post-revolutionary governments employ the state administrative apparatus to control strikes, unionization, and individual worker grievances from the 1930s through the early 1990s? Did administrative regulation of labor participation vary with shifts in presidential policy or economic conditions? Second, did Mexico's governing political elite exercise tighter control over some forms of labor participation than others? If there were differences in the extent of state administrative control among these three forms of labor participation, what implications did they have for organized labor's political and economic bargaining leverage? Third, in what ways can this investigation illuminate the relationship between state-centered and society-centered sources of elite control over mass participation in postrevolutionary Mexico?

Presidential labor policy is the principal state-centered variable in this analysis. The federal executive's power is preponderant in political decision making in Mexico. Thus one might reasonably expect that the extent of state administrative control over worker actions would vary considerably over time as different presidential administrations pursued divergent policies toward labor. Although in practice it is often difficult to characterize a particular administration's overall approach as "liberal" or "conservative," the substantially different labor policies adopted by administrations from the 1930s through the early 1990s provide ample basis on which to test this proposition.

Lázaro Cárdenas (1934–40), for example, opened a new era in state-labor relations by offering outspoken support for workers' efforts to organize unions and negotiate collective contracts. Although he adopted more restrained policy positions after 1938 (including, for example, blocking efforts by the Confederation of Mexican Workers to unionize federal government employees and peasants) as conservative opposition to popular mobilization intensified, Cárdenas is generally recognized as the most pro-labor president in Mexican history. Similarly, Luis Echeverría (1970–76) promoted a "democratic opening" *(apertura democrática)* by permitting greater freedom of action for opposition labor and political groups. He also expanded government-subsidized worker housing, granted government employees a forty-hour workweek, and enacted several emergency wage hikes to compensate workers for price increases.[2]

In contrast, the Manuel Ávila Camacho (1940–46), Miguel Alemán (1946–52), Gustavo Díaz Ordaz (1964–70), Miguel de la Madrid (1982–88), and Carlos Salinas de Gortari (1988–94) administrations pursued generally conservative policies toward labor. Arguing that Mexico's entry into World War II on the side of the Allies required national unity and an end to the intense political conflict that had characterized the Cárdenas period, Ávila Camacho promoted worker-employer collaboration. He also tightened procedural requirements for strike petitions, imposed harsh penalties on strikers causing "moral or physical violence or coercion," and amended federal labor law in 1943 to restrict further workers' right to strike. The government distributed basic commodities at subsidized prices, and in 1943 it granted an emergency wage increase to lowest-paid workers and created a national health care system, the Instituto Mexicano del Seguro Social (IMSS). But most workers' real wages fell significantly between 1941 and 1946 as the Ávila Camacho administration imposed a de facto wage freeze during a period of high inflation.

Alemán continued his predecessor's conservative labor policies as part of a more general effort to stimulate capital accumulation and rapid industrialization. Between 1948 and 1951 his administration acted decisively to defeat a major labor opposition movement and oust opposition elements from major industrial unions that challenged Alemán's support for an accommodationist labor leadership and a pro-business economic development strategy. The Díaz Ordaz administration's support for the "stabilizing development" *(desarrollo estabilizador)* policies that had been adopted in the mid-1950s produced rising real wages, and the president made a major concession to organized labor by initiating a significant reform of the federal labor code. Yet the administration's overall tone was set by the suppression of a 1965 strike by medical workers and the brutal repression of the 1968 student and popular movement.

The de la Madrid administration, in turn, imposed stringent controls on wage increases, cut public-sector employment and social spending, and sharply reduced subsidies for basic commodities, mass transportation, electricity, natural gas, and gasoline as part of a concerted program to reduce inflation. At the same time, de la Madrid systematically undercut organized labor's bargaining leverage on a broad range of economic and political issues. Salinas de Gortari, a principal architect of de la Madrid's austerity policies, accelerated the process of neoliberal economic reform. The massive employment cuts and contract and work rule changes that accompanied the privatization or closure of major state-owned enterprises sapped the strength of Mexico's most important industrial unions, and in a number of high-profile labor conflicts the government intervened decisively to undercut union bargaining strength in the workplace and ensure outcomes acceptable to employers. State labor officials strongly enforced a wage ceiling on a case-by-case basis. In support of these policies, Salinas simultaneously sought to undermine the political position of some traditional labor leaders and support those who were more receptive to his calls for greater attention to productivity and flexible workplace relations.

The Adolfo Ruiz Cortines (1952–58), Adolfo López Mateos (1958–64), and José López Portillo (1976–82) administrations pursued more mixed policies toward labor and are labeled "moderate" presidencies for the purpose of this analysis. Ruiz Cortines prevented the resurgence of opposition groups in major national industrial unions, but his administration's general success in controlling inflation permitted both continuous economic growth and rising real wages after the mid-1950s in a period known as "stabilizing development." Similarly, López Mateos (minister of labor and social welfare, 1952–58) repressed a national strike by railroad workers in March 1959 which threatened to paralyze the country. In 1963 he also enacted legislation which, while clarifying their legal status, severely restricted public-sector workers' rights to form unions and strike. At the same time, however, he was responsible for creating a social security institute for federal government employees and implementing the 1917 constitution's provision for worker profit sharing. López Portillo maintained tight control over wage increases during 1976–77 as part of an International Monetary Fund–supervised stabilization program, and he enacted an electoral reform in 1977 despite stiff opposition from the "official" organized labor movement. But the petroleum-led 1978–81 economic boom later permitted the López Portillo administration to raise some wages and increase government social spending.

If shifts in presidential labor policy systematically affected the extent to which state administrative arrangements were used to restrict labor participation from the 1930s through the early 1990s, one would expect significant differences in the degree of control that liberal, moderate, and conservative administrations maintained over strikes, union formation, and worker demand articulation. There may also have been important differences over time in the degree of control exercised depending upon the form of labor participation involved. For example, because limiting labor mobilization is more important to preserving political stability and the governing elite's decision-making autonomy on economic issues than constraining individual worker demands, one might expect postrevolutionary governments to have maintained tighter controls on strikes than on workers' grievances filed before conciliation and arbitration boards. If shifts in presidential labor policy do not explain well the observed differences in strike frequency, the percentage of union registration petitions approved or the time a union required to win legal recognition, or the outcome and resolution time of worker grievances before conciliation and arbitration boards, then other, primarily society-centered explanations must also be considered.

Labor Strikes

Recognition of the right to strike was perhaps the most significant legacy of the 1917 constitution's Article 123. Because they are collective actions, strikes represent workers' most important means of bringing strong pressure to bear on private-sector employers or, in the case of state-owned enterprises, on the federal government in negotiations over wages, fringe benefits, working conditions, employment policies, and other socioeconomic issues. In some instances, strikes may also serve as the principal vehicle for workers' political protests.[3] Federal labor law does not formally permit "political" strikes, but the timing of coordinated strike actions on more narrowly economic issues can have significant political consequences. Moreover, Article 123 allows workers to strike "to achieve equilibrium among the diverse factors of production, harmonizing the rights of labor with those of capital," thus permitting unions to mobilize in response to a general deterioration in economic circumstances.[4]

This section reports the results of analyses of officially recorded strikes and strike petitions in federal- and local-jurisdiction industries between 1938 and 1993. Although wildcat strikes (paros) and other unauthorized forms of worker protest are not reported in government sources, official data on strikes and strike petitions represent the best available indicators of labor mobilization. Data on other possible measures of the level and impact of labor mobilization (such as the number of workers involved in strikes, working time lost as a result of strikes, or financial losses attributable to strikes) are incomplete for the period examined here.[5]

Previous studies of labor strikes in Mexico have argued that presidential labor policy is the principal determinant of the level of strike activity. After examining the period from 1920 through 1963, González Casanova concluded that "presidential policy—in its broad outlines—determines whether there is a larger or smaller number of strikes and strikers."[6] He specifically argued that liberal administrations permitted larger numbers of strikes and that conservative governments constrained labor mobilization. However, González Casanova failed to note that in the period before 1938 government statistics did not always differentiate between strike petitions *(emplazamientos)* and actual strikes,[7] making it difficult to formulate meaningful comparisons between strike activity during the 1920s and much of the 1930s and during later periods. Nor did he distinguish between strikes in federal- and local-jurisdiction economic activities. It is likely that government policy regarding strikes in nationally important federal-jurisdiction industries differed significantly from that toward labor mobilization in less crucial economic activities.

Table 5.1 presents data concerning federal-jurisdiction strikes and strike petitions and local-jurisdiction strikes for the period from 1938 to 1993. One of the most noteworthy features of these data is that, with the exceptions of 1943–45 and 1964–67, there were substantially fewer legally recognized strikes in federal-jurisdiction industries than in local-jurisdiction economic activities.

Both organizational and political factors account for this difference. Workers in many federal-jurisdiction industries are organized in one or several large national unions.[8] Thus strikes by railroad, petroleum, electrical, telephone, and mining and metalworking workers—even though highly disruptive because of the number of workers and the economic activities involved—are likely to be fewer in number than strikes by workers in local-jurisdiction activities, who are overwhelmingly organized in smaller, enterprise- or plant-specific unions.[9] More important, however, state administrative controls are often more tightly enforced in strategically important federal industries than in local-jurisdiction activities. The fact that Ministry of Labor and Social Welfare (STPS) officials, and sometimes the president as well, are actively involved in mediating major labor conflicts in federal-jurisdiction economic activities increases the probability that national political considerations will influence their outcome, including whether or not strikes occur.

Evidence of three kinds supports this conclusion. First, the percent-

TABLE 5.1   Labor Strike Petitions and Strikes, 1938–1993

Presidential Administration	Year	Federal-Jurisdiction Strike Petitions	Federal-Jurisdiction Strikes	Local-Jurisdiction Strikes
Cárdenas	1938	140	32	287
	1939	153	35	268
	1940	184	15	342
Ávila Camacho	1941	117	17	125
	1942	133	19	79
	1943	858	569	197
	1944	1,103	734	153
	1945	263	107	113
	1946	NA	24	183
Alemán	1947	NA	13	117
	1948	NA	34	54
	1949	NA	35	55
	1950	NA	28	54
	1951	NA	17	127
	1952	NA	29	84
Ruiz Cortines	1953	NA	20	142
	1954	NA	18	75
	1955	NA	13	122
	1956	NA	10	149
	1957	NA	10	183
	1958	NA	11	729
López Mateos	1959	NA	18	361
	1960	NA	52	325
	1961	NA	42	331
	1962	NA	23	702
	1963	1,244	36	468
	1964	1,532	46	16
Díaz Ordaz	1965	1,127	40	27
	1966	NA	73	18
	1967	1,661	45	33
	1968[a]	145	39	117
	1969	1,361	40	104
	1970	1,512	NA	NA
Echeverría	1971	1,632	36	168
	1972	2,176	33	174
	1973	5,557	57	NA
	1974	5,182	55	337
	1975	2,155	84	236
	1976	6,299	107	547

TABLE 5.1   continued

Presidential Administration	Year	Federal-Jurisdiction Strike Petitions	Federal-Jurisdiction Strikes	Local-Jurisdiction Strikes
López Portillo	1977	5,033	128	476
	1978	5,572	87	758
	1979	6,021	141	795
	1980	5,757	93	1,339
	1981	6,589	108	1,066
	1982	16,095	675	1,971
de la Madrid	1983	13,536	230	978
	1984	9,052	221	548
	1985	8,754	125	489
	1986	11,579	312	903
	1987	16,141	174	949
	1988	7,730	132	518[b]
Salinas de Gortari	1989	6,806	118	757[b]
	1990	6,395	149	NA
	1991	7,006	136	NA
	1992	6,814	156	NA
	1993	7,531	155	NA

Sources: Federal-jurisdiction strikes and strike petitions: For 1938–71, Secretaría del Trabajo y Previsión Social, Memoria de labores, 1942–1943, 238; 1946–1947, 107; 1948–1949, 123; 1950–1951, 123; 1954, n.p.; 1958, n.p.; 1962, n.p.; 1966, 161; 1967, 225–26; 1968, 181; 1969, n.p.; 1970–1971, n.p.; for 1972–91, Salinas de Gortari, Cuarto informe de gobierno, 1992: Anexo (1992), 347; for 1992–93, Junta Federal de Conciliación y Arbitraje internal documents.

Local-jurisdiction strikes: For 1938–72, this is the difference between total national strikes reported in Secretaría de Industria y Comercio, Dirección General de Estadística, Anuario estadístico (various years), and federal-jurisdiction strikes. For 1974–89, Anuario estadístico, 1980, 153; 1984, 580; 1985, 540; 1988–89, 702; 1991, 765.

Note: NA = Not available.

[a] Information on federal-jurisdiction petitions may be incomplete for 1968.

[b] Data for local-jurisdiction strikes are incomplete (information for the Federal District is missing) for 1988–89.

age of strike petitions recognized as legal *(existente)* strikes in federal-jurisdiction industries between 1938 and 1993 was generally low; the recognition rate varied over time, but this change was unrelated to shifts in the political character of different presidential administrations. The data in table 5.1 show that on average 32.0 percent of the strike petitions filed in the years between 1938 and 1945 were declared legal strikes by federal labor authorities. The highest strike recognition rates for the entire 1938–93 period occurred between 1943 and 1945 (annual rates of 66.3 percent,

66.5 percent, and 40.7 percent, respectively) during the conservative Ávila Camacho presidency, which had enacted legislation that raised the procedural barriers to strikes.[10] At no time between 1938 and 1945 were fewer than 8.2 percent (in 1940) of strike petitions recognized as legal strikes.

In marked contrast, on average only 2.2 percent of all federal-jurisdiction strike petitions filed in the years between 1963 and 1993 were recognized as legal strikes.[11] The strike recognition rate during this period ranged from a low of 1.0 percent in 1973 to a high of 4.2 percent in 1982. A union may file a strike petition in the normal course of bargaining over wages or contract terms so that legal requirements are fulfilled in the event that negotiations with the employer fail to produce satisfactory results. If negotiations are concluded successfully, the petition is withdrawn. As a result, state labor officials actually rule on only some unknown proportion of all strike petitions.[12] Yet the fact that the percentage of petitions recognized as legal strikes was so consistently low over such a long period strongly suggests that state authorities maintained tight control over labor mobilization, independent of the efforts by government-allied labor leaders to limit rank-and-file mobilization. It is noteworthy in this regard that on average the conservative Díaz Ordaz administration recognized a slightly higher proportion of strike petitions (3.0 percent)[13] than did the Echeverría administration (1.9 percent).

Second, although the volume of strike petitions in federal-jurisdiction economic activities fluctuated with changing economic circumstances, there was no significant relationship between the number of legally recognized strikes and shifting economic conditions. Table 5.2 reports the results of a regression analysis of federal-jurisdiction strike petitions filed between 1941 and 1993. Several different independent variables were tested in order to determine which economic factors had the strongest impact on year-to-year changes in the number of strike petitions, including the annual rate of inflation, changes in real wage levels (measured as the real minimum daily wage in Mexico City), and annual variations in real gross domestic product. Only inflation had a statistically significant effect, though this effect was weak.[14] The estimated coefficient for this variable means that an increase of one percentage point in the rate of inflation produced a 0.02 percent increase in the number of federal-jurisdiction strike petitions.

The variance in strike petitions explained by the model depicted in table 5.2 is small (an adjusted R^2 of only .144). This may reflect the fact that a union's decision to file a strike petition is often motivated by concerns (contract violations, for example) unrelated to macroeconomic conditions. Nevertheless, these results do have interesting political implications. They indicate that during the 1941–93 period labor organizations in federal-jurisdiction industries did use the strike petition process to signal their

TABLE 5.2   Analysis of Covariance in the Incidence of Federal-Jurisdiction Strike Petitions, 1941–1993

Variable	Estimated Coefficient	Standard Error	T-Value
Inflation	.02	.01	2.45[a]
Presidential administration[b]			
Liberal	−.19	.42	−.28
Conservative	−.57	.31	−1.85
Constant	8.54	.48	17.93[c]

$R^2 = .227$
Adjusted $R^2 = .144$
$N = 32$
Degrees of freedom $= 29$
Durbin-Watson statistic $= 2.61$

Note: These are the results of a two-stage least squares analysis. The dependent and independent variables were first transformed by the Cochrane-Orcutt iterative technique to correct for autocorrelation; this operation reduced the number of observations from 33 to 32. The regression analysis used natural logs of the dependent variable (the number of strike petitions in federal-jurisdiction economic activities) and one independent variable, the annual rate of inflation (see table 6.1 for inflation data and a discussion of how the inflation rate was calculated). The analysis was limited to the 1941–93 period (that is, beginning with the Ávila Camacho administration) because it was not possible to calculate a rate of inflation for 1938 and 1939 on the basis of the available data. Similarly, the analysis excluded 1968 because the information on federal-jurisdiction strike petitions for that year appears to be incomplete.

[a] Significant at the .05 level.

[b] These are dummy variables representing presidential policy toward labor. "Liberal" is coded 0 (not liberal) and 1 (liberal); "conservative" is coded 0 (not conservative) and 1 (conservative). For the purposes of this analysis, the Echeverría administration (1971–76) was characterized as having a liberal policy toward labor, and the Ávila Camacho (1941–46), Alemán (1947–52), Díaz Ordaz (1965–70), de la Madrid (1983–88), and Salinas de Gortari (1989–93) administrations were characterized as having conservative policies toward labor. The constant represents three moderate administrations, the Ruiz Cortines (1953–58), López Mateos (1959–64), and López Portillo (1977–82) presidencies. The time periods in parentheses after each president's name indicate the way in which the petition data were grouped by presidential administration.

[c] Significant at the .001 level.

discontent when rising inflation threatened workers' economic position. The relationship between the incidence of strike petitions and fluctuations in the rate of inflation was particularly close during the 1980s (see figure 5.1).[15] However, the volume of petitions remained comparatively high during the Salinas administration even as the annual rate of inflation declined. Perhaps this indicates that labor organizations' principal motives for threatening to strike shifted somewhat during this period from concern over inflation to opposition to the negative consequences of rapid industrial restructuring (for example, large-scale layoffs, forced modifications in

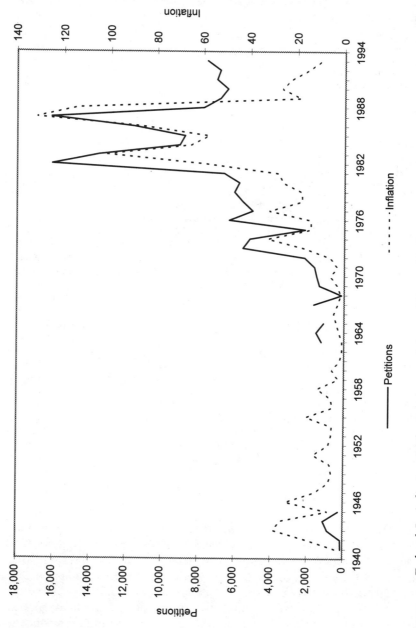

FIGURE 5.1 Federal-Jurisdiction Strike Petitions and Annual Rate of Inflation, 1941–1993. *Sources:* Tables 5.1, 6.1.

TABLE 5.3 Analysis of Covariance in the Incidence of Federal-Jurisdiction Strikes, 1938–1993

Variable	Estimated Coefficient	Standard Error	T-Value
Federal-jurisdiction strike petitions	.57	.15	3.81[a]
Presidential administration[b]			
Liberal	−.24	.47	−.52
Conservative	.32	.37	.85
Constant	−.11	1.30	−.09

$R^2 = .339$
Adjusted $R^2 = .276$
$N = 35$
Degrees of freedom = 32
Durbin-Watson statistic = 1.87

Note: These are the results of a two-stage least squares analysis. The dependent and independent variables were first transformed by the Cochrane-Orcutt iterative technique to correct for autocorrelation; this operation reduced the number of observations from 36 to 35. The regression analysis used natural logs of the dependent variable (the number of strikes in federal-jurisdiction economic activities) and one independent variable, the number of strike petitions in federal-jurisdiction economic activities. The analysis excluded 1968 because the information on federal-jurisdiction strike petitions for that year appears to be incomplete.

[a] Significant at the .001 level.

[b] These are dummy variables representing presidential policy toward labor. "Liberal" is coded 0 (not liberal) and 1 (liberal); "conservative" is coded 0 (not conservative) and 1 (conservative). For the purposes of this analysis, the Cárdenas (1938–40) and Echeverría (1971–76) administrations were characterized as having liberal policies toward labor, and the Ávila Camacho (1941–46), Alemán (1947–52), Díaz Ordaz (1965–70), de la Madrid (1983–1988), and Salinas de Gortari (1989–93) administrations were characterized as having conservative policies toward labor. The constant represents three moderate administrations, the Ruiz Cortines (1953–58), López Mateos (1959–64), and López Portillo (1977–82) presidencies. The time periods in parentheses after each president's name indicate the way in which the petition and strike data were grouped by presidential administration.

contract terms and work rules, and so forth) in both the public and private sectors.

In contrast, neither fluctuations in the rate of inflation nor changes in other economic variables (real minimum wages and real economic growth rates) had a statistically significant, direct impact on the number of legally recognized strikes in federal-jurisdiction industries. During the period between 1938 and 1993, the best predictor of the number of strikes in a given year was the number of strike petitions filed (see table 5.3).[16] The estimated coefficient for this variable means that a 1 percent increase in petitions produced a 0.57 percent rise in strikes. Although the variance explained is again modest (an adjusted R^2 of .276), these results indicate that state labor authorities were somewhat sensitive to labor pressure registered in the form

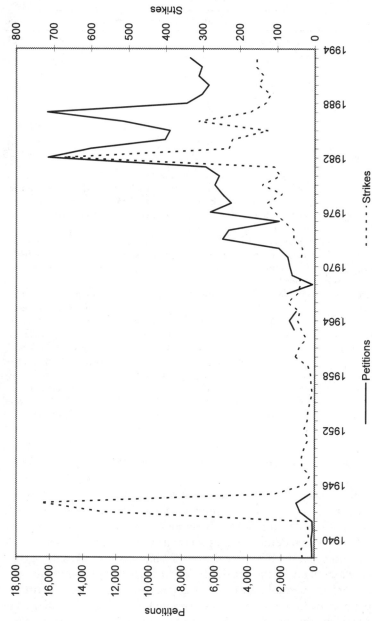

FIGURE 5.2 Federal-Jurisdiction Strike Petitions and Strikes, 1938–1993. *Source:* Table 5.1.

of increased strike petitions. A graphic presentation of the data on strike petitions and strikes (see figure 5.2) shows that this relationship was quite consistent over the 1938–93 period. However, as noted above, the strike recognition rate remained very low, with little year-to-year fluctuation, in the years after 1963.

Third, neither the number of federal-jurisdiction strike petitions nor the number of legally recognized strikes varied consistently with shifts in presidential labor policy. As tables 5.2 and 5.3 show, the estimated coefficients for the variables representing presidential term are not statistically significant. There is no strong a priori reason for believing that presidential policy determines the volume of strike petitions, although it is certainly possible that labor organizations might increase or decrease the number of strike petitions they file in response to a president's actions. (For example, the sharp increase in federal-jurisdiction petitions in 1973–74 came when the Confederation of Mexican Workers urged its affiliates to file strike petitions to protest the Echeverría administration's support for opposition labor groups and the government's relative hostility toward "official" unions.)[17] However, analysts such as González Casanova have identified variations in presidential labor policy as a key factor determining the number of strikes. The coefficients reported in table 5.3 suggest that liberal and conservative administrations did differ somewhat from each other, but during the period between 1938 and 1993 neither liberal nor conservative presidencies had an impact on strikes that differed significantly from that of moderate administrations (represented by the constant).

In conclusion, the data examined in this section indicate that postrevolutionary governments generally maintained strong control over strikes in federal-jurisdiction economic activities, regardless of changes in the political character of different presidential administrations.[18] There were, of course, some periods during which the number of legally recognized strikes rose sharply. In 1943–44, for example, textile and mining workers mobilized strongly in support of their demands for wage increases to compensate for the effects of rising inflation, producing in 1944 a larger number of federal-jurisdiction strikes (734) than at any other time during the 1938–93 period.[19] Similarly, the highest number of strikes in federal- and local-jurisdiction industries combined (2,646) came in 1982 as Mexico fell into severe economic crisis. Yet it is important to emphasize the causal process involved. Unions in nationally important federal-jurisdiction industries generally filed a larger number of strike petitions when the rate of inflation rose, and a higher volume of petitions led to some increase in strikes. But state labor authorities were interposed between changing economic conditions and workers' ability to mobilize collectively behind their demands. This explains why the number of strikes in federal-jurisdiction industries declined in 1987–88 even as Mexico recorded the highest rates of inflation since the revolution. Stated succinctly, state administrative review of strike petitions was a key point of political control.

Labor Union Registration

The stability of authoritarian rule in postrevolutionary regimes depends in part on political elites' ability to control access to organization as a political resource. Legal restrictions on union formation, for example, potentially give governing elites the ability to shape their base of mass support, undercutting class loyalties and creating organizations heavily dependent on them. The administrative capacity to limit and order sociopolitical pluralism in the labor sector may also increase government decision makers' relative autonomy in policy formulation and implementation.

In Mexico, labor unions form in one of two ways. When a new enterprise or work site opens in an economic activity already dominated by an existing national industrial union, workers are normally organized as a local section of that union. There is generally no question regarding the identity of the union responsible for forming the new section unless there is substantial doubt regarding the jurisdictional classification of the economic activity involved, or unless a recently formed national union is still in the process of consolidating its position among workers in an industry. Only a small proportion of all unions formed in Mexico are local sections of national industrial unions. More frequently, employees at new work sites are organized as affiliates of state and regional labor federations. Because the state or regional affiliates of different national labor confederations often represent workers in similar economic activities in the same geographical area, union formation and the determination of a union's confederative linkage are often intensely political issues in which state labor authorities can play a decisive role.

In both circumstances, however, legal recognition of the new organization is the capstone of union formation. In federal-jurisdiction industries, the Ministry of Labor and Social Welfare's Associational Registry, located in the STPS headquarters in Mexico City, is responsible for approving registration requests; state-level Juntas Locales de Conciliación y Arbitraje have responsibility for registering unions in local-jurisdiction economic activities. Because there are no data available which would permit an examination of union registration in the latter case, this analysis only focuses on union registration in federal-jurisdiction industries.

The Associational Registry's review of union applications is a bureaucratic process whose duration and outcome are subject to numerous influences. Administrative circumstances such as the personnel resources available to the Associational Registry, registry directors' personal ties to particular labor confederations, and labor lawyers' efficacy in handling registration applications could all have a significant impact in this regard.[20] Similarly, the characteristics of the labor organizations seeking legal recognition might also influence whether they receive official registration and the time it takes. Factors such as the experience of union organizers, the legal resources available to a union (not necessarily dependent on its size alone), and the extent to which major confederations supervise their affiliates closely during the registration process may also be important.

It is also quite possible that a particular presidential administration's orientation toward labor might influence the union registration process, both because union formation in federal-jurisdiction economic activities is sometimes politically sensitive and because the presidential appointee in charge of the Associational Registry has exclusive legal authority over the process. The absence of a formal appeal mechanism offers union representatives few alternative courses of action if registry officials manipulate the process to achieve partisan political goals.[21]

It is possible, then, for registry officials to support a government-allied confederation among several rival organizations competing to unionize a particular work site, to speed the registration of a favored labor organization, or to delay registration so as to hamper the activities of a dissident group. They might also respond to a particular administration's political preferences by permitting the formation of a rival union within a work force already organized by a legally constituted union, thus threatening the targeted union's right to negotiate a collective contract and undermining its bargaining leverage vis-à-vis the employer. Similarly, a union might be denied legal recognition because of its political opposition to the government or to "official" labor organizations, or an existing union might lose its registration for similar reasons (although federal labor law states that a union's registration can be canceled only when the union is dissolved, or when it no longer meets formal registration requirements).

A significant number of all union registration applications in federal-jurisdiction activities fail to receive official approval, either because they do not meet the stated legal requirements or because of political considerations such as those discussed above. The proportion of applications turned down by registry officials averaged 21.3 percent per year between 1935 and 1971, ranging from 4.0 percent in 1941 to 68.7 percent in 1969 (see table 5.4). Although data are very incomplete for the Cárdenas administration (and were not published at all after 1971), change in the rejection rate between 1935 and 1971 was not closely associated with shifts in presidential labor policy. The two highest annual rejection rates came during administrations known for their conservative labor policies (48.0 percent

TABLE 5.4   Federal-Jurisdiction Union Registration Applications, 1935–1971

Presidential Administration	Year[a]	Applications Received[b]	Applications Rejected[c]	Annual Rejection Rate (%)	Rejection Rate for Presidential Term (%)
Cárdenas	1935	394	31	7.9	
	1936	NA	NA	NA	
	1937	NA	NA	NA	10.5
	1938	NA	NA	NA	
	1939	NA	NA	NA	
	1940	175	29	16.6	
Ávila Camacho	1941	200	8	4.0	
	1942	136	19	14.0	
	1943	133	11	8.3	10.1
	1944	NA	NA	NA	
	1945	162	28	17.3	
	1946	237	22	9.3	
Alemán	1947	246	118	48.0	
	1948	316	22	7.0	
	1949	211	22	10.4	17.1
	1950	223	17	7.6	
	1951	115	13	11.3	
	1952	79	11	13.9	
Ruiz Cortines	1953	210	16	7.6	
	1954	88	19	21.6	
	1955	106	35	33.0	17.0
	1956	104	4	3.8	
	1957	98	34	34.7	
	1958	94	11	11.7	

in 1947 during the Alemán presidency, and 68.7 percent in 1969 during the Díaz Ordaz administration), but disapproval rates during the remainder of the Alemán administration were quite similar to those registered in 1935 and 1940 under Cárdenas. Moreover, the average rejection rate during the comparatively liberal López Mateos presidency (29.7 percent) was nearly twice as high as that corresponding to the Alemán administration (17.1 percent).

Rather than varying with changes in presidential labor policy, the rate of approval for union registration applications steadily fell over time. The proportion of applications rejected rose from 10.1 percent under Ávila Camacho, to 17.1 percent under Alemán, to 17.0 percent under Ruiz Cortines, to 29.7 percent under López Mateos, to 32.3 percent under Díaz Ordaz.

TABLE 5.4   continued

Presidential Administration	Year[a]	Applications Received[b]	Applications Rejected[c]	Annual Rejection Rate (%)	Rejection Rate for Presidential Term (%)
López Mateos	1959	95	29	30.5	
	1960	78	25	32.1	
	1961	132	26	19.7	29.7
	1962	120	35	29.2	
	1963	NA	NA	NA	
	1964	137	52	38.0	
Díaz Ordaz	1965	123	34	27.6	
	1966	81	18	22.2	
	1967	109	28	25.7	32.3
	1968	90	26	28.9	
	1969	67	46	68.7	
	1970	NA	NA	NA	
Echeverría	1971	327	93	28.4	28.4

Source: Secretaría del Trabajo y Previsión Social, *Memoria de labores,* various years. No data concerning rejected applications were published after 1971.

Note: NA = not available.

[a] For 1935, data are for period from August 1, 1934, to July 31, 1935; for 1940–52 and 1971, data are for period from September 1 to August 31 (e.g., September 1, 1939–August 31, 1940); for 1953, data are for period from September 1, 1952, to December 31, 1953; for 1954–69, data are for calendar year.

[b] Applications received from all unions, federations, and confederations. The total does not include applications for the formation of local sections in legally registered unions. Applications from unions not in federal-jurisdiction economic activities are excluded from this total and from calculation of the annual rejection rate.

[c] Applications rejected in a given year may have been filed in a previous year.

Given the relatively low proportion of the economically active population which is unionized in Mexico and the fact that more federal-jurisdiction unions were registered during the Díaz Ordaz and Echeverría administrations than in any six-year period since Cárdenas,[22] it is unlikely that this change resulted from the saturation of the labor force by existing labor organizations and the consequent rejection of applications made by potential rivals. However, on the basis of the information available, it is impossible to determine whether an increase over time in rejection rates resulted from the more stringent enforcement of legal criteria, opposition by existing unions to the official recognition of additional labor organizations, an attempt by state authorities to limit the number of legally registered unions, or some other factor. Nor do the official data on application rejections permit one to conclude what role political considerations played in the registration process.

Qualitative data, however, show that political factors have often been crucial considerations in state labor authorities' review of registration applications. The following three cases, selected to illustrate the different conditions under which politicization of the *registro* process occurs and the forms it takes, demonstrate that state authorities have used their legal authority to further diverse political goals:[23]

1. The Cárdenas administration delayed the registration of the Federación de Sindicatos Independientes de Nuevo León (Nuevo León Federation of Independent Unions, FSINL) for nearly four years because it threatened to strengthen the political position of conservative business groups in the industrial city of Monterrey. Cárdenas's progressive economic and political policies won him widespread support among workers and peasants, and Cárdenas played an important role in the formation of the Confederation of Mexican Workers (CTM). These actions produced serious conflict between Monterrey industrialists and the Cárdenas administration. In order to obstruct CTM-led unionization in the area, local business leaders supported the formation of company-controlled unions *(sindicatos blancos)* affiliated with the FSINL.[24] Cárdenas administration labor officials countered this effort by delaying the FSINL's registration, thus preventing it from legally representing its affiliates. The federation's application reached the Associational Registry on May 30, 1936, but labor authorities did not grant it official registration until February 12, 1940.

2. In early 1944 the Ávila Camacho administration used the registration process to create internal opposition groups within the Mexican Railroad Workers' Union (STFRM).[25] The STFRM was founded after a long drive to unite numerous craft organizations into a single national union. However, loyalties to these older groups, as well as some elements' resentment of higher union dues and more centralized governance in the new national organization, continued to be an important source of internal union discontent. Railroad managers and state labor authorities exploited these divisions by authorizing the registration of separate unions representing train crews *(trenistas)* and boilermakers *(caldereros)*. By doing so, the Ávila Camacho government sought to undercut STFRM opposition to Mexican National Railroads' (FNM) efforts to restructure work rules and contract terms. Internal division significantly weakened union leaders' bargaining position, and railroad managers successfully implemented major administrative reforms to improve operating efficiency. The dissident worker movements finally lost their registration in June 1946 just prior to a presidential arbitration decision ending the conflict.

3. In 1983 and 1984 the de la Madrid administration used the union registration process to undercut the CTM's ability to protest harsh government austerity policies in the wake of the 1982 debt crisis. State labor authorities favored rival labor confederations (especially the Revolutionary Confederation of Workers and Peasants, CROC, and the Mexican Regional Labor Confederation, CROM) in their unionization efforts.[26] In return, these organizations opposed the CTM's call for a general strike, accepted wage increases smaller than those sought by the CTM, and openly backed the government's economic austerity program. In the context of a national economic crisis that in itself reduced labor's bargaining leverage, the resulting internal divisions prevented the organized labor movement from presenting a united front in negotiations with the de la Madrid administration.

Although these examples are indicative of the circumstances under which state authorities can manipulate the union registration process to achieve different political goals, an analysis of the politics of union registration in Mexico based on selected cases in the historical record leaves unanswered a number of important questions. For example, has the CTM's status as an Institutional Revolutionary Party (PRI) sector organization and the country's most politically influential labor confederation been reflected in its share of all union registrations? To what extent does the registration process respond to the general labor policies of different presidential administrations? Is a president's support for, or opposition to, the CTM or other major labor confederations evident in an organization's performance in the registration process (measured in terms of the length of time between application and formal recognition)? Is CTM support for the established regime during periods of political and economic crisis rewarded in an expedited registration process for its affiliates? If political considerations such as these are not generally significant, what other factors (for instance, a union's size or its geographical or sectoral location) might explain differences in the time required for a union to receive official recognition?

The remainder of this section addresses these questions by examining systematically union registrations in federal-jurisdiction economic activities between 1934 and 1976 (see appendix A for a description of the data set on which this analysis is based). State labor authorities gave legal recognition to an average of 528 organizations in each of the seven presidential administrations during this period, although they registered more organizations under the Cárdenas (771 cases) and Díaz Ordaz (877 cases) administrations than at any other time.[27] The mean size of all labor unions registered was 170 workers.[28] In general, union registrations were highly concentrated in terms of geographical location and economic activity. The Federal District (26.4 percent) and the states of Veracruz (12.6 percent) and Puebla (9.0 percent) together accounted for 48.0 percent of all registrations ($N = 2,514$), reflecting the traditional concentration of economic activity in these areas. No other state accounted for more than 4.4 percent (the state of México) of all registrations. Similarly, general cargo and passenger transportation (by train, ship, airplane, truck, and bus) (26.4 percent) and the textile (23.5 percent) and mining (5.1 percent) industries together represented 55.0 percent of all registrations ($N = 2,519$). No other activity accounted for more than 4.1 percent (construction) of total registrations.

The Confederation of Mexican Workers' dominant role in the national labor movement was evident in the distribution of union registrations between 1934 and 1976. Of the 2,335 cases for which information is available, 29.6 percent (690) were registered as CTM affiliates. In comparison, the CROM and CROC accounted for only 11.9 percent (279) and 8.2 percent (191), respectively, of all unions registered in federal-jurisdiction industries during these years; only 4.4 percent (103) of all unions registered during this period were affiliated with the General Confederation of Workers (CGT). It is especially noteworthy that 24.0 percent of all unions registered were affiliated with a wide variety of industry-specific and regional labor organizations and that 21.9 percent of all unions registered had no affiliation with *any* major confederation (though they may have subsequently established such ties). Because of the key roles that the CTM and other national confederations play in labor matters, one would have anticipated a higher degree of concentration in affiliation patterns. Yet the four most important national confederations (the CTM, CROC, CROM, and CGT) together accounted for only 54.1 percent of all unions registered during the period under investigation.

The CTM, CROC, and CROM all maintained a national presence during the 1934–76 period, with important numbers of affiliates registered in every major region. However, most affiliates of these three confederations were located in the Federal District and Center[29] regions, a reflection of the extent to which economic activity has traditionally been concentrated in the Mexico City metropolitan area and surrounding states. The proportion of total affiliates ($N = 2,334$) located in these areas ranged from 54.1 percent for the CROM, to 50.0 percent for the CROC, to 40.0 percent for the CTM, indicating the CTM's stronger presence in other parts of the country. The CGT, with the weakest national presence (it had no affiliates registered in the Pacific South[30] during the 1934–76 period), had 81.6 percent of its affiliates concentrated in the Federal District and Center regions. Yet once again, it is surprising that even in the Federal District—the center of national political power—CTM affiliates were fewer in number (and only represented 17.8 percent more workers) than unions registered without ties to a federation or confederation.[31]

In some states, a single confederation controlled the lion's share of union registrations. CTM affiliates represented 50 percent or more of all unions registered in the states of Chiapas, Quintana Roo, Sinaloa, and Tamaulipas. CROM affiliates similarly dominated the registration process in Colima and Tlaxcala. The absence of major industrial centers in these states may have reduced competition among different confederations to unionize new work sites; with the partial exceptions of Sinaloa and Tamaulipas, these states lacked a diversified industrial economy, and there were relatively few federal-jurisdiction unions (generally of small size) registered in them between 1934 and 1976. In some cases, however, these patterns reflected durable local political alliances. For example, Agapito González Cavazos, the CTM leader in Matamoros, Tamaulipas, dominated local labor politics from the 1950s through the early 1990s and effectively barred other national confederations from establishing a significant presence in the area.[32] In Tlaxcala, the CROM's strong presence in the textile industry (the state's principal industrial activity) dated from the 1920s.

The CTM, CROC, CROM, and CGT all registered affiliates in a broad range of economic activities, although the CTM had a larger share of its affiliates in transportation, communication, heavy manufacturing, and extractive activities than did other major labor organizations. (The CGT's affiliates were most highly concentrated, with 71.8 percent in light industry, construction, and services.) However, a more differentiated analysis of affiliates' identity shows that a large proportion of a particular confederation's membership was often concentrated in one or two industries. For example, 38.7 percent of all CROM affiliates were in the textile industry. The textile and cargo transportation industries together accounted for 51.3 percent of all CROM affiliates, 42.9 percent of CROC unions, and 32.9 percent of CTM affiliates. Conversely, a single confederation sometimes dominated the registration process in a particular industry, a phenomenon that was especially common when there were only a few unions registered in a given activity over the 1934–76 period. The CTM, for instance, accounted for 50 percent or more of the unions registered in the rubber processing, pharmaceutical, and bottling industries and in municipal services.

Because the data recorded by the Associational Registry pertain only to approved registrations, it is impossible to ascertain the extent to which such political considerations as a union's confederative ties (whether it was associated with the CTM, another major labor organization, or not) influenced the success of a particular application. Nor can one determine whether a particular confederation's dominance in a given industry or region resulted from state labor officials' open support for its unionization activities, the confederation's organizational work and its actual support among workers, or some combination of both factors.

It is possible, however, to test for politicization of the registration process (that is, whether the registration process was influenced by political factors external to the administrative review of a union's compliance with stipulated legal criteria) in an area of great importance—the time required for a union's registration application to be approved. Until it gains official recognition, a union cannot legally negotiate a contract with an employer or otherwise represent its members' interests. Moreover, a decision by state labor authorities to facilitate or delay a union's registration is a subtle but important means of introducing political considerations into the registration process. Manipulating the registration process in this way would presumably involve less potential political risk to state labor authorities than actually denying official recognition to a union. If the union registration process in Mexico was regularly subject to political intervention by state authorities during the 1934–76 period, it is likely to be evident in variations in the time required for the approval of registration applications.

For all 2,443 cases of union registration between 1934 and 1976 for which information is available,[33] an average of 224 days elapsed between the filing of a union's application and its final approval. The time required ranged from 1 to 9,103 days (24.9 years), with 13.2 percent of all cases requiring more than a year.[34] The wheels of labor administration turned so slowly that a major reform of federal labor law in April 1970 included a formal limitation on the time permitted the Associational Registry to review a union's application.[35] Since then, if the Associational Registry fails to act within 60 days after a union has submitted all required documentation, the law requires that the union's registration be granted automatically 3 days after the applicant requests it. This new requirement does not, however, appear to have resolved the problem of lengthy delays in the registration process.[36]

If the registration process is consistently politicized, one might hypothesize that the time required for union recognition would vary most significantly by presidential term and by confederative affiliation. (The impact of presidential labor policy might have been particularly important in this regard in the period before a formal limit was placed on the time permitted registry officials to act on an application.) Because of the federal executive's predominant role in national policymaking, one might reasonably expect the Cárdenas and Echeverría administrations' more liberal policies toward organized labor to have encouraged expedited union registration procedures, either because of presidential instructions to this effect or because these administrations may have devoted additional resources to the Associational Registry. In contrast, the Ávila Camacho, Alemán, and Díaz Ordaz administrations' more conservative policies toward labor might have included deliberate delays in the registration process. If shifts in presidential labor policy directly affected the length of the union registration process, then one might predict that the Ruiz Cortines and López Mateos administrations would fall somewhere between more liberal and conservative presidencies.

Although the CTM's position as the country's most politically influential confederation would presumably have permitted its affiliates to win registration more quickly than unions linked to other labor confederations, differences in presidential policy toward the CTM might also have produced variations in the time required for its affiliates to receive official recognition. For example, Cárdenas actively backed the formation and expansion of the CTM as a means of mobilizing labor support for his socioeconomic reform program. Alemán supported the CTM's more pragmatic leadership in its struggle against the leftist opposition Coalition of Worker and Peasant Organizations for control of the labor movement in 1947–48, and Díaz Ordaz authorized long-awaited reforms in the federal labor law as a reward to the CTM for backing the government when it was challenged by the 1968 student and popular movement. In contrast, Ruiz Cortines supported the CROC and López Mateos helped organize the National Workers' Central in 1960 as politically acceptable counterweights to the CTM. Moreover, Echeverría publicly criticized the leadership of "official" organizations such as the CTM in an attempt to encourage the emergence of a new generation of labor leaders. His administration also permitted (and at times encouraged) the formation of labor unions outside such "official" bodies as the Labor Congress.

However, the analysis-of-variance results reported in table 5.5 only partly confirm these hypotheses. Presidential term and confederative linkage had a statistically significant influence on the time required for union registration, but in both cases partial eta values (a measure of the strength of association between the independent and dependent variables, adjusted for other independent variables, interaction effects, and a covariate, union size) are modest—.12 for presidential term and .08 for confederative affiliation. The mean time required for union registration was lower in the pro-labor Echeverría administration than for the entire 1934–76 period but higher in the even more progressive Cárdenas administration (adjusted deviations from the grand mean of −.13 and .07, respectively). State labor officials approved union registration applications nearly as quickly during the conservative Alemán presidency as under Echeverría, and the mean registration time was the same under Ávila Camacho and Cárdenas. Only the Díaz Ordaz and Echeverría administrations (adjusted deviations from the grand mean of .29 and −.13, respectively) conformed to the predicted

TABLE 5.5   Analysis of Variance in the Time Required for Union Registration in Federal-Jurisdiction Industries, 1934–1976: Main Effects and Interaction Effects

Variable	Adjusted Deviation from Grand Mean[a]	Partial eta[b]	Significance of F
Main Effects			
Presidential Term		.12	.001
Cárdenas (1934–40)	.07		
Ávila Camacho (1940–46)	.07		
Alemán (1946–52)	−.05		
Ruiz Cortines (1952–58)	.03		
López Mateos (1958–64)	.13		
Díaz Ordaz (1964–70)	.29		
Echeverría (1970–76)	−.13		
Confederative Affiliation[c]		.08	.056
CTM	.10		
CROC	.16		
CROM	.13		
CGT	−.04		
Independent	−.07		
Other	.05		
Region[d]		.14	.000
Pacific North	.17		
North	.02		
Center	.02		
Gulf	.14		
Pacific South	.16		
Federal District	−.10		
Economic Activity[e]		.07	.048
Light manufacturing, construction, services	0		
Transportation and communications	.10		
Heavy manufacturing, extractive activities	.04		
Federations and confederations	.20		

pattern, and even in these two instances the deviations from the mean were modest.

The CTM actually required somewhat *more* time to register its affiliates than the overall 1934–76 average (an adjusted deviation from the grand mean of .10). Of the major national confederations included in this analysis, only the CROC's affiliates took longer to win official recognition. The politically marginal CGT and unaffiliated unions (listed as "Independent" in table 5.5) both fared better than the CTM in this regard. Even the diverse array of industry-specific and regional labor organizations (grouped as "Other" in table 5.5) required less registration time than did CTM

TABLE 5.5 continued

Variable	Adjusted Deviation from Grand Mean[a]	Partial eta[b]	Significance of F
Interaction Effects			
Presidential term by affiliation	.16		.042
Presidential term by region	.18		.007
Presidential term by activity	.13		.062
All other interaction effects	.19		NS
eta = .365			
eta[2] = .133			

Note: Analysis of variance is based on logged dependent variable (time, in days, between a union's application for official recognition at the Ministry of Labor and Social Welfare's Associational Registry and its final registration). NS = Not statistically significant.

[a] Grand mean = 2.07 (or 224.4 days); N = 2,226.

[b] The regression method was used to adjust for the effects of other independent variables, interaction effects, and the covariate, union size.

[c] The full names of the confederations listed are CTM (Confederation of Mexican Workers), CROC (Revolutionary Confederation of Workers and Peasants), CROM (Mexican Regional Labor Confederation), CGT (General Confederation of Labor).

[d] The states in each region listed are Pacific North (Baja California, Baja California Sur, Nayarit, Sinaloa, Sonora), North (Chihuahua, Coahuila, Durango, Nuevo León, San Luis Potosí, Tamaulipas, Zacatecas), Center (Aguascalientes, Guanajuato, Hidalgo, Jalisco, México, Michoacán, Morelos, Puebla, Querétaro, Tlaxcala), Gulf (Campeche, Quintana Roo, Tabasco, Veracruz, Yucatán), Pacific South (Chiapas, Colima, Guerrero, Oaxaca).

[e] The industries grouped in each economic activity are light manufacturing, construction, and services (the textile, sugar, food processing, pulp and paper, pharmaceutical, shipbuilding, and construction industries; municipal services; fishing; lumbering; and general commercial and manufacturing activities); transportation and communications (railroad, air, and other forms of cargo and passenger transportation; radio; television; and motion picture production); heavy manufacturing and extractive activities (the mining, metalworking, petroleum, electrical power generation, rubber, petrochemical, cement, and automobile manufacturing industries).

affiliates, suggesting that CTM affiliates' performance cannot be attributed to the geographical and sectoral heterogeneity of the confederation's membership.

Of the four variables included in this analysis, region had the most important impact on registration time (a partial eta value of .14). Unions located in the Federal District received official recognition substantially faster than those in other regions, indicating that even in federal-jurisdiction industries, geographical proximity to the Ministry of Labor and Social Welfare speeded the registration process. The economic activity in which unions were organized also had a statistically significant effect on registration time, but this was due to the longer times required (an adjusted deviation from the grand mean of .20) for federations and confederations to receive official recognition. The formation of such organizations might have raised particularly sensitive political issues that resulted in delays in the registration process, although it is also possible that these delays reflected the administrative difficulties involved in verifying necessary documentation for organizations whose members could have been dispersed among different industries, employers, and locations.[37]

The statistical results presented in table 5.5 show that individual independent variables are of only modest value in predicting union registration time. The partial eta values for two-way interaction effects indicate that registration time can be better predicted when both presidential term and either confederative affiliation, region, or economic activity are known. The substantively most interesting of these interactions is between presidential term and confederative linkage, and an analysis of parameter values (a measure of the effect of different categories of the independent variable on the dependent variable) suggests that there may have been several occasions during the 1934–76 period when presidential policy toward a particular labor organization influenced the time required for its affiliates to receive official recognition. For example, CROC affiliates won registration faster than average and CTM affiliates received recognition more slowly than average during the 1952–58 period, indicating that the Ruiz Cortines administration may have facilitated the CROC's unionization efforts in the years immediately after its formation in order to bolster its role as a counterweight to the CTM. Similarly, CROC affiliates and unaffiliated unions won registration more quickly, and CTM, CROM, and CGT affiliates more slowly, than average during the López Mateos administration, perhaps also indicating a presidential policy of selective support for particular labor organizations. However, only one of these specific interactions between presidential term and confederative affiliation was statistically significant (a coefficient of .16, significant at the .10 level): CTM affiliates required significantly more time than average to win official registration during the Alemán administration, even though one would have predicted an opposite result based on Alemán's strong defense of the CTM in its struggle with opposition labor groups for political control of the organized labor movement.[38]

The four independent variables included in this analysis together explain only 13.3 percent of variance in registration time. On the basis of this examination, one must conclude that factors such as presidential labor policy and confederative affiliation generally did not account well for variations in the time required for a union to win official recognition in nationally important federal-jurisdiction industries, economic activities in which one would have expected political considerations to be particularly important.

Worker Demand Resolution

Tripartite conciliation and arbitration boards are the principal state administrative channels for the resolution of individual worker grievances not settled in private negotiations between workers and employers. Delegates to Mexico's 1916–17 Constitutional Convention viewed the creation of institutional arrangements that permitted practical experience to guide the administration of labor legislation as one of their major achievements in the labor field, and the composition of conciliation and arbitration boards allows labor representatives to play a significant role in shaping the procedural and substantive criteria that govern the labor justice system. At least in principle, these boards (*juntas*) provide an effective forum for the redress of workplace grievances even when an employee's own union leadership is unresponsive.

This section examines two sets of questions concerning the articulation of individual worker demands through state administrative structures. First, how do conciliation and arbitration boards operate in practice, and how does their operation affect workers' ability to seek redress of individual grievances? Second, what impact does presidential labor policy have on this process? For example, does the volume of cases, the substance of individual grievances, or their form and time of resolution vary in accordance with major shifts in presidential labor policy? To what extent is the grievance resolution process before conciliation and arbitration boards responsive to the political preferences of different presidential administrations?

The Conciliation and Arbitration System: An Overview

The volume of cases handled by federal and local (state-level) conciliation and arbitration boards has varied considerably over time. Data for the period from 1939 through 1963 show that juntas resolved as many as 15,127 worker grievances at the federal and local levels in 1962, whereas they resolved as few as 9,073 cases in 1950.[39] Federal and local boards resolved an average of 12,240 cases per year over the entire 1939–63 period.[40] Because these cases involved such diverse issues as workers' petitions for reinstatement, work-related accident compensation, pension adjustment, and the return of wages withheld by the employer in a disciplinary matter, one would not expect a close relationship between the total number

TABLE 5.6   Work Conflicts Resolved, by Presidential Administration, 1939–1963

Presidential Administration	Total Conflicts	Federal Conflicts	Form of Conflict Resolution (Percentage of Total)			
			Conciliation	Arbitration	Private Settlement	Worker Withdrawal
Cárdenas (1939–40)						
Low	12,451	6,386	10.1	17.6	51.5	4.6
High	12,664	6,461	23.8	19.0	54.8	14.7
Annual average	12,558	6,424	17.0	18.3	53.2	9.7
Ávila Camacho (1941–46) [a]						
Low	11,837	4,037	3.9	15.8	42.1	11.1
High	14,281	6,735	9.8	19.9	60.0	19.1
Annual average	12,189	5,891	6.0	18.1	54.7	15.5
Alemán (1947–52) [b]						
Low	9,073	3,616	5.7	6.2	43.1	15.6
High	10,491	5,205	11.7	19.5	60.8	24.5
Annual average	9,428	4,583	7.7	14.4	50.4	19.4
Ruiz Cortines (1953–58)						
Low	9,775	4,473	2.3	6.8	49.5	14.8
High	14,186	7,426	14.8	18.2	66.6	23.4
Annual average	12,946	6,303	5.0	10.3	59.7	19.7
López Mateos (1959–63)						
Low	13,045	4,346	3.0	7.9	61.0	18.0
High	15,127	5,747	5.2	9.3	64.7	20.2
Annual average	14,140	4,837	3.9	8.4	62.7	19.2
Annual average for 1939–63 period	12,240	5,508	7.5	13.4	56.6	17.6

Source: Secretaría de Industria y Comercio, Dirección General de Estadística, Anuario estadístico, 1939–71.

Note: Data on form of work conflict resolution are for both local- and federal-jurisdiction economic activities. Minor resolution categories are not listed; as a result, the "annual average" rows do not add to 100.0 percent.

[a] Data on total work conflicts are incomplete for 1946.

[b] Data on total work conflicts are incomplete for 1947 and missing for 1952; data on form of work conflict resolution are missing for 1952.

of grievances resolved and shifts in economic variables such as the inflation rate or the real minimum wage. No such relationship existed at the national level during the period from 1941 to 1963.[41]

However, the volume of worker grievances might well be influenced by presidential labor policy. A particular administration's reputation for pro-labor policies might foster expectations of speedy grievance resolution and a favorable decision from conciliation and arbitration boards, encouraging workers to articulate their demands through the labor justice system. Alternatively, a conservative administration's support for enterprise economic restructuring might produce a larger number of junta cases as workers seek reinstatement in their former jobs, payment of separation indemnities, and so forth.

There is, in fact, some evidence that the Cárdenas administration favored workers in their cases before conciliation and arbitration boards,[42] and this perception may have accounted for the large number of workers filing grievances in the late 1930s. Table 5.6 shows that juntas resolved an annual average of 12,558 individual work conflicts in 1939 and 1940, the last two years of Cárdenas's pro-labor presidency.[43] The average number of work conflicts resolved remained quite high during the Ávila Camacho administration, probably because of the large volume of grievances initially filed during the Cárdenas presidency. The general level of conciliation and arbitration board activity declined somewhat thereafter, reaching its lowest level in the entire 1939–63 period during the conservative Alemán administration—a time when government support for economic restructuring in major industries might have been expected to produce the opposite effect. The number of worker grievances handled by these boards rose again during the moderate Ruiz Cortines and López Mateos administrations, reaching average levels even higher than the level reached during the Cárdenas administration. There was no major difference between federal- and local-jurisdiction work conflicts in these trends.

The grievance resolution process before federal and state-level conciliation and arbitration boards includes the following steps: presentation of the worker's demand; investigation of the dispute by board members and testimony by the conflicting parties and relevant witnesses; a formal decision regarding the case; and enforcement of the board's ruling.[44] Federal labor law and conciliation and arbitration board internal guidelines have always emphasized that the grievance resolution process should be flexible, permitting a board to reach a decision that takes into account all available evidence and reflects the particularities of an individual case. Each stage of the process normally requires a separate meeting (scheduled at legally specified intervals) between the parties involved in the dispute and the junta's president, sectoral (labor and capital) representatives on the board, and administrative staff members. The junta's president and his or her auxiliary are legally empowered to conduct most such meetings if no sectoral representative is present; federal labor law requires that at least one sector's representative(s) be present only for a board's final ruling on a case.[45] If neither the worker nor the employer attends a scheduled meeting, the board normally suspends review of the case until one of the parties takes further action; the board terminates a case only when neither party pursues the grievance for a period of six months.[46] All affected parties may examine and appeal board rulings at each step. Labor law and conciliation and arbitration board guidelines protect the conflicting parties' rights and maintain procedural flexibility in a great diversity of worker-employer disputes, but the result is a complex, time-consuming, often legalistic process that is very susceptible to delay.[47]

The labor justice system was created with the intention that a worker could prepare and present his or her own case, and much of the grievance resolution process involves oral argument.[48] In practice, however, most workers pursuing grievances before conciliation and arbitration boards are represented by counsel—either a union representative or union attorney, a lawyer from the Procuraduría Federal de la Defensa del Trabajo (Federal Labor Legal Defense Office),[49] or a private attorney.[50] Interviews with Junta Federal de Conciliación y Arbitraje (Federal Conciliation and Arbitration Board, JFCA) officials indicate that the effectiveness of conciliation efforts varies considerably from one special junta and industry to another; in some areas, cases regularly end in a private settlement, whereas in others grievances are normally resolved by a formal board decision (laudo).

The character of the grievance resolution process is also shaped by the occupational backgrounds of junta staff members, which have become increasingly homogeneous over time. The original operating guidelines for federal conciliation and arbitration boards (published in 1927–28) set very general requirements for junta members, specifying only that government representatives be Mexican citizens, literate and of legal age, and that they not have a criminal record or be a priest or minister.[51] However, the 1931 federal labor law stipulated that the presidents of the Federal Conciliation and Arbitration Board, state-level conciliation and arbitration boards, JFCA special juntas, and their administrative general secretaries all be attorneys with a specialization in labor law.[52] The 1970 federal labor law went even further, requiring that JFCA special junta presidents' administrative assistants and most other professional staff members also be attorneys with particular expertise in labor law.[53]

The common legal background of junta professional staff members creates distinctive workplace values in the labor court system. Discussions among staff members often concern recent substantive and procedural changes in federal labor law, and "Licenciado" (a reference to the *licencia-tura* professional degree) is the standard form of personal address. There is necessarily some turnover among professional personnel with each change in presidential administration, but there appears to be considerable conti-nuity in the case of special junta presidents. For example, before serving as JFCA president during the period from 1980 to 1994, Lic. Miguel Ángel Pino de la Rosa had served on a total of six special juntas and had been president of three of them.[54] A common occupational background empha-sizing specialized expertise in labor law and distinctive workplace values establish the sociological basis for organizational cohesion and consider-able institutional autonomy in the day-to-day operations of conciliation and arbitration boards.[55] This is especially important in the demand reso-lution process because government representatives hold the deciding vote.

Administrative delay is the principal difficulty with grievance reso-lution by conciliation and arbitration boards.[56] In some instances these delays are quite extraordinary. In December 1976, for example, the Federal Conciliation and Arbitration Board reported that fourteen of its sixteen special juntas had a combined backlog of 26,401 cases (the backlog ranged from 425 cases for Special Board 15 [with jurisdiction over the automobile manufacturing, chemical, pharmaceutical, and pulp and paper industries] to 3,341 cases for Special Board 14 [with jurisdiction over decentralized federal agencies and the National Autonomous University of Mexico]).[57] Some 71.9 percent of the cases under review in December 1976 had been filed in 1975 or earlier, and 18.5 percent of the cases awaiting resolution had been initiated in 1971 or earlier—and thus had been under review for at least five years. Even more remarkable, 4 cases dated from the 1930s, 37 cases (0.1 percent of the total) from the 1940s, 212 cases (0.8 percent of the total) from the 1950s, and 2,149 cases (8.1 percent of the total) from the 1960s.

Delays of this length—and the widely shared perception that the labor justice system operates very slowly—may account in part for the form in which individual work conflicts were resolved between 1939 and 1963 (see table 5.6).[58] An average of only 13.4 percent of the federal- and local-jurisdiction grievances settled during this period were resolved through formal arbitration procedures involving a vote by junta members. This pro-portion was never larger than 19.9 percent (1942), and in 1951 it was only 6.2 percent. Formal conciliation by juntas also played a very limited role in the resolution of such cases. On average, only 7.5 percent of all individual work conflicts were settled in this manner between 1939 and 1963, with a high of 23.8 percent in 1940 and a low of 2.3 percent in 1956.

By far the most common means of resolving individual worker griev-ances before conciliation and arbitration boards during the 1939–63 period was private agreement among the parties in dispute. An annual average of 56.6 percent of all cases was settled in this manner, although this proportion ranged between 42.1 percent in 1946 and 66.6 percent in 1957. The prospect of long, potentially costly legal proceedings may well have encouraged workers to seek such private settlements rather than await a formal junta ruling on their cases, although these decisions also presumably reflected grievants' evaluation of the strength of their cases. Even more revealing, 17.6 percent of all cases terminated during the 1939–63 period ended in grievants' voluntary withdrawal of unresolved demands *(desistimiento)*, with a low of 4.6 percent ending in this manner in 1940 and a high of 24.5 percent in 1948. For most of the 1939–63 period, the means by which individual work conflicts were resolved varied little under different presidential administrations. However, government-sponsored conciliation produced a substantially higher proportion of settlements during the Cárdenas administration than in subsequent presidential administrations. In addition, a smaller percentage of cases ended in worker withdrawal during the pro-labor Cárdenas presidency than in subsequent administrations.

Railroad Worker Grievance Resolution

Grievances filed before the Federal Conciliation and Arbitration Board by Mexican National Railroads (FNM) employees were analyzed in order to determine more precisely the kinds of demands made by workers, their pattern of resolution, and the possible impact of political variables such as presidential labor policy on worker demand articulation through state administrative structures. By focusing on demands filed by workers at a single firm over the period from 1934 to 1975, it is possible to evaluate the impact of economic conditions, managerial policies, and changes in union governance on patterns of demand articulation and resolution. Moreover, if shifts in presidential policy have a direct impact on conciliation and arbitration boards' handling of individual worker demands, this effect is especially likely to be evident in the case of railroad workers because of the industry's strategic economic importance. The volume of demands filed by railroad workers is sufficiently large to permit statistically valid testing of the significance of this relationship.

A total of 2,081 cases were selected for analysis from the more than 62,000 demands filed by FNM employees between 1934 and 1975 (see appendix B for details on sampling procedures).[59] FNM workers filed an average of 1,504 demands per year during this period before two special juntas (nos. 1 and 14) devoted exclusively to FNM conflicts. Case volume fluctuated somewhat from one year to another, ranging from a high of 2,648 cases in 1959 (following the López Mateos administration's repression of the Vallejo movement) to a low of 714 cases in 1971. The number of demands filed each year did not vary consistently with shifts in presidential labor policy. Nevertheless, case volume did increase from 1,400 per year under Cárdenas to 1,580 per year under Ávila Camacho, a time when railroad workers came under intense government and managerial pressures over contract terms and work rules. Yet the average number of cases then declined somewhat to 1,503 per year during the even more conservative Alemán administration, before rising to 1,945 per year during the Ruiz Cortines presidency—a period when FNM workers faced less open government hostility than under Alemán, although they continued to suffer negative effects from railroad modernization and declining real wages.

A total of 9.9 percent of the cases in the sample involved formal agreements (convenios) between workers and railroad management legally registered with the JFCA.[60] Of the 207 convenios filed, 71 addressed the terms of a worker's retirement. Another 21 cases in the sample were administrative petitions filed by the railroad workers' union or individual workers involving such issues as workplace regulations. The Mexican Railroad Workers' Union (STFRM) appeared as a grievant or co-grievant in 124 cases (52 convenios and 72 grievances; 6.0 percent of all cases in the sample).

Of the 1,853 grievances in the sample, 780 (42.1 percent) involved employment issues (see table 5.7, Sample 1). The most common employment grievance (568 cases) concerned workers' petitions for reinstatement following dismissal from their jobs, although a substantial number of cases involved workers seeking promotion, the recognition of seniority rights, and so forth (212 cases). An additional 360 grievances (19.4 percent) involved workers' claims for wage and benefit payments, including compensation for overtime, additional payments due following a promotion, medical expenses, and so forth. Some 277 cases (14.9 percent) involved workers petitioning for retirement, and 213 cases (11.5 percent) resulted from either railroad employees seeking indemnity payments following work-related accidents or a worker's heirs petitioning for contractually specified benefits following his death on the job. Disciplinary issues (workers petitioning for the cancellation of demerits or, more frequently, for wages withheld by management for a disciplinary infraction) produced 154 demands (8.3 percent).[61]

One might hypothesize that the incidence of employment, wage and benefit, and disciplinary grievances would vary according to shifts in worker-employer relations at Ferrocarriles Nacionales de México and changes in the political independence and governance of the Mexican Railroad Workers' Union. The number of such demands would be expected to decline during the Worker Administration (May 1938 through December 1940), increase during the 1940s and early 1950s as railroad administrators

TABLE 5.7 Railroad Worker Grievances before the Federal Conciliation and Arbitration Board, 1934–1975

Grievance Type	Sample 1[a]		Sample 2[a]	
	Cases	Percentage	Cases	Percentage
Employment issues[b]	780	42.1	72	43.1
Wage and benefit issues[c]	360	19.4	47	28.1
Retirement petitions	277	14.9	6	3.6
Indemnity claims[d]	213	11.5	22	13.2
Disciplinary issues[e]	154	8.3	11	6.6
Miscellaneous issues[f]	69	3.7	9	5.4
Total	1,853	99.9[g]	167	100.0

[a] Sampling procedures are discussed in appendix B.

[b] Demands for reinstatement following dismissal; promotion; and recognition of seniority rights.

[c] Demands for wage and fringe benefit increases, pension adjustment, compensation for overtime work, pay differentials following a promotion, and payment of medical expenses.

[d] Claims for payment of work-related accident or death indemnity.

[e] Petitions for cancellation of demerits or return of wages withheld for disciplinary infractions.

[f] Includes worker demands for expense reimbursement (funeral costs, travel expenses), union petitions for creation or elimination of job positions, demands that contract be enforced, and various administrative petitions.

[g] Total does not add to 100.0 percent because of rounding.

sought to reduce employment levels and curtail the STFRM's contractual authority and bargaining power, and increase again in 1959 and subsequent years as management sought to restore control following the 1958–59 national railroad strikes. Similarly, wage and benefit cases might vary in frequency with changes in railroad workers' economic circumstances.[62]

However, figure 5.3 shows only a weak overall relationship between fluctuations in these grievance types and changes in the character of worker-employer relations at FNM, union governance (vertical lines mark the key dates of 1938–40, 1948, and 1958), or the real wages and benefits earned by railroad workers. The volume of cases involving employment issues did generally fall during the Worker Administration (a time when union officials were in charge of the company) and increase between 1942 and 1946, but these cases also declined in frequency during 1947–48 and the early 1950s even in those years when FNM management reduced the size of the labor force (see table 4.1). They rose sharply in the mid-1950s at a time when FNM employment remained stable. Employment grievances declined in 1958 (perhaps reflecting more forceful union lobbying efforts under Vallejo's leadership) and increased in 1959 as reinstatement petitions were filed in the wake of the government's forcible resolution of the railroad

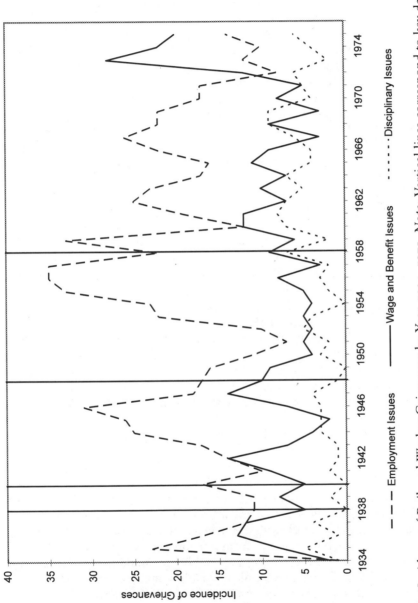

FIGURE 5.3 Incidence of Railroad Worker Grievances by Year, 1934–1975. *Note*: Vertical lines correspond to key dates in the history of Ferrocarriles Nacionales de México and the Mexican Railroad Workers' Union. *Source*: Table 5.5.

- - - Employment Issues   —— Wage and Benefit Issues   · · · · · Disciplinary Issues labor crisis and the restoration of a far more conservative union leadership. But they fell again in 1960 and remained at a reduced level during the 1960s and early 1970s at a time when railroad management once again sought to reduce work force levels.

There was also a weak relationship between the incidence of wage and benefit grievances and shifts in railroad workers' real earnings (see table 4.1 and figure 5.3). These grievances rose in 1942 and 1946–47 when workers' real wages and benefits were falling, and the number of such grievances jumped sharply in the early 1970s as FNM employees sought increased wage and benefit payments during a period of accelerating inflation. However, the number of these cases also fell in 1943–45 at a time when real earnings were in sharp decline. Their continuous decline in 1948–50 during a period of great economic pressure on railroad workers is particularly noteworthy.

The volume of disciplinary cases was never as great as that of employment and wage and benefit grievances. The incidence of these demands predictably declined during the Worker Administration, and they were generally more common in the 1960s and early 1970s during a period in which accommodationist union leaders and management exercised tight control over the rank and file. But these cases also decreased in number in 1949 at a time when one would have predicted a sharp upturn in them. If the incidence of such grievances were positively associated with conservative departures in worker-employer relations and the political orientation of the union leadership, the number of these cases should have declined in 1958 (when the union was led by democratically elected leaders committed to protecting rank-and-file interests) and risen in 1959 (when more politically conservative union leaders regained control with government support). Instead, disciplinary cases rose in number in 1958 and declined in 1959.

It is possible, however, that the JFCA's institutional structure in the railroad transportation sector produced a negative correlation between conservative shifts in worker-employer relations and the political character of union leadership, on the one hand, and the frequency of disciplinary demands filed before Special Boards 1 and 14. The majority of JFCA special juntas are responsible for resolving grievances in two or more industries. As a consequence, a worker filing a demand may well have his or her case heard by a labor representative from a union and industry different than his or her own. However, because Special Boards 1 and 14 are exclusively devoted to resolving grievances filed by FNM employees, and because the national executive committee of the Mexican Railroad Workers' Union exercises significant influence over the selection of candidates to serve as elected labor representatives on these two boards, the political character of the union leadership may directly affect the criteria employed by labor representatives in reviewing cases. As a consequence, a worker dismissed from his or her job for politically motivated reasons might reasonably conclude that he or she has little chance of prevailing in circumstances in which the junta's employer and labor representatives might *both* oppose his or her claim. A potential grievant might, therefore, never enter the labor justice system. The available archival evidence does not indicate whether the special juntas' labor representatives were replaced in 1948 and 1958–59 following changes in the STFRM's governance. If a change in union leadership did result in the election of new labor representatives, then this change in the boards' composition might help explain why the frequency of disciplinary grievances declined in 1949, rose in 1958 when the union was again democratically governed, and fell in 1959.

Because FNM is a state-owned enterprise in which the general director is appointed by the president, it is difficult to distinguish completely between changes in railroad management's policies toward labor and shifts in presidential policy toward railroad workers or organized labor more generally. Nevertheless, figure 5.4 (vertical lines demarcate presidential terms) shows that the incidence of different railroad worker grievances did not vary consistently with shifts in presidential policy. Employment-related demands rose sharply during the Ávila Camacho administration as the government sought to restructure industrial relations at FNM, but the frequency of these grievances fell just as precipitously under Alemán despite the administration's aggressive efforts to curtail union power—a policy that presumably would have led to an increase in reinstatement cases. Employment demands rose again during the Ruiz Cortines administration even though presidential policy toward railroad workers and organized labor more generally was substantially more moderate than under the preceding administration. Nor did variations in the incidence of wage and benefit and disciplinary demands closely parallel shifts in presidential policy. The only exception was the upturn in wage and benefit demands in the early 1970s under Echeverría, when workers may have hoped that a pro-labor administration would give them relief from inflationary pressures.

A more detailed analysis of railroad worker grievances before the Federal Conciliation and Arbitration Board offers new insight into the operation of the labor justice system in Mexico.[63] A subset of 205 cases was selected for intensive examination from the larger sample of FNM demands (see appendix B for sampling procedures). A total of 38 of these cases (18.5 percent) were *convenios* between workers and FNM management registered with the JFCA. Of the 167 grievances in this sample, 72 (43.1 percent) involved employment issues, 47 (28.1 percent) were claims

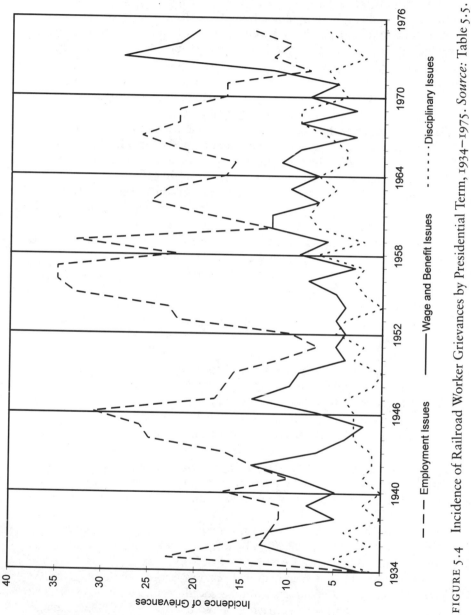

FIGURE 5.4 Incidence of Railroad Worker Grievances by Presidential Term, 1934–1975. *Source:* Table 5.5.

for wage and benefit payments, 22 (13.2 percent) were accident and death indemnity claims, 11 (6.6 percent) involved disciplinary issues, and 6 (3.6 percent) were workers' petitions for retirement (see table 5.7, Sample 2). Thus, with the exception of wage and benefit cases, the distribution of grievance types in this subset generally paralleled that in the larger sample of railroad cases.[64]

Some 90.4 percent of these grievances were filed by individual workers; 8.4 percent were group demands filed by from 2 to 21 workers, and 1.2 percent cited the Mexican Railroad Workers' Union as a co-grievant ($N = 167$). The period of time workers had been employed on the railroads at the time they filed their grievances ranged from 1 to 52 years and averaged 25.4 years. The great majority of workers (77.2 percent) were represented during the demand resolution process by either union officials or union attorneys (the STFRM maintains its own legal department), although a number of grievants had private lawyers (19.2 percent) and some workers (3.6 percent) handled their own cases.[65] Most demands were filed by workers employed at major railroad sites in the Federal District (20.5 percent of all cases, $N = 127$) and in the Center (33.9 percent) and North (33.1 percent) of the country.[66] Workers sought a financial award in 90.4 percent of all cases. Archival records included clear evidence of employer opposition to the worker's grievance in 64.8 percent of all cases ($N = 165$). Given FNM's perpetual financial difficulties, it is not surprising that railroad managers were twice as likely to oppose the worker's demand when money was at stake.[67] Female employees accounted for only 18 grievances (10.8 percent), and all but 5 of these cases involved a widow or heir seeking a death indemnity or pension payment for a deceased male worker.[68]

The parties in dispute employed the junta grievance resolution process for diverse purposes. In several reinstatement cases, the worker filed a demand before the JFCA while simultaneously pursuing his or her demand through the union-management Comisión Mixta de Apelaciones Disciplinarias (Joint Disciplinary Appeals Commission). If the worker was reinstated as a result of this internal administrative review, he or she then withdrew the demand lodged before the JFCA.[69] In 3 of the 11 cases involving petitions for death indemnity payments, railroad managers did not object to the widow's or heir's claim, but they sought a formal JFCA ruling in order to avoid future legal controversies over the identity of the deceased worker's legitimate heirs.[70]

The outcome of the grievance resolution process favored workers in 53.6 percent of all cases ($N = 166$),[71] either because of a junta ruling in favor of the grievant (33 cases) or because the conflicting parties reached a settlement generally favorable to the worker's interests (56 cases). Workers fared best in cases involving reinstatement or retirement petitions. The 77 cases ending on terms favorable to the employer included 41 instances in which a junta ruled in favor of railroad management, 24 cases in which the worker desisted in the course of the grievance resolution process, and 12 grievance cases that the JFCA terminated because one of the parties failed to pursue the case (thus leaving unchanged the situation the grievant had attempted to reverse). Railroad managers were most successful in cases involving wage and benefit claims—some of the same kinds of cases in which FNM was most likely to oppose the grievant actively. Only in cases concerning accident and death indemnity claims did workers generally win (in 17 of 22 such cases, 77.3 percent) against active employer opposition, which may have been due in part to the strong protection that federal labor law provides workers in such instances. Workers represented by union officials or union lawyers won 60.2 percent of their grievances, whereas workers represented by private attorneys won only 28.1 percent of their cases.[72]

The special juntas hearing FNM employee grievances issued a formal ruling in only 74 of the cases (44.3 percent) in Sample 2. Only 12.2 percent of these rulings were unanimous decisions; the others were split decisions in which the junta president voted with the representative of either the STFRM or Ferrocarriles Nacionales. In none of the Sample 2 cases did the labor representative vote against the grievant in a split decision, although in two cases the labor representative did write a separate opinion concerning his views on the case.[73] The average resolution time for cases ending in a formal board ruling was 1,541 days (4.2 years), ranging from 30 to 6,295 days. In a total of 31 cases, either the worker or the employer sought an injunction (amparo) from the Supreme Court against a junta ruling (not necessarily the final decision). However, only 7 (22.6 percent) of these appeals were granted,[74] and in all 7 cases the Supreme Court supported the employer's claim.

A favorable JFCA decision, however, did not necessarily ensure the worker that Ferrocarriles Nacionales de México management would comply promptly with the board's ruling—particularly when a financial award was at stake, even during the Worker Administration. For example, Gilberto Saavedra filed a demand in May 1947 for promotion to a position to which his seniority as a carpenter entitled him. He finally received a favorable junta decision in August 1958, but he did not receive a payment for back wages (4,146 pesos, U.S.$332) until December 1963.[75] Similarly, in May 1954 three employees each filed claim to two hours' pay for work performed at a higher job classification. The special junta did not issue a ruling until 1971, by which time accumulated interest had greatly inflated the value of the original claim. When the employer's request for an injunction against the junta's decision was turned down by the Supreme Court in

1972, the junta made financial awards to the workers ranging from 143,200 to 185,330 pesos (U.S.$11,456 to U.S.$14,826). Even then the company apparently still refused to pay because in 1978 FNM renewed its effort to secure an injunction. Thus the workers' initially small financial claim remained unresolved twenty-four years later.[76]

One of the most noteworthy characteristics of the labor justice system is the length of time required for cases to be resolved. The average resolution time for all Sample 2 cases (whether the case ended in a formal junta ruling, a private settlement, or the worker's decision to drop the case) was 1,122 days (3.1 years), ranging from a minimum of 3 days to a maximum of 8,668 days (23.7 years). Only slightly more than half (56.0 percent, $N = 166$) of the grievances were resolved in two years or less.[77] A total of 28 cases (16.9 percent) required more than six years, and in 10 grievance cases (6.0 percent) it took the JFCA more than ten years to bring the case to conclusion.[78] In 3 of these cases, the worker died before his case was resolved.

In some instances, the length of the delay bore little relationship to the apparent complexity of the case. For example, Demetrio Rivera, a mechanic in FNM's Puebla repair facilities, waited from July 1941 until August 1948 for a special junta to rule against his claim that FNM management was liable for the theft of some of his tools, which he valued at 85 pesos.[79] FNM managers offered no real opposition to Genaro Lomelín Rayón's January 1944 claim to a promotion as an office worker, but the special junta hearing the case took until September 1956 to issue a unanimous ruling in his favor.[80] A dispute in which railroad managers argued that FNM had overpaid Gerardo Hernández Vargas's law scholarship by 262 pesos dragged on from May 1944 until June 1967; the junta finally declared the case inactive in February 1968.[81] In contrast, it took Manuel Castañeda Flores less than three years (from June 1970 until April 1973) to win a favorable ruling on his seemingly dubious claim that FNM was financially liable for the loss of his right index and middle fingers while attempting on company property to repair his car's engine before beginning his shift.[82]

It is not surprising that employer opposition to a worker's grievance increased the time required for the case to be resolved. Of the 58 grievances in which railroad managers did not actively oppose the worker's claim, 36 (62.1 percent) were resolved in six months or less, and 46 cases (79.3 percent) were resolved in one year or less. In contrast, only 10 (9.3 percent) of the 107 cases involving employer opposition were resolved in six months or less. Only 17 of these grievances (15.9 percent) were resolved in one year or less; 67 of these cases (62.6 percent) required more than two years.

There was also a relationship between the grievant's choice of legal representation and the length of resolution time. Forty-one of the 129 cases (31.8 percent) in which the worker was represented by a union representative or a union lawyer were resolved in six months or less, and 52 cases (40.3 percent) were resolved in two years or less. In contrast, 25 of the 32 cases (78.1 percent) in which the worker was represented by a private attorney required more than a year to resolve, and 20 (62.5 percent) of these grievances required more than two years to resolve. It is possible that the delay involved in resolving some of these cases resulted from private attorneys purposely dragging out JFCA proceedings, without a correspondingly greater success rate. For example, it is interesting to note that 3 of the 28 cases lasting more than six years were handled by the same private law firm.[83] At a minimum, private attorneys would have had an incentive to continue promoting a grievance long after it became clear the worker would not win.[84]

The grievant's decision to retain private counsel bore some relationship to the type of demand and FNM's tendency to offer (and perhaps management's reputation for posing) active opposition in cases in which money was at stake. Some 62.5 percent of the cases in which the worker was represented by a private attorney involved a potential financial award (demands for promotion, recognition of seniority, wages and benefits, an accident indemnity, and disciplinary actions in which wages had been withheld). But another 37.5 percent of these cases involved reinstatement petitions, cases in which FNM often offered little opposition and which were often resolved comparatively quickly by private accord between the worker and railroad managers (see below). Thus the grievant's decision to retain private counsel may often have reflected personal preferences, union leaders' political hostility toward a worker, or the poor professional reputation of the union lawyers then available.

These factors are important because there was a relationship between the final outcome and the length of time required to resolve a case. Most private settlements (87.5 percent of the 56 cases resolved in this manner) occurred within the first year after the grievance was filed. Similarly, the likelihood of the worker's desisting increased as the grievance resolution process dragged on (54.2 percent of the 24 cases ending in this fashion did so after two years had passed). More significant, of the 48 cases lasting two years or more in which special juntas made formal rulings, the employer received a favorable ruling in 29 instances (60.4 percent).

FNM managers used the delay normally involved in resolving grievances before the JFCA to their advantage. In 32 of the 53 reinstatement cases (60.4 percent), railroad managers offered no opposition to the worker's demand, and in 34 of these cases (64.2 percent) the grievant reached a settlement with management in which he or she was permitted to return to work—usually in exchange for dropping his or her demand for back wages.[85] As a result, 52.8 percent of these cases were resolved in six months or less. In these instances Ferrocarriles Nacionales de México in effect used the junta system as a means of disciplining workers—firing the employee and allowing him or her to file a grievance before the JFCA but knowing that the worker was more likely to concede a claim for back pay than to persist for years in a grievance resolution process whose ultimate outcome was uncertain. This tactic also allowed FNM managers to dismiss a worker temporarily without paying him or her constitutionally mandated severance pay. Management's reliance on this strategy may account in part for the fact that employment issues represented the single most common kind of grievance in Samples 1 and 2.

A central question in this analysis of railroad worker demand articulation through state administrative structures is whether presidential labor policy had a significant impact on either the time required or the outcome of the grievance resolution process. Because an individual worker's grievance before a conciliation and arbitration board is not nearly as politically significant as a major strike or a particularly sensitive union registration case, one would not expect direct presidential intervention to shape the timing or outcome of the case except in truly exceptional circumstances. The substantial time that juntas require to examine a case and produce a formal ruling also makes it difficult for a particular presidential administration to influence the handling of individual worker grievances because some cases filed during a given president's administration would not be concluded until after he left office. (Some 16.9 percent of all the cases in Sample 2 had resolution times of more than six years.)

Nevertheless, other considerations suggest that the grievance resolution process might be sensitive to policy shifts from one presidential administration to another. The head of the Federal Conciliation and Arbitration Board is appointed by the president to a six-year term that coincides with the length of his own administration, and the biographical information that is available concerning past JFCA presidents strongly suggests that those who have held this high-profile post (under the 1970 federal labor law, they have the same administrative rank as a Supreme Court justice)[86] have been well connected politically.[87] Since the passage of the 1970 federal labor law, JFCA sectoral representatives are elected to six-year terms that overlap with its president's.[88] The JFCA president can by law assume direction of a particular special junta if the case before it is of sufficient importance. Moreover, interviews with JFCA officials indicate that professional staff members are fully aware of the political importance of different

TABLE 5.8   Analysis of Variance in the Time Required for Railroad Worker Grievance Resolution before the Federal Conciliation and Arbitration Board, 1934–1975

Variable[a]	Unstandardized Coefficient	Standard Error	T-Value	Significance Level
Presidential Administration				
Cárdenas (1934–40)	−.37	.36	−1.02	.312
Ávila Camacho (1940–46)	.12	.37	.34	.738
Alemán (1946–52)	.05	.44	.11	.910
Ruiz Cortines (1952–58)	−.60	.35	−1.71	.090
López Mateos (1958–64)	−.42	.34	−1.22	.226
Díaz Ordaz (1964–70)	−.72	.35	−2.06	.043
Employer Opposition[b]	1.24	.22	5.74	.000
Legal Representation				
Union representation or union attorney	.41	.46	.89	.380
Private attorney	1.17	.52	2.26	.026
Constant[c]	4.50	.53	8.51	.000

$R^2 = .415$
Adjusted $R^2 = .359$
$N = 103$
Model degrees of freedom = 9

Note: Analysis of variance is based on logged dependent variable (time, in days, between a worker's initiation of grievance proceedings before the Federal Conciliation and Arbitration Board and the final resolution of the case, whether the case ended in a formal board ruling, a private settlement, or the worker's decision to drop the case); mean = 5.33 (or 364.2 days). Only those cases that were both initiated and resolved during the same six-year presidential term are included in this analysis.

[a] Main effects; two-way interaction effects are not statistically significant.

[b] Variable is coded 1 (railroad management actively opposed worker's grievance) and 2 (no apparent employer opposition).

[c] Constant is derived from dropped categories for presidential term (Echeverría administration, 1970–76), employer opposition (railroad management offered no significant opposition to worker's petition), and legal representation (employee represented himself or herself). Because grievance resolution times might be expected to be shorter under Echeverría's generally pro-labor administration, when railroad management did not actively oppose a grievant's petition, and when no attorney was involved in the case, the constant represents those conditions under which worker grievances could be expected to be resolved comparatively quickly.

kinds of grievances, and some emphasize the extent to which the JFCA president leaves a personal mark on the grievance resolution process during his tenure.[89]

The 103 cases in Sample 2 which were initiated and resolved during a single presidential term were analyzed to test for the possible impact of shifts in presidential policy on the demand resolution process. Grouping grievance cases in this manner constitutes the strictest test of presidential policy impact, although it necessarily excludes from the analysis cases filed late in a given administration and cases with especially long resolution times. The mean resolution time for these 103 cases was 364 days; the grievance resolution process produced outcomes favorable to workers in 69 of these cases (67.0 percent).

The results reported in table 5.8 indicate that presidential policy did not have a significant impact on the time required for the JFCA to resolve individual FNM employee grievances between 1934 and 1975. There was a statistically significant relationship between presidential term and grievance resolution time only during the Díaz Ordaz presidency, and contrary to what one would hypothesize, railroad worker grievances were resolved more quickly (the unstandardized coefficient for the Díaz Ordaz administration is −.72) during this conservative presidency than during Echeverría's pro-labor administration. The absence of a stronger relationship between presidential term and resolution time may have been due to the fact that delays resulting from the normal operation of a complex legal bureaucracy, or delays due to the failure of workers or FNM managers to promote legal proceedings aggressively, are little influenced by presidential priorities.

In contrast, active employer opposition to a grievant's petition and the involvement of a private attorney had strong, statistically significant impacts on the length of time required for a case to be resolved (unstandardized coefficients of 1.24 and 1.17, respectively, significant at the .000 and .026 levels). Yet despite the strength of these two relationships, the three independent variables examined in table 5.8 together explain only 35.9 percent of the variance in demand resolution times.

Table 5.9 summarizes the results of a probability analysis of the outcome of railroad worker grievance cases before the Federal Conciliation and Arbitration Board between 1934 and 1975. Employer opposition and resolution time were generally the most important factors determining whether a case was resolved on terms favorable to the worker or to FNM management. Workers were more likely to prevail in the grievance resolution process when railroad managers offered no active opposition (an unstandardized coefficient of 2.23, significant at the .000 level), whereas a case was more likely to end on terms favorable to the employer when the grievance resolution process was lengthy (an unstandardized coefficient of −1.10, also significant at the .000 level).

Although presidential policy made no substantial difference in the length of time required to resolve JFCA cases, several presidential administrations did have an important impact on the outcome of the grievance resolution process. For example, compared with the pro-labor Echeverría presidency, cases initiated and resolved during the Ruiz Cortines and Díaz

TABLE 5.9   Probit Analysis of the Outcome of the Railroad Worker Grievance Resolution Process before the Federal Conciliation and Arbitration Board, 1934–1975

Variable	Unstandardized Coefficient	Standard Error	T-Value	Significance Level
Presidential Administration				
Cárdenas (1934–40)	−2.35	.75	−3.12	.002
Ávila Camacho (1940–46)	−1.25	.88	−1.42	.159
Alemán (1946–52)	−.29	.78	−.37	.715
Ruiz Cortines (1952–58)	−1.80	.70	−2.57	.012
López Mateos (1958–64)	−1.13	.67	−1.69	.094
Díaz Ordaz (1964–70)	−1.33	.64	−2.08	.041
Employer Opposition [a]	2.23	.59	3.77	.000
Resolution Time [b]	−1.10	.28	−3.90	.000
Constant [c]	4.89	1.83	2.67	.009

chi^2 = 71.76
N = 103
Prob chi^2 (8) = .000

Note: Dependent variable is coded 0 (outcome favorable to employer) or 1 (outcome favorable to worker). The outcome is defined as favorable to the employer when the board ruled in favor of railroad management, when the worker desisted in the course of the grievance resolution process, or when the board terminated a grievance because one of the two parties failed to pursue the case (thus leaving unchanged the situation the grievant had sought to reverse). The outcome is defined as favorable to the worker when the board ruled in his or her favor or when a private settlement was reached which was generally favorable to the worker's interests. Only those cases that were both initiated and resolved during the same six-year presidential term are included in this analysis.

[a] Variable is coded 1 (railroad management actively opposed worker's grievance) and 2 (no apparent employer opposition).

[b] Logged variable (time, in days, between a worker's initiation of grievance proceedings before the Federal Conciliation and Arbitration Board and the final resolution of the case, whether the case ended in a formal board ruling, a private settlement, or the worker's decision to drop the case).

[c] Constant is derived from the dropped category for presidential term (Echeverría administration, 1970–76).

Ordaz administrations were more likely to end on terms favorable to railroad management even after the effects of employer opposition and resolution time are taken into account (unstandardized coefficients of −1.80 and −1.33, respectively, significant at the .012 and .041 levels). These results conform to these administrations' more conservative labor policies.

It is more difficult, however, to explain why the Cárdenas administration had an independent effect on the grievance resolution process more favorable to railroad management (an unstandardized coefficient of −2.35, significant at the .002 level) than the Echeverría administration. It is possible that, despite Cárdenas's generally pro-labor policies and reports of conciliation and arbitration boards' overall support for workers during his administration, government representatives on the Federal Conciliation and Arbitration Board during this period favored FNM management in grievance cases in an effort to limit financial awards to employees and thus reduce the company's operating losses. Alternatively, it is possible that Cárdenas's pro-labor policies encouraged workers to file demands before the JFCA even though their grievances were not substantively strong. At a minimum, these results show that even Cárdenas's policy toward labor was not so uniformly favorable as some analysts have suggested.

Conclusion

The creation of state administrative structures in the labor sector was a key dimension of state building in postrevolutionary Mexico. Postrevolutionary governments' institutional initiatives in this area paralleled their other efforts to centralize political authority and expand the state's regulatory capacity, making the state apparatus a crucial instrument of political control. Increasingly centralized administrative authority over labor issues gave the national political elite the capacity to regulate strikes, union formation, and even such aspects of worker-employer relations as the resolution of individual worker grievances. From the perspective of the postrevolutionary political elite, exercising effective state authority in these areas was necessary to preserve national political stability and promote economic development.

It is essential, however, to distinguish between the *capacity* that the state administrative apparatus offers political elites to restrict different forms of labor participation, and the extent to which they actually exercise political control through these structures.[90] One should certainly not underestimate the impact that legal restrictions on the rights to strike or organize unions might have on workers' attitudes or actions. Yet this chapter has demonstrated that during the period between the 1930s and the early 1990s the extent of state administrative control over labor did vary depending upon the kind of labor participation at issue. Moreover, the degree of control varied significantly over time.

During this period postrevolutionary governments imposed the tightest restrictions on strikes. The degree of control exercised through state administrative structures was particularly great in politically important federal-jurisdiction economic activities. Only a minuscule proportion of federal-jurisdiction strike petitions received official approval between the early 1960s and the early 1990s. Although changes in the volume of strike petitions in federal-jurisdiction industries generally paralleled shifts in the rate of inflation, there was no close relationship between the number of legally recognized strikes and changing economic conditions. State administrative controls had an important impact on workers' ability to mobilize in defense of their economic interests.

The data examined in this chapter indicate that Mexico's governing political elite exercised less uniform control over union registration and individual worker demands filed before conciliation and arbitration boards in federal-jurisdiction industries. The mandatory union registration requirement often constitutes a very real barrier to workers' organizational efforts, as evidenced by the significant proportion of registration petitions rejected by state labor officials. Moreover, the historical record contains numerous instances in which state labor authorities manipulated the registration process to further their political goals.

But an analysis of Associational Registry data for the 1934–76 period shows that presidential labor policy and confederative affiliation generally did not account well for variations in the time required for a union to receive official recognition, even though one would have expected political factors such as these to be particularly important in these key economic activities. Of course, the data examined here shed no light on the political considerations that determine which confederation unionizes a particular work site and files a registration petition. And if they were available, systematic data concerning unions whose registration applications were rejected, or more detailed information regarding the political identity of some unions that did receive official recognition, might alter the conclusion that the registration process was not consistently affected by political considerations. Still further investigation might also show that administrative conditions at the Associational Registry, or societal factors such as the characteristics of the labor organizations seeking registration (though not their size, confederative affiliation, or sectoral location), are more important explanations than presidential labor policy of the time required for unions to receive official recognition.

Presidential labor policy did have some impact on the handling of individual worker demands filed with conciliation and arbitration boards. Data concerning the overall number of demands resolved by juntas in federal- and local-jurisdiction industries between 1939 and 1963 indicate that government-sponsored conciliation efforts were more effective and fewer grievance cases ended in worker withdrawal during Cárdenas's pro-labor presidency than during subsequent administrations. Analysis of grievances filed by railroad workers before the Federal Conciliation and Arbitration Board between 1934 and 1975 also shows that several presidential administrations had an important impact on the outcome of the demand resolution process. However, fluctuations in the number of worker grievances resolved by conciliation and arbitration boards between 1939 and 1963 did not correspond closely to changes in the political character of different administrations. Nor did presidential policy have a significant impact on the time required for railroad grievances to be resolved. The analysis of railroad worker grievances suggests that administrative conditions at the JFCA and actions by labor organizations themselves (for example, whether a union vigorously supports a worker in often lengthy demand resolution proceedings by providing financial support or legal counsel) may be more important determinants of the length of the grievance resolution process.

The fact that in federal-jurisdiction industries state authorities exercised tighter political control over labor strikes than over the union registration process reflects the overall character of Mexico's postrevolutionary authoritarian regime. Control over labor mobilization has been crucial to preserving national political stability, limiting intra-elite factionalism, and managing economic adjustment crises. Yet the heterogeneity of Mexico's governing coalition and the diffuseness of postrevolutionary political beliefs produced a long-term elite commitment to the inclusion of mass actors in the political process. Although ensuring the political loyalty of major unions has been a top priority, no presidential administration has sought to block entirely workers' ability to organize. Indeed, the governing political elite's relative decision-making autonomy on labor issues depends in part on the ability to balance competing interests by exploiting (and sometimes creating) divisions within the labor movement. This approach is viable so long as limited but real sociopolitical pluralism exists in the labor sector. Thus successive presidential administrations have sought to balance their need to prevent extreme labor factionalism against their strategic interest in constraining the potential influence of a united organized labor movement. The failure of the Confederation of Mexican Workers to account for a larger share of union registrations in federal-jurisdiction industries over the 1934–76 period, the persistence of several rival national confederations competing for support, and the substantial number of unions registered which were not affiliated with any major confederation may all be consequences of this policy, although the available registration data do not provide sufficient basis on which to distinguish between intervention by state labor authorities to shape different confederations' overall strength and their actual support among workers.

The extent of state administrative control over different forms of labor participation varied over time in the period from the 1930s to the early 1990s. For the most part, however, important changes in the degree of control did not coincide closely with shifts in the political character of different presidential administrations. For example, there was no close relationship between the number of legally recognized strikes in federal-jurisdiction economic activities and changes in presidential labor policy; indeed, state labor authorities generally maintained tight control over worker mobilization in these industries regardless of whether overall presidential policy toward labor was liberal, moderate, or conservative. The rejection rates for both strike petitions and union registration applications increased steadily over time, without regard to variations in presidential labor policy. Nor, for the period examined, did variations in presidential policy have any significant effect on the length of union registration or individual worker demand resolution processes or the number or type of worker grievances filed by FNM employees before the Federal Conciliation and Arbitration Board. Thus despite the central importance of the federal executive in many aspects of national decision making and the president's crucial role in determining the outcome of major strikes or particularly important union registration petitions, this analysis suggests that there are limits to state-centered explanations of political control over organized labor in postrevolutionary Mexico.

Finally, this analysis also indicates why society-centered factors are important to understanding patterns of labor participation in Mexico. For example, the collaborative strategies adopted by state-subsidized labor organizations such as the CTM help explain why the number of federal-jurisdiction strike petitions declined in 1977 despite sharply rising inflation; organized labor and business agreed to limit their economic demands during this period under the terms of a government-negotiated "Alliance for Production." Similarly, an analysis of railroad worker grievances before conciliation and arbitration boards suggests that the political character of union leadership, and its impact on the criteria employed by a junta's labor representative, may influence a worker's decision to pursue his or her grievance through the labor justice system. In instances in which a particular junta has jurisdiction over several industries, the resources available to different unions and the degree of union leaders' commitment to rank-and-file interests may also influence the length and outcome of the grievance resolution process before conciliation and arbitration boards.

CHAPTER SIX

Labor Politics and Import-Substituting Industrialization: From Coalition Maintenance to Labor Insurgency

Beginning in the early 1940s, Mexican decision makers embraced import-substituting industrialization as their principal strategy for promoting rapid economic growth. Pursuit of this approach, whose goal was to supply national demand with domestically manufactured consumer durable goods and intermediate products rather than with foreign imports, led the Ávila Camacho (1940–46), Alemán (1946–52), and Ruiz Cortines (1952–58) administrations to enact new policies to promote domestic industry. These included higher tariff barriers, direct import controls, and tighter government restrictions on foreign direct investment. Unlike their counterparts in Argentina and Brazil, Mexican policymakers had by the late 1950s realized their double goals of producing steady economic expansion and rising per capita income while at the same time controlling inflation.

Many analysts subsequently noted that, over the longer term, import-substitution policies created a number of enduring problems that contributed to serious economic difficulties in the 1970s and 1980s. These negative consequences included excessive dependence on imports of intermediate and capital goods, overvalued exchange rates and chronic balance-of-payments problems, inefficient domestic industries producing high-cost consumer products for a heavily protected national market, and a very limited capacity to export manufactured goods.[1] Moreover, the pattern of growth often characterized as the "Mexican miracle" contributed to greater economic and social inequality. Yet in the 1940s, the strategy of import-substituting industrialization enjoyed both broad support within Mexico's governing coalition and the endorsement of such respected international organizations as the United Nations Economic Commission for Latin America. The fact that other major Latin American countries were simultaneously committed to import-substitution policies imbued them with even greater legitimacy.

Mexico's successful pursuit of "stabilizing development" depended in large measure on effective political control over organized labor. The defeat of opposition elements based in powerful national industrial unions in 1947–51 and the consolidation of the Confederation of Mexican Workers' (CTM) political dominance in the labor movement were key developments in this regard. In conjunction with administrative restrictions on different forms of labor participation (especially strikes), reliable support from the "official" labor movement gave government officials a high degree of decision-making autonomy in economic matters.

At the same time, sustained economic expansion and the characteristics of import-substituting industrialization together reinforced the governing elite's social pact with organized labor. Economic growth produced new sources of employment, and especially after the mid-1950s rising real wages and expanding social welfare benefits significantly improved many workers' standard of living. Because they were protected from import competition, private-sector firms could maintain comfortable profit margins despite rising wages. The ability of labor leaders to deliver substantial resources to their members strengthened their position within government-allied unions. Active state regulation of economic affairs and an expanding public sector made it easier for major labor organizations to translate their political importance into social and economic policy gains.

Despite this convergence of interests between Mexico's political elite and leading elements of the labor movement, import-substituting industrialization sometimes produced changes in workplace conditions that threatened to undermine state-subsidized labor organizations' control over the rank and file. In the automobile industry, for example, the shift from assembly operations to manufacturing in the 1960s and 1970s transformed the in-plant industrial relations environment. "Official" unions, typically more dependent on political alliances for their influence than on effective workplace organization, were often unable to adapt to the problems posed by a larger work force and more conflictive workplace relations. In some automobile companies the breakdown of existing labor controls permitted rank-and-file opposition movements to win power. These reform movements sought increased participation for the rank and file in union affairs and heightened worker influence over different aspects of the production process. For many workers, democratic unionism promised increased leadership responsiveness in resolving workplace conflicts and more effective representation of worker interests in a changing industrial environment.

Although attempts by internal opposition groups to oust entrenched local union leaders did not always succeed, the emergence of dissident movements in almost all the major automobile workers' unions reflected changes in the labor relations context produced by rapid expansion of a key manufacturing industry. Thus while import-substituting industrialization helped sustain a national alliance between Mexico's governing political elite and organized labor, in some sectors it eroded the very bases of labor control on which this alliance ultimately depended. These changes contributed to the "labor insurgency" of the early 1970s, a period of sustained political challenge to the pattern of state-labor relations consolidated in the late 1940s and early 1950s.

This chapter analyzes the relationship between political control over labor and import-substituting industrialization. The first section briefly examines successive presidential administrations' efforts to promote domestic industrialization in the 1940s and 1950s and the principal economic consequences of this development strategy. It gives special emphasis to the ways in which the characteristics of import-substituting industrialization reinforced the alliance between Mexico's governing elite and the "official" labor movement. The second section focuses on union democratization in the automobile manufacturing industry in the 1960s and 1970s. It examines both the emergence of democratizing rank-and-file movements in the industry during these years and the consequences of this process for workers' participation in union affairs and their control over the production process. Like chapter 4's examination of railroad workers' involvement in labor opposition movements in the 1940s, this case study illustrates the ways in which changes in workplace industrial relations affect workers' and unions' political actions.

Import-Substituting Industrialization and State-Labor Relations

In the years after 1940, Mexican economic policymakers pursued rapid industrial expansion as their principal development goal. They shifted to an import-substituting strategy in response to the favorable economic conditions created by World War II, particularly growth in demand for domestic manufactured goods caused by the wartime disruption of imports and the financial resources then available owing to increased external demand for traditional Mexican exports.[2] Their ability to do so rested in part on important institutional innovations in the 1920s and 1930s, including the creation of the Banco de México (1925) and a government investment bank, Nacional Financiera, S.A. (1934), and expansion of the Ministry of Finance's decision-making authority. State ownership or majority state control of railroad transportation, electrical power generation, and petroleum production also provided an important basis for increased public investment and state intervention in economic affairs.

The Ávila Camacho, Alemán, and Ruiz Cortines administrations adopted a number of policies specifically designed to promote national industry. These included strong tariff protection for domestic producers, an import licensing system, and tax concessions for manufacturing firms.[3] In 1944–45 the Ávila Camacho government formally limited foreign equity participation in Mexican firms to 49 percent and reserved "strategic" industries exclusively for national investors, though strong U.S. resistance prevented strict enforcement of these restrictions. Legislation enacted in 1950–51 strengthened the federal executive's control over economic policymaking, and beginning in 1954 the government provided incentives for foreign firms to purchase a proportion of their inputs from national producers.[4] In addition, Mexican policymakers maintained a fixed, increasingly overvalued exchange rate between 1941 and 1948, which encouraged large-scale imports of machinery and equipment. The textile industry was an early beneficiary of these policies, but the iron and steel, cement, pulp and paper, and chemical industries also grew rapidly during the 1940s and early 1950s. The initial successes of this development strategy laid the basis for expanded production of consumer durable goods beginning in the mid-1950s.[5]

The import-substituting industrialization project rested on strong political foundations. The 1910–20 revolution and Cárdenas's land reform in the 1930s destroyed large landowners' political power, thus eliminating a potential source of opposition to protectionist measures. Equally important, however, import-substitution policies enjoyed widespread support within Mexico's governing coalition. Domestic manufacturers were the most prominent beneficiaries of tariff protection and other policies stimulating industrial production, and by the late 1940s they constituted a powerful lobby in support of import substitution. The creation of the Cámara Nacional de la Industria de Transformación (National Chamber of Manufacturing Industries, CNIT) in December 1941 formally marked their entrance into national politics.[6]

The labor movement, too, was firmly committed to the broad goal of state-led industrialization.[7] Organized labor advocated a revolutionary nationalist program that privileged state action to promote economic development and social justice. In May 1946, for example, the CTM issued a call for import and export controls, state regulation of the banking system to promote agricultural modernization and industrialization, and price controls.[8] Given the intensity of national political conflict in the 1930s and many Mexican private firms' vigorous opposition to unionization and worker mobilization, it is not surprising that labor organizations believed their goals could best be achieved by expanding the public sector. Labor especially championed the nationalization of foreign enterprises in key industries.[9] It did so both for ideological reasons and because a growing public sector would create significant numbers of comparatively well paid, more easily unionized jobs.

Labor's most prominent proponent of these policies was Vicente Lombardo Toledano, secretary-general of the Confederation of Mexican Workers between 1936 and 1941. Lombardo Toledano gradually lost political power within the CTM during the 1940s, but his ideological influence remained largely intact and strongly shaped the views of his successor, Fidel Velázquez, and other CTM leaders. When in early 1945 U.S. representatives at the Inter-American Conference on Problems of War and Peace (the "Chapultepec conference," held in Mexico City) called on Latin American countries to reduce tariff barriers and welcome foreign investment, Lombardo Toledano joined with CNIT representatives in sharply criticizing what they perceived to be an attempt to block Latin American industrial development. In April 1945 the CTM and CNIT formed an "Industrial Labor Pact" to promote worker-employer cooperation and thereby further industrialization. Moreover, in August 1945 the CTM issued a plan for national industrialization that closely paralleled earlier CNIT proposals.[10]

The Economic Consequences of Import-Substituting Industrialization

Import-substituting industrialization policies stimulated rapid economic growth. Mexico's gross domestic product rose by an average of 6.3 percent per year in real terms between 1940 and 1965. Nonagricultural activities' share of gross domestic product (GDP) rose from 75.6 percent in 1940 to 82.6 percent in 1965, and manufacturing activities' share of GDP increased from 18.0 percent to 25.3 percent over the same period. Substantial public investment in roads, dams, and irrigation projects helped commercialize agricultural production and facilitated the expansion of the domestic consumer market. Per capita GDP grew by 117.2 percent in real terms between 1940 and 1965.[11]

Successive presidential administrations' commitment to rapid economic expansion based on import-substituting industrialization did, however, create or aggravate a number of socioeconomic problems. Export growth, still strong in the 1945–50 period, fell significantly in the early 1950s.[12] Federal government expenditures on education and social welfare programs lagged far behind economic investment and administrative expenditures; indeed, not until the López Mateos administration (1958–64) did the proportion of federal government expenditures devoted to social programs again reach the level attained under Cárdenas.[13] Over time, stag-

TABLE 6.1   Minimum Daily Wage and Annual Rate of Inflation, 1938–1993

Year	Nominal Minimum Daily Wage in Mexico City (Pesos)	Annual Rate of Inflation[a] (%)	Real Minimum Daily Wage Index for Mexico City[b] (1939 = 100)
1938	2.50		
1939	2.50		100.0
1940	2.50	3.3	96.8
1941	2.50	3.2	94.0
1942	2.50	15.6	81.2
1943	2.50	29.7	62.4
1944	3.60	27.1	70.8
1945	3.60	6.6	66.4
1946	4.50	24.6	66.8
1947	4.50	12.3	59.6
1948	4.50	6.6	55.6
1949	4.50	5.2	52.8
1950	4.50	5.9	50.0
1951	4.50	13.0	44.4
1952	6.70	6.6	60.0
1953	6.70	5.4	56.8
1954	8.00	5.1	64.4
1955	8.00	16.0	55.6
1956	11.00	4.8	73.2
1957	11.00	5.7	69.2
1958	12.00	11.4	67.6
1959	12.00	2.4	66.0
1960	14.50	5.2	76.0
1961	14.50	1.8	74.4
1962	17.50	0.9	89.2
1963	17.50	0.9	88.4
1964	21.50	2.2	106.4
1965	21.50	3.4	102.8
1966	25.00	4.5	114.4
1967	25.00	2.8	111.2
1968	28.25	1.5	124.0
1969	28.25	3.0	120.4
1970	32.00	5.9	128.4
1971	32.00	3.1	124.8
1972	38.00	6.0	139.6
1973	41.43	17.1	130.0
1974	57.70	32.7	136.4
1975	63.40	14.3	131.2
1976	87.65	14.3	158.8

TABLE 6.1   continued

Year	Nominal Minimum Daily Wage in Mexico City (Pesos)	Annual Rate of Inflation[a] (%)	Real Minimum Daily Wage Index for Mexico City[b] (1939 = 100)
1977	106.40	32.1	146.0
1978	120.00	18.1	139.2
1979	138.00	18.2	135.6
1980	163.00	26.3	126.8
1981	210.00	28.0	129.6
1982	322.00	58.9	123.2
1983	489.00	101.9	92.4
1984	748.00	65.4	85.6
1985	1,155.00	57.7	84.0
1986	2,065.00	86.2	80.4
1987	4,661.00	131.8	78.4
1988	7,882.50	114.2	62.0
1989	9,293.33	18.6	61.6
1990	10,990.00	26.7	57.6
1991	12,615.00	22.7	53.6
1992	13,330.00	15.5	49.2
1993	14,270.00	9.8	48.0

Sources: Nominal minimum daily wage in Mexico City: For 1938–45, 1948–49, and 1952–85, Instituto Nacional de Estadística, Geografía e Informática (INEGI), Estadísticas históricas de México (1985), 1:170; for 1946–47 and 1950–51, Confederación de Trabajadores de México, Memoria de la Asamblea Nacional del Salario Mínimo (1953), 107; for 1986–93, Nacional Financiera, S.A., internal documents.

Annual rate of inflation: For 1939–78, INEGI, Estadísticas históricas de México, 2:766; for 1979–93, Salinas de Gortari, Quinto informe de gobierno, 1993: Anexo (1993), 261, and Nacional Financiera, S.A., internal documents.

Note: For the period 1938–71, minimum wages were set only in even-numbered years. Minimum wages increased more than once each year during 1973–74, 1976, and 1982–93; annual values are the mean of all increases during a given year.

[a] For 1940–78, annual percentage increase in the worker cost-of-living index for Mexico City; for 1979–93, annual percentage increase in the national consumer price index (yearly average). No cost-of-living data are available before 1939.

[b] Nominal minimum daily wage in Mexico City deflated by the annual rate of inflation.

nating agricultural production produced greater inequality in rural areas, a growing need to import basic foodstuffs, a high rate of rural-to-urban migration, and land invasions and rural violence.

Income inequality also worsened. The wealthiest 20 percent of Mexican families increased their share of total family income from 59.8 percent in 1950 to 63.7 percent in 1968. In contrast, the share of family income held by the poorest 60 percent shrank from 24.6 percent to 18.4 percent over the same period.[14] The proportion of national income accruing to labor as wages, salaries, and benefits declined steadily from 52.1 percent in 1940 to 40.2 percent in 1947, stabilized between 1948 and 1952, and then increased gradually through the early 1960s. However, labor's share of national income did not regain its 1940 level until 1966 (53.1 percent).[15]

More specifically, some urban and industrial workers suffered significant economic losses during the early stages of industrialization. To stimulate industrial growth, government policymakers substantially expanded credit and tolerated rapid price increases in order to mobilize financial resources.[16] As a result, the rate of inflation (the annual increase in the cost of living for workers in Mexico City) rose by an average of 12.2 percent per year between 1941 and 1955, with the period of worst inflation coming during and immediately after World War II (see table 6.1). In the context of strong government resistance to wage increases and some labor organizations' willingness to limit salary demands, high inflation rates produced a sharp, almost continuous fall in the real value of the minimum wage. Real minimum wages fell by 48.3 percent between 1940 and 1950, before rising again in the early 1950s (see the real-minimum-wage index for Mexico City in table 6.1).[17] Government efforts to slow the decline in real wages by regulating prices (including the creation of a National Price Commission in January 1951) had little effect.

It is difficult to determine the precise impact of declining real minimum wages on urban workers' economic well-being. Some analysts conclude that a fall in the inflation-adjusted value of the minimum wage may have been partially offset by a movement of actual wages paid upward toward the legal minimum. Similarly, because of substantial migration from rural to higher-wage urban employment (especially migration from the countryside to areas such as Mexico City and Monterrey) during this period, real income per worker may have risen nationally despite a decline in the average real wage earned by nonagricultural workers.[18] This effect would presumably have been greatest in those economic activities with relatively low skill barriers to rural migrants, such as manufacturing, construction, and unskilled services (including domestic service).[19]

It is important to note, however, that labor market segmentation (based on educational requirements or institutional barriers to entry, including contract-defined distinctions between permanent and temporary employment and contract clauses in some industries giving first preference in hiring to the children of workers already employed) placed a limit on intersectoral occupational mobility. Labor market segmentation and the limited effectiveness of compensatory government welfare programs meant that important numbers of urban and industrial workers were exposed to the full impact of government wage restraint and high inflation. The strength of labor protests against inflation and deteriorating economic conditions in the early postwar years certainly indicates that some urban and industrial workers saw their standard of living fall significantly.[20]

Economic Development Strategy and Mexico's Social Pact

The ability of economic decision makers to pursue policies that promoted rapid industrialization and capital accumulation at the expense of some workers' welfare depended on effective political control over labor mobilization. However, the strategic need to preserve the labor peace won by dramatic state action in the late 1940s and early 1950s eventually spurred the Ruiz Cortines administration to rein in inflation. The most important cause of inflation in the early postwar period was the persistent balance-of-payments deficit, a situation produced by high domestic demand for imports of consumer and capital goods and declining exports. The balance-of-payments deficit quickly exhausted financial reserves accumulated during World War II and forced devaluations of the peso in 1948 and 1949. These measures, however, aggravated inflationary pressures by raising the price of imported goods while failing to win more than temporary balance-of-payments relief. The prospect of ever more severe inflation/devaluation cycles, the growing policy influence of conservative economists at the Banco de México and the Ministry of Finance, consumer protests against rising prices, and strong signals from international financial agencies that Mexico's future access to external investment credits depended on currency stability all combined to stiffen decision makers' resolve to stabilize the economy.[21]

The turning point came following yet another devaluation of the peso in April 1954, when a sharp increase in inflation threatened to undermine the labor peace achieved after the 1947–51 crisis. The Ruiz Cortines administration's efforts to stabilize national finances by cutting public investment had provoked a recession in 1953 and aroused strong private-sector opposition. In its continuing search for a solution to the balance-of-payments problem, the government announced a 44.5 percent currency devaluation (the exchange rate fell from 8.65 to 12.5 pesos to the U.S. dollar) in an attempt to expand exports to the U.S. market. The devaluation did produce a temporary increase in exports, but it also sparked widespread labor discontent.

The labor movement had no advance notice of the devaluation. The CTM and other major labor organizations publicly endorsed the government's action, but they quickly protested the measure's inflationary impact.[22] Throughout the early 1950s, the Confederation of Mexican Workers had repeatedly condemned the rising cost of rent, food, clothing, electricity, and transportation. CTM secretary-general Fidel Velázquez called inflation the principal problem confronting the working class, and the CTM both strongly supported government legislation in 1950–51 establishing price controls on basic commodities and called for strict enforcement of them. As early as October 1951, CTM leaders reported growing rank-and-file pressure for wage increases to offset rising prices. Yet minimum wages (which, despite inflationary pressures, were renegotiated only every two years) remained frozen in the Federal District and other key areas in the late 1940s and early 1950s.[23] In the weeks following the devaluation on April 17, 1954, then, the CTM leadership renewed its demand for energetic government efforts to control price increases and limit business profits. Other major labor organizations reacted similarly. The Mexican Regional Labor Confederation (CROM), for example, called for wage increases equal to the size of the devaluation.

The Ruiz Cortines administration's initial response to accelerating inflation and growing labor dissatisfaction was modest in scope.[24] In June 1954 the government granted a 10 percent wage increase to public-sector workers (federal government employees, military personnel, and employees of state-owned enterprises earning less than nine hundred pesos per month), awarded tax-exempt status to union-operated and enterprise-based commodity distribution centers, and sought to improve the production and distribution of foodstuffs. At the same time, President Ruiz Cortines urged private firms to grant their employees a similar 10 percent wage increase. Business organizations agreed to do so, but the CTM protested that workers had suffered at least a 24 percent loss in purchasing power. The confederation told its affiliates to demand a 25 percent wage hike in the hope that they could win at least a 21 percent increase. CTM leaders called for a general strike on July 12 if the government failed to meet its demand.

The CTM pressured state labor authorities by instructing its affiliated unions to file thousands of coordinated strike petitions before federal- and local-jurisdiction conciliation and arbitration boards.[25] Although the confederation had never conducted a general strike and its organizational strength varied considerably from one state and industry to another, its threat was more credible than it might have been several years before because Velázquez had contained the CTM's factional rivalries for the first time since 1936. He had also negotiated "unity pacts" with a number of other labor organizations, including several national industrial unions that had earlier seceded from the confederation. Moreover, the CTM's bargaining position may have been further strengthened by the fact that worker dissatisfaction with deteriorating economic conditions had given additional electoral strength to the dissident *henriquista* movement during the 1952 elections. General Miguel Henríquez Guzmán's Federación de Partidos del Pueblo (Federation of People's Parties) had won 16 percent of the vote, proving to be the most serious challenger to the PRI's presidential candidate since the governing party's formation in 1929.[26]

Yet the CTM's strike proposal did not receive unanimous support from other labor organizations. Some confederations preferred a more cautious approach. Indeed, the Revolutionary Confederation of Workers and Peasants (CROC) openly opposed a strike. CROC secretary-general Luis Gómez Z. (who won national political prominence in the late 1940s as a leader of the anti-inflation struggle but had served a prison term in 1948–49 for his opposition activities) dismissed the CTM's call for "revolutionary struggle" as demagoguery.

The CTM, despite its rhetoric, adopted a pragmatic approach to political bargaining that would become its stock-in-trade when confronted with a major economic challenge: after pressuring state labor authorities with public declarations and coordinated strike petitions, CTM leaders repeatedly postponed the date of the threatened general strike and relied on affiliated unions to win the best settlements they could manage on a case-by-case basis. Conflicts in the textile and electrical power industries lasted for some time. By mid-July, however, most unions had negotiated new wage agreements. Wage increases ranged in size from 10 percent in the petroleum industry to 30 percent in the restaurant and hotel industry, averaging about 20 percent nationally. On the whole, the CTM had achieved its objectives.

The successful resolution of the 1954 devaluation crisis placed Mexico on the path of sustained, low-inflation economic growth. Maintaining a stable exchange rate became an article of faith for Mexican policymakers, even though it contributed to persistent balance-of-payments problems. The Banco de México also mobilized domestic savings by raising the reserve requirements for commercial banks, thus avoiding the inflationary effects of continuing government deficits by requiring private banks to finance public debt. State investment banks channeled credit to priority industries, and high interest rates discouraged capital flight and stimulated private-sector investment. These heterodox policies, pursued by successive presidential administrations from the late 1950s through the 1960s, were labeled "stabilizing development."[27]

Explanations for this shift in economic strategy must necessarily include such factors as strong institutional support from the Banco de México and the Ministry of Finance for conservative monetary and fiscal policies (reinforced by close ties between Mexican economic officials and international financial agencies), as well as Mexico's considerable success at attracting foreign investment to promote sustained economic expansion. However, the Ruiz Cortines administration's need to preserve labor peace was also a crucial element. The 1947–51 labor crisis was only recently past, and memories of the way in which the labor opposition had used widespread popular discontent with inflation to mobilize working-class support were still fresh. Maintaining workers' electoral support and preserving the CTM's leading position in the labor movement were of vital political importance, giving CTM leaders significant bargaining leverage. Indeed, the potential risk of renewed labor unrest probably had more impact on government decision makers than the specific tactics the CTM employed to back up its wage demands.

The economic success of import-substituting industrialization from the late 1950s through the early 1970s underpinned the governing political elite's strategic alliance with organized labor. Low-inflation economic growth produced an upturn in real wage levels. Despite some year-to-year fluctuation, the index value for the real minimum wage in Mexico City rose from a near postwar low of 55.6 in 1955 to 76.0 in 1960, 102.8 in 1965, and 128.4 in 1970. The index reached its highest level during the entire post-1940 period (158.8) in 1976 (see table 6.1).[28] At the same time, the proportion of federal government investment going to social spending (education, health care, housing, training programs, and so forth) rose from 11.4 percent in 1941 to 23.1 percent in 1976. One consequence was that the coverage of government health and welfare programs (especially those directed toward unionized employees in the formal sector) expanded dramatically from the 1940s to the 1970s.[29]

The general characteristics of import-substituting industrialization also reinforced the social pact with labor. Government price controls on many goods increased producers' incentive to control labor costs, but the probability of continued economic expansion undoubtedly reassured them that higher wage payments could be recouped in future sales to a growing consumer market. Moreover, because tariffs and other import controls created a highly protected domestic market, companies had little reason to fear that wage increases would erode profits or cause them to lose market share to lower-wage foreign competitors. Protectionist policies and, until late 1976, a fixed exchange rate also helped stabilize the environment for worker-employer negotiations by insulating the economy from external shocks.

Other aspects of Mexican development strategy during this period also strengthened the political elite's alliance with labor. The size of the public sector and the extent of state regulatory intervention in economic affairs enhanced "official" labor organizations' ability to barter political support for policy concessions.[30] By mobilizing its affiliates in electoral support of the Institutional Revolutionary Party and by backing the government during political crises, the CTM in particular was able to win compensation in the form of higher minimum wages, favorable legislation on social welfare issues, or labor law reform. By reiterating key demands over a period of years, the national CTM leadership attempted to set the agenda for government policy innovation at those subsequent moments when the confederation's bargaining position was strongest. For example, in the early 1960s the López Mateos administration finally acted on labor's longstanding demand for worker profit sharing, which had been formally guaranteed by the 1917 constitution. This initiative followed the CTM's strong progovernment stance during the political crisis created by the railroad worker protest movement in 1958–59. Some viewed the 1963 reform legislation as López Mateos's bid to refurbish his pro-labor image after army troops broke a national railroad strike in March 1959,[31] but it also represented partial compensation for CTM support during a period of serious labor unrest.

Many such policy concessions won by the CTM and other "official" labor organizations benefited Mexican workers in general. However, politically favored unions often enjoyed privileged access to state-subsidized housing, health care, financial credit, retirement funds, and so forth. For example, the CTM served as the labor sector's official representative on the governing boards of the Mexican Social Security Institute and government agencies responsible for providing workers with subsidized housing and financial credit, positions that it used to benefit its own affiliates. Preferential access to publicly financed social welfare benefits of this kind strongly reinforced the position of government-allied labor leaders by giving them the material means to build and sustain rank-and-file support. The politicized distribution of social welfare benefits certainly contributed to labor movement corruption in some instances. Yet the long-term survival of many of Mexico's most prominent labor leaders cannot be explained without noting that, in many cases, they were able to use political connections to improve the living standards of their members. At the same time, of course, reliance on the selective, politicized distribution of economic resources made these labor leaders more heavily dependent on the state, and it therefore reduced their incentive to develop stronger representational arrangements in the workplace.

Political bargaining between the Confederation of Mexican Workers and the López Portillo (1976–82) administration illustrates these points. Wage restraint was a central element in López Portillo's 1977–78 economic stabilization program, and the key to controlling wage increases on a national scale was the CTM's agreement to moderate its economic demands. The impact of this policy on workers' economic welfare was dramatic: real minimum wages fell by 12.3 percent between 1976 and 1978 (see table 6.1). As a partial reward for CTM loyalty, in January 1977 the López Portillo administration established a worker-controlled financial institution, the Banco Obrero (Workers' Bank). By doing so, the government satisfied a demand the CTM had voiced since at least 1951.[32] The institution's motto was "A Bank for All." However, rival labor organizations accused the CTM of creating a financial reserve for its own benefit. CTM affiliates contributed most of the bank's operating capital. In addition, they controlled the administrative council responsible for allocating loans. Fidel Velázquez served as "general adviser" to the bank.[33]

Industrialization and Workplace Change: Union Democratization in the Automobile Industry and Its Consequences for Labor Participation

Import-substituting industrialization produced sustained economic growth from the early 1940s into the 1970s, and in general it reinforced the social pact between organized labor and Mexico's governing political elite. In some sectors, however, rapid industrial change transformed workplace relations and sparked rank-and-file challenges to the political control exercised by state-subsidized labor organizations. The automobile industry experienced significant political change in the 1960s and 1970s as workers in several firms overthrew entrenched labor leaders and instituted more democratic forms of union governance. Specific measures of democratic unionism included the election of key union officers and their accountability to members, regularly held general assemblies, an enhanced role for the general assembly in internal decision making, procedural safeguards for workers' union rights, and opportunities for the emergence of identifiable and relatively stable internal opposition groups. By 1975 workers in five of the seven principal vehicle manufacturing firms had won control over the selection of union leaders and other aspects of internal union decision making.[34]

Challenges to established mechanisms of labor control in some automobile workers' unions formed part of the broader "labor insurgency" (insurgencia obrera) that swept Mexico in the 1970s. This was a heterogeneous movement in which economic and political struggles were frequently linked. In addition to higher wages and benefits and improved working conditions, worker reform movements often sought greater union democracy and political autonomy from such "official" confederations as the CTM, as well as from the Labor Congress and the Institutional Revolutionary Party.[35] The most prominent elements in the labor insurgency were opposition groups within national industrial unions. The "Tendencia Democrática" (Democratic Tendency) was a dissident movement within the Sindicato Único de Trabajadores Electricistas de la República Mexicana (General Union of Mexican Electrical Workers, SUTERM) led by Rafael Galván. The Movimiento Sindical Ferrocarrilero (Railroad Workers' Union Movement, MSF) was an opposition group of railroad workers led by Demetrio Vallejo, the principal leader of the 1958–59 railroad worker protests who had been released from prison in 1971.[36] The Sindicato Único de Trabajadores de la Industria Nuclear (Nuclear Industry Workers' Union, SUTIN) and newly formed university unions were also important at the national level. Because of their mobilizational capacity, strong leadership, and ideological identification with the precepts of revolutionary nationalism, these groups constituted the core of diverse labor protest movements and attracted widespread support from the political Left.

Yet the labor insurgency also drew considerable strength from workers in the manufacturing, commercial, and service sectors. Unions in these economic activities varied considerably in size, with the largest and most influential organizations concentrated in the automobile, steel, metalworking, chemical, electrical products, rubber processing, air transportation, and textile industries.[37] Although not as prominent in national affairs as the Democratic Tendency or the MSF, newly democratic or politically autonomous unions in these areas often played an important role in local and regional politics. In many cases (the Volkswagen union in Puebla and the Nissan union in Cuernavaca, for instance), they had sufficient members and financial resources to serve as the focal point for locally or regionally important protest movements. The Unidad Obrera Independiente (Independent Worker Unit, UOI, led by Juan Ortega Arenas, a labor lawyer with national political connections and ambitions) gained considerable importance in the mid- and late 1970s by grouping some 120 plant- and company-level unions representing more than 100,000 workers.[38] Similarly, Línea Proletaria (Proletarian Line, LP), a Maoist-influenced group committed to grassroots organization, direct democracy, and mobilization around workplace demands, played a prominent role among telephone workers, metalworkers, and teachers in the late 1970s and early 1980s.[39]

Opposition labor currents prospered during the early and mid-1970s in part because of the Echeverría administration's (1970–76) "democratic opening" policy *(apertura democrática).* President Luis Echeverría's call for a national dialogue and his more flexible approach to political opposition were attempts to distance himself from the conservative Díaz Ordaz administration (1964–70) and his own role as minister of the interior in the violent repression of the 1968 student and popular movement. His political reform initiatives (freeing political prisoners, lowering the minimum-age requirement for election to the federal Congress, and easing the legal requirements for opposition party formation) sought to defuse an increasingly severe crisis of public confidence in the regime, a crisis that was manifested in part by declining rates of voter turnout and by the rise of armed urban and rural guerrilla movements in 1968–71.

At the same time, Echeverría recognized that Mexico's post-1940 economic development strategy had produced a very unequal pattern of income distribution and growing popular discontent. He responded to these problems by decreeing emergency wage hikes that increased workers' purchasing power despite rising inflation; reforming the federal labor code in September 1974 to permit the annual renegotiation of both minimum wages and wages set by collective contract; expanding social welfare programs (including the creation of the Instituto del Fondo Nacional de la Vivienda para los Trabajadores [National Worker Housing Institute, INFONAVIT] in January 1972); reducing the workweek for government employees to forty hours; and raising the share of enterprise profits going to workers under the national profit-sharing program.[40]

Echeverría's democratic opening policy had particularly important consequences for reformist elements in the labor movement. Echeverría encouraged organizational and political pluralism in the labor movement by openly criticizing traditional labor leaders such as Fidel Velázquez and by tolerating (and sometimes encouraging) the emergence of reformist labor groups not affiliated with the Labor Congress.[41] These opposition groups—including the Democratic Tendency, the UOI, and the Frente Auténtico del Trabajo (Authentic Labor Front, FAT, a Christian Democratic labor organization formed in 1960)—frequently allied with dissident union factions seeking to break their ties to confederations such as the CTM, offering them political contacts, financial assistance, and an organizational framework for mobilizing public support for union demands.[42] Rank-and-file opposition movements often met with stiff employer resistance, and in some instances strikes and other protest movements encountered police repression.[43] It was especially significant, however, that Echeverría administration labor officials permitted the legal recognition of unions not affiliated with "official" confederations. At times, the Ministry of Labor and Social Welfare even supported attempts by dissident factions to win control in local unions and separate from major national confederations. Growing inflationary pressures compelled Echeverría to make peace with the CTM after 1973 in order to secure its cooperation in restraining rank-and-file economic demands, but dissident union groups continued their organizational activities throughout his presidency.

Despite the overall importance of Echeverría's political orientation for the labor insurgency of the 1970s, an examination of union democratization in the automobile manufacturing industry shows that significant change in workplace industrial relations was the most consistently important factor explaining the breakdown of traditional mechanisms of labor control. Focusing on the workplace origins of rank-and-file demands for union democracy contributes to a deeper understanding of Mexican labor politics during this period. It also makes an important contribution to the general literature on union democracy.[44]

Labor Control in the Mexican Automobile Manufacturing Industry

The Mexican automobile industry was founded in the 1920s and 1930s when several automobile firms built assembly plants in the Mexico City area. The first companies to begin operations in Mexico as part of international expansion programs or in response to tariff protection offered to local vehicle assembly were Ford (in 1925), General Motors (in 1937), and Fábricas Auto-Mex, a Mexican firm assembling Chryslers (in 1938). By 1961 twelve firms were engaged in automobile assembly, and seven other companies imported already-assembled vehicles. At the time, however, no significant automobile manufacturing was performed in Mexico. The automobile manufacturing decree published in 1962 thus marked a dramatic change in the industry.[45] Between 1965 and 1975, the automobile industry's (vehicles and auto parts) share of gross domestic product in manufacturing rose from 3.6 percent to 6.9 percent (at constant 1960 prices). Over this same period, the annual production of cars and trucks rose from 102,485 to 352,193 vehicles. Similarly, the value of automobile industry production rose at an average rate of 15.5 percent per year between 1965 and 1974, faster than all other economic activities except the petrochemical industry.[46] Seven firms dominated the industry: Auto-Mex/Chrysler, Diesel Nacional (National Diesel, DINA), Ford, General Motors, Nissan, Volkswagen, and Vehículos Automotores Mexicanos (Mexican Automotive Vehicles, VAM).[47]

Automobile workers' unions in the vehicle manufacturing industry have historically formed part of the heterogeneous labor confederations that group the majority of organized workers in Mexico.[48] All are enterprise- or plant-level unions, and those unions established at Auto-Mex (1938), VAM (1946), DINA (1955), and Nissan (1966) were all initially affiliated with federations linked to the Confederation of Mexican Workers. The Ford union (1932) was affiliated with the Federación de Obreros del Distrito Federal (Federal District Workers' Federation) until 1936, when it temporarily joined the General Confederation of Workers (CGT). In 1938 it became part of the recently formed CTM. Similarly, the General Motors union (1936) was initially associated with the CGT's Federación Obrera Local del Distrito Federal (Federal District Local Labor Federation), but it joined the Revolutionary Confederation of Workers and Peasants (CROC) when that organization was formed in 1952. The Volkswagen union was also originally linked to the CGT in the state of México, but company managers arranged to transfer the union's affiliation to the CTM when Volkswagen began manufacturing operations in Puebla in 1966.

Ties to federations and confederations constituted a crucial element of political control over automobile workers, preventing local union members from selecting their own leaders freely and circumscribing their actions in negotiations with company managers. Federation officials often appointed plant-level labor leaders, whose unpaid status made them vulnerable to co-optation and who generally remained responsible to the federation's leaders rather than to the union membership. Union statutes generally gave federation leaders or their local representatives broad legal authority over union affairs. By refusing to convene general assemblies or hold regular union elections, they could deprive dissident workers of organizational space in which to challenge incumbent union officials. Reliable support from company managers and state labor authorities, as well as provisions in union statutes and the separation exclusion clause included in labor contracts, provided federation officials with a strong defense against rank-and-file opposition movements. Moreover, federation representatives were often legally responsible for negotiating collective contracts with management. This arrangement permitted little or no rank-and-file input into the bargaining process, and many workers complained that contract clauses covering hiring, wage rates, and different aspects of the production process disregarded worker interests and protected managerial prerogatives. Only the General Motors union in the Federal District enjoyed both a democratic tradition dating from the 1940s and considerable organizational autonomy in its relationship with the CROC.

In those automobile workers' unions in which democratic reform movements eventually triumphed, the new union leadership usually acted quickly to redefine the character of local union ties to government-allied state or national labor organizations. Between 1961 and 1975, three automobile workers' unions broke their ties with the CTM (DINA in 1961, Volkswagen in 1972, and Nissan in 1972), and a fourth substantially redefined this relationship (Ford in 1975) in an effort to increase local union autonomy. Only the VAM union, which shifted its affiliation to the Confederación Obrera Revolucionaria (Revolutionary Labor Confederation, COR) in 1973 after an internal split in the CTM's Federación de Trabajadores del Distrito Federal (Federal District Workers' Federation, FTDF), altered its external ties without experiencing a significant internal democ-

TABLE 6.2 Political Status of Principal Automobile Workers' Unions, 1961–1975

Automobile Company and Plant Sites	Former Confederation Affiliation	New Confederation Affiliation	Democratic Governance
Auto-Mex/Chrysler			
Federal District	CTM (1938)	No change	No
Toluca (México)	CTM (1968)	No change	No
Diesel Nacional			
Ciudad Sahagún (Hidalgo)	CTM (1955–61)	UOI (1961)	Yes (1961)
Ford			
Federal District	CTM (1938)	No change[a]	Yes (1975)
Tlanepantla (México)	CTM (1962)	No change[a]	Yes (1975)
Cuautitlán (México)	CTM (1964)	No change[a]	Yes (1975)
General Motors			
Federal District	CROC (1952)	No change	Yes (1940s)
Toluca (México)	CTM (1965)	No change	No
Nissan			
Cuernavaca (Morelos)	CTM (1966–72)	UOI (1972)	Yes (1971)
Vehículos Automotores Mexicanos			
Federal District	CTM (1946–73)	COR (1973)[b]	No
Volkswagen			
Puebla (Puebla)	CTM (1966–72)	UOI (1972)[c]	Yes (1972)

Sources: These data are drawn from Aguilar García, *La política sindical en México* (1982), 105–14; Middlebrook, "Political Economy of Mexican Organized Labor" (1982), 251–52, 278–309; Roxborough, *Unions and Politics in Mexico* (1984), 76–104.

Note: This table includes data only on plant sites and unions established as of 1975. The full names of the organizations listed are CTM (Confederation of Mexican Workers); CROC (Revolutionary Confederation of Workers and Peasants); UOI (Independent Worker Unit); and COR (Revolutionary Labor Confederation).

[a] In 1975 Ford workers were reorganized into a single union affiliated with the CTM.

[b] In 1979 the VAM union reestablished ties with the CTM.

[c] In 1981 the Volkswagen union broke its ties with the UOI.

ratization movement. Although the DINA, Volkswagen, and Nissan unions subsequently joined the Independent Worker Unit in order to increase their bargaining leverage vis-à-vis employers, the character of these external linkages remained a source of intense union debate. Table 6.2 summarizes these changes in the political status of automobile workers' unions between 1961 and 1975.

Sources of Union Democratization among Automobile Workers

Given the multiple obstacles that they faced, what factors explain the emergence and frequent success of democratic reform movements in the automobile manufacturing industry during the 1960s and 1970s?

Most analysts emphasize the impact of Echeverría's democratic opening policy on labor opposition movements in the industry.[49] At Volkswagen and Nissan, presidential labor policy did facilitate union democratization.[50] The involvement of opposition labor elements (Ortega Arenas at Volkswagen, Ortega Arenas and the FAT at Nissan) encouraged nascent reform groups and channeled worker dissatisfaction with established union practices into overt opposition to the CTM. Moreover, the Volkswagen and Nissan unions encountered no government opposition to the democratic election of new union leaders or their decision to break ties with the CTM and join the UOI.[51]

In other cases, however, presidential labor policy was neither a necessary nor a sufficient condition for union democratization. At DINA, an internal reform movement came to power in 1961 despite persistent opposition from both federal labor authorities and national and state CTM leaders. At Chrysler, company managers defeated worker opposition movements in 1969–70 and 1975 under two different presidents (Díaz Ordaz and Echeverría) with sharply divergent labor policies. Nor did the activities of the UOI, the FAT, or federal labor authorities have any apparent impact on the Ford union's decision to redefine the character of its association with the CTM in the mid-1970s. And Echeverría's democratic opening policy failed to spark internal opposition movements in two other CTM-affiliated automobile workers' unions, the VAM union in Mexico City and the General Motors union in Toluca.

A second explanation of union democratization in the automobile industry focuses on the relative strength or weakness of the state-level labor federations with which individual unions were affiliated. Roxborough has argued that where state federation leaders were politically strong and attentive to rank-and-file concerns, plant-level democratization movements either failed to emerge or were successfully defeated by entrenched union leaders (often acting in consort with company managers). Conversely, where state labor federations were weak, democratic reform movements triumphed and frequently broke established federation ties.[52]

Because state federation leaders commonly have the legal authority to negotiate directly with an employer over contract and wage issues and frequently have strong political ties to state governors or national political figures, they can often successfully block dissident movements in company-

or plant-level unions. For example, Roxborough presents convincing evidence that the CTM-affiliated union at the General Motors Toluca plant escaped the wave of democratization movements sweeping the automobile industry by virtue of strong leadership in both the local union and the state-level federation. Four brothers from a working-class family dominated the CTM hierarchy in the state of México in the 1970s. They all held important posts in CTM unions, state and local government, or both. One brother led the state-level metalworkers' union with which the General Motors union was affiliated, while another headed the General Motors union itself.[53] This closely knit network of union and political authority may well have prevented the emergence of rank-and-file opposition. Conversely, considerable disarray in the CTM's state federation in Morelos may have allowed a prodemocracy movement to win control in the Nissan union in Cuernavaca.[54]

Other cases, however, indicate that focusing on the strength or weakness of state-level labor federations does not adequately explain union democratization in the automobile industry. The CTM state federations in Hidalgo and Puebla energetically resisted losing their large, economically prosperous automobile workers' unions, and both the Puebla and Federal District federations were led by experienced, politically influential labor leaders. Indeed, the secretary-general of the CTM's state federation in Puebla, Blas Chumacero, was one of the most prominent labor leaders in Mexico. He had been a confidant of Fidel Velázquez since the late 1930s and had held more national political offices that any other Mexican labor leader. When preparing to expand manufacturing operations in Puebla, Volkswagen managers negotiated the transfer of its work force's union affiliation from the General Confederation of Workers to the CTM specifically to ensure that the strength of Chumacero's federation would prevent the outbreak of labor unrest.[55] They were soon disappointed.

Although these interpretations sometimes offer valuable insights, they provide only a partial explanation for union democratization in the automobile manufacturing industry. Neither presidential labor policy nor variation in the strength of state labor federations adequately explains the timing of such movements or why, in the same national political context, democratic reform movements emerged within some unions but not in others.[56] It is insufficient, however, simply to argue that a more complete understanding of union democratization requires attention to the internal dimensions of this process. Almost by definition, the emergence and consolidation of democratic governance in a particular union are shaped by a host of highly specific circumstances. A parsimonious explanation of these processes must demonstrate that a pattern of internal change exists across different cases and over time.

TABLE 6.3   Growth of Major Automobile Manufacturing Firms, 1960–1975

Year	Total Workers	Workers per Firm	Total Remunerations[a] (Millions of Pesos)	Remunerations per Worker (in Pesos)
1960	5,610	801	148.1	26,399
1965	15,853	2,265	441.6	27,855
1970	23,506	3,358	1,130.5	48,094
1975	36,822	5,260	3,475.0	94,372

Source: Author's calculations based on internal documents of the Asociación Mexicana de la Industria Automotriz.

Note: The firms measured are Auto-Mex/Chrysler, Ford, General Motors, Nissan, Vehículos Automotores Mexicanos, Volkswagen, and Diesel Nacional.

[a] Wages, salaries, fringe benefits, and distributed profits (if any), in millions of pesos. All financial amounts are listed in pesos at nominal prices, with 12.5 pesos equal to 1 U.S. dollar from 1960 to 1975.

This criterion is better met by focusing on changes in workplace industrial relations and their consequences for union democratization. The characteristics of automobile production changed significantly as the industry shifted from assembly activities to manufacturing operations following the 1962 decree. In the seven leading companies that are the focus of this analysis, the average number of workers per firm rose from 801 in 1960 to 3,358 in 1970. By 1975 this average was 5,260, reaching 9,515 at Volkswagen (see tables 6.3 and 6.4). The average automobile worker's annual earnings (wages, fringe benefits, and profits distributed under the 1963 profit-sharing law) rose from U.S.$2,112 in 1960 to U.S.$3,848 in 1970; by 1975 average annual earnings had reached U.S.$7,550.[57] Although there are no data available on the value of production at the firm level, the number of vehicles (cars and trucks up to 13,500 kilograms) produced by these seven firms rose from an average of 14,193 per firm in 1965 to 50,098 per firm in 1975. The average number of vehicles produced per worker rose from 6.3 in 1965 to 9.5 in 1975.[58]

By 1970, then, the vehicle manufacturing industry had become a highly capital-intensive activity with large and growing worker concentrations per firm and rising worker productivity. These changes had three important consequences for workplace relations and established mechanisms of labor control. First, sharply increased worker concentrations per firm posed special challenges for the informal, paternalistic labor relations arrangements that had long prevailed in the industry. Most labor relations analysts concur that large worker concentrations in manufacturing activities such as the automobile industry require institutionalized procedures for con-

TABLE 6.4   Workers Employed by Major Automobile Manufacturing Firms, 1960–1975

Firm	1960	1965	1970	1975
Auto-Mex/Chrysler	1,024	2,411	3,999	5,649
Diesel Nacional (DINA)	1,362	2,002	4,080	7,622
Ford	1,029	3,931	4,437	4,418
General Motors	1,480	4,330	4,325	4,991
Nissan	15	200	1,067	2,735
Vehículos Automotores Mexicanos (VAM)	450	1,158	1,982	1,892
Volkswagen	250	1,821	3,625	9,515

Source: Internal documents of the Asociación Mexicana de la Industria Automotriz.
Note: These totals include both blue-collar and white-collar workers.

flict resolution which are capable of addressing the day-to-day grievances arising from a complex, closely integrated production process. Paternalistic responses to workplace problems based on the supervisor's personal relationship with the worker are no longer adequate in a modern manufacturing environment.[59]

Second, as manufacturing activities accelerated, automobile companies placed greater emphasis on controlling overall labor costs and transferring employees freely among different work areas in order to increase the efficiency of production processes. These issues were particularly important to management because the Ministry of Industry and Commerce administered both production quotas and price controls on finished vehicles between 1962 and 1977. Production quotas preserved a minimum market share for firms with Mexican capital, and price controls encouraged firms to contain costs and achieve greater production efficiency.[60] As a result, wage and fringe benefit costs and control over disposition of the labor force within the workplace became central issues in bargaining between workers and employers. Union officials, in turn, came under increased pressure to win larger economic benefits for workers and control the sometimes arbitrary movement of workers on the plant floor.

Third, the transition to vehicle manufacturing produced new workplace grievances and increased worker discontent with established union practices. In comparison with craft system technologies (activities requiring that workers possess considerable skill at manipulating physical materials with tools, such as printing) and continuous process technologies (activities characterized by automatic, centralized control of an integrated production system, such as petroleum refining), in the 1960s and 1970s mass-production industries such as automobile manufacturing generally involved relatively unskilled and highly standardized production techniques, a significant degree of repetitiveness in work tasks, and considerable subdivision of the production process.[61] The characteristics of work in an automobile manufacturing plant during this period—particularly reduced social interaction among workers due to the noise level, the close attention required by the pace of the assembly line, restricted physical activity, and limited contact with all but immediate work supervisors—produced considerable worker alienation.[62] The concerns typically voiced by Mexican automobile workers (which focused on the intensity and repetitiveness of assembly-line work, conflicts with supervisors, and the need for enhanced job safety measures) conformed closely to this general characterization of work in mass-production industries in the 1960s and 1970s.

Because workers sometimes viewed entrenched CTM leaders as allies of the employer, grievances arising from a more conflictive industrial environment frequently produced worker demands for more democratic union representation. A review of the available (albeit sometimes incomplete) evidence suggests broad similarities across different automobile workers' unions in terms of worker complaints with local union leaders and their conduct of union business.[63] The complaints workers voiced typically concerned such issues as union leaders' open collaboration with management to prevent rank-and-file protests; their failure to secure improved wages and fringe benefits, better working conditions, or restraints on the arbitrary movement of workers on the plant floor; malfeasance in the administration of union dues and strike funds; manipulation of general assemblies and elections; exploitation of temporary workers (including the sale of job openings) and labor leaders' failure to improve employment security; and the dismissal of workers advocating more assertive actions toward employers or a change in union governance. For many workers, union democracy promised increased union autonomy in negotiations with management, regular election of union officials by secret balloting, greater leadership accountability to the rank and file, an expanded role for the general assembly in internal union decision making, and meaningful grievance procedures that included departmental delegates distributed throughout the workplace. In sum, although workers attached considerable importance to procedural issues such as effective member participation in union affairs through the general assembly, they also viewed union democratization as a means of increasing their bargaining effectiveness with company managers and resolving a wide range of workplace problems.

The Crisis of Traditional Unionism in the Automobile Industry

Changes in workplace industrial relations assumed particular importance in the context of traditional labor relations arrangements. The top-down orientation of the "official" labor movement in Mexico frequently results in a crucial gap between labor leaders and workers. Traditional union leaders are often more intent upon winning local, state, or national political office than attending to day-to-day workplace grievances. The arrangement developed to address this problem is the plant delegate system *(delegado de planta)*. The *delegado de planta* is an individual chosen by the federation or local labor union leader to attend to workers' daily concerns and avoid worker-employer conflicts at the work site in exchange for a share of union dues, political rewards, or both. In many instances, plant delegates are not selected from among the regular work force at a particular plant. Their approach to worker-employer relations typically is personal and unstructured, and they vary considerably in their skill and dedication in resolving workplace problems.[64]

The plant delegate system was firmly entrenched in the Auto-Mex/Chrysler (Federal District) and Ford unions. In the case of Auto-Mex/Chrysler, the plant delegate also served continuously as union secretary-general from 1942 until his death in 1965. Although a formal union structure existed, actual decision-making authority and day-to-day responsibility for resolving workplace grievances rested with the plant delegate, who reported directly to the leader of Section 23 of the Federal District Workers' Federation.[65] At Ford, a single plant delegate handled worker-employer relations in all three of Ford's separate manufacturing plants. Although he was not originally a Ford worker and never held union office, he maintained close contact with (and control over) workers. In formal terms, CTM control lay in the legal requirement that federation section leaders (who also held the post of secretary-general in the two different Ford unions) sign the collective contract for each manufacturing plant. In practical terms, however, CTM control depended on the longtime plant delegate's highly personalistic, but skillful, resolution of workplace problems and his ability to limit internal opposition. The plant delegate thus served as a crucial intermediary between Ford management and the CTM until his death in 1975.[66]

Plant delegates also played an important role at DINA, Volkswagen, and Nissan, albeit for shorter periods of time. In the case of DINA, the same plant delegate was active from the union's formation in 1955 until 1961. He shared responsibility with local union officials for negotiating, signing, and administering the collective work agreement, and he was in charge of resolving day-to-day workplace conflicts.[67] In both the Volkswagen and Nissan cases, the CTM's main tie with workers was a plant delegate (who in both cases also served as union secretary-general) brought in by the leader of the respective state labor federation to handle union affairs in these newly established manufacturing facilities. The Volkswagen *delegado de planta* was very successful at maintaining strict control over the rank and file during the Puebla plant's first years of activity, but his Nissan counterpart was quite ineffective in resolving workplace grievances. His office was located in the CTM state federation's headquarters in downtown Cuernavaca rather than at the plant, and he failed to maintain close supervision over daily developments in the workplace.[68]

In all these cases, the breakdown of the plant delegate system opened the way for major rank-and-file challenges to established patterns of union governance and CTM control over local union affairs.[69] For instance, several months after DINA's plant delegate left Ciudad Sahagún for personal reasons in early 1961, a protracted struggle for union leadership spiraled out of control as reformist groups mobilized widespread worker support for an opposition candidate when the incumbent secretary-general attempted to win reelection by fraudulent means, in apparent violation of an implicit internal agreement to rotate union offices among CTM loyalists on a regular basis. Concerted efforts by both state and national CTM leaders and Ministry of Labor and Social Welfare officials to restore order (and to back the incumbent secretary-general's position) only fueled anti-CTM dissidence. By early 1962, a new, democratically elected union leadership had successfully consolidated its position and ended the union's ties to the CTM.

At both Auto-Mex/Chrysler and Ford, the death of longtime plant delegates opened traditional labor relations arrangements to worker challenges, although the crises were resolved quite differently in the two cases. At Auto-Mex/Chrysler, the plant delegate's death in 1965 disrupted the established system of labor control just as the company began a major expansion program, which culminated with the construction of a manufacturing plant in Toluca in 1968. Open labor strife erupted in the union's Toluca section in late 1969 as workers protested wages and working conditions that were considerably less favorable than those at the Mexico City plant. When Auto-Mex/Chrysler managers dismissed the protest organizers, the dissident movement rapidly expanded its agenda to include reform of a number of union practices. These included the sale of job openings for union leaders' private gain, the questionable and undocumented use of union dues, union leaders' censorship of worker participation in general assemblies, union leaders' open collaboration with management, and the extensive use of one-day work contracts. In the end, however, forceful and sustained opposition by CTM leaders, state government labor authorities, and especially company managers defeated the rank-and-file challenge. In 1970 Auto-Mex/Chrysler imposed the company's chief production manager as union secretary-general to ensure future labor peace.

In contrast, the death of the Ford plants' delegate in 1975 sparked an internal reform process that ended with the unification of the three Ford plants' labor forces in a single union and a substantial increase in the new union's organizational autonomy. The former plant delegate had relied on a number of assistants at the different plant sites, but none of them was able to fill his position. Faced with a severe disruption in the established system of labor relations and the possibility that the breakdown of traditional control mechanisms might lead to the emergence of a more combative, "independent" union, Ford managers acted quickly to group the work force in one union under a single, more easily administered collective contract. Simultaneously, CTM representatives and management personnel responded to increasing rank-and-file pressures by developing formalized procedures for resolving grievances. They included section-level labor delegates elected by employees in different workplace divisions who could address more effectively the demands of a large industrial labor force. In addition, after 1975 the union broke its links to CTM-affiliated federations and established direct ties to the national CTM. In this process, the union achieved significantly greater autonomy vis-à-vis the CTM and Ford management.

In other instances, established labor control arrangements failed for reasons other than the death or departure of a plant delegate. At Volkswagen, the rapidly expanding work force and the union's growing political and economic importance tempted the plant delegate to wrest power from the CTM state federation leader in order to gain personal control over union membership dues. In the ensuing struggle, a democratic reform group succeeded in winning office. In the Nissan union, an opposition (but not anti-CTM) coalition succeeded in convening union elections in 1971 in which the incumbent secretary-general–plant delegate was defeated. The state CTM federation leader accepted this change because of the union leader's demonstrated inability to maintain control over the work force, but the turnover in union leadership offered an opportunity for anti-CTM activists to develop a political base within the union. In both cases, then, conflicts that challenged elements of the established system of labor control offered internal opposition groups (aided by Ortega Arenas, the FAT, or both) the opportunity to mobilize accumulated discontent among the rank and file and take power. Victorious reformers then established more democratic forms of union governance and broke ties with the CTM.

Although the specific circumstances surrounding the crisis of traditional unionism in these five cases varied considerably, a pattern emerges from this analysis of automobile workers' unions. The dramatic increase in work force size and the transformation in workplace labor relations resulting from the automobile industry's shift to manufacturing in the 1960s and 1970s laid the basis for challenges to traditional means of labor control. When the plant delegate system was seriously disrupted under substantially different workplace conditions, rank-and-file challenges often quickly followed. The new industrial relations context also precluded re-creating labor relations arrangements based on paternalism. It is particularly significant in this regard that newly democratic automobile workers' unions moved swiftly to establish formal structures for resolving workplace conflicts.

The time between the breakdown of the plant delegate system and internal challenges to incumbent union leaders was usually a matter of weeks or months. Only in Auto-Mex/Chrysler did a longer period of time pass, and only in DINA did the challenge to established labor controls and the CTM's presence occur before the rapid expansion of automobile manufacturing activities. DINA had experienced substantial growth in its labor force between 1955 and 1960. The threat of a plant shutdown following the abrogation of a licensing agreement with Fiat, combined with major contract concessions to management in 1960, led dissident workers to challenge the incumbent union leadership and CTM control.

Evidence concerning the three cases in which significant internal challenges did not emerge during the 1960s and 1970s—General Motors (Federal District), General Motors (Toluca), and VAM—further supports the workplace-based interpretation of union democratization presented here. As previously noted, the General Motors (Federal District) union enjoyed both an established democratic tradition and substantial autonomy vis-à-vis the CROC. The growth of the General Motors labor force occurred in the context of a democratically accountable union executive committee and department-level union representatives actively involved in resolving worker grievances. Although such procedures did not exist at the General Motors plant in Toluca, the union's strong, politically influential leadership and its close ties to the state-level metalworkers' union and government authorities prevented the emergence of a rank-and-file opposition movement. In the case of the VAM union, several factors worked against the generalization of workplace grievances: an effective plant delegate, a sophisticated strategy of employer paternalism, a comparatively small labor force, and an incentive wage system (in which wage scales were tied to a complex set of productivity measures that rewarded workers in narrowly defined workplace units according to their own productivity).[70]

Consequences of Union Democratization in the Automobile Industry

What were the political and economic consequences of union democratization in the automobile manufacturing industry? The remainder of this section evaluates systematically the extent of changes produced by union democratization in three major areas: worker participation in union affairs; worker-employer relations, including promotion procedures and employment conditions, rules governing the production process, and conflict resolution procedures; and union mobilizational activities. By comparing the performance of different unions in these distinct areas (especially by examining data for the same firm before and after union democratization occurred), this analysis demonstrates both the broad significance of the political controls that state-subsidized labor organizations maintain on worker mobilization and demand articulation in Mexico and the sometimes dramatic changes wrought by union democratization.

It is important to note, however, that union democratization in the automobile manufacturing industry did not necessarily improve workers' economic welfare. A careful examination of different measures (average yearly wage increases in different firms from the late 1960s through the mid-1970s, and total wages and benefits earned by automobile workers in the mid-1970s) shows that democratic unions did not perform noticeably better than their industry counterparts.[71] In some instances newly democratic unions did win wage increases above the industry average in their initial contract negotiations, in large part because they were more inclined to strike in support of their demands. But several other factors were more important than the character of union governance in explaining differences in automobile workers' wage increases and income levels during this period. These included the length of time different firms had operated in Mexico (older firms had a higher proportion of their work force in upper wage categories as a result of seniority promotions over time); whether manufacturing facilities were located in low- or high-wage areas; and corporate policies concerning compensation (whether company managers placed greater emphasis on wage compensation or fringe benefits).

Worker Participation in Union Affairs

The triumph of rank-and-file reform movements in several automobile workers' unions substantially increased opportunities for worker participation in union affairs. Union democracy has often been identified with regularized turnover among union officeholders,[72] and by this criterion the transformation of union politics in the automobile manufacturing industry produced very significant change. There was a complete turnover in union leadership at Diesel Nacional, Volkswagen, and Nissan. Moreover, the data presented in table 6.5 show that, from the mid-1960s through the mid-1970s, union officials were *least* likely to be reelected to more than one term at DINA, Nissan, General Motors, and Volkswagen (in that order). At DINA, for example, only 14.8 percent of the individuals elected to union office between 1967 and 1977 held more than one position (or served more

TABLE 6.5 Leadership Change in Major Automobile Workers' Unions, 1964–1977

Union	Number of Individuals Elected to Union Office, by Number of Times Elected						Total Union Positions Contested	% of Total Positions Held by Reelected Officials
	1	2	3	4	5	6		
Auto-Mex/Chrysler (Federal District) (1967, 1970–77)	10	0	0	0	0	0	10	0
Diesel Nacional (DINA) (1967–77)	46	4	0	0	0	0	54	14.8
Ford (1967–71, 1973–77)	49	12	2	1	0	0	83	41.0
General Motors (Federal District) (1967–77)	32	4	2	0	0	0	46	30.4
Nissan (Cuernavaca) (1966–76)	23	3	1	0	0	0	32	28.1
Vehiculos Automotores Mexicanos (VAM) (1964–76)	2	2	0	1	2	1	26	92.3
Volkswagen (1968–76)	15	4	0	0	0	0	23	34.8

Sources: Data for the DINA and General Motors unions are from the Ministry of Labor and Social Welfare's Associational Registry records of regular union elections. Data for all the remaining unions but Auto-Mex/Chrysler are from the list of union officials included in collective contracts for each firm; this information may be partially incomplete. Data for Auto-Mex./Chrysler are from the union's social and cultural magazine, *Justicia Social* 1 (Aug. 1974): 5–7.

than one term in the same position) on the union's executive committee. In contrast, 92.3 percent of those individuals holding office at Vehículos Automotores Mexicanos between 1964 and 1976 were reelected, and one official was reelected six times. At Auto-Mex/Chrysler, the defeat of a rank-and-file challenge to CTM control in 1969–70 resulted in the installation of the firm's production manager as union secretary-general. The new executive committee members selected in 1970 served without interruption through 1977, which accounts for the "zero reelection" result reported in table 6.5.

Union democratization also produced other reforms that increased members' opportunities for participation in union affairs.[73] Union statutes were substantially revised (or new ones adopted) to provide for regular election of union officers and their accountability to members, improve procedural safeguards on workers' union rights, increase rank-and-file participation in general assemblies, and expand the general assembly's role in internal union decision making. The election of departmental delegates produced a differentiated representational structure that greatly increased these unions' mobilizational capabilities in negotiations with company managers. Moreover, in cases such as General Motors and Nissan, open competition for union office led over time to the emergence of relatively stable, identifiable political factions that regularly competed for leadership positions.[74]

Democratically elected union officials generally proved more assertive than their predecessors in defense of members' interests, both in the resolution of individual and collective demands within the firm and in grievance proceedings before state agencies such as the Mexican Social Security Institute (IMSS) and labor conciliation and arbitration boards.[75] At Diesel Nacional, for example, the union general assembly frequently responded to an unjustified dismissal by voting special financial support for the worker and his or her dependents until the situation could be rectified.[76] Furthermore, DINA union officials often filed a formal grievance before the Federal Conciliation and Arbitration Board (JFCA) in order to win the worker's reinstatement. Union officials supervised each stage in the demand presentation process, and the union's resources permitted the worker greater access to legal counsel than he or she could otherwise have afforded. Designated union representatives were normally available to make formal presentations to JFCA authorities on the worker's behalf. They also helped the grievant meet various administrative deadlines throughout the often lengthy dispute resolution process. Such actions by union officials at DINA and other democratic unions substantially improved automobile workers' effective access to the labor justice system.

There were, however, other areas of union activity which were less affected by democratization. Government-allied union leaders in Mexico have often been accused of corruption, especially of stealing union funds and selling job openings to applicants. Yet union democratization did not necessarily end these practices in the Mexican automobile industry. The democratic histories of both the DINA and General Motors unions, for instance, include examples of union officials' theft of membership dues, payoffs from company managers to union officeholders in exchange for their toleration of contract violations, and the sale of employment openings. Elected officials in these unions have also employed the separation exclusion clause in collective contracts to deprive political opponents of their union membership and jobs.[77]

Worker-Employer Relations

Changes in workplace labor-management relations were among the most important consequences of union democratization in the automobile industry. These changes can best be evaluated by examining whether (and to what degree) labor unions exercised influence over three key dimensions of worker-employer relations: promotion procedures and policies affecting employment security; rules governing the production process; and plant-level conflict resolution procedures. Contracts are a generally reliable indicator of labor relations practices, especially the extent of union involvement. Although modifications in these different areas did not always occur at the same pace, a comparison of collective contracts for the seven principal firms engaged in vehicle manufacturing during the 1970s shows that workers in unions with more democratic governance—DINA, Nissan, General Motors, and Volkswagen—generally enjoyed more favorable contract terms in each of these areas than did VAM or Chrysler workers. The Ford union frequently held an intermediate ranking during this period. The results of a content analysis of collective labor agreements in all seven firms appear in table 6.6.

Promotion Procedures and Employment Security: Of the three different dimensions of worker-employer relations examined here, union democratization had the most significant impact on contract-stipulated promotion procedures and employment conditions. Contracts negotiated by democratic automobile workers' unions in the 1970s generally described different positions and category levels in considerable detail and provided for union participation in the elaboration of the personnel hierarchy *(escalafón)*, thus reducing employers' ability to make arbitrary promotion decisions based on favoritism or other such considerations. At DINA, Nissan, and Volkswagen, for example, a union-appointed board supervised all promotion decisions, and at Nissan the board's members even received paid leave from their regular jobs while engaged in such work.[78] Collective contracts at these three firms carefully defined promotion procedures and permitted union participation in all job category changes. At General Motors, not only did union representatives participate in all promotion decisions, but the contract also set the percentage share of the total work force employed at different category levels.[79] The General Motors contract guaranteed promotion to the next job category after a worker met stipulated seniority requirements.[80] The Volkswagen contract required that vacancies be advertised and that promotion decisions be publicly announced, provisions designed to limit arbitrary actions by work supervisors.[81]

In marked contrast, the Chrysler contract permitted the union no role whatsoever in promotions. Nor did it specify the criteria on which promotion decisions were made. In the case of VAM, the union had only a limited role in promotions. It provided a framework through which workers seeking promotion to a higher job category could test their qualifications, and previously employed workers and union members were assured preference in promotions to either permanent jobs or administrative and supervisory positions. But the VAM contract did not define promotion criteria, and company managers retained broad discretion in making promotion decisions.

Contract provisions regulating the hiring and promotion of temporary workers and the benefits they receive have historically been a key issue in labor-management negotiations in the Mexican automobile industry. Whereas permanent workers *(trabajadores de planta)* are entitled to a constitutionally mandated separation indemnity (three months' salary plus twenty days' pay per year of seniority, in addition to other benefits that may be provided by a particular firm's labor contract) if they are dismissed, temporary workers *(trabajadores eventuales)* are hired only for a limited time period or a defined task.[82] A firm may in fact employ a temporary worker continuously over a period of many years—without the worker automatically gaining *planta* status—simply by renewing his or her short-term contract. (For example, some of the General Motors *eventuales* who received permanent positions in August 1957 had between ten and seventeen years' experience at the company.)[83] Temporary workers generally do not receive the full range of contract benefits available to permanent workers, and at the end of a contract period they can be dismissed without receiving an indemnity payment regardless of their length of employment by a company. Nor is their period of employment necessarily counted as accumulated seniority if they do finally gain a permanent position.

A company with a large proportion of temporary employees in its work force can respond quickly and flexibly to changing market conditions (seasonal variations in demand, temporary disruptions in the supply of ma-

TABLE 6.6 Comparative Evaluation of Workplace Relations in Major Mexican Automobile Manufacturing Firms, 1972–1977

	Chrysler (Federal District) (1977)	DINA (1976)	Ford (1977)	General Motors (Federal District) (1977)	Nissan (1976)	VAM (1972)	Volkswagen (1976)
Promotion Procedures and Employment Security							
Union participation in hiring and promotions	0	4	2	3	4	2	4
Specification of promotion criteria	0	4	2	4	4	1	4
Automatic promotion of temporary workers or other limitations on their number	0	4	2	4	4	0	0
Other job security provisions	1	3	3	4	3	2	1
Subtotal	1	15	9	15	15	5	9

Production Process

Union participation in determination of production rate	0	4	2	1	4	2	0
Union control over work force distribution within plant	1	4	2	4	3	0	3
Equalization of wage categories	0	4	2	3	4	2	0
Union participation in occupational health and safety measures	0	4	4	4	4	4	4
Subtotal	1	16	10	12	15	8	7

Conflict Resolution Procedures

Specification of procedures, labor-management authorities, time periods for resolution of workplace conflicts	1	4	4	4	2	3	4
Total	3	35	23	31	32	16	20

Source: Labor contracts for the firms and years indicated.

Note: The numerical values listed in the table refer to the following code:

0 = No special benefits or provisions beyond those specified by federal labor law

1 = Very limited measures

2 = Moderate protection or union participation

3 = Extensive protection or active union participation

4 = Very extensive protection or active union participation in formal institutional mechanisms or specified procedures

TABLE 6.7 Comparative Evaluation of Workplace Relations at Diesel Nacional (DINA), Nissan, and Volkswagen, 1960–1976

	DINA (1960)	DINA (1976)	Nissan (1966)	Nissan (1976)	Volkswagen (1968)	Volkswagen (1976)
Promotion Procedures and Employment Security						
Union participation in hiring and promotions	2	4	0	4	0	4
Specification of promotion criteria	2	4	0	4	0	4
Automatic promotion of temporary workers or other limitations on their number	0	4	0	4	0	0
Other job security provisions	2	3	2	3	0	1
Subtotal	6	15	2	15	0	9
Production Process						
Union participation in determination of production rate	2	4	1	4	0	0
Union control over work force distribution within plant	0	4	0	3	0	3
Equalization of wage categories	4	4	0	4	0	0
Union participation in occupational health and safety measures	0	4	0	4	0	4
Subtotal	6	16	1	15	0	7
Conflict Resolution Procedures						
Specification of procedures, labor-management authorities, time periods for resolution of workplace conflicts	4	4	0	2	1	4
Total	16	35	3	32	1	20

Source: Labor contracts for the firms and years indicated.
Note: The numerical values listed in the table refer to the following code:
0 = No special benefits or provisions beyond those specified by federal labor law
1 = Very limited measures
2 = Moderate protection or union participation
3 = Extensive protection or active union participation
4 = Very extensive protection or active union participation in formal institutional mechanisms or specified procedures

terials, and so forth) by varying the length of *eventuales'* job contracts or by dismissing them on short notice without incurring the cost of separation indemnities. During the 1970s, for example, Chrysler regularly hired a number of temporary workers on one-day contracts to cover temporary absences created when permanent workers fell ill or were on vacation. These workers waited each morning outside Chrysler's Mexico City plant for an opportunity to work that day.[84]

Automobile workers' unions have long sought to limit employers' flexible use of temporary labor. In the 1970s all seven unions in the vehicle manufacturing industry had, as part of their general personnel procurement authority, the legal right to select those temporary workers the firm required to fill employment openings. However, only democratic unions won contract provisions limiting the number of *eventuales* and regulating the terms of their employment. Tables 6.6 and 6.7 show that over time the DINA (1960–76), Nissan (1966–76), and General Motors (1977) unions significantly redefined contract terms governing temporary workers. In addition to limiting the proportion of *eventuales* in the labor force (14 percent at DINA and 10 percent at Nissan in 1976) or guaranteeing them automatic promotion and job security after a specified period (three years in the case of General Motors' 1977 contract), contract settlements in these three firms frequently required the firm to grant permanent positions to a substantial number of temporary workers.[85] At General Motors, company managers regularly offered during the 1950s and 1960s to increase the proportion of *planta* positions in the work force in lieu of larger wage increases.[86] Management's strategy was sound so long as the domestic automobile market expanded rapidly, but when sales slumped in 1976–77, the company was unable to reduce the size of its work force without making substantial indemnity payments to the *planta* workers it dismissed.

Ford and especially Volkswagen were exceptions to this pattern in the 1970s. Despite major changes in other contract provisions following the consolidation of more democratic governance, Volkswagen managers retained in 1976 virtually unrestricted control over the hiring and remuneration of temporary workers.[87] At Ford, as well as at VAM and Chrysler, company managers continued to exercise broad flexibility concerning *eventuales*.[88] Neither the absolute number of these workers nor their proportion of the total labor force was limited, and temporary workers' employment conditions were regulated by individual contracts rather than by the collective labor agreement covering permanent workers.[89]

The more democratic automobile workers' unions also won more advantageous contract provisions concerning other forms of job security, although differences among firms were less significant in this area than in the case of promotion policies (see table 6.6). Contracts in effect at General Motors and Nissan in the mid-1970s safeguarded workers' jobs in the event that the firm moved its manufacturing operations to another location.[90] The General Motors and DINA contracts also required that some or all of existing positions be filled when vacancies occurred. In the case of Nissan, the contract stipulated that the least senior workers were to be laid off first, and it required that dismissed workers be given preference when hiring resumed.[91]

Collective contracts at other firms gave workers less employment security. Both the Ford and the VAM contracts in effect in the mid-1970s provided some protection for the existing labor force in the event the company relocated its manufacturing operations. The VAM contract expressly recognized seniority as the criterion determining the order in which layoffs occurred.[92] However, neither the Volkswagen nor the Chrysler contracts contained any job security provisions beyond those required by federal labor law (that is, that permanent workers receive an indemnity payment upon dismissal). Nor did either contract obligate company managers to fill vacancies as they occurred.[93]

The changes that democratization produced in workplace policies regarding promotions and employment security can best be demonstrated by comparing contracts negotiated at different firms before and after changes in union governance. Table 6.7 presents the results of a content analysis of collective labor contracts in effect at DINA, Nissan, and Volkswagen in the early and mid-1960s and in the mid-1970s. In the first year examined for each company (DINA, 1960; Nissan, 1966; Volkswagen, 1968), the contract was negotiated while the union was still affiliated with the CTM. By 1976 union democratization movements had triumphed in all three cases, the unions had broken with the CTM, and labor-management negotiations had produced substantial changes in contract provisions concerning promotions and job security.

Although the 1960 DINA contract required that employment openings be advertised within the plant, stressed seniority and technical ability as the principal criteria for advancement, established a labor-management committee to evaluate candidates for promotion, and offered workers moderate job security, the 1976 contract included significant improvements in each of these areas.[94] The 1966 Nissan and 1968 Volkswagen contracts contained no provisions whatsoever regarding union participation in promotion decisions, the criteria according to which promotion decisions would be made, or limitations on the number of temporary workers. By 1976, however, democratic unions at these two firms had made very significant gains in these areas, although the Volkswagen union continued to lag behind its democratic counterparts on job security issues. The job security provisions added to the Nissan contract between 1966 and 1976 were particularly noteworthy. In addition to limitations on management's use of temporary workers, the union won the company's agreement to reaccommodate those workers affected if specific production areas were eliminated in the course of plant modernization.[95]

Rules Governing the Production Process: Rules governing the production process are typically among the most controversial worker-employer issues. Manufacturing company managers consider their control over the rate of assembly-line production and the flexible movement of personnel among different work areas (whether to cover temporary labor shortages or to reorganize production on short notice) to be crucial to maintaining a cost-efficient production process capable of responding to changing market conditions. In contrast, workers try to regularize the rate of production so as to avoid speed-ups, and they generally attempt to restrict managers' authority to shift personnel arbitrarily among different work areas and employment categories. Most blue-collar workers also seek to eliminate minor wage differentials among different job levels on the grounds that they increase tensions in the workplace. Moreover, occupational health and safety measures and working conditions are of vital importance to workers.

To what extent were democratic automobile workers' unions able to increase their control over these different aspects of the production process? Table 6.6 shows that democratic unions at DINA, Nissan, General Motors, and Ford were most successful at extending their influence in these areas. The exception to this pattern was again the Volkswagen union. The fact that the Volkswagen union generally made less headway in contract negotiations over production process rules than over promotion procedures reflected company managers' vigorous defense of their prerogatives on matters crucial to manufacturing efficiency. Indeed, the Volkswagen union's performance on most production process issues was little better than that of unions at VAM and Chrysler.

The DINA and Nissan unions were clearly the industry leaders in this area. By the mid-1970s these unions had compelled company managers to create special labor-management commissions in which union officials participated in time-and-motion studies that defined "normal" work rhythms and detailed the content of newly created positions. The Nissan union made particularly rapid progress on these and similar issues in the years after seceding from the CTM, but at the time the DINA union enjoyed the most advantageous contract terms in the industry. For example, the DINA contract placed strict limitations on the movement of personnel among different production areas. Company managers could make personnel transfers of up to five days in length in order to cover vacancies due to illness or vacation leave, but permanent changes in work force distribution required the formal approval of the union's committee on promotions.

There was considerably less variation among different firms in terms of union participation in workplace health and safety measures. Contract provisions governing occupational health and safety issues were particularly detailed at Nissan and Volkswagen, but union representatives at DINA, Nissan, Volkswagen, Ford, and VAM all participated with managers in joint occupational health and safety commissions that examined working conditions and devised measures to prevent accidents and work-related illnesses. At General Motors this commission was composed solely of union members. Only Chrysler lacked such a commission; indeed, collective contracts in effect at Chrysler in the mid-1970s made no specific provision for attention to occupational health and safety matters.

The data in table 6.7 show that changes in worker influence over the production process at DINA, Nissan, and Volkswagen were closely linked to union democratization. For example, although the 1960 DINA contract promised "equal pay for equal work,"[96] the pay scale in effect at Diesel Nacional at this time emphasized minute wage differentials among different job classifications, in practice violating contractual safeguards. The elimination of most such differentials by the mid-1970s was a major union accomplishment. Similarly, although the 1966 Nissan contract referred to "normal work in terms of quantity and quality," the union had no formal role in decisions over production rates.[97] Under democratic leadership, the union quickly won institutionalized influence in this area. At Volkswagen, the contract negotiated under the CTM in 1968 gave the union no role whatsoever in decisions over production rates or the movement of employees among different work areas; indeed, the contract explicitly assigned complete control over these issues to management, stating that "the greatest possible efficiency" was the only criterion by which these decisions would be made.[98] Moreover, none of the contracts negotiated before democratization movements triumphed at DINA, Nissan, and Volkswagen permitted union participation in occupational health and safety matters, underscoring the significance of democratic unions' gains in these areas by the mid-1970s.

Conflict Resolution Procedures: Finally, in nearly all cases, union democratization produced important changes in contractually specified workplace conflict resolution procedures (see table 6.6). In the years following the triumph of rank-and-file reform movements, unions at DINA, Volkswagen, General Motors, and Ford institutionalized conflict resolution procedures by creating a system of section- and department-level delegates responsible for resolving workers' daily grievances. The collective contracts in force in these companies in the mid-1970s not only recognized these delegates' role, but they also established orderly procedures for resolving problems and specified time limits within which conflicts were to be addressed at the section, department, and plant level. VAM was the only company not represented by a democratic union which recognized significant union rights in the grievance resolution process.

Contracts at DINA, Volkswagen, General Motors, and Ford outlined disciplinary procedures in considerable detail and guaranteed union representatives' formal participation in the application of sanctions. At Volkswagen, for example, the contract set aside a time each day during working hours for the resolution of workplace problems, and it provided for regular meetings between the union's executive committee and personnel managers.[99] At Volkswagen and DINA, the contract required managers to keep written records of disciplinary proceedings.[100] The Ford contract did not set specific time periods for disciplinary investigations and grievance resolution by union and management representatives (it referred only to "a reasonable period"), but it did impose an overall thirty-day limit on investigations and the application of disciplinary sanctions.[101] Only the Nissan union lagged behind its democratic counterparts in institutionalizing such procedural guarantees. The union's 1976 contract accredited various labor representatives and working groups involved in conflict resolution below the union executive committee. However, it provided no other details concerning the procedures to be followed in resolving workplace grievances. Even so, the Nissan union had greater influence in this area than did the Chrysler union. Chrysler's contract limited the union's formal role in grievance resolution to the "investigation" of the problem and "agreement" concerning the application of disciplinary measures.

DINA's contract guaranteed the union a strong, institutionalized role in workplace-level conflict resolution as early as 1960, although these provisions were not fully implemented.[102] However, the Nissan and Volkswagen cases again show the important impact that union democratization had over time in this area. The 1966 Nissan contract included no clause at all that specifically addressed conflict resolution procedures. Nor did the 1968 Volkswagen contract establish detailed procedures or institutional arrangements for resolving workplace grievances. Yet as noted above and as summarized in table 6.7, by 1976 both unions had made substantial progress in this area. The extensive conflict resolution procedures that the Volkswagen union put in place in a short period of time were particularly noteworthy.

Union Mobilizational Activities: Strikes and Alliance Formation

Of the various dimensions of union behavior examined here, none is more closely linked to union democratization than mobilizational activities—especially strikes and union alliance formation. With few exceptions, strikes in the vehicle manufacturing industry during the 1960s and 1970s were closely associated with union democratization and the erosion of "official" labor organizations' control over local unions. Similarly, unions that ended or substantially altered their relations with government-allied confederations were the most active in forging interunion alliances and cooperative ties.

Labor Strikes: Strike activity in the automobile manufacturing industry was very limited before 1970 (see table 6.8).[103] The earliest known case was a wildcat strike at Ford in 1938, which ended abruptly when Ford managers fired the dozen or so workers who headed the protest movement. The strike that occurred at DINA in 1962 following the union's break with the CTM was declared nonexistent by the Federal Conciliation and Arbitration Board on the grounds that the union had failed to meet various procedural requirements. Similarly, the wildcat strike at Auto-Mex/Chrysler's Toluca plant in 1969–70 was vigorously opposed by both local CTM leaders and company managers; it ended with the forced dismissal of a large number of blue-collar workers.

The strike waged by General Motors workers in February 1965 was an important departure in the automobile industry, and it marked a turning point in labor-management relations at General Motors. General Motors workers had discussed the possibility of filing a strike petition in support of their contract demands as early as July 1947, although they viewed this action with some trepidation.[104] Even when the union finally did file its first strike petition in May 1959 as part of contract negotiations with the firm, the very limited preparations that union leaders took suggest that they did not consider a strike likely.[105] The 1965 strike lasted only two days, but it was preceded by the formation of a strike committee to coordinate union activities and the creation of a strike fund. Union members later judged that the strike was only partially successful. However, it ended union hesitation regarding strikes and offered important lessons concerning the need for adequate advance preparations.[106]

Strike activity in the automobile manufacturing industry in the 1970s was closely linked to the advance of democratic unionism. The unions most likely to strike were the democratic DINA, General Motors, Nissan, Ford, and Volkswagen unions. In contrast, neither the VAM nor the Chrysler unions struck during this period, although another brief wildcat strike oc-

TABLE 6.8   Strike Activity in the Mexican Automobile Manufacturing
Industry, 1938–1980

Union	Years in Which Strikes Occurred
Auto-Mex/Chrysler (Federal District and Toluca)	1969–70,[a] 1975[a]
Diesel Nacional (DINA)	1962, 1973, 1974, 1976, 1977, 1978, 1979
Ford	1938,[a] 1976, 1977, 1978, 1980
General Motors (Federal District)	1965, 1973, 1975, 1976, 1977, 1979, 1980
Nissan (Cuernavaca)	1972, 1973, 1974, 1976, 1977, 1978
Vehículos Automotores Mexicanos (VAM)	None
Volkswagen	1974, 1976, 1977, 1978

Sources: Author's interviews with a staff official of the International Metalworkers' Federation, 10 May 1977, Mexico City; General Motors labor relations manager, 11 July 1977, Mexico City; Diesel Nacional union official, 5 Aug. and 20 Aug. 1977, Ciudad Sahagún, Hidalgo; coordinator of Independent Worker Unit, 30 Nov. and 2 Dec. 1977, Mexico City; Roxborough, *Unions and Politics in Mexico* (1984), table 2.4; Aguilar García, *La política sindical en México* (1982), 157, table 39.

[a] Wildcat strike.

curred at Chrysler in 1975. Even though the López Portillo administration generally pursued a more conservative labor policy than did its predecessor, the DINA (1977, 1978, 1979), General Motors (1977, 1979, 1980), Ford (1977, 1978, 1980), Volkswagen (1977, 1978), and Nissan (1977, 1978) unions continued to strike in support of their wage and contract demands.

Union Alliance Formation: Forging ties with other labor organizations can significantly increase a union's mobilizational capacity and bargaining leverage. Although such linkages can be particularly valuable for enterprise- or plant-level unions, interunion cooperation of this kind was quite limited throughout much of the history of the Mexican automobile industry. However, the emergence of democratic unions at several manufacturing firms in the 1960s and 1970s led to significantly expanded efforts to develop organizational linkages among automobile workers' unions, as well as between automobile workers and other labor groups, student organizations, and opposition political parties. The initiative for such cooperative relationships came from both automobile workers' unions themselves and from these other sociopolitical actors. Strike movements most frequently created both the need and the opportunity for alliance formation.

In the 1970s the most important focus for economic and political cooperation among newly democratic automobile workers' unions was the Independent Worker Unit (UOI). The DINA, Volkswagen, and Nissan unions were all formally affiliated with the UOI at different times, and the UOI was also active among workers at General Motors and Ford.[107] Interunion cooperation through the UOI was particularly important during strikes at DINA (1974, 1976, 1978) and Nissan (1974, 1976). DINA workers on strike in 1974 and 1976 received financial support from approximately thirty UOI affiliates. Although economic solidarity payments did not fully replace workers' regular pay, they were both economically and politically important. For example, the Volkswagen union contributed 80,000 pesos (U.S.$6,400) per week during DINA workers' 1974 strike, an amount that when combined with other contributions permitted all DINA workers two payments of 100 pesos each. When DINA union officials later offered to repay this amount, Volkswagen union leaders stated that they preferred future assistance from the DINA union during their own contract negotiations.

In addition, the International Metalworkers' Federation (IMF) was active among automobile workers during this period.[108] During the 1960s and 1970s the IMF offered advice and assistance on a number of different problems to the DINA, Ford, Nissan, and Volkswagen unions. However, the organization's closest ties were with the General Motors union.[109] Beginning with the union's 1965 strike and during contract negotiations in 1973, 1975, and 1977, the IMF offered General Motors workers economic assistance and information concerning the company's activities in Mexico and other countries. During a lengthy strike in 1977, it pressured General Motors management in Detroit to resolve several issues in the workers' favor and contributed 132,000 pesos (U.S.$5,818) to the union's strike fund. Moreover, throughout the 1960s and 1970s, IMF staff officials conducted collective bargaining and leadership training seminars in Mexico and other Latin American countries to which they regularly invited union representatives (mainly members of the executive committee) from General Motors' Mexico City plant. These activities further strengthened linkages between the IMF and the General Motors union.

Strikes in the automobile industry both encouraged interunion alliance formation and offered other sociopolitical actors an opportunity to strengthen ties with automobile workers. University student groups supported strikes at DINA in 1974 and Nissan in 1976.[110] Opposition labor groups such as the Authentic Labor Front (FAT) and opposition parties such as the Partido Mexicano de los Trabajadores (Mexican Workers' Party) and the Partido Socialista de los Trabajadores (Socialist Workers' Party) all sought to forge ties with democratic unions at DINA, Ford, General Motors, Nissan, and Volkswagen during the 1970s. However, these unions were reluctant to compromise their hard-won autonomy—and increase the risk of government opposition to their actions—by establishing formal affiliations with such groups.

Conclusion

The rapid economic growth that Mexico achieved from the 1940s through the 1970s depended in large part on effective political control over organized labor. The governing elite's administrative capacity to regulate different forms of labor participation (especially strikes), combined with reliable support from state-subsidized organizations such as the CTM, generally limited labor demands and gave decision makers considerable leeway to formulate and implement economic policies. At the same time, sustained economic expansion and the characteristics of import-substituting industrialization reinforced the governing elite's social pact with labor. The labor movement endorsed import-substitution policies for two reasons. First, the central features of this development strategy (active state regulation of socioeconomic affairs, state ownership or majority control of strategic economic activities, restrictions on foreign investment) conformed to its revolutionary nationalist preferences. Second, a highly protected economy with a prominent public sector maximized organized labor's ability to translate its national political importance into higher wages, better contract terms, and improved social welfare benefits in state-owned enterprises. The ability of government-allied labor leaders to deliver substantial resources to union members strengthened their position within their organizations.

At the national level, the characteristics and economic success of import-substituting industrialization strengthened the ruling elite's alliance with organized labor. Yet in some cases, industrialization produced significant changes in workplace conditions which threatened state-subsidized labor organizations' control over workers. In the automobile industry, for example, CTM-affiliated federations exercised strong political control for many years, limiting workers' participation in local union affairs and circumscribing their negotiations with company managers. Provisions in union statutes and collective contracts gave federation leaders and their handpicked local representatives tight control over the rank and file. Their position was backstopped by the CTM's national political connections and, in some cases, the willingness of federal and state labor authorities to defend incumbent union leaders against internal challenges when they occurred. The plant delegate system served the interests of both federation leaders and automobile company managers; the former received substantial economic benefits in the form of a share of workers' mandatory union dues and the political advantages that accrued from representing a sizeable industrial labor force at the local, state, and national levels, while the latter enjoyed favorable contract terms and labor discipline.

However, the shift from assembly operations to vehicle manufacturing in the 1960s and 1970s transformed the in-plant industrial relations environment, generating new workplace grievances and increasing worker dissatisfaction with established union practices. Because workers often viewed incumbent CTM leaders as allies of company managers, grievances arising from a more conflictive workplace environment frequently produced demands for more democratic, accountable union leadership. In several companies the death or departure of longtime plant delegates precipitated a crisis in the established means of labor control. Rank-and-file reform movements sometimes succeeded in ousting incumbent union leaders and taking office. Once in power, union reformers acted quickly to break or substantially redefine their ties with the CTM and to institute more democratic forms of governance. These changes permitted significantly increased rank-and-file participation in union decision making. Over time, democratic unions' greater mobilizational capacity and more assertive bargaining with employers also generally produced collective work agreements that gave workers stronger influence over promotion procedures, the conditions of employment, workplace conflict resolution procedures, and the production process.

This case study of the automobile manufacturing industry in the 1960s and 1970s underlines why both state-centered and society-centered approaches are important to understanding the bases of elite control over labor and patterns of political change in Mexico's authoritarian regime. The political dominance of CTM-affiliated federations in the automobile industry depended heavily upon the state subsidies they received, including in some instances government officials' strong support against rank-and-file challenges. Yet focusing only on the state-centered variable of presidential labor policy—whether different presidential administrations opposed or favored worker-led democratization movements—does not adequately explain why democratic reform initiatives triumphed in some automobile workers' unions in the 1960s and 1970s and not in others. Presidential labor policy was an important factor in some cases. However, a satisfactory explanation of this phenomenon must also address the impact of industrial change on state-subsidized labor organizations and traditional mechanisms of labor control such as the plant delegate system.

CHAPTER SEVEN

Labor Politics under Economic Stress
in the 1980s: Economic Crisis, Industrial
Restructuring, and the Consequences
for Workers

Mexico's post-1982 economic crisis had serious, lasting consequences for workers. Heavy government borrowing from international creditors in the late 1970s and early 1980s produced high, ultimately unsustainable levels of indebtedness, leading to financial collapse in 1982. As part of the broad financial stabilization and economic adjustment program that it adopted in response to the crisis, the administration of President Miguel de la Madrid (1982–88) sharply limited wage increases, cut government social spending, relaxed price controls on many basic commodities, and reduced or eliminated government subsidies for mass transportation, electricity, natural gas, and gasoline. These policies caused a dramatic fall in real wages and a sharp decline in workers' standard of living. Government statistics registered an increase in unemployment only in the immediate aftermath of the 1982 debt shock (from 4.2 percent of the economically active urban population in 1982 to 6.3 percent in 1983 and 5.7 percent in 1984).[1] However, unemployment in some sectors and regions remained significantly higher throughout the 1980s because of economic retrenchment in the private sector and the government's decision to close unprofitable state-owned enterprises.

Moreover, the severity of the crisis compelled economic policymakers to reorient Mexico's development strategy. The de la Madrid administration reduced state participation in the economy, and by cutting tariffs and nontariff barriers to imports it encouraged Mexican firms to increase their international competitiveness. In order to stabilize government finances and promote economic efficiency, de la Madrid reduced government production and consumption subsidies in many areas and began to privatize state-owned enterprises. The de la Madrid administration also attempted to stimulate industrial growth and expand the share of manufactured exports in foreign trade by lowering tariff barriers on imports of capital goods and by relaxing restrictions on direct foreign investment. Limiting wage increases in order to make workers' low compensation a basis of international economic comparative advantage was a key element in this new strategy. De la Madrid's handpicked successor, President Carlos Salinas de Gortari (1988–94), accelerated still further the pace of economic liberalization.

Economic crisis and the shift in national development strategy sparked an extensive process of industrial restructuring. Under de la Madrid, the number of state-owned or state-controlled enterprises and public investment funds shrank from 1,155 in 1982 to 412 in 1988.[2] In preparing state-owned companies for sale to private investors, the government often forced upon workers significant cuts in wages and fringe benefits and contract changes that substantially reduced unions' influence in enterprise affairs. A similar process also began in private firms. In many industries, employers (often with strong government support) cut employment, reduced wages and benefits, and attempted to increase productivity by rewriting contracts and redefining work rules.

The fundamental reorientation of national development strategy which de la Madrid initiated and Salinas vigorously pursued challenged the bases on which Mexico's social pact had rested since the 1950s. Organized labor benefited in multiple ways from the economic environment created by import-substituting industrialization, especially from extensive state regulation of the economy and the highly protected domestic market in which private-sector firms operated. The closing or privatization of state-owned enterprises eroded what had long been the principal advantage of some of Mexico's largest and most influential unions: the ability to use their political leverage to win concessions from state managers in negotiations over wage and fringe benefit levels and contract terms. Industrial restructuring in the public and private sectors undermined the mobilizational capacity and bargaining leverage of government-allied and more politically independent unions alike. In fact, in the automobile manufacturing industry, the labor organizations that bore the brunt of transnational firms' aggressive efforts to reorganize the industry and shift toward export production were the democratic unions that arose in the 1960s and 1970s.

The first part of this chapter examines Mexico's post-1982 economic crisis and organized labor's response to the challenges it engendered, focusing especially on the crucial period between 1983 and 1987. The crisis revealed, like no other political or economic moment since the late 1940s, both the importance of state administrative controls on labor participation and the consequences of "official" labor organizations' heavy dependence on state subsidies. Some groups gained temporary advantage from the de la Madrid administration's efforts to block united labor action in the years immediately after the debt crisis erupted. Moreover, the Confederation of

Mexican Workers (CTM) and other major labor organizations won economic concessions from the government that cushioned some of their affiliates from the worst effects of the crisis. Indeed, industrial restructuring in such activities as automobile manufacturing even benefited the CTM by severely eroding the position of more politically independent unions. In general, however, the 1980s economic crisis significantly weakened the labor movement and its social pact with Mexico's governing political elite.

The second section returns to the case of the automobile manufacturing industry in order to evaluate in greater depth the impact of industrial restructuring in the 1980s on union organizations, workers' economic welfare, and opportunities for workplace participation. This analysis shows that changes in market conditions and presidential labor policy offered companies an opportunity to redefine the terms of worker-employer interaction, thereby placing enterprise- and plant-level democratic unions on the defensive. Industrial restructuring in the automobile manufacturing industry began earlier and proceeded more rapidly than in other economic activities in which transnational firms played a less prominent role or which were less closely linked to export markets. However, many of the changes that occurred in the automobile industry in the 1980s (including firms' efforts to introduce post-Fordist industrial relations measures in order to increase managerial control, lower production costs, and improve product quality) were later replicated in other sectors. More generally, this discussion demonstrates the extent to which unions may find their hard-won bargaining leverage undermined as key Mexican industries become more fully integrated into the global economy.

Economic Challenges to Organized Labor in the 1980s

Workers paid a heavy price under the Mexican government's post-1982 economic stabilization program. Faced with an inflation rate averaging 88.0 percent per year between 1982 and 1988 (and reaching an annual rate of 177 percent in January 1988), the de la Madrid administration imposed stringent controls on wage increases. As a result, the inflation-adjusted value of the daily minimum wage in Mexico City fell by 49.7 percent between 1982 and 1988, with the sharpest fall in 1983.[3] The administration also departed from long-established practice by employing the percentage increase in the official minimum wage not as a reference point for contract negotiations conducted by individual unions and firms but as a limit on annual wage increases. The state's position as the single largest employer significantly increased the effectiveness of wage restraint as a means of controlling inflation.

At the same time, the de la Madrid administration sharply cut government social spending. Total federal government spending on education and health services fell by a cumulative 29.6 percent and 23.3 percent, respectively, between 1983 and 1988.[4] In combination, the government's adjustment policies produced an extremely rapid decline in workers' income. The wage share of national income declined from 43.2 percent in 1982 to 34.6 percent in 1987.[5] Moreover, income distribution became more unequal, and the proportion of the population living below the extreme poverty line rose.[6]

Workers' changing consumption patterns closely reflected these difficult economic conditions. The cost of a basket of basic foodstuffs for a working-class family in Mexico City (corn tortillas, bread, pasta, wheat flour, cookies, crackers, rice, beef, pork, fresh and frozen fish, fresh milk, eggs, vegetable oil, seasonal fruits, fresh vegetables, beans, and sugar) rose from 123.7 pesos per day in 1981 to 897.5 pesos per day in 1984. In contrast, the legal minimum daily wage rose only from 210 pesos in 1981 to 748 pesos in 1984. A 1984 survey by the National Institute for the Consumer found that even over a three-month period (March–May), working-class families significantly reduced their consumption of bread, beans, rice, eggs, sugar, fruits, and vegetables. They substituted foods of generally lower nutritional value for previously consumed high-nutrition products (rice replaced by pasta, milk by coffee, sugar by *piloncillo* [a traditional sweetener made of unrefined sugar, sold in cone-shaped cakes], vegetables by beans, fish by pasta, and so forth), and some families stopped buying meat, fish, and fruit altogether.[7]

There were important regional and sectoral variations in the impact of the economic crisis. Industrial centers such as Mexico City, Guadalajara, and Monterrey suffered comparatively high rates of unemployment, whereas employment in the *maquiladora* (in-bond manufacturing) industry along the U.S.-Mexican border grew steadily. Similarly, workers in relatively privileged jobs faced particularly severe pressures because employment in the manufacturing sector as a whole fell by 11.8 percent between 1980 and 1989. Employment declined even more sharply (by 48.0 percent between 1981 and 1990) in public-sector manufacturing firms.[8]

These variations reflected in part the historical heterogeneity of the Mexican working class: the mix of labor-intensive and capital-intensive employment, wide variations in work force concentration and productivity, geographical differences in rates of unemployment, and great disparities in working conditions, wage and fringe benefit levels, and educational achievement. Nevertheless, the dramatic fall in real economic growth rates after 1982 (which had averaged 5.5 percent per year from 1970 to 1977 and 8.4 percent per year from 1978 to 1981 during a petroleum-led economic boom, but fell to an average of −0.1 percent per year from 1982 to 1988) underlined the generally adverse conditions that workers faced.[9]

Organized Labor's Response

The Confederation of Mexican Workers, often working through the Labor Congress, took the lead in shaping the "official" labor movement's response to the multiple challenges posed by economic crisis. In December 1982 the CTM announced that, in exchange for government social programs to protect workers' purchasing power and a modest increase in the legal minimum wage, it would support the newly inaugurated de la Madrid administration's call for wage restraint as a necessary part of a stabilization program designed to control inflation.[10] This was a familiar CTM response. It had taken the same position under similar, if less dire, economic circumstances following the 1954 and 1976 peso devaluations, and in both instances government-CTM cooperation had contributed to quick economic recovery and increased the confederation's political capital.

The CTM's decision to back the de la Madrid stabilization plan in part reflected the fact that controlling inflation was a high priority for the labor movement. Moreover, in an effort to secure labor support, the de la Madrid government enacted constitutional reforms that formally recognized the "social sector" (union-owned enterprises, for example) and guaranteed workers access to adequate housing and health care. The administration also revised the federal labor law to permit negotiations over minimum-wage levels whenever economic conditions required. These measures persuaded the CTM and other Labor Congress members to endorse the government's "Program for the Production, Supply, and Control of Essential Consumption Goods," which both government and labor representatives characterized as a "solidarity pact" designed to stabilize wages and prices. But this government-labor stabilization pact lasted only five days.[11] Labor leaders were stunned when in January 1983 the de la Madrid administration violated the terms of the agreement by relaxing price controls on a wide range of basic consumer goods.

In early 1983 the CTM hierarchy came under intense criticism from state and local labor leaders as rank-and-file discontent with increased unemployment, limited wage increases, and rapidly rising prices (particularly for basic commodities) grew. The high level of labor discontent in part reflected the sharp reversal of worker expectations brought about by the sudden onset of national economic crisis, as well as the perception that labor's sacrifices during the 1976–77 recession had never been fully compensated during the ensuing petroleum boom. Indeed, the depth of worker dissatisfaction was already evident by the end of the López Portillo presidency (1976–82): the number of strike petitions filed in federal-jurisdiction economic activities more than doubled between 1981 and 1982, and the number of legally declared strikes in these industries was six times higher in 1982 than in the preceding year. The volume of strike petitions in federal-jurisdiction activities declined somewhat but remained very high in 1983 (see table 5.1). Thus de la Madrid's "Programa Inmediato de Reordenación Económica" ("Immediate Program for Economic Reordering," PIRE)[12] met almost immediate resistance from unions in many sectors, even as the CTM and the Labor Congress backed its broad goals.

With rank-and-file discontent growing, and under pressure to preserve its political leadership in the labor movement, the CTM adopted a more militant line. It called upon the government to index wage and price increases, and it sought a formal labor-government agreement establishing firm guidelines for managing the economic crisis. The confederation backed up its demands by appealing for support from other labor organizations, holding for the first time a joint May Day parade with politically independent university workers' unions and the Trotskyist Partido Revolucionario de los Trabajadores (Revolutionary Workers' Party). More important, it threatened a general strike if the de la Madrid administration failed to act favorably on its demands. In May and June 1983 the CTM brought pressure on the administration by coordinating a national wave of some fourteen thousand strike petitions.[13] President de la Madrid, however, sharply rebuffed the CTM's demands. He stated pointedly, "As president, I pledge that the national interest is above all other considerations; my position will not be affected by old styles of negotiation or pretensions to influence."[14]

State labor authorities used their administrative power over the union registration process to harass the CTM and remind the confederation of its dependence on state subsidies. They favored rival labor confederations (particularly the Revolutionary Confederation of Workers and Peasants, CROC, and the Mexican Regional Labor Confederation, CROM) in their unionization drives. In return, these organizations opposed the CTM's general strike proposal, accepted wage increases smaller than those sought by the CTM leadership, and openly backed the government's austerity policies.[15] Previous administrations had also manipulated the union registration process to achieve specific political objectives. Yet this strategy was even more effective at a time when economic conditions themselves seriously reduced labor's bargaining leverage. Government actions exacerbated divisions within the labor movement, and the Labor Congress proved unable to agree on the CTM's proposal for wage indexation. In June 1983 the CTM and the Labor Congress won an increase in the legal minimum wage (15.6 percent, far short of the 50 percent increase they had demanded) that was only slightly greater than the 12.5 percent increase the government had announced in December 1982.[16]

Most CTM affiliates reached agreements with employers before their June 1983 strike deadlines, and others struck but reached quick settlements after receiving modest wage increases. Some unions, however, aggressively pursued their demands. The de la Madrid administration took a particularly hard line in response to strikes by unions representing university employees and the Nuclear Industry Workers' Union (SUTIN). The university unions were compelled to suspend their strike without achieving a wage increase, and most nuclear power workers lost their jobs when the strike failed and the government closed Mexican Uranium, the state-owned firm in which they were employed.[17] These unions had often been at the forefront of past labor mobilizations. State labor authorities' handling of these strikes and other major labor conflicts seriously undermined unions' capacity to resist declining real wages and industrial restructuring in major state-owned enterprises. By eroding the influence of potential allies, the government's response also made it much more difficult for the CTM to build broad labor support for its policy positions.

The de la Madrid administration's response to the June 1983 labor mobilization epitomized its hard-line policy toward strikes. On average, the de la Madrid government approved only 1.8 percent of the strike petitions filed in federal-jurisdiction economic activities between 1983 and 1988. The recognition rate showed minimal year-to-year variation, ranging from 1.1 percent in 1987 to 2.7 percent in 1986. As a result, even though the volume of strike petitions remained high, the number of legally recognized strikes actually fell during the worst period of economic contraction, from a historical high of 675 in 1982 to 230 in 1983 (see table 5.1). The volume of both strike petitions and strikes declined in 1984–85 (the rate of inflation slowed somewhat in these years and there was modest economic growth, although real wages continued to fall) and rose in 1986 during a period of renewed recession. However, the number of strikes fell again between 1986 and 1987 even though the number of petitions increased sharply during 1987—the year that registered the highest annual inflation rate in Mexico's postrevolutionary history.

Tight state controls on labor mobilization and continued government intransigence prevented leading labor organizations from winning significant policy changes. In late 1983 the de la Madrid administration rejected the Labor Congress's proposal to suspend the value-added tax, freeze rents, and renegotiate collective contract terms and wage levels semiannually. Although the government later offered organized labor some very modest concessions (including postponing an increase in transportation fares), the de la Madrid austerity plan remained firmly in place.[18] In early 1984 the

CTM again threatened to call a general strike to secure an emergency wage increase, yet despite a wave of strike petitions filed by individual affiliates, no national mobilization occurred.

The CTM was eventually forced to shift the focus of its demands. Rather than merely opposing the government's austerity measures, in 1985 the confederation began to promote an alternative policy that would both protect workers from the effects of high inflation and reaffirm its historical role as an advocate of socially equitable development. The CTM's proposals included several demands that it had advanced since at least the late 1970s, including price-indexed wage increases, improved worker profit-sharing arrangements, and the nationalization of the food products industry. However, beginning in 1985 it placed new emphasis on protecting the "social wage." Specifically, it called for the creation of additional union-owned enterprises (especially union-owned stores providing access to basic commodities at low cost) that would form the core of an expanded social sector. The CTM identified the social sector as a key ideological and programmatic legacy of the Mexican revolution.[19]

A united Labor Congress backed this agenda, and the de la Madrid administration offered some concessions.[20] What was most important, however, was that the CTM's 1985 proposals signaled the "official" labor movement's willingness to negotiate with the government within parameters defined by the PIRE. By confining their demands to social welfare measures designed to ease the impact of economic crisis on workers, the CTM and the Labor Congress indicated both their commitment to a more conciliatory approach than they had adopted in 1983 and their desire to shape the broader debate on national development strategy. Nevertheless, their approach left in place the centerpiece of the de la Madrid stabilization program and the principal source of the economic difficulties workers suffered: nominal wage increases substantially lower than the rate of inflation.

The collapse of the Mexican stock market in November 1987 provoked renewed capital flight and forced the de la Madrid administration to devalue sharply the peso. This action unleashed a new wave of inflation and jeopardized the turn toward more conciliatory labor-government relations. In mid-December the Labor Congress threatened to mobilize its members in a general strike if the government did not immediately enact both an emergency wage hike (ranging in size from 46 percent in central Mexico to 133 percent along Mexico's border with the United States, where the inflation rate was highest) and a 32 percent national increase in minimum daily wages in January 1988, the date when the minimum wage would next be revised. State labor authorities and the private sector initially rejected these demands, insisting that any wage increase be negotiated by individual unions on a company-by-company basis.[21] However, as negotiations dragged on and the strike deadline neared, government officials agreed to control basic commodity prices, provide the Labor Congress with coupons that would permit its affiliated workers access to essential foodstuffs, and eliminate income taxes for workers earning up to twice the legal minimum wage.[22]

Faced with the imminent danger of hyperinflation, President de la Madrid expanded the scope of these negotiations on December 4, 1987, by calling for concerted labor-business action to resolve the country's economic problems. Private-sector representatives indicated that they were willing to reach a cooperative agreement with labor so long as the administration backed labor-business efforts to control inflation with cuts in government spending. The Labor Congress's conditions for supporting such an agreement were a 46 percent emergency wage increase retroactive to November 18 (the date of the devaluation); subsequent wage increases on a monthly basis; private-sector commitments to reinvest profits and emphasize job creation; effective government price controls; and a government guarantee that the process of industrial restructuring then under way would not increase unemployment or erode workers' legal rights.[23]

The CTM in particular was strongly opposed to further cuts in government spending and the continued sale of state-owned enterprises to private investors, and it lobbied vigorously for wage indexation.[24] Some internal dissension again surfaced within the labor movement (the CROC once more sided with the de la Madrid administration, arguing that the threatened general strike was ill advised). However, after complicated negotiations, government, labor, peasant, and business representatives signed the "Pacto de Solidaridad Económica" ("Economic Solidarity Pact," PSE) on December 15, 1987.[25]

The pact offered some concessions to labor, but they generally failed to meet the Labor Congress's principal demands.[26] Workers received only a modest emergency wage hike (a 15 percent increase in wages set by collective contract in December 1987, which was not retroactive as the Labor Congress had insisted) and a 20 percent increase in minimum wages in January 1988.[27] The de la Madrid administration also agreed to take several measures designed to rein in inflation, including controlling government deficit spending and making further cuts in import tariffs that would lower the cost of some consumer goods. Yet at the same time, the government also raised prices for public-sector goods and services (including electricity and gasoline) and basic commodities by as much as 80 percent.

Assessing the Economic Gains and Losses for Labor

The Economic Solidarity Pact proved to be a turning point in Mexico's economic adjustment program. The rate of inflation declined significantly in 1988 (from a monthly rate of 15.5 percent in January to 0.6 percent in September), and as a result President de la Madrid renewed the pact at regular intervals throughout the remainder of his term. The newly inaugurated Salinas administration reached a similar economic stabilization agreement with labor, business, and peasant organizations (known as the "Pacto para la Estabilidad y el Crecimiento Económico" ["Pact for Stability and Economic Growth," PECE]), which was also periodically renewed. The most important contribution these agreements made was to lower the annual rate of inflation from 131.8 percent in 1987 to 26.7 percent in 1990.[28] The negotiation of both these pacts and external debt rescheduling agreements also permitted the government to accelerate the pace of neoliberal economic reform after 1987.

Labor support for the *pactos* was crucial because it created the political conditions for successful economic stabilization in Mexico. However, the Economic Solidarity Pact and the subsequent agreements negotiated with the de la Madrid and Salinas administrations had mixed consequences for labor. Both the CTM and the Labor Congress had long demanded vigorous government action to control inflation, and the PSE and PECE did formally recognize organized labor's continuing importance in the governing coalition. Yet the concessions the de la Madrid administration made to labor under the original *pacto* appear to have been due more to organized labor's political importance during the 1987–88 presidential campaign than to a significant recovery of labor's longer-term bargaining leverage.

Even these modest gains had a very significant price: continued wage discipline by the Confederation of Mexican Workers and the Labor Congress. The wage increases authorized under the terms of the PSE in 1987–88 did not compensate workers for the post-1982 decline in real wages.[29] Moreover, the de la Madrid administration eliminated the pact's original provision for wage indexation (effective after March 1, 1988, until inflation fell to 2 percent per month) in February 1988 when the government stabilized the exchange rate and tightened price controls.[30] The pact did not require substantial changes in private-sector behavior,[31] nor did it alter the de la Madrid administration's commitment to promote broad economic transformation by privatizing state-owned firms.

Although the *pactos* produced some general benefits for workers (including lower inflation and reductions in income and value-added taxes) and had specific advantages for CTM or Labor Congress affiliates (expanded access to subsidized foodstuffs, worker housing, and financial credits, and government support for union-owned enterprises), they failed miserably to compensate workers for the effects of government wage policy during the 1980s. *Every* available indicator of wage performance recorded a decline during the period from 1983 through 1988. Total real wage income fell by a cumulative 40.0 percent during this same period. Total real nonwage income also declined, though by a lower 6.9 percent. Real average wages in the manufacturing sector fell by a cumulative total of 32.0 percent during 1983–88, before rising again in 1989.[32] Precipitous declines in real wages were a key reason why overall private consumption per capita in Mexico fell by a total of 11.1 percent between 1983 and 1988.[33]

Explaining Labor Strategy

The CTM's bargaining strategy during the worst years of economic crisis, then, did not depart from its long-established negotiating style. The CTM has conventionally pursued its goals through pragmatic intra-elite bargaining rather than open confrontation with state authorities. This negotiating pattern reflects the fact that organized labor's membership in Mexico's postrevolutionary governing coalition traditionally ensured it a degree of policy influence, as well as the reality of state administrative controls on labor participation and government-allied unions' heavy dependence on state subsidies. The CTM has sometimes threatened a general strike if the government fails to meet its economic demands. Yet the confederation has never led a nationally coordinated strike action. Instead, the CTM typically coordinates a wave of strike petitions to demonstrate its mobilizational potential and pressure state authorities, but then it relies upon individual affiliates to negotiate separately with employers to win the highest wage and benefit increase they can manage. The CTM's historical reluctance to pursue more aggressive collective action in support of workers' interests is one of the most noteworthy aspects of state-labor relations in Mexico.

The "official" Mexican labor movement's response to the challenges of the 1980s contrasted sharply with the tactics adopted by organized labor in other major Latin American countries when confronted with similar economic reverses in the wake of the 1982 debt crisis. Argentina's Confederación General de Trabajo (General Confederation of Labor, CGT), for example, led eight general strikes between December 1983 and early 1987 to protest the Alfonsín government's austerity program, its policy on foreign debt, its relations with the International Monetary Fund, and its efforts to oust entrenched labor leaders from major unions.[34] Even in Brazil, where broad labor support for the transition to civilian rule in 1985 made unions more hesitant to challenge a newly installed democratic government, the organized labor movement called brief general strikes in 1986 and 1987 to protest sharp price increases and higher unemployment.[35]

What explains leading Mexican labor organizations' continued pursuit during the 1980s of bargaining tactics that manifestly failed to protect workers' socioeconomic interests, and their apparent reluctance to challenge the de la Madrid administration more forcefully in order to promote their economic agenda? Prolonged economic crisis, especially higher unemployment rates in some industries and regions and greater job instability, undermined workers' capacity for resistance. At the same time, state labor authorities' tight control over strikes (especially in federal-jurisdiction industries) and their manipulation of the union registration process weakened unions' bargaining position and undercut labor movement unity. These factors may have effectively ruled out the option of more confrontational tactics. At the same time, the fact that some labor organizations (including the CTM) increased their political representation in the federal Chamber of Deputies during these years may have convinced key labor leaders that they would be positioned to recoup short-term losses at a later date.[36]

However, an explanation of organized labor's strategy during the worst years of the 1980s crisis must also address elements other than state administrative controls on different forms of labor participation, government-allied unions' continued dependence on state subsidies, and the impact of the economic crisis itself on labor's bargaining leverage. The two most important additional considerations are major labor organizations' internal weaknesses and the political beliefs of key labor leaders.

Despite its long political dominance in the Mexican labor movement, the CTM in the 1980s continued to suffer from significant organizational weaknesses that limited its mobilizational potential. Problems such as the comparatively small average size of CTM-affiliated unions and the concentration of CTM members in nonstrategic economic activities, the heterogeneous membership of CTM affiliates, and the frequent lack of effective representational structures linking local labor leaders with rank-and-file union members all compounded the CTM's difficulties in responding more effectively to government economic policies that harmed workers' interests. These organizational problems were of long standing, but the severity of the economic challenges confronting the CTM in the 1980s underscored their importance as never before.

The comparatively small average size of CTM unions is mainly a reflection of the dispersion of the Mexican working class as a whole. A 1978 analysis of the Labor Congress showed that the CTM's 731,015 members (32.7 percent of all unionized workers) were divided among 4,987 separate organizations.[37] The average size of CTM unions (147 members) was half the national average of 287 members per union (see table 4.2). Only 13.4 percent of the confederation's members were organized in more powerful national industrial unions, and only 12.2 percent of its affiliates worked in such key industries as electrical power generation (6.7 percent), the steel and metalworking industries (1.6 percent), the chemical industry (1.2 percent), the rubber industry (0.9 percent), automobile manufacturing (0.7 percent), mining (0.3 percent), and the petrochemical industry (0.1 percent).[38] The CTM's membership in the automobile industry increased in the 1980s as it won control over newly established export facilities in central and northern Mexico (see below), but declining employment in the manufacturing sector as a whole prevented the confederation from making similar advances in other important industrial activities. Although the CTM represented more unionized workers in the politically sensitive Federal District than any other single labor organization, the small average size of its affiliated unions and their concentration in nonstrategic industries constrained the confederation's ability to mobilize even this membership in support of its economic and political agenda.

The general weakness of representational arrangements at the workplace level also reduced the CTM's capacity to mobilize its members and closely coordinate their actions. The top-down orientation of the "official" labor movement and the resulting disjuncture between many labor leaders and rank-and-file union members necessitate arrangements such as the plant delegate system. The frequent absence of more formal workplace representational structures providing institutionalized opportunities for workers to participate in union affairs makes it easier for CTM leaders to control workers, but it also limits the national CTM leadership's ability to coordinate mobilization strategies effectively.

The CTM's national leadership has over the years taken some steps to correct these weaknesses. For example, in the early 1980s the CTM opened a union leadership training school, the Centro Obrero de Estudios Superiores (Labor Center for Advanced Studies), in Cuernavaca, Morelos, to provide selected candidates with instruction in economics, labor law, negotiating strategies, and leadership skills and thereby improve the quality of local union officials' performance in the workplace. Similarly, for many years Fidel Velázquez advocated the creation of national industrial unions that unite all workers in a single economic activity. In both instances, however, opposition from traditional state and regional federation leaders committed to established ways of conducting union affairs limited the effectiveness of reform efforts. Because Velázquez maintained broad unity within the CTM by generally respecting these leaders' autonomy, the national confederation had only a limited ability to impose reforms of this kind.

The political beliefs of key labor leaders also appear to have played an important role in shaping the "official" labor movement's response to economic crisis. Because of the hierarchical organization of the Mexican labor movement and the long dominance of Fidel Velázquez and his close allies over the CTM, his personal political views had a greater impact in this regard than those of any other union leader. Velázquez owed his personal success to the social and institutional changes produced by the Mexican revolution, and during his lifetime he witnessed a general improvement in working-class standards of living. As a result, he had an abiding loyalty to the postrevolutionary political order. As a seasoned political pragmatist, he preferred a conciliatory approach to resolving problems rather than mobilized confrontation with state authorities or the private sector. In part because of his personal experiences,[39] Velázquez understood that personal and organizational discipline was essential if organized labor was to preserve its long-term position in the established regime.

However, Velázquez also had other reasons to be wary of mass political mobilization. Because the CTM's membership is heterogeneous and sometimes only loosely organized, broad-based mobilization might offer political and labor rivals an opportunity to expand their own bases by making inroads in CTM-affiliated unions, perhaps leading to their secession. Moreover, loss of control over its members during a general strike would have deprived the CTM of its principal resource—its capacity to constrain rank-and-file demands—in negotiations with government officials during a period of economic crisis. Velázquez's apparent reluctance to endorse more aggressive labor action in the 1980s, then, may have reflected in part his sense that such tactics would only further erode the confederation's already weakened position.

It is more difficult to judge the degree to which Velázquez's advancing age may have affected either his willingness to challenge the de la Madrid administration's economic policies or his conduct of CTM affairs. Throughout the 1980s he remained in good physical and mental health, maintained an active schedule of private and public meetings, and traveled frequently throughout Mexico and abroad on CTM business. Moreover, in early 1992 Velázquez accepted another six-year term as CTM secretary-general. Nevertheless, some observers who knew Velázquez well over a long period recognized in the late 1980s that he was then a less forceful leader than in earlier years.[40]

State administrative controls on labor participation (especially strikes), internal organizational weaknesses, and the political orientation of key labor leaders together help explain why Mexico's "official" labor movement failed to oppose more aggressively the austerity measures and economic restructuring program implemented by the de la Madrid administration. The principal consequence was that the 1980s crisis produced a drop in Mexican workers' real wages nearly twice as severe as the Latin American average.[41] At the same time, however, it is important to note that the CTM's unflagging commitment to compromise and negotiated settlement of its differences with government policymakers permitted it to survive one of the most difficult periods in its history, a time when the combined effects of economic crisis and conservative government labor policies hurt some labor organizations even more badly. Indeed, as the next section shows, the CTM's continued position as the country's single most important labor organization permitted it to reap some organizational and political rewards from industrial restructuring.

Industrial Restructuring in the Automobile Industry: Democratic Unionism on the Defensive

The transformation in union politics and workplace labor relations that occurred in the automobile industry during the 1980s and early 1990s exemplified the challenges that Mexican workers faced as a result of the shift from import-substituting to export-led industrialization. Because automobile production is dominated by transnational firms facing global pressures to adopt more innovative production technologies and more flexible labor relations, industrial restructuring began earlier and proceeded more quickly in automobile manufacturing than in many Mexican industries. Nevertheless, parallel processes were also under way in other areas (including the telecommunications, steel, rubber, textile, and banking industries) during this period.[42] Developments in automobile manufacturing firms demonstrated that union democracy remains an important determinant of workers' capacity to influence the character of industrial change. Yet this case also shows the limits of enterprise- and plant-level worker action in an economic context that exposes labor to significant new challenges.

The Legacies of Union Democratization

The emergence and consolidation of democratic unionism in several automobile firms in the 1960s and 1970s posed significant challenges for employers. More frequent strikes and democratic unions' assertiveness in collective bargaining made the normal conduct of labor relations much more difficult. Even more important, however, increased union influence over the production process and limitations on the movement of personnel among different departments constrained managers' ability to respond flexibly to day-to-day shifts in production requirements. Similarly, a decline in the proportion of temporary workers (those employees hired for less than sixty days or for a specific task) in the labor force reduced firms' capacity to respond quickly to changing market conditions by dismissing redundant workers without paying costly separation indemnities. These issues were important in part because, as noted in chapter 6, the Ministry of Industry and Commerce administered both production quotas and price controls on finished vehicles from 1962 to 1977. As a result, wage and fringe benefit costs and control over the distribution of workers on the shop floor were of central importance to employers. Managers in automobile manufacturing firms with democratic unions responded to these challenges by vigorously contesting worker demands for increased wages and fringe benefits, employment security (especially the automatic promotion of temporary workers to permanent positions), and union influence over promotions and the production process. But over time, they were generally compelled to make important concessions in these areas.

However, General Motors and Nissan managers attempted to regain lost bargaining leverage through a different strategy: opening new manufacturing facilities in which the work force was affiliated with the Confederation of Mexican Workers, whose national political connections and generally cooperative attitude toward management permitted these companies to exercise strong control over plant-level labor relations. In what became an important precedent in the industry, General Motors founded an engine manufacturing plant in Toluca in 1965 and negotiated with the CTM to unionize the new labor force. By doing so, General Motors took advantage of government investment incentives for manufacturing operations established outside the highly congested Mexico City area, and it was able to hire workers at the lower wage rates prevailing in the region. Even more important, company managers eliminated union influence over various aspects of the production process, regained flexibility over the movement of personnel among different production areas and the use of temporary workers, and sharply reduced seniority-based labor costs by hiring a new work force. Although the union at General Motors' Federal District facility (affiliated with the CROC) went on strike to prevent management from abrogating a contract clause dating from 1955 that gave it legal representation of workers in any new plant established in the country, company managers won the union's acquiescence on this key point and settled the strike after only two days by offering to increase the number of permanent positions at the Federal District plant.[43] In 1978 Nissan replicated General Motors' stratagem by establishing a CTM-affiliated plant in Lerma, thus removing the labor force at its foundry operations from the legal control of the democratic union at its assembly plant in Cuernavaca. Both the General Motors and the Nissan work forces in the state of Mexico subsequently remained under tight CTM control, and neither plant experienced serious labor-management conflict.[44]

Despite gains by democratic unions and a recession in 1975–76, the Mexican automobile industry generally prospered during the 1970s. The value of automobile industry production grew at an average rate of 10.3 percent per year during 1975–81, and over the same period the automobile industry's (vehicles and auto parts) share of gross domestic product in manufacturing increased to 7.5 percent (at constant 1970 prices).[45] The total production of cars and trucks rose to 587,460 vehicles in 1981.[46] Automobile manufacturing in Mexico remained comparatively inefficient because of the number of firms producing a wide range of models destined primarily for a restricted national market. However, the 1978–81 petroleum-led economic boom greatly expanded domestic demand and temporarily eased such problems.

Economic Crisis and the Shift toward Export Production: The Political and Economic Consequences of Industry Reorganization

The onset of economic crisis in 1982 struck the automobile industry hard. The total production of cars and trucks fell by 51.6 percent between 1981 and 1983, and despite a partial recovery thereafter, the level of production in 1987 (395,258 vehicles) remained only slightly above that achieved in 1975.[47] Total employment in the seven principal vehicle manufacturing firms fell from 60,388 persons in 1981 to 51,676 persons in 1986, a decline of 14.4 percent; blue-collar employment (obreros) fell almost as sharply (by 12.5 percent) over this same period.[48] The dramatic contraction of the domestic market forced Ford to close two of its three plants in the Mexico City area between 1983 and 1986. Renault, which had acquired Vehículos Automotores Mexicanos (VAM) and Diesel Nacional's passenger car operations in 1983, stopped manufacturing vehicles in Mexico in 1986.

The crisis in the domestic automobile market compelled both the government and transnational firms to reassess the future of the industry. In September 1983 the de la Madrid administration issued a decree designed to improve industry efficiency by sharply limiting the number of permitted makes and models (beginning in 1987 each firm was limited to a single make and five models), increasing the domestic content for all automotive vehicles (to 60 percent for the 1987 model year), and encouraging exports.[49] Transnational firms in the vehicle manufacturing industry had long resisted constraints on the number of makes and models produced, but they had begun export production (especially engines and other automotive parts) in the late 1970s.[50] With the domestic market in crisis, these companies aggressively expanded automotive exports. Annual exports of finished vehicles rose from 15,819 to 155,983 units between 1982 and 1987, and exports of engines increased from 320,301 to 1,431,733 over the same period.[51] By the late 1980s, automobile companies operating in Mexico were firmly committed to export production.

The shift toward exports produced a significant spatial reorganization of the vehicle manufacturing industry. Chrysler (Ramos Arizpe, four-cylinder engines), General Motors (Ramos Arizpe, six-cylinder engines and automobiles), and Nissan (Aguascalientes, four-cylinder engines) opened new plants in central and northern Mexico in 1981. In some cases these facilities had originally been planned when hope for increasing domestic automobile sales was bright, but after 1982 they were dedicated primarily to export production. Ford (Chihuahua, four-cylinder engines, 1983; Hermosillo, automobiles, 1986) soon followed with its own export-production plants.[52] These northern sites were chosen mainly because of their geographical proximity to the United States, the intended export market, and the investment incentives available for locating new manufacturing facilities outside the Mexico City metropolitan area. For example, Ford received large subsidies from both federal and state governments for its Hermosillo plant,[53] and several firms used debt-equity swaps to finance their new operations.[54] Equally important, however, the construction of these plants in central and northern Mexico offered automobile companies important political advantages.

The Restoration of CTM Preeminence

By negotiating for the CTM to represent workers at these plants, transnational firms won far-reaching managerial control over industrial relations and the production process, and they placed democratic unionism on the defensive in the automobile industry. Chrysler's Ramos Arizpe labor force became part of the Sindicato Nacional de Trabajadores de la Industria Automotriz Integrada, Similares y Conexos de la República Mexicana (National Union of Automotive Industry Workers, the union formed to represent all three Chrysler plants in Mexico), while Ford's Chihuahua and Hermosillo work forces were organized as local sections of the Sindicato Nacional de Trabajadores de Ford Motor Company (National Union of Ford Motor Company Workers). Neither Chrysler nor Ford managers had any incentive to seek alternatives to their established CTM-affiliated national unions to organize the new northern plants. The Chrysler union (still led in the 1980s by Hugo Díaz, the former production manager the company had installed as union secretary-general in 1970) had not permitted a serious outbreak of rank-and-file discontent since 1969–70, and despite the Ford union's success in winning very favorable contract terms during the 1970s and early 1980s, Ford managers saw important advantages in preserving unified union representation of its workers.[55]

General Motors, on the other hand, was determined that its engine and automobile manufacturing plants at Ramos Arizpe have no organizational ties to the democratic, assertive union at its Federal District plant. In 1980 the Federal District union fought a bitter 106-day strike (the longest in the history of the Mexican automobile industry) for legal control of the General Motors sites in northern Mexico. However, management eventually prevailed, and the Federación Regional de Sindicatos de Saltillo (Regional Federation of Saltillo Unions, affiliated with the CTM's state federation in Coahuila) organized workers in the two facilities as separate plant-level unions.[56] Similarly, Nissan's labor force at its Aguascalientes plant was organized as part of the CTM's state federation in Aguascalientes.

Following the CTM's loss of influence in the industry in the 1960s and 1970s, the confederation's national leaders reformulated their approach to local-level labor relations in the new automobile plants established in central and northern Mexico. In particular, they made a concerted effort to upgrade the quality of CTM representatives. Local union advisers in these plants were often graduates of the confederation's Labor Center for Advanced Studies in Cuernavaca, where they acquired specialized expertise and the leadership skills necessary to manage a more educated labor force.[57] Moreover, national CTM leaders recognized the importance of establishing formal representational structures at the plant level, including elected union executive committees. Elected union representatives may demonstrate considerable autonomy from the CTM in internal decision making, but they enjoy much greater legitimacy vis-à-vis the rank and file than the appointed plant delegates traditionally in charge of local affairs in CTM-affiliated unions. Thus the national CTM leadership's clear preference was for local governance arrangements that permitted the effective representation of workers' economic interests while preserving overall CTM control.[58]

Nevertheless, national CTM leaders were not always able to impose their preferences on the confederation's constituent organizations. In practice, therefore, there was considerable diversity in the representational arrangements established at the new export-production plants. At all four General Motors and Ford northern plants during the 1980s, workers enjoyed important opportunities to participate in local union affairs.[59] There was regular turnover in elected union officials; rival slates of candidates often competed in union elections; and general assemblies were commonly held. Workers at each of the four plants received copies of the plant's collective labor contract for their inspection. On several occasions in the early

1980s, internal opposition movements overturned the executive committees at the General Motors–Ramos Arizpe engine and automobile manufacturing plants in disputes over the incumbents' conduct of union business. In addition, in 1986 the unions at these General Motors facilities established systems of departmental delegates in order to give the rank and file a larger role in union affairs. Rank-and-file opponents also succeeded in overthrowing the local executive committees at Ford's Chihuahua and Hermosillo facilities when the union leadership failed to respond to workers' economic and personnel concerns.[60]

Moreover, unions at all four Ford and General Motors plants exercised a degree of autonomy vis-à-vis their respective national union or state-level federation. In each case, the company provided paid full-time leave for several executive committee members (ranging from two in the General Motors plants to three at Ford-Chihuahua and four at Ford-Hermosillo) to facilitate union work. Although the national union took a leading role in contract and wage negotiations at the Ford plants, local union representatives were also involved. Indeed, the labor contract at Ford-Chihuahua provided three local representatives (in addition to three local executive committee members) paid full-time leave during contract revisions. At General Motors' Ramos Arizpe facilities, the state CTM federation was represented by trained union advisers who assisted the local executive committee in contract and wage negotiations.

In contrast, the CTM maintained tight control over workers at the Chrysler–Ramos Arizpe and Nissan-Aguascalientes plants through more traditional means.[61] Plant delegates appointed by the national union served as the principal intermediaries between workers and company managers at Chrysler–Ramos Arizpe, and the head of the CTM's Aguascalientes state federation also served as secretary-general of the Nissan-Aguascalientes union. Local union representatives were not involved in contract and wage negotiations at either plant during the 1980s. Nor were labor contracts distributed to workers. In short, the CTM reproduced in these two plants the traditional control mechanisms that served CTM and management interests so well before the wave of democratization movements which swept the industry in the 1960s and 1970s. These arrangements did not face serious rank-and-file challenges at either Chrysler–Ramos Arizpe or Nissan-Aguascalientes during the 1980s.

Despite this diversity in local union structures, CTM officials were united in their opposition to internal dissent. The separation exclusion clause generally included in Mexican labor contracts provides incumbent union leaders with a strong defense against rank-and-file challenges because the employer is legally required to dismiss any worker who is expelled from the officially recognized union. CTM officials and company managers colluded to fire the entire union executive committee at General Motors' Ramos Arizpe engine plant in 1985 when these local leaders aggressively pressed economic demands. Similarly, incumbent union leaders at Ford's Hermosillo plant compelled management to dismiss four activist workers in 1987.[62]

Maintaining control over automobile workers in these export-production plants served the interests of both company managers and CTM officials. For employers, the unionization of a labor force under CTM auspices offered greater stability in day-to-day labor relations and fewer political risks than did a nonunion work force. The representational monopoly that federal labor law confers on a legally recognized union made it more difficult for rival labor and political groups to establish a presence in the workplace, and incumbent union leaders could readily use the separation exclusion clause to defend their position against internal challengers. For CTM leaders, representation of an important industrial labor force constituted a major political and economic resource. Workers at automobile plants often constituted a significant proportion of a state federation's total membership, and a larger membership base increased the federation's political influence at state and national levels. In addition, the CTM derived important economic benefits from the automatic deduction of workers' union dues. In some cases, CTM affiliation offered federation leaders special opportunities for financial gain. For example, labor contracts at all three Chrysler plants in Mexico in the 1980s required that workers' life insurance policies be subscribed from a firm selected by the leadership of Section 23 of the CTM's Federal District Workers' Federation.[63]

The Economic Consequences of Industry Reorganization

In addition to construction subsidies and reliable control over worker-employer relations under CTM auspices, transnational firms gained other important economic advantages by founding new manufacturing facilities in central and northern Mexico. Because these plants were generally located in low-wage areas without significant concentrations of heavy manufacturing, companies were able to hire workers at wage and fringe benefit levels substantially below those in established automobile plants in and around Mexico City. For example, in 1988 workers' daily wages at General Motors' and Nissan's new plants were approximately 40 percent lower than in their older facilities in and around Mexico City. An analysis of collective contracts for the automobile industry shows that both the range and level of fringe benefits normally available to individual workers also differed significantly between older and newer plants.[64] Because seniority-based fringe benefit payments are smaller for newly hired labor forces, automobile companies' total labor costs were also lower than in older manufacturing facilities. Moreover, during the 1980s the work-week was from one to eight hours longer in the newer export-production plants than in a given firm's facility in central Mexico.

Workers at the Ford and General Motors export-production plants lobbied strenuously for improved wages and fringe benefits. Indeed, disparities in wage and benefit levels between newer and older manufacturing facilities became an important issue in worker-employer negotiations at Ford and General Motors.[65] Wage and contract negotiations at these plants were normally accompanied by formal strike petitions, and workers at Ford-Chihuahua (in 1983, 1986, and 1988), Ford-Hermosillo (in 1987), and General Motors–Ramos Arizpe (automobiles and engines in 1982, and automobiles in 1986) struck for periods ranging from eleven to thirty-nine days in support of their economic demands.[66] But because workers at these plants were originally hired at wage and benefit levels far below those prevailing at older manufacturing facilities, this gap will close only gradually even if workers enjoy some success in bargaining with employers.

Events at Ford's Cuautitlán plant in 1987 bluntly demonstrated how the shift toward export production and state authorities' support for industrial restructuring dramatically altered the terms of worker-employer bargaining.[67] In July 1987, workers at the plant demanded payment of the 23 percent national emergency wage increase the de la Madrid government had recently authorized. Although Ford had granted the increase to its workers in Chihuahua and Hermosillo, company managers refused to do so at Cuautitlán. They argued that if the plant was to remain competitive in national and international markets, the union local had to make economic concessions and accept changes in work rules designed to increase productivity and bring labor costs into line with those at the company's northern facilities and other Mexican producers. When the union suspended work in support of its demands, Ford managers ended the bitter sixty-one-day strike by firing the entire Cuautitlán labor force, temporarily closing the plant (with the tacit support of the CTM's Fidel Velázquez and the de la Madrid administration, which was willing to permit this politically sensitive action in the name of greater industry efficiency), and then rehiring twenty-five hundred of its original workers under terms that were very favorable to management. These dramatic actions allowed Ford to implement contract modifications that greatly increased production flexibility and permitted it to recover its considerable separation indemnity costs in a single year. After October 1987, wage and fringe benefit levels at Cuautitlán were much closer to those at Ford's northern plants.

Angry workers ousted the union secretary-general who had signed the new contract, and a significant proportion of the Cuautitlán work force fought for several years to restore previous wage and benefit levels and contract terms. They staged work stoppages and held street demonstrations in downtown Mexico City, prompting Ford managers to fire the protest leaders. One worker was killed and nine were wounded in January 1990 when some two hundred armed CTM strikebreakers forcibly attempted to oust workers who had stopped production by occupying the plant. Police finally ended the plant occupation, and Ford fired large numbers of workers in February 1990. However, despite the fact that dissenting workers overthrew a second union secretary-general and drew national and international attention to their cause, they made little progress toward realizing their core demands (a revised contract and the reinstatement of workers who had been fired). An attempt to break ties with the CTM and join a rival labor confederation met stiff resistance from CTM leaders, Ford management, and Ministry of Labor and Social Welfare officials. Dissident workers eventually won the right to hold a formal vote on the matter, but the June 1991 vote in which the CTM narrowly retained control over the Cuautitlán contract was held under conditions (open ballots signed by workers in the presence of Ford representatives and a large police force) that favored the company and the CTM.

Post-Fordist Labor Relations and Transnational Firms' Search for Flexible Production

Transnational firms' attempts to redefine workplace industrial relations were a core element of the restructuring process in the Mexican automobile manufacturing industry. Beginning in the early 1980s, Ford, General Motors, Nissan, Volkswagen, and Chrysler all implemented post-Fordist labor relations arrangements at their production facilities throughout Mexico.[68] The initiative for this new approach to industrial relations in the Mexican automobile industry usually came from each company's home office. However, local managers perceived such arrangements as quality circles and work teams to be important elements in their campaign to maximize production efficiency, diffuse worker-employer tensions by improving communications and increasing worker participation in production decisions, and achieve internationally competitive levels of quality control in export programs. This section examines different automobile firms' use of post-Fordist strategies and their relative significance in the managerial drive for flexible production.

Individual firms introduced post-Fordist arrangements in different combinations at their various manufacturing facilities.[69] For example, Ford first established quality circles at its Cuautitlán plant in 1981–82; work teams were introduced in the mid-1980s. Ford-Chihuahua employed work teams, quality circles, and worker rotation among different production areas after the plant opened in 1983.[70] General Motors introduced work teams (with eight to twelve workers in each one) and quality circles at its Ramos Arizpe automobile and engine plants in 1985; similar measures were adopted at its Toluca and Federal District plants later the same year. Nissan created quality circles at its Aguascalientes, Lerma, and Cuernavaca plants in 1983 as part of its "Shop Floor Management Reform Program." Work teams (with six to eight persons in each team) followed in 1987–88. By 1987 Volkswagen had also organized work teams and quality circles in some departments. Chrysler implemented both work teams and quality circles at its Toluca facility in the mid-1980s but only work teams at its Ramos Arizpe plant.[71]

In contrast to the gradual incorporation of post-Fordist concepts at most production facilities, Ford created a fully integrated new labor relations system at its Hermosillo plant when it opened in 1987. The system (designed in collaboration with its Japanese partner, Mazda) featured flexible work rules, regular job rotation, broadly defined job classifications, work teams, and quality circles. Promotions were based not on seniority but on demonstrated technical proficiency and proven versatility at different tasks, and the requirements for promotion included mandatory rotation among specified production areas. An individual's work team, area supervisor, union representative, and training coordinator (in that order) were all required to approve promotion to a higher job level.[72] A worker first had to attempt to resolve a grievance through his or her work group and production specialist before taking the problem to a union representative.[73] Ford managers sought to reduce workplace tensions and motivate workers so that they functioned well in a state-of-the-art manufacturing environment, maintaining internationally competitive productivity and quality levels.

The ease with which firms were able to implement post-Fordist arrangements in different manufacturing plants during the 1980s depended mainly upon the character of union governance and labor force characteristics.[74] General Motors faced no resistance to these measures at its Ramos Arizpe facilities, where a young work force without significant industrial experience was organized by CTM-affiliated unions. These were the only General Motors plants in Mexico where management introduced "pay by knowledge" compensation arrangements and a nonseniority promotion system in the 1980s. In marked contrast, the older and more experienced, democratically governed labor force at General Motors' Federal District plant resisted managers' efforts to redefine work rules and downplay the established role of seniority. The local union also perceived work teams and quality circles to be a threat to its own authority. As a result, General

Motors managers were unable during the 1980s to introduce there compensation and promotion systems like those in place in Ramos Arizpe.

Similarly, Nissan managers encountered no serious obstacles to the introduction of post-Fordist arrangements at either their Aguascalientes or Lerma plants, where workers were organized by the CTM. However, a combative, democratic union representing an older work force at the company's Cuernavaca plant vigorously resisted the adoption of flexible work rules and the creation of work teams after 1987. When company managers proposed a Japanese-style program of thirteen physical exercises before work each morning, the union demanded that attendance be voluntary and that participating workers be paid overtime. This kind of persistent union resistance also initially limited the adoption of post-Fordist strategies at Volkswagen's Puebla plant.[75]

Where they were implemented, company managers were convinced that post-Fordist industrial relations arrangements contributed to increased communications on the shop floor and improved quality control. For example, Ford managers argued that a new approach to industrial relations was necessary at the Hermosillo facility because extensive automation and the complexity of computer-assisted technologies demanded more cooperative, flexible workplace relations. The use of post-Fordist arrangements helped Ford's Chihuahua plant win the company's coveted "Q1" award for quality in 1987.[76] In the case of General Motors, this approach helped the Toluca engine plant and the Ramos Arizpe automobile plant achieve the highest levels of quality control in the company's global network of manufacturing facilities.[77] The use of post-Fordist approaches also remedied specific problems at General Motors. The introduction of work teams at the Ramos Arizpe automobile and engine plants in 1985 led to a sharp decline in industrial accidents and substantially reduced personnel turnover. As a result, the team concept was welcomed by workers.[78]

However, during the 1980s the principal source of managerial flexibility in organizing the production process lay in the labor contracts companies negotiated with CTM-affiliated unions rather than in post-Fordist arrangements such as work groups. Table 7.1 presents a content analysis of labor contracts for the five principal transnational firms operating in the Mexican automobile manufacturing industry in the late 1980s. The central question examined here is whether, and to what degree, labor unions exercised influence over three key areas of industrial relations: promotion procedures and policies affecting employment security, rules governing the production process, and plant-level conflict resolution procedures.

The absence of a single national automobile workers' union in Mexico and the heterogeneity of CTM affiliates permitted considerable variation

TABLE 7.1 Comparative Evaluation of Workplace Relations in Major Mexican Automobile Manufacturing Firms, 1985–1988

	Chrysler			Ford		General Motors				Nissan			Volkswagen
	Federal District Toluca	Ramos Arizpe	Cuau-titlán	Chihua-hua	Hermo-sillo	Federal District	Toluca	Ramos Arizpe (Autos)	Ramos Arizpe (Engines)	Cuerna-vaca	Lerma	Aguas-cal-ientes	Puebla
Promotion Procedures and Employment Security													
Union participation in hiring and promotions	0	0	3	0	1	4	0	2	1	4	0	0	3
Specification of promotion criteria	0	0	0	2	4	4	1	2	2	4	0	0	4
Automatic promotion of temporary workers or other limitations on their number	0	1	1	0	0	4	2	0	1	4	0	0	2
Other job security provisions	1	1	1	1	0	4	2	2	2	4	0	0	2
Subtotal	1	2	5	3	5	16	5	6	6	16	0	0	11
Production Process													
Union participation in determination of production rate	0	0	1	0	1	3	1	1	1	4	0	0	2

Union control over work force distribution within plant	0	0	0	0	4	0	2	2	0	4
Equalization of wage categories	1	1	4	1	3	4	1	3	1	3
Union participation in occupational health and safety measures	0	0	3	1	4	0	0	4	0	4
Subtotal	1	1	8	2	14	5	4	13	2	13
Conflict Resolution Procedures										
Specification of procedures, labor-management authorities, time periods for resolution of workplace conflicts	0	0	4	1	3	1	1	4	1	4
Total	2	3	17	6	33	11	11	33	3	28

Sources: 1988 labor contracts for Chrysler–Ramos Arizpe, Ford-Hermosillo, General Motors–Toluca, General Motors–Ramos Arizpe (both automobile and engine plants), Nissan-Cuernavaca, and Nissan-Aguascalientes; 1987 labor contracts for Chrysler–Federal District, Chrysler-Toluca, Ford-Cuautitlán, General Motors–Federal District; 1986 labor contracts for Ford-Chihuahua and Volkswagen-Puebla; 1985 labor contract for Nissan-Lerma.

Note: The numerical values listed in the table refer to the following code:

0 = No special benefits or provisions beyond those set by federal labor law

1 = Very limited measures

2 = Moderate protection or union participation

3 = Extensive protection or active union participation

4 = Very extensive protection or active union participation in formal institutional mechanisms or specified procedures

in labor contracts among both different firms and a single firm's separate production facilities. However, the data presented in table 7.1 indicate that democratically governed unions affiliated with labor organizations other than the CTM generally had greater influence over promotion procedures and the conditions of employment, the production process, and workplace conflict resolution than did CTM affiliates.[79] In the late 1980s, the unions at General Motors–Federal District and Nissan-Cuernavaca played a very active role in hiring and promotion decisions. At Nissan's Cuernavaca plant, for example, the sons and brothers of union members received preference in hiring. In both plants, union delegates had equal representation with management on the commission that supervised promotions; seniority was the principal criterion affecting promotion decisions. At General Motors' Federal District facility, the union had won contractual terms that specified the percentage of the work force in different skill classifications and wage levels, thus guaranteeing regular promotion for workers and preventing management from holding employees at low-level classifications.[80]

Similarly, the unions at General Motors–Federal District and Nissan-Cuernavaca had won job security provisions for workers which were far more favorable than the separation benefits provided by federal labor law. At General Motors' Federal District facility, the contract imposed heavy financial penalties on the company if managers closed the plant, and management could not reduce the number of permanent (*planta*) positions during the life of the contract. A worker whose employment at the plant was interrupted for up to ninety days could return to his or her former job without loss of seniority.[81] Unions at both plants were also actively involved in protecting workers' occupational health and safety, and they had succeeded in creating institutionalized conflict resolution procedures (workers' rights, time periods for grievance resolution, and other issues were all clearly defined) in which union representatives were fully involved.[82]

Even more important, these democratic unions had in different ways won broad influence over the production process itself. Over time, unions at the General Motors–Federal District and Nissan-Cuernavaca plants had negotiated contractual restrictions on management's use of temporary workers by limiting the permitted number of *eventuales*, by requiring their automatic promotion to *planta* positions after a specified period, or both. These contract provisions increased the union's bargaining leverage by limiting the firm's flexible use of labor and by preventing company managers from manipulating *eventuales'* job insecurity to their political advantage in negotiations with the union.[83]

In addition, the General Motors and Nissan unions participated extensively in decisions affecting the rate of production. The General Motors–

Federal District contract required that one meter be maintained between vehicles on the assembly line, and any changes in the work pace required advance approval from the union. At Nissan-Cuernavaca, union representatives met regularly with company managers on a special commission charged with maintaining a "normal" work rate, and the contract obligated management to train union representatives in time-and-motion procedures in order to allow them to make informed judgments in this area.[84] Finally, the General Motors–Federal District and Nissan-Cuernavaca unions exercised considerable influence over the movement of workers among different production areas, thus limiting managerial discretion in the organization of production. Contracts at these plants stipulated the conditions under which such transfers were permitted (generally limiting them to one to three days) and guaranteed workers the wage corresponding to the new position.[85]

Unions at all other automobile plants in Mexico exercised considerably less influence in these areas. Indeed, the contracts at Chrysler's three production facilities and Nissan's Aguascalientes and Lerma plants provided company managers with virtually unrestricted control over hiring and promotions, the use of temporary workers, the determination of production rates, and the movement of employees among different departments on the shop floor. Even though the CTM's reformulated approach to labor relations at Ford's and General Motors' northern export-production plants permitted workers new opportunities to participate in union affairs, local unions had little control over promotion procedures and the conditions of employment, the production process, or conflict resolution procedures. Tight CTM control over contract negotiations in these plants reduced the prospects that workers might eventually increase their influence vis-à-vis management in these areas; after all, company managers and CTM federation leaders successfully preserved a labor contract highly favorable to management interests at General Motors' Toluca facility from 1965 through the late 1980s.

Until 1992, contract terms and worker-employer relations at Volkswagen's Puebla plant more closely resembled those at General Motors–Federal District and Nissan-Cuernavaca than those at the newer, CTM-organized production facilities in central and northern Mexico (see table 7.1). The Volkswagen union had been somewhat less successful than its General Motors–Federal District and Nissan-Cuernavaca counterparts at improving workers' employment security or gaining influence over the rate of production. Nevertheless, it played a very active role in hiring and promotion decisions, exercised strong influence over the movement of workers among different production areas within the plant, and inhibited management's use of temporary workers by winning contract provisions requiring

Volkswagen to pay a bonus to *eventuales* who were not rehired at the end of their contracts.[86] During the 1980s Volkswagen managers had pressured the union for contract concessions that would grant them more flexible control over the use of labor and the production process. However, the fact that Volkswagen (alone among Mexican automobile producers) had not geographically dispersed its production facilities increased the combative, democratically governed union's capacity to resist these pressures. In 1987 the Volkswagen union waged a successful fifty-seven-day strike to prevent management from imposing extensive contract modifications and wage and personnel cuts.[87]

The Volkswagen union also initially appeared to prevail in contract negotiations in 1992. A brief strike ended on July 2 with a new labor-management agreement that made no significant changes in contract terms and gave workers a 20 percent wage increase. However, midlevel union officials soon discovered that the union's senior leadership had also signed a side agreement *(convenio)* with company representatives that completely redefined established work rules at Volkswagen, making twenty-five-member work teams the central element in the industrial relations system. The agreement made training, demonstrated skill in a given job assignment, and rotation among different work areas (that is, factors other than seniority) the principal criteria in promotions. More remarkable still, the *convenio* gave Volkswagen the unrestricted right to alter any existing contract provision in order to make the new system of work teams successful.[88] Apart from the fact that it was kept secret, what outraged the union's elected department and section delegates was that the side agreement threatened to undermine their authority to resolve worker-employer grievances on the shop floor (the work teams were to be headed by company-appointed administrative personnel *[empleados de confianza]*, who under federal labor law were not subject to union control) and simultaneously to increase their work load (the number of workers for which each delegate was responsible rose from 100 to 379).[89]

In late July 1992, department and section delegates led a rank-and-file revolt against the incumbent union secretary-general which shut down manufacturing operations.[90] Volkswagen managers responded to the intra-union struggle with a lockout, and they petitioned the Federal Conciliation and Arbitration Board (JFCA) for the right to abrogate the collective work agreement and suspend the existing terms of employment at the plant. In a highly controversial ruling issued on August 17, 1992, the board found that the internal union conflict constituted force majeure and therefore approved Volkswagen's petition. The company, in a reenactment of Ford's actions at Cuautitlán in 1987, immediately fired all 14,200 workers and imposed a new contract. Although Volkswagen later selectively rehired workers without a cut in wages or fringe benefits, they lost accumulated seniority rights. Moreover, the new contract dramatically increased managerial control over the production process, the transfer of workers among different departments, and the hiring and promotion of employees. The union also lost legal control over any new production facility that Volkswagen might establish in Mexico, opening the way for the company to preserve future bargaining leverage vis-à-vis its Puebla union by replicating the stratagem so successfully employed by other automobile firms.

At the same time, the union adopted new statutes that extended the term of the incumbent secretary-general and increased the executive committee's authority over union affairs. Francisco Hernández Juárez, leader of the Mexican Telephone Workers' Union, played a key role in smoothing the adoption of the new contract and negotiating changes in union governance. His efforts were rewarded when, after a delay of more than two years, the Ministry of Labor and Social Welfare granted official recognition to his Federación de Sindicatos de Empresas de Bienes y Servicios (Federation of Goods and Services Unions, FESEBES). The grateful leaders of the Volkswagen union brought their substantial membership into the FESEBES in December 1992.

The JFCA's decision in this highly publicized conflict reflected the Salinas de Gortari administration's strong support for industrial restructuring. In the early 1990s Volkswagen was Mexico's largest vehicle manufacturer, with a 1991 production of more than 200,000 cars. It exported both cars and auto parts to Germany. Even more important, in 1991 the company had announced an ambitious U.S.$1.1 billion expansion program featuring its Puebla facility as the base for export production for the entire North American market. The preamble to the July 1992 labor-management *convenio* justified the introduction of post-Fordist industrial relations arrangements by referring to the proposed North American Free Trade Agreement, thus explicitly linking the company's demands for contract flexibility to one of the Salinas administration's highest political priorities.

The Volkswagen case underscored the importance that transnational firms attached to contract flexibility. In addition to facilitating the introduction of post-Fordist labor relations arrangements, contract flexibility offers firms two other major advantages. First, the absence of contractually specified union participation in decisions affecting the production process greatly simplifies company managers' work and significantly increases the opportunity costs of collective worker resistance to managers' day-to-day actions. In firms with little union influence over workplace relations, supervisors need not negotiate with union representatives on such issues as the movement of personnel on the shop floor, hiring temporary workers, or introducing new technologies or other changes in the production process. Second, flexible contract terms may be even more important than low wages to production efficiency in capital-intensive, highly automated plants because they permit managers to utilize labor fully. In facilities of this kind, labor costs generally represent a low proportion of the total product value added in the manufacturing process, yet high depreciation and start-up costs make it imperative that managers avoid work stoppages or other labor disruptions that reduce the productivity of capital.[91]

Shaiken's study of Ford's Chihuahua engine plant offers the best available test of the relative importance during the 1980s of post-Fordist arrangements and labor contract terms in providing flexible managerial control over the production process. In planning the Chihuahua facility, Ford managers carefully studied Japanese automobile firms' manufacturing techniques and adopted from them such concepts as broadly defined job classifications, job rotation, and promotion based on the mastery of specified tasks rather than seniority.[92] However, when asked to assess the factors that accounted for the facility's high efficiency and internationally competitive product quality, plant supervisors emphasized the great flexibility that the existing contract gave them to control the production process and move employees among different work areas as needed. One industrial relations manager even argued that the contract provided the plant "more flexibility than any other [company] plant in the world."[93] When negotiating the work agreement, Ford's CTM-affiliated union accepted the company's calls for far-reaching managerial flexibility in the new plant. During the 1980s the union had only a limited presence on the shop floor—prompting one plant manager to remark, "As far as I'm concerned there is no union here."[94]

Conclusion

The economic crisis of the 1980s had enduring consequences for Mexican workers in general and the organized labor movement in particular. Under the pressures of financial collapse and prolonged economic stagnation, the de la Madrid administration significantly reduced the consumption subsidies and social welfare benefits on which the working-class population had depended for an important proportion of its total income. The impact was immediately evident in the form of declining real wages and incomes and a substantial erosion of workers' standard of living. Equally important, economic crisis compelled the de la Madrid administration to reorient Mexican development strategy, a shift that led to rapid industrial restructuring in both the public and private sectors. Privatization of state-owned enterprises and economic reorganization in private companies often led to lower wage and fringe benefit levels, job losses, and the erosion or abrogation of contract rights that unions had won over the course of many years.

The consequences of the shift from import-substituting industrialization to export-oriented production were especially visible in the automobile industry, where transnational firms (backed, most notably in the Ford-Cuautitlán and Volkswagen cases, by strong government support) aggressively redefined contract terms and work rules in order to expand their control over the production process and increase manufacturing efficiency.

Most labor organizations emerged from the 1980s in a substantially weaker position vis-à-vis both private enterprise and the state. Not only did prolonged economic stagnation reduce unions' market-based bargaining leverage with employers, but the privatization of state-owned firms also undermined major national unions' ability to use their political importance to achieve their economic goals. Strong state action against strikes led by unions representing nuclear power, electrical power generation, and airline pilots in 1987–88 seriously eroded (and in the case of the SUTIN, eliminated) their capacity to serve as leaders of broader labor protest movements.[95] In the automobile industry as well, industrial restructuring and actions by state labor authorities undercut the position of democratic unions that had played a prominent part in the labor insurgency of the early and mid-1970s. The vulnerability of automobile workers was accentuated by the fact that their unions are enterprise- or plant-specific, a form of union organization that substantially increases the obstacles to industry-wide labor mobilization. But in the face of determined state support for rapid restructuring in a key export industry, it is unlikely that even a democratically governed national automobile workers' union would have been an adequate guarantee of rank-and-file interests on the shop floor.

The Confederation of Mexican Workers and other leading labor organizations were unable to prevent cutbacks in consumption subsidies and welfare benefits, the decline in workers' real wages, the privatization of state-owned firms, or the shift away from industrial production for a protected domestic market. As a result, developments during the 1980s eroded some of the underlying conditions and much of the substantive content of the social pact that had existed between organized labor and the governing political elite since the 1950s. Nevertheless, as the CTM's role in the automobile industry during this period demonstrated, state-subsidized labor organizations retained their significance as important instruments of political control over workers. They therefore proved crucial to the success of both government economic stabilization policies and private employers' efforts to restructure workplace industrial relations and increase their competitiveness in a more open economy. Thus even as its social content changed, there remained a core reason for the governing elite to preserve an alliance with organized labor.

CHAPTER EIGHT

Conclusion: Labor Politics and Regime Change in Mexico

The successful consolidation of a governing coalition in which organized labor was a major partner infused Mexico's postrevolutionary authoritarian regime with remarkable resilience. This is a key reason why urban and industrial workers' entry into national politics was among the most important consequences of Mexico's 1910–20 social revolution. The overthrow of the Díaz regime offered workers unprecedented opportunities to organize unions and build alliances to achieve their political and socioeconomic objectives. In addition, organized labor's presence in the political arena helped redefine the character of elite-mass interactions by creating new opportunities for the competitive mobilization of support and by reformulating standards of political legitimacy. But as in most revolutionary situations, mass mobilization and structural transformation in Mexico gave rise to a new form of authoritarian rule as the revolutionary leadership strove to expand and centralize political power. Establishing effective political control over organized labor was a crucial step in this process.

Mexican politics in the 1990s still reflected the legacy of strategies that revolutionary leaders pursued to institute political control over worker participation. As chapter 2 demonstrated, successive presidential administrations significantly expanded the state's administrative capacity to mediate labor participation. Most working-class organizations viewed favorably the growth of state authority over labor affairs, a position that was reinforced by the inclusion of Article 123 and its broad guarantees of labor rights in the 1917 federal constitution. Labor groups considered state involvement essential to implementing constitutionally mandated reforms at a time when most workers lacked sufficient bargaining leverage in the workplace to realize their political and social rights. Moreover, agencies such as conciliation and arbitration boards (on which workers themselves participated) offered workers important channels outside the workplace through which to redress their grievances.

Yet labor support for state activism was selective. Workers sought government action to compel employers to recognize unions, sign collective contracts, and improve wages and working conditions, but they opposed laws and regulations that restricted their autonomy in relation to the state. Although the labor movement won some important concessions, it lacked sufficient influence to prevail in many of the debates that occurred during and after the revolution concerning the appropriate extent of state involvement in labor-capital relations. Over time, Mexico's governing political elite was able to impose legal restrictions on such centrally important forms of worker participation as union formation, internal union activities, and strikes. These restrictions—backed by the political elite's effective control over the means of coercion and state officials' willingness to use force when necessary to achieve their objectives—established the de jure and de facto parameters of labor action.

At the same time, the new ruling elite forged a durable alliance with major elements of the organized labor movement. Many working-class organizations, especially those with a base in key industries that gave them a relatively strong labor market position and considerable bargaining leverage with employers, were wary of ties to state authorities or political parties which might compromise their autonomy. However, triumphant revolutionary leaders' acceptance of labor as a legitimate political force, their advocacy of revolutionary nationalist ideals and their willingness to make some policy concessions on matters of vital importance to workers, and their harsh opposition to labor radicals all encouraged the emergence of pragmatic labor leaders open to a close collaborative relationship with the governing elite. At different times, two dominant national labor organizations—the Mexican Regional Labor Confederation (CROM) during the 1920s and the Confederation of Mexican Workers (CTM) from 1936 onward—gave specific form to labor's alliance with the political elite. In particular, CTM membership in Mexico's "official" governing party symbolized labor support for the postrevolutionary order.

Participation in Mexico's postrevolutionary governing coalition permitted many labor organizations to win both significant material benefits for their members (including access to government-financed housing, health care, low-cost consumer goods, and a legally mandated share of enterprise profits) and representation in important elective and administrative offices. However, the combination of state administrative controls on labor participation, selective repression, and many unions' heavy dependence on state-provided legal, financial, and political subsidies allowed the ruling political elite to define (and redefine) the terms of its alliance with labor. The principal value that labor organizations have had historically for Mexico's ruling political elite is their capacity to constrain workers' eco-

nomic demands and block worker mobilization during periods of actual
or potential economic and political instability. For this reason, the ability
of "official" labor organizations to preserve their preferential access to
state resources has depended primarily on their willingness to control the
actions of rank-and-file union members. Understanding the political role
played by the state-subsidized labor movement is, then, especially important to unraveling the paradox of social revolution in the Mexican case—
that is, to explaining how revolutionary mass mobilization gave rise to a
durable authoritarian regime in which the governing elite has maintained a
strong base of popular support while simultaneously imposing significant
constraints on mass participation.

Characterizing Mexico as a postrevolutionary authoritarian regime
highlights the distinctive features of Mexican authoritarianism and points
to the value of both state-centered and society-centered explanations of
elite political control over labor participation. The introductory chapter in
this book defined postrevolutionary authoritarian regimes as a distinctive
form of authoritarian rule on the basis of the prominence of mass actors in
the governing coalition, the legitimating role of political ideas associated
with the revolutionary experience, and the dual importance of a hegemonic party and a strong, interventionist state. Chapter 1 also developed
an analytic framework that identified limitations on mobilization, sociopolitical pluralism, and demand articulation as the principal dimensions
of elite control over mass participation in postrevolutionary authoritarian
regimes. These categories are relevant to the study of mass politics in authoritarian regimes in general. However, because the crisis of participation
is particularly acute in revolutionary situations, the specific strategies that
revolutionary leaders adopt in response to this challenge often differ significantly from the approaches that elites in other authoritarian regimes
pursue to control mass participation.

In the Mexican case, control over lower-class actors has rested primarily on the ruling elite's exercise of state power. In the labor sector, state
administrative capacity to regulate worker-employer relations and enforce
legal restrictions on different forms of worker participation contributed
greatly to the governing elite's relative decision-making autonomy. The
analysis in chapter 5 of labor strikes, union formation, and worker grievances filed before conciliation and arbitration boards demonstrated the
central importance of the state administrative apparatus as an instrument
of elite control over labor participation. Between the late 1930s and the
early 1990s the degree of control exercised through administrative structures varied depending upon the form of worker participation at issue.
(For example, there was much tighter control over strikes than over union
formation or individual worker demands filed before conciliation and arbi-

tration boards.) In some areas, the extent of state administrative control also varied over time.

Yet chapter 5 also revealed the limits of a state-centered explanation of elite control over worker participation. Because Mexico's authoritarian regime originated in a broad process of popular mobilization and because mass actors historically played a major role in the postrevolutionary governing coalition, it is important to focus as well on the character and actions of labor organizations themselves. The case studies of union politics in the railroad transportation (chapter 4) and automobile manufacturing (chapters 6 and 7) industries showed how significant state-subsidized labor organizations have been to the preservation of elite political control in Mexico. In both sectors, government-allied labor leaders were frequently able to use their political connections and command over organizational space to defeat opposition challenges, block worker mobilization, and circumscribe worker negotiations with employers. Rank-and-file challenges to entrenched progovernment labor leaders sometimes succeed, but state-subsidized labor organizations constitute an effective means of political control because successful challenges are generally limited in scope.

"Official" labor organizations have the capacity to function in this way principally because of their links to the state. The requirement that state labor authorities certify the election of union leaders, the legal sanction that government approval gives to undemocratic provisions in union statutes, "official" unions' ability to use privileged access to publicly funded social welfare programs as patronage resources, and especially government officials' willingness to defend (often through the use of force, if necessary) progovernment labor leaders have all helped sustain the alliance between accommodationist labor leaders and the ruling political elite. At the same time, however, it is important to note that ties between major labor organizations and Mexico's "party of the revolution" have reinforced this alliance in important ways. The party lacks the institutional capacity to block independent worker mobilization or otherwise exercise direct control over labor. But by providing progovernment union leaders with preferential opportunities for political mobility and by symbolically reaffirming the labor movement's national importance, ties to the governing party have bolstered labor support for the postrevolutionary order. Moreover, for many years the "official" party embodied a shared elite-mass consensus in favor of revolutionary nationalism, ideas that further bonded labor to the regime. In summary, by identifying both the state apparatus and "official" labor organizations as important instruments of elite political control, by distinguishing between labor organizations' links to the state and to the governing party (and thereby permitting a nuanced analysis of the relative importance of these ties), and by accenting the role that revolutionary nationalist ideas have played in cementing labor support for the regime, the concept of postrevolutionary authoritarian rule contributes significantly to the study of Mexican politics.

This chapter examines the shifting terms of the alliance between organized labor and the Mexican political elite in the late 1980s and early 1990s, focusing in particular on the relationship between labor politics and the prospects for democratic regime change in Mexico. The point of departure for this analysis is the "official" labor movement's continued loyalty to Mexico's authoritarian regime despite sustained efforts by the Salinas de Gortari administration (1988–94) to limit labor's national influence. Even though the labor movement suffered significant reverses, major labor organizations—conspicuously unlike their counterparts in most other authoritarian regimes—opposed electoral and party reforms. Rather than pushing for a democratic opening that might have increased labor's opportunities to resist more effectively unfavorable government economic policies, the Confederation of Mexican Workers and other labor groups sought to preserve core elements of the established regime. The "official" labor movement's resistance to regime democratization was one important reason why the scope and speed of economic transformation exceeded the extent and pace of political opening in Mexico during the late 1980s and early 1990s.

Following an examination of the most important developments affecting organized labor during the Salinas administration, this chapter addresses three sets of questions concerning labor politics and the prospects for democratic transition in Mexico. First, in what ways did the character of Mexico's postrevolutionary authoritarian regime change during the 1980s and early 1990s? Viewed from the vantage point of the early 1990s, in what areas did the legacy of postrevolutionary authoritarian rule remain strong? Second, what is the broader relationship between labor politics and democratic regime change in postrevolutionary contexts? Is the "official" Mexican labor movement's resistance to political opening unique, or are there parallels in labor's response to democratic regime change in other postrevolutionary contexts? What can be learned from comparing the Mexican experience with other such instances of regime change? Third, how likely is it that the Mexican organized labor movement will become an active proponent of democratization? What changes would be necessary for this to occur, either within the labor movement or in Mexican politics more broadly?

The concept of postrevolutionary authoritarian rule makes significant contributions to the examination of these issues. Although Mexico experienced a number of important political changes during the 1980s and early 1990s, it did not undergo a successful transition from authoritarian to democratic rule. One of the most difficult questions raised by the Mexican case, then, is how to assess the extent and potential implications of change in a highly institutionalized, durable authoritarian regime. Focusing on those elements that define postrevolutionary authoritarianism as a distinctive form of authoritarian rule establishes analytic bench marks against which to evaluate shifts in the configuration of the Mexican regime's governing coalition, the evolving content of ideas that the political elite invokes to legitimate its rule, and the changing roles over time of the "official" party and the state. Equally important, the concept of postrevolutionary authoritarian rule facilitates comparative analysis by identifying other cases in which democratic regime change presented special challenges to organized labor movements that had formed part of postrevolutionary governing coalitions. The Nicaraguan and Russian experiences, for example, offer valuable comparative insights into some of the dilemmas that political and economic opening pose for the Mexican labor movement.

Mexico in the 1990s: State-Labor Relations in a Neoliberal Era

The social pact between organized labor and the governing political elite, already significantly weakened by de la Madrid's orthodox stabilization policies and the shift in national development strategy, eroded still further in the late 1980s and early 1990s. During the 1987 presidential succession, CTM leaders and other important labor figures backed the candidacy of Alfredo del Mazo, a former governor of the state of México and at the time minister of energy, mines, and state-controlled industry. CTM leaders considered del Mazo more sympathetic to their basic policy preferences than other leading contenders, and they hoped that under a del Mazo presidency organized labor could recoup past economic losses.[1] However, when Institutional Revolutionary Party (PRI) officials announced in October 1987 that Carlos Salinas de Gortari (minister of programming and budget during 1982–88 and a principal architect of de la Madrid's adjustment strategy) would be the party's presidential nominee, many labor leaders concluded that neoliberal economic policies would remain firmly in place.

As a result, some prominent labor leaders broke ranks and publicly questioned whether workers would vote for Salinas.[2] Joaquín ("La Quina") Hernández Galicia, the powerful de facto leader of the Mexican Petroleum Workers' Union (STPRM), took the even more serious step of giving political and financial support to the opposition candidacy of Cuauhtémoc Cárdenas, son of former president Lázaro Cárdenas who had nationalized the oil industry in 1938.[3] Because traditional labor leaders apparently failed to deliver the sectoral vote in the July 1988 presidential election (their discontent with Salinas apart, it is an open question whether labor leaders in any country could have convinced their members to support a party responsible for years of declining real wages and significant job losses in key industries), and because a number of prominent labor candidates failed to win election,[4] organized labor's relationship with the newly inaugurated Salinas administration was severely strained. Equally important, because his victory was so narrow and intensely disputed, Salinas had strong incentives to identify and build a new political coalition to support his policies. His decision to use army troops to arrest Hernández Galicia (the archetypal Mexican union boss widely known for his use of corruption and coercion to control his fiefdom) in January 1989 on charges of illegal firearms possession bluntly served notice of his intention to do so.[5]

More generally, overlapping developments in three areas further undermined the social pact that had long existed between organized labor and the governing elite. First, Salinas named to prominent positions in his administration political technocrats whose mentalities and ideological preferences differed sharply from those of traditional PRI politicians.[6] Control over key posts by young, often foreign-educated technocrats increased discontent within the political elite because traditional politicians (sometimes referred to as *dinosaurios*) believed that their opportunities for mobility and policy influence were blocked. Labor leaders were particularly concerned that technocrats failed to appreciate the role played by organizations such as the CTM in preserving political stability. Individuals rising to high national office in the 1980s and early 1990s on the basis of their educational achievements and technical expertise were members of a generation far removed from the violent political and social upheaval that produced the Mexican regime. Their backgrounds and expectations differed dramatically from those of the aging leaders of the "official" labor movement, the only major actor in national politics still led in the early 1990s by individuals personally linked to the 1910–20 revolutionary experience. In this sense, the continued weakening of the social pact with labor reflected the inevitable consequences of generational change in Mexico's governing political elite.

Second, the Salinas administration's neoliberal policy initiatives broadly challenged labor interests. In principle, Salinas sought to reduce state intervention in socioeconomic affairs and increase the role of market forces in determining wages, employment levels, and working conditions. He maintained that these matters should appropriately be negotiated directly by workers and employers themselves, with minimal state involvement.[7] Salinas administration practice, however, often departed sharply from this broad philosophical orientation. For instance, legal restrictions on many aspects of labor participation remained firmly in place. Tight administrative control limited the average number of strikes in federal-jurisdiction industries to 143 per year between 1989 and 1993, an average of 2.1 percent of the strike petitions filed by unions during this period (see table 5.1).

In precedent-setting cases such as the July–August 1992 Volkswagen conflict,[8] state labor authorities also intervened decisively to undercut union bargaining strength in the workplace and ensure an outcome acceptable to company managers. Similarly, during a wave of strikes in the textile industry in mid-1992, the Salinas administration supported employers' attempts to vitiate the terms of the industrywide *contrato-ley* by negotiating wage and productivity agreements on a company-by-company basis. Moreover, because the January 1989 "Pact for Stability and Economic Growth" (PECE, renamed the Pacto para la Estabilidad, Competitividad y Empleo ["Pact for Stability, Competitiveness, and Employment"] in October 1992) set upper limits on company-level wage increases, wage settlements more frequently reflected the result of government-controlled negotiations with major labor and business organizations than the free play of market forces. State labor officials strongly enforced the wage ceiling on a case-by-case basis.

At the same time, Salinas undermined the political position of some traditional labor leaders and supported those who were more receptive to his calls for greater attention to productivity, enterprise modernization, and flexible workplace relations.[9] The most sensational case was the arrest and imprisonment of Hernández Galicia. However, in 1989 Salinas also responded to political pressures created by a massive rank-and-file protest movement against Carlos Jonguitud Barrios, de facto leader of the National Education Workers' Union (SNTE) since 1972, by forcing him to resign. At least initially, the new union secretary-general, Elba Esther Gordillo Morales, was better positioned than her predecessor to negotiate with the National Coordinating Committee of Education Workers, the opposition teachers' movement that had aggressively promoted union democracy, higher wages, and teachers' rights since the late 1970s. Yet as in the case of state-owned Petróleos Mexicanos (PEMEX)—where the ouster of Hernández Galicia and the government-supported installation of a more accommodating union leadership paved the way for the reorganization of PEMEX into several subsidiary enterprises, far-reaching contract and work rule modifications, and massive job cuts—leadership change in the SNTE permitted the Salinas administration to implement important policy changes. In May 1992 the union signed an agreement with the government that decentralized Mexico's public education system, a change long resisted by the previous SNTE leadership because it threatened to weaken the national union's bargaining power by forcing individual union locals to negotiate directly with state governments over wages and working conditions.[10]

One of the principal beneficiaries of Salinas's effort to identify new bases of labor support was Francisco Hernández Juárez, secretary-general of the Mexican Telephone Workers' Union (STRM). Salinas identified the STRM's 1989 restructuring agreement with Teléfonos de México as a model of successful worker-management cooperation *(concertación)*.[11] Under the terms of this accord, the union agreed to link wage increases to improvements in productivity and to accept more flexible work rules; in exchange, the company preserved most union jobs (though the company increasingly hired new workers through nonunionized subsidiaries) and gave the STRM 4.4 percent of its stock.

Moreover, Salinas backed Hernández Juárez's creation in April 1990 of the Federación de Sindicatos de Empresas de Bienes y Servicios (Federation of Goods and Services Unions, FESEBES). This new organization eventually grew to include approximately one hundred thousand workers in the telecommunications, airline, electrical power generation, tramway, film and television, and (after the 1992 Volkswagen conflict) automobile industries.[12] The CTM lobbied against granting the FESEBES official registration, which it did not receive until September 1992—apparently as partial compensation for the role that Hernández Juárez played in resolving the bitter Volkswagen dispute. Salinas's support for the FESEBES alternative waned as the 1993 presidential succession neared and his need increased for political support from organizations such as the CTM. However, his prominent backing for Hernández Juárez's initiatives fueled rivalries within the national labor leadership during the early years of his administration.

Measures that deprived traditional labor leaders of their control over important public welfare programs accompanied Salinas's other actions. Among the most important of these was a reform of the government-subsidized worker housing fund which sharply constrained union leaders' influence over this program. The CTM had long dominated the administration of the National Worker Housing Institute (INFONAVIT), generally limiting access to the program to union members and distributing a large proportion of finished housing units to its own affiliates.[13] Moreover, individual CTM leaders derived multiple benefits from the program: they purchased land and sold it to INFONAVIT at inflated prices; they often owned or received kickbacks from the construction companies responsible for building housing; and they selectively distributed completed housing units to loyal supporters in order to strengthen their political position. Previous government attempts to depoliticize access to INFONAVIT housing had failed to break union control. In September 1992, however, the Salinas administration pushed through legislation against CTM opposition that substantially reduced union influence over the distribution of housing units. The new rules gave each worker direct control over use of money in his or her INFONAVIT account. Each employee was free to use these funds to secure a mortgage on any house or apartment available on the open market. In addition, INFONAVIT ended its direct involvement in housing construction.[14]

The third cause for the organized labor movement's diminishing influence during the late 1980s and early 1990s was the continuing decline in its own organizational and mobilizational strength. As noted in earlier chapters, the alliance between organized labor and the governing political elite which was consolidated in the late 1940s and early 1950s was never equal. Unchallenged control over the means of coercion and well-developed state administrative capacity permitted different presidential administrations to define (and redefine) their relations with labor, while the labor movement's internal weaknesses generally constrained its own bargaining leverage. Yet the terms of this relationship became increasingly one-sided in the 1980s and early 1990s because of the cumulative impact of structural adjustment policies and industrial restructuring in the public and private sectors. Privatization of additional state-owned enterprises under Salinas was especially damaging to organized labor's position. Massive employment cuts in the mining, steel, metalworking, petroleum, and railroad industries and in port facilities (more than four hundred thousand jobs were lost in the state sector between 1983 and 1993) sapped the strength of Mexico's most important industrial unions, reducing their membership and undermining wage levels and contract terms.[15]

One indicator of unions' declining negotiating effectiveness is that, even under the *pacto* agreements signed after 1987, the index value of the real minimum daily wage in Mexico City fell by 22.6 percent between 1988 and 1993 (see table 6.1).[16] Real average wages in manufacturing industries rose by 28.1 percent between 1989 and 1992.[17] However, despite an average annual 2.5 percent increase in labor productivity between 1980 and 1992, in 1992 the real hourly compensation of Mexican production workers in the manufacturing sector was only three-quarters of what it had been in 1979.[18]

Major labor organizations did retain in the late 1980s and early 1990s sufficient strength to delay some policy changes and block others, sometimes securing important concessions in the process.[19] For example, aggressive lobbying by the Confederation of Mexican Workers defeated proposals made at the PRI's September 1990 and March 1993 national assemblies to eliminate sector organizations within the party. Instead of adopting an entirely new, territorial structure for an envisioned "party of citizens," the PRI remained organized around a combination of territorial and sectoral bodies.[20]

Similarly, the CTM withheld for nearly two years its endorsement of the "National Accord for the Elevation of Productivity and Quality," which was designed by the Salinas administration to promote more flexible workplace labor relations and thereby increase enterprise productivity. The CTM sought the government's commitment that greater productivity would lead to higher wages and that government and business would back labor support for higher productivity by expanding worker training programs. To secure final CTM approval in May 1992, the government finally conceded that the terms of any such agreements signed by individual unions and companies would not legally supersede collective contracts. In addition, the Salinas administration agreed to an employer-funded retirement savings program (employers were required to contribute a sum equal to 2 percent of their workers' wages) for the nearly ten million workers affiliated with the Mexican Social Security Institute (IMSS). The CTM-controlled Banco Obrero was to administer a significant proportion of these retirement funds.[21]

Moreover, the CTM blocked Salinas administration efforts to reform the federal labor code. The CTM itself had initiated discussions of labor law reform in 1987–88, and in early 1989 the Ministry of Labor and Social Welfare established a tripartite commission to begin discussion of the matter. In August 1989 the Chamber of Deputies held formal hearings to elicit testimony from experts in the field. However, the Salinas administration's demonstrated intention to limit or eliminate many established labor prerogatives, the fact that business interests were politically influential in the Salinas government, and the labor movement's weakened bargaining position all made the CTM fear it might have little influence over the final terms of new national labor legislation. Organized labor could not prevent the Salinas administration from interpreting and applying existing law in such a way as to provide employers in practice with the flexibility to redefine workplace industrial relations they sought to incorporate into law. But under pressure from the CTM, the Ministry of Labor and Social Welfare suspended formal discussions of labor law reform in January 1992.[22]

In the sextuple rhythm of Mexican politics, the CTM's political influence increased somewhat toward the end of the Salinas administration as the all-important presidential succession process reached its conclusion.[23] Yet overall, when confronted by an administration determined to redefine important aspects of the state's relationship with labor, the "official" labor movement was in a weaker political and economic position in the early 1990s than at any time since the late 1920s and early 1930s. Indeed, organized labor's declining influence in national politics marked an important shift in regime dynamics. The following section assesses both changes in the character of the Mexican regime during the 1980s and early 1990s and the legacies of postrevolutionary authoritarian rule.

The Legacies of Postrevolutionary Authoritarianism in Mexico

Unlike many other countries in Latin America, eastern Europe, and Africa, Mexico did not experience during the 1980s and early 1990s a successful transition from authoritarian to democratic rule. For this reason, the main challenge confronting analysts in this case is to evaluate the extent and potential implications of changes within a highly institutionalized authoritarian regime. The concept of postrevolutionary authoritarian rule facilitates this effort by focusing attention on three issues of crucial significance for the future of the Mexican regime: the position of mass actors in the governing coalition, shifts in the content of ideas that the political elite invokes to legitimate the established regime, and the evolving role of the "official" party and a powerful, still highly centralized state.

Changes in the Configuration of Mexico's Governing Coalition

Business interests assumed new prominence in Mexico's governing coalition in the 1980s and early 1990s. López Portillo's nationalization of the banking industry in September 1982 profoundly disturbed government relations with the private sector. In an effort to restore business confidence and encourage private-sector investment, the de la Madrid administration enacted constitutional reforms in December 1982 which in principle limited state ownership to specified strategic activities (communications, petroleum and basic petrochemicals, nuclear energy, railroad transportation, and banking).[24] Even more important, de la Madrid initiated a program of deregulation and privatization which gradually convinced Mexican entrepreneurs that the government was committed to an economic development strategy in which the private sector would play a leading role.

Salinas won widespread approval from domestic and foreign investors by accelerating the pace of neoliberal economic reform. The number of state-owned enterprises and public investment funds continued to decline, from 412 in 1988 to 232 in 1992. Indeed, Salinas was responsible for some of the largest and most politically significant privatizations, including banks and investment houses, telecommunications, air transportation, mining companies, steel producers, sugar mills, toll roads, and port facilities.[25] Coupled with more effective control over inflation, further price deregulation, additional cuts in tariff and nontariff barriers to imports, and liberalized terms for foreign investment, these measures boosted business confidence and transformed Mexican entrepreneurs from limited partners in a predominantly state-led development model into leading promoters of economic growth. Privatization, market opening and export promotion, and North American economic integration were especially favorable to the interests of financiers and large manufacturers. These groups were a major source of political support for the Salinas administration.

This shift in the configuration of Mexico's governing coalition came at the expense of organized labor. As noted above, Salinas attempted to undermine the position of some traditional labor leaders and construct new alliances in the labor movement by negotiating separate, often highly personal deals with individual unions in such key sectors as telecommunications, education, and electrical power generation.[26] At times his efforts encountered strong resistance from Fidel Velázquez and the CTM. However, by restricting the role of sector organizations in the PRI and by threatening traditional labor prerogatives in a number of areas, the government somewhat reduced the CTM's room for political maneuver.[27]

But even as its social content changed significantly, the alliance between the governing political elite and representatives of the organized working class survived. For example, labor representation in the PECE and labor leaders' presence in the Mexican working groups negotiating the North American Free Trade Agreement (NAFTA) formally acknowledged the "official" labor movement's continued importance. Labor's alliance with the national political elite retained much of its old form in the early 1990s in part because of the longevity of Fidel Velázquez and his skill at protecting some established CTM prerogatives, which increased the potential political costs to Salinas of an even more aggressive assault on the labor movement. Even more significant, however, Salinas remained dependent on state-subsidized labor organizations for support in two crucial areas: effective economic policy management and orderly presidential succession. Mexico's successful economic stabilization and structural adjustment program in the 1980s and early 1990s rested centrally on policymakers' ability to impose large, sustained cuts in real wages and fringe benefits. For most observers, this was the feature that primarily distinguished Mexico's stabilization and adjustment program from far less effective efforts in other Latin American countries.[28] Such policies could not have been implemented without the collaboration of a labor leadership willing to limit rank-and-file economic demands.

The single most important political process in authoritarian Mexico—the incumbent president's transfer of concentrated authority to his self-designated successor—remained equally dependent upon the discipline and loyalty of the "official" labor movement. The signal achievement of Mexico's postrevolutionary political leadership was the institutionalization of peaceful presidential succession, something that typically remains beyond the reach of governing elites in other authoritarian regimes and which eventually contributes (often decisively) to their demise. For Salinas no less than for any of his predecessors, control over this process depended on the labor movement's continued allegiance to the established rules of the game. Despite the erosion of its political influence, in the early 1990s the Confederation of Mexican Workers still claimed a membership of five million workers organized in eleven thousand affiliated unions.[29] Even if these totals were greatly inflated, control over a substantial mass membership made the continued political allegiance of "official" labor organizations vitally important to Salinas's ability to transfer power smoothly to his successor. Indeed, unforeseen events made labor's loyalty especially valuable in 1994: Luis Donaldo Colosio Murrieta, the former minister of social development whom Salinas had picked in November 1993 as the PRI's presidential candidate, was assassinated on March 23, 1994, following a campaign rally in Tijuana. In the tumultuous days that followed, Salinas struggled to control a visibly contested succession process that finally led to the designation of Ernesto Zedillo Ponce de León (former minister of programming and budget, minister of education, and Colosio's campaign manager) as the PRI's new candidate.

Developments under Salinas thus recalled the close relationship in postrevolutionary Mexico between concentrated political power and a disciplined labor movement dependent upon state support. Explanations of the CROM's disintegration as a dominant labor confederation in the late 1920s and early 1930s typically focus on Morones's personal corruption, the violence (including assassination) which he and his allies employed against opponents, and his overweening political ambitions. The CTM in the 1930s and 1940s certainly enjoyed a number of significant advantages over the CROM. These included a federal labor law supportive of unionization on a national scale, a broader membership base formed during the intense popular mobilizations of the late 1930s, support from leftist groups such as the Mexican Communist Party (which for both domestic and international reasons continued to back CTM unity even after the confederation's leadership sought a closer, less independent relationship with state officials and adopted more conservative policies), and more politically astute leadership.

Yet the most important difference between these experiences concerns the amount and concentration of political power exercised by Mexico's governing elite in the late 1920s and in subsequent periods. The political distance between 1928 (the end of the CROM's unquestioned dominance in the labor movement) and 1948 (the date of the *charrazo* in the Mexican Railroad Workers' Union and the beginning of sustained government efforts to displace opposition leaders in national industrial unions, thereby consolidating the political position of the CTM's more accommodationist leadership) was very great indeed. The CROM lost its privileged position in part because, in the political vacuum created by the assassination of Obregón in 1928, its national political alliances collapsed. The next two decades witnessed the creation of an "official" party capable of uniting disparate factions and winning national and state elections, the beginning of orderly presidential succession, and the consolidation of civilian rule (Ávila Camacho was the last revolutionary general to become president). Government actions in the late 1940s and early 1950s to ensure CTM dominance in the labor movement were thus an essential element in a broader process of postrevolutionary political institutionalization. CTM strength in later years depended centrally on the concentrated political power of the federal government; at the same time, labor movement discipline under CTM leadership bolstered the governing elite's decision-making autonomy in economic affairs and helped sustain Mexico's authoritarian regime. Whatever the CTM's eventual fate as a confederation, the reciprocal relationship that it long embodied may well endure so long as Mexico's authoritarian regime remains in place and state-subsidized labor organizations retain their capacity to control rank-and-file demands.

Political Ideas and Regime Legitimation: From "Revolutionary Nationalism" to "Social Liberalism"

Mexican presidents from the 1920s through the 1980s legitimated their rule by invoking the heterogeneous corpus of political ideas emanating from the 1910–20 revolutionary struggle. Indeed, with the exceptions of Cárdenas in the 1930s and Echeverría in the 1970s, these "governments of the revolution" ("la revolución hecho gobierno") made no particular effort to articulate special guiding principles to justify their policies. Yet in the same way that his neoliberal agenda broke with many established precedents, Salinas sought to reformulate inherited postrevolutionary ideas to support his political position. The close identification of his principal political opponent, Cuauhtémoc Cárdenas, with the traditional precepts of revolutionary nationalism made it imperative that Salinas define a distinctive ideological framework to legitimate his policy initiatives. His administration's strong showing in the 1991 midterm elections (a significant recovery from the PRI's disastrous performance in the 1988 presidential election) offered him a relatively secure political position from which to do so.

Salinas's effort to reformulate inherited postrevolutionary beliefs occurred in two stages. First, in his annual address to Congress in November 1991, Salinas argued that Mexican nationalism should not be identified with an immutable set of policy positions, such as a large state-owned sector or economic protectionism. He maintained that the practical meaning of nationalism changes with historical conditions and that new circumstances require different responses to promote national interests and defend Mexican sovereignty.

> Ours is a nationalism that is recognizable in all its historical stages, linked not to particular formulas of power or production but to the national interest and the values and culture that define us. . . . That is why we should reject deformations that see in nationalism "sacred" positions, frozen in time, consisting of yesterday's public policies that today are ineffective. . . . Nationalism is what strengthens the nation. It is not the mourning of formulas and traits of other times which, in the context of the world today, weaken rather than invigorate [the nation], which make it more vulnerable, less viable.[30]

Thus Salinas maintained that, in the 1990s, Mexico's national interests were best served by policies that opened the economy to trade and investment in order to promote growth and increase competitiveness, North American economic (but not political) integration, and the promotion of social cohesion through the elimination of poverty.

Second, in a speech to ranking members of the Institutional Revolutionary Party in March 1992, Salinas articulated a doctrine of "social liberalism" as the ideological basis for his policy program. According to Salinas, social liberalism represents an alternative to both state capitalism and libertarianism. He argued that the state should regulate social and economic activities in order to eradicate injustice and prevent such abuses as the formation of monopolies, but that as a general principle the state should not own means of production and thereby suffocate private initiative. Salinas contrasted his vision of a "solidaristic state" committed to promoting social justice and democratic rights with Mexico's past tradition of a paternalistic, bureaucratic state with an "excessively" large role in economic production.[31]

There were, of course, obvious parallels between Salinas's definition of social liberalism and some of the political ideas associated with Mexico's revolutionary experience. In essence, he highlighted the liberal, constitutional elements of postrevolutionary beliefs, reaffirming the state's responsibility for promoting social justice while criticizing the state-led, protectionist model of economic development traditionally associated with revolutionary nationalism. By referring to his program as "the reform of the revolution," Salinas sought to ground his ideas firmly in that earlier tradition. One might even argue that Salinas's strong emphasis on social justice themes reaffirmed the continuing vitality of the most important political ideas embodied in the Mexican revolution, ideas whose survival into the 1990s depended in large part on the continued presence of mass organizations such as the CTM which were committed to defending them. Nevertheless, his characterization of social liberalism broke clearly with the revolutionary tradition in a fundamental way: it did not reaffirm the legitimacy of *collective* social rights.

The doctrine of social liberalism may not outlive its role as a conjunctural justification for Salinas administration policies. Salinas's articulation of social liberalism as a guiding philosophy reflected both the political dominance of neoliberal economic reformers in the late 1980s and early 1990s and the declining influence of mass actors in the governing coalition. By stressing the liberal content of postrevolutionary ideas while omitting traditional references to collective social rights (whereas many previous presidents might have employed terms such as "social classes," in his March 1992 address Salinas referred only to "popular groups"), Salinas recognized political values more frequently associated with the urban middle class than with workers or peasants. This shift in ideological emphasis complemented Salinas's forceful efforts to eliminate the established political privileges of groups such as organized labor. Over the longer term, it may stand as an important moment in the redefinition of the ideological discourse of the Mexican revolution.

Party and State in Neoliberal Mexico

Although the "official" Institutional Revolutionary Party remains the most enduring symbol of Mexico's postrevolutionary authoritarian order, elections and the party system became increasingly competitive during the 1980s and 1990s. Over time, urbanization, higher educational levels, generational change, and political actions by community-based social movements all undermined the PRI's capacity to mobilize electoral support through traditional clientelist arrangements. The control that sectoral organizations exercised over their mass constituencies became less and less reliable. As a result, the PRI faced greater challenges in winning electoral support in the Mexico City metropolitan area and other major urban centers. In the mid-1980s these problems were exacerbated by dissension within the party over the appropriate direction of national development policy (pitting supporters of neoliberal reforms against nationalist-populist advocates of a stronger state role in promoting socially equitable economic growth) and the desirability of more rapid political liberalization (pitting PRI reformers against labor leaders, state and local party bosses, and other elements in the party whose position was threatened by political opening). These divisions led in 1986–87 to the most serious intra-elite schism since the early 1950s, the PRI's disastrous showing in the 1988 general elections (under pressure from a left-nationalist opposition coalition led by Cuauhtémoc Cárdenas, the PRI's official—and much disputed—share of the presidential vote shrank to a new low of 50.7 percent), and the formation of Cárdenas's Partido de la Revolución Democrática (Party of the Democratic Revolution, PRD) in 1989.

Mounting challenges to the governing party led PRI leaders in the early 1990s to enact internal organizational reforms that lessened the influence of established sectoral organizations and strengthened the PRI's territorial structure at the state and local levels. Their goal was to forge closer ties to urban popular movements, community-based organizations, professional groups, and so forth, thus enabling the PRI to respond to the increasing complexity of Mexican society and to compete more effectively for electoral support in urban areas. In September 1990 party reformers also made membership nominally voluntary, thus ending in principle the governing party's long tradition of enlisting members indirectly through sector-affiliated mass organizations such as labor unions.[32] As noted above, opposition from the CTM and other party traditionalists blocked plans to eliminate functionally defined sectors altogether. The CTM vigorously opposed such a change because it would reduce political mobility opportunities for labor leaders and threaten labor organizations' ability to use influence within the party to shape public policy decisions.

During the 1980s, opposition parties began to play a much more significant role in national politics. Despite resistance from elements such as the CTM (which feared that stronger opposition parties would challenge its affiliates' control over union members), legislation enacted after 1977 eased the requirements for party formation and increased opposition parties' proportional representation in federal and state legislatures.[33] Moreover, it expanded opposition parties' access to public campaign financing and the mass media. By permitting these parties to supervise polling sites, requiring that voters carry fraud-proof identification cards, and establishing tighter control over voter registration lists, reform measures also made it more difficult (though certainly not impossible) for PRI party bosses to commit electoral fraud. These changes and the growing prominence of opposition parties eroded the PRI's electoral dominance in many parts of the country. Even though their organizational links to civil society often remained weak, opposition parties on both the political Left and Right established a strong presence in some regions. State and local elections in many areas thus became increasingly competitive; nomination by the PRI no longer guaranteed a candidate's election. Indeed, in 1989 the center-right Partido

Acción Nacional (National Action Party, PAN) broke the ruling party's monopoly on state governorships by winning the gubernatorial election in Baja California. During the early 1990s PAN candidates also won control of the governorships of Chihuahua and Guanajuato, and the PAN controlled a substantial number of municipal governments.

Yet despite these changes, the PRI's overall electoral dominance remained intact. Modest rates of economic growth after 1989 and Salinas's strong political leadership aided the party's electoral recovery in the early 1990s.[34] Widespread public approval of the Programa Nacional de Solidaridad (National Solidarity Program, PRONASOL, a program combining government financial support and citizen involvement in local actions to improve community access to water and sewer systems, education, health care, and housing) and Salinas's close personal identification with the program, were significant factors in this regard. However, PRI victories in some hotly contested elections were due principally to government officials' continued resort to fraud. Government and PRI leaders also successfully exploited (and wherever possible, encouraged) internal divisions in opposition parties over strategy and leadership selection. Even more serious, opposition party activists (especially members of the PRD) often encountered threats and physical intimidation, and a number of *cardenistas* were killed or "disappeared."

By 1993, Salinas judged the PRI's position sufficiently strong to permit him to implement a new round of political reform in order to increase the legitimacy of electoral outcomes. This legislation increased the size of the federal Senate and guaranteed that opposition parties would control at least one-quarter of its seats; eliminated the "governability clause" enacted in 1986 (which ensured the PRI majority representation in the federal Chamber of Deputies even if it failed to win a similar share of the national vote); placed overall limits on campaign spending and loosely regulated private campaign financing; reduced somewhat the government's control over electoral authorities; and permitted independent verification of voter registration procedures and national election observers.[35]

In the wake of the January 1994 peasant-based guerrilla insurgency in Chiapas, the Salinas government came under still greater domestic and international pressure to speed the pace of political liberalization. The result was yet another round of electoral reform. Legislation adopted in May 1994 further limited direct government and PRI influence over the Instituto Federal Electoral (Federal Electoral Institute); permitted foreign visitors to witness federal elections; banned the use of public funds and government personnel to benefit the PRI; and established a special prosecutor to pursue those accused of electoral fraud.[36] Taken together, the four electoral reform laws enacted in 1990, 1993 (two different sets of changes), and

1994 formally established much more equal terms of interparty competition. Nevertheless, in practice the PRI retained considerable advantages over opposition parties as a result of its long incumbency.

The liberalization of electoral processes contrasted dramatically with continued, strong state control over nonelectoral forms of mass participation.[37] The practical impact of state controls on strikes, union formation, and worker demand articulation was arguably greater in the late 1980s and early 1990s than in previous years because many labor organizations had been weakened by economic crisis and industrial restructuring. Indeed, the de la Madrid and Salinas administrations' vigorous efforts to broaden the tax base and increase the efficiency of tax collection substantially strengthened the state's extractive capacity.[38] Combined with continued controls on nonelectoral mass participation, the fiscally responsible, regulatory state taking shape in the late 1980s and early 1990s promised to be an even more powerful state.

In sum, despite important changes, the legacies of postrevolutionary authoritarianism were still strong in Mexico in the early 1990s. The further erosion of the governing elite's social pact with labor, Salinas's efforts to reorient the ideological justification for PRI rule, and the increasing competitiveness of elections and the party system were significant developments with important long-term implications. Yet many important features of Mexican authoritarianism remained firmly in place. The "official" organized labor movement's opposition to political liberalization was especially noteworthy, raising broader comparative questions concerning the relationship between labor politics and democratization in postrevolutionary regimes.

Labor Politics and Democratization in Postrevolutionary Contexts
Contending Perspectives on Labor's Role in Democratization

Recent scholarship outlines two principal perspectives on the question of labor's role in democratization. Rueschemeyer, Stephens, and Stephens adopt a "relative class power" approach to the study of democratization in their far-ranging comparative work *Capitalist Development and Democracy*. The authors' examination of historical cases of democratization in advanced capitalist countries (European countries and Australia, Canada, New Zealand, and the United States) and Latin America focuses on the relative power of different social classes and the structure of class coalitions, the strength and autonomy of the state apparatus and its interrelations with civil society, and the impact of transnational power relations (interstate political, military, and economic relations and transnational cultural flows) on domestic political change. They conclude that the initial emergence and subsequent consolidation of democracy in different historical and geographical contexts are primarily the result of significant shifts in the balance of power among different classes and class coalitions: "[C]apitalist development is associated with democracy because it transforms the class structure, strengthening the working and middle classes and weakening the landed upper class."[39]

More specifically, Rueschemeyer, Stephens, and Stephens maintain that the working class has been a crucial—and historically quite consistent—force in favor of political democracy because "those who have only to gain from democracy will be its most reliable promoters and defenders."[40] In the course of their analysis, they argue that the capacity of the working class to play this historical role depends on its relative size and organizational density, its organizational and ideological autonomy vis-à-vis the state and dominant classes, the ready availability of political allies (especially middle-class groups committed to democratization), and political parties capable of articulating these interclass alliances.[41]

Valenzuela's essay titled "Labor Movements in Transitions to Democracy" examines the political impact of labor movements on transitions from authoritarian to democratic rule. In contrast to Rueschemeyer, Stephens, and Stephens' broad focus on the structural forces shaping relative class power and their consequences for democracy, Valenzuela analyzes the shifting positions of specific sociopolitical actors during the dynamic process of regime change. In particular, he addresses the issue of whether labor strikes and demonstrations during politically fluid, potentially unstable transition periods advance (by increasing the political costs of repression for hard-line elements in ruling groups) or endanger (by heightening fears of social and economic disruption, thereby motivating soft-liners to side with hard-liners and restore authoritarian order) the democratization process. Valenzuela's expectation that organized labor generally favors democratic regime change parallels Rueschemeyer, Stephens, and Stephens' argument that the working class is the most historically consistent force in favor of democracy. Yet Valenzuela cautions that, in some circumstances, labor movement behavior can have a significant destabilizing effect on political transitions.[42]

For the purposes of this discussion, the central issue is how applicable these different analytic approaches are to the study of labor and regime change in postrevolutionary authoritarian contexts. Two sets of questions arise. First, how do labor movements in postrevolutionary contexts respond to the prospect of political liberalization or democratization? In what ways is their reaction similar to, or different from, that of labor movements in other types of authoritarian regimes? Second, if labor's response to regime change in postrevolutionary contexts is in any way distinctive, how applicable are insights from the more general literature on labor and democratization to the study of this phenomenon? What additional factors must be considered?

There are important reasons why organized labor in postrevolutionary authoritarian regimes might resist some aspects of democratic transition. First, because of its key position in most postrevolutionary governing coalitions, the labor movement almost certainly secured institutional advantages and material benefits that may be endangered by political liberalization or democratization. These include, for example, sectoral representation in the governing party or privileged political access to important elective and administrative positions. Labor might also benefit from institutional arrangements or legal provisions that strengthen employees' bargaining position in the workplace. Similarly, the labor movement probably received significant material benefits from postrevolutionary governments, perhaps including subsidized access to consumer goods and social welfare programs that provide workers with housing, education, and health care. Of course, postrevolutionary authoritarian regimes impose major constraints on labor actions, and workers' privileged political access may be of more symbolic than real importance. Yet unless their value to workers is undercut by the political harshness of authoritarian rule, these institutional advantages and material benefits potentially offer powerful reasons for labor movements to resist processes of regime change which jeopardize them.

Second, the distinctive political ideas or ideologies that legitimate postrevolutionary regimes may heighten workers' identification with the established order. In most instances the depth of these loyalties varies with the chronological distance from the revolutionary transformation, declining over time as memory of the revolution fades and rival political ideas intrude on workers' consciousness. Workers' identification with postrevolutionary beliefs is likely to be strongest where governing elites legitimate their rule by reference to a coherent ideology such as Marxism-Leninism that gives special historical place to the working class, and where ruling elites rely heavily on an official ideology to legitimate their rule and mobilize worker participation for government-specified ends. The strength of workers' ideological support for the postrevolutionary order may also depend on the overall political character of the regime, particularly whether it is relatively open and provides meaningful opportunities for worker participation or whether it is harshly repressive.

In considering organized labor's response to regime change in postrevolutionary contexts, it is important to distinguish between the reactions of labor leaders and those of rank-and-file workers, as well as between labor's response to initial regime liberalization and to subsequent stages of democratization. Many authoritarian rulers seek some accommodation with labor, often creating institutions whose principal purpose is to restrict worker participation but which simultaneously foster a dependent stratum of labor leaders with a personal stake in preserving the status quo. It would not be surprising, then, for some incumbent labor leaders to resist significant political change. Labor's response to regime change in postrevolutionary contexts would be distinctive only if a substantial proportion of the rank and file shares labor leaders' loyalty to the institutional, policy, and ideological legacies of the established order. Similarly, even though organized labor might resist the initial liberalization of a postrevolutionary authoritarian regime in order to protect its past gains, the labor movement might later support democratization if the process of regime change offers it expanded opportunities to organize and mobilize behind its political and socioeconomic demands. Labor's reaction could vary considerably in these different periods depending upon the kinds of challenges arising to labor's political and economic interests and the capacity of worker organizations to resolve them satisfactorily.

To what extent does recent scholarship on labor's role in democratization address the position of organized labor in postrevolutionary contexts?

Rueschemeyer, Stephens, and Stephens recognize some exceptions to their argument that organized labor historically favors democratic change. They state that "exceptions to the pro-democratic posture of the working class occurred where the class was initially mobilized by . . . a hegemonic party linked to the state apparatus," and they acknowledge that "the conditions under which the social construction of working-class interests takes a non-democratic form—as it did in Leninism[—]" merit special attention.[43] Mexico is the principal empirical referent that Rueschemeyer, Stephens, and Stephens offer in support of these points. In their discussion of Mexico, they note "the strong opposition of the leadership of the PRI-linked unions to the process of political liberalization."[44] They also correctly emphasize the significance of state-constructed barriers to the independent political organization of workers for the long-term process of regime change in Mexico. However, Rueschemeyer, Stephens, and Stephens stop short of suggesting that postrevolutionary authoritarian regimes might constitute a general class of exceptions to their argument concerning labor's historically consistent support for democratization.

Valenzuela shares with Rueschemeyer, Stephens, and Stephens the overarching assumption that organized labor generally supports transitions from authoritarian to democratic rule. He emphasizes that labor generally sees in regime change the opportunity to recoup economic losses, rebuild worker organizations, and redefine industrial relations systems. Valenzuela notes, however, that labor organizations sponsored by governing elites in "syndically mild and politically open" authoritarian regimes (which he labels "populist authoritarianisms") may view the transition process with considerable suspicion. From the perspective of labor organizations in such situations, democratization threatens "to displace the ruling authorities in favor of a new elite that has no association with the labor movement and to shift economic policies in a way which is detrimental to workers."[45] Defensive mobilization may occur as the labor movement strives to protect past policy gains and secure its position in the new political order. Valenzuela offers as examples the cases of the Argentine labor movement after the fall of Juan Perón in 1955 and the Peruvian labor movement after General Francisco Morales Bermúdez replaced the populist General Juan Velasco Alvarado in 1975. He further suggests that Mexico's labor movement might react similarly if the Institutional Revolutionary Party lost power to the political Right.

Valenzuela's systematic distinctions concerning different authoritarian regimes' treatment of labor and his attention to the implications these policies have for labor movement behavior during regime transitions are important conceptual advances. His typology does not, however, admit the possibility that labor movements might resist some aspects of regime change in syndically mild but politically closed authoritarian regimes, such as the former Soviet Union. Moreover, there are important differences between labor's position in postrevolutionary authoritarian regimes and "populist authoritarianisms." The most important of these is that the representational advantages, legal safeguards, and material benefits available to labor in most postrevolutionary contexts are the historical product of broad-based popular mobilization, not limited concessions extended to workers by authoritarian elites seeking to preempt labor activism. Nor do most populist-authoritarian regimes recognize workers' collective social rights as part of their efforts to foster rank-and-file support for the incumbent regime. As a result, with the possible exception of Peronism, workers' political identification with the established order is likely to be stronger (though not necessarily unqualified) in postrevolutionary authoritarian regimes than in other instances of authoritarian rule.[46]

Organized Labor and Regime Change in Nicaragua and Russia

Developments in Nicaragua and Russia in the late 1980s and early 1990s support the view that, because of organized labor's distinctive position in postrevolutionary authoritarian regimes, the labor movement's role in the transition process is significantly different in these contexts than in other instances of democratic regime change. These two cases were selected to highlight similarities and differences in organized labor's historical position in both comparatively open and politically closed postrevolutionary authoritarian regimes.[47] Regime change in Nicaragua and Russia roughly coincided in time, although democratization occurred more quickly in Nicaragua during the period examined here. Equally important in terms of the comparative significance of these cases, political opening generally preceded economic reform in Nicaragua and especially Russia. This is one reason why these two countries offer valuable insights into some of the challenges that a different sequencing of economic and political liberalization poses for the Mexican organized labor movement. Moreover, focusing on examples drawn from different geographical and cultural contexts illustrates how the concept of postrevolutionary authoritarian rule helps identify relevant cases with which the Mexican regime can be usefully compared.

In Nicaragua, organized urban and industrial workers were a central part of the broad-based, Sandinista-led revolutionary coalition that seized power in July 1979.[48] The Frente Sandinista de Liberación Nacional (Sandinista Front for National Liberation, FSLN, formed in 1961) organized numerous workplace-level labor committees during the late 1970s as the revolutionary movement gained force, and they became the principal base for the Central Sandinista de Trabajadores (Sandinista Workers' Central, CST) formed in 1979. Unionization proceeded rapidly under Sandinista rule; the unionized proportion of the salaried work force rose from 11 or 12 percent in 1979 to 56 percent in 1986. Although the CST faced rival labor organizations linked to opposition political parties on both the Left and Right, it was by far the largest confederation in postrevolutionary Nicaragua, representing four-fifths of all industrial unions. It especially benefited from government opposition to the formation of more than one union in each workplace, "closed shop" provisions, and the automatic payroll deduction of union dues, as well as from state-imposed obstacles to the formation and legal registration of non-Sandinista unions. The CST, along with other mass organizations representing rural workers, agricultural producers, and women, represented a crucial base of popular support for the revolutionary government.

Although labor organizations gained strength in the workplace and were prominently represented in national government, the FSLN imposed significant political constraints on the Sandinista Workers' Central. Local unions played an important role in workplace negotiations over working conditions and some fringe benefit issues, and members of CST affiliates elected their own representatives at the local level. However, the FSLN

National Directorate appointed regional and national CST officials. The CST was subject to "party discipline," and Sandinista Base Committees operated in the workplace (although party control at the enterprise-level was not always strong enough to prevent wildcat strikes). The Sandinista government, facing both domestic opposition and intense U.S. government hostility during the Reagan and Bush administrations, declared states of emergency that officially banned strikes from 1981 until July 1984 (when restrictions were lifted in preparation for national elections) and again from October 1985 until the FSLN's electoral defeat in February 1990. Moreover, under Sandinista rule the Ministry of Labor had broad authority to approve or reject collective bargaining agreements.

In spite of these political restrictions and the serious reverses that workers suffered under economic stabilization programs after 1985, the CST continued to back the Sandinista government and its policies. The government won labor support in part because, as real wages fell, it sought to protect the "social wage" by expanding workers' access to education, health care, and housing. But more important, many workers believed that even though they faced significant restrictions on their actions, Sandinista rule offered the best long-term guarantee of their class interests. This perception was no doubt strengthened by the Sandinistas' advocacy of collective social rights for workers (an important element in the FSLN's broader ideological justification for its claim to the legitimate exercise of political authority) and by vivid memories of the recent revolutionary struggle that had brought the Sandinistas and their working-class allies to power. Economic hardship and the political and social costs of the U.S.-backed Contra war did erode labor support for the government. Yet postelection opinion polls indicated that as many as half of all workers (and a clear majority among state-sector employees) voted for the FSLN in the February 1990 general elections.

The electoral victory of the Unión Nacional Opositora (National Opposition Union, UNO) in 1990 and the transition to a competitive democracy posed significant challenges for Sandinista labor organizations. In the absence of government financial subsidies and political support, direct ties between the CST and the FSLN weakened.[49] Moreover, President Violeta Barrios de Chamorro's administration sought to undermine CST power by recognizing more than one union in each workplace and by ending the automatic payroll deduction of union dues. The Chamorro government also suspended public-sector employees' right to collective bargaining. At the same time, UNO-allied labor organizations (especially the Congreso Permanente de Trabajadores [Permanent Congress of Workers], formed in 1987 by anti-Sandinista unions) received significant financial and logistical assistance from the U.S. National Endowment for Democracy, the U.S.

Agency for International Development, and the American Institute for Free Labor Development (AIFLD).

Despite these reverses, the Sandinista Workers' Central remained both the most important labor organization in Nicaragua and a significant base for Sandinista political influence. In April 1990 pro-Sandinista unions established a loose alliance in the Frente Nacional de Trabajadores (National Workers' Front). They continued to register more affiliates than their political rivals, and the CST and other labor organizations mobilized strongly against the UNO government's orthodox economic stabilization policies. The successful demonstration of their power in national strikes in May and July 1990 won important policy concessions, primarily in the form of *concertación* agreements that provided workers with somewhat greater protection against inflation and unemployment while contributing to macroeconomic stabilization. One of the most telling concessions to labor was the UNO government's agreement to grant workers up to 25 percent ownership in privatized state enterprises. (Sectoral negotiations produced even higher worker shares in enterprises in some economic activities.) These developments suggested that, because of the organizational and ideological legacies of Nicaragua's postrevolutionary authoritarian regime, unionized workers retained the capacity to exert strong economic and political pressure on public policy in a democratic context.

Organized labor was subject to much stricter political control in the former Soviet Union than in postrevolutionary Nicaragua, yet labor unions were also of vital importance in the Soviet system.[50] In the decade after the October 1917 revolution, debates raged concerning the appropriate role of trade unions under communism. The view that eventually triumphed held that unions should perform dual functions, both increasing productivity to meet state needs and defending workers against unscrupulous factory managers. The Communist Party of the Soviet Union (CPSU) significantly tightened control over union activities in the late 1920s as Stalin promoted industrialization at the cost of union autonomy, and in 1938 the Tenth Trade Union Congress consolidated the overall pattern of party-union relations that would prevail during the next fifty years.

Party organization penetrated the labor movement down to the local production unit. CPSU representatives participated directly in the preliminary selection of candidates for elected union office, and union officials formed part of the hierarchical *nomenklatura* system. Nevertheless, in both principle and practice, local union leaders remained substantially accountable to the rank and file. Particularly in heavy manufacturing enterprises in older industrial regions, unions played a key role in defending workers' interests on the shop floor. From the mid-1920s onward, unions assumed direct responsibility for distributing social welfare benefits (including pensions, worker housing, and so forth) to workers.

Despite the politically closed character of the Soviet regime and very strict controls on strikes, workers benefited from important legal guarantees. Labor rights and obligations were codified in enterprise-level collective agreements. In addition, the 1970 Fundamental Principles of Labor Legislation (made binding on plant managers by republic-level labor codes) established a complex dispute mediation process that included labor-management grievance committees and recourse to appellate courts. Legal protection against such managerial abuses as the unjustified dismissal of a worker was particularly effective.

Moreover, the Soviet system formally guaranteed workers' rights to employment, a healthy work environment, and a legal wage. As one analyst observed, "Legitimated by its claims of proletarian power, the Soviet state could not ignore basic issues of worker living standards, nor could it fail to define an essential place for workers within Soviet society."[51] Of course, actual workplace conditions did not always conform to official standards. Nor were social services and other resources distributed equally to all segments of the working class. Worker discontent with wage levels and the workplace environment was the principal cause of the strikes and other labor protests that did occur, many of which were brutally repressed even as Soviet authorities acted to correct the factors that had motivated them. Yet the concept of a "social contract," strongly reinforced by the central position that Marxism-Leninism defined for workers, was broadly accepted in the former Soviet Union.

Workers' institutional advantages and the ideologically sanctioned concept of collective social rights shaped trade union responses to the program of economic and political liberalization that Mikhail Gorbachev promoted between 1985 and 1991. Strategically placed unions with the potential to gain materially from export production (coal miners, for example) supported enterprise reform and the greater union autonomy that it promised.[52] In general, however, economic reforms (especially government efforts to raise productivity and impose unfavorable wage, price, and employment policies) significantly increased labor discontent. In the less repressive climate created by Gorbachev's policy of political liberalization (glasnost), worker protests erupted with growing frequency. Worker mobilization accelerated still further following the failure of hard-line Communists' attempted coup d'état and the final collapse of CPSU rule in August 1991. The fact that much of the economy remained under state control meant that strikes placed direct political pressure on the government. Indeed, prolonged strikes in such strategic industries as coal mining, metalworking, and transportation in 1991–92 repeatedly threatened Boris Yeltsin's capacity to promote price liberalization, enterprise privatization, and political democratization in Russia.

The common theme in many of these labor protests was workers' commitment to defending egalitarian income policies, guaranteed employment, favorable work rules, and other social benefits extended to them under the Soviet regime.[53] For example, in 1990–91 different labor organizations opposed enterprise reforms that took away workers' right to elect their own managers. Equally important as workers' impassioned defense of their prerogatives, government officials felt constrained in the formulation and implementation of neoliberal economic policies by their fear of violating the established social contract. The pattern repeated often in the late 1980s and early 1990s was for the Gorbachev and Yeltsin administrations to decree price liberalizations or propose worker layoffs, encounter labor resistance in the form of strikes or union protests, and then grant (though they did not always deliver) compensatory wage and benefit increases or job creation programs that substantially undermined the effect of the government's original policy initiative.

As in Nicaragua, democratic regime change in the former Soviet Union also posed serious political and organizational challenges to the existing trade union movement. Worker representation in the Supreme Soviet fell sharply when its members were elected democratically in 1989, leading labor groups to call for special mechanisms to guarantee their future political representation. The All-Union Central Council of Trade Unions (AUCCTU), which had grouped some 98 percent of the labor force, came under growing pressure to defend rank-and-file interests more vigorously. In October 1990 the AUCCTU dissolved to form the General Confederation of Trade Unions of the USSR (GCTU, with affiliates [Federations of Independent Trade Unions] in all the former republics). It sought to bolster its authority by demanding full employment, minimum income policies, and price-indexed wage and pension increases. Yet in several important cases in 1989–91 (especially widespread coal miners' strikes), worker mobilization quickly outpaced the established union leadership and led to the formation of influential independent labor organizations representing coal miners, air traffic controllers, and airline pilots. Union membership became voluntary, and the Yeltsin administration ended the automatic payroll deduction of union dues. Ties between the leadership of the Federation of Independent Trade Unions of Russia (FITU-R, the GCTU's largest affiliate)[54] and its members were weak, sustained principally by the organization's continued control over the distribution of social welfare benefits.

Government officials responded to labor challenges by enacting new legislation in October 1989 that granted unions the right to strike (except in defense, energy, transportation, communications, and health care industries) while establishing mandatory conflict mediation processes. Additional legislation adopted in early 1991 banned "political" strikes and strikes in the transportation sector, and it gave the president special authority to postpone or suspend strike actions. Workers' mobilizational capacity was sufficiently strong, however, and governmental authority was so weak in the late 1980s and early 1990s that much of this legislation was effectively ignored. In an effort to build greater labor support for economic reform, in January 1992 the Yeltsin administration created the Russian Tripartite Commission on the Regulation of Social and Labor Relations, with representatives from major labor organizations, employer/manager associations, and the government. The commission secured only marginally greater labor discipline, but at least in the short term it preserved the GCTU's role as centralized labor representative in policymaking. Despite the weakness of many labor organizations, mobilized workers retained the capacity to disrupt the economy and, in all likelihood, to influence such issues as future employment levels in privatized enterprises and the state's role in economic affairs.

The Nicaraguan and Russian cases suggest, then, that organized labor's response to democratic regime change is significantly different in postrevolutionary contexts than in other instances of authoritarian rule. Because postrevolutionary authoritarian regimes generally develop distinctive ideologies that give workers a special place in postrevolutionary society and offer the labor movement important institutional advantages and material benefits, labor has a stronger interest in preserving elements of the status quo than it does in most other authoritarian regimes. This is the case despite the onerous restrictions that postrevolutionary authoritarian regimes impose on some forms of labor participation, particularly strikes but often other labor actions as well. Moreover, support for important elements of the old regime extends beyond incumbent labor leaders to include a substantial proportion of the rank and file. In Nicaragua, continued labor support for Sandinista rule was undoubtedly due in large part to the relative proximity of the revolutionary experience and workers' accurate perception that an opposition electoral victory would endanger major social and political conquests. Yet even in Russia, despite the political harshness of Soviet rule, a highly developed sense of collective social rights (a major product of Soviet communism) motivated workers to mobilize powerfully to preserve key features of the postrevolutionary regime. In neither case did the labor movement inevitably or unequivocally support a democratic transition.

Organized labor's actions during these transitions did not indicate unqualified working-class support for authoritarianism.[55] Rather, the dilemmas that democratic transition poses for the labor movement in post-revolutionary contexts simply compel a reconsideration of broad generalizations concerning labor's role in political liberalization or democratization. Although in the long run unionized workers may benefit as both citizens and consumers from democratic governance and economic liberalization, their short-term losses may be considerable. This is particularly so in historical settings in which processes of political democratization and economic liberalization are closely linked. In Nicaragua and Russia, workers' perceptions of democracy were strongly colored by fears of neoliberal economic reforms that threatened to increase unemployment, reduce real wages and fringe benefits, and alter work rules. Their preference for statist solutions was particularly strong because of the ideological focus of the old regime. In both cases, too, the end of postrevolutionary rule deprived labor organizations of some important institutional privileges, including mandatory union membership and the automatic payroll deduction of union dues. Union leaders in Nicaragua had comparatively strong ties to the rank and file (most leaders survived the first round of national union elections held after the FSLN defeat in 1990),[56] and in both countries labor organizations in strategically important sectors often had sufficient bargaining leverage to cushion their members from the worst consequences of market reforms. But most Nicaraguan and Russian trade unions were poorly prepared in organizational terms to defend their members' interests in a more competitive political and economic environment. Building stronger labor organizations remains a major challenge for workers in both cases.

Although the labor movement's capacity to influence the social character of a new democratic regime depends in the first instance on its overall strength,[57] it may also vary with the sequencing of political and economic liberalization. The pace and scope of political transformation exceeded the speed and extent of economic reform in Nicaragua and especially Russia. In these cases, worker mobilization occurred in a more open political environment with some of labor's institutional advantages still in place and a large state sector intact. Unionized workers derived considerable bargaining advantage from surviving representational and legal safeguards and from the political impact of strikes in the public sector.[58] In contrast, extensive economic restructuring under continued authoritarian rule seriously undermined the Mexican organized labor movement's bargaining power by reducing the size of the more easily mobilized work force in the state sector and by promoting contract and work rule changes that often weakened strong, combative unions. For this and other reasons examined in the final section of this chapter, the Mexican labor movement may well play a less prominent role in a future democratic transition than did its Nicaraguan and Russian counterparts.

Dilemmas of Change in Mexican State-Labor Relations

What factors will shape the future character of state-labor relations in Mexico? How likely is it that the organized labor movement will become an active proponent of democratization? What changes would be necessary for this to occur, either within the labor movement or in the Mexican regime more broadly? The literature on labor and democratic regime change and the preceding examination of the Nicaraguan and Russian experiences suggest that three factors will have an important influence on organized labor's future political role in Mexico. These factors are: (1) the changing characteristics of the Mexican labor movement, especially its future size, composition, organizational strength, and bargaining effectiveness at the national and workplace levels; (2) labor organizations' relations with other sociopolitical actors, particularly political parties; and (3) labor organizations' relationship with the state, especially the extent of state authorities' political control over labor participation. This final section examines probable medium-term developments in each of these areas and their potential implications for labor's role in democratic regime change in Mexico.

Changes in the Labor Movement's Size, Composition, Organizational Strength, and Bargaining Effectiveness

The shift away from import-substituting industrialization, the closure or privatization of many state-owned enterprises, and related changes in the structure of the Mexican economy and in industrial organization hold important implications for the future size, composition, organizational strength, and bargaining effectiveness of the labor movement. Despite overall growth in the economically active population, employment in the manufacturing sector fell during the 1980s and early 1990s.[59] The decline was both a short-term consequence of the post-1982 economic crisis and the result of a broad shift in Mexican industrial strategy, away from the manufacture of consumer durable goods and intermediate products for the national market and toward the more specialized production of automotive vehicles, auto parts, chemicals and petrochemicals, light manufactured goods (including shoes and apparel), and food products for export. Employment in some manufacturing industries may continue to fall as, in a

liberalized trade environment, imports of foreign manufactured goods fulfill an increasingly large share of national consumer demand. This change,
coupled with a sharp, permanent cut in the number and size of state-owned
enterprises, limits the potential for labor movement expansion in the areas
that had for several decades been the most important focus of union activity.

The most dynamic manufacturing activity during most of the 1980s
and early 1990s was the in-bond processing *(maquiladora)* industry concentrated along the U.S.-Mexican border and in northern states. The industry grew from 620 firms employing 119,546 workers in 1980 to 1,708
companies with 447,606 employees in 1990,[60] and it is likely to remain an
important source of manufacturing growth. Some of these companies employ relatively large numbers of workers.[61] However, employment conditions (including high rates of worker turnover and frequent plant closings),
labor force characteristics (a large proportion of the labor force consists
of young workers without much union experience), and a long history of
collaboration between company managers and state labor officials have
all made the industry notoriously hostile to effective union action. Unions
rarely have any presence on the shop floor, and labor organizations committed to improving wage levels and working conditions have long been a
distinct minority in the industry. Indeed, with the exception of Matamoros,
Nuevo Laredo, and Reynosa in the state of Tamaulipas, unionization rates
in the *maquiladora* industry are very low.[62] These conditions will, at best,
change slowly. As a result, future employment growth in *maquiladora*-style
light manufacturing activities will not in the short term increase very substantially either the size or the negotiating strength of the Mexican labor
movement.

Moreover, future economic expansion is likely to be concentrated in
sectors that are much more difficult to unionize than heavy industry and
state-owned firms. Commercial activities and the service sector expanded
significantly during the 1980s and early 1990s.[63] They are likely to remain
important areas of job creation. Yet the number of employees per firm is
typically lower in these areas than in manufacturing, and employment in
some service activities (tourism, for example) is predominantly temporary.
Both factors are significant obstacles to worker organization. It is unlikely,
therefore, that unions formed in these activities could ever play a leading
role in national labor politics.

Sectoral changes such as these have been accompanied by a northward shift in the geographical locus of economic activity, a trend that the
North American Free Trade Agreement is likely to accelerate. This development has three important implications for the organized labor movement.
First, the emergence of new poles of economic growth in north-central

and northern Mexico and the relative decline of established manufacturing centers like Mexico City (the consequence of such factors as employers' desire to locate production closer to their principal export market, tighter environmental restrictions on industrial development in the heavily polluted Mexico City metropolitan area, and employers' interest in locating new production sites outside traditional areas of union strength) further disperse the labor force, potentially making coordination of union actions even more difficult. Second, the northward shift in the location of new enterprises and potential union activity, away from the political center in Mexico City, reduces the national political leverage that labor organizations derive from strikes and other forms of mobilization. Third, entrepreneurs in northern states have historically been even more resistant to unionization than their counterparts in central Mexico, and except in the case of *maquiladora* plants in some areas along the U.S.-Mexican border, they have particularly opposed unionization drives by confederations closely allied with the national political leadership in Mexico City. The northern industrial city of Monterrey, for example, is the center of company-controlled "white" unions *(sindicatos blancos)* in Mexico. The owners of large manufacturing firms in Monterrey have successfully combined a well-developed tradition of employer paternalism (comparatively high wages and fringe benefits and an extensive network of company-sponsored social, educational, and recreational activities for workers and their families) with ruthless opposition to independent labor organizing in order to maintain a skilled, highly productive, and politically quiescent work force.[64]

As a result of shifts in the sectoral composition and geographical location of economic activity, the unionized proportion of the economically active population is likely to decline in future years.[65] These changes have already weakened some national confederations, and they may continue to do so. Serious fragmentation of the CTM and the Labor Congress as a result of leadership struggles, or sustained government hostility toward particular national confederations, would further accelerate this trend. Even if workers in some strategically important economic activities (especially those organized in national industrial unions) prove capable of defending their particular economic and workplace interests, continued decline in the organizational strength of major confederations is likely to undercut further the labor movement's negotiating effectiveness at the national level. Labor's declining bargaining leverage was particularly evident in the 1980s and early 1990s in its reduced capacity to articulate and promote broad policy initiatives concerning such issues as federal labor legislation, minimum wages, social welfare programs, and national health and safety standards.

Enacting progressive legislation in these areas has depended historically on the strength of national organizations (the most important of which was the Confederation of Mexican Workers) capable of defining a programmatic agenda for labor. The most recent labor efforts to formulate a broad statement of policy goals both occurred in the turbulent 1970s; in retrospect, they constituted the labor movement's last coherent effort to advance an economic development strategy based on the principles of revolutionary nationalism. In April 1975 the opposition Democratic Tendency issued its "Declaration of Guadalajara" calling for union democracy, wage increases, social welfare improvements, and nationalist economic reforms. The CTM, in conjunction with other labor organizations, subsequently developed and publicized in 1978 and 1979 an even more elaborate program of redistributive economic reform. The CTM undertook this initiative as part of its efforts to revitalize its image in the wake of the labor insurgency of the early and mid-1970s. At the same time, CTM leaders sought to respond to the political challenges posed by both the 1977 political reform (especially the prospect that leftist parties would seek to undermine the confederation's control over its members) and the Consejo Coordinador Empresarial's (Business Coordinating Council) May 1975 founding declaration of principles, which rejected direct state responsibility for the production of goods and services and only reluctantly recognized the legitimacy of a mixed economy.

The most innovative proposal the CTM made in the late 1970s and early 1980s was its call for legal recognition of a distinct social sector consisting of worker-owned companies, small producers' associations, and member-operated enterprises such as cooperatives. Paralleling the Democratic Tendency's earlier statist demands, the CTM also called for the nationalization of a broad range of economic activities, including food production and the pharmaceutical, textile, construction, petrochemical, and steel industries.[66] The de la Madrid administration formally recognized the social sector in its 1982 constitutional reforms defining the composition of the Mexican economy. However, the greater significance of these labor proposals was that they often became the point of reference for specific demands made by unions and opposition political groups. In marked contrast, neither "official" organizations such as the CTM nor dissident unions proved capable in the late 1980s and early 1990s of formulating a coherent, autonomous programmatic response to the far-reaching economic transformations that confronted Mexican workers.[67]

Just as labor organizations will be challenged to maintain their bargaining effectiveness at the national level, they will also face new dilemmas in the workplace. In an increasingly open economy, employers will have even stronger incentives to maintain tight control over their work forces and resist union influence over the production process than they did when they could more easily pass higher production costs on to consumers in a highly protected domestic market. These pressures may be particularly strong in less capital-intensive enterprises producing primarily for export, firms whose international comparative advantages lie in low-wage labor and weakly organized, complacent unions. Moreover, some companies (including leading firms in the automobile and consumer electronics industries) began in the 1980s to experiment with work teams, quality circles, and similar arrangements as part of their efforts to increase managerial flexibility and promote production efficiency. Post-Fordist industrial relations approaches posed new challenges to traditional forms of union representation. Indeed, in some instances employers adopted them for the express purpose of weakening ties between democratically elected union leaders and their members.

The multiple dilemmas that will confront the Mexican labor movement during the 1990s and beyond demand a new generation of labor leaders committed to strengthening union organizations in the workplace and at industry and national levels, ensuring the effective representation of rank-and-file interests, and responding to the needs of a more educated labor force. Too frequently in the past labor leaders have been part of the problem, obstructing rank-and-file initiatives by negotiating "protection contracts" that gave legal sanction to almost unlimited employer prerogatives and workplace practices of questionable legality. Rapid economic change, new production technologies, and innovative forms of workplace organization may well provide both the stimulus and the opportunity for leadership renewal. This, however, will necessarily be a slow, uneven process, all the more so because many employers find undemocratic forms of union organization highly functional. Labor leadership change would probably occur more quickly and be more far-reaching in scope in a more fully competitive political environment. But so long as significant controls on labor participation remain in place in an authoritarian regime, state officials will continue to influence the selection of union leaders. Equally important, many labor leaders may still see greater potential for personal gain in maintaining close relations with the governing political elite than in representing the interests of rank-and-file union members.

Links between Labor Organizations and Political Parties

Analysts such as Rueschemeyer, Stephens, and Stephens emphasize the importance that links with other sociopolitical actors have in shaping labor's role in transitions from authoritarian to democratic rule. The availability of prodemocratic allies, particularly in the urban middle class, strengthens labor organizations' capacity to promote political opening and redistributive reform. Political parties are particularly important mediating institutions in this regard, providing an organizational framework for solidifying cross-class alliances and articulating programmatic positions that appeal to broad constituencies. For these reasons, the nature of the party system and the character of labor's ties to parties are key factors influencing the labor movement's impact on regime change.

Forging strong links between labor organizations and parties committed to promoting democratization is always a challenge under authoritarian rule, but it is especially difficult in postrevolutionary authoritarian regimes. The hegemonic or single party whose formation often helps consolidate postrevolutionary rule typically establishes close ties with labor organizations. The general character of party-labor relations and the degree of direct political control which the "party of the revolution" exercises over unions depend on the party's ideological orientation, its organizational characteristics, and the tasks it performs. In Marxist-Leninist regimes such as the former Soviet Union, for example, the official party's leading role precluded altogether the development of opposition party-labor ties. But even in postrevolutionary settings in which rival parties exist, the governing party's dominant position may seriously weaken links between labor and other political organizations. For many workers, ties to political parties may carry the taint of the authoritarian past even after postrevolutionary rule collapses. This explains in part why labor-party ties in Russia remained tenuous in the early 1990s, with many workers preferring at least in the short term to defend their interests through trade union–based strategies. Even in Nicaragua, where the proximity of the revolutionary experience helped preserve links between unions and the Sandinistas, some labor organizations sought to increase their autonomy vis-à-vis the FSLN when the party compromised on labor issues in order to preserve a working relationship with the UNO government.[68]

In Mexico as well, a long history of hegemonic party rule often makes unions reluctant to form alliances with partisan political organizations. The state administrative apparatus, not the governing party, has been the principal instrument of elite control over labor participation. Nevertheless, the PRI's close identification with authoritarian rule and the tradition of party membership through affiliated mass organizations (at least until 1990, the statutes of many government-allied unions formally required members to belong to the PRI) make union-party ties a frequent source of concern among the rank and file. Unions that have seceded from confederations such as the CTM have often taken the additional step of revising their statutes to eliminate the requirement of PRI membership or have otherwise announced their separation from the governing party. Having struggled hard to win their autonomy from state-subsidized federations or confederations, these unions have been understandably reluctant to risk their independence by developing close ties to political parties. Some opposition parties' inclination to subordinate immediate union interests to their partisan priorities, the limited ability of opposition parties to serve as effective interlocutors with government officials, and state authorities' hostility to such opposition party–union alliances all make labor organizations doubly hesitant to form links of this kind.

The task of building stronger labor-party ties is further complicated in Mexico by the shifting priorities of those parties on the political Left which might serve as the most logical vehicles for articulating labor interests in the national arena. From the 1920s through the 1970s, most leftist parties identified themselves closely with the urban working class and the peasantry, seeking in different ways to establish close relations with unions and peasant organizations. Following the repression of the 1968 student and popular movement, former student activists intensified their organizing work among blue-collar employees, peasants, and the urban poor. The scope and importance of the labor insurgency of the early and mid-1970s reinforced this identification because leftist activists played important roles in union democratization movements and other protests in a broad range of economic activities. The unionization of university academic staff and nonacademic employees had a particularly important impact on the thinking of leftist party leaders, many of whom were heavily involved in university politics.

In the late 1970s, however, major leftist parties began to devote greater attention to electoral strategies. They did so in response to the 1977 political reform and the increased opportunities it offered for opposition parties to participate in elections and gain representation in federal, state, and local government. The Mexican Communist Party (which disbanded in 1981 to form, along with other leftist parties, the Partido Socialista Unificado de México [Mexican Unified Socialist Party, PSUM]) was among the most prominent advocates of this strategic reorientation.

Some leftist groups questioned the merit of this policy. They took the position that, in a political context in which governing elites maintained tight limits on political competition, electoral involvement would divide opposition forces and fruitlessly absorb scarce resources that might be better devoted to grassroots organizing.[69] These elements sought to develop nonparty sectoral organizations (the most important of which were "coordinating committees" [coordinadoras] created in the late 1970s and early 1980s to unite autonomous regional organizations in loose national networks)[70] which would both defend popular actors' immediate interests and promote societal democratization. Nevertheless, by the mid-1980s electoral strategies became dominant on the Left. This tendency was reinforced by the significant weakening of more politically independent labor organizations under the weight of state repression and economic crisis, a development that reduced the number of opposition parties' potential allies in the labor movement. The most prominent party on the Left, the *cardenista,* Party of the Democratic Revolution, fully embraced an opposition strategy centered on elections. Although the PRD supported strikes and other forms of labor protest,[71] it made only limited efforts to establish long-term ties to worker organizations.

Whether or not leftist parties' commitment to electoral participation successfully promotes democratization, it may have significant implications both for the role that labor organizations play in an eventual political transition and for the social character of a new democratic regime. Organized labor is rarely able to initiate regime change, and as a consequence of the economic transformations discussed in the preceding section, it is especially unlikely to do so in Mexico. Although opposition leadership in a future Mexican transition is most likely to come from the urban middle class, strong links to opposition political parties would increase labor's capacity to support movement toward democracy. Close ties to opposition parties would also expand labor's opportunities to influence the character of social and economic policies adopted by a democratically elected government. A more competitive post-transition political environment would perhaps encourage labor organizations to form closer links to political parties, but they would be more likely to achieve equality in this relationship if these ties were developed before the transition occurs.

Workers, Unions, and the State

Neither economic changes affecting the future size, composition, and organizational strength of the labor movement nor the character of labor ties to opposition parties offers much reason for optimism concerning organized labor's independent capability to promote democratization in Mexico. The greatest obstacle, however, lies in political controls on worker participation. Limitations on workers' rights to organize and strike are keystones of authoritarian rule. The issue is not merely the content of the federal labor code, although complex administrative procedures and mandatory state approval for both union formation (and the requirement that unions subsequently register with state authorities all changes in their statutes and leadership) and strikes often pose real obstacles to rank-and-file initiative. Rather, the main problem is the concentration of political power in the state administrative apparatus, which makes it possible for state labor officials to apply legal requirements arbitrarily in order to block strikes, rank-and-file opposition movements within unions, and other forms of worker protest.

It also gives rise to such phenomena as the preemptive unionization of workplaces by "official" organizations, a tactic often encouraged by employers seeking to avoid politically independent union representation. The successful transition to democratic rule via fully competitive elections may not in itself remedy all these problems; indeed, restrictive legal controls on some forms of labor participation survived democratic transitions in Brazil and Chile in the 1980s.[72]

At least in principle, a more fully democratic political environment would increase workers' opportunities to pressure for the removal of legal controls in such areas as union formation and strikes, as well as to hold state officials more directly accountable for their administration of labor law. Some administrative regulation of union formation, union activities, and strikes is, of course, appropriate in a democracy, and it is highly probable that a future revision of Mexico's federal labor code will leave some restrictions in place. The greater risk that labor law reform holds for organized labor's long-term interests is that—in the name of promoting democracy in the labor movement and preventing abuses like those frequently committed by union officials under authoritarian rule—basic legal provisions underpinning workers' bargaining strength in the workplace will be eliminated.

Organized labor's capacity to influence labor law reform could be limited by the weakness of its ties to opposition political parties. Internal divisions within the labor movement may also prevent it from presenting a united front in legislative debates. More important, however, the outcome of public policy debate on this issue is likely to be strongly shaped by the growing influence of business interests in Mexican politics. The approval of NAFTA may make the putative requirements for promoting production efficiency and international competitiveness the decisive criteria in future labor code reform.

It is no doubt true that some provisions in the 1970 federal labor law pose obstacles to economic efficiency. These include industrywide collective bargaining agreements (the *contrato-ley*), permanent employee *(planta)* status and other legal regulations governing the length and terms of employment, the requirement that workers be compensated for the forty-eight-hour legal workweek rather than the actual time worked, an employer's obligation to sign a collective contract when requested to do so by a legally recognized union, and mandatory compensation for unjustified dismissal. But because future economic trends may further weaken Mexican workers' market-based bargaining leverage, labor law provisions such as these are crucial instruments through which unions might safeguard their status as significant social actors. Similarly, even though the separation exclusion clause in contracts has often been abused, it provides union officials with an important legal defense against employers' efforts to co-opt workers and thereby undermine union discipline.

The prospects for preserving organized labor's role in the workplace and in national policymaking and for promoting democratic regime change in Mexico would both be enhanced if the removal of major state controls on labor participation occurred in conjunction with the democratization of the labor movement. The consolidation of political democracy depends in part on the progressive extension of democratic social relations. Yet advances in societal democratization remain tenuous so long as political power is concentrated in the state apparatus. Continued authoritarian rule encourages governing elites to build undemocratic social networks in order to sustain themselves in power, while simultaneously making such alliances a compelling option for those social forces without strong, autonomous bases of influence. In the Mexican case, some significant liberalization of state controls on nonelectoral mass participation must necessarily come first. Organized labor is unlikely to initiate this process, but substantial changes in this area might quickly win significant labor support for democratic reformers, greater freedom for worker organization and mobilization, and increased opportunities for labor organizations to forge new alliances with other sociopolitical actors nationally and perhaps internationally. Just as a state-subsidized labor movement long supported authoritarian rule in Mexico, organized labor's political alignment following an initial political transition will be a major factor influencing the social character and stability of a future democratic regime.

Union Registration Data for Federal-Jurisdiction Industries

The data set for the analysis of union registration in federal-jurisdiction economic activities (chapter 5) is the actual record of union registrations maintained by the Ministry of Labor and Social Welfare's Associational Registry. With the exception of occasional missing values, the information on each case (the dates of each union's formation, application for registration, and formal registration; links to federations or confederations, if any; geographical location; economic sector; membership size; type of union, as specified in federal labor law; and the date on which the union's registration was canceled, if applicable) is quite complete for the period between November 30, 1934, and December 1, 1964 (the Cárdenas through López Mateos administrations). The data after June 4, 1965, are less complete; the cases for which at least partial data are available represent 22.1 percent of total registrations between this date and November 30, 1976, the end of the Echeverría administration. For the entire 1934–76 period, then, the data set contains at least partial information for 84.0 percent of all registrations. It was not possible to gather data for later years.

In the statistical analysis accompanying the text, cases are grouped in different six-year presidential terms according to the date on which formal recognition was granted. For example, the first union registered after November 30, 1934, is included in the Cárdenas administration, even though it applied for registration at an earlier date. Grouping cases in this manner means that statistical measures of the impact of presidential policy on registration time are conservative because a given administration is credited with some cases initiated in previous periods. An analysis of variance in which only those cases initiated *and* concluded within a six-year term are credited to a given administration did not produce substantially different results.

Railroad Worker Case Sampling Procedures

Records of individual worker grievances in the Federal Conciliation and Arbitration Board's (JFCA) archives in Mexico City are filed alphabetically by grievant's last name under the number of the special junta that examined the case. Because it was impossible to determine the total number of demands filed by Ferrocarriles Nacionales de México (FNM) employees in a given year before actually counting the file cards listing the grievant's name and case number, it was necessary to estimate the number of cases for a particular year and then select cases at regular intervals. For the years 1936, 1938, and 1940–75, the estimated total was divided by 50 to compile a sample of 50 cases per year; slightly more cases were selected for 1934 (71), 1935 (58), 1937 (60), and 1939 (56) before this standard sampling method was established. This method produced a sample of 2,145 cases, although choosing the same number of cases for each year biased the sample in favor of years when fewer grievances were filed. All but 7 cases were subsequently dropped from the 1934 total (those filed before November 30, the date on which the Cárdenas presidency began), leaving a total sample of 2,081 cases.

The file cards selected in this way contained the grievant's name, the nature of the demand, the date on which the case was filed, the number of the special junta hearing the case, and the case's sequential number among all demands filed before a particular special junta in a given year, as well as an identifying code necessary to locate the actual case record in the JFCA archives.

Although this sample provides valuable insight into the kinds of grievances filed by railroad workers before the JFCA between 1934 and 1975, difficulties in actually locating case records in the JFCA archives meant that it was impractical to conduct a more detailed analysis of railroad worker demands on the basis of this sample. A smaller sample was selected for this purpose. Using a random numbers table, 5 demands were selected from the cases for each year in the original sample, producing a second sample of 209 cases for the 1934–75 period. Cases filed before November 30, 1934, were also subsequently deleted, leaving a final sample of 205 cases. Because of difficulties encountered in locating some archival records, the final sample includes only 2 grievances for 1964 and 1 case for 1965.

The cases in this second sample were located in the JFCA's archives; when a case could not be found, a replacement case was selected from the same year using a random numbers table. The following information was compiled: the name of the worker(s) filing the demand and the number of grievants involved (whether a single worker, a group of workers, or the Mexican Railroad Workers' Union, STFRM); the number of the special junta hearing the case; the nature of the grievance and whether a monetary award was sought; the date on which the case was filed and the date when the JFCA reached its final decision; the date on which the employee began work on the railroads, when this information was reported; the state in which the worker was employed at the time the demand was filed, when this information was available; the grievant's legal representation (whether the worker represented himself or herself, was represented by an STFRM official or an STFRM attorney, or was represented by private counsel); whether Ferrocarriles Nacionales de México (or, in some cases, the union) actively contested the case; the outcome of the case (a formal decision by the special junta; a private settlement by the worker and the employer; the worker failed to pursue the grievance; or the special junta terminated the case because the worker and/or the employer failed to pursue the grievance for a specified period of time); in cases involving a formal junta decision, whether the ruling favored the worker or the employer and the vote of the three-person board; the size of the special junta's financial award to the grievant, when this information was available; whether the worker or employer sought a legal injunction *(amparo)* from the Supreme Court against the special junta's action, and whether an injunction was granted; and whether the grievant died while his or her case was under review.

In cases in which either the worker or FNM sought an injunction against a JFCA action, the date of the special junta's initial decision was used for the purposes of computing a case's duration. However, if the JFCA reopened a case as the result of Supreme Court action and subsequently issued a new ruling, this second date was used to calculate the case's duration.

Information concerning the amount of JFCA financial awards to grievants proved very difficult to use. For example, in pension adjustment cases the worker sometimes received a single payment, whereas in other cases the worker's monthly pension was increased by a specified amount. At other times, the case record noted the amount of the final award but not the amount the grievant had sought. Given these problems of comparability, monetary settlements were excluded from the analysis of railroad worker grievances.

NOTES

Chapter 1: Introduction

1. See Huntington, *Political Order in Changing Societies* (1968), chaps. 1, 3, esp. 143–46. See also Weiner, "Political Participation" (1971), and Bendix and Rokkan, "Extension of Citizenship to the Lower Classes" (1964).

2. Skocpol, *States and Social Revolutions* (1979), 4, and chap. 1 passim.

3. See Huntington, *Political Order*, chap. 5.

4. For a methodologically sophisticated comparative analysis of the impact of organized labor on regime change in Latin America, see Collier and Collier, *Shaping the Political Arena* (1991).

5. See Scott, *Mexican Government in Transition* (1964), esp. 15–30, 195–96, 300. Almond and Powell, *Comparative Politics* (1966), 271, called Mexico a "partially mobilized democratic system." Even in the 1970s, Apter, *Introduction to Political Analysis* (1977), 375, termed Mexico a polyarchy, along with Australia, Canada, Denmark, France, Great Britain, Israel, New Zealand, Norway, Sweden, and the United States.

6. Linz, "Totalitarian and Authoritarian Regimes" (1975), 358 n. 8, concludes that in efforts to classify different regimes as democratic or not, "the most debated case is Mexico." For a summary of the earlier debate concerning the character of the Mexican regime, see Needleman and Needleman, "Who Rules Mexico?" (1969).

7. See Purcell, *Mexican Profit-Sharing Decision* (1975), 4–5, 12, and Smith, *Labyrinths of Power* (1979), 50, 56–57.

8. Both Purcell, *Mexican Profit-Sharing Decision,* and Smith, *Labyrinths of Power,* frame their discussion of Mexico in terms of ideas originally developed in Linz, "An Authoritarian Regime: Spain" (1964), leading them to stress style of rulership and elite mentalities. O'Donnell at one time characterized Mexico as a bureaucratic-authoritarian regime, a model he developed on the basis of his analysis of military-led authoritarian regimes in Argentina and Brazil; see "Corporatism and the Question of the State" (1977), 53, 80–81. For O'Donnell's later views on this comparison, see "Introduction to the Latin American Cases" (1986), 5–6. With some qualifications, Kaufman, "Mexico and Latin American Authoritarianism" (1977), 194–95, and Cardoso, "On the Characteristics of Authoritarian Regimes in Latin America" (1979), 38–39, also applied the bureaucratic-authoritarian label to Mexico.

9. Cambodia is an exception to this argument, even though the Khmer Rouge's brutal rule blocked independent sociopolitical organization and political mobilization. In this case, social revolution gave rise to a totalitarian regime without a preceding or succeeding period of postrevolutionary authoritarian rule.

10. This definition draws upon Krasner, "Structural Causes and Regime Consequences" (1982), 186; Collier, *New Authoritarianism in Latin America* (1979),

402–3; O'Donnell, *Bureaucratic Authoritarianism* (1988), 6, 24; Cardoso, "Characteristics of Authoritarian Regimes," 38.

11. Linz, "Totalitarian and Authoritarian Regimes," 179–80, distinguishes among various authoritarian regime subtypes on the basis of "the degree or type of limited political pluralism under such regimes and the degree to which such regimes are based on political apathy and demobilization of the population or limited and controlled mobilizations." He subsequently identifies and examines (285–350) bureaucratic-military authoritarian regimes, organic statism, mobilizational authoritarian regimes in postdemocratic societies, postindependence mobilizational authoritarian regimes, racial and ethnic "democracies," "defective" and "pretotalitarian" political situations and regimes, and post-totalitarian authoritarian regimes.

12. In terms of Linz's various subtypes of authoritarian rule, postrevolutionary regimes most closely parallel postindependence mobilizational regimes. However, the founding experiences that give rise to these two forms of authoritarian rule are quite different. With the exception of Algeria, where the independence struggle approached a social revolution in the mobilization of lower-class elements, mass social forces have generally played only a limited role in independence movements and nationalist elites' subsequent consolidation of political power. As a result, mass actors have generally not retained their political importance over time in postindependence mobilizational regimes. See ibid., 321–26.

13. Ibid., 266–69.

14. Huntington, *Political Order,* 270, emphasizes the importance of both nationalism and socioeconomic appeals in revolutionary mass mobilization.

Of course, developments in Ethiopia and the former Soviet Union in the late 1980s and early 1990s demonstrated that in societies deeply divided along ethnic, linguistic, or religious lines, nationalist sentiment may eventually help undermine postrevolutionary authoritarian regimes.

15. Linz, "Totalitarian and Authoritarian Regimes," 266, 269–71, 279.

16. Huntington, "Social and Institutional Dynamics of One-Party Systems" (1970), 6–7.

17. Linz, "Totalitarian and Authoritarian Regimes," 185, 333, notes the diffuseness of the line separating totalitarian and authoritarian regimes.

18. Perlmutter, *Modern Authoritarianism* (1981), 2–4 and passim, emphasizes the importance of state structures in "modern" (that is, mass-based) authoritarian regimes.

19. This definition of the state draws upon Skocpol, *States and Social Revolutions,* 29; O'Donnell, "Corporatism," 50; and Hamilton, *Limits of State Autonomy* (1982), 6–7. See also Weber, *Economy and Society* (1978), 1:54–56; 2:901–4.

20. The focus here on mobilization activities (strikes, demonstrations, election campaigns, solidarity actions, and so forth) specifically does not include prior or preparatory developments such as consciousness raising. These latter aspects of mobilization are referred to in the text as mobilizational capabilities or capacities. For an analysis that combines these two dimensions in examining political mobilization, see Waterman, "Reasons and Reason" (1981), 554–89.

21. Huntington, "Dynamics of One-Party Systems," links the fate of modern authoritarian regimes to that of one-party systems, noting that "the one-party system is the principal modern form of authoritarian government" and that "the fate of authoritarianism in modern society depends upon the viability of the one-party system in modern society" (4).

22. For comments on the differential impact of such controls, see O'Donnell, "Corporatism," 48, and Schmitter, *Interest Conflict and Political Change in Brazil* (1971), 110, 150, 159, 239. On the importance of organizational involvement in political participation, see Nie and Verba, "Political Participation" (1975), 49–55.

23. Womack, "Mexican Revolution" (1986), 107–10.

24. The character of the Mexican revolution remains a source of controversy. For a review of the debate and an insightful analysis of this question, see Knight, "Mexican Revolution" (1985).

25. Ibid., 14–15, 17–26.

26. See Knight, *Mexican Revolution* (1986), 1:55–68, for a discussion of Madero, his political agenda, and his support among rising middle-class elements.

27. Knight, *Mexican Revolution*, 1:62–63, 138–39; Hart, *Revolutionary Mexico* (1987), chaps. 3, 6. Carr, *El movimiento obrero y la política en México* (1976), 1:64–66, summarizes Madero's limited public statements on labor issues. On Mexican Liberal Party activities in support of worker protests, see Hernández, "El magonismo en México" (1980).

28. See Knight, *Mexican Revolution*, 1:78–127, 150–70, for an excellent overview of the origin and varieties of agrarian revolt during this period. See also Tutino, *From Insurrection to Revolution in Mexico* (1986).

29. Knight, "The Working Class and the Mexican Revolution" (1984), 65–71, argues that workers played a less important role than peasants in the revolutionary struggle because the urban working class had weaker ties to village communities and was more fully integrated into the market (and therefore had a vested interest in continued industrial production).

30. Hart, *Revolutionary Mexico*, chap. 2. See also Carrera Stampa, *Los gremios mexicanos* (1954).

31. Walker, "Porfirian Labor Politics" (1981), 259; Carrera Stampa, *Los gremios mexicanos*, 283, 288.

32. For discussions of economic change during the Porfiriato, the emergence of an urban working class, and the composition of the industrial labor force, see Anderson, *Outcasts in Their Own Land* (1976), chap. 2 and appendix B; Basurto, *El proletariado industrial en México* (1975), chaps. 1–2; and Carr, *El movimiento obrero*, 1:16–24. Ruiz, *Labor and the Ambivalent Revolutionaries* (1976), 6, calculates that industrial workers constituted 16 percent of the work force in 1910.

33. On anarchists' organizational successes and anarchism's appeal to artisans, see Hart, *Anarchism and the Mexican Working Class* (1978), 104, 108, 123, 127, 178. See also Leal and Woldenberg, *Del estado liberal a los inicios de la dictadura porfirista* (1980), 156, 164.

34. Leal and Woldenberg, *Del estado liberal*, 178–201. See Díaz, "Satiric Penny Press for Workers" (1990), for an excellent discussion of the working-class

press and the formation of workers' political attitudes in the decades before the revolution.

35. Leal and Woldenberg, *Del estado liberal,* 233–43.

36. Hart, *Revolutionary Mexico,* 55–60. Walker, "Porfirian Labor Politics," 264, reports 119 Congreso Obrero affiliates throughout the country in 1900, but he offers no estimate of total membership.

37. Walker, "Porfirian Labor Politics," 262, 264; Carr, *El movimiento obrero,* 1:26–36; Lear, "Workers, *Vecinos,* and Citizens" (1993), 66–67, 69–71, 80–81.

38. Some strikes did occur, however; see Anderson, *Outcasts,* appendix A. Carr, *El movimiento obrero,* 1:34–36, discusses the typical motivations for labor strikes.

39. Rodea, *Historia del movimiento obrero ferrocarrilero* (1944), xxix, 153. Ruiz, *Labor,* 18, estimates that the various railroad worker organizations had 21,000 members in 1910.

40. Katz, "Mexico" (1986), 65; Knight, *Mexican Revolution,* 1:129–30, 143; Anderson, *Outcasts,* 303–12; Ruiz, *Labor,* chap. 2.

41. Anderson, *Outcasts,* 242–50, 254–72, discusses early efforts by elite factions to recruit labor support in the 1910 presidential election.

42. Carr, *El movimiento obrero,* 1:67–69.

43. Womack, "Mexican Revolution," 88–89, 94; Knight, *Mexican Revolution,* 1:408, 424–25, 433, 436, 440; Hart, *Revolutionary Mexico,* 241, 257–58, 271.

44. The COM's predecessor, the Casa del Obrero, was formed in September 1912. The COM was affiliated with the anarchist International Association of Workers; Hart, *Revolutionary Mexico,* 271. Araiza, *Historia de la Casa del Obrero Mundial* (1963), provides a documentary history of the formation of the COM and its activities.

45. Lear, "Workers, *Vecinos,* and Citizens," 109, 122, 170; see Hart, *Revolutionary Mexico,* 303–4.

46. On working-class violence during this period, see Knight, *Mexican Revolution,* 1:132–33, 208–18.

47. Hart, *Revolutionary Mexico,* 307–8. Hart estimates that during the revolution as many as 15,000 industrial and urban workers participated in fighting nationwide. Knight, *Mexican Revolution,* 1:430–31, notes that Coahuila coal miners and railroad workers formed militias as early as 1911–12. Womack, "Mexican Revolution," 114, estimates the size of the "Red Battalions" at 5,000 workers, while Carr, *El movimiento obrero,* 1:89, estimates their size at 4,000–8,000 workers.

On the different political, ideological, and economic factors leading to the COM-Carranza alliance, including some urban workers' anticlericalism and their distrust of religiously conservative *zapatistas,* see the excellent analysis by Carr, *El movimiento obrero,* 1:83–95.

48. Knight, *Mexican Revolution,* 2:424–25, 430.

49. Womack, "Mexican Revolution," 118, 125, 135; Hart, *Revolutionary Mexico,* 317–18; Lear, "Workers, *Vecinos,* and Citizens," 178–83. Knight, *Mexican Revolution,* 2:427, notes that demands for payment in hard currency were the basis for many labor protests throughout the country in 1915–17.

50. This discussion draws on Womack, "Mexican Revolution," 133–34, 136, 143; see also González Casanova, *En el primer gobierno constitucional* (1980), 33. On the formation of the CROM, see Rivera Castro, *En la presidencia de Plutarco Elías Calles* (1983), 17–19.

51. Córdova, *La ideología de la revolución mexicana* (1973), 16, 18, 21, 27. On the origins and content of liberalism in nineteenth-century Mexico, see Hale, *Transformation of Liberalism in Late Nineteenth-Century Mexico* (1989), chap. 1.

52. Womack, *Zapata* (1970), 55 n. 4, notes the extent to which Madero's political ideas were influenced by the Progressive movement in the United States.

53. Of course, prerevolutionary protest movements had also contributed to the emergence of social justice concerns in national political debates. See Anderson, *Outcasts*, 320–24.

54. For a discussion of Carranza's and Francisco Villa's adoption of socioeconomic reform proposals in order to secure mass support, see Womack, "Mexican Revolution," 98–99, 113.

55. Córdova, *La ideología*, 22.

56. Hart, *Revolutionary Mexico*, 243–45, 255–57, 259, 263, 274, 325. See also Katz, *Secret War in Mexico* (1981), 7, 10–11, on nationalist resentment of foreign investors. Anderson, *Outcasts*, 252–54 and chap. 6, and Lear, "Workers, *Vecinos*, and Citizens," 104, discuss workers' resentment of foreigners' presence in supervisory capacities. On ties between the Díaz regime and domestic and foreign capitalists, see Hamilton, *Limits of State Autonomy*, 48–52.

57. Turner, *Dynamics of Mexican Nationalism* (1968), 202–16.

58. Meyer, "Mexico" (1986), 158.

59. Córdova, *La ideología*, 31; Knight, "Mexican Revolution," 6; Meyer, "Mexico," 165.

60. On the nationalist content of working-class demands for social justice in the decade before the revolution, see Anderson, *Outcasts*, 324–28; Carr, *El movimiento obrero*, 1:35–36, 40; and Adleson, "Cultural Roots of the Oil Workers' Unions in Tampico" (1992), 49, 54. Tutino, "Revolutionary Confrontation" (1990), 62, observes that shared nationalist opposition to foreign firms underpinned the alliance between Carranza's Constitutionalist forces and the Casa del Obrero Mundial. Rodea, *Historia*, 335–410, discusses in detail the process of "Mexicanization" on the railroads.

Knight, *Mexican Revolution*, 1:145, insists that the examples cited here were exceptions and that workers in general did not evidence strong antiforeign sentiment during the early stages of the revolution. Knight, *U.S.-Mexican Relations* (1987), 24, also notes that some foreign investors—especially petroleum and railroad companies—successfully manipulated their enclave status to win support from local populations and work forces.

61. Meyer, "Mexico," 156–57; Hart, *Revolutionary Mexico*, 11, 45, 48, 50, 96–100. Katz, *Secret War*, 6–10, suggests that popular defense of local and regional autonomy against the centralizing effects of the Porfiriato was a key dynamic in the revolution.

62. Turner, *Mexican Nationalism*, 15–21, 101–55, 163–69, 216–31. See also

Schmidt, *Roots of Lo Mexicano* (1978), chaps. 2–4. On foreign intervention in the revolution, see esp. Katz, *Secret War*.

63. Córdova, for example, notes that respect for political liberties has been subject to the pragmatic needs of economic development. *La ideología,* 35–36, 226.

64. See, for example, Calles, "Policies of Mexico Today" (1926). See also Meyer, "Mexico," 172–73, and Bennett and Sharpe, "The State as Banker and Entrepreneur" (1980), 168–74.

65. Less serious military uprisings occurred in 1927, 1929, and 1938.

66. Meyer, "Mexico," 160–61, 165, 169; Córdova, *La ideología,* 368–79; Hamilton, *Limits of State Autonomy,* 76; Lieuwin, *Mexican Militarism* (1968), chaps. 2–4. For an examination of the modern Mexican military, see Ronfeldt, *Modern Mexican Military* (1984).

67. Meyer, "Mexico," 173–74; Córdova, *La ideología,* 351–67; Hamilton, *Limits of State Autonomy,* 79–80.

68. Hamilton, *Limits of State Autonomy,* 69–74.

69. Córdova, *La ideología,* 247; see also 27–28, 214, 218, 230.

70. See Benjamin, "Laboratories of the New State" (1990), for an excellent overview of the gradual centralization of political power in the 1920s and early 1930s.

71. The definitive study of political parties during and after the revolution and the circumstances surrounding the formation of the PNR is Garrido, *El partido de la revolución institucionalizada* (1982); see esp. chaps. 1–2. See also Lajous Vargas, *Los orígenes del partido único* (1979); Fuentes Díaz, *Los partidos políticos en México* (1954); and Furtak, *El partido de la revolución* (1978).

72. Garrido, *El partido,* 92, notes the existence of at least 148 parties in 28 states in 1929. He refers to the PNR as "a confederation of caciques" (103).

73. Regional and local bosses remained strong in Tamaulipas and Yucatán well into the 1930s, and the regionally dominant Partido Veracruzano del Trabajo (Veracruz Labor Party) did not officially disband until 1946, when the PRM became the PRI. I am grateful to John Womack, Jr., for his comments on these points.

In Oaxaca, regional political powers held sway into the 1960s; see Rubin, "Popular Mobilization and the Myth of State Corporatism" (1990), 252–55.

74. Garrido, *El partido,* 73, 112, 120, 164, 256, 324.

75. The best analyses of Mexico's political elite are Smith, *Labyrinths of Power,* and Camp, *Mexico's Leaders* (1980). For an examination of changes in elite composition and behavior, see Middlebrook, "Dilemmas of Change in Mexican Politics" (1988), 122–34.

76. Calles made this distinction explicit in December 1928 when organizing support for the party; see Dulles, *Yesterday in Mexico* (1961), 410.

77. Garrido, *El partido,* 187, 276, 295, 297, 348.

78. Under Cárdenas the PRM played an active role in promoting agrarian reform and the nationalization of the petroleum industry, which helped forge ties between groups such as organized labor and the "official" party. After 1940, however, the party's principal responsibility was the mobilization of popular support during elections. See ibid., 301, 307, 309, 311, 340, 348.

79. This interpretation differs from those analyses of postrevolutionary Mexican politics which emphasize the "official" party's role as the principal instrument of elite control over mass actors, as well as from those studies that credit both the state apparatus and the party with exercising this function without differentiating clearly between them. See, for example, Huntington, *Political Order*, 318–21; Hansen, *Politics of Mexican Development* (1971), chaps. 5, 7; Smith, *Labyrinths of Power*, 49–62; Hamilton, *Limits of State Autonomy*, 35–37; Levy and Székely, *Mexico* (1987), 60, 91, 106; Collier and Collier, *Shaping the Political Arena*, 202, 224, 242, 416–19.

80. See Domínguez, introduction to *Mexico's Political Economy* (1982), 9–17.

81. The principal exceptions are political culture interpretations of Mexican politics, which maintain that organized labor's behavior is strongly influenced by cultural orientations that discourage aggressive demands. From this perspective, both labor leaders and workers fail to press social and economic demands or initiate widespread labor mobilization because they form part of a national political culture that seemingly emphasizes the importance of enduring sociopolitical hierarchies, established authority relationships, and personal loyalties. They are said to share psychological predispositions to conform to existing cultural norms. See Padgett, *Mexican Political System* (1976), 119–21, 125, 131, 147, 233, 314, and Hansen, *Politics of Mexican Development*, 142, 165, 183–97, 224.

There are, however, a number of difficulties with a culturalist approach. At the most general level, there are important problems in arriving at meaningful national generalizations regarding the impact of political culture on labor behavior given the possibility of significant regional or subregional variations in value structures and the ordering of relevant political orientations. Culturalist interpretations also appear to understate considerably the significance of both individual protests and collective mobilization in the historical development of the Mexican organized labor movement.

82. This study departs from common practice in that it does not characterize the Mexican regime or state-labor relations in Mexico as "corporatist." There are two reasons for not doing so. First, the term has come to be used indiscriminately to describe such diverse features of the Mexican regime as the sectoral organization of the governing party, the state's legal authority to structure interest representation (for example, the requirement that unions receive formal state recognition before they can negotiate a collective contract or otherwise legally represent their members), government support for the formation of relatively inclusive labor organizations (such as the Confederation of Mexican Workers in the late 1930s and the Labor Congress in the mid-1960s) and business associations, and the selective distribution of social welfare benefits to progovernment mass organizations. Under some stricter definition, aspects of state-labor relations or mass politics in Mexico (including, for example, the sectoral composition of the governing party and the labor-government-business composition of labor conciliation and arbitration boards) would merit use of the term *corporatism*. However, because of the many connotations the word has acquired in analyses of Mexican politics, greater clarity of meaning can be achieved by avoiding it.

Second, discussions of corporatism in the Latin American context privilege the state in the analysis of state-society relations, emphasizing the importance of the state apparatus as an instrument of political control while downplaying the influence of societal factors on the characteristics of mass participation. Much of the literature on this subject implicitly assumes, moreover, that state-society relations closely approximate the ideal-typical form labeled "state corporatism" by Schmitter, "Still the Century of Corporatism?" (1974). One of the goals of this study is to determine the limits of state-centered explanations of labor participation in Mexico. It leaves open to empirical investigation such questions as how and to what extent state officials employ administrative structures and legal restrictions to limit different forms of labor participation, and it highlights the interaction between the state apparatus and labor organizations themselves as mechanisms of political control. By not labeling state-labor relations in Mexico as corporatist, this study seeks to avoid inappropriate connotations that might obscure the effort to understand in historical context major changes in state-society relations.

83. For the purposes of this study, the term *national political elite* refers to those individuals occupying major national office: presidents, cabinet and subcabinet officials, directors of major state-owned enterprises, leaders of the governing "party of the revolution," governors, members of the federal Chamber of Deputies and Senate, and ambassadors. See Smith, *Labyrinths of Power*, 15.

Some workers (and other individuals from working-class families) rose to national elective or appointive office in the decades after the 1910–20 revolution. However, the proportion of workers in the national political elite was always small. Chapter 3 discusses worker political mobility in the postrevolutionary period.

84. Collier and Collier, *Shaping the Political Arena*, 46.

Chapter 2: State Structures and Political Control

1. González Casanova, *La democracia en México* (1976), 29–43, examines this issue in detail. For other analyses of the federal executive's central position in postrevolutionary Mexican politics, see Cosío Villegas, *El sistema político mexicano* (1976); Goodspeed, "El papel del jefe del ejecutivo en México" (1955); Calderón, *Génesis del presidencialismo en México* (1972); Carpizo, *El presidencialismo mexicano* (1979).

2. Córdova, *La ideología de la revolución mexicana* (1973), 46, 49–50, 53–63, 68, 215, 262.

3. Article 925 of the 1871 Federal District penal code established penalties (fines and incarceration) for those convicted of exercising "physical or moral violence" in an attempt to alter wage levels or working conditions. The text is reproduced in Trueba Urbina, *Evolución de la huelga* (1950), 53.

4. Anderson, *Outcasts in Their Own Land* (1976), 33–37, 302.

5. Ibid., 127, 143–44, 150–51, 212–21, 229–35. See also Knight, "The Working Class and the Mexican Revolution" (1984), esp. 57–58.

6. Díaz's 1907 arbitration decree (*laudo*) and subsequent additions to it on working conditions in the Puebla textile industry addressed such issues as child

labor, working hours, paid holidays, wages, disciplinary measures, workplace health and safety, and grievance resolution procedures. In 1907–8 the Díaz administration also considered labor legislation providing for the mandatory arbitration of strikes (and harsh penalties for workers involved in strikes producing physical damage, injuries, or deaths) and an accident compensation law. However, these measures were not enacted. See Anderson, *Outcasts*, 151–52, 207–8, 217–20.

The violent suppression of the Río Blanco textile strikes produced a shift in business and Catholic elites' attitudes regarding the need for labor legislation, though those favoring social legislation to address working-class problems remained in the minority. Ibid., chap. 5, esp. 180–81, 184–88.

7. On the relationship between state capacity and state autonomy, see Evans and Rueschemeyer, "The State and Economic Transformation" (1985), esp. 50–60.

8. Attention to this process is absent, for example, in Collier and Collier, *Shaping the Political Arena* (1991), even in cases in which "the principal agency involved in the incorporation project was the state" (163).

9. Oszlak, "Historical Formation of the State in Latin America" (1981), 26–27, refers to the importance of state-society interactions during the process of state formation, but his discussion focuses primarily on the nineteenth century. Similarly, Veliz, *Centralist Tradition of Latin America* (1980), examines the historical formation of centralized states in Latin America ("political centralism") and argues that states promoted and shaped industrialization. However, he does not suggest that the social classes produced by industrialization influenced the form or character of the state.

10. Leal and Woldenberg, *Del estado liberal* (1980), 222–23; Moreno Toscano, "Los trabajadores y el proyecto de industrialización" (1980), 345.

11. See Knight's very suggestive comments on this point in "Working Class," 58–61.

12. The anarchosyndicalist Confederación General de Trabajadores (General Confederation of Workers, CGT) opposed any state involvement in worker-employer relations, although the actions of CGT affiliates often departed significantly from this principle. See Tamayo, *En el interinato de Adolfo de la Huerta* (1987), 150–52, 154.

Like their counterparts in Mexico, worker organizations in Argentina and Brazil generally supported state intervention in labor affairs in order to compensate for their weak bargaining position in the workplace. See Korzeniewicz, "Labor Unrest in Argentina" (1993), 37–38, and French, *Brazilian Workers' ABC* (1992), 32–33.

13. Franco G. S., "El papel del derecho del trabajo" (1987), appendix 1, lists the various measures enacted between 1900 and 1916. Bensusán Areous, "Institucionalización laboral en México" (1992), 81–88, notes the influence of Belgian, British, French, and U.S. social legislation on labor laws enacted during this period.

14. Quoted in Franco G. S., "Labor Law and the Labor Movement in Mexico" (1991), 106.

15. Remolina Roqueñi, *Evolución de las instituciones y del derecho del trabajo* (1976), 11–21. The first effort to create a separate labor department occurred

under interim-president Francisco de la Barra (1911), but the Chamber of Deputies failed to act on the proposal. The department's functions would have been limited to gathering information on labor-related matters.

16. For brief discussions of Department of Labor activities, see Bensusán Areous, "Institucionalización laboral," 65–66; Carr, *El movimiento obrero y la política en México* (1976), 1:69–70; Ruiz, *Labor and the Ambivalent Revolutionaries* (1976), 33–36, 40–41, 56–59, 64–66; Lear, "Workers, *Vecinos,* and Citizens" (1993), 117–18, 121, 123, 136; Shabot, *Los orígenes del sindicalismo ferrocarrilero* (1982), 249–56, 262–70.

17. In 1915 Carranza had reformed the 1857 constitution to permit the federal legislature to regulate labor affairs throughout the country, and in 1916 he issued another decree declaring that mandatory labor laws were solely of federal jurisdiction. See Remolina Roqueñi, *Evolución,* 17, 29–30, 33.

18. See Rocha Bandala and Franco, *La competencia en materia laboral* (1975), 35–38. The final proposal that Carranza submitted to the convention for debate included provisions for an eight-hour day, a weekly day of rest, and prohibitions against work at night by women and children.

19. See Moreno, *El congreso constituyente* (1967), 37–53.

20. See Carr, *El movimiento obrero,* 1:123. The Gran Orden Mexicana de Conductores, Maquinistas, Garroteros y Fogoneros (Great Mexican Order of Conductors, Engineers, Brakemen, and Firemen, formed in 1916) was one of the few labor organizations to lobby the Constitutional Convention in favor of labor rights. In addition to appealing for the "Mexicanization" of railroad personnel, the Gran Orden called for the creation of tripartite arbitration boards, free access to education, an eight-hour workday, a prohibition against the employment of children under the age of fourteen, retirement and work-related accident benefits, the right to strike, and inexpensive worker housing. See Rodea, *Historia del movimiento obrero ferrocarrilero* (1944), 193–94.

21. Franco G. S., "El papel del derecho del trabajo," appendix 2, presents the original text of Article 123 and lists subsequent amendments to it. Bensusán Areous, "Institucionalización laboral," 94–109, 112–15, summarizes developments leading up to the adoption of Article 123 and initial business and labor reaction to it.

22. Remolina Roqueñi, *Evolución,* 12–14, 15, 17, 20, 25–27.

23. Ibid., 32–33.

24. Ibid., 33, 43–49. Only Morelos and Tlaxcala failed to produce legislation codifying the provisions of Article 123.

State labor laws enacted during this period are compiled in Secretaría de Industria, Comercio y Trabajo, Departamento del Trabajo, *Legislación del trabajo* (1928). Bensusán Areous, "Institucionalización laboral," chap. 3, provides a summary evaluation of this legislation. However, virtually nothing is known about the impact of these state-level labor codes on worker-employer relations or on the development of the organized labor movement during this period.

25. For examples of the problems summarized here and responses by unions and employers, see González Casanova, *En el primer gobierno constitucional* (1980), 56–59, 100–101, 130; Bensusán Areous, "Institucionalización laboral,"

113–14, 208; Ruiz, *Labor*, 149–50; Saragoza, *Monterrey Elite and the Mexican State* (1988), 135.

Because of its involvement in major labor conflicts in states such as Puebla and Veracruz, and because of the role played by federal labor inspectors throughout the country, the actual scope of ministry involvement in labor affairs exceeded its formal authority during the late revolutionary period and the 1920s.

26. Remolina Roqueñi, *Evolución*, 63–64; Tamayo, *En el interinato*, 29–31, 33. On the defeat of the 1921 proposal (which would have created a separate Ministry of Labor, thus satisfying a condition of the 1919 electoral pact between the CROM and Álvaro Obregón), see Collier and Collier, *Shaping the Political Arena*, 207. The 1922 proposal was apparently formulated initially by the Alianza de Ferrocarrileros Mexicanos (Mexican Railroad Workers' Alliance); Rodea, *Historia*, 232.

Perhaps because its opponents feared that it would pave the way for a national labor code, efforts to enact a labor law for the Federal District and federal territories encountered stiff resistance between 1919 and 1926. In the mid-1920s, fears that the proposed law would extend CROM influence also fueled opposition to it. See de la Cueva, *Derecho mexicano del trabajo* (1964), 1:137–38; Bensusán Areous, "Institucionalización laboral," 208–13; *Excélsior*, 14 Dec. 1926, 4; 16 Dec. 1926, 4; 31 Dec. 1926, 3.

27. Remolina Roqueñi, *Evolución*, 65–67. For evidence concerning evolving business, labor, and political opinion during these years regarding the desirability of a federal labor code, see Bensusán Areous, "Institucionalización laboral," 241, 249–53.

28. The CROM's relations with former president Obregón soured during the Calles administration (1924–28) as Calles consolidated his alliance with organized labor and Obregón sought to strengthen his political ties with peasant-based organizations linked to the Partido Nacional Agrarista (National Agrarian Party, PNA). At issue were CROM efforts to organize in rural areas. Members of the PNA congressional delegation strongly opposed proposals for a federal labor law on the grounds that it would expand the CROM's undemocratic control over the labor movement. Antonio Díaz Soto y Gama, an anarchist leader and *agrarista* who was a prominent member of the Chamber of Deputies throughout the 1920s, was particularly committed to impeding CROM expansion. See Carr, *El movimiento obrero*, 2:117–23, and Rivera Castro, *En la presidencia de Plutarco Elías Calles* (1983), 104.

29. Saragoza, *Monterrey Elite*, 156; Bensusán Areous, "Institucionalización laboral," 149–50; Mario de la Cueva, interview with author, 11 Jan. 1978, Mexico City.

30. Carr, *El movimiento obrero*, 2:77–78; Saragoza, *Monterrey Elite*, 126.

31. Rocha Bandala and Franco, *La competencia*, 160–61. The reforms affected Article 73 (x) and Article 123's preamble and clause 29.

32. Carr, *El movimiento obrero*, 2:74–78. The CROM's role during the 1920s is examined in chapter 3 of this book.

33. For general discussions of labor opposition to the 1929 proposal, see Córdova, *En una época de crisis* (1980), 45–46, 49; Guadarrama, *Los sindicatos y la*

política en México (1981), 182; Loyola Díaz, *Conflictos laborales en México* (1980), 51–53. Córdova notes (53–55) that some labor groups favored quick passage of the 1929 initiative.

34. See the last section of this chapter for a more detailed discussion of evolving legal provisions concerning union formation, union activities, and the right to strike.

35. Saragoza, *Monterrey Elite*, 157, suggests that Portes Gil viewed the proposed legislation as a vehicle to punish the CROM.

Vicente Lombardo Toledano, a prominent member of the CROM during this period, claimed that prohibitions against unions' involvement in religious and, especially, political affairs were quite common in state-level labor legislation. See his *La libertad sindical en México (1926)* (1974), 208.

36. Saragoza, *Monterrey Elite*, 159–65; Bensusán Areous, "Institucionalización laboral," 262–79. U.S. firms especially opposed provisions such as those requiring that at least 70 percent of a firm's employees be Mexican citizens, that supervisory personnel (managers, doctors, foremen, and so forth) speak Spanish, and that employers receive permission from conciliation and arbitration boards and give one month's notice to workers before closing a business. See *New York Times*, 10 July 1929, 14.

37. Córdova, *En una época de crisis*, 109–12. The labor codes in Yucatán, Veracruz, Durango, Puebla, and Sonora were cited as especially favorable to workers' interests. In recognition of labor's concerns on this issue, the Ley Federal del Trabajo ("Transitorios," #13) guaranteed that contracts providing workers with benefits more advantageous than those in the law itself would remain in effect unless they were revised with the consent of the workers and employers affected.

38. *Revista Mexicana del Trabajo* 4 (July–Aug. 1957): 154; 5 (Sept.–Oct. 1958): 559, 561–63. The origin and significance of exclusion clauses, an important legal subsidy for unionization, are discussed in more detail in chapter 3 of this book.

For discussions of the positions taken by labor organizations during the 1931 legislative debates, see Córdova, *En una época de crisis*, 112–16; Bensusán Areous "Institucionalización laboral," 312–18; Garrido, *El partido de la revolución institucionalizada* (1982), 131.

39. Saragoza, *Monterrey Elite*, 166.

40. In practice, the federal government strongly influences the labor policies of state governments, especially on matters with implications extending beyond the boundaries of a single state. The Ley Orgánica de la Administración Pública Federal (sec. 1, art. 40) gives the Ministry of Labor and Social Welfare authority to ensure state governments' compliance with both Article 123 and the provisions of federal labor law wherever they apply. See Franco G. S., "Labor Law," 117.

Proposals to give the federal government exclusive jurisdiction over labor matters appeared as early as August 1934; see Córdova, *En una época de crisis*, 185–86. Mexico joined the International Labour Organisation in September 1931 following enactment of the federal labor law.

41. Córdova, *En una época de crisis*, 81–87, 90–94, discusses the impact of the economic crisis in Mexico and reproduces sections of congressional commen-

tary on the political significance of the new federal labor law. Bensusán Areous, "Institucionalización laboral," 374, notes that the government's failure in 1931 to implement Article 123 guarantees of worker housing and enterprise-level profit sharing reflected its preoccupation with the economic viability of private firms.

42. Medin, *El minimato presidencial* (1982), 55, 64; Saragoza, *Monterrey Elite*, 166–67; Córdova, *En una época de crisis*, 96.

43. Córdova, *En una época de crisis*, 94–95, 98.

44. Secretaría de Industria, Comercio y Trabajo, *Proyecto de Ley Federal del Trabajo* (1931), "Exposición de motivos," x.

45. Excerpt from the report by the congressional study commission on legislation creating the Departamento Autónomo del Trabajo, quoted in Remolina Roqueñi, *Evolución*, 81.

46. Secretaría de Industria, Comercio y Trabajo, Departamento del Trabajo, *Legislación del trabajo*, p. 5 of introduction by Vicente Lombardo Toledano.

47. Remolina Roqueñi, *Evolución*, 81–87. The Ministry of Industry, Commerce, and Labor disappeared shortly thereafter; its economic functions became the responsibility of a new Secretaría de la Economía Nacional (Ministry of the National Economy).

48. Ibid., 110–14.

49. Article 2 of "Reglamento interior de la Secretaría del Trabajo y Previsión Social," *Diario Oficial de la Federación*, 9 Apr. 1957, 8.

50. "Reglamento interior," chaps. 17 and 18, respectively.

51. Wilkie, *Mexican Revolution* (1973), 170–71, shows that neither the Autonomous Department of Labor nor the Ministry of Labor and Social Welfare was ever a large outlet for social expenditures. Their share of actual federal budgetary expenditures only ranged from 0.1 percent to 0.6 percent between 1933 and 1963.

52. For an overview of the STPS's administrative evolution through 1957, see Secretaría del Trabajo y Previsión Social, *Evolución histórica de la Secretaría del Trabajo y Previsión Social* (1957).

53. Federal-jurisdiction industries, while strategically important in political and economic terms, represent a small proportion of the unionized labor force. In 1979, for example, they accounted for only 15.9 percent of the unionized labor force; 84.1 percent of unionized workers were employed in local-jurisdiction economic activities. See Zazueta and de la Peña, *La estructura del Congreso del Trabajo* (1984), table 2.6.

54. Rocha Bandala and Franco, *La competencia*, 15–28; de la Cueva, interview with author, 11 Jan. 1978, Mexico City.

55. Although the 1915 Yucatán system was apparently the model for the juntas created by the Constitutional Convention, there had been earlier legislative precedents for such boards at the federal level. These included several proposals made between 1913 and 1915 to create boards composed of worker and employer representatives to set minimum wages and regulate labor conflicts. For details, see Remolina Roqueñi, *Evolución*, 37–38.

De la Cueva, *Derecho mexicano del trabajo*, 2:890–903, maintains that the juntas created at the convention were in fact a synthesis of precedents found in other countries' labor justice systems. For example, the tripartite representational formula had precedents in the labor legislation of Belgium, France, and Germany.

56. Article 25 of the "Ley del trabajo de Yucatán," 14 May 1915, reproduced in Rocha Bandala and Franco, *La competencia,* 23.

57. In the early 1900s the Progressive movement in the United States advanced parallel arguments in its call for informal, "sociological" arbitration tribunals and legal procedures. See Harrington, *Shadow Justice* (1985), chaps. 1–2.

58. Quoted in de la Cueva, *Derecho mexicano del trabajo,* 2:906.

59. One labor organization, the Great Mexican Order of Conductors, Engineers, Brakemen, and Firemen, called for the convention to create arbitration boards on which worker representatives would equal the combined number of government and employer representatives. Apparently they were to operate on an ad hoc basis to resolve conflicts at the request of the workers and employers involved. See Rodea, *Historia,* 194.

60. See Article 123, clauses 9, 18–21.

61. Rocha Bandala and Franco, *La competencia,* 52–53, 84; de la Cueva, interview with author, 11 Jan. 1978, Mexico City. Rocha Bandala and Franco quote selections from the constitutional debates to support this interpretation.

Although there was long discussion at the convention concerning the need for a special article on labor and the issues to be addressed in it, apparently the only sections of Article 123 which were formally debated before final adoption were clauses 3 and 18 on, respectively, working hours for minors and strikes. See Rocha Bandala and Franco, *La competencia,* 75.

62. See, for example, Article 5 of the decree establishing juntas in the Federal District and federal territories, reproduced in Remolina Roqueñi, *Evolución,* 36.

63. Clause 20 read: "Differences or conflicts between capital and labor will be submitted to a conciliation and arbitration board formed by an equal number of worker and employer representatives, and one from the government." Clause 21 stated: "If the employer refuses to submit his differences to arbitration or accept the verdict pronounced by the board, the labor contract will be terminated and he will be obliged to compensate the worker with the payment of three months' salary, in addition to bearing responsibility for the result of the conflict. If the refusal is on the part of the workers, the labor contract will be terminated."

64. See Rocha Bandala and Franco, *La competencia,* 92–131, for a selection of the most important of these cases. Among other considerations, the Supreme Court argued that giving juntas authoritative powers would in effect create a rival court system, and that worker and employer representatives on them lacked the necessary legal training to conduct grievance cases properly; de la Cueva, interview with author, 11 Jan. 1978, Mexico City.

De la Cueva, *Derecho mexicano del trabajo,* 2:909, notes that because some of the Supreme Court justices involved in these cases had been delegates at the Constitutional Convention, their arguments were considered an accurate interpretation of its intentions.

65. The court's decision in *La Corona, S.A.* is reproduced in Rocha Bandala and Franco, *La competencia,* 132–42. The court found that the juntas fell under the

states' constitutional authorization to legislate on matters in which the boards did not conflict with other tribunals operating in the states. The court thus reversed its earlier position in finding that the boards did not constitute "special tribunals," which were prohibited by Article 13 of the 1917 constitution.

66. See de la Cueva, *Derecho mexicano del trabajo*, 2:910; Bensusán Areous, "Institucionalización laboral," 121.

67. See González Casanova, *En el primer gobierno constitucional*, 31, 76; Rodea, *Historia*, xxxiv; de la Cueva, interview with author, 11 Jan. 1978, Mexico City. For an example of employer opposition to the creation of conciliation and arbitration boards, see Adleson, "La adolescencia del poder" (1982), 95, 98–99.

The anarchosyndicalist General Confederation of Workers opposed the presence of government representatives on juntas, preferring direct action by workers to resolve disputes. See Bensusán Areous, "Institucionalización laboral," 121.

68. Clark, *Organized Labor in Mexico* (1934), 101, 247.

69. Rocha Bandala and Franco, *La competencia*, 156–57; Remolina Roqueñi, *Evolución*, 51–58, 61; "Reglamento de las Juntas Federales de Conciliación y Arbitraje," *Diario Oficial de la Federación*, 27 Sept. 1927, 6–13. Regional conciliation boards operated on an ad hoc basis. The JFCA began operation with five special branches (*juntas especiales*) for different federal-jurisdiction industries.

70. Secretaría de Industria, Comercio y Trabajo, *Del trabajo y la previsión social* (1928), 103–4, 526–27; Lombardo Toledano, *La libertad sindical*, 266; Rodea, *Historia*, 489–91. Rodea reports that the government representative on the JFCA who wrote the decision against the Confederation of Transport and Communications Workers was none other than Reynaldo Cervantes Torres, a CROM loyalist who had initially declared the strike illegal in his capacity as head of the Ministry of Industry, Commerce, and Labor's Labor Office. The labor representative on the JFCA was also a CROM member.

71. For example, subsequent legislative initiatives eliminated the national Labor Court included in the 1928 Ministry of the Interior *proyecto*. See Secretaría de Gobernación, *Código Federal del Trabajo (Proyecto)* (1928), bk. 2, chap. 6.

72. The plan for enterprise-level mixed commissions closely resembled similar proposals made in Germany in the 1880s. See Rimlinger, *Welfare Policy and Industrialization* (1971), 112–30.

73. The five-tier junta system also included state-level and federal conciliation and arbitration boards. See Secretaría de Industria, Comercio y Trabajo, *Proyecto de Código Federal de Trabajo* (1929), bk. 2, chaps. 1–9; bk. 3, sec. 2, chap. 7.

74. See Secretaría de Industria, Comercio y Trabajo, *Ley Federal del Trabajo* (1931), title 8, chaps. 1–6, 10; title 9.

75. The 1970 federal labor law permitted (art. 600 [IV]) federal conciliation boards to arbitrate definitively all conflicts under their jurisdiction which involved financial matters involving less than three months' salary. It also allowed (art. 595) for the creation of ad hoc federal conciliation boards (*juntas federales de conciliación accidentales*) to resolve specific disputes. See Trueba Urbina and Trueba Barrera, *Ley Federal del Trabajo* (1988).

76. Following the creation of the JFCA with five special branches in 1927,

other *juntas especiales* were established in 1933 (one), 1936 (one), 1944 (seven), and 1975 (two). These additional juntas were created in parallel (though not simultaneously) with the extension of federal labor jurisdiction over additional economic activities.

77. See *Ceteme*, no. 700, 26 Feb. 1965, 6; no. 871, 15 June 1968, 2; no. 936, 20 Sept. 1969, 3; no. 1092, 14 Oct. 1972, 1; *Excélsior*, 22 Aug. 1976, 1. The perception that there is greater opportunity for political influence on the labor justice system at the state level is shared by some Federal Conciliation and Arbitration Board personnel and Mexican legal authorities. Author's interviews with JFCA *junta especial* president, 26 Oct. 1977, Mexico City, and de la Cueva, 11 Jan. 1978, Mexico City.

The CTM's own influence on local-level juntas has sometimes been criticized by government labor authorities; see *Tiempo*, 29 Feb. 1952, 43–44.

78. State governors have lobbied strenuously against such a change. De la Cueva, interviews with author, 11 Jan. and 28 Apr. 1978, Mexico City.

79. Franco G. S., "Labor Law," 107 n. 4.

80. On the role of the JFCA in the petroleum conflict, see Ashby, *Organized Labor and the Mexican Revolution under Lázaro Cárdenas* (1963), 211–14, 228, 231–33. The railroad dispute is examined in chapter 4 of this book.

81. Conciliation and arbitration boards have jurisdiction over individual and collective conflicts between workers and employers, among workers, among unions, between unions and workers (whether or not the workers are unionized), among employers, and between unions and the state. Franco G. S., "Labor Law," 117. Franco G. S., 118, also briefly discusses other conflict resolution authorities in Mexico.

82. Trueba Urbina and Trueba Barrera, *Ley Federal del Trabajo*, art. 469.

83. See the text of Article 123, clause 21, in note 63.

84. For an example of vigorous internal union competition among railroad workers to serve on the JFCA, see *Unificación Ferroviaria* (newspaper published by the Mexican Railroad Workers' Union), no. 194, 1 Dec. 1944, 2; no. 195, 15 Dec. 1944, 4; no. 196, 1 Jan. 1945, 2.

Although the railroad workers' union leadership attached great importance to JFCA elections, this enthusiasm was not necessarily shared by rank-and-file union members—resulting in low turnout for elections to choose junta representatives. *Unificación Ferroviaria*, no. 242, 16 Jan. 1947, 2.

Other evidence of the importance that labor organizations attach to junta elections appears in *Ceteme*, no. 370, 4 Oct. 1958, 5, and the author's interviews with a JFCA *junta especial* labor representative, 8 Nov. 1977, Mexico City, and with a JFCA senior administrator, 26 June 1978, Mexico City. For evidence that some employers also attach great importance to junta representation, see Saragoza, *Monterrey Elite*, 131.

85. *Unificación Ferroviaria*, no. 310, 31 Dec. 1950, 6.

86. Carr, *El movimiento obrero*, 2:25–26, 156; Hart, *Anarchism and the Mexican Working Class* (1978), 170–71; Malpica Uribe, "Las Juntas de Conciliación y Arbitraje en Puebla" (1980), 129–31.

CROM control of the Federal District's Junta Central de Conciliación y Arbitraje apparently produced decisions overwhelmingly in favor of workers. For data concerning cases resolved in 1925, see Centro de Estudios Históricos del Movimiento Obrero Mexicano, "La Junta Central de Conciliación y Arbitraje" (1980), 15.

87. Medin, *El minimato presidencial,* 62. There was no legal basis for the government's removal of the CROM representatives.

88. Hernández Chávez, *La mecánica cardenista* (1979), 123–24. Hernandez Chávez notes that President Portes Gil contributed simultaneously to the erosion of CROM strength and the rise of the Velázquez faction's Federación Sindical de Trabajadores del Distrito Federal by nullifying the December 1928 elections held to select worker representatives to the Junta Central de Conciliación y Arbitraje in the Federal District, which the CROM had won.

89. For information on the CTM's "national assembly" of junta representatives, see *Ceteme,* no. 794, 24 Dec. 1966, 1; no. 921, 7 June 1969, 1; no. 978, 18 July 1970, 7; no. 991, 24 Oct. 1970, 2. Fidel Velázquez regularly addressed these meetings.

At least for the JFCA and the Federal District's Junta Central de Conciliación y Arbitraje, the CTM also organized a supervisory board (*jurado de responsabilidades*) chaired by a senior confederation leader (including Jesús Yurén and Alfonso Sánchez Madariaga) to coordinate the actions of its junta representatives. See *Ceteme,* no. 12, 15 Dec. 1950, 7; no. 477, 3 Dec. 1960, 1, 6; no. 792, 10 Dec. 1966, 1, 2; no. 896, 7 Dec. 1968, 4; no. 998, 12 Dec. 1970, 2.

For data concerning CTM majority control of the JFCA in the late 1970s, see Middlebrook, "Political Economy of Mexican Organized Labor" (1982), 174–78.

90. Trueba Urbina and Trueba Barrera, *Ley Federal del Trabajo,* art. 378 (I).

91. Franco G. S., "Labor Law," 108, discusses this phenomenon and uses the cases of medical students and university employees to show how specific political problems have been resolved by creating separate legal regulations.

92. For a discussion of the juridical-constitutional basis for this distinction and the evolution of special legal provisions for government employees, see ibid., 108–9.

93. A 1983 reform of the federal constitution's Article 115 gave state legislatures the authority to regulate labor matters involving the employees of state governments. Ibid., 109.

94. Legislation detailing the provisions of Apartado "B" was published in the *Diario Oficial de la Federación* on December 28, 1963. For a discussion of the special legal status of bank employees before 1990, see Franco G. S., "Labor Law," 109 n. 7.

95. Several authorities on Mexican labor law note that there is no specific legal justification for the requirement that federal-jurisdiction unions be registered by the Ministry of Labor and Social Welfare rather than by the Federal Conciliation and Arbitration Board. See Franco G. S., "Labor Law," 112 n. 11, and Trueba Urbina and Trueba Barrera, *Ley Federal del Trabajo,* "Commentary" on art. 365.

96. Trueba Urbina and Trueba Barrera, *Ley Federal del Trabajo,* title 7, chap. 2.

The minimum age for union membership was originally twelve years (art. 239). See also de la Cueva, *El nuevo derecho mexicano del trabajo* (1979), 2:336–46.

Federal law recognizes five different types of unions: craft unions (*sindicatos gremiales*, representing workers in a single occupation or profession); company unions (*sindicatos de empresa*, composed of workers employed by the same firm); industrial unions (*sindicatos industriales*, formed by workers employed by two or more firms in the same economic activity); national industrial unions (*sindicatos nacionales de industria*, representing workers employed by one or more firms in the same economic activity in two or more states or federal territories); and "mixed" unions (*sindicatos de oficios varios*, formed by workers employed in different economic activities in a given municipality when fewer than twenty workers are employed in each of these activities). See Trueba Urbina and Trueba Barrera, *Ley Federal del Trabajo*, art. 360.

97. Bensusán Areous, "Institucionalización laboral," 213–21, summarizes the union registration requirements in state labor codes enacted between 1918 and 1928. For earlier historical precedents, see Carrera Stampa, *Los gremios mexicanos* (1954), 148, and Leal and Woldenberg, *Del estado liberal*, 152–53.

Unlike some of the state labor laws adopted after 1917, the 1931 federal code did not establish any time limit within which state authorities were required to act on a union's request for official recognition; see Bensusán Areous, "Institucionalización laboral," 214–15. This omission may have contributed to lengthy delays in the registration process, a phenomenon examined in chapter 5 of this book.

98. De la Cueva, *Derecho mexicano del trabajo*, 2:420.

99. Ibid., 422; *Revista Mexicana del Trabajo* 4 (Jan.–Apr. 1957): 19–20 (reproducing the prologue to the final draft of the 1931 federal labor law).

100. Archivo General de la Nación, Labor Section, packet 1234, file 5 (Act #9, 28 Nov. 1928, of the Convención Obrero-Patronal, pp. 1, 7), and packet 1275, case no. 8/071/22, pt. 7, pp. 10–12.

101. Bensusán Areous, "Institucionalización laboral," 150–55, 214, 303–6, 354. For a more general discussion of such bargains, see Zapata, "Las organizaciones sindicales" (1979), 211–12, and Stepan, *The State and Society* (1978), 87.

102. See Shafer, *Mexican Business Organizations* (1973), 21–63.

103. Archivo General de la Nación, Labor Section, packet 1275, case no. 8/071/22, pt. 7, p. 12.

104. Ibid., pp. 9–17, 63; packet 1234, file 5 (Act #9, 28 Nov. 1928, of the Convención Obrero-Patronal), pp. 64–66, 68–70. The CROM accepted the parallel prohibition against union involvement in religious affairs, although it argued that loss of a union's official registration was an inappropriate penalty.

105. This discussion draws on Trueba Urbina and Trueba Barrera, *Ley Federal del Trabajo*, arts. 359, 371–73, 376. Foreigners cannot serve as union officers.

106. Secret balloting is one of the statutory changes that union reform movements sometimes introduce after they come to power. For the case of the National Education Workers' Union, see *Páginauno*, 7 Dec. 1992, 8.

107. Trueba Urbina and Trueba Barrera, *Ley Federal del Trabajo*, art. 371 (VIII).

108. De la Cueva, *Derecho mexicano del trabajo,* 2:452, notes that labor authorities are not obligated to recognize new union leaders in the conduct of union business if their election was not properly reported.

109. Trueba Urbina, *Evolución de la huelga,* is the classic study of the historical evolution of strike legislation in Mexico. Carr, *El movimiento obrero,* 1:33, notes that legislation similar to the Federal District penal code existed in other states as well.

110. Clause 18 also prohibited strikes during wartime by employees of military-industrial enterprises (*establecimientos fabriles militares*) owned by the federal government. On the political origins of this provision (the temporary suspension of work at the Fábrica Nacional de Armas as a consequence of the July–August 1916 general strike in Mexico City, which some government officials said threatened the position of the Constitutionalist army at a time when U.S. troops were in northern Mexico), see de la Cueva, *Derecho mexicano del trabajo,* 2:844, and Carr, *El movimiento obrero,* 1:100–101. The prohibition was lifted in December 1938.

111. Secretaría de Gobernación, *Código Federal del Trabajo,* art. 276.

112. Ibid., arts. 268(v), 271, 275.

113. For labor organizations' reactions at the Worker-Employer Convention, see Archivo General de la Nación, Labor Section, packet 1234, file 5 (Act #10, 29 Nov. 1928, pp. 4–6; Act #11, 3 Dec. 1928, pp. 2–4), and packet 1275, case no. 8/071/22, pt. 7, pp. 16–17, 23–25, 28.

114. See especially the comments made by Aarón Sáenz (then minister of industry, commerce, and labor) in May 1931, quoted in Bensusán Areous, "Institucionalización laboral," 305.

115. This discussion draws on Trueba Urbina and Trueba Barrera, *Ley Federal del Trabajo,* arts. 443, 450, 920–24, 926–39.

116. De Buen L., *Derecho del trabajo* (1992), 2:894; Franco G. S., "Labor Law," 112.

117. Trueba Urbina and Trueba Barrera, *Ley Federal del Trabajo,* art. 925, defines public service employees as those working in firms in the communications, transportation, electrical power generation, natural gas, water distribution, and food services (when an entire branch of service is affected) industries, as well as those employed in hospitals and health care centers and in cemeteries.

118. Evidence in support of the claim that the strike is nonexistent must be submitted within five days, and the junta in question is required to rule on this matter within twenty-four hours after it receives such evidence. If either the worker or employer representative fails to participate in the board's ruling on the claim, that person's vote is ceded to the junta president. Trueba Urbina and Trueba Barrera, *Ley Federal del Trabajo,* art. 930.

Article 123 of the 1917 constitution referred only to legal (*lícita*) or illegal (*ilícita*) strikes. The possibility that state authorities might declare a strike nonexistent was introduced in the 1929 Portes Gil *proyecto* (art. 330).

119. León and Marván, *En el cardenismo* (1985), 163, 166, 208.

120. See, for example, "Decreto que reforma la Ley Federal del Trabajo," *Diario Oficial de la Federación,* 10 Apr. 1941, 3–5; "Decreto que adiciona los artícu-

los 5, 11 y 13, y reforma el 12 de la Ley de Prevenciones Generales, de 11 de junio de 1942, relativo a la suspensión de garantías," *Diario Oficial de la Federación,* 20 Sept. 1943, 1–2; and Bensusán Areous, "Construcción y desarrollo del derecho laboral" (1985), 66. For a discussion of additional wartime legislation restricting political activities, see Stevens, "Legality and Extra-Legality in Mexico" (1970).

Chapter 3: The Challenge of Mass Participation and the Origins of Mexico's State-Subsidized Labor Movement

1. An early chronicler of the revolution, Ernest Gruening, wrote that "the most palpable product of the Mexican Revolution [was] the labor movement." *Mexico and Its Heritage* (1928), 335.

2. This discussion draws on Hart, *Anarchism and the Mexican Working Class* (1978), 16–17, 21, 24, 49, 55, 58, 75–76, 116, 120, 123–24, 126, 133, and Leal and Woldenberg, *Del estado liberal a los inicios de la dictadura porfirista* (1980), 242, 244.

3. Walker, "Porfirian Labor Politics" (1981), 258, 260–62, 264–66, 272, 279.

4. See Hart, *Anarchism,* 135, on the COM's initial organizational successes.

5. See Díaz, "Satiric Penny Press for Workers" (1990), 498–99, 514, 516–17.

6. See Anderson, *Outcasts in Their Own Land* (1976), 73, 103–4, on labor involvement in electoral activities in the 1900–1910 period.

7. Instituto Nacional de Estadística, Geografía e Informática, *Estadísticas históricas de México* (1985), 1, tables 6.1, 6.2.

8. Guadarrama, *Los sindicatos y la política en México* (1981), 80.

9. Reynolds, *Mexican Economy* (1970), appendix table E.12, p. 406.

10. Guadarrama, *Los sindicatos,* table 6.

11. This discussion draws on Hart, *Anarchism,* 127, 132–33, 136–38, 152, 154–55, 159, and Lear, "Workers, *Vecinos,* and Citizens" (1993), 136–37, 149–50, 160.

12. González Casanova, *En el primer gobierno constitucional* (1980), 22.

13. Carr, *El movimiento obrero y la política en México* (1976), 1:84–85, 90–92; Knight, "The Working Class and the Mexican Revolution" (1984), 52–58; Hart, *Anarchism,* 131; Lear, "Workers, *Vecinos,* and Citizens," 139–40, 150–51. Carr, however, notes (1:82–83) that some labor leaders were attracted to the *zapatistas'* radicalism.

14. González Casanova, *En el primer gobierno constitucional,* 47–48; Lear, "Workers, *Vecinos,* and Citizens," 183–84.

15. Morones served as secretary-general of the CROM from its founding in May 1918 until 1943, when he was replaced by Antonio J. Hernández.

16. Quoted in Carr, *El movimiento obrero,* 1:134. See also González Casanova, *En el primer gobierno constitucional,* 43, 65, 70–72, 78.

17. Carr, *El movimiento obrero,* 1:141–44; González Casanova, *En el primer gobierno constitucional,* 104–5. Carr notes that the existence of the 1919 secret pact between the CROM and Obregón was not known until 1930. Its text is reproduced in Araiza, *Historia del movimiento obrero mexicano* (1975), 4:45, 48.

The CROM also played a key role in organizing labor parties in several states in 1920. Garrido, *El partido de la revolución institucionalizada* (1982), 41.

18. Carr, *El movimiento obrero,* 1:127–29, 141, 144. On the formation of the CGT and its early bases of support, see Rivera Castro, *En la presidencia de Plutarco Elías Calles* (1983), 114–35; Tamayo, *En el interinato de Adolfo de la Huerta* (1987), chap. 3; Hart, *Anarchism,* 159–62; and Baena Paz, "La Confederación General de Trabajadores" (1976). The CGT initially included Communist-influenced groups that joined with anarchosyndicalists to protest "state-influenced" unionism; they seceded from the CGT in late 1922 in response to a doctrinal dispute.

19. This discussion draws on Carr, *El movimiento obrero,* 1:187, 202–3; 2:34, 41–43, 100–101. See also Rivera Castro, *En la presidencia de Plutarco Elías Calles,* 26–27.

20. Tamayo, *En el interinato,* 275–83. The CROM also appealed to its U.S. ally, the American Federation of Labor, to disrupt at customs and port facilities arms shipments to de la Huerta, and simultaneously to lobby the U.S. government to permit the Obregón government to purchase military supplies in the United States. See Lombardo Toledano, *La libertad sindical en México (1926)* (1974), 96–97.

21. Gruening, *Mexico,* 359, notes that a demonstration organized by the CROM in Mexico City in August 1926 represented an important sign of political support for the Calles government at the beginning of the Cristero rebellion. Bensusán Areous, "Institucionalización laboral" (1992), 179–82, discusses CROM strike policy in the early 1920s. Some CROM affiliates vigorously resisted the national leadership's policy on strikes; see Gamboa Ojeda, "La CROM en Puebla" (1980), 55–56. For a discussion of shifts in the regime's base of mass support in the early 1920s, see Collier and Collier, *Shaping the Political Arena* (1991), 207–11.

22. The following three paragraphs draw on Carr, *El movimiento obrero,* 1:134, 154–55, 178–79, 180, 183–86; 2:5–6, 64–90. For a discussion of the political opposition provoked by growing CROM influence, see Collier and Collier, *Shaping the Political Arena,* 219–24.

23. Basurto, *El proletariado industrial en México* (1975), 203–4. Carr, *El movimiento obrero,* 2:6–7, reports that in 1925 only some 15,000 CROM members actually paid dues. He further suggests that even an estimated total confederation membership of 600,000 in 1925 (100,000 of which were peasants) may be too high.

24. An important Catholic workers' movement emerged in Mexico before 1910, leading to the formation of the Confederación Nacional Católica del Trabajo (Catholic National Confederation of Labor) in Guadalajara in 1922. However, the Calles administration greatly undermined the Catholic labor movement as part of the government's campaign against the Cristero movement (a conservative revolt by agrarian groups in west-central Mexico linked to the Catholic Church hierarchy) in the late 1920s. See Tamayo, *En el interinato,* chap. 4, and Carr, *El movimiento obrero,* 2:97–100.

25. Lombardo Toledano, *La libertad sindical,* 105, 163, 243, 247; Secretaría de Industria, Comercio y Trabajo, *Del trabajo y la previsión social* (1928), 39; Córdova, *En una época de crisis* (1980), 171.

26. Meyer, *Estado y sociedad con Calles* (1977), 78–79; Buve, "Tlaxcala" (1990), 252, 259; Benjamin, "Laboratories of the New State" (1990), 77–78, 81.

27. The data on work force concentration in the textile industry are from Gua-darrama, *Los sindicatos,* 80. See esp. Gamboa Ojeda, "La CROM en Puebla," on employers' and government officials' resistance to union organizing.

28. See Lombardo Toledano, *La libertad sindical,* 166–73.

29. Most studies of the CROM (for example, Guadarrama, *Los sindicatos,* chap. 3) offer little basis for differentiating between affiliates formed as the result of workplace unionization efforts and unions created by political fiat, which may or may not have received rank-and-file support. Gamboa Ojeda, "La CROM en Puebla," is an important exception.

30. This discussion draws on Carr, *El movimiento obrero,* 1:154–55, 180–82; 2:7–9, 18–19, 30–31; Dulles, *Yesterday in Mexico* (1961), 193, 238, 281; Tamayo, *En el interinato,* 95, 103–4.

31. CROM members José María Elizalde, Vicente Lombardo Toledano, Matías Rodríguez, and Ezequiel Salcedo served as governor in, respectively, Aguas-calientes, Puebla, Hidalgo, and Zacatecas in the mid-1920s. (Lombardo Toledano and Salcedo only served very brief terms.) In addition, *laboristas* (not necessarily CROM members) served as governors in México and Querétaro during this period. See Basurto, *El proletariado industrial,* 224; Gruening, *Mexico,* 389; and Camp, *Mexican Political Biographies* (1991).

Four of the 8 labor leaders who served in the federal Senate between 1920 and 1928 were affiliated with the CROM's Mexican Labor Party (PLM), and 50 of the 52 labor leaders who served in the federal Chamber of Deputies between 1922 and 1928 were PLM members (of these 50, 29 were members of the CROM). See Ba-surto, *El proletariado industrial,* appendix. Information concerning CROM labor attachés is from Secretaría de Industria, Comercio y Trabajo, *Del trabajo,* chart following p. 55.

32. Carr, *El movimiento obrero,* 1:156–57; 2:19–28; González Casanova, *En el primer gobierno constitucional,* 83; Tamayo, *En el interinato,* 65–68; Rivera Castro, *En la presidencia de Plutarco Elías Calles,* 20–22, 112–13, 122–26, 142, 155. There was also resistance to the CROM among miners and telephone and tramway workers.

33. *Excélsior,* 15 Dec. 1926, 1, 10; Rodea, "La huelga de 1926–1927" (1988), 16–25, 32–33. Morones's attempts to undermine other railroad strikes in the 1920s alienated many workers from the CROM; Miguel Ángel Velasco, interview with author, 10 Jan. 1978, Mexico City. On the CROM's role among railroad workers during this period, see Rivera Castro, *En la presidencia de Plutarco Elías Calles,* 155–60; Guadarrama, *Los sindicatos,* 101, 104, 139–43; Bensusán Areous, "Insti-tucionalización laboral," 187–92.

The extent of CROM influence among railroad workers has been vigorously debated. Guadarrama, *Los sindicatos,* 104, suggests that the CROM's Federación Nacional Ferrocarrilera (National Railroad Federation, FNF) may have grouped as many as 13,685 railroad workers in December 1926, compared with the politically independent Confederación de Sociedades Ferrocarrileras de la República Mexi-cana's (Confederation of Mexican Railroad Societies) 28,000 members. Morones's position as minister of industry, commerce, and labor would have easily permitted the CROM to inflate its membership totals, but if these data are accurate, then the railroad industry would be a partial exception to the CROM's generally unsuccessful efforts to organize workers in strategically important economic activities.

Rodea, *Historia del movimiento obrero ferrocarrilero* (1944), 249, predictably downplays the extent of CROM influence, estimating that the FNF had no more than 3,000 members. He notes, however, that the last of the CROM-affiliated railroad worker organizations were not formally disbanded until July 1938 (635).

34. The discussion in the following three paragraphs draws on Carr, *El movimiento obrero,* vol. 2, chap. 4; Medin, *El minimato presidencial* (1982), 17, 61–64; Córdova, *En una época de crisis,* 38–41, 59–61, 134; Loyola Díaz, *Conflictos laborales en México* (1980), 13–21, 53–55; Dulles, *Yesterday in Mexico,* 411.

35. Garrido, *El partido,* 59; Córdova, *En una época de crisis,* 12–16. Some CROM affiliates supported Obregón's reelection, thus increasing factional divisions within the confederation; see Loyola Díaz, *Conflictos laborales,* 16.

36. Garrido, *El partido,* 104.

37. See *Boletín del Archivo General de la Nación* 2, nos. 2–3 (Apr.–Sept. 1978): 26. The data presented in this study of labor confederation size do not include all industrial activities, and they exclude peasants and rural workers.

38. Medin, *El minimato presidencial,* 61–63; Carr, *Marxism and Communism in Twentieth-Century Mexico* (1992), 44–45. Government support for the PCM ended after Escobar's military revolt in 1929, which the party was falsely accused of supporting.

39. Córdova, *En una época de crisis,* 58–59, 72, 77; Garrido, *El partido,* 76, 84. Three presidents held office between 1928 and 1934: Emilio Portes Gil (1928–30), Pascual Ortiz Rubio (1930–32), and Abelardo L. Rodríguez (1932–34).

40. See Córdova, *En una época de crisis,* chap. 3, on the effects of economic depression on workers. The Departamento Autónomo del Trabajo, *Memoria de labores, 1935,* 73, estimated that there were a total of some 500,000 unionized workers in both federal- and local-jurisdiction industries in 1934–35. The total had remained essentially unchanged since 1929. Guadarrama, *Los sindicatos,* table 12.

41. On the Mexican Communist Party's organizational activities during the 1920s and 1930s, see Rivera Castro, *En la presidencia de Plutarco Elías Calles,* 137–51; Córdova, *En una época de crisis,* 71–72, 139; Garrido, *El partido,* 104–5; Márquez Fuentes and Rodríguez Araujo, *El Partido Comunista Mexicano* (1973), 99–105, 127–28; Anguiano, *El estado y la política obrera del cardenismo* (1975), 34–35; Carr, "Mexican Communist Party" (1987); Campa S., *Mi testimonio* (1978), 51, 57. On the Comité Pro-Unidad Obrera y Campesina and doctrinal shifts by the PCM, see León González and Marván, *En el cardenismo* (1985), 71–72, 99–123, and Carr, *Marxism and Communism,* 43–46, 57–58.

42. See Cuarto Congreso Ferrocarrilero, "Libro de actas" (1932), 1:9–12A, 13A, 24–25, 58, 59A, 60A, 69–70, 72–72A, 76, 80–85, 111, 135–35A, 137–39; 2:8–8A, 146; Secretaría de Industria, Comercio y Trabajo, *Del trabajo,* 102–3; Dulles, *Yesterday in Mexico,* 512–13.

43. Velasco, interview with author, 10 Jan. 1978, Mexico City; Campa S., *Mi testimonio,* 103, 143; Córdova, *En una época de crisis,* 84, 125–26; León González and Marván, *En el cardenismo,* 150; Rodea, *Historia,* 258, 267, 272–79, 552–54; Navarrete, *Alto a la contrarrevolución* (1971), 182–84.

44. See León González and Marván, *En el cardenismo,* 33, 70–71, on other worker initiatives in the early 1930s to promote labor movement unity.

Railroad workers had also been active in the late 1920s and early 1930s in organizing regional labor alliances. The Confederación de Transportes y Comunicaciones, for example, played a key role in founding the Cámara del Trabajo del Distrito Federal. See Cuarto Congreso Ferrocarrilero, "Libro de actas," 2:146–48A.

45. However, formal recognition of national industrial unions as a separate legal category came later, in a 1956 reform of the federal labor code. See de la Cueva, *El nuevo derecho mexicano del trabajo* (1979), 2:329.

46. On Lombardo Toledano's background and beliefs, see Wilkie and Monzón de Wilkie, *México visto en el siglo veinte* (1969), chap. 4; Chassen de López, *Lombardo Toledano* (1977); Millon, *Lombardo* (1964).

47. Mexican Communist Party activists were, however, excluded from the convention at which the CGOCM was formed; see Chassen de López, *Lombardo Toledano,* 159. On the formation of the FSTDF, see Loyola Díaz, *Conflictos laborales,* 48–49.

48. Chassen de López, *Lombardo Toledano,* 158–64. On the CGOCM's origins and goals, see Córdova, *En una época de crisis,* 154–58, 163–67; León González and Marván, *En el cardenismo,* 44–47; Hernández Chávez, *La mecánica cardenista* (1979), 126–27.

In December 1934 the CGOCM claimed 962 affiliated organizations and 234,471 individual members, which would have made it the largest single labor organization in the country. Either this claim was grossly inflated, or the CGOCM's membership consisted predominantly of peasants and rural workers. The Departamento Autónomo del Trabajo's 1935 survey of labor organizations in the petroleum, mining, transportation, electrical power generation, and textile industries— the most heavily unionized industrial activities—credited the CGOCM with only 148 affiliates and 20,533 members, about half the CROM's total membership at the time. Both organizations were eclipsed by the size of autonomous unions. See *Boletín del Archivo General de la Nación* 2, nos. 2–3 (Apr.–Sept. 1978): 26.

49. Palacios, "México en los años treinta" (1977), 529. See *Boletín del Archivo General de la Nación* 2, nos. 2–3 (Apr.–Sept. 1978): 26–30, for a detailed summary of labor organizations in the transportation, textile, electrical power, petroleum, and mining sectors in 1935.

50. Chassen de López, *Lombardo Toledano,* 136–37. Many of these grievances were filed by workers dismissed during a period of economic stagnation.

51. On the PNR's efforts to win support from labor groups, see ibid., 143–44, 155–56.

52. Velasco, interview with author, 10 Jan. 1978, Mexico City; *Unificación*

Ferroviaria, no. 2, 1 Feb. 1934, 32, 37; *Boletín del Archivo General de la Nación* 2, nos. 2–3 (Apr.–Sept. 1978): 26–27. Transportation workers (mainly railroad workers) represented 69.4 percent of the CNT's membership in key industries in 1935.

53. Córdova, *En una época de crisis*, 70–71, 73, 135–39, 159, 168–69; Chassen de López, *Lombardo Toledano*, 155–56, 163; Garrido, *El partido*, 171; Lajous Vargas, *Los orígenes del partido único* (1979), 146; Velasco, interview with author, 10 Jan. 1978, Mexico City. Some CNT leaders denied that the organization was linked to the PNR or that it received government financial support. See Cuarto Congreso Ferrocarrilero, "Libro de actas," 2:144–44A, 148A–50.

54. For a perceptive discussion of these issues, see Córdova, *La política de masas del cardenismo* (1974), esp. 29–30, 38–39, 54–56, 64.

55. Garrido, *El partido*, 126.

56. For a selection of Cárdenas's statements on these issues before and after taking office, see Ashby, *Organized Labor and the Mexican Revolution under Lázaro Cárdenas* (1963), 20–24.

57. See the excerpt quoted in León González and Marván, *En el cardenismo*, 28.

58. See Hernández Chávez, *La mecánica cardenista*, appendix 3, for data on strikes in federal-jurisdiction industries in 1935.

59. Calles's statement may have been prompted in part by the fact that the May 1935 strike against the Mexican Telephone and Telegraph Company (a subsidiary of the American Telephone and Telegraph Company) affected a firm in which he owned a large block of stock. See Ashby, *Organized Labor*, 25.

60. Calles argued that spiraling social and political conflict might soon lead to the same degree of polarization which had threatened the presidency of Ortiz Rubio (1930–32), a particularly ominous comparison because in those circumstances Calles had successfully maneuvered to oust the weakened Ortiz Rubio and impose a successor.

61. The CROM and the CGT together formed the Alianza de Trabajadores Unificados (Alliance of Unified Workers) to back Calles and oppose "communism"; León González, introduction to *La constitución* (1986), 13.

62. Cornelius, "Nation Building, Participation, and Distribution" (1973), esp. 417–62. The texts of Calles's June 1935 declaration to the national press and the responses from Cárdenas and various labor organizations, as well as the CNDP's founding documents, are reproduced in Instituto Nacional de Estudios Históricos de la Revolución Mexicana, *La constitución de la Confederación de Trabajadores de México* (1986).

63. Departamento Autónomo del Trabajo, *Memoria de labores, 1935*, 5–10 (the "mission statement" for the department); *1936*, 220; *1937*, 173–74; Secretaría del Trabajo y Previsión Social, *Evolución histórica* (1957), table titled "Erogaciones anuales del gobierno federal en la administración nacional del trabajo."

64. Secretaría de la Economía Nacional, Dirección General de Estadística, *Anuario estadístico, 1941*, 394. The most heavily unionized industries were elec-

trical power generation (93.3 percent), communications and transportation (77.2 percent), manufacturing (49.0 percent), and construction (33.6 percent). Basurto, *Del avilacamachismo al alemanismo* (1984), appendix table 3.

65. Author's calculations based on data presented in *Anuario estadístico, 1939,* 274, 280; *1941,* 398, 402. For detailed information concerning the geographical distribution and membership of federal-jurisdiction unions registered during the Cárdenas period, see Secretaría del Trabajo y Previsión Social, *Memoria de labores, 1940–1941,* 170–71.

Only data on annual registrations (not cumulative totals) are available for local-jurisdiction labor organizations. The *Anuario estadístico, 1939,* 272, refers to the frequent creation and disappearance of these unions.

66. Quoted in León González and Marván, *En el cardenismo,* 81; see also 79, 139, and Córdova, *La política de masas,* 62–63. Durán, *Lázaro Cárdenas* (1972), 183–99, presents Cárdenas's major policy statements on labor during the 1930s.

67. The text of convention debates appears in Instituto Nacional de Estudios Históricos de la Revolución Mexicana, *La constitución.* See also Confederación de Trabajadores de México, *C.T.M., 1936–1941* (1941); Salazar, *La CTM* (1956); Salazar, *Historia de las luchas proletarias* (1956).

68. León González and Marván, *En el cardenismo,* 162–63, 186.

69. Ibid., 55–58, 141, 145, 181.

70. This discussion of the 1937 split in the CTM draws on Hernández Chávez, *La mecánica cardenista,* 148–58, 162; Anguiano, *El estado y la política obrera del cardenismo,* 111–13; Campa S., *Mi testimonio,* 119, 125–26, 135; Ashby, *Organized Labor,* 83–85; Chassen de López, *Lombardo Toledano,* 238; López Villegas-Manjarrez, *La CTM* (1983), 21–22; Yañez Reyes, *Génesis de la burocracia sindical cetemista* (1984), 224 n. 11, 235, 237–38, 250–51, 279–82, 286–88, 304–33.

71. See Hernández Chávez, *La mecánica cardenista,* table 4 and appendix 4, for a list of labor organizations leaving the CTM, those remaining, and their respective memberships.

72. Ibid., table 5.

73. Confederación de Trabajadores de México, *C.T.M., 1936–1941,* 471.

74. Federal labor authorities recorded a total of 982 federal-jurisdiction and 3,850 local-jurisdiction labor organizations among urban and industrial workers in December 1937, for a national total of 4,832 labor unions. There were 316,191 federal-jurisdiction and 300,372 local-jurisdiction employees in urban and industrial economic activities, for a national total of 616,563. On the basis of the total memberships claimed publicly by the CTM (945,913), the CROM (50,000), and the CGT (30,000), the CTM's urban and industrial worker membership could have totaled no more than 536,563 (that is, the total national organized worker population minus the total CROM and CGT memberships—although it is unlikely that the CTM grouped all remaining unionized workers). These data suggest that the CTM's peasant membership may have been as high as 409,350, or 43.3 percent of its stated total membership. These are the author's calculations based on data presented in Departamento Autónomo del Trabajo, *Memoria de labores, 1938,* 263, 321, and Ashby, *Organized Labor,* 79.

75. Garrido, *El partido*, 263; Córdova, *La política de masas*, 133–34; Anguiano, *El estado y la política obrera del cardenismo*, 59–60.

76. See Ashby, *Organized Labor*, 49, 72–73, 76, 82, and Chassen de López, *Lombardo Toledano*, 206–10. The CTM's action program contained several items that would address peasant needs, including proposals for reforms in agrarian legislation, expanded credit for rural producers, the abolition of high land rent payments, and additional land distribution. On earlier efforts by the CROM to organize rural workers, see Rivera Castro, *En la presidencia de Plutarco Elías Calles*, 35–37, 40–41, 48–49, 72–73, and Carr, "Mexican Communist Party," 383.

León González and Marván, *En el cardenismo*, 182–86, argue that the CTM in fact failed to address seriously the problem of peasant organization. They explain the lack of extensive joint worker-peasant organization in terms of the relatively few peasant representatives at the CTM's 1936 inaugural congress, the absence of a clear plan by supporters of such joint organizations, and the opposition of some key peasant leaders to this approach.

77. See Parkes, *History of Mexico* (1950), 402–3; Prewett, *Reportage on Mexico* (1941), 162; Chassen de López, *Lombardo Toledano*, 211–15, esp. 213; Córdova, *La política de masas*, 163–64. For a discussion of Cárdenas's agrarian reform program and his policies toward the peasantry, see Córdova, *La política de masas*, 93–122.

78. León González and Marván, *En el cardenismo*, 187–88.

79. Carr, "Mexican Communist Party," 396, 403–4. Garrido, *El partido*, 204, 261, notes that for some time many peasant groups maintained affiliations with both the CTM and the CNC; also see Carr, ibid., 373, 374 n. 6, 393, and 399 on this point. The CTM continued to raid CNC members into the late 1940s. *Tiempo*, 4 Apr. 1947, 3.

80. Garrido, *El partido*, 210, 212, 219, 230.

81. See ibid., 233–42, on the process leading to the creation of the PRM.

82. See *Boletín del Archivo General de la Nación* 2, nos. 2–3 (Apr.–Sept. 1978): 26.

83. Garrido, *El partido*, 89, 103, 118, 121, 125–32, 137, 141, 165, 171, 173.

84. Ibid., 189–90.

85. A preference for statist action figured prominently, for example, in the action program outlined by the "CROM *depurada*" in 1933. See Córdova, *En una época de crisis*, 156.

86. For a discussion of the reorganization of the PNR as the PRM and the new party's organizational structure, see Furtak, *El partido de la revolución* (1978), 41–45, and Córdova, *La política de masas*, 146–76. Garrido, *El partido*, 298–99, notes that de facto the PRM had a dual organizational structure, retaining the PNR system of geographically defined linkages to state and local political bosses.

The military sector was dissolved by President Manuel Ávila Camacho in 1940. When the Confederación Nacional de Organizaciones Populares (National Confederation of Popular Organizations, CNOP) was formed in 1943 to represent the "popular" (middle-class) sector, members of the armed forces were individually integrated into this organization. Garrido (306) notes that in later years military officers regularly headed the ruling party, and at least one was named to the Supreme Court.

87. For discussions of the relationship between earlier efforts to create a "popular front" in Mexico and the formation of the PRM, see Garrido, *El partido,* 219–27; Weyl and Weyl, *Reconquest of Mexico* (1939), 346; Chassen de López, *Lombardo Toledano,* 231–32, 236, 242–46; Anguiano, *El estado y la política obrera del cardenismo,* 11–22.

88. Weyl and Weyl, *Reconquest of Mexico,* 350.

89. Garrido, *El partido,* 240, 269.

90. Ibid., 334, 336.

91. This discussion draws on Hernández Chávez, *La mecánica cardenista,* 191–99, 204–6; Garrido, *El partido,* 279, 288, 290, 299; and Durand Ponte, *La ruptura de la nación* (1986), 31, 36. I am also grateful to John Womack, Jr., for his comments on these points.

92. The CROM, a significant proportion of SME members, and a few other labor groups (including some railroad, mine, telephone, and tramway workers) supported Almazán. Camacho, *El futuro inmediato* (1980), 44; Durand Ponte, *La ruptura,* 37–38; Loyola Díaz, *El ocaso del radicalismo revolucionario* (1991), 33.

93. See Franco G. S., "Labor Law and the Labor Movement in Mexico" (1991), 113–14, and Departamento Autónomo del Trabajo, *Memoria de labores, 1937,* 173.

In 1926 President Calles endorsed the principle that contract terms negotiated by the union representing the largest number of employees in a workplace should apply to all workers; see Lombardo Toledano, *La libertad sindical,* 243. Presidents Portes Gil, Ortiz Rubio, and Rodríguez agreed that there should be a single majority union in each workplace. See Archivo General de la Nación, Labor Section, packet 1234, file 5 (Act #9, 28 Nov. 1928, of the Convención Obrero-Patronal), 14; *Revista Mexicana del Trabajo* 4 (Jan.–Apr. 1957): 18–20; Junta Federal de Conciliación y Arbitraje, case no. 8.1/320 (72) "46"/1214, pp. 30–32. Subsequent administrations generally adopted this precedent.

94. On this point see Córdova, *En una época de crisis,* 95. This discussion of the historical origin of exclusion clauses follows de la Cueva, *Derecho mexicano del trabajo* (1964), 2:369–75. See also Fajardo Ortiz, "El movimiento sindical y la cláusula de exclusión" (1955).

95. State labor codes that permitted exclusion clauses in contracts sometimes referred to them as "union consolidation clauses," in reference to their obvious importance for unionization.

96. Bensusán Areous, "Institucionalización laboral," 311; Clark, *Organized Labor in Mexico* (1934), 137.

97. *Revista Mexicana del Trabajo* 4 (July–Aug. 1957): 139.

98. Rodea, *Historia,* 541–43, and *Unificación Ferroviaria,* no. 2, 1 Aug. 1934, 224–27.

99. For evidence of the Cárdenas administration's support for the addition of exclusion clauses to collective contracts and opposition to the official registration of *sindicatos blancos,* see Departamento Autónomo del Trabajo, *Memoria de labores, 1936,* 15, 220, and León González and Marván, *En el cardenismo,* 160–61.

100. Rodea, *Historia*, 542; Navarrete, *Alto a la contrarrevolución*, 173–78.

101. See, for example, Garrido, *El partido*, 300, 357, and Basurto, *Del avilaca-machismo*, 108.

102. For evidence of state financial subsidies to other labor organizations, see, for the CGT, Basurto, *Del avilacamachismo*, 59–60; for the CROC, Ugalde, *Power and Conflict in a Mexican Community* (1970), 43; for the Confederation of Mexican Workers and Peasants, López Villegas-Manjarrez, *La CTM*, 115.

Perhaps the most ingenious defense of the longstanding government practice of providing selective financial support for labor organizations' activities was that offered by Gudelio Morales, secretary-general of the Confederación de Transportes y Comunicaciones in 1932 and a founder of the Cámara del Trabajo del Distrito Federal. In defending the Cámara against charges made at the STFRM's founding convention that it had received government financial support, he replied, "And is not the state's money also the people's money?" See Cuarto Congreso Ferrocarrilero, "Libro de actas," 2:151.

103. The CTM's 1936 statutes are reproduced in Confederación de Trabajadores de México, *C.T.M., 1936–1941*, 66–80. Dues provisions are outlined in arts. 56–57, 59–60.

One further indication of the founders' resolve to maintain the confederation's economic self-sufficiency was their directive to all National Committee for Proletarian Defense (CNDP) member organizations to cede their office equipment to the CTM. These organizations were also to pay the CTM all outstanding debts owed to the CNDP. Similarly, the CTM levied a special quota of 0.02 pesos per affiliated union member then employed, payable by March 31, 1936, to cover the costs of organizing the national executive committee. See ibid., 80 ("Transitorios," #3).

104. Confederación de Trabajadores de México, *C.T.M., 1936–1941*, 208–9. By March 31, 1937, only 258 affiliates had paid their monthly dues in full (346). The national headquarters had to cancel its telephone service because it could not pay the bill.

105. Ibid., 222–23. See also 822 for comments regarding the dangers to the CTM of relying on external financial support.

106. This analysis draws on financial information presented in, for 1936–40, Confederación de Trabajadores de México, *C.T.M., 1936–1941*, 208–9, 216–17, 342–45, 361, 390–93, 406, 436–41, 545, 668–69, 822–24, 861, 915–16, 949, 992–93, 1061; for 1950, *Ceteme* (the confederation's official newspaper), 19 July 1950, 7; 1 Oct. 1950, 7; 1 Jan. 1951, 7; for 1956–67, *Ceteme*, 8 Nov. 1967, 4.

107. For representative comments on this problem, see *Ceteme*, 19 July 1950, 7; 9 July 1954, 3; 24 Feb. 1957, 9; 13 June 1959, 1; 18 Sept. 1965, 7.

108. *Ceteme*, 19 July 1950, 7; 4 June 1954, 8; 17 Aug. 1957, 2; 9 Jan. 1965, n.p.; 18 Sept. 1965, 7. Annual confederation dues were raised from 1.00 to 3.65 pesos per member in 1950. They were apparently raised to 4.00 pesos per year in 1954, and they remained at that level until at least 1965.

109. *Tiempo*, 7 Feb. 1972, 14.

110. *Ceteme*, 23 Sept. 1972, 2.

111. *Diario Oficial de la Federación*, 6 Nov. 1942, 2; Confederación de Traba-

jadores de México, *C.T.M., 1936–1941*, 454. The CTM had been given the 4,100-square-meter property in September 1937 even though the formal expropriation did not occur until 1942. At that time it was valued at 471,851 pesos (U.S.$131,070).

112. In July 1951, Fidel Velázquez told a meeting of CTM officials, "[T]he Confederation cannot live on public charity; it cannot live always on government assistance, nor should it live on such assistance." Partido Revolucionario Institucional, *CTM* (1986), 3:603.

113. Purcell, *Mexican Profit-Sharing Decision* (1975), 22, provides the lower estimate; the higher estimate was obtained during the author's interview with a former CTM senior adviser, 18 Jan. 1978, Mexico City. The CTM also presumably receives revenue (perhaps a considerable amount) from union-owned enterprises.

Fagen and Tuohy, *Politics and Privilege in a Mexican City* (1972), 48, refer to small financial subsidies provided by the Jalapa, Veracruz, municipal government in the 1960s to the CTM's local, state, and national organizations.

114. These episodes of state intervention in support of the CTM are discussed in more detail in chapter 4 of this book.

115. See Garrido, *El partido*, 143.

116. For an example from Matamoros, Tamaulipas, see Quintero Ramírez, "Reestructuración sindical en las maquiladoras mexicanas" (1992), 240–42, 373.

117. Smith, *Labyrinths of Power* (1979), table 3.3. Some 11.5 percent of elites during this period came from peasant families.

118. Ibid., table 3.6. This percentage includes those listed as workers and half of those listed in the worker/peasant "labor leader" category.

119. Camp, *Mexico's Leaders* (1980), 77.

120. Smith, *Labyrinths of Power*, table 5.4. Smith's data show that of the 135 "labor" elites in the 1946–71 cohort, 85.9 percent rose no higher than federal deputy. Some 13.3 percent became governors, federal senators, subcabinet officials, or members of the PRI national executive committee. Only one individual (0.7 percent) rose to a higher position (table 8.4).

121. Information concerning the organizational affiliation of labor leaders elected to the Congress is not consistently available for the period since the mid-1970s. However, data on the organizational affiliation of PRI candidates suggest that the CTM preserved its dominance in this area from the late 1970s through the late 1980s. CTM affiliates held 64 percent of all PRI labor sector candidacies in 1979, 67 percent in 1982, 71 percent in 1985, and 68 percent in 1988. Reyes del Campillo, "El movimiento obrero en la Cámara de Diputados" (1990), table 3.

122. Durand Ponte, "Confederation of Mexican Workers" (1991), 91, suggests that the CTM's share of labor seats in the federal Chamber of Deputies may have declined to 25.9 percent in 1973–76, before recovering to about 50 percent in 1979–82. In 1979 the CTM also controlled 56 percent of the labor positions on the National Minimum Wage Commission. The CTM controlled seven state governorships between 1973 and 1991. *La Jornada*, 27 May 1991, 12.

123. The FSTSE claimed political representation through the "popular" sector.

124. *La Jornada*, 27 May 1991, 12; Camp, *Mexican Political Biographies* (1982), 335–43.

Chapter 4: Turning Point

1. Basurto, *Del avilacamachismo al alemanismo* (1984), 29–35.

2. See Scott, *Mexican Government in Transition* (1964), 140–43; Hansen, *Politics of Mexican Development* (1971), 113–16; Purcell, *Mexican Profit-Sharing Decision* (1975), 20–25; Kaufman, "Mexico and Latin American Authoritarianism" (1975), 211–12.

3. Basurto, *Del avilacamachismo*, 217, 220; Durand Ponte, "Relaciones entre estructura y coyuntura" (1984), 20–23.

Medina, *Civilismo y modernización del autoritarismo* (1979), 162–70, is a partial exception; his analysis notes the economic restructuring dimension of Alemán's assault on the railroad workers' union. Roxborough, "Mexico" (1992), 214–15, offers a nuanced evaluation of the interplay between domestic and international influences on Alemán's labor policies.

4. For analyses of restructuring efforts at state-owned Petróleos Mexicanos (PEMEX) during this period, see Cuéllar Vázquez, "Golpe al Sindicato de Trabajadores Petroleros" (1984), 104, 107, 113, 117, and esp. Loyola Díaz *El ocaso del radicalismo revolucionario* (1991), 67–74, 185–213. Basurto, *Del avilacamachismo*, 226–70, examines labor conflicts in the mining industry in the 1940s and early 1950s, but he does not address possible economic restructuring dimensions of labor developments in these sectors.

5. Collier and Collier, *Shaping the Political Arena* (1991), 404–13; Basurto, *Del avilacamachismo*, 15–21; Medina, *Del cardenismo al avilacamachismo* (1978), 283–344.

6. Garrido, *El partido de la revolución institucionalizada* (1982), 317, 326–27; Basurto, *Del avilacamachismo*, 52–53. In 1942 the CPN briefly attracted support from the SITMMSRM and STFRM. López Villegas-Manjarrez, *La CTM* (1983), 32–33.

The CTM did, however, continue to pressure for minimum-wage increases during this period. *Tiempo*, 17 Sept. 1943, 43; 1 Oct. 1943, 33; 7 Jan. 1944, 38.

7. Durand Ponte, *La ruptura de la nación* (1986), 66–68; López Villegas-Manjarrez, *La CTM*, 39–44; *Tiempo*, 12 June 1942, 4–5; 12 May 1944, 9; 3 Sept. 1948, 5–6.

The National Worker Council apparently survived until at least 1948 as a loose coordinating organization for the CROM, CGT, CPN, and COCM. Hernández C., "Del pacto de sindicatos industriales a la represión" (1979), 931.

8. There is no careful examination of this crucial period in the CTM's development. For a general discussion that overemphasizes the degree of organizational centralization in the CTM, see Yañez Reyes, *Génesis de la burocracia sindical cetemista* (1984), chap. 4. Gutiérrez G., "Grupos sindicales y división interna" (1988), 10–23, and Ventura Rodríguez, "La consolidación de la FTP-CTM" (1988), outline the way in which the Velázquez group consolidated its influence in, respectively, the states of Nuevo León and Puebla.

9. Basurto, *Del avilacamachismo*, 26, 56–57; Garrido, *El partido*, 315–18. On tensions within the CTM in 1942 and 1943 over the reelection of Velázquez, see *Tiempo*, 11 Dec. 1942, 9; 19 Feb. 1943, 9; 26 Feb. 1943, 9.

10. For basic biographical information on Velázquez, see *Ceteme*, 10 Dec. 1954, 1, 4; 8 Nov. 1967, 1; Velasco, *Fidel Velázquez* (1986), 75; Amilpa Trujillo, *Fidel Velázquez* (1991), 93–94, 107. There is no serious biography of Velázquez, but some useful information concerning his life and beliefs appears in Mejía Prieto, *El poder tras de las gafas* (1980), 51–52, 57, 59–60, 75–76; Velasco, *Fidel Velázquez* 11, 16, 80, 98–99, 113–14, 149; Guerrero Tapia, *Y después de mí* (1987), 27–30; Sánchez González, *Fidel* (1991), 15–16, 27–28.

11. Basurto, *Del avilacamachismo*, 315–17; León González and Marván, *En el cardenismo* (1985), 145–46; Miguel Ángel Velasco, interview with author, 10 Jan. 1978, Mexico City.

Velázquez's actions were a sharp contrast to the views he expressed in his inaugural address as CTM secretary-general on March 1, 1941: "I am not a communist, but I admire the communists because they are revolutionaries like me. Since we are all members of the CTM, I must coexist with them" (quoted in *Ceteme*, 8 Nov. 1967, 1).

12. For example, the members of this group organized unions in the Mexico City area representing milkmen, street cleaners and paving workers, transport workers, hotel and restaurant workers, bricklayers, textile workers, and so forth. Many of these unions were grouped in the Federation of Federal District Workers' Unions (FSTDF), formed in February 1929 when the "five little wolves" ("los cinco lobitos") seceded from the CROM. Velázquez and Alfonso Sánchez Madariaga both served on the executive committee of the General Confederation of Mexican Workers and Peasants (CGOCM), organized by Lombardo Toledano in October 1933 to unite former CROM affiliates. See *Ceteme*, 10 Dec. 1954, 1; 21 Jan. 1955, 3; 24 Feb. 1961, 5; 8 Nov. 1967, 1; *Unificación Ferroviaria*, no. 240, 16 Dec. 1946, 3; Hernández Chávez, *La mecánica cardenista* (1979), 128–30; León González and Marván, *En el cardenismo*, 172.

13. Garrido, *El partido*, 317; Basurto, *Del avilacamachismo*, 31–34; Durand Ponte, *La ruptura*, 64.

14. "Decreto que reforma la Ley Federal del Trabajo," *Diario Oficial de la Federación*, 10 Apr. 1941, 3–5.

15. "Decreto que aprueba la suspensión de las garantías individuales consignadas en varios artículos constitucionales," *Diario Oficial de la Federación*, 2 June 1942, 2; "Ley de Prevenciones Generales relativa a la suspensión de garantías individuales," *Diario Oficial de la Federación*, 13 June 1942, 1–6; "Decreto que adiciona los artículos 5, 11 y 13, y reforma el 12 de la Ley de Prevenciones Generales, de 11 de junio de 1942, relativo a la suspensión de garantías," *Diario Oficial de la Federación*, 20 Sept. 1943, 1–2. Restrictions on political rights were in effect between June 1, 1942, and October 10, 1945.

In early 1941 the Ávila Camacho administration also revised the federal penal code to include the crime of "social dissolution." This provision was originally designed to curtail the activities of Axis agents, but it was occasionally used later as the grounds on which to arrest and imprison leaders of popular movements (including Demetrio Vallejo, the leader of a national railroad worker strike in March 1959). See Bensusán Areous, "Construcción y desarrollo del derecho laboral" (1985), 66–67.

16. Author's calculations based on data presented in Instituto Nacional de Estadística, Geografía e Informática, *Estadísticas históricas de México* (1985), vol. 1, table 9.1 (p. 311).

17. "Reglamento de la fracción III del artículo 111 de la Ley del Trabajo," *Diario Oficial de la Federación,* 31 Dec. 1941, 3–5; "Decreto que congela los precios de diversos artículos en los lugares que se especifican," *Diario Oficial de la Federación,* 21 Sept. 1943, 1–13; "Ley de compensación de emergencia al salario insuficiente," *Diario Oficial de la Federación,* 24 Sept. 1943, 4–8.

18. The CTM's alliance with the CNIT also helped guard its flank against criticisms from more conservative business organizations, which strongly opposed unions' involvement in electoral politics and called for even more restrictive strike legislation. López Villegas-Manjarrez, *La CTM,* 85–87.

19. Basurto, *Del avilacamachismo,* 46–47, 72–73, 76–80. Some local STFRM sections held protests against price increases in March–April 1943 and May 1946. See *Unificación Ferroviaria,* no. 226, 16 May 1946, 11, and Campa S., *Mi testimonio* (1978), 176–77, 179–84.

20. *Unificación Ferroviaria,* no. 214, 1 Dec. 1945, 1; no. 220, 16 Feb. 1946, 1; no. 226, 16 May 1946, 1, 11; no. 228, 16 June 1946, 3, 7.

21. A list of the CTM's principal affiliates appears in *Unificación Ferroviaria,* no. 203, 1 June 1945, 5.

22. Gómez Z.'s candidacy was supported by the principal national industrial unions. *Unificación Ferroviaria,* no. 245, 1 Mar. 1947, 7. On developments during this period, see López Villegas-Manjarrez, *La CTM,* 95–105, 112–13; Gómez Z., *Sucesos y remembranzas* (1979), 1:300–303; Campa S., *Mi testimonio,* 124–26, 132–38, 198.

Lombardo Toledano played an ambivalent role in these events. He generally sided with critics of the CTM's relationship with the government and the "official" party, but in the name of labor movement unity, he supported Amilpa in the 1947 elections. Some observers believe that he took these contradictory positions in exchange for the Velázquez faction's promise to support his initiative to form a new political party representing labor interests. However, when Lombardo Toledano founded the Partido Popular (Popular Party) in 1948, Velázquez and other CTM leaders refused to give their support. See Durand Ponte, "Relaciones entre estructura y coyuntura," 22; López Villegas-Manjarrez, *La CTM,* 96–98, 120–21; Velasco, interview with author, 27 Apr. 1978, Mexico City; *Tiempo,* 10 Oct. 1947, 6.

23. The proposed reforms would have permitted strikes only with the express consent of the Ministry of Labor and Social Welfare, limited strike demands to clauses in existing collective contracts, and submitted all strikes to compulsory arbitration. See Durand Ponte, "Relaciones entre estructura y coyuntura," 22–23. These modifications were vigorously backed by conservative business organizations. Basurto, *Del avilacamachismo,* 105–7.

24. *Tiempo,* 10 Oct. 1947, 6; 31 Oct. 1947, 11; Rivera Flores, "Unión General de Obreros y Campesinos de México" (1984), 44–45. When the Party of the Mexican Revolution (PRM) was reorganized as the PRI in January 1946, the former's

system of indirect party membership via ties to affiliated mass organizations was replaced by direct, individual party membership. CTM affiliates' collective affiliation with the "official" party had been obligatory since January 1938. Garrido, *El partido*, 239, 247.

25. See, for example, Cuéllar Vázquez, "Golpe al Sindicato de Trabajadores Petroleros," 112, and *Tiempo*, 21 Nov. 1947, 37; 9 Jan. 1948, 4–6.

26. Córdova, *La política de masas del cardenismo* (1974), 163, 165; *Unificación Ferroviaria*, no. 245, 1 Mar. 1947, 6.

27. Report by a federal inspector attending the "Labor Unity Congress" ("Congreso Constituyente de Unidad Obrera"), cited by a former railroad union activist in an interview with the author, 22 June 1978, Mexico City. The convocation for the meeting was first published in the STFRM's newspaper, *Unificación Ferroviaria*.

The CTM apparently tried to block STFRM participation in this initiative by reviving tensions among train crew personnel (*trenistas*), who had seceded from the STFRM in 1944. *Excélsior*, 21 Apr. 1947, 9. The next section in this chapter discusses this secession episode in more detail.

28. Carr, *Marxism and Communism in Twentieth-Century Mexico* (1992), 147. The PCM's legal registration was revoked in 1949.

29. Luis Gómez Z., "A los trabajadores de México," *Unificación Ferroviaria*, no. 245, 1 Mar. 1947, 7. He wrote, "I am not, nor have I ever been, a member of the Communist Party. I am not a communist."

30. *Unificación Ferroviaria*, no. 245, 1 Mar. 1947, 6–7. Each participating organization (including the individual sections of national industrial unions) had one delegate; those organizations with more than three hundred members had two delegates. In addition to those labor organizations listed in the text, national unions representing employees at soft-drink bottling companies and Nacional Monte de Piedad (the government-operated system of pawnshops) attended the congress. Many of the regional and local labor groups in attendance apparently represented secessionist elements from the CTM in the states of Aguascalientes, Baja California, Campeche, Chiapas, Coahuila, Durango, Guerrero, Hidalgo, Puebla, Tamaulipas, Veracruz, and Zacatecas.

31. See the CUT's statement in *Excélsior*, 25 Apr. 1947, 12.

32. The SITMMSRM had left the CTM in 1942, and the STPRM initially seceded in July 1946 when the confederation refused to support its strike in demand of a wage increase. See Roxborough, "The Mexican Charrazo" (1986), 31; López Villegas-Manjarrez, *La CTM*, 94, 97; *Excélsior*, 19 July 1946, 4–6; Cuéllar Vázquez, "Golpe al Sindicato de Trabajadores Petroleros," 105, 114.

Durand Ponte, "Relaciones entre estructura y coyuntura," 22, suggests that Gómez Z. established this alliance because the CUT lost strength after the secession of the SITMMSRM and the Alianza de Tranviarios (Tramway Workers' Alliance), the result of a conflict over Gómez Z.'s "antidemocratic" leadership style.

33. *Unificación Ferroviaria*, no. 266, 16 Jan. 1948, 1, 11; *Tiempo*, 16 Jan. 1948, 5. The pact was signed in the presence of two officials from the Ministry of Labor and Social Welfare, and President Alemán sent his personal greetings.

34. In November 1947 the CTM withdrew from the Confederación de Trabajadores de América Latina (Latin American Workers' Confederation, CTAL,
founded in 1938 under the leadership of Lombardo Toledano) and the leftist World
Federation of Trade Unions. At the same time, it established ties with the U.S.
American Federation of Labor. In January 1951 the CTM joined the International
Confederation of Free Trade Unions. See López Villegas-Manjarrez, *La CTM,* 107,
121, and Camacho, *El futuro inmediato* (1980), 50.

35. Despite their many differences, the CUT and CTM affiliates cooperated
to oppose Alemán's proposed labor law reforms restricting the right to strike, and
to support minimum-wage increases. See *Unificación Ferroviaria,* no. 257, 1 Sept.
1947, 1, and *Tiempo,* 2 Jan. 1948, 28.

36. *Unificación Ferroviaria,* no. 268, 16 Feb. 1948, 3; no. 269, 1 Mar. 1948, 1;
no. 271, 1 Apr. 1948, 1–2, 5; no. 273, 1 May 1948, 12; no. 278, 15 July 1948, 8.

The CUT, STFRM, SITMMSRM, STPRM, SME, Alianza de Obreros y Campesinos de México (Alliance of Mexican Workers and Peasants), and the Confederación Nacional de Electricistas (National Confederation of Electricians) petitioned
to join the CTAL in March 1948.

37. These membership totals were listed as part of the COOC's campaign
to prevent Fernando Amilpa from serving as Mexico's delegate to the International Labor Conference in San Francisco, California, in June 1948. See *Unificación
Ferroviaria,* no. 276, 16 June 1948, 1, 7; no. 280, 16 Aug. 1948, 1. It is not clear
whether the membership reported for the CUT included the STFRM; if so, then
railroad workers were counted twice in the COOC total. Leal and Talavera, "Organizaciones sindicales" (1977), table 2, p. 1260, cite a CUT membership of 98,189
workers in 1948, although it is not clear whether this was before or after progovernment leaders seized control of the STFRM in October 1948 and ended its ties to
the CUT.

38. Author's calculations based on data presented in Talavera and Leal, "Organizaciones sindicales," table 2, p. 1260. Leal and Talavera report all members of
the Coalition of Worker and Peasant Organizations as CUT affiliates.

The CTM reported a total of 1.3 million members in 1941; Confederación de
Trabajadores de México, *C.T.M., 1936–1941* (1941), 1098–1146. Its 1947 national
congress was attended by delegates from 3,426 affiliated unions, which claimed a
total of 1.1 million members. *Tiempo,* 4 Apr. 1947, 3.

39. Carr, *Marxism and Communism,* 166, presents evidence that by 1945–46
the CTM had also lost considerable support in such key states as Jalisco, Puebla,
and Veracruz.

40. *Tiempo,* 27 Aug. 1948, 3–4.

41. *Tiempo,* 3 Sept. 1948, 6; Alonso, *El movimiento ferrocarrilero* (1975), 92–
93.

42. Sindicato de Trabajadores Ferrocarrileros de la República Mexicana
(STFRM), *Acuerdos tomados por la Tercera Convención General Extraordinaria*
(1947), accords #202 and #204.

43. *Unificación Ferroviaria,* no. 280, 16 Aug. 1948, 1; no. 281, 1 Sept. 1948,

1–2, 4; *Tiempo,* 27 Aug. 1948, 3–4; Valentín Campa S., interview with author, 12 Apr. 1978, Mexico City. See also King, *Mexico* (1970), 33–34.

44. In 1947, for example, the Mexican Railroad Workers' Union led labor protests in the Federal District against the rising cost of living and proposed a national work stoppage as part of its anti-inflation campaign. See *Tiempo,* 17 Oct. 1947, and Campa S., *Mi testimonio,* 179–80.

45. Alonso, *El movimiento ferrocarrilero,* 75; *Unificación Ferroviaria,* no. 282, 16 Sept. 1948, 2; Campa S., *Mi testimonio,* 199–201.

46. *Unificación Ferroviaria,* no. 284, 16 Oct. 1948, 3; Alonso, *El movimiento ferrocarrilero,* 80, 85. At its October 1948 national council meeting, the CTM expressed support for the recent devaluation of the peso. *El Universal,* 8 Oct. 1948, 10.

47. Antonio Martínez Baez (minister of national economy, August 1948–November 1952), interview with author, 22 June 1992, Mexico City.

48. Rodea, *Historia del movimiento obrero ferrocarrilero* (1944), provides the best historical account of early railroad workers' organizations (the first of which, U.S. railroad brotherhoods, appeared about 1875), major labor conflicts and other formative experiences leading to the creation of the STFRM, and the STFRM's early activities. Rodea served as a STFRM attorney in the 1940s and prepared his study with union assistance. See also Alzati, *Historia de la mexicanización de los Ferrocarriles Nacionales de México* (1946), and Shabot, *Los orígenes del sindicalismo ferrocarrilero* (1982).

49. Rodea, *Historia,* 628. This membership figure slightly exceeded the total number of railroad workers (69,667) reported in 1943 by the Secretaría de Comunicaciones y Obras Públicas (SCOP), Departamento de Ferrocarriles en Explotación, *Estadística de los ferrocarriles y tranvías de concesión federal, 1947,* 125.

The STFRM's membership thus accounted for about half of all unionized transportation workers in 1943. There were more unionized workers in the textile and mining (*minas metálicas*) industries than in railroad transportation in 1943, but they were not organized in a single union. For data concerning the sectoral distribution of unionized workers at the time, see Secretaría de la Economía Nacional, Dirección General de Estadística, *Anuario estadístico, 1943–1945,* 431–33.

50. Rodea, *Historia,* 335–410, 673; Alzati, *Historia de la mexicanización,* 165–260, 299.

51. See Rodea, *Historia,* 247–49, 258, 469, 475, 505, 534, on railroad workers' struggles with CROM-affiliated organizations.

STFRM's constitution ("Acta Constitutiva") permitted the union to negotiate solidarity pacts or similar alliances with other labor organizations so long as they did not have "affiliations or tendencies of a political or religious character." See Cuarto Congreso Ferrocarrilero, "Libro de actas" (1932), 2:158.

52. For a description of typical Mexican railroad employees' work clothing, see Cedillo Vázquez, *¡Vaaamonos!* (1979), 86.

53. The discussion in this and the following two paragraphs draws especially on the author's interviews with Velasco, 10 Jan. 1978 and 27 Apr. 1978, Mexico City. Velasco became a union organizer in 1919 in Jalapa, Veracruz, and was a mem-

ber of the Mexican Communist Party from 1927 until he was expelled in 1943. He served on the party's Central Committee in 1929, and he was the PCM's candidate (and Fidel Velázquez's principal rival) for the key position of secretary of organization and propaganda on the CTM's first national executive committee. Between 1936 and 1941 he served as the CTM's secretary of education and cultural problems. Velasco was actively involved in organizational work leading to the formation of the STFRM, and he had close ties among railroad workers from the 1920s through the 1950s.

See also Campa S., *Mi testimonio,* 27, 37, 39–40, 64, 226, and Gómez Z., *Sucesos,* 1:235–38, 323–24, 347.

54. Morones's conduct in the 1921 and 1926–27 strikes was the object of widespread hostility among railroad workers and significantly compromised the CROM-affiliated National Railroad Federation's efforts to win rank-and-file support. The 1921 strike was directed by a "tripartite committee" composed of the CROM (with Morones as its representative), the CGT, and the CSFRM. Morones apparently negotiated privately with the Obregón administration to end the conflict against the wishes of striking railroad workers. During the 1926–27 conflict, Morones in his capacity as minister of industry, commerce, and labor recruited strikebreakers from rival CROM railroad worker organizations to undermine the bargaining position of the Confederation of Transport and Communications Workers. Velasco, interview with author, 10 Jan. 1978, Mexico City; Campa S., *Mi testimonio,* 33–39; Rodea, *Historia,* 469, 474–76, 478; Rivera Castro, *En la presidencia de Plutarco Elías Calles* (1983), 55–60.

55. Campa was secretary-general of the PCM's Unitary Mexican Union Confederation (CSUM) in 1936 and a participant at the CTM's founding congress. Laborde was secretary-general of the PCM between 1929 and 1940.

The 1926–27 strikes failed both as a result of government opposition and because some of the CTC's affiliates (formed along specialized occupational lines) refused to back a national strike.

56. It claimed between eight hundred and fifteen hundred railroad workers as members in 1938–39, but this number declined very sharply after Campa and Laborde were expelled from the PCM in 1940. See Carr, *Marxism and Communism,* 52 n. 14, 76, and table 2.

57. See ibid., 149, on the ASU's ties to railroad workers.

58. Velasco, interview with author, 10 Jan. 1978, Mexico City; Carr, *El movimiento obrero y la política en México* (1976), 1:192–95, 197, 202. See also *Boletín del Archivo General de la Nación* 2, nos. 2–3 (Apr.–Sept. 1978): 3, 15–16.

59. Rodea, *Historia,* 240–41, 264–65.

60. SCOP, *Estadística de ferrocarriles, 1953,* 15, and Secretaría de la Economía Nacional, *Anuario estadístico, 1951–1952,* 758.

61. A letter dated November 13, 1942, from the Ministry of Labor and Social Welfare to the STFRM executive committee reported that 15,411 union members (20.5 percent) were employed by railroad companies other than Ferrocarriles Nacionales. The largest of these lines was the Ferrocarril Mexicano, which em-

ployed 3,692 union members. See Secretaría del Trabajo y Previsión Social (STPS), Registro de Asociaciones (cited hereafter as "RA") case no. 10/611-1.

62. See Rodea, *Historia*, 635, and Junta Federal de Conciliación y Arbitraje [JFCA] case no. A/938/6190 (419). This JFCA document, dated July 28, 1938, lists the CROM's affiliates among railroad workers.

CROM affiliates among railroad workers survived until 1938 because the STFRM could not apply the separation exclusion clause against workers who were not STFRM members; see Navarrete, *Alto a la contrarrevolución* (1971), 176. The STFRM's control over the Worker Administration gave it sufficient bargaining leverage vis-à-vis minority labor groups to force them to join the STFRM. Gill, *Los ferrocarrileros* (1971), 125.

63. The government created Ferrocarriles Nacionales de México by fusing the two largest railroads in the country, the Ferrocarril Nacional de México and the Ferrocarril Central Mexicano, in which the Díaz administration had held majority ownership since 1906. For the history of railroad development in Mexico and a discussion of FNM's financial problems after 1908, see Fuentes Díaz, *El problema ferrocarrilero* (1951), esp. 64–120, and Ortiz Hernán, *Los ferrocarriles de México* (1974).

64. Adler, "La administración obrera en los Ferrocarriles Nacionales de México" (1988), is the best study of the Worker Administration. On developments leading up to its creation, see Ashby, *Organized Labor and the Mexican Revolution under Lázaro Cárdenas* (1963), 122–23; Rodea, *Historia*, 510–11; Velasco, interview with author, 10 Jan. 1978, Mexico City; de la Peña, "La expropiación de los Ferrocarriles Nacionales de México" (1937).

65. In the late 1930s, FNM operated about 60 percent of the national railroad transportation system. Loyola Díaz, *El ocaso*, 57.

66. "Ley que crea la Administración Nacional Obrera de los Ferrocarriles," *Diario Oficial de la Federación*, 30 Apr. 1938, 1–4.

67. The Worker Administration apparently sought to hold wage and benefit payments to 48.0 percent of total expenditures; *Ferronales* (magazine published by Ferrocarriles Nacionales de México), 15 June 1941, 2, and 1 Jan. 1942, 9.

68. *Ferronales*, 1 June 1940, "Suplemento," 2.

69. *Ferronales*, 1 Jan. 1940, 2–3; 1 June 1940, "Suplemento," 4–5.

70. *Ferronales*, 1 Aug. 1940, 7, and 15 June 1941, 3.

71. "Ley que crea la Administración de los Ferrocarriles Nacionales de México," *Diario Oficial de la Federación*, 31 Dec. 1940, 27–29. FNM's new administrative structure initially featured a government-appointed general director and a seven-member executive board that included three STFRM and four government representatives. Two of the government representatives appointed in January 1941, Pablo M. Hernández and Juan Gutiérrez, were former railroad workers; see *Ferronales*, 15 Jan. 1941, 2. Gutiérrez had been STFRM secretary-general in 1936–37.

72. This discussion is based on information in Villafuerte, *Ferrocarriles* (1959), 34, 50, 54, 157, 202; Ortiz Hernán, *Los ferrocarriles de México*, 220; SCOP, *Estadística de ferrocarriles, 1944*, 61, 67; *1947*, 17, 22, 26, 29, 47, 49. For additional

details on FNM modernization programs after 1941, see *Ferronales*, 15 June 1941, 1–3; 15 Sept. 1941, 1; 15 Jan. 1942, 1; 15 Sept. 1942, 1; 15 Sept. 1943, 2; 15 Jan. 1944, 8–9; 15 Aug. 1945, 6; 15 Apr. 1946, 6–7; 15 Sept. 1946, 2.

Nearly half of all the freight handled by FNM between January and March 1944 was war-related matériel. *Ferronales*, 15 Aug. 1944, 1.

73. The 10 percent tax on gross company income (implemented in 1923 to meet FNM debt obligations and finance repairs of physical damage sustained during the revolution) remained in effect, but these payments were apparently regularly postponed. They added to FNM's long-term debt. See *Ferronales*, 15 Sept. 1949, 13; *Unificación Ferroviaria*, no. 232, 16 Aug. 1946, 4, 11; JFCA case no. 8.1/302 (72) "48"/797 (cited hereafter as " 'Conflicto económico' case"), vol. 1, no. 2 ("Anexo No. 6," p. 3), and vol. 3, no. 2 (B), pp. 19, 21, and (F), p. 1.

74. The number of rented cars doubled between 1940–41 and 1946; Villafuerte, *Ferrocarriles*, 203. The rental cost of U.S.-owned railroad cars as a proportion of total FNM expenditures peaked at 5.6 percent in 1944; author's calculation from data presented in table 4.1 and *Ferronales*, 15 Apr. 1947, 5.

75. In December 1940 the government eliminated the FNM's legal requirement to maintain an operating coefficient of at least .85. Adler, "La administración obrera," 120.

76. *Ferronales*, 15 Apr. 1942, 2–3. The government had granted a wage increase to the lowest-paid railroad workers in early 1941, but average wage and benefit expenditures per worker remained unchanged in nominal terms between 1940 and 1941. *Ferronales*, 15 Feb. 1942, 22–23.

77. *Unificación Ferroviaria*, no. 187, 15 Aug. 1944, 3; Rodea, *Historia*, 612–13; STPS, *Memoria de labores, 1943–1944*, 196. The average weekly wage for all railroad workers (not just FNM employees) rose from 35.6 pesos in 1940 and 1941 to 40.5 pesos in 1942 and 50.8 pesos in 1943. Railroad workers' average wages during this period were generally higher than those for workers in the textile, mining, and metalworking industries, but about half to two-thirds those of petroleum workers.

78. Author's calculation based on data presented in *Unificación Ferroviaria*, no. 190, 1 Oct. 1944, 1; no. 191, 15 Oct. 1944, 5.

79. *Tiempo*, 4 Oct. 1946, 5–6; *Unificación Ferroviaria*, no. 262, 16 Dec. 1947, 6; STFRM, *Acuerdos tomados por la Tercera Convención*, accord #215. Data concerning total 1941–47 wage increases are *especialidad* averages.

80. *Ferronales*, 15 Feb. 1942, 21; 15 July 1942, 1–2. The Ávila Camacho administration's decision to do so partly reflected its desire to take advantage of wartime cooperation with the United States to modernize the country's railroad transportation network. Beginning in November 1942, a specially created United States Railway Mission supervised rehabilitation work on the Mexican National Railroads. The U.S. government agreed to underwrite the cost of war-related railroad modernization projects, and the U.S. Export-Import Bank loaned Mexico funds for the purchase of additional railroad equipment and construction materials. U.S. financial support for the government's railroad modernization program was conditioned on improvements in FNM operating efficiency. See *Ferronales*,

15 Sept. 1943, 2; 15 Sept. 1949, 13; Quintana, Crespo de la Serna, and Rosado Aragón, "Estudio sobre los Ferrocarriles Nacionales de México" (1943), 75; *Tiempo,* 12 May 1944, 34; and U.S. Department of State, "Rehabilitation of Certain Mexican National Railways." Executive Agreement Series 289, Nov. 1942.

Binational railroad cooperation during World War II included the large-scale use of Mexican workers (57,370 by July 1944) to maintain railroad lines in the United States. STPS, *Memoria de labores, 1943–1944,* 45.

81. Ramírez's upward political mobility began when a grateful Obregón made him chief of military trains and later governor of Jalisco. Dulles, *Yesterday in Mexico* (1961), 40.

82. The basic contract terms then in effect were those that had been adopted in July 1925, September 1936, and April and October 1937. JFCA case no. C/939/7000.

Substantially cutting employment would have been very costly in the short term because each dismissed worker would have received a separation indemnity payment equal to three months' salary plus twenty days' salary for each year of service; see *Ferronales,* 15 June 1944, "Suplemento," 20. Seniority-based payments would have been large because of many railroad workers' advanced length of service.

83. Under the existing contract, workers with more than sixty-one demerits on their service records were subject to dismissal, but workers who had clean service records for a specified period of time could have them removed (five demerits canceled for thirty days' satisfactory work, and twenty-five demerits canceled after maintaining a clean record for one year). Workers could also have demerits canceled for other reasons, including keeping equipment clean and avoiding accidents. Workers with more than twenty years' seniority received special consideration in disciplinary proceedings. See JFCA case nos. C/939/7000 and 8.1/315.1 (19) "42"/1116.

84. The collective contract in effect in 1943 stipulated that candidates for administrative positions had to be railroad workers with at least fifteen years' seniority and at least two years' full-time service immediately prior to the appointment, that they have worked in the regional or service division where the administrative opening occurred, and that they had not "defrauded the interests of the Worker Administration or railroad workers." See Quintana et al., "Estudio," 66.

85. See ibid., 54–58, for Ramírez's complete proposal.

86. *Ferronales,* 15 Feb. 1943, 1–2.

87. Quintana et al., "Estudio," 50–51, 58–60, 196–97.

88. *Ferronales,* 15 Feb. 1943, 3.

89. Quintana et al., "Estudio," 61–74; *Excélsior,* 11 June 1943, 1, 8.

90. The STFRM had long protested the construction of trunk roads parallel to railroad lines, which undercut the railroads' freight and passenger business. See, for example, Cuarto Congreso Ferrocarrilero, "Libro de actas," 2:79–80A; *Unificación Ferroviaria,* no. 253, 1 July 1947, 1; no. 258, 16 Sept. 1947, 1.

91. Villafuerte, *Ferrocarriles,* 160, 162.

92. *Ferronales,* 15 Aug. 1949, 1. For a general discussion of railroad freight

rates, see Villafuerte, *Ferrocarriles,* 214–32. The STFRM based its argument on its own study of FNM's financial situation, published in July 1943; see Gill, *Los ferrocarrileros* (1971), 137–40.

93. Piña, "Las pérdidas de los F.F.C.C.N.N." (1952), 4–6. The data cited by Piña cover the period 1939–51 and show that FNM received 21.91 pesos in income per 1,000 ton-kilometers for transporting mineral ores and semirefined metals, for which the actual transportation cost was 40.91 pesos per 1,000 ton-kilometers. *Unificación Ferroviaria,* no. 261, 1 Nov. 1944, 5, lists other products on which FNM suffered transportation losses.

94. *Unificación Ferroviaria,* no. 204, 16 June 1945, 4.

95. Author's calculations based on data presented in SCOP, *Estadística de ferrocarriles, 1944,* 67, 73, 105–9.

96. Inorganic products (primarily mineral ores and metal products) accounted for 82.2 percent of total FNM freight losses between January 1942 and December 1947. Author's calculations based on data presented in "Conflicto económico" case, vol. 2, no. 2, pp. 1–2.

97. For example, the Cárdenas administration's announcement in 1938 that it intended to raise FNM freight rates (by 20 to 100 percent for different minerals, and by 10 to 20 percent for other products) prior to the creation of the Worker Administration drew intense criticism from national business organizations and the governors of nine central and northern states whose economies depended heavily on mining. The SITMMSRM also opposed the measure on the grounds that the reduced export competitiveness of mineral products would increase unemployment and produce downward pressure on miners' wages. In the end the Cárdenas administration dropped the proposal. See Adler, "La administración obrera," 107–8.

98. Ávila Camacho formally responded to the union leadership's compromise proposals on March 15, 1943, calling them laudable but insufficient; *Ferronales,* 15 Apr. 1943, 1–2. Shortly thereafter, the government severely restricted railroad workers' access to complimentary travel passes; see "Prevenciones generales sobre pases o pasajes libres de cargos que expidan las empresas ferrocarrileras de jurisdicción federal," *Diario Oficial de la Federación,* 15 May 1943, 8.

99. The discussion in these two paragraphs draws on Gómez Z., *Sucesos,* 1:228–29, 232–38; Rodea, *Historia,* 614–16; Loyola Díaz, *El ocaso,* 102–11, 123–24; *Tiempo,* 14 Jan. 1944, 8; 28 Jan. 1944, 8; 4 Feb. 1944, 7; 18 Feb. 1944, 10; 22 Feb. 1944, 32; 31 Mar. 1944, 33; *Unificación Ferroviaria,* no. 185, 15 July 1944, 8; no. 193, 16 Nov. 1944, 3; no. 203, 1 June 1945, 5; no. 213, 15 Nov. 1945, 1–2, 7; no. 227, 1 June 1946, 8; no. 231, 1 Aug. 1946, 1, 4, 8; *El Universal,* 19 Nov. 1943, 11; 25 Nov. 1943, n.p.; STPS, RA case nos. 10/614-2 (correspondence from the early 1940s between Ministry of Labor and Social Welfare and other government officials and the STFRM and/or Ferrocarriles Nacionales) and 10/611-2 (correspondence from the STFRM to Ministry of Labor and Social Welfare and other government officials concerning union elections in the early 1940s).

100. The bases of *trenista* disaffection were of long standing. Although they were in favor of forming a stronger national union, *trenistas* had openly expressed their concerns regarding loss of contract benefits and organizational autonomy at

the STFRM's founding convention. Cuarto Congreso Ferrocarrilero, "Libro de actas," 1:9, 19A, 41, 103A, 169A, 170A, 175, 182A, 183A, 184. Both the CROM's organizational presence among train crews in the 1920s and 1930s and the PCM's general lack of organizational success among them suggest that *trenistas* may have been particularly concerned about leftist influence in the STFRM in the early and mid-1940s.

In 1934 Cavazos had played a leading role in a secessionist movement by *trenista* personnel. *Tiempo*, 4 Jan. 1944, 8.

101. See Rodea, *Historia*, 65, 67, 69, 622, 636–39, for the names and occupational backgrounds of STFRM secretaries-general.

102. Gómez Z.'s supporters were accused of robbing substantial numbers of ballots in Mexico City, Monterrey, Aguascalientes, Gómez Palacio (Durango), and Empalme (Sonora); RA case no. 10/614-2. According to a contemporary account, the CTM's Fidel Velázquez was sufficiently concerned by such charges that he considered intervening in the situation, even though the CTM actively supported Gómez Z.'s candidacy. *Tiempo*, 14 Jan. 1944, 8.

103. Fidel Velázquez served as a principal contact with some STFRM elements during Ávila Camacho's negotiations to form a coalition executive committee in February 1944; RA case no. 10/614-2. See *Unificación Ferroviaria*, no. 182, 25 May 1944, 1, for the membership of this second coalition committee.

104. Both groups applied for registration on February 22, 1944, and received it on May 12, 1944. The *trenistas* claimed 7,499 members, and the *caldereros* listed 2,415 members. For the geographical distribution of the organizations' membership, see STPS, *Memoria de labores, 1943–1944*, 89–94.

For information concerning the evolution of the conflict, see *Tiempo*, 5 June 1942, 32; 21 Jan. 1944, 8; 17 Mar. 1944, 7–8; 12 May 1944, 8–9; *Unificación Ferroviaria*, no. 182, 25 May 1944, 1, 7; no. 184, 30 June 1944, 8; no. 186, 31 July 1944, 1, 8; no. 189, 30 June 1944, 8; no. 192, 1 Nov. 1944, 8; no. 194, 1 Dec. 1944, 1; no. 196, 1 Jan. 1945, 1, 7; no. 201, 2 Apr. 1945, 2; no. 202, 1 May 1945, 1; no. 205, 16 July 1945, 1, 4; no. 215, 16 Dec. 1945, 1, 2; no. 217, 1 Jan. 1946, 2; no. 231, 1 Aug. 1946, 1, 4.

105. On the importance of occupational community as a basis for political solidarity among workers, see Marks, *Unions in Politics* (1989), 24–33.

106. See JFCA case nos. 8.1/305 (72) "44"/823 (the demand for contract representation filed by *trenistas*), esp. pp. 3–5, and 8.1/305 (72) "44"/825 (the demand for contract recognition filed by *caldereros*), esp. pp. 2–4. Many of these issues arose in the debates preceding the STFRM's formation in 1933. See Cuarto Congreso Ferrocarrilero, "Libro de actas," 1:58–60A, 69–70, 72, 103A, 111, 135–35A, 138–39; 2:47, 109–12.

107. *Tiempo*, 28 Jan. 1944, 8; RA case nos. 10/611-2 and 10/614-2; JFCA case no. 8.2/305 (72) "44"/407, p. 4. On rising discontent among *trenistas* in the early 1940s, see Loyola Díaz, *El ocaso*, 91–93, 95–97, 101–2.

108. The STFRM reported that the secession of *trenistas* and *caldereros* reduced union dues by about 35 percent. *Unificación Ferroviaria*, no. 191, 15 Oct. 1944, 2; no. 195, 15 Dec. 1944, 2.

109. The *trenista* and *calderero* examples sparked short-lived secessionist movements among workers at Compañía Pullman in February–March 1944 and among train dispatchers in August 1944. *Unificación Ferroviaria*, no. 188, 1 Sept. 1944, 8; no. 189, 15 Sept. 1944, 1; no. 193, 16 Nov. 1944, 2.

110. *Unificación Ferroviaria*, no. 195, 15 Dec. 1944, 1; no. 196, 1 Jan. 1945, 1, 7; no. 200, 1 Mar. 1945, 1; no. 213, 15 Nov. 1945, 7; *Tiempo*, 28 Jan. 1944, 8.

Efforts to establish secessionist groups (with management support) began in some local STFRM sections as early as 1942. Hernández, *Andanzas de un ferrocarrilero* (1951), 303.

The secessionist organizations were also encouraged and assisted by Alfredo Navarrete (a former train conductor and STFRM secretary-general in 1934–35 who was later expelled from the union, and who at the time was leader of the conservative National Proletarian Confederation) and Luis N. Morones. See *Unificación Ferroviaria*, no. 182, 25 May 1944, 1, 7; no. 203, 1 June 1945, 1, 5, 7; no. 213, 15 Nov. 1945, 2; no. 215, 16 Dec. 1945, 5; *Tiempo*, 5 June 1942, 32; Camacho, *El futuro inmediato*, 47; Loyola Díaz, *El ocaso*, 156.

111. *Excélsior*, 19 July 1949, 1; *Unificación Ferroviaria*, no. 213, 15 Nov. 1945, 7; *Ferronales*, 15 Oct. 1945, 10.

112. *Tiempo*, 17 Mar. 1944, 7–8; *Unificación Ferroviaria*, no. 193, 16 Nov. 1944, 1; no. 215, 16 Dec. 1945, 3–4; no. 226, 16 May 1946, 2; *Ferronales*, 15 Dec. 1945, 1; 15 July 1945, 1; Hernández, *Andanzas*, 316–17; Loyola Díaz, *El ocaso*, 148–49. The partially successful national *paro* in December 1945 resulted from a government decision to allow other workers to substitute for dissident *trenistas* and *caldereros* if they called work stoppages in support of their demands.

113. Two factors made the government's legal recognition of these separatist organizations particularly remarkable. First, in the course of its long struggle with minority labor groups, the STFRM had won legal recognition of its position as the majority organization among railroad workers. Both Presidents Rodríguez and Cárdenas had issued decisions (*laudos*) to this effect, and the STFRM's contracts with FNM after 1934 gave it sole representational rights even if the majority of workers in a particular *especialidad* seceded; see Ferrocarriles Nacionales de México, S.A., "Cláusulas de exclusión" (13 June 1934), arts. 2–3. Despite a long legal battle, neither the *trenistas* nor the *caldereros* ever won separate collective work agreements.

Second, granting legal recognition to these separatist groups risked disrupting wartime railroad service. Their attempt to paralyze rail traffic in December 1945 led to presidential arbitration of the internal union conflict and the cancellation of legal registration for both *trenistas* and *caldereros*. All but the two organizations' top leaders were eventually reinstated with full back pay. A copy of President Manuel Ávila Camacho's arbitration decision ending the dispute (dated July 19, 1946) and supporting documentation concerning the STFRM conflict are included in JFCA case no. 8.1/320 (72) "46"/1214; see esp. pp. 14–80. On government-mediated negotiations to end the conflict and STFRM concessions prior to presidential arbitration, see *Unificación Ferroviaria*, no. 186, 31 July 1944, 1, 8; no. 194, 1 Dec. 1944, 1; no. 205, 16 July 1945, 1, 4; no. 212, 1 Nov. 1945, 3; no. 213, 15 Nov. 1945, 2;

no. 214, 1 Dec. 1945, 1; no. 216, 20 Dec. 1945, 1; *Excélsior,* 19 July 1944, 1, 13.

The available materials do not shed much light on the political calculations behind the Ministry of Labor and Social Welfare's tremendously sensitive decision to register the two secessionist organizations. It is possible, however, that the two groups won registration because they had the support of General Maximino Ávila Camacho, who was the president's brother, minister of communications and public works (the cabinet position with jurisdiction over railroad transportation) from 1941 until his death in February 1945, and a prominent political conservative who was strongly opposed to leftist influence in the labor movement. Campa S., *Mi testimonio,* 174–77, and the author's interviews with a railroad engineer active in the *trenista* secession movement (27 Apr. 1978, Mexico City) and a former railroad union activist (22 June 1978, Mexico City) indicate that Maximino Ávila Camacho was the groups' principal political sponsor, apparently as part of a potential 1946 presidential bid. After his death, the groups were supported by Ezequiel Padilla (minister of foreign relations, 1940–45) in an effort to marshal support for his own presidential candidacy in 1946. On the groups' connection with Padilla, see *Unificación Ferroviaria,* no. 229, 1 July 1946, 1, and Cedillo Vázquez, *De Juan Soldado a Juan Rielero* (1963), 36.

The STFRM later charged that the government gave legal recognition to the dissident organizations because they agreed to accept the terms of FNM's Circular GG-96; see *Unificación Ferroviaria,* no. 210, 1 Oct. 1945, 3; no. 215, 16 Dec. 1945, 5. There is no independent basis on which to confirm this claim, though the dissident groups apparently did have advance knowledge of Circular GG-96; see Loyola Díaz, *El ocaso,* 122.

114. "Decreto que reforma los artículos 5, 6, 8 y 18 de la ley de 31 de diciembre de 1940, que creó la Administración de los Ferrocarriles Nacionales de México," *Diario Oficial de la Federación,* 11 Mar. 1944, 5–6. This decree also added to FNM's executive board one representative each from two major business organizations, the Confederación de Cámaras Industriales (CONCAMIN) and the Confederación de Cámaras Nacionales de Comercio (CONCANACO), while reducing the STFRM's representation from three to two members. The decree was suspended on September 30, 1945. For a statement of Ávila Camacho's goals, see *Ferronales,* 15 Oct. 1944, 1, 9–12.

Medical expenses constituted a significant cost because until August 1975 FNM operated its own health care system. Employees of most other railroad companies in Mexico were affiliated with the newly established Instituto Mexicano del Seguro Social. *Ferronales,* Mar. 1976, 9.

115. See Administración de los Ferrocarriles Nacionales de México, *Suplemento de la Circular GG-96,* 5 June 1944; *Ferronales,* 15 May 1944, 1–2; *Unificación Ferroviaria,* no. 182, 25 May 1944, 4.

116. *Tiempo,* 12 May 1944, 37.

117. *Unificación Ferroviaria,* no. 182, 25 May 1944, 1–2, 6; no. 196, 1 Jan. 1945, 3. The STFRM's response to Circular GG-96 appears in *Unificación Ferroviaria,* no. 182, 25 May 1944, 4.

118. *Ferronales,* 15 Aug. 1944, "Suplemento," 5; 15 Oct. 1944, 12; *Tiempo,* 1 Sept. 1944, 4.

119. The system was inaugurated on November 7, 1944, "Railroad Workers' Day." The program's goal was to open a store in each STFRM local section, but the network of outlets expanded only slowly. See "Decreto que crea las 'Tiendas Ferronales' para la venta de artículos de primera necesidad a los trabajadores de los Ferrocarriles Nacionales de México," *Diario Oficial de la Federación,* 24 Oct. 1944, 10–11; *Ferronales,* 15 Nov. 1944, 1–2; *Unificación Ferroviaria,* no. 186, 31 July 1944, 2; no. 200, 1 Mar. 1945, 1, 4; no. 242, 16 Jan. 1946, 3. The system was in operation at least as late as 1955; see Alberto Rangel Escalera, "El informe presidencial y los Ferrocarriles Nacionales," *Excélsior,* 17 Sept. 1955.

120. SCOP, *Memoria, Septiembre 1943–Agosto 1944,* 179; *Unificación Ferroviaria,* no. 195, 15 Dec. 1944, n.p.; "Conflicto económico" case, vol. 2, no. 1 (C) ("Anexo Número 1: Situación económica y financiera"), p. 12.

121. The accomplishments of the "Plan Alemán de Rehabilitación Ferroviaria" are effusively summarized in FNM, *Cien años de ferrocarriles* (1952). See also *Ferronales,* 15 Apr. 1952, 6–11.

122. See Villafuerte, *Ferrocarriles,* 50, 54, 58, 86, 157; Ortiz Hernán, *Los ferrocarriles de México,* 219; SCOP, *Estadística de ferrocarriles, 1947,* 22; *1953,* 27, 33, 39, 69, 159; *Ferronales,* 15 Oct. 1949, 7.

123. *Tiempo,* 14 Mar. 1947, 42–43; *Unificación Ferroviaria,* no. 246, 16 Mar. 1947, 1. The Ministry of Communications and Public Works published a study in April 1947 reporting that these rate increases were insufficient to restore FNM's profitability. See Cortés A., "Golpe al movimiento ferrocarrilero" (1984), 81.

124. *Ferronales,* 15 Feb. 1947, 4, 5, 8; 15 Oct. 1947, 30.

125. *Unificación Ferroviaria,* no. 258, 16 Sept. 1947, 5; no. 298, 31 Dec. 1949, 6.

126. *Unificación Ferroviaria,* no. 253, 1 July 1947, 1; no. 258, 16 Sept. 1947, 1, 5; no. 259, 1 Oct. 1947, 1; no. 261, 1 Nov. 1947, 1, 5; no. 262, 16 Dec. 1947, 6. See also STFRM, *Acuerdos tomados por la Sexta Gran Convención Ordinaria* (1946), accord #715, and *Acuerdos tomados por la Tercera Convención,* accord #215.

127. *Ferronales,* 15 Mar. 1948, 17; 15 Apr. 1950, 2–3. At least one *especialidad* (train dispatchers) received an additional wage increase at another time. JFCA case no. 8.1/303.3 (72) "48"/779.

128. The growth in FNM's labor force in 1947 (see table 4.1) may have been due in part to the June 1946 addition to the FNM operating system of workers employed by the Ferrocarril Mexicano and the Compañía Terminal de Veracruz. See *Unificación Ferroviaria,* no. 226, 16 May 1946, 1, 5.

129. The total cost of the wage increase that Ávila Camacho granted FNM employees in October 1946 was forty-five million to fifty million pesos. Although the government planned a fully compensating increase in railroad mining tariffs, mining products were excluded from the 10–15 percent rate increase enacted on some items because the Ministry of Finance was concerned about the effect such a measure would have on the mining industry, which at the time suffered from the decline in demand that followed the end of World War II. See "Conflicto económico"

case, vol. 1, no. 2 ("Anexo Número 6"), p. 4; vol. 2, no. 1 (C) ("Anexo Número 1: Situación económica y financiera"), p. 12; vol. 3, no. 2 (A), p. 2A; *Tiempo,* 4 Oct. 1946, 5–6.

130. "Conflicto económico" case, vol. 3, no. 2 (A), p. 1A.

131. This discussion of the *charrazo* and the context in which it occurred draws on JFCA case no. 8.1/315.1 "49"/569 ("Valentín Campa Salazar v. STFRM y Ferrocarriles Nacionales," cited hereafter as "Campa case"), pp. 38, 70–78, 81–93, 124–25, 409–16; Campa S., interview with author, 12 Apr. 1978, Mexico City; Velasco, interview with author, 27 Apr. 1978, Mexico City; *Unificación Ferroviaria,* no. 268, 16 Feb. 1948, 6, 8, 11; no. 283, 1 Oct. 1948, 1; no. 284, 16 Oct. 1948, 1–2, 4, 5, 7–8; no. 285, 30 Nov. 1948, 1, 15; no. 288, 28 Feb. 1949, 2, 10; *Tiempo,* 8 Oct. 1948, 6–7; 15 Oct. 1948, 1–2; 22 Oct. 1948, 3; 5 Nov. 1948, 1–3; Gómez Z., *Sucesos,* 1:323, 328–30; Cedillo Vázquez, *De Juan Soldado,* 38–40. Medina, *Civilismo y modernización,* 162–70; Alonso, *El movimiento ferrocarrilero,* 74–98; and Gill, *Los ferrocarrileros,* 148–51, provide general summaries of these events.

132. See Carr, *Marxism and Communism,* 171, regarding support from Campa and Laborde for Díaz de León. As late as July 1948, Gómez Z. and Díaz de León (whose full name was Jesús Díaz de León Díaz de León) had worked together during STFRM contract negotiations with the Ferrocarril Sud-Pacífico. *Tiempo,* 16 July 1948, 36.

133. Accountants from the attorney general's office began their investigation on September 24, 1948. Díaz de León's original complaint questioned the use of 647,042 pesos in union funds, but the investigation quickly focused on those monies used in the organization of the CUT. (The 206,250.21 pesos in question represented 43.2 percent of the STFRM's "extraordinary expenditures" during the period January–November 1947.) Díaz de León later claimed that he called for government action only after his requests for an internal investigation concerning the use of STFRM funds were repeatedly ignored by the union's finance secretary and the national oversight committee. See *Unificación Ferroviaria,* no. 264, 16 Dec. 1947, 11; no. 283, 1 Oct. 1948, 1; *El Universal,* 8 Oct. 1948, 9; Hernández, *Andanzas,* 365; Campa case, pp. 97–98.

134. Díaz de León's February 9, 1949, report to the STFRM membership concerning his first year in office included a detailed statement of his charges; see Campa case, pp. 97–130.

135. *Unificación Ferroviaria,* no. 268, 16 Feb. 1948, 4; no. 280, 16 Aug. 1948, 2; no. 281, 1 Sept. 1948, 9, 11; no. 282, 16 Sept. 1948, 2; no. 283, 1 Oct. 1948, 2.

136. Campa case, pp. 34A, 35, 406–7A, 415–15A, 417A, 419A; *Unificación Ferroviaria,* no. 284, 16 Oct. 1948, 4; Gómez Z., *Sucesos,* 1:304–5, 329–30.

137. STFRM, *Acuerdos tomados por la Sexta Gran Convención,* accord #593; *Estatutos del Sindicato de Trabajadores Ferrocarrileros de la República Mexicana aprobados por la Sexta Convención Ordinaria* (1946; cited hereafter as "STFRM statutes for 1946"), art. 189(b).

138. *Tiempo,* 5 Nov. 1948, 1–3.

139. President Alemán created the "Comisión para el estudio de los problemas económicos y financieros de los Ferrocarriles Nacionales de México" in October

1947, although it apparently did not begin work until January 1948. *Unificación Ferroviaria,* no. 261, 1 Nov. 1947, 1. It included representatives from the Ministry of Finance, the Ministry of Communications and Public Works, FNM management, and the STFRM. The commission was generally known as the "Comisión Tripartita," although some documents refer to it as the "Comisión Cuadripartita." The STFRM's request for the commission was prompted by Ferrocarriles Nacionales' announcement in 1947 that it might initiate "economic conflict" proceedings before the Federal Conciliation and Arbitration Board. See STFRM, *Acuerdos tomados por la Tercera Convención,* accord #62, and Hernández, *Andanzas,* 339–53.

140. Campa case, p. 112; *Unificación Ferroviaria,* no. 282, 16 Sept. 1948, 4. The commission's estimates of the budgetary savings to be realized by various operational reforms are summarized in "Conflicto económico" case, vol. 1, no. 2 ("Anexo Número 6"), pp. 10–11.

141. Quoted in *Auto dictado por la H. Junta Federal de Conciliación y Arbitraje, con fecha 16 de Noviembre de 1948, en relación con el Conflicto de Orden Económico planteado por los Ferrocarriles Nacionales de México* (no publisher or date), 5. A full copy of the commission's report does not appear in any of the JFCA files examined for this period.

142. Campa case, pp. 54–55, 114; *El Universal,* 4 Oct. 1948, 8. There was much general discontent among railroad workers in 1947–48 because of FNM's lengthy delays in paying workers, a consequence of the company's increasingly precarious financial situation. On several occasions employees suspended work in protest. See STFRM, *Acuerdos tomados por la Tercera Convención,* accords #110 and #121; *Unificación Ferroviaria,* no. 267, 31 Jan. 1948, 1; no. 281, 1 Sept. 1948, 2; no. 283, 1 Oct. 1948, 2; *Ferronales,* 15 Feb. 1948, 24; 15 Oct. 1948, 9. Similar problems also gave rise to work stoppages on the Ferrocarril Sud-Pacífico and the Ferrocarril del Noroeste in 1948. Hernández C., "Del pacto de sindicatos industriales," 903–8.

143. See JFCA case nos. 8.1/315.1 (19) "42"/1116 and 8.1/315.1 (19) "44"/38, and Gómez Z., *Sucesos,* 1:305.

144. *El Universal,* 6 Oct. 1948, 8.

145. Campa case, pp. 100, 126, 407A; *Unificación Ferroviaria,* no. 268, 16 Feb. 1948, 4. For specific examples of STFRM actions in support of other labor groups during this period, see *Unificación Ferroviaria,* no. 277, 1 July 1948, 3, 6; no. 279, 1 Aug. 1948, 6.

The STFRM received a substantial amount of union dues (4.1 million pesos in 1946, equal to U.S.$845,361 at the prevailing exchange rate), making it a very wealthy union by Mexican standards. See *Unificación Ferroviaria,* no. 242, 16 Jan. 1947.

146. Campa case, pp. 75, 409A; *Tiempo,* 12 Nov. 1948, 16.

147. It is possible, of course, that the Alemán administration orchestrated the entire affair from the beginning. Campa S., *Mi testimonio,* 200–201, claims that Alemán felt personally betrayed when Gómez Z. allowed a major protest against the July 1948 devaluation to proceed on August 21, 1948, in Mexico City. Similarly, Velasco (interview with the author, 27 Apr. 1978, Mexico City) believed that

Díaz de León turned on his former political mentor in exchange for government support that permitted him to establish his own unchallenged control over the union, and perhaps for material rewards as well. Carr, *Marxism and Communism,* 171, notes that Díaz de León had close ties to Colonel Carlos Serrano, the Alemán aide who directed the secret police force in the October 14 assault on STFRM headquarters.

148. See, for example, midlevel union officials' public declaration in support of the national executive and oversight committees. *El Universal,* 6 Oct. 1948, 8.

149. *El Universal,* 5 Oct. 1948, 17.

150. Hernández, *Andanzas,* 364–76, reproduces the text of the national oversight committee's decision.

151. Gómez Z. and other former executive committee (and CUT) officials were arrested in October 1948; Gómez Z. was released from prison in May 1949. Campa avoided capture and was not arrested until November 1949; he was released from prison in January 1952. See Gómez Z., *Sucesos,* 1:331, 344, 351; Campa S., *Mi testimonio,* 93, 213; Campa case, pp. 401, 422. On the role of the Federal Security Directorate, see Carr, *Marxism and Communism,* 145, and Alonso, *El movimiento ferrocarrilero,* 84.

Campa's formal railroad ties ended with a separation indemnity payment from Ferrocarriles Nacionales in 1957, but Gómez Z. returned as STFRM secretary-general in 1962–64 and 1965–68. He concluded his railroad career as FNM general manager between 1973 and 1982. See *Excélsior,* 6 May 1988, 18.

152. Gómez Z., *Sucesos,* 1:328; author's interview with a railroad engineer active in *trenista* secession movement, 27 Apr. 1978, Mexico City. Díaz de León had earlier offered to reduce union dues in general. *El Universal,* 8 Oct. 1948, 9.

Regular national STFRM dues from 1933 until 1950 were 1.2 percent of a worker's monthly salary; see *Unificación Ferroviaria,* no. 4, 1 Mar. 1934, 67; no. 184, 30 June 1944, 1. For special dues and other deductions during this period, see STFRM, *Acuerdos tomados por la Sexta Gran Convención,* accord #625 (art. 283).

153. Campa case, pp. 100, 104, 106–9, 126–27. Díaz de León's attack on his union opponents dripped with populist disdain: "But neither do I think it just that our comrades' money be employed to create a new class of wealthy union leaders, real opportunists ["verdaderos arribistas del movimiento obrero"] who live in opulence and look down on their former working-class comrades—individuals who, stretched out in their comfortable surroundings, dictate manifestos in which they speak of union rights, international conferences, and democratic ideals, all the while belching of exotic whiskies and sumptuous foods. They think they belong to a neobourgeois caste because they no longer have the same economic needs felt by their former brothers in poverty." See *El Universal,* 4 Oct. 1948, 8. Díaz de León did not identify Gómez Z. by name in this statement.

In the course of justifying his action against Gómez Z. and Campa, Díaz de León exaggerated the size of STFRM dues payments to the CUT, claiming that they totaled 300,000 pesos for January–June 1948. *El Universal,* 8 Oct. 1949, 9.

154. Campa case, p. 113.

155. Díaz de León's nickname was "El Charro." For examples of his partici-

pation in rodeos (including a photograph of him on horseback captioned "¡Charro en verdad!"), see *Unificación Ferroviaria*, no. 295, 30 Sept. 1949, 7, and Gómez Z., *Sucesos*, 1: 323–24. The first anniversary of the STFRM takeover was celebrated with "un festival charro" at the "La Tapatía" ranch and a special "Balance depurador" ("Housecleaning Report") supplement in *Unificación Ferroviaria*, no. 286, 31 Oct. 1949, 11.

156. By the first week of November, Díaz de León was sufficiently confident of his position that he took time to trade cars, purchasing a 1941 Buick. *Excélsior*, 27 Jan. 1949, 3.

157. Alonso, *El movimiento ferrocarrilero*, 86–87, 89; *Tiempo*, 5 Nov. 1948, 1–3.

158. Velasco, interview with author, 27 Apr. 1978, Mexico City; López Villegas-Manjarrez, *La CTM*, 103. I am grateful to Barry Carr for his comments regarding the PCM's attitude toward Campa and Gómez Z.

The Mexican Electricians' Union (SME) also continued to back Díaz de León because it believed that he was defending railroad workers' contract rights against government attack. *Unificación Ferroviaria*, no. 287, 31 Jan. 1949, 1, 11–12.

159. Compare STFRM statutes for 1946, arts. 160–87 (esp. arts. 163, 168), with *Estatutos aprobados por la Cuarta Convención General Extraordinaria* (cited hereafter as "STFRM statutes for 1949"), arts. 124–28, 136 (b, c, d), and p. 166 (sample ballot). The system of indirect elections was apparently repealed in 1964 by the Novena Convención Nacional Ferrocarrilera. *Unificación Ferroviaria*, n.s., no. 36, 2 Feb. 1965, 1.

160. STFRM statutes for 1949, arts. 27, 29.

161. See, for example, *Unificación Ferroviaria*, no. 286, 31 Dec. 1948, 13; no. 293, 31 July 1949, 2, 5, 9, 12; no. 294, 31 Aug. 1949, 2, 5, 11, 14; no. 308, 31 Oct. 1950, 5; no. 309, 30 Nov. 1950, 10; no. 310, 31 Dec. 1950, 8; *Tiempo*, 12 Nov. 1948, 16; Alonso, *El movimiento ferrocarrilero*, 93.

162. See, respectively, accord #108 (5 Mar. 1949) cited in *Unificación Ferroviaria*, no. 293, 31 July 1949, 2, and accord #415 cited in *Unificación Ferroviaria*, no. 293, 31 July 1949, 5; no. 294, 31 Aug. 1949, 14. The former union officials expelled at this time are named in Campa case, p. 54.

163. Compare STFRM statutes for 1946, art. 188(f), with STFRM statutes for 1949, arts. 146–47.

164. David Vargas Bravo, Ricardo Velázquez Vázquez, and Samuel Ortega Hernández were elected STFRM secretary-general for the periods 1951–54, 1954–57, and 1957–60, respectively. Vargas Bravo was a senator from San Luis Potosí during 1952–58; Velázquez Vázquez served as federal deputy from the Federal District during 1955–58; and Ortega Hernández represented the state of Tlaxcala as federal deputy (1955–58) and senator (1958–64). Alfredo Navarrete, who was STFRM secretary-general in 1934–35 and backed Díaz de León in 1948–49, served as federal deputy from the state of México in 1952–55. Following his rehabilitation and return to union politics, Luis Gómez Z. served as senator from Aguascalientes (1964–70) and held national PRI positions (1969–70). Lists of STFRM union officials appear in RA case no. 10/611-1; information concerning elective positions is from Camp, *Mexican Political Biographies* (1982).

165. See, for example, *Tiempo*, 23 Nov. 1951, 12–13; *Unificación Ferroviaria*, n.s., no. 21, 9 Nov. 1963, 1; no. 24, 3 Feb. 1964, 20; no. 48, 2 Feb. 1966, "Suplemento politico" section, 1; no. 59, 1 Jan. 1967, 1; no. 118, Feb. 1972, 24; Ortega Aguirre, "El movimiento ferrocarrilero" (1977), 246.

166. Secretaría de Industria, Comercio y Trabajo, *Ley Federal del Trabajo* (1931), title 9, chap. 7, arts. 570–83. The Cárdenas (1934–40) and Alemán administrations had initiated similar JFCA proceedings in, respectively, 1940 and 1946–47 to win significant union concessions in the petroleum industry. Medina, *Civilismo y modernización*, 153, 157–58.

167. The text of President Alemán's November 12 policy statement appears in *Ferronales*, 15 Nov. 1948, 4. Alemán referred specifically to the Tripartite Commission's August 1948 report as the basis for directing Ferrocarriles Nacionales to initiate JFCA proceedings.

The other steps that Alemán took at this time to stem FNM losses and modernize the railroad transportation system included government financing of FNM's short-term debt, the use of the 10 percent tax on FNM gross income for the purchase of equipment and material and for new construction, and a reform of FNM's tariff structure which raised transportation rates for ores and metal products by 65 percent; see *Ferronales*, 15 Apr. 1950, 2–5, for an overview of Alemán's reforms. The government also enacted a new administrative statute (*ley orgánica*) for Ferrocarriles Nacionales on December 30, 1948, which strengthened the general manager's operational authority. The text of this statute appears in *Ferronales*, 15 Feb. 1949, 6–9.

168. This paragraph summarizes material in "Conflicto económico" case, vol. 1, nos. 2 (pp. 1–2, 5–6, 19–37; "Anexo Número 3," p. 1; "Anexo Número 5," pp. 5–8; "Anexo Número 6," p. 9), 6, 7, 12 (pp. 10–35, 37, 42–52). Ferrocarriles Nacionales estimated that the contract and work rule modifications it proposed would result in savings of approximately fifty-seven million pesos per year.

In addition to the proposals summarized in this paragraph, FNM's petition to the Federal Conciliation and Arbitration Board sought detailed modifications in work rules for various railroad occupational specialties. In the case of train crews, for instance, railroad managers sought savings in wages and fuel costs by revising established agreements concerning the circumstances under which crews could double engines or divide trains when climbing steep grades. See ibid., vol. 1, no. 8, 9 (A–F), 10, 11 (A–F).

169. Díaz de León claimed that, as part of his vigorous defense of union interests, he wrested a commitment from Alemán not to cut wage or employment levels. He may have secured a promise to this effect, but the strategy that FNM managers pursued in 1948—seeking contract and work rule concessions, although not immediate wage or employment reductions—did not differ significantly from the approach that management adopted in 1943–44. The decision to cancel all workers' disciplinary demerits as a Christmas bonus in 1948 was also presumably part of FNM managers' effort to limit union resistance to their restructuring initiative. See *Ferronales*, 15 Jan. 1949, 18.

170. Because of his supposedly vigorous defense of union privileges, *Unifica-*

ción Ferroviaria's front-page headline on December 31, 1948 (no. 286), referred to Díaz de León as "champion of the railroad workers' cause" ("paladín de los rieleros").

171. "Conflicto económico" case, vol. 1, no. 2, various pages. (This document and its six appendices were the STFRM's principal refutation of FNM charges.) See also vol. 1, no. 3 (STFRM statement to the JFCA technical commission, dated 13 Jan. 1949), p. 6, and no. 12, pp. 2–7.

172. "Conflicto económico" case, vol. 1, no. 1 (JFCA decision memorandum dated 23 Nov. 1948), pp. 1A–3A; no. 3 (STFRM petitions dated 13, 14 Dec. 1948); vol. 2, no. 1(C), pp. 2–5.

173. "Conflicto económico" case, vol. 1, no. 5 ("Informe y dictamen, relativos al conflicto de orden económico de los Ferrocarriles Nacionales de México, rendidos por los c. peritos oficiales Antonio Manero, Ing. Manuel J. Zevada e Ing. Lorenzo Pérez Castro"), pp. 23–28, 31–43, 58, 66–67, 91–98. An internal FNM evaluation committee registered similar criticisms of the company's administrative procedures and accounting system in May 1947; see ibid., vol. 3, no. 2(A), pp. 1–1A, 4A, 5, 10A–11A.

174. "Conflicto económico" case, vol. 1, no. 5, pp. 34, 43, 72–73, 78–79, 82, 98, 122, 129, 145. Data that the STFRM later submitted to the JFCA as part of its critique of the commission's report showed that, while materials expenditures remained roughly constant as a proportion of FNM income over the 1938–47 period, wages and other forms of compensation increased from 58.0 percent of FNM income in 1938 to 75.2 percent in 1947. The increase was apparently due mainly to rising employment levels. See ibid., vol. 2, no. 1(C), pp. 28, 41.

175. For example, on November 18, 1948, members of the ousted STFRM national executive committee filed a legal brief with the JFCA challenging Díaz de León's right to represent the union in the economic conflict proceedings. See "Conflicto económico" case, vol. 1, no. 14 (statement by Pineda et al. to JFCA), pp. 1–3.

176. Camp, *Mexican Political Biographies* (1982), 145–46.

177. *Auto dictado por la H. Junta,* 4–5, and "Conflicto económico" case, vol. 1, no. 1 (JFCA decision memorandum dated 23 Nov. 1948), pp. 4A–6. The JFCA used the Tripartite Commission's criticism of established contract clauses to justify its November 16 ruling. On December 14, 1948, Díaz de León petitioned the Supreme Court for an injunction (*amparo*) against the JFCA's actions, but his request was denied on January 12, 1949. "Conflicto económico" case, vol. 1, no. 4, pp. 1–2.

178. See, for example, the detailed critique of the JFCA-appointed technical commission's report that the union filed on February 12, 1949, in "Conflicto económico" case, vol. 2, no. 1(C); no. 2 (A). In these documents, the STFRM presented extensive statistical data to show that FNM financial losses in the 1940s were principally due to tariff rates that failed to cover transportation costs, particularly in the case of mining products.

179. The January 6 and February 25, 1949, *convenios* are included in vol. 2 of the "Conflicto económico" case as, respectively, nos. 1(D) and 3(A). For a detailed

summary of FNM contract clauses prior to November 1948, the modifications sought by FNM managers, and the revised clauses adopted in January 1949, see vol. 3, no. 2(B). The JFCA approved the January and February 1949 *convenios* and formally ended the economic conflict proceedings on March 17, 1949.

180. *Unificación Ferroviaria*, no. 287, 31 Jan. 1949, 1, 2.

181. *Ferronales*, 15 Aug. 1950, 11.

182. *Tiempo*, 26 Jan. 1951, 12–13. Little is known of Díaz de León's activities after his term as STFRM secretary-general ended in 1951. Stevens, *Protest and Response in Mexico* (1974), states that he "owned a prosperous dairy farm in the Federal District which, it was alleged, supplied milk to government institutions at inflated prices" (105). Cedillo Vázquez, ¡*Vaaamonos!* 135, reports that Díaz de León later became a hotel owner in Acapulco.

183. *Unificación Ferroviaria*, no. 293, 31 July 1949, 1; no. 305, 31 July 1950, 9. For the tone of union demands during this period, see ibid., no. 296, 31 Oct. 1949, 3; no. 301, 31 Mar. 1950, 5; no. 302, 30 Apr. 1950, 6.

184. See *Ferronales*, 15 Sept. 1950, 14–5; 15 Oct. 1952, n.p.; *Unificación Ferroviaria*, no. 304, 30 June 1950, 4; SCOP, *Memoria, Septiembre 1948–Agosto 1949*, 237.

The government implemented additional rate increases in 1951–52. SCOP, *Memoria, Septiembre 1951–Agosto 1952*; see 119, and Secretaría de Comunicaciones y Transportes, *Memoria, Diciembre 1952–Septiembre 1953*, n.p. As a result, FNM remained solvent throughout the 1950s. *Ferronales*, 15 May 1958, 10.

185. Information concerning rank-and-file discontent after the *charrazo* appears in *Unificación Ferroviaria*, no. 297, 30 Nov. 1949, 7; no. 301, 31 Mar. 1950, 2; no. 310, 31 Dec. 1950, 3, 5; Cedillo Vázquez, ¡*Vaaamonos!* 9; author's interview with a railroad engineer active in the *trenista* secession movement, 27 Apr. 1978, Mexico City. The Fourth Special National Convention increased regular union dues to 5 percent of a worker's monthly salary, effective in 1950. See STFRM statutes for 1949, arts. 93–94, and *Unificación Ferroviaria*, no. 307, 30 Sept. 1950, 5.

186. The 1958–59 railroad worker movement, led by Demetrio Vallejo, has received considerable attention. For examinations of this protest movement and extensive bibliographical citations, see Alonso, *El movimiento ferrocarrilero*, 99–124; Pellicer de Brody and Reyna, *El afianzamiento de la estabilidad política* (1978), 157–214; Ortega Aguirre, "El movimiento ferrocarrilero," 1–242; Stevens, *Protest and Response*, 99–126; Gill, *Los ferrocarrileros*, 161–209.

187. Basic information concerning these cases appears in Cuéllar Vázquez, "Golpe al Sindicato de Trabajadores Petroleros," 99–125; Gaitán Riveros, "El movimiento minero" (1984), 127–65; Molina A., *La caravana del hambre* (1978), 17–21.

In 1949 the Alemán administration also denied legal recognition to Lombardo Toledano's General Union of Mexican Workers and Peasants (UGOCM), which proposed to group the remnants of an antigovernment labor opposition. See Rivera Flores, "Unión General de Obreros y Campesinos de México" (1984), 49–55; Medina, *Civilismo y modernización*, 173.

188. Cuéllar Vázquez, "Golpe al Sindicato de Trabajadores Petroleros," 121; Gaitán Riveros, "El movimiento minero," 141–45, 148, 152.

189. These SITMMSRM statutes were still in effect in the late 1970s. Bizberg, *Estado y sindicalismo en México* (1990), 128–29.

190. Other Latin American governments made similar assaults on labor radicalism during these years. See Bethell and Roxborough, *Latin America between the Second World War and the Cold War* (1992).

191. On tensions between Amilpa and Velázquez during the transition, see *Tiempo*, 13 Jan. 1950, 1; 3 Feb. 1950, 2–3.

192. *Ceteme*, 21 Dec. 1951, 1; 29 Nov. 1954, 1.

193. *Ceteme*, 8 Apr. 1956, 6–7; 9 Apr. 1956, 2; 20 Oct. 1956, 4; 28 June 1958, 8. For a discussion of the CTM's internal dynamics, see Camacho, *El futuro inmediato*, 116–18.

194. This discussion draws on Durand Ponte, "Confederation of Mexican Workers" (1991), 87–88; Pellicer de Brody and Reyna, *El afianzamiento de la estabilidad política*, 64–77; and *Tiempo*, 9 May 1952, 7.

195. Camacho, *El futuro inmediato*, 57.

196. See, for example, the initiatives described in *Ceteme*, 12 Jan. 1951, 3–4, and 4 May 1953, 2.

197. Evidence concerning the BUO's membership over time appears in *Ceteme*, 14 Jan. 1955, 1, 5; 28 Jan. 1955, 1; 1 July 1955, 1; 26 Feb. 1959, 1; 16 Jan. 1960, 5; 24 Feb. 1961, 10; 24 Apr. 1965.

198. On developments leading up to the formation of the Labor Congress, see Durand Ponte, "Confederation of Mexican Workers," 88–89; Camacho, *El futuro inmediato*, 101–5. Zazueta and de la Peña, *La estructura del Congreso del Trabajo* (1984), provide an exhaustive analysis of the Labor Congress's structure and membership.

199. On CTM membership in the late 1970s, see Camacho, *El futuro inmediato*, 106 n. 5.

200. *Proceso*, 13 July 1981, 11.

201. See de la Garza Toledo, "Independent Trade Unionism in Mexico" (1991), 170, for labor organizations that were not CT members.

202. Nevertheless, it is worth noting that Fidel Velázquez perceived a direct connection between the 1919 CROM-Obregón pact and subsequent state-labor collaboration. In the course of an extended interview given in 1990, Velázquez said, "And that pact [the CROM-Obregón agreement], well, we here in the CTM put it back into effect with the governments of the revolution . . . that pact exists." Quoted in Amilpa Trujillo, *Fidel Velázquez*, 71–72.

203. For selected examples, see Camacho, *El futuro inmediato*, 111, and Portillo Ceballos, *La CTM* (1986), 83–85. Bizberg, "La crisis del corporativismo" (1990), 707, notes that the mobilization of labor support in favor of the PRI was easiest in such sectors as petroleum production, mining, and the sugar industry, where worker residential communities (*colonias*) were relatively cohesive and at times geographically isolated.

204. This issue is examined in greater detail in chapter 6 of this book.

205. Author's calculation based on data presented in Secretaría de Industria y Comercio, Dirección General de Estadística, *Anuario estadístico, 1951–1952*, 420; *1953, 71*; *1970–1971*, 49, 359; Zazueta and de la Peña, *La estructura del Congreso del Trabajo*, tables 2.4, 7.1. Of course, unionization rates vary greatly from one industry to another. For various examples, see Garavito Elías, "Así les fue a los trabajadores" (1990), table 8.29.

206. For a discussion of the specific ways in which incumbent union officials can maintain their control over the rank and file, see Camacho, "Control sobre el movimiento obrero en México" (1976).

Chapter 5: State Structures, Political Control, and Labor Participation

1. This chapter does not examine another important dimension of labor mobilization in Mexico, participation in elections. The best study of this subject, based on data from opinion surveys conducted in 1979–81, is Davis, *Working-Class Mobilization and Political Control* (1989).

2. This summary of presidential labor policies draws in part on Reyna and Trejo Delarbre, *De Adolfo Ruiz Cortines a Adolfo López Mateos* (1981), 49–50, 60, 73–76, 94–95, 152–53, 155–60; Fernández Christlieb and Rodríguez Araujo, *En el sexenio de Tlatelolco* (1985), 127 and passim.

3. See Zapata, *El conflicto sindical en América Latina* (1986), 15–19, for an excellent discussion of the range of possible motives for strikes.

4. Trueba Urbina and Trueba Barrera, *Ley Federal del Trabajo* (1988), art. 450(i). The de la Madrid administration, however, interpreted federal labor law so as to make this more difficult. Franco G. S., "Labor Law and the Labor Movement in Mexico" (1991), 115–16.

5. Data concerning workers on strike and estimated financial losses due to strikes are available only for the period between 1938 and 1962 for federal-jurisdiction industries, and for the period between 1938 and 1958 for local-jurisdiction industries; see the Secretaría del Trabajo y Previsión Social's (STPS) *Memoria de labores* and the Secretaría de Industria y Comercio's (SIC) *Anuario estadístico* for these years. For an analysis of strike activity during the 1935–77 period which pools data concerning the number of workers on strike, see Zapata, *El conflicto sindical*, 113–18.

6. González Casanova, *La democracia en México* (1976), 27–28. See also Zapata, "Labor and Politics" (1989), 181–85.

7. See Secretaría de Industria y Comercio, Dirección General de Estadística, *Anuario estadístico, 1939*, 330–33, and *1941*, 379. Even worse, Carr, *El movimiento obrero y la política en México* (1976), 2:41, states that strike data for the period between 1925 and 1928 are incomplete because strikes declared by unions other than the government-allied Mexican Regional Labor Confederation (CROM) often were not legally recognized and therefore were not included in official statistics.

8. Exceptions include the textile, bottling, food products, pulp and paper, and pharmaceutical industries and maritime zone activities.

9. Even in industries with numerous unions, a few strikes can cause widespread disruption. In 1958, for example, two strikes in the textile industry closed 247 plants in Puebla and Tlaxcala, and in 1962, two strikes in the textile industry affected 320 different plants. In 1960, two strikes in the sugar industry affected 78 different mills (*ingenios*). See STPS, *Memoria de labores, 1962*, n.p.

10. Despite these high recognition rates, there is evidence that wartime restrictions on strikes altered some unions' behavior. Railroad workers, for example, resorted to unauthorized work stoppages (*paros*) to register their discontent with wages and working conditions. Some of these work stoppages occurred despite opposition from the national leadership of the Mexican Railroad Workers' Union (STFRM). See, for example, *Ferronales*, 15 Jan. 1942, 15; 15 Sept. 1944, 1; *El Popular*, 7 Sept. 1944, 1; 9 Sept. 1944, 1; *Excélsior*, 7 Sept. 1945, 1; *Unificación Ferroviaria*, no. 225, 1 May 1946, 4; Sindicato de Trabajadores Ferrocarrileros de la República Mexicana (STFRM), *Acuerdos tomados por la Sexta Gran Convención Ordinaria* (1946), accords #313, 319, 683, 715.

11. Data for 1968 are excluded from this and subsequent calculations involving petitions because the number of federal-jurisdiction strike petitions reported by official sources for this year is so much at variance with the general pattern for the 1960s (including 1967 and 1969) that it is of questionable reliability.

12. There is no reason to believe that the petitions withdrawn introduce any systematic bias in the kinds of cases adjudicated by state labor authorities.

13. This average is calculated from data available for 1965, 1967, and 1969 only.

14. The inflation rate used in this analysis is calculated from official data on the cost of living for workers (1941–78) and consumers (1979–93) in Mexico City (see table 6.1). There were certainly regional variations in the inflation rate during the 1941–93 period, but the Mexico City metropolitan area contained the largest working-class population in the country during these years. Moreover, because no national price index existed before 1968, these are the only consistent inflation indicators available for the entire period under examination.

15. Tests to determine whether changes in real minimum wages or the annual rate of inflation had a lagged effect on the incidence of strike petitions (that is, to determine whether shifts in wage levels or the rate of inflation in one year influenced the volume of strike petitions in the following year) failed to produce statistically significant results. An analysis using data for only the 1963–93 period (years when the information on federal-jurisdiction strike petitions was consistently available) did not produce results substantially different from those reported in table 5.2.

16. Because of the absence of data on the annual rate of inflation before 1940, the analysis of the relationship between economic variables and federal-jurisdiction strikes was restricted to the 1941–93 period (that is, beginning with the Ávila Camacho administration). When preliminary results showed that economic variables had no statistically significant impact on the number of strikes during these years, the time period under examination was extended to 1938–93 in order to encompass part of the Cárdenas administration. The statistical results for the model depicted in table 5.3 do not differ substantially for the 1941–93 period.

Zapata, *El conflicto sindical,* 119, 126–27, found no relationship between national strike activity in Mexico and either the size of the unionized population or changes in real minimum wages.

17. However, the data in table 5.1 do not indicate that unions consistently filed coordinated strike petitions in an attempt to exert influence during presidential successions. During the 1938–93 period there was only one presidential succession year (1976) when a very substantial increase in the volume of federal-jurisdiction strike petitions might be attributed to political factors rather than to changing economic conditions. The fact that the number of petitions remained comparatively high in subsequent years suggests that, even in this instance, unions responded mainly to generally higher inflation rates.

18. An analysis of covariance in the incidence of legally recognized strikes in local-jurisdiction economic activities between 1941 and 1989 produced no statistically significant results. Neither economic variables (changes in the rate of inflation, real-minimum-wage levels, and real-economic-growth rates), presidential labor policy, nor the volume of federal-jurisdiction strikes had a significant impact on year-to-year changes in strike activity in these industries. Because data concerning the number of strike petitions filed in local-jurisdiction economic activities are missing for most of the 1938–93 period, it was impossible to test for the relationship between petitions and legally recognized strikes.

19. In 1943, 557 (97.9 percent) of the total 569 strikes were in the textile industry, principally in the Federal District and Puebla. In 1944, 565 (77.0 percent) of the total 734 strikes were in the textile industry and 158 (21.5 percent) were in the mining industry; see STPS, *Memoria de labores, 1943–1944,* 193; *Memoria de Labores, 1946–1947,* 107. The STPS's *Memoria de labores, 1948–1949,* 123, states that the large number of strikes registered in 1944 was due to the fact that "large unions filed strike petitions for each of their local sections"; see also *Memoria de labores, 1946–1947,* 107. One of the unions involved was the Mexican Mining and Metalworkers' Union (SITMMSRM), which led a forty-day strike (the only nationwide strike in its history) against foreign-owned mining companies. Its demands included the signing of an industrywide collective bargaining agreement. See Carr, *Marxism and Communism in Twentieth-Century Mexico* (1992), 131, and Durand Ponte, *La ruptura de la nación* (1986), 94, 96, for details.

20. Although employers or union leaders may occasionally bribe registry officials to influence the registration process, there is no evidence to suggest that this has been a widespread problem.

21. In both the 1929 Portes Gil and 1931 Ortiz Rubio labor code *proyectos,* a union denied official recognition could appeal the decision to the minister of industry, commerce, and labor. The decision to exclude this provision from the 1931 federal labor law was justified on the rather ingenuous grounds that, because any union that fulfilled the specified registration criteria would be granted official recognition, there was no need for an appeal process.

22. See below for the number of federal-jurisdiction unions registered during different presidential administrations.

23. For other references to the political use of the registration process at the

federal and state levels, see Franco G. S., "Labor Law," 113–14; Basurto, *Del avi-lacamachismo al alemanismo* (1984), 31, 33; Carr, *Marxism and Communism*, 173.

24. Pozas, *Industrial Restructuring in Mexico* (1994), 76.

25. See chapter 4 of this book for a detailed discussion of the context in which this episode occurred.

26. See *Proceso*, 25 July 1983, 20–23; 25 June 1984, 12–15; *Unomásuno*, 18 Jan. 1984, 3; 26 June 1984, 3.

27. The totals for the other presidential terms were Ávila Camacho, 472; Alemán, 432; Ruiz Cortines, 330; López Mateos, 313; Echeverría, 498. These totals include employers' organizations, which are excluded from subsequent calculations. Note that these totals do not conform to those in the following analysis because some data are missing.

28. The major confederations' affiliates varied somewhat in average size. CTM affiliates averaged 177 members, while the CROC and CROM averaged 90 and 96 members, respectively. The General Confederation of Workers (CGT) averaged only 57 members per union. Unions registered without a federative or confederative affiliation averaged 181 members, strongly suggesting that this category represents an important section of the working class in major economic activities. The 548 industry-specific and regional labor organizations for which membership data are available (of a total 560 such organizations) averaged 237 workers per union.

29. The Center region includes the states of Aguascalientes, Guanajuato, Hidalgo, Jalisco, México, Michoacán, Morelos, Puebla, Querétaro, and Tlaxcala.

30. The Pacific South region includes the states of Chiapas, Colima, Guerrero, and Oaxaca.

31. The CTM registered 145 unions representing 76,691 workers in the Federal District during the 1934–76 period, while 194 unaffiliated unions representing 65,106 workers were registered in the Federal District.

32. Quintero Ramírez, "Reestructuración sindical en las maquiladoras mexicanas" (1992), 240–44.

33. Although some data are available for 1977–78, they have been excluded here because a principal focus of this analysis is variation in the time required for registration by six-year presidential term.

34. Four unions were granted registration on the same day on which they applied. The longest delay involved an unaffiliated union representing thirty-nine medical workers in Veracruz, which applied for registration in 1932 but did not receive approval until 1957. (It has not been possible to determine the reasons for this extraordinary delay.) Nine unions registered during the 1934–76 period experienced delays of more than three thousand days.

35. Both the CTM and the Labor Congress proposed a thirty-day time limit, but records of negotiations preceding the adoption of the 1970 labor code do not indicate whether the proposal for a time limit on the registration period originated in the organized labor movement. See Confederación de Trabajadores de México, "Ante-proyecto de Ley Federal del Trabajo" (1968), 228–34, and Federación de Trabajadores del Distrito Federal, "Proposiciones del Congreso del Trabajo en relación al anteproyecto de la Ley Federal del Trabajo" (1968), art. 380.

Mario de la Cueva, who headed the commission appointed in 1967 to prepare a draft of the new labor code, notes that some labor representatives resisted a proposal that the mandatory union registration process be replaced by simple administrative notification of a union's formation. They argued that this would permit the proliferation of fictitious unions. See de la Cueva, *El nuevo derecho mexicano del trabajo* (1979), 2:342.

36. Trueba Urbina and Trueba Barrera, *Ley Federal del Trabajo*, art. 366. Only 35.4 percent of the 226 unions seeking and receiving official recognition after April 1, 1970, were registered within the mandatory sixty-day period. Only 24.8 percent of all cases registered between November 30, 1934, and March 31, 1970, would have met this deadline. Associational Registry records do not indicate whether unions registered after 1970 actually received official recognition automatically once the specified time period had elapsed. However, given the great variation in actual registration times in the post-1970 period, this does not appear to have occurred.

37. Some 10.6 percent of all registrations ($N = 2,520$) granted between 1934 and 1976 were to federations and confederations, some of which were associated with larger organizations such as the CTM. The size of this category indicates how fragmented organizationally the Mexican labor movement is. In the most extreme case, 18.3 percent of all CROC affiliates registered during this period were smaller federations or confederations in specific industries or geographical areas.

38. The CTM's share of union registrations fell below its 1934–76 average of 29.6 percent twice in the years after 1940, in 1946–52 (25.9 percent) when it lost an important part of its membership to the opposition Coalition of Worker and Peasant Organizations, and in 1970–76 (24.2 percent) as a result of Echeverría's efforts to undermine the CTM's position.

39. SIC, *Anuario estadístico*, various years. These totals correspond to the number of work conflicts resolved in a given year for both federal- and local-jurisdiction economic activities. Information concerning the number of demands initiated each year is available only for federal-jurisdiction industries for 1939–43, 1954–65, and 1972–75. For information on work conflicts settled in federal-jurisdiction industries between 1924 and 1932, see Clark, *Organized Labor in Mexico* (1934), 239.

40. SIC, *Anuario estadístico*, various years. Data are incomplete for 1946–47 and are missing for 1952.

41. See Middlebrook, "Political Economy of Mexican Organized Labor" (1982), chap. 4, figures 4, 5.

42. Ashby, *Organized Labor and the Mexican Revolution under Lázaro Cárdenas* (1963), 24, 74. Clark, *Organized Labor in Mexico*, 257, reports that in the late 1920s and early 1930s state-level conciliation and arbitration boards were known for their pro-labor attitudes. See also Gruening, *Mexico and Its Heritage* (1928), 378, and Comisión Nacional del Salario Mínimo, *Memoria de la Comisión Nacional del Salario Mínimo* (1934), table following p. 188.

43. There are no data available regarding the national total of work conflicts initiated or resolved between 1935 and 1938. The number of local-jurisdiction work

conflicts *initiated* and the number of federal-jurisdiction work conflicts *resolved* are reported in SIC, Dirección General de Estadística, *Anuario estadístico, 1939,* 304, 317, 328.

44. This discussion of conciliation and arbitration board procedures draws on the author's interviews with Junta Federal de Conciliación y Arbitraje (JFCA) officials, 25–26 Oct., 8–9 Nov. 1977, and 18, 26 June 1978, México City and Toluca, México; author's field notes, JFCA, 27 Oct. 1977, Mexico City. For the legal provisions concerning demand resolution by conciliation and arbitration boards, see Trueba Urbina and Trueba Barrera, *Ley Federal del Trabajo,* arts. 591–647, 685–794, esp. 751–85.

45. Trueba Urbina and Trueba Barrera, *Ley Federal del Trabajo,* art. 620 (II, III). This provision, new to the 1970 labor code, was adopted to expedite the grievance resolution process.

46. Ibid., art. 773.

47. Clark, *Organized Labor in Mexico,* 242–60, suggests that state-level conciliation and arbitration boards operated in an extremely informal manner in the late 1920s and early 1930s. Grievance proceedings before the Federal Conciliation and Arbitration Board, including votes on the merits of a worker's case, are also sometimes remarkably informal. Author's field notes, Junta Federal de Conciliación y Arbitraje, 27 Oct. 1977, Mexico City.

48. To facilitate workers' access to conciliation and arbitration boards and promote the correct preparation of their grievance petitions, in 1949 the STPS's Federal Labor Legal Defense Office prepared for free distribution a "Worker-Employer Petition Form" ("Formulario de juicios obrero patronales") that summarized relevant provisions in federal labor law and Supreme Court jurisprudence. The booklet included preformulated petitions (with blank pages on which a worker could note the factual circumstances particular to his or her case) appropriate for a broad range of substantive grievances.

49. This office was created by the 1931 federal labor law; see Secretaría de Industria, Comercio y Trabajo, *Ley Federal del Trabajo* (1931), arts. 407–13. The office, part of the Ministry of Labor and Social Welfare, provides free legal assistance to workers requesting it. The ministry's annual *Memoria de labores* (renamed *Informe de labores* in 1987) regularly carries information concerning these activities.

50. Observations of proceedings before the JFCA suggest that a corps of "court attorneys" exists, lawyers who regularly represent workers in grievance cases and are well known to junta staff members. Author's field notes, Junta Federal de Conciliación y Arbitraje, 27 Oct. 1977, Mexico City.

51. Secretaría de Industria, Comercio y Trabajo, Junta Federal de Conciliación y Arbitraje, *Reglamento de las juntas federales de conciliación y arbitraje* (1928), art. 27. Article 26 established the same requirements for sectoral representatives.

52. Secretaría de Industria, Comercio y Trabajo, *Ley Federal del Trabajo,* arts. 397–98.

53. Trueba Urbina and Trueba Barrera, *Ley Federal del Trabajo,* arts. 626–30. The size of the administrative and clerical staff for each special junta varies with

its jurisdictional responsibilities and normal case load. For example, in December 1976 four of the sixteen JFCA special juntas listed professional staffs ranging in size from two to nine members, with an average seniority at the JFCA ranging from 5.7 to 19 years. Junta Federal de Conciliación y Arbitraje internal documents, December 1976.

54. Pino de la Rosa, interview with author, 26 Oct. 1977, Mexico City.

55. Junta clerical workers do not necessarily share the same standards as professional staff members. Clerical workers generally receive low salaries, and one junta sectoral representative reported that they frequently insist upon receiving gratuities from workers' and employers' attorneys as the price for promptly preparing summaries of board proceedings. Author's interview with JFCA sectoral representatives, 9 Nov. 1977, Mexico City.

56. There is no time limit for the resolution of grievances. However, federal labor law does provide for the punishment of junta professional staff members who fail to conduct business expeditiously. See Trueba Urbina and Trueba Barrera, *Ley Federal del Trabajo,* arts. 640–43.

Junta officials argue that the failure of one or both parties in dispute to promote the case actively is a principal source of such delay. Author's interviews with JFCA special junta presidents, 25–26 Oct. 1977, Mexico City.

The delays involved in the demand resolution process sometimes encourage the parties in dispute to bribe JFCA clerical staff to expedite the handling of their cases. Author's field notes, Junta Federal de Conciliación y Arbitraje, 26 June 1978, Mexico City.

57. Junta Federal de Conciliación y Arbitraje internal documents, December 1976. The fact that Special Board 15 had the smallest backlog undoubtedly was in part due to the fact that it had only been created in 1975.

Similar problems have existed since the JFCA's formation in 1927. In 1942, STPS officials reported that the JFCA handled 1,137 conflicts in its first year of operation. Some 1,248 unresolved cases had accumulated by 1932, a total that grew to 4,355 cases in 1936 and 18,259 cases in 1940. See STPS, *Memoria de labores, 1941–1942,* 221–22.

58. Only scattered information is available concerning the time that local-jurisdiction conciliation and arbitration boards require to resolve grievances. Carrillo V., "Evolution of the *Maquiladora* Industry" (1991), 233, reports that resolution times averaged 16.5 months for grievances filed by workers in local-jurisdiction industries in the Tijuana, Baja California, area between 1967 and 1983, with considerable variation by industry.

59. At least 62,234 demands were filed by FNM employees between 1934 and 1975. Case reference cards (on which this count is based) appear to be incomplete for 1938 and 1975.

Railroad workers filed at least 5,889 additional demands against a variety of smaller railroad lines during the period from 1934 to 1975, including the Ferrocarril Mexicano, Ferrocarril del Pacífico, Ferrocarril Mexicano al Pacífico, Ferrocarril Chihuahua al Pacífico, Ferrocarril Occidental de México, Ferrocarril Noroeste de

México, Ferrocarriles Unidos de Yucatán, Ferrocarriles Unidos del Sureste, Ferro-carril Sud-Pacífico, Ferrocarril Coahuila y Zacatecas, Ferrocarril Tijuana y Tecate, Compañía Pullman, Compañía Terminal de Veracruz, and nineteen others. Archi-val records for these smaller firms appear to be incomplete for the period from 1945 through 1964.

60. The number of *convenios* registered with the JFCA declined sharply after 1940. The sample contains no such cases at all for 1943–55, although there was a slight upturn in the number of *convenios* filed from the late 1950s through 1975. It is not possible to determine on the basis of available information why such cases should have been so common during the Cárdenas administration, although this was a period when the Mexican Railroad Workers' Union negotiated important contract clauses and work rules with FNM.

61. Some cases that came before the JFCA involved more dramatic issues. In December 1976 Special Board 1 reported two difficult cases in progress involving train accidents, one of which occurred on October 5, 1972, and resulted in the death of two hundred passengers and the injury of more than fifteen hundred others. In a third case, two workers who had been fired were charged with the murder of a union official in Matías Romero, Oaxaca. Junta Federal de Conciliación y Arbitraje internal documents, December 1976.

62. There is less reason to expect accident and death indemnity grievances, retirement petitions, or some miscellaneous demands (petitions for expense re-imbursement, union efforts to create or eliminate individual job positions) to fluc-tuate in association with political factors such as the character of union governance or presidential labor policy. In fact, no such relationship could be discerned in the analysis of demand frequency.

The number of cases involving accident and death indemnity claims rose steadily from 1934 through 1945 (a period of heavy railroad use) and generally declined throughout the late 1940s and 1950s (a period during which substantial resources were devoted to equipment modernization). However, the upturn in such cases in the late 1960s and early 1970s cannot be explained in similar terms.

The frequency of cases involving union efforts to enforce contract terms might well vary according to changes in railroad conditions and presidential policy. How-ever, there were only twenty-nine of these demands in the 1934–75 sample, making it difficult to interpret the significance of year-to-year fluctuations.

63. Only two previous studies have examined the grievance resolution process before the Federal Conciliation and Arbitration Board. Meyers, *Mexican Industrial Relations* (1979), summarized the type of grievances filed before the JFCA in 1976, and he made useful observations concerning the board's operations. However, be-cause only about 15 percent of the cases he sampled had been decided, Meyers could say little about how cases were resolved. Roxborough, *Unions and Politics in Mexico* (1984), 145–54, examined grievance cases filed by automobile workers in the mid-1970s, focusing particularly on the impact of democratic unionism on the conduct and outcome of the grievance resolution process.

64. The number of retirement petitions is smaller in Sample 2 than in Sample 1

because some cases bearing this label in the JFCA archives proved upon examination to be retirement *convenios* rather than grievances, which also explains the higher proportion of *convenios* in Sample 2 than in Sample 1.

As a consequence of the smaller number of retirement petitions in Sample 2, other grievance types constitute a disproportionate share of the total cases in the sample. See note 78 for comments on the implications of the disproportionate number of wage and benefit cases in Sample 2.

65. Three cases in which a worker began by representing himself or herself but later retained counsel were included in the union representative/lawyer or private attorney categories.

STFRM officials and STFRM lawyers supposedly represent workers in grievance proceedings without charge, which almost certainly accounts for the large proportion of grievants with this form of legal representation. In practice, however, it is likely that a worker would have provided his or her union counsel with some financial compensation, though this could have been significantly less costly than retaining a private attorney.

66. The Center region includes such major railroad sites as Aguascalientes, Guadalajara, Guanajuato, Puebla, and Querétaro, while the North includes Torreón, Monterrey, and San Luis Potosí. The Gulf (Veracruz) and Pacific South regions each accounted for 6.3 percent of the cases in Sample 2. See table 5.5 for the states composing these different regions.

67. In three cases, the worker charged the STFRM with complicity with railroad management and listed the union as a codefendant.

68. These five grievances were filed by a nurse, a hospital cleaning woman, an office employee, and two secretaries.

69. See, for example, JFCA case nos. 8.1/315.1 (16) "42"/831, 8.1/315.1 "45"/497, 8.1/315 "51"/733, 8.1/315.1 (17) "54"/117, 8.14/315.1 (29) "55"/980, 8.1/315.1 (19) "57"/248, 8.1/315.1 (29) "57"/686, 8.14/315.1 (29) "58"/459.

70. JFCA case nos. D/938/8111; 8.4/317.1 (72) "62"/27; 8.1/317.1 (29) "66"/184.

71. The last case in the sample had not yet been resolved when this information was compiled. Thus Sample 2 consists of 166 cases for some parts of this analysis.

One cannot conclude that the success rate of FNM employees is representative of other workers' experience before conciliation and arbitration boards. In addition to the fact that the STFRM had the resources to make union attorneys available to grievants, FNM workers enjoyed other important advantages when appearing before juntas: a long union tradition of dealing with such cases; an extremely detailed collective contract that gave workers extensive legal protection; and separate juntas devoted to the railroad industry, which meant that board members were fully versed in railroad contract issues and that juntas' labor representatives were fellow railroad workers. Many unionized workers do not have these advantages, and nonunionized workers may find it even more difficult to pursue their grievances in the labor justice system.

72. The higher success rate for union representatives and union attorneys than

for private attorneys could have been due to their greater familiarity with the junta system or the issues raised by different cases. Alternatively, grievants may have contracted private attorneys when informed by the STFRM that their cases were weak.

73. See JFCA case nos. 8.4/303 (29) "62"/369 and 8.4/315.1 (8) "63"/223.

The STFRM attached great importance to the discipline of its representatives on the JFCA. See *Unificación Ferroviaria*, no. 194, 1 Dec. 1944, 2, for discussion of a case in which the STFRM's national oversight committee sanctioned a junta representative who, in violation of a formal union resolution, voted against the reinstallation of a worker fired for collaborating with the de la Huerta rebellion in 1923.

74. *Amparo* petitions are addressed to the Supreme Court's Fourth Chamber (Cuarta Sala), which was created in December 1934 to hear labor-related cases. Workers filed twelve *amparo* petitions and FNM filed nineteen. For examples of cases involving successful appeals, see JFCA case nos. F/937/1654, 8.14/305.1 (17) "56"/430, and 8.4/305.5 (8) "62"/466.

75. JFCA case no. 8.15/305.4 (18) "47"/271.

76. JFCA case no. 8.1/303 (26) "54"/333. JFCA case no. 8.1/323 (72) "51"/ 394 is a similar case. JFCA officials acknowledge FNM's inclination to file continuous appeals to delay payment of financial awards. Interview with special junta president, Junta Federal de Conciliación y Arbitraje, 26 Oct. 1977, Mexico City.

77. The historical record contains little evidence concerning railroad workers' own estimates of the time required to conclude grievance proceedings. However, in the late 1940s the STFRM estimated that the JFCA required an average of two years to resolve grievances involving death, professional injury, and reinstatement; see *Unificación Ferroviaria*, no. 298, 31 Dec. 1949, 3. For a typical STFRM complaint concerning delays in JFCA decisions and the resulting backlog of cases, see *Unificación Ferroviaria*, no. 258, 16 Sept. 1947, 5.

78. Of these 28 cases, 4 were initiated under Cárdenas, 7 under Ávila Camacho, 9 under Alemán, 5 under Ruiz Cortines, and 3 under López Mateos. Nineteen cases ended in formal junta decisions; in 8 other cases the worker desisted, and in 1 case a private settlement was reached between the worker's widow and railroad management. There is no apparent pattern in these 28 cases in terms of the kind of grievance raised, and in 16 of the 19 cases involving a formal junta ruling, no obvious reason appears in the archival records to explain such long delays.

Sample 2 may overestimate the average resolution time for all railroad worker grievances because it contains a disproportionate number of wage and benefit grievances—cases in which FNM was most likely to resist, thus lengthening the average resolution times for this grievance type. In contrast, the sample may underestimate the proportion of railroad grievance cases with extremely long resolution times because only terminated cases filed in the JFCA archives could be sampled.

79. JFCA case no. 8.1/303 (18) "41"/730.

80. JFCA case no. 8.1/305.3 "44"/62.

81. JFCA case no. 8.1/303.7 "44"/590.

82. JFCA case no. 8.4/315 (29) "70"/114.

83. See JFCA case nos. I/940/2942; 8.1/313 (29) "41"/29; 8.1/305.3 "48"/537.

84. See JFCA case no. 8.1/303.7 "44"/590. However, a private attorney represented the grievant in only 8 of the 28 cases requiring more than six years for resolution; the other 20 cases were handled by a union representative or a union attorney.

85. See, for example, JFCA case no. 8.1/300 (3) "74"/321.

86. Trueba Urbina and Trueba Barrera, *Ley Federal del Trabajo,* art. 612.

87. Examples include Lic. José Cantú Estrada (1933), Dr. Mario de la Cueva (1946), Lic. Fernando Zertuche Muñoz (1974–76), and Lic. Juan Francisco Rocha Bandala (1976–80). See Camp, *Mexican Political Biographies* (1982), 48, 79, 320–21, for biographical entries for Cantú Estrada, de la Cueva, and Zertuche Muñoz. Rocha Bandala served as a legal adviser to both the Institutional Revolutionary Party and the Confederation of Mexican Workers, as well as holding diverse administrative positions in the federal government, before becoming JFCA president.

88. Trueba Urbina and Trueba Barrera, *Ley Federal del Trabajo,* art. 667. Representatives may be reelected to these positions. Under the terms of the 1931 labor law, sectoral representatives were elected to two-year terms, although they could be reelected. Secretaría de Industria, Comercio y Trabajo, *Ley Federal del Trabajo,* art. 390.

89. Interviews with JFCA officials, 25 Oct. and 9 Nov. 1977, Mexico City.

90. Some of the literature on state-labor relations in Latin America does not make this distinction clearly. In the case of state regulation of union formation, for example, analysts often cite examples of selective state intervention to deny opposition labor groups official sanction or to reward labor allies with legal recognition. For the most part, however, they do not examine the extent to which state authorities intervene to order interest representation in the labor sector, the conditions under which formal controls on associability are actually employed, or the extent to which state intervention of this kind varies over time, across economic sectors, or in connection with other government policies toward labor. See Buchanan, "State Corporatism in Argentina" (1985); Collier and Collier, "Inducements versus Constraints" (1979); Dix, *Colombia* (1967); Epstein, "Control and Co-optation of the Argentine Labor Movement" (1979); McCoy, "Labor and the State in a Party-Mediated Democracy" (1989); Mericle, "Corporatist Control of the Working Class" (1977).

Chapter 6: Labor Politics and Import-Substituting Industrialization

1. See, for example, Thorp, "Reappraisal of the Origins of Import-Substituting Industrialization" (1992), and Hirschman, "Political Economy of Import-Substituting Industrialization in Latin America" (1968).

2. The discussion in this and the following paragraph draws especially upon King, *Mexico* (1970), 16–43, and Reynolds, *Mexican Economy* (1970), 36–43, 76. On industrial development during the 1930s and the initial process of import substitution, see Cárdenas, *La industrialización mexicana durante la gran depresión* (1987), chaps. 5, 6.

3. A 1942 reciprocal trade agreement with the United States partially limited Mexico's freedom to enact protective tariffs. This agreement ended in 1951. See King, *Mexico*, 31–32, 75.

4. Thorp, "Reappraisal," 192–93; Mosk, *Industrial Revolution in Mexico* (1975), 89–90; Whiting, *Political Economy of Foreign Investment in Mexico* (1992), 71–73.

5. Consumer durable goods are conventionally defined as those items designed to last at least three years, such as electrical appliances and automobiles. See Villarreal, "Policy of Import-Substituting Industrialization" (1977), 71, 73–74, for estimates of the effective rate of protection on imported goods.

6. See Mosk, *Industrial Revolution*, chaps. 2–3, for an early discussion of this "new group."

7. One of the early precedents for this position was the Mexican Labor Party's call in 1920 for protective tariffs and national development of heavy industry. González Casanova, *En el primer gobierno constitucional* (1980), 120.

8. *Unificación Ferroviaria*, no. 226, 16 May 1946, 1, 11.

9. Basurto, *Del avilacamachismo al alemanismo* (1984), 84–86; Mosk, *Industrial Revolution*, 101.

10. Mosk, *Industrial Revolution*, 27–28, 102, 105.

11. Reynolds, *Mexican Economy*, tables 1.1, 1.4, 2.1, 2.2.

12. Thorp, "Reappraisal," table 6.

13. Wilkie, *Mexican Revolution* (1973), tables 1.4, 2.1. The administrative expenditures category includes the military budget, the cost of servicing the public debt, and general administrative expenditures.

14. Felix, "Income Distribution Trends in Mexico" (1982), table 2.

15. United Nations Economic Commission for Latin America and Nacional Financiera, S.A., "La política industrial en el desarrollo de México" (1971), statistical appendix, table 13.

16. Kaufman, *Politics of Debt in Argentina, Brazil, and Mexico* (1988), 63.

17. Because an especially large proportion of Mexico's working-class urban population lived in the Mexico City area during these years, the worker cost-of-living index for Mexico City is an appropriate measure of inflation for this period. For a critical evaluation of the price indices used to deflate wages in table 6.1 and a discussion of possible alternatives, see Bortz, "Industrial Wages in Mexico City" (1984), 92–97, 102–4, and chap. 2 passim.

Real wage indices calculated by other analysts differ somewhat in their year-to-year variation, but they show the same general pattern. See King, *Mexico*, table 2.10, and Gregory, *Myth of Market Failure* (1986), table 7.1. Bortz, "Industrial Wages," appendix 2, table 2, presents real-wage data for manufacturing activities in the Federal District which show a substantial decline in workers' real wages between 1939 and 1946, with a sustained upturn in wage levels occurring after 1952.

The concept of a minimum wage was first outlined in Article 123 of the 1917 constitution. The 1931 federal labor law specified that minimum wages were to be set by municipal-level "mixed" commissions (composed of labor, business, and municipal government representatives) operating under the administrative supervision of state-level conciliation and arbitration boards. However, in September 1933 President Rodríguez made state-level conciliation and arbitration boards directly responsible for setting wages, although municipal-level tripartite commissions continued to conduct initial economic analyses and make wage recommendations. He also created the Comisión Nacional del Salario Mínimo (National Minimum Wage Commission). Beginning in January 1934, these state-level juntas established new minimum wages every two years, with differences in wage levels reflecting variations in the cost of living between urban and rural areas in different zones. A subsequent reform of the federal labor code in 1962 gave authority for determining minimum-wage levels in different zones to special regional commissions, whose recommendations were submitted to the National Minimum Wage Commission (renamed the Comisión Nacional de los Salarios Mínimos) for final approval. See Secretaría de Industria, Comercio y Trabajo, *Ley Federal del Trabajo* (1931), title 8, chap. 9; Comisión Nacional de los Salarios Mínimos, *Memoria de la Comisión Nacional del Salario Mínimo* (1934), 276–79; Bensusán Areous, "Construcción y desarrollo del derecho laboral en México" (1985), 48.

18. See King, *Mexico*, 26–27; Felix, "Income Distribution," 275; and esp. Gregory, *Myth of Market Failure*, 222–31.

19. For survey data concerning occupational mobility into semiskilled and skilled manual work in large industrial firms during Monterrey's rapid industrial expansion in 1940–55, see Balán, Browning, and Jelín, *Migración, estructura ocupacional y movilidad social* (1973), 189.

20. Basurto, *Del avilacamachismo*, table 3, calculates that real wages in major industries fell by 14.6 percent in real terms between 1945 and 1955. Real wages rose in electrical power generation and mining, but they declined in manufacturing, construction, and petroleum production.

21. See Kaufman, *Politics of Debt*, 63–75, for an excellent analysis of financial stabilization in Mexico during the mid-1950s.

22. This discussion of the CTM's anti-inflation campaign in the early 1950s, its internal situation, and the political bargaining following the 1954 devaluation draws on CTM documents reproduced in Partido Revolucionario Institucional (PRI), *CTM* (1986), 3:524, 549–51, 554, 562, 577, 581–85, 595–97, 608, 611, 625–29, 637; 4:1, 91–105, 136–38, 143–50, 160, 176–82, 194–200, 203, 206–9; Pellicer de Brody and Reyna, *El afianzamiento de la estabilidad política* (1978), 83–103, 106; and Aguilar García, "En un período de unidad monolítica" (1990), 261–64, 320, 322, 325.

23. For official minimum wages in different regions during this period, see Instituto Nacional de Estadística, Geografía e Informática (INEGI), *Estadísticas históricas de México* (1985), 2:168–77. In late 1951, the CNIT supported the labor movement's call for higher wages on the grounds that greater consumer purchasing power would stimulate economic growth. *Tiempo*, 28 Dec. 1951, 34–37.

24. Everett, "Role of Mexican Trade Unions" (1967), table 18, presents month-to-month inflation rates for early 1954.

25. The CTM claimed that its affiliates filed 31,854 strike petitions and that 173 strikes occurred; see PRI, *CTM*, 209. Other sources, however, reported far fewer petitions and strikes. See Pellicer de Brody and Reyna, *El afianzamiento de la estabilidad política*, 97, and table 5.1 in this book.

26. Pellicer de Brody and Reyna, *El afianzamiento de la estabilidad política*, 48–55.

27. Kaufman, *Politics of Debt*, 65, 68–71.

28. This did not mean, however, that labor organizations accepted minimum-wage levels as adequate compensation. See Fidel Velázquez's acid criticism of the 1958–59 minimum wage in *Ceteme*, 4 Jan. 1958, 1.

The cost-of-living index for workers in Mexico City that was used to deflate nominal wages in table 6.1 may overestimate the inflation rate between 1970 and 1975; see Bortz, "Industrial Wages," 135. As a result, real wages may have increased more rapidly during these years than indicated in table 6.1.

29. Zapata, *El conflicto sindical en América Latina* (1986), 126–27.

30. The Mexican Petroleum Workers' Union (STPRM) was one of the most notable examples. The STPRM translated the strategic importance of the petroleum industry and its political dominance in oil-producing areas into a union empire. In the late 1980s, the STPRM's holdings included hospitals, schools, supermarkets, farms and ranches, gasoline stations, auto repair shops, funeral parlors, and appliance, furniture, and clothing stores. *New York Times*, 15 Jan. 1989, 1.

31. Purcell, *Mexican Profit-Sharing Decision* (1975), 58, 66.

32. PRI, *CTM*, 3:603, 605–6, 614–19. The Cárdenas administration had established a Banco Nacional Obrero de Fomento Industrial (National Worker Bank for Industrial Development) in 1937 as one of several credit institutions designed to promote economic growth and industrialization; see Confederación de Trabajadores de México, *C.T.M., 1936–1941* (1941), 453. It is not clear when this institution was disbanded. For a discussion of still earlier antecedents, see Remolina Roqueñi, *Evolución de las instituciones y del derecho del trabajo* (1976), 75–76.

33. See Middlebrook, "Political Economy of Mexican Organized Labor" (1982), 231–34, for details.

34. See Middlebrook, "Union Democratization in the Mexican Automobile Industry" (1989), for citations to the extensive literature on this subject.

35. This discussion draws on de la Garza Toledo's excellent analysis of this phenomenon in "Independent Trade Unionism in Mexico" (1991).

36. For analyses of the Democratic Tendency, see Gómez Tagle and Miquet Fleury, "Integración o democracia sindical" (1976), esp. 152–54, 170–71; Trejo Delarbre, "Cronología de la Tendencia Democrática" (1978); and Bizberg, *Estado y sindicalismo en México* (1990), 305–18. For information on the MSF, see *Punto Crítico*, no. 13, Jan. 1973, 10; no. 69, 31 Jan. 1977, 19.

37. For case studies of labor actions in the automobile, metalworking, rubber, chemical, airline transportation, and food processing industries, see Aguilar García, *Los sindicatos de industrias dinámicas* (1988).

38. Ortega Arenas, interviews with author, 30 Nov. and 2 Dec. 1977, Mexico

City; author's interview with a staff official of the International Metalworkers' Federation, 2 June 1977, Mexico City; Leal, "Las estructuras sindicales" (1985), 86–88.

39. Carr, "Labor and the Political Left in Mexico" (1991), 142–43; Bizberg, *Estado y sindicalismo*, 17, 272–75, 282–85.

40. For an overview of Echeverría's reform program in the labor sector, see Basurto, *En el régimen de Echeverría* (1983), 9, 32, 34, 36–45; Molina, "Notas sobre el estado y el movimiento obrero" (1977); and Galindo, "El movimiento obrero en el sexenio echeverrista" (1977). Echeverría's emergency wage hikes produced an increase in the index value of the real minimum wage in Mexico City from 124.8 in 1971 to 158.8 in 1976; see table 6.1. See also Arriaga Lemus, Velasco Arregui, and Zepeda Miramontes, "Inflación y salarios en el régimen de LEA" (1977).

41. In a speech delivered in December 1970 shortly after his inauguration, Echeverría asked rhetorically, "And how can we speak of democracy in Mexico if, when electing a union executive committee, the process is not democratic?" Quoted in Bizberg, *Estado y sindicalismo*, 311.

42. For an examination of the FAT, see Méndez and Quiroz, "El FAT" (1991).

43. See de la Garza Toledo, "Independent Trade Unionism," 160–61, figure 7.3.

44. Most explanations of union democratization, based largely on research conducted in advanced industrial societies, focus on the internal organizational characteristics of labor unions and the availability of formal or informal arrangements that permit opposition groups to mobilize support and contest control of union leadership. Much of this literature assumes that opposition movements seek to realize the potential of formally democratic decision-making procedures. Relatively little attention has been devoted to changes in workplace relations as a source of demands for increased worker control over internal union decision making, especially in an authoritarian regime in which political elites are committed to maintaining controls on worker participation. See Edelstein and Warner, *Comparative Union Democracy* (1976), chap. 3; Hemingway, *Conflict and Democracy* (1978), chaps. 1–2; Martin, "Union Democracy" (1968); Anderson, "Comparative Analysis of Local Union Democracy" (1978), 278–95; Lipset, Trow, and Coleman, *Union Democracy* (1956), 15, 77–91, 452–69. However, Martin, "Union Democracy," 211, 216, notes that rapid technological change may encourage the emergence of democratic reform movements in unions.

45. The 1962 decree required companies to increase the share of nationally produced components in automobile manufacturing to 60 percent, regulated the price of vehicles manufactured in Mexico in accordance with international market prices, and set annual production quotas for each firm (varying according to each firm's prior market penetration, compliance with the terms of the decree, and share of national capital participation). For the full text of the decree, see *Diario Oficial de la Federación*, 25 Aug. 1962. For a discussion of the automobile industry's early history and the implementation of the 1962 decree, see Bennett and Sharpe, *Transnational Corporations versus the State* (1985), chaps. 3, 5, and Jenkins, *Transnational Corporations and the Latin American Automobile Industry* (1987).

46. Asociación Mexicana de la Industria Automotriz, *La industria automotriz en cifras, 1976* (1977), 13, 58–59, 170; Vázquez Tercero, *Una década de política sobre industria automotriz* (1975), 14, 19.

47. Of these seven firms, Ford Motor Company, S.A., General Motors de México, S.A. de C.V., Nissan Mexicana, S.A. de C.V., and Volkswagen de México, S.A. de C.V. were wholly owned subsidiaries of transnational corporations. Chrysler purchased 33 percent of Fábricas Auto-Mex in 1959, and in 1971 it increased its holdings to 90.5 percent and changed the firm's name to Chrysler de México, S.A. Chrysler later expanded its equity share to 99.3 percent. Until 1983, Vehículos Automotores Mexicanos, S.A. de C.V. was 60 percent state owned, with 40 percent of equity held by the American Motors Corporation; in 1983 Vehículos Automotores Mexicanos was purchased by Regie Nationale des Usines Renault. Prior to 1978, Diesel Nacional, S.A. (DINA) was wholly state owned; in 1978 Regie Nationale des Usines Renault purchased 40 percent of equity. In 1982 DINA (which produced trucks, buses, and engines) and Renault de México, S.A. de C.V. (which produced passenger cars) were divided; DINA was subsequently reorganized into five separate enterprises, and in 1983 Renault de México was wholly purchased by Regie Nationale des Usines Renault. Although these seven firms were the largest producers and employers, the Mexican automobile industry included several other companies manufacturing heavy trucks and buses and a large auto parts industry. For details, see Vázquez Tercero, *Una década,* 16–17, and Bennett and Sharpe, *Transnational Corporations,* 129–34, 176–78.

48. For details concerning the formation and affiliation of individual automobile workers' unions, see Middlebrook, "Political Economy," 278–309; Roxborough, *Unions and Politics in Mexico* (1984), 76–104; Aguilar García, *La política sindical en México* (1982), 105–14.

The CTM-affiliated unions evidenced the greatest degree of organizational dispersion. The VAM and Auto-Mex/Chrysler unions were affiliated with Sections 9 and 23, respectively, of the CTM's powerful Federal District Workers' Federation (FTDF). When General Motors established its Toluca subsidiary in 1965, its work force was unionized as Section 9 of the CTM's Sindicato Nacional de Trabajadores de la Industria Metalúrgica. The DINA and Nissan unions were organized within the CTM's state federations in Hidalgo and Morelos, respectively. Workers at Ford's original manufacturing and assembly plant at La Villa (in the Federal District) were represented by the Unión de Obreros y Empleados de la Industria Automovilística del Distrito Federal and affiliated with the FTDF's Section 15, which grouped workers from a large number of electrical products and metalworking firms. Workers at the Ford assembly plant in Tlanepantla and the motor manufacturing plant at Cuautitlán (established in 1962 and 1964, respectively) in the state of México were represented by the CTM's Unión Sindical de Trabajadores de la Industria Metálica del Estado de México. Each of the three Ford plants had a separate collective contract.

49. See, for example, Roxborough, *Unions and Politics,* 32–33; Aguilar García, *La política sindical,* 37, 69, 71; Bizberg, "Política laboral y acción sindical en México" (1984), 169; and Basurto, *En el régimen de Echeverría,* 9.

50. This discussion of developments in individual unions is based on information presented in Middlebrook, "Political Economy," 284–86, 289–90, 292, 294–96, 302, 304, 308; Roxborough, *Unions and Politics,* 78–80, 100, 108; and Aguilar García, *La política sindical,* 79, 109.

51. The Echeverría administration's tolerance of labor dissent was especially important in the Volkswagen case. CTM state federation leaders vigorously protested when their control was challenged by a rank-and-file reform movement, but they were unable to pressure federal labor officials to support their position.

52. Roxborough, *Unions and Politics,* 82–102, 104, 107.

53. Ibid., 82.

54. Author's interview with a former Nissan union official, 26 Feb. 1978, Cuernavaca, Morelos.

55. Information concerning Blas Chumacero's political record comes from Basurto, "La influencia de la economía y el estado en las huelgas" (1962), appendix 2, and Camp, *Mexican Political Biographies* (1982), 69. Camp notes that between 1940 and 1979 Chumacero served as a federal deputy more frequently than any other Mexican. Information concerning Volkswagen managers' strategy is from the author's interviews with a former governor and federal senator with ties to the automobile industry, 21 June 1977, Mexico City; a Volkswagen labor relations employee, 13 Sept. 1977, Puebla; and a staff official from the International Metalworkers' Federation, 18 Jan. 1978, Mexico City.

56. Middlebrook, "Union Democratization," 76–77, evaluates the possible impact of a third factor—deteriorating national economic conditions—on labor opposition movements in the automobile industry. This analysis shows that total worker income in the industry rose during the early and mid-1970s. In any event, by the time that economic growth slowed and inflation rose, reform movements had already triumphed in the DINA, Volkswagen, and Nissan unions.

57. By way of comparison, the national average was 215 workers per union in the late 1970s; author's calculation based on data presented in Zazueta and de la Peña, *La estructura del Congreso del Trabajo* (1984), tables 2.4, 7.1. Per capita GDP was equivalent to U.S.$365 in 1960, U.S.$737 in 1970, and U.S.$1,463 in 1975; author's calculations based on data presented in INEGI, *Estadísticas históricas,* vol. 1, table 9.1.

58. Author's calculations based on data presented in table 6.3 and in Asociación Mexicana de la Industria Automotriz, *La industria automotriz en cifras, 1976,* 58–59.

59. Clack, *Industrial Relations in a British Car Factory* (1967), 21, 23–24, 36, 42–43, and esp. 96. See also McPherson, *Labor Relations in the Automobile Industry* (1940), chap. 5, esp. 48–49.

60. Bennett and Sharpe, *Transnational Corporations,* 117, 149, 210. During this period, production efficiency in vehicle manufacturing depended significantly on labor costs. Fullan, "Industrial Technology and Worker Integration in the Organization" (1970), 1031.

61. Fullan, "Industrial Technology," 1028, offers a comparative analysis of

these factors. For other discussions of workplace relations in the automobile industry during this period, see Bloomfield, *World Automotive Industry* (1978), 113–14,
and Faunce, "Automation in the Automobile Industry" (1958), 402–3.

62. Fullan, "Industrial Technology," 1031, 1034–35; Faunce, "Automation in
the Automobile Industry," 402–3. For a discussion of working conditions in the
Brazilian automobile industry at this time, see Humphrey, *Capitalist Control and
Workers' Struggle* (1982), 82–84, 100–104.

Although this general characterization of automobile manufacturing may have
been correct, considerable diversity existed in workplace relations within a single
automobile plant; see Clack, *Industrial Relations,* 16. Moreover, according to
Clack, not all studies concluded that these workplace conditions resulted in worker
dissatisfaction (13).

63. For a more detailed discussion of these issues in the context of specific automobile workers' unions, see Middlebrook, "Political Economy," 279–89, 293–96,
298–99, 302–4, and Roxborough, *Unions and Politics,* 77–78, 88. For a compelling
examination of the relationship between the industrial environment in Mexican
automobile manufacturing plants and worker grievances, see Quiroz, "Proceso de
trabajo en la industria automotriz" (1980), 65–72. Anderson, "Comparative Analysis," 284, suggests that the failure of incumbent union leaders to satisfy membership
demands in collective bargaining may increase pressures for union democracy.

64. For references to plant delegates in the *maquiladora* (in-bond processing)
industry, see Quintero Ramírez, "Reestructuración sindical en las maquiladoras
mexicanas" (1992), 381–82, 388–95.

65. This discussion is based on the author's interview with a staff official from
the International Metalworkers' Federation, 22 June 1978, Mexico City; *Justicia
Social* 1, no. 1 (Aug. 1974), the first issue of the Chrysler union's cultural and social
affairs magazine; and Fojo de Diego, "Estudio de un conflicto industrial" (1973),
1–2.

66. This discussion is based on the author's interviews with staff officials of
the International Metalworkers' Federation, 2 June 1977 and 18 June 1978, Mexico
City, and an analysis of Ford labor contracts. See also Roxborough, *Unions and
Politics,* 78–79.

67. This discussion is based on the author's interviews with a former DINA
worker, 11 Aug. 1977, Ciudad Sahagún, Hidalgo, and a staff official from the
International Metalworkers' Federation, 18 Jan. 1978, Mexico City.

68. This discussion of the Volkswagen case is based on the author's interviews
with a Volkswagen labor relations official, 13 Sept. 1977, Puebla, and a staff official
of the International Metalworkers' Federation, 20 June 1978, Mexico City; see
also Montiel, *Proceso de trabajo* (1991), 151–58. Information concerning Nissan
is from the author's interview with a former Nissan union official, 26 Feb. 1978,
Cuernavaca.

69. The discussion of these cases is based on the same materials cited in notes
65–68.

70. This discussion of the VAM case is based on the author's interview with

a staff official of the International Metalworkers' Federation, 18 Jan. 1978, Mexico City; Roxborough, *Unions and Politics*, 93–94; and Quiroz, "Proceso de trabajo," 67–68.

71. See Middlebrook, "Political Economy," 356–68.

72. See, for example, Lipset, Trow, and Coleman, *Union Democracy*, chaps. 1, 18. Of course, leadership turnover in regular elections may also occur in what are generally undemocratic unions. Between 1955 and 1961, for example, union leadership at Diesel Nacional circulated among a number of CTM loyalists; there was little continuity among union officeholders, but CTM supporters maintained tight control over internal union affairs. Author's interview with a former DINA worker, 11 Aug. 1977, Ciudad Sahagún, Hidalgo.

73. These summary observations are based on the author's interviews with Diesel Nacional union officials, 29 June 1977 and 9 Apr. 1978, Mexico City and Ciudad Sahagún, Hidalgo, respectively; a Nissan union official, 26 Feb. 1978, Cuernavaca; and a staff official of the International Metalworkers' Federation, 25 Apr. 1978, Mexico City, as well as on the author's field notes (5 Aug. 1977, 20 Aug. 1977, 30 Aug. 1977, 22 Nov. 1977, 4 Feb. 1978, and 6 Feb. 1978) on union activities at DINA.

74. However, the issue of union democracy did not disappear from the political agenda. In August 1975, for example, dissident General Motors workers at the Federal District plant accused the incumbent secretary-general of failing for more than two years to convene a general assembly meeting, even though union statutes required the general assembly to meet monthly. See *El Día*, 21 Aug. 1975, 2.

75. These comments are based on the author's interviews with Junta Federal de Conciliación y Arbitraje officials, 25–26 Oct. 1977, Mexico City, and a staff official of the International Metalworkers' Federation, 25 Apr. 1978, Mexico City, as well as on the author's field notes on Junta Federal de Conciliación y Arbitraje proceedings (27 Oct. 1977) and an Unidad Obrera Independiente meeting (30 Jan. 1978).

76. These comments are based on the author's interviews with DINA union officials, 2 Sept. 1977 and 9 Apr. 1978, Ciudad Sahagún, Hidalgo, as well as the author's field notes on a DINA union general assembly, 12 Sept. 1977.

77. Author's interviews with a DINA union activist, 11 Aug. 1977, Ciudad Sahagún, Hidalgo, and a staff official of the International Metalworkers' Federation, 25 Apr. 1978, Mexico City.

78. Nissan 1976 contract, "Transitorios," #10.

79. General Motors 1977 contract, clauses 10–11.

80. Ibid., clause 10.

81. Volkswagen 1976 contract, p. 27, "Reglamento de escalafón," A(c).

82. The 1970 federal labor law limited temporary workers' contracts to sixty days, although they could be for periods as short as one day and could be renewed without limit. For a discussion of the evolution of legal provisions regulating the employment of temporary workers, see de la Cueva, *El nuevo derecho mexicano del trabajo* (1977), 1:225–27.

A January 1953 reform of the federal labor code increased the size of separation indemnity payments from three months' salary (the amount specified by Article 123 of the 1917 constitution and the 1931 federal labor law) to three months' salary plus twenty days' pay per year of seniority. Aguilar García, "En un período de unidad monolítica," 257.

83. Secretaría del Trabajo y Previsión Social, Registro de Asociaciones (cited hereafter as "RA") case no. 10/6298-2, 448 (7 Aug. 1957).

84. Author's field notes (28 May 1977) based on observations of Chrysler's Mexico City manufacturing plant.

85. See, for example, the 1976 DINA contract, "Transitorios," #2.

86. General Motors management awarded particularly large numbers of permanent positions in 1956, 1957, 1969, and 1975. See, respectively, RA case nos. 10/6298-2, pp. 232–33; 3/498; 9/2251; and 14 (15 Mar. 1975), p. 2.

87. There was, however, some change compared with the 1968 contract (clause 20), which explicitly gave company managers complete control in this area. In the 1976 contract, Volkswagen management agreed to grant the union the same privileges regarding the hiring of temporary workers which it had with other personnel.

88. The 1977 Ford contract (clauses 6–7) did give preference in hiring to those temporary workers with prior experience in the firm, and they received regular fringe benefits.

89. The status of temporary workers led to a rare protest movement at Chrysler's Federal District plant in 1975. Some three hundred Chrysler *eventuales* occupied the CTM's national headquarters building to protest the Chrysler union secretary-general's practice of selling employment openings and to demand permanent jobs. See *El Universal*, 6 June 1975, 1.

An examination of different automobile firms' production and employment levels during the 1960s and 1970s (data for 1966–76 made available to the author by the Asociación Mexicana de la Industria Automotriz) reveals how important the flexible use of temporary labor was to these companies. By retaining the capacity to hire or dismiss temporary workers as necessary, Ford, VAM, Chrysler, and Volkswagen were all able to adjust employment levels quickly when market conditions changed. Firms with contract restrictions on the use of *eventuales* had greater difficulty in this regard.

90. General Motors 1977 contract, clause 19(b). The General Motors union was particularly concerned that the company would close its overcrowded, technologically outmoded assembly plant in the Federal District. It won provisions protecting all permanent workers' jobs for the life of the contract.

91. Nissan 1976 contract, clause 18.

92. VAM 1972 contract, clause 30.

93. Volkswagen 1976 contract, clauses 2, 20; Chrysler 1977 contract, clauses 10, 19.

94. DINA 1960 contract, clause 15; 1976 contract, clause 16.

95. Other job security provisions at Nissan included partial indemnity payments for temporary workers who were dismissed and the guarantee that dismissed workers would retain their seniority and be given preference when new employment openings appeared. See the Nissan 1976 contract, clause 14.

96. DINA 1960 contract, clause 45.

97. Nissan 1966 contract, clause 15.

98. Volkswagen 1968 contract, clause 43; see also clauses 10, 31, 59.

99. Volkswagen 1976 contract, clause 15.

100. Volkswagen 1976 contract, clause 5, and DINA 1976 contract, clause 26, respectively.

101. Ford 1977 contract, clause 70.

102. DINA's 1958–60 contract called for both the creation of a Joint Commission for Conflict Resolution to serve as the principal forum for union-employer consultation and attention to workplace problems within specified time limits. A government labor inspector was to head the commission when it considered economic conflicts or strikes. However, this commission never became fully operational, and it was disbanded in 1960. See DINA 1960 contract, clauses 94, 97, and Junta Federal de Conciliación y Arbitraje case no. 8.9/312 (29) "59"/694 (4 Dec. 1959).

103. The discussion of strikes in this section is based on the sources listed in table 6.8.

104. RA 10/6298-1, p. 199; 2/126 (17 Oct. 1955).

105. RA 10/6298-3, pp. 577–78 (14 May 1959); 3/660 (26 Aug. 1959); RA 10/6298-1, p. 163; 6/1357 (6 Jan. 1965).

106. RA 10/6298-6, p. 1372 (18 Jan. 1965); 6/1423 (17 Feb. 1965); 10/6298-7, p. 1621 (5 Feb. 1966); 9/2199 (5 Dec. 1968); 11/2714, pp. 2722, 2730 (30 Jan. 1971).

107. Information concerning the UOI and its activities in the automobile industry is from the author's interviews with the UOI's director, Juan Ortega Arenas, 30 Nov., 2 Dec. 1977, Mexico City, and a staff official of the International Metalworkers' Federation, 2 June 1977, Mexico City. See also Aguilar García, *La política sindical,* 110, 113.

108. For a discussion of the IMF's membership, organizational structure, history, and activities, see Willatt, *Multinational Unions* (1974), 101–5. The IMF is known in Latin America as the Federación Internacional de Trabajadores de la Industria Metalúrgica (FITIM).

109. The discussion here is based on the author's interviews with IMF staff officials, 10 May 1977, 2 June 1977, 24 June 1977, 18 Jan. 1978, 20 June 1978, Mexico City, and on minutes of General Motors union general assemblies in RA 6/1387 (2 Feb. 1965); 6/1480 (23 June 1965); 6/1500 (11 Aug. 1965); 7/1625 (5 Feb. 1966); 7/1673–4 (2 Apr. 1966); 7/1699 (14 May 1966); 10/2448 (4 Apr. 1970); 12 (9 Mar. 1974), p. 10; 14 (9 Oct. 1976), pp. 2–3; 14 (11 Mar. 1977), pp. 1–2; 14 (3 Apr. 1977), pp. 1–3.

110. This discussion draws on the author's interviews with a staff official of the International Metalworkers' Federation, 18 Jan. and 25 Apr. 1978, Mexico City; a Nissan union official, 26 Feb. 1978, Cuernavaca; and a senior DINA company official, 28 June 1978, Mexico City; author's field notes based on a DINA union meeting, 22 Nov. 1978, Ciudad Sahagún, Hidalgo.

Chapter 7: Labor Politics under Economic Stress in the 1980s

1. Lustig, *Mexico* (1992), table 3.3.

The absence of unemployment insurance in Mexico may have compelled workers to seek lower-quality jobs at lower pay, or to seek jobs in the informal sector, rather than risk unemployment. Even so, the government's very loose definition of employment (those employed at least one hour during the week of reference, even if the work was not remunerated) may account for the conspicuously low urban unemployment rate at a time of persistent economic stagnation and industrial restructuring in the public and private sectors. For details on how unemployment data are compiled, see *El Mercado de Valores* 53 (15 Feb. 1993): 23–27.

2. Valdés Ugalde, "From Bank Nationalization to State Reform" (1994), table 9.2.

3. Author's calculations based on data presented in table 6.1; here and in chapter 8, the inflation rate is the annual percentage increase in the Banco de México's national consumer price index. The data presented here may actually underestimate the extent of real wage decline because, at least in the early 1980s, as much as 54 percent of the economically active urban population may have earned less than the legal minimum. See Carr, "Mexican Left, the Popular Movements, and the Politics of Austerity" (1986), 3.

Labor code reforms in January 1983 permitted increases in minimum wages as economic conditions required, and additional reforms in 1985 reduced the number of minimum-wage zones to three (centered on Mexico City, Guadalajara, and Monterrey). In practice, minimum wages were revised every six months from June 1983 until late 1986; during 1987 they were revised every three months to compensate for a high, rising inflation rate. Under the terms of a 1988 reform of federal labor law, either the Ministry of Labor and Social Welfare, unions representing at least 51 percent of unionized workers, or employers representing at least 51 percent of the work force can solicit a revision in minimum wages whenever economic conditions demand.

Despite these changes, Ros, "Mexico's Stabilisation and Adjustment Policies" (1986), shows that minimum-wage adjustments fully compensated for consumer price increases only once (in January 1985) between January 1983 and January 1986.

4. Lustig, *Mexico*, table 3.7. Per capita social spending fell even more, by 40.2 percent during the 1983–88 period.

5. Álvarez Béjar, "Economic Crisis and the Labor Movement in Mexico" (1991), table 2.1. The wage share of national income fell even more in the early 1990s, reaching 27.9 percent in 1992. *El Día*, 10 Dec. 1992, 1.

6. Lustig, *Mexico*, 92–93.

7. Álvarez Béjar, "Economic Crisis," 35.

8. De la Garza Toledo, "Restructuring of State-Labor Relations in Mexico" (1994), tables 8.5 and 8.8.

9. Calculations based on data presented in Instituto Nacional de Estadística, Geografía e Informática, *Estadísticas históricas de México* (1986), vol. 1, table 9.1,

and Salinas de Gortari, *Cuarto informe de gobierno: Anexo* (1992), 142.

10. This discussion draws in part on Ortega Aguirre, "La CROC y la política salarial" (1992), 4–6.

11. Durand Ponte, "Confederation of Mexican Workers" (1991), 95–98; Zamora, "La política laboral del estado mexicano" (1990), 128, 131–32.

12. The PIRE called for a sharp reduction in government deficit spending, lower import tariffs and fewer barriers to trade, exchange rate adjustments, the reduction or elimination of public consumption subsidies in different areas, and wage controls designed to limit inflationary pressures.

13. Durand Ponte, "Confederation of Mexican Workers," 99.

14. *Unomásuno*, 10 June 1983; quoted in Aziz Nassif, *El estado mexicano y la CTM* (1989), 269.

15. For details, see *Proceso*, 25 July 1983, 20–23; 25 June 1984, 12–15; *Unomásuno*, 18 Jan. 1984, 3; 26 June 1984, 3.

16. In June 1983 the government signed a crisis management agreement with the Labor Congress, but it did not include a wage indexation clause and the CTM abstained. Aziz Nassif, *El estado mexicano*, 268.

17. Cook, "Restructuring and Democracy in Mexico" (1991), 17; Sánchez Díaz, *El "nuevo" revisionismo en el sindicalismo* (1990), 91–124. For a discussion of the de la Madrid administration's equally tough handling of earlier strikes by electrical power and telephone workers, see Franco G. S., "Labor Law and the Labor Movement in Mexico" (1991), 115–16.

18. Carr, "Mexican Left," 5; Álvarez Béjar, "Crisis in Mexico" (1986), 54–55.

19. The document, titled "Los trabajadores ante la situación económica nacional: Opciones para el desarrollo," was published in *El Día*, 11 Apr. 1985, 12; 12 Apr. 1985, 12; 13 Apr. 1985, 12. The CTM also sought expanded government social welfare programs, including expanded production and subsidized distribution of essential foodstuffs, worker housing programs, and increased financing for worker credit facilities.

In 1984 the CTM controlled as many as four hundred enterprises in agriculture, fishing, manufacturing, retailing, and transportation. Carr, "Mexican Left," 6.

20. The de la Madrid administration promised increased funding for union-owned consumer cooperatives and worker housing programs, expanded access to basic commodities, preferential access to credit, and an increase from 8 to 10 percent in worker profit sharing. For details, see *El Día*, 30 Apr. 1985, 6–7; Zamora, "La política laboral," 128.

21. *La Jornada*, 1 Dec. 1987, 3; 2 Dec. 1987, 1, 8; 3 Dec. 1987, 1.

22. *La Jornada*, 4 Dec. 1987, 1, 28–29.

23. *La Jornada*, 5 Dec. 1987, 1, 5, 14; 6 Dec. 1987, 1, 8.

24. Author's interview with a former government labor official in the de la Madrid administration, 22 Oct. 1988, Mexico City.

25. *La Jornada*, 7 Dec. 1987, 1, 16; 8 Dec. 1987, 1, 14; 9 Dec. 1987, 1; 11 Dec. 1987, 11–12; 12 Dec. 1987, 11; 15 Dec. 1987, 1.

26. For additional details concerning the plan and its implementation, see *El Mercado de Valores* 47 (21 Dec. 1987), "Pacto de Solidaridad Económica" supple-

ment; 48 (1 Feb. 1988): 5–7; Whitehead, "Political Change and Economic Stabilization" (1989).

27. The Labor Congress won some additional benefits when the PSE was renegotiated in August 1988. These included the government's decision to eliminate a 6 percent value-added tax on medicines and processed foods, a 30 percent income tax reduction for individuals earning up to four times the Federal District minimum wage, and expanded access to government credit facilities for workers. See *El Mercado de Valores* 48 (1 Sept. 1988): 3–4.

28. See table 6.1. For the first time since the early 1970s, the rate of inflation fell to single digits in 1993.

29. For examples of labor protests because the PSE failed to improve workers' economic welfare, see *Excélsior*, 19 Feb. 1988, 1; 29 Mar. 1988, 1, 12; 17 May 1988, 1; *El Cotidiano*, no. 22 (Mar.–Apr. 1988): 51.

30. *New York Times*, 13 June 1988, 30.

31. On the difficulties experienced in securing business compliance with the pact, see *Mexico Journal*, no. 26 (4 Apr. 1983): 13.

32. Lustig, *Mexico*, tables 3.2, 3.4; Ros, "Mexico in the 1990s," table 3.1.

33. Lustig, *Mexico*, table 3.2.

34. *New York Times*, 16 Mar. 1984, 3; 25 Apr. 1984, 5; 4 Sept. 1984, 9; 14 Oct. 1984, IV, p. 4; 24 May 1985, 7; 30 Aug. 1985, 3; 25 Jan. 1986, 36; 16 Feb. 1986, IV, p. 3; 7 Apr. 1986, IV, p. 12; 14 June 1986, 5; 27 Jan. 1987, 9. See also Pozzi, "Argentina, 1976–1982" (1988), 115, 125–35, and Manzetti and Dell'Aquila, "Economic Stabilisation in Argentina" (1988), 20–21.

35. *New York Times*, 4 Mar. 1986, IV, p. 23; 28 Nov. 1986, D5; 29 Nov. 1986, 1; 13 Dec. 1986, 3; 13 June 1987, 33. See also Payne, "Working Class Strategies in the Transition to Democracy in Brazil" (1991).

36. Reyes del Campillo, "El movimiento obrero en la Cámara de Diputados" (1990), tables 2–4.

It is, of course, possible that major organizations such as the CTM won unpublicized benefits that allowed labor leaders to protect rank-and-file union members more effectively than the available data indicate, though this seems unlikely. The information available does not permit one to determine whether the de la Madrid government rewarded continuing CTM discipline by permitting its affiliates larger wage and fringe benefit increases or systematically better access to social welfare programs than other major labor organizations.

37. Zazueta and de la Peña, *La estructura del Congreso del Trabajo* (1984), table 7.7, p. 463. This is the last date for which data such as these are available.

38. Ibid., table 7.12, p. 463, and 7.18, pp. 486–87. See also Aguilar García, *Los sindicatos nacionales* (1985), 125–31.

39. Mejía Prieto, *El poder tras de las gafas* (1980), 93, presents circumstantial evidence to suggest that the Mexican government's harsh response to Velázquez's support in the early 1930s for such radical actions as the general strike may have led him to moderate his tactics.

40. Author's interviews with government labor officials closely identified with the CTM, 29 Oct. 1987 and 15 Oct. 1988, Mexico City.

41. Sheahan, *Conflict and Change in Mexican Economic Strategy* (1991), table 2.

42. See, for example, de la Garza Toledo, *Reestructuración productiva y respuesta sindical* (1993), 94–122, 156–62; Gutiérrez Garza, ed., *Reconversión industrial y lucha sindical* (1989); and Mondragón, "Contratos-ley y sindicatos" (1993).

43. Carrillo V. and García, "Etapas industriales y conflictos laborales" (1987), 325.

44. The only exception was the six-day wildcat strike that workers at Nissan's Lerma plant staged in 1979 to protest union leaders' actions. Roxborough, *Unions and Politics in Mexico* (1984), 48.

45. Author's calculations based on data presented in Asociación Mexicana de la Industria Automotriz (AMIA), *La industria automotriz de México en cifras: Edición 1986* (1986), 6.

46. Ibid., 54–55.

47. Ibid., and AMIA *Boletín* 265 (Jan. 1988): 23. The 1987 production figure includes tractor-trailers and passenger buses. Automotive production grew rapidly in the late 1980s and early 1990s, reaching a total of 1,083,091 vehicles (cars, trucks, and buses) in 1992. AMIA *Boletín* 325 (Jan. 1993): 30.

48. AMIA internal documents.

49. "Decreto para la racionalización de la industria automotriz," *Diario Oficial de la Federación,* 15 Sept. 1983, 3–9. The decree also barred eight-cylinder engines and required that one-fourth of each firm's production be "austere" cars without extra equipment. Under the terms of the decree, firms could produce an additional model only if half its production was exported and if the model was self-sufficient in foreign exchange terms. Transnational firms used this provision to increase export production dramatically.

50. See Dombois, "La producción automotriz y el mercado del trabajo" (1985), 48–50, and Bennett and Sharpe, "Transnational Corporations and the Political Economy of Export Promotion" (1979), for discussions of initial export promotion efforts in the late 1970s.

51. Tsunekawa, "Dependency and Labor Policy" (1989), table 2.13. A total of 383,374 finished vehicles were exported in 1992. AMIA *Boletín* 325 (Jan. 1993): 35.

52. Renault constructed a four-cylinder engine plant in Gómez Palacio, Durango, in 1985. This discussion focuses on Chrysler, Ford, General Motors, Nissan, and Volkswagen because of their greater importance in the Mexican automobile manufacturing industry during the 1980s.

For data on total investment and installed capacity in these new facilities, see Tsunekawa, "Dependency and Labor Policy," 67–68. Nissan added vehicle assembly operations to its Aguascalientes plant in 1992. *New York Times,* 16 Nov. 1993, C1.

53. Carrillo V., "Restructuración en la industria automotriz en México" (1991), 491.

54. *South,* no. 84 (Oct. 1987): 7; AMIA *Boletín* 253 (Jan. 1987): 1–2.

55. Author's interview with a Ford labor relations manager, 25 Oct. 1988, Mexico City.

56. Arnulfo Arteaga (an authority on labor relations in the Mexican automobile industry), interview with author, 18 Oct. 1987, Mexico City.

57. Tsunekawa, "Dependency and Labor Policy," 286; Arteaga, interview with author, 16 Oct. 1987, Mexico City.

58. Author's interview with former Ministry of Labor and Social Welfare official, 2 Oct. 1987, Mexico City.

59. This discussion is based on an analysis of Junta Federal de Conciliación y Arbitraje (JFCA) internal documents and the author's interviews with Arteaga, 16 and 18 Oct. 1987, Mexico City.

60. Carrillo V., "Restructuración," 516; La Jornada, 21 Oct. 1988, 10.

61. This discussion is based on JFCA internal documents and Tsunekawa, "Dependency and Labor Policy," 284.

62. Arteaga, interview with author, 18 Oct. 1987, Mexico City, and Tsunekawa, "Dependency and Labor Policy," 276, 286.

63. Labor contracts for Chrysler's Federal District (1987, clause 60), Toluca (1987, clause 60), and Ramos Arizpe (1988, clause 45) plants.

64. For data on average daily wages at Mexican automobile manufacturing plants in 1988, see Middlebrook, "Politics of Industrial Restructuring" (1991), table 1. Information concerning fringe benefits is from JFCA internal documents.

65. Author's interview with a Ford labor relations manager, 25 Oct. 1988, Mexico City, and Arteaga, interview with author, 18 Oct. 1987, Mexico City.

66. Tsunekawa, "Dependency and Labor Policy," 276–78; La Jornada, 21 Oct. 1988, 10; JFCA internal documents; Arteaga, interview with author, 16 Oct. 1987, Mexico City. No strike occurred at either Chrysler–Ramos Arizpe or Nissan-Aguascalientes in the 1980s.

67. This discussion draws in part on the author's interviews with a Ford labor relations manager, 6 Nov. 1987 and 21 Oct. 1988, Mexico City, and Comité de Observadores Independientes, "Recuento sindical en Ford Motor Company" (1991). For more detailed accounts of events at Ford-Cuautitlán between 1987 and 1991, see Middlebrook, "Reestructuración industrial y política sindical" (1990), 52–55, and La Botz, Mask of Democracy (1992), 148–58.

68. Post-Fordist labor relations arrangements challenge such mainstays of traditional industrial unionism as seniority, contractually specified job definitions designed to protect the rights of individual workers, and union representatives' role in the resolution of workplace grievances. For discussions of the post-Fordist model, see Kenney and Florida, "Beyond Mass Production" (1988); Dohse, Jürgens, and Malsch, "From 'Fordism' to 'Toyotism'?" (1985); and Sabel, Work and Politics (1982), esp. 209–16.

69. This discussion is based on the author's interviews with Ford (25 Oct. 1988), General Motors (28 Oct. 1988), and Nissan (27 Oct. 1988) labor relations managers in Mexico City; Carrillo V., "Restructuración," table 5; La Jornada, 28 July 1987, 13.

70. Shaiken (with Herzenberg), Automation and Global Production (1987), 59, 63.

71. No information is available for Chrysler's Federal District plant.

72. Ford-Hermosillo labor contract (1988), clause 12.

73. Ibid., clause 9.

74. This discussion is based on the author's interviews with General Motors (28 Oct. 1988) and Nissan (27 Oct. 1988) labor relations managers in Mexico City and on internal Nissan documents.

75. Montiel, "Volkswagen" (1987), 12.

76. Author's interview with a Ford labor relations manager, 25 Oct. 1988, Mexico City; Carrillo V., "Restructuración," 501.

77. Author's interview with a General Motors labor relations manager, 28 Oct. 1988, Mexico City.

78. Arteaga, interview with author, 14 Oct. 1988, Mexico City.

79. Before October 1987, the Ford-Cuautitlán union enjoyed contract terms in these areas equivalent to those at General Motors–Federal District and Nissan-Cuernavaca. Compare the data presented in table 7.1 with those in Middlebrook, "Reestructuración industrial," table 1.

80. General Motors–Federal District labor contract (1987), clauses 4, 9, 10; Nissan-Cuernavaca labor contract (1988), clauses 7, 12, 62, 86.

81. General Motors–Federal District labor contract (1987), clauses 5, 10(e), 19bis, 27; Nissan-Cuernavaca labor contract (1988), clauses 14, 16.

In early 1992 General Motors finally announced the closing of its aging, technologically outmoded Federal District plant. Company managers stated that they did so because of Mexico City's increasingly stringent environmental laws. However, by shifting the plant's vehicle production to a new facility in Silao, Guanajuato, General Motors was also able to renegotiate its labor contract and hire a new work force organized by the CTM.

82. Labor contracts for General Motors–Federal District (1987), clauses 19bis, 30, 49, 50, 62, 75, 81; Nissan-Cuernavaca (1988), clauses 1, 50, 54–60, 95, 96, 103, 106.

83. Labor contracts for General Motors–Federal District (1987), clauses 10(e), 20, 31, 33; Nissan-Cuernavaca (1988), clauses 7, 20, 21, 23, 24.

84. Labor contracts for General Motors–Federal District (1987), clauses 80, 85; Nissan-Cuernavaca (1988), clauses 13, 17, 18, 101.

85. Labor contracts for General Motors–Federal District (1987), clauses 18, 85; Nissan-Cuernavaca (1988), clause 13.

86. Volkswagen labor contract (1986), clauses 2, 14, 19, 24, 28, 33–37, 44, 45, 50, 60, 65, 84, 92; JFCA internal documents; Dombois, "La producción automotriz y el mercado del trabajo" (1986), 68.

87. See Middlebrook, "Reestructuración industrial," 55–57; Montiel, "Volkswagen"; Montiel, "¿Una modernización con pies de barro?" (1992), 50–51.

88. JFCA case no. III-2144/92, esp. clauses 1, 4, 11, 15.

89. Montiel, "¿Una modernización?" 57.

90. This discussion of the 1992 Volkswagen conflict draws on Montiel, "¿Una modernización?"; Quiroz and Méndez, "El conflicto de Volkswagen" (1992); Pries, "Contexto estructural y dinámica de acción" (1992); Economist, 22 Aug. 1992, 31–32; El Financiero International, 3 Aug. 1992, 17 Aug. 1992, 31 Aug. 1992.

91. Shaiken (with Herzenberg), *Automation and Global Production,* 25–26, 42; Shaiken, interview with author, 14 Oct. 1988, Mexico City; the author's interview with a Nissan labor relations manager, 27 Oct. 1988, Mexico City; Ebel, "Social and Labour Implications of Flexible Manufacturing Systems" (1985), 134.

92. Shaiken (with Herzenberg), *Automation and Global Production,* 45, 49, 59, 61–63. Ford's Chihuahua facility is not identified by name in this study.

93. Ibid., 48.

94. Ibid., 61; see also 22, 42, 44, 47, 48.

95. For discussions of the SME and airline pilots cases, see respectively Cook, "Mexican State-Labor Relations" (1994), 11, and La Botz, *Mask of Democracy,* 90–100.

Chapter 8: Conclusion

1. Author's interview with a del Mazo adviser, 6 June 1991, La Jolla, California. Del Mazo had served as president of the CTM-dominated Banco Obrero in the late 1970s.

2. *La Jornada,* 5 Oct. 1987, 6; 12 Oct. 1987, 1; 16 Oct. 1987, 7; 19 Oct. 1987, 4; *Unomásuno,* 21 Oct. 1987, 5.

3. The opposition that Hernández Galicia mounted against Salinas's candidacy was reportedly motivated in part by the latter's opposition (in his capacity as minister of programming and budget) to STPRM control over a substantial proportion of PEMEX contracts, which the union then let to subcontractors at a profit. See *New York Times,* 11 Jan. 1989, 6; *Latin American Regional Report: Mexico and Central America,* 15 Feb. 1989; Bizberg, "La crisis del corporativismo mexicano" (1990), 715, 717. Collier, *Contradictory Alliance* (1992), 137.

4. In an unprecedented reversal of electoral fortunes, 30 of the 101 candidates representing Labor Congress affiliates failed to win election. Reyes del Campillo, "El movimiento obrero en la Cámara de Diputados" (1990), 158.

5. *New York Times,* 11 Jan. 1989, 6; 12 Jan. 1989, 1, 6.

6. See Middlebrook, "Dilemmas of Change in Mexican Politics" (1988), 122–29, for an overview of this subject. The term *political technocrat* is used by Camp in "The Political Technocrat in Mexico" (1985).

7. Salinas de Gortari, interview with author, 8 Dec. 1992, Mexico City.

8. This case is discussed in detail in chapter 7 of this book.

9. See Méndez and Quiroz, "Organización obrera" (1990), 48, for a summary of Salinas's proposals for a new style of trade unionism.

10. On administrative reorganization and employment and contract changes in PEMEX, see *Proceso,* 15 May 1989, 22–24; 19 Aug. 1991, 31; Barbosa, "Los retos del sindicalismo petrolero" (1993). On the circumstances surrounding leadership change in the SNTE and its consequences, see Cook, *Organizing Dissent* (1993), 93–98.

11. Cook, "Restructuring and Democracy in Mexico" (1991), 28–30; de la Garza Toledo, *Reestructuración productiva y respuesta sindical* (1993), 109–10, 160–65, 171–76; Vázquez Rubio, "Por los caminos de la productividad" (1990); Solís, "La modernización de Teléfonos de México" (1992); *El Financiero Interna-*

tional, 5 Oct. 1992, 13. Contract changes at Teléfonos de México also benefited management by permitting the privatized firm to hire a larger proportion of future employees through its nonunionized subsidiaries.

12. *El Financiero International,* 18 May 1992, 14; *La Jornada,* 23 June 1992, 15. In his rise to power in 1976 as leader of a successful opposition movement within the STRM, Hernández Juárez had similarly benefited from presidential support.

13. *Proceso,* 16 Jan. 1977, 10–13.

14. *News* (Mexico City), 25 Feb. 1992, 2, 4; *Economist,* 14 Mar. 1992, 49–50; Carstens, "How to Get a Leg Up—and a Foot in the Door" (1993); *El Financiero,* 11 Feb. 1993, 45. The 1992 legislation required an employer to deposit each month a sum equal to 5 percent of a worker's salary. Workers earning more than 2.5 times the minimum wage were to make an additional 1 percent contribution to their accounts. A corollary political advantage to the Salinas administration was that mandatory housing contributions substantially increased bank assets, thus benefiting Salinas's political allies in the financial sector. Advance word of these measures led investors to bid up the value of banks scheduled for privatization, providing a financial windfall for the government as well. *Economist,* 14 Mar. 1992, 50.

15. Data concerning cumulative job losses in the state sector appear in the *New York Times,* 27 Oct. 1993, A1–6. The reprivatization of the banking industry had similarly adverse effects on employment. *Proceso,* 28 Sept. 1992, 12–15.

16. Official minimum-wage levels remained important because wages in many sectors were defined as multiples of the legal minimum.

17. Instituto Nacional de Estadística, Geografía e Informática (INEGI) internal documents.

18. Shaiken, "Myths about Mexican Workers" (1993), 12–13 (citing U.S. Bureau of Labor Statistics and Banco de México data).

19. In addition to the examples discussed here, the CTM also received government support in highly politicized conflicts at Ford-Cuautitlán, Tornel Rubber Company, and the Modelo Brewery, in which union dissidents openly challenged the confederation's control. On the Tornel and Modelo conflicts, see La Botz, *Mask of Democracy* (1992), 131–47.

20. As of late 1993, the PRI was organized around a National Front of Citizens' Organizations, an Urban Popular Territorial Movement, a Worker-Peasant Pact, and other organizations. The Worker-Peasant Pact, signed in June 1992 between the CTM and the National Peasants' Confederation (CNC), was designed to promote productivity and increase consumer access to commodities. For details, see Rodríguez Guillén and Mora Heredia, "El agotamiento del autoritarismo con legitimidad" (1993), 27.

For a discussion of the CTM's success in the late 1940s and again in 1965 at blocking PRI reforms that threatened to diminish the influence of sectoral organizations in internal party decision making and their share of elective positions, see Middlebrook, "Political Change and Political Reform in an Authoritarian Regime" (1981), 18.

21. *El Financiero International,* 18 May 1992, 13–14; Lovera, "Las reformas a la Ley Federal del Trabajo," *La Jornada Laboral,* 31 Jan. 1992, 1, 8. For a sum-

mary of the productivity accord's principal provisions, see Méndez and Quiroz, "Productividad, respuesta obrera y sucesión presidencial" (1993), 71–73.

In August 1993 Salinas agreed in principle to compensate future productivity gains with wage increases. He did so in response to U.S. pressures during final bargaining over the North American Free Trade Agreement. See *New York Times,* 29 Sept. 1993, A1; 4 Oct. 1993, C1–2.

22. Author's interviews with a CTM representative, 23 Apr. 1992, Ventura, California, and Néstor de Buen L. (a prominent authority on Mexican labor law), 8 Dec. 1992, Mexico City. For business organizations' proposals for labor law reform, see *Proceso,* 21 Oct. 1991, 17, and Confederación Patronal de la República Mexicana, "Propuestas preliminares" (1989).

23. In addition to the examples cited in the text, the Salinas administration acceded to CTM demands for an increase in the number of INFONAVIT housing units distributed to workers, and it rejected a proposal from business organizations to privatize the Mexican Social Security Institute (IMSS). In a further concession to labor, the government required employers to increase their financial contributions to the IMSS. See Romero Miranda, Méndez, and Bolívar Espinoza, "Muchos cambios legales que agitan las aguas políticas" (1993), 65–69.

24. Valdés Ugalde, "From Bank Nationalization to State Reform" (1994), 223.

25. Ibid., tables 9.2, 9.3. The data on state-owned enterprises refer to firms with either majority or minority state participation, decentralized public agencies, and public investment funds.

26. See Cook, "Mexican State-Labor Relations" (1995), 9–12, for specific examples.

27. One conventional indicator of different sector organizations' influence in party affairs is the proportion of PRI nominations they receive for congressional seats. The labor sector's share fell from 21.5 percent in 1988 to 15 percent in 1991. See Reyes del Campillo, "El movimiento obrero," 145, and Cornelius, "Mexico's Incomplete Democratic Transition" (1993), 40–41.

28. See, for example, Lustig, *Mexico* (1992), 38–45, and Ros, "Mexico in the 1990s" (1994), 72–73, 76, 78.

29. Press reports of the CTM's estimated membership in the early 1990s ranged from 3.5 million to 5.5 million workers. See the *News,* 23 Feb. 1992, 1, and the *Economist,* 14 Mar. 1992, 49, respectively, for the lower and higher estimates. Note that these totals were much higher than those reported by independent analysts in the late 1970s (see table 4.2).

30. Salinas de Gortari, *Tercer informe de gobierno, 1991* (1991), 5.

31. The text of Salinas's March 4, 1992, address to the PRI was published in the party's journal under the title "Liberalismo social: Nuestro camino." See *Examen* 35 (Apr. 1992): 19–22.

32. See Pimentel González and Rueda Castillo, "Reforma del PRI" (1991), 29–30. The Labor Congress formally agreed in December 1990 to end its practice of automatically affiliating union members with the PRI. La Botz, *Mask of Democracy,* 41.

33. On the origins and content of the 1977 political reform and its implications

for political liberalization in Mexico, see Middlebrook, "Political Liberalization in an Authoritarian Regime" (1986).

34. The PRI's share of seats in the federal Chamber of Deputies rose from 49.2 percent in 1988 to 61.5 percent in 1991. Cornelius, "Mexico's Incomplete Democratic Transition," table 4.

35. Zaldívar Lelo de Larrea, "La propuesta priísta de reforma política" (1993); *New York Times,* 14 Sept. 1993, A4; 19 Sept. 1993, 11.

36. Author's communication with a Federal Electoral Institute official, 16 May 1994.

37. One possible exception concerned the Salinas administration's November 1991 reform of the *ejido* sector, lands distributed to peasants as part of Mexico's agrarian reform program. The reform legislation reduced the intervention of government agencies (especially the Ministry of Agrarian Reform and Banrural, long the principal source of low-cost agricultural credits for peasant producers) in the economic life of rural communities, while simultaneously limiting the powers of *ejido* executive committees (*comisariados ejidales*) and expanding the authority of the general assembly of *ejido* members. Peasants' economic dependence on government agencies and the extensive powers of *comisariados ejidales* (whose election formally required formal validation by state authorities) had long served as key instruments of political control in the countryside.

38. *New York Times,* 26 Feb. 1990, C4. One important consequence of these reforms was to increase the proportion of government income tax revenue from business sources, which rose from 36.2 percent of the total in 1982 to 41.3 percent in 1990; author's calculations from data presented in Salinas de Gortari, *Cuarto informe de gobierno, 1992: Anexo (1992),* 162.

39. Rueschemeyer, Stephens, and Stephens, *Capitalist Development and Democracy* (1992), 7.

40. Ibid., 57.

41. Ibid., 50, 59, 202, 270–74.

42. Valenzuela, "Labor Movements in Transitions to Democracy" (1989), esp. 449–51.

43. Rueschemeyer et al., *Capitalist Development and Democracy,* 8, 59.

44. Ibid., 282; see also 218–19, 223 on Mexico. See 59, 184, 282–83 for brief references to Argentina as another such exception, where unions sought to preserve "a Peronist regime, democratic or not."

Rueschemeyer, Stephens, and Stephens do not include Nicaragua in this category, classifying Sandinista rule between 1984 and 1990 as a case of "restricted democracy." In this characterization, they apparently chose to emphasize the political inclusion of popular sectors under the Sandinista regime, in effect downplaying the importance of other elements in their definition of democracy (especially "responsibility of the state apparatus to the elected parliament" and "the freedoms of expression and association as well as the protection of individual rights against arbitrary state action"). See 43–44, 246.

45. Valenzuela, "Labor Movements," 462.

46. In the case of Peru between 1977 and 1980, labor organizations opposed specific anti-labor policies adopted by the Morales Bermúdez government (especially wage controls and state of emergency legislation) while supporting an accelerated transition from military rule to democracy. See Haworth, "Political Transition and the Peruvian Labor Movement" (1989), 207–8.

47. How to characterize the Sandinista regime remains a subject of debate. For a concise overview of political developments between 1979 and 1990, see Williams, "Dual Transitions from Authoritarian Rule: Popular and Electoral Democracy in Nicaragua" (1994).

48. This discussion of the Nicaraguan case draws on Stahler-Sholk, "Nicaragua" (1987), 549, 553, 555–58, 571, and "Labor/Party/State Dynamics in Nicaragua" (1992), 2, 4–7, 9, 11–15, 17–18, 22–31; Quandt, *Unbinding the Ties: The Popular Organizations and the FSLN* (1993), 8, 14, 17–18, 25–27, 47–48.

49. The transition to democratic rule prompted extensive debate concerning the appropriate relationship between the FSLN and mass organizations. See Quandt, *Unbinding the Ties,* 10–11.

50. This background discussion of the Soviet case draws on Ruble, *Soviet Trade Unions* (1981), 9–26, 47–49, 57, 61, 65–71, 105, and Connor, *Accidental Proletariat* (1991), 200, 208–9, 211–14, 220, 223–24, 238–40, 243, 245, 259, 266–67.

51. Ruble, *Soviet Trade Unions,* 1.

52. See Cook, *Soviet Social Contract* (1993), chap. 6, for a differentiated analysis of labor responses to the Gorbachev reforms.

53. This discussion of labor politics in Russia in the early 1990s draws on Connor, *Accidental Proletariat,* 271–84, 290–93, 298, 301, 319–20, and "Labor Politics in Post-Communist Russia" (1993), 2, 11–12, 17, 27; Cook, "State-Labor Relations and the Soviet Collapse" (1993), 2, 4–6, 8–14, 17, 19–22, 23, and "Russia's Labor Relations" (1993), 2–3, 6, 9, 11, 20.

54. In the early 1990s, the GCTU devoted itself primarily to coordinating labor issues among the former Soviet republics.

55. Despite some worker opposition to political reform in the Soviet Union in 1989–90, major labor organizations opposed hard-line Communists' attempted coup d'état in August 1991 (though they did not call protest strikes, as Yeltsin requested). See Connor, *Accidental Proletariat,* 293, and "Labor Politics," 14.

56. Stahler-Sholk, "Labor/Party/State Dynamics," 15.

57. For discussions of factors determining labor strength, see Valenzuela, "Labor Movements," 453–54, and Cameron, "Social Democracy, Corporatism, Labour Quiescence" (1984), 164–65.

58. For a discussion of this relationship in the Russian case, see Cook, "State-Labor Relations," 22, and "Russia's Labor Relations," 4–5, 16–17.

59. Data reported in Salinas de Gortari, *Cuarto informe de gobierno,* 1992.: *Anexo,* 353, indicate that employment in the largest manufacturing firms fell between 1981 and 1990. Public-sector manufacturing employment fell particularly significantly (152).

60. Ibid., 309. INEGI internal documents show that the value of *maquiladora* production grew by an average annual rate of 4.2 percent between 1981 and 1991, faster than any other manufacturing activity.

61. In 1990, *maquiladoras* in the cities of Matamoros, Ciudad Juárez, and Chihuahua averaged, respectively, 422, 447, and 491 workers per plant. Quintero Ramírez, "Reestructuración sindical en las maquiladoras mexicanas" (1992), 160.

62. For an overview of labor organization in the *maquiladora* industry, see Quintero Ramírez, "Tendencias sindicales en la frontera norte de México" (1993). On collaboration between local conciliation and arbitration boards and employers to block strikes and workers' demands, see Quintero Ramírez, "Reestructuración sindical," 210–12, 219.

63. Salinas de Gortari, *Cuarto informe de gobierno,* 1992, *Anexo,* 18, 352.

64. María de los Angeles Pozas (an authority on worker-employer relations in Monterrey), interview with author, 17 June 1993, Monterrey.

65. There are no data available on union membership as a proportion of the economically active population in the early 1990s. The proportion presumably declined in the 1980s as a consequence of job losses in the heavily unionized public sector and in private firms. The last reliable information available places this proportion at 16.3 percent in 1978; see Zazueta and de la Peña, *La estructura del Congreso del Trabajo* (1984), tables 2.4, 7.1.

66. See Confederación de Trabajadores de México, *Memoria: Reunión nacional para la reforma económica* (1978), 15–16, 202–10, 219–33; *El Día,* 26 Feb. 1979, 7; Casar, "El proyecto del movimiento obrero organizado" (1982), esp. 34–37; Marván L., "El proyecto nacional de las organizaciones obreras" (1985). The CTM's other demands included a constitutional guarantee of the right to remunerative employment, unemployment insurance, a forty-hour workweek with pay for fifty-six hours, an increase in the share of enterprise profits distributed to workers under the 1963 profit-sharing law, expansion of the social security system and the INFONAVIT worker housing program, and employer-financed worker training programs.

67. For an excellent examination of different labor strategies since the 1970s, see Cook, "Restructuring and Democracy in Mexico," esp. 31–34.

68. Connor, "Labor Politics," 17–18; Stahler-Sholk, "Labor/Party/State Dynamics," 20–22, 30.

69. For an overview of this debate, see Carr, *Marxism and Communism in Twentieth-Century Mexico* (1992), 284–85, 295–97, and Cook, *Organizing Dissent,* chap. 1.

70. The most important *coordinadoras* were the National Coordinating Committee of Education Workers (Coordinadora Nacional de Trabajadores de la Educación, CNTE, formed in 1979 to represent prodemocracy forces within the National Education Workers' Union, SNTE), the "Plan de Ayala" National Coordinating Committee (Coordinadora Nacional Plan de Ayala, CNPA, formed in 1979 to represent peasants and small farmers), and the National Coordinating Committee of the Urban Popular Movement (Coordinadora Nacional del Movimiento Urbano Popular, CONAMUP, founded in 1981).

71. The CTM vehemently opposed PRD involvement in labor conflicts such as that at Tornel Rubber Company. La Botz, *Mask of Democracy*, 135–40.

72. Valenzuela, "Labor Movements," 464–65, notes the importance of industrial relations legislation in regime transitions. On the Brazilian case, see Keck, "New Unionism in the Brazilian Transition" (1989), 257–59, 284–85.

BIBLIOGRAPHY

Adler, Ruth. 1988. "La administración obrera en los Ferrocarriles Nacionales de México." *Revista Mexicana de Sociología* 50 (3): 97–124.

———. 1992. "Worker Participation in the Administration of the Petroleum Industry, 1938–1940." In *The Mexican Petroleum Industry in the Twentieth Century*, edited by Jonathan C. Brown and Alan Knight. Austin: University of Texas Press.

Adleson, S. Lief. 1982. "La adolescencia del poder: La lucha de los obreros de Tampico para definir los derechos del trabajo, 1910–1920." *Historias* 2 (Oct.–Dec.): 85–101.

———. 1992. "The Cultural Roots of the Oil Workers' Unions in Tampico, 1910–1925." In *The Mexican Petroleum Industry in the Twentieth Century*, edited by Jonathan C. Brown and Alan Knight. Austin: University of Texas Press.

Aguilar García, Francisco Javier. 1978. "El sindicalismo del sector automotriz, 1960–1976." *Cuadernos Políticos* 16:44–64.

———. 1980. "Historia sindical de General Motors y la huelga de 1980." *A: Revista de Ciencias Sociales y Humanidades* 1 (1): 91–105.

———. 1982. *La política sindical en México: Industria del automóvil*. Mexico City: Ediciones Era.

———. 1985. "Los sindicatos nacionales." In *Organización y sindicalismo*. Vol. 3 of *El obrero mexicano*, edited by Pablo González Casanova, Samuel León González, and Ignacio Marván. Mexico City: Siglo Veintiuno Editores.

———, ed. 1988. *Los sindicatos de industrias dinámicas*. Vol. 3 of *Los sindicatos nacionales en el México contemporáneo*, edited by Francisco Javier Aguilar García. Mexico City: GV Editores.

———. 1990. "En un período de unidad monolítica: Consolidación del sindicalismo institucional, 1953–1957." In *Historia de la CTM, 1936–1990: El movimiento obrero y el estado mexicano*, edited by Francisco Javier Aguilar García. 2 vols. Mexico City: Universidad Nacional Autónoma de México.

Almond, Gabriel A., and G. Bingham Powell, Jr. 1966. *Comparative Politics: A Developmental Approach*. Boston: Little, Brown.

Alonso, Antonio. 1975. *El movimiento ferrocarrilero en México, 1958–1959*. 2nd ed. Mexico City: Ediciones Era.

Álvarez Béjar, Alejandro. 1986. "Crisis in Mexico: Impacts on the Working Class and the Labor Movement." In *The Mexican Left, the Popular Movements, and the Politics of Austerity*, edited by Barry Carr and Ricardo Anzaldúa Montoya. La Jolla: Center for U.S.-Mexican Studies, University of California, San Diego.

———. 1987. *La crisis global del capitalismo en México, 1968–1983*. Mexico City: Ediciones Era.

———. 1991. "Economic Crisis and the Labor Movement in Mexico." In *Unions,*

Workers, and the State in Mexico, edited by Kevin J. Middlebrook. La Jolla: Center for U.S.-Mexican Studies, University of California, San Diego.

Alzati, Servando A. 1946. *Historia de la mexicanización de los Ferrocarriles Nacionales de México.* Mexico City: Editorial Beatriz de Silva.

Amilpa Trujillo, Fernando. 1991. *Fidel Velázquez: Mi amigo Amilpa.* Mexico City: Colección Testimonios Contemporáneos.

Anderson, John C. 1978. "A Comparative Analysis of Local Union Democracy." *Industrial Relations* 17 (3): 278–95.

Anderson, Rodney D. 1976. *Outcasts in Their Own Land: Mexican Industrial Workers, 1906–1911.* DeKalb: Northern Illinois University Press.

Anguiano, Arturo. 1975. *El estado y la política obrera del cardenismo.* Mexico City: Ediciones Era.

Apter, David E. 1977. *Introduction to Political Analysis.* Cambridge, Mass.: Winthrop Publishers.

Araiza, Luis. 1963. *Historia de la Casa del Obrero Mundial.* Mexico City: N.p.

———. 1975. *Historia del movimiento obrero mexicano.* 4 vols. 2nd ed. Mexico City: Ediciones Casa del Obrero Mundial.

Arriaga Lemus, María de la Luz, Edur Velasco Arregui, and Eduardo Zepeda Miramontes. 1977. "Inflación y salarios en el régimen de LEA." *Investigación Económica* 3:211–40.

Arteaga, Arnulfo. 1987. Interviews with author. Mexico City, 16, 18 Oct.

———. 1988. Interviews with author. Mexico City, 11, 14 Oct.

Ashby, Joe C. 1963. *Organized Labor and the Mexican Revolution under Lázaro Cárdenas.* Chapel Hill: University of North Carolina Press.

Asociación Mexicana de la Industria Automotriz. *Boletín,* various years. Mexico City.

———. 1976. *La industria automotriz en cifras, 1976.* Mexico City: AMIA.

———. 1986. *La industria automotriz de México en cifras: Edición 1986.* Mexico City: AMIA.

Aziz Nassif, Alberto. 1989. *El estado mexicano y la CTM.* Mexico City: Centro de Investigaciones y Estudios Superiores en Antropología Social.

Baena Paz, Guillermina. 1976. "La Confederación General de Trabajadores, 1921–1931." *Revista Mexicana de Ciencias Políticas y Sociales* 83: 113–86.

Balán, Jorge; Harley L. Browning; and Elizabeth Jelín. 1973. *Migración, estructura ocupacional y movilidad social: El caso de Monterrey.* Mexico City: Universidad Nacional Autónoma de México.

Barbosa, Fabio. 1993. "Los retos del sindicalismo petrolero." *El Cotidiano* 56 (July): 33–39.

Barrios, Elías. 1938. *El escuadrón de hierro: Páginas de historia sindical.* Mexico City: Editorial Popular.

Basurto, Jorge. 1962. "La influencia de la economía y del estado en las huelgas: El caso de México." Escuela Nacional de Ciencias Políticas y Sociales, Universidad Nacional Autónoma de México, Mexico City.

———. 1975. *El proletariado industrial en México, 1850–1930.* Mexico City:

Instituto de Investigaciones Sociales, Universidad Nacional Autónoma de México.

———. 1983. *En el régimen de Echeverría: Rebelión e independencia.* Vol. 14 of *La clase obrera en la historia de México,* edited by Pablo González Casanova. Mexico City: Siglo Veintiuno Editores.

———. 1984. *Del avilacamachismo al alemanismo, 1940–1952.* Vol. 11 of *La clase obrera en la historia de México,* edited by Pablo González Casanova. Mexico City: Siglo Veintiuno Editores.

Bazán, Lucía. 1980. "El sindicalismo independiente de Nissan Mexicana." In vol. 3 of *Memorias del encuentro sobre historia del movimiento obrero,* edited by Centro de Investigaciones Históricas del Movimiento Obrero. Puebla: Universidad Autónoma de Puebla.

Bendix, Reinhard, with Stein Rokkan. 1964. "The Extension of Citizenship to the Lower Classes." In Reinhard Bendix, *Nation-Building and Citizenship: Studies of Our Changing Social Order.* New York: John Wiley & Sons.

Benjamin, Thomas. 1990. "Laboratories of the New State, 1920–1929: Regional Social Reform and Experiments in Mass Politics." In *Provinces of the Revolution: Essays on Regional Mexican History, 1910–1929,* edited by Thomas Benjamin and Mark Wasserman. Albuquerque: University of New Mexico Press.

Bennett, Douglas C., and Kenneth E. Sharpe. 1979. "Transnational Corporations and the Political Economy of Export Promotion: The Case of the Mexican Automobile Industry." *International Organization* 33 (2): 177–201.

———. 1980. "The State as Banker and Entrepreneur: The Last-Resort Character of the Mexican State's Economic Intervention, 1917–1976." *Comparative Politics* 12 (2): 165–89.

———. 1985. *Transnational Corporations versus the State: The Political Economy of the Mexican Auto Industry.* Princeton: Princeton University Press.

Bensusán Areous, Graciela. 1985. "Construcción y desarrollo del derecho laboral en México." In *El derecho laboral.* Vol. 4 of *El obrero mexicano,* edited by Pablo González Casanova, Samuel León, and Ignacio Marván. Mexico City: Siglo Veintiuno Editores.

———. 1992. "Institucionalización laboral en México: Los años de la definición jurídica, 1917–1931." Ph.D. diss., Facultad de Ciencias Políticas y Sociales, Universidad Nacional Autónoma de México.

Bergquist, Charles. 1986. *Labor in Latin America: Comparative Essays on Chile, Argentina, Venezuela, and Colombia.* Stanford: Stanford University Press.

Bethell, Leslie, and Ian Roxborough, eds. 1992. *Latin America between the Second World War and the Cold War, 1944–1948.* Cambridge: Cambridge University Press.

Bizberg, Ilán. 1984. "Política laboral y acción sindical en México, 1976–1982." *Foro Internacional* 25 (2): 166–89.

———. 1990. *Estado y sindicalismo en México.* Mexico City: El Colegio de México.

———. 1990. "La crisis del corporativismo mexicano." *Foro Internacional* 30 (4): 695–735.

Bloomfield, Gerald. 1978. *The World Automotive Industry.* Vancouver, British Columbia: David and Charles.

Bolívar Espinoza, Augusto, Luis Méndez Berrueta, and Miguel Ángel Romero Miranda. 1993. "Los síntomas de la víspera." *El Cotidiano* 56 (July): 60–68.

Bortz, Jeffrey. 1980. "Problemas de la medición de la afiliación sindical." *A: Revista de Ciencias Sociales y Humanidades* 1 (1): 29–66.

———. 1984. "Industrial Wages in Mexico City, 1939–1975." Ph.D. diss., Department of History, University of California–Los Angeles.

Brachet-Márquez, Viviane. 1992. "Explaining Sociopolitical Change in Latin America: The Case of Mexico." *Latin American Research Review* 27 (3): 91–122.

Brandenburg, Frank. 1964. *The Making of Modern Mexico.* Englewood Cliffs, N.J.: Prentice-Hall.

Buchanan, Paul. 1985. "State Corporatism in Argentina." *Latin American Research Review* 20 (1): 61–95.

Buve, Raymond Th. J. 1990. "Tlaxcala: Consolidating a Cacicazgo." In *Provinces of the Revolution: Essays on Regional Mexican History, 1910–1929,* edited by Thomas Benjamin and Mark Wasserman. Albuquerque: University of New Mexico Press.

Calderón, José María. 1972. *Génesis del presidencialismo en México.* 2nd ed. Mexico City: Ediciones El Caballito.

Calles, Plutarco E. 1926. "The Policies of Mexico Today." *Foreign Affairs* 5 (1): 1–5.

Camacho, Manuel. 1976. "Control sobre el movimiento obrero en México." In *Las fronteras del control del estado mexicano,* edited by Centro de Estudios Internacionales, El Colegio de México. Mexico City: El Colegio de México.

———. 1980. *El futuro inmediato.* Vol. 15 of *La clase obrera en la historia de México,* edited by Pablo González Casanova. Mexico City: Siglo Veintiuno Editores.

Cameron, David R. 1984. "Social Democracy, Corporatism, Labour Quiescence, and the Representation of Economic Interest in Advanced Capitalist Society." In *Order and Conflict in Contemporary Capitalism,* edited by John H. Goldthorpe. New York: Oxford University Press.

Camp, Roderic A. 1980. *Mexico's Leaders: Their Education and Recruitment.* Tucson: University of Arizona Press.

———. 1982. *Mexican Political Biographies, 1935–1981.* Rev. ed. Tucson: University of Arizona Press.

———. 1985. "The Political Technocrat in Mexico and the Survival of the Political System." *Latin American Research Review* 20 (1): 97–118.

———. 1991. *Mexican Political Biographies, 1884–1935.* Austin: University of Texas Press.

Campa S., Valentín. 1978. *Mi testimonio: Memorias de un comunista mexicano.* Mexico City: Ediciones de Cultura Popular.

———. 1978. Interview with author. Mexico City, 12 Apr.

Campuzano Montoya, Irma. 1990. "El impacto de la crisis en la CTM." *Revista Mexicana de Sociología* 52 (3): 161–90.

Cárdenas, Enrique. 1987. *La industrialización mexicana durante la gran depresión.* Mexico City: El Colegio de México.

Cardoso, Fernando Henrique. 1979. "On the Characteristics of Authoritarian Regimes in Latin America." In *The New Authoritarianism in Latin America,* edited by David Collier. Princeton: Princeton University Press.

Carpizo, Jorge. 1979. *El presidencialismo mexicano.* 2nd ed. Mexico City: Siglo Veintiuno Editores.

Carr, Barry. 1976. *El movimiento obrero y la política en México, 1910–1929.* 2 vols. Mexico City: SepSetentas.

———. 1986. "The Mexican Left, the Popular Movements, and the Politics of Austerity, 1982–1985." In *The Mexican Left, the Popular Movements, and the Politics of Austerity,* edited by Barry Carr and Ricardo Anzaldúa Montoya. La Jolla: Center for U.S.-Mexican Studies, University of California, San Diego.

———. 1987. "The Mexican Communist Party and Agrarian Mobilization in the Laguna, 1920–1940: A Worker-Peasant Alliance?" *Hispanic American Historical Review* 67 (3): 371–404.

———. 1991. "Labor and the Political Left in Mexico." In *Unions, Workers, and the State in Mexico,* edited by Kevin J. Middlebrook. La Jolla: Center for U.S.-Mexican Studies, University of California, San Diego.

———. 1992. *Marxism and Communism in Twentieth-Century Mexico.* Lincoln: University of Nebraska Press.

Carrera Stampa, Manuel. 1954. *Los gremios mexicanos: La organización gremial en Nueva España, 1521–1861.* Mexico City: Ibero Americana de Publicaciones.

Carrillo V., Jorge. 1991. "The Evolution of the *Maquiladora* Industry: Labor Relations in a New Context." In *Unions, Workers, and the State in Mexico,* edited by Kevin J. Middlebrook. La Jolla: Center for U.S.-Mexican Studies, University of California, San Diego.

———. 1991. "Restructuración en la industria automotriz en México." *Estudios Sociológicos* 9 (Sept.–Dec.): 483–525.

Carrillo V., Jorge, and Patricia García. 1987. "Etapas industriales y conflictos laborales: La industria automotriz en México." *Estudios Sociológicos* 5 (May–Aug.): 303–40.

Carstens, Catherine Mansell. 1993. "How to Get a Leg Up—and a Foot in the Door." *Hemisfile* 4 (Mar.–Apr.): 3–4.

Casar, Ma. Amparo. 1982. "El proyecto del movimiento obrero organizado en la LI legislatura." *Estudios Políticos,* n.s., 1 (Oct.–Dec.): 33–45.

Cedillo Vázquez, Luciano. 1963. *De Juan Soldado a Juan Rielero: El pueblo lucha.* Mexico City: Publicaciones Mexicanas.

———. 1979. *¡Vaaamonos! Luchas, anécdotas y problemas de los ferrocarrileros.* Mexico City: Ediciones de Cultura Popular.

Centro de Estudios Históricos del Movimiento Obrero Mexicano. 1980. "La Junta

Central de Conciliación y Arbitraje." *Historia Obrera* 5 (May): 15–16.
Ceteme (Mexico City).
Chassen de López, Francie R. 1977. *Lombardo Toledano y el movimiento obrero mexicano, 1917–1940.* Mexico City: Editorial Extemporáneos.
Clack, Garfield. 1967. *Industrial Relations in a British Car Factory.* Department of Applied Economics, University of Cambridge, Occasional Papers 9. Cambridge: University of Cambridge.
Clark, Marjorie Ruth. 1934. *Organized Labor in Mexico.* Chapel Hill: University of North Carolina Press.
Coleman, Kenneth M., and Charles L. Davis. 1983. "Preemptive Reform and the Mexican Working Class." *Latin American Research Review* 18 (1): 3–31.
Collier, David, ed. 1979. *The New Authoritarianism in Latin America.* Princeton: Princeton University Press.
Collier, Ruth Berins. 1992. *The Contradictory Alliance: State-Labor Relations and Regime Change in Mexico.* Berkeley: International and Area Studies, University of California, Berkeley.
Collier, Ruth Berins, and David Collier. 1979. "Inducements versus Constraints: Disaggregating 'Corporatism.'" *American Political Science Review* 73 (4): 967–86.
———. 1991. *Shaping the Political Arena: Critical Junctures, the Labor Movement, and Regime Dynamics in Latin America.* Princeton: Princeton University Press.
Comisión Nacional del Salario Mínimo. 1934. *Memoria de la Comisión Nacional del Salario Mínimo.* Mexico City: Comisión Nacional del Salario Mínimo.
Comité de Observadores Independientes. 1991. "Recuento sindical en Ford Motor Company." *La Otra Cara de México* 21 (May–June): 4–5.
Confederación de Trabajadores de México. 1937. *Informe del comité nacional, 1936–1937.* Mexico City: N.p.
———. 1941. *C.T.M., 1936–1941.* Mexico City: Talleres Gráficos Modelo.
———. 1953. *Memoria de la Asamblea Nacional del Salario Mínimo.* Mexico City: N.p.
———. 1968. "Ante-proyecto de Ley Federal del Trabajo." Mexico City. Mimeographed.
———. 1978. *Memoria: Reunión nacional para la reforma económica.* Mexico City: N.p.
Confederación Patronal de la República Mexicana. 1989. "Propuestas preliminares que la Confederación Patronal de la República Mexicana presenta para la discusión del anteproyecto de una nueva Ley Federal del Trabajo." Mexico City. Mimeographed.
Connor, Walter D. 1991. *The Accidental Proletariat: Workers, Politics, and Crisis in Gorbachev's Russia.* Princeton: Princeton University Press.
———. 1994. "Labor Politics in Post-Communist Russia: A Preliminary Assessment." In *The Social Legacy of Communism,* edited by James R. Miller and Sharon L. Wolchik. Cambridge: Cambridge University Press.

Contreras, José Ariel. 1977. *México, 1940: Industrialización y crisis política.* Mexico City: Siglo Veintiuno Editores.

Contreras Suárez, Enrique, and Gilberto Silva Ruiz. 1972. "Los recientes movimientos obreros mexicanos pro-democracia sindical y el reformismo obrero." *Revista Mexicana de Sociología* 34 (3–4): 845–79.

Cook, Linda J. 1993. "Russia's Labor Relations: Consolidation or Disintegration?" Department of Political Science, Brown University. Mimeographed.

———. 1993. *The Soviet Social Contract and Why It Failed: Welfare Policy and Workers' Politics from Brezhnev to Yeltsin.* Cambridge: Harvard University Press.

———. 1993. "State-Labor Relations and the Soviet Collapse." Department of Political Science, Brown University. Mimeographed.

Cook, Maria Lorena. 1991. "Restructuring and Democracy in Mexico: Twenty Years of Trade Union Strategies, 1970–1990." Paper presented at the International Congress of the Latin American Studies Association, April, Washington, D.C.

———. 1993. "Organizing Dissent: Unions, the State, and the Democratic Teachers' Movement in Mexico." School of Industrial and Labor Relations, Cornell University. Typescript.

———. 1995. "Mexican State-Labor Relations and the Political Implications of Free Trade." *Latin American Perspectives* 22 (1): 77–94.

Córdova, Arnaldo. 1973. *La ideología de la revolución mexicana: La formación del nuevo régimen.* Mexico City: Ediciones Era.

———. 1974. *La política de masas del cardenismo.* Mexico City: Ediciones Era.

———. 1980. *En una época de crisis, 1928–1934.* Vol. 9 of *La clase obrera en la historia de México,* edited by Pablo González Casanova. Mexico City: Siglo Veintiuno Editores.

Cornelius, Wayne A. 1973. "Nation Building, Participation, and Distribution: The Politics of Social Reform under Cárdenas." In *Crisis, Choice, and Change: Historical Studies of Political Development,* edited by Gabriel A. Almond, Scott C. Flanagan, and Robert J. Mundt. Boston: Little, Brown.

———. 1993. "Mexico's Incomplete Democratic Transition." Paper presented at the annual meeting of the International Studies Association, March, Acapulco, Mexico.

Cortés A., Guadalupe. 1984. "Golpe al movimiento ferrocarrilero, 1948." In *Las derrotas obreras, 1946–1952,* edited by Víctor Manuel Durand Ponte. Mexico City: Instituto de Investigaciones Sociales, Universidad Nacional Autónoma de México.

Cosío Villegas, Daniel. 1976. *El sistema político mexicano.* Mexico City: Cuadernos de Joaquín Mortiz.

Cuarto Congreso Ferrocarrilero. 1932. "Libro de actas." Mexico City: N.p.

Cuéllar Vázquez, Angélica. 1984. "Golpe al Sindicato de Trabajadores Petroleros de la República Mexicana (STPRM), en 1949." In *Las derrotas obreras, 1946–1952,* edited by Víctor Manuel Durand Ponte. Mexico City: Instituto de Investigaciones Sociales, Universidad Nacional Autónoma de México.

Davis, Charles L. 1989. *Working-Class Mobilization and Political Control: Venezuela and Mexico.* Lexington: University Press of Kentucky.

Davis, Charles L., and Kenneth M. Coleman. 1986. "Labor and the State: Union Incorporation and Working-Class Politicization in Latin America." *Comparative Political Studies* 18 (4): 395–417.

de Buen L., Néstor. 1992. *Derecho del trabajo.* 2 vols. Mexico City: Editorial Porrúa.

———. 1992. Interview with author. Mexico City, 8 Dec.

de la Cerda Silva, Roberto. 1961. *El movimiento obrero en México.* Mexico City: Instituto de Investigaciones Sociales, Universidad Nacional Autónoma de México.

de la Cueva, Mario. 1964. *Derecho mexicano del trabajo.* 2 vols. Mexico City: Editorial Porrúa.

———. 1977–79. *El nuevo derecho mexicano del trabajo.* 2 vols. Mexico City: Editorial Porrúa.

———. 1978. Interviews with author. Mexico City, 11 Jan. and 28 Apr.

de la Garza Toledo, Enrique. 1991. "Independent Trade Unionism in Mexico: Past Developments and Future Perspectives." In *Unions, Workers, and the State in Mexico,* edited by Kevin J. Middlebrook. La Jolla: Center for U.S.-Mexican Studies, University of California, San Diego.

———. 1993. *Reestructuración productiva y respuesta sindical en México.* Mexico City: Universidad Nacional Autónoma de México and Universidad Autónoma Metropolitana.

———. 1994. "The Restructuring of State-Labor Relations in Mexico." In *The Politics of Economic Restructuring: State-Society Relations and Regime Change in Mexico,* edited by Maria Lorena Cook, Kevin J. Middlebrook, and Juan Molinar Horcasitas. La Jolla: Center for U.S.-Mexican Studies, University of California, San Diego.

de la Peña, Moisés T. 1937. "La expropiación de los Ferrocarriles Nacionales de México." *El Trimestre Económico* 4:195–226.

Departamento Autónomo del Trabajo. *Memoria de labores,* various years. Mexico City.

Dexter, Lewis A. 1970. *Elite and Specialized Interviewing.* Evanston, Ill.: Northwestern University Press.

Día, El (Mexico City).

Diario Oficial de la Federación (Mexico City).

Díaz, María Elena. 1990. "The Satiric Penny Press for Workers in Mexico, 1900–1910: A Case Study in the Politicisation of Popular Culture." *Journal of Latin American Studies* 22 (Oct.): 497–526.

Dix, Robert H. 1967. *Colombia: The Political Dimensions of Change.* New Haven: Yale University Press.

Dohse, Knuth, Ulrich Jürgens, and Thomas Malsch. 1985. "From 'Fordism' to 'Toyotism'? The Social Organization of the Labor Process in the Japanese Automobile Industry." *Politics and Society* 14 (2): 115–46.

Dombois, Rainer. 1985. "La producción automotriz y el mercado del trabajo en un país en desarrollo: Un estudio sobre la industria automotriz mexicana." Research paper 85–206, International Institute for Comparative Social Research/ Labor Policy, Berlin.

————. 1986. "La producción automotriz y el mercado del trabajo en un país en desarrollo: Los mercados internos del trabajo y las relaciones industriales." Research paper 86–216, International Institute for Comparative Social Research/ Labor Policy, Berlin.

Domínguez, Jorge I. 1982. Introduction to *Mexico's Political Economy: Challenges at Home and Abroad*, edited by Jorge I. Domínguez. Beverly Hills, Calif.: Sage Publications.

Dulles, John W. F. 1961. *Yesterday in Mexico: A Chronicle of the Revolution, 1919–1936*. Austin: University of Texas Press.

Dunlop, John T. [1958] 1971. *Industrial Relations Systems*. Reprint, Carbondale: Southern Illinois University Press.

Durán, Leonel, ed. 1972. *Lázaro Cárdenas: Ideario político*. Mexico City: Ediciones Era.

Durand Ponte, Víctor Manuel. 1984. "Relaciones entre estructura y coyuntura en el análisis del movimiento obrero." In *Las derrotas obreras, 1946–1952*, edited by Víctor Manuel Durand Ponte. Mexico City: Instituto de Investigaciones Sociales, Universidad Nacional Autónoma de México.

————. 1986. *La ruptura de la nación: Historia del movimiento obrero mexicano desde 1938 hasta 1952*. Mexico City: Instituto de Investigaciones Sociales, Universidad Nacional Autónoma de México.

————. 1990. "Corporativismo obrero y democracia." *Revista Mexicana de Sociología* 52 (3): 97–110.

————. 1991. "The Confederation of Mexican Workers, the Labor Congress, and the Crisis of Mexico's Social Pact." In *Unions, Workers, and the State in Mexico*, edited by Kevin J. Middlebrook. La Jolla: Center for U.S.-Mexican Studies, University of California, San Diego.

Ebel, Karl-H. 1985. "Social and Labour Implications of Flexible Manufacturing Systems." *International Labour Review* 124 (2): 133–45.

Ebergenyi Magaloni, Ingrid. 1986. *Primera aproximación al estudio del sindicalismo ferrocarrilero en México, 1917–1936*. Mexico City: Instituto Nacional de Antropología e Historia.

Eckstein, Harry. 1975. "Case Study and Theory in Political Science." In *Strategies of Inquiry*. Vol. 7 of *Handbook of Political Science*, edited by Fred I. Greenstein and Nelson W. Polsby. Reading, Mass.: Addison-Wesley Publishing Company.

Economist (London).

Edelstein, J. David, and Malcolm Warner. 1976. *Comparative Union Democracy: Organization and Opposition in British and American Unions*. New York: John Wiley & Sons.

Epstein, Edward C. 1979. "Control and Co-optation of the Argentine Labor Movement." *Economic Development and Cultural Change* 27 (3): 445–65.

Erickson, Kenneth Paul. 1977. *The Brazilian Corporative State and Working-Class Politics*. Berkeley and Los Angeles: University of California Press.

Erickson, Kenneth Paul, and Kevin J. Middlebrook. 1982. "The State and Organized Labor in Brazil and Mexico." In *Brazil and Mexico: Patterns in Late
Development,* edited by Sylvia A. Hewlett and Richard S. Weinert. Philadelphia: Institute for the Study of Human Issues.

Evans, Peter B., and Dietrich Rueschemeyer. 1985. "The State and Economic Transformation: Toward an Analysis of the Conditions Underlying Effective Intervention." In *Bringing the State Back In,* edited by Peter B. Evans, Dietrich
Rueschemeyer, and Theda Skocpol. Cambridge: Cambridge University Press.

Everett, Michael David. 1967. "The Role of the Mexican Trade Unions, 1950–1963."
Ph.D. diss., Department of Economics, Washington University.

Excélsior (Mexico City).

Fagen, Richard R., and William S. Tuohy. 1972. *Politics and Privilege in a Mexican
City.* Stanford: Stanford University Press.

Fajardo Ortiz, Sergio. 1955. "El movimiento sindical y la cláusula de exclusión."
Lic. thesis, Facultad de Derecho y Ciencias Sociales, Universidad Nacional
Autónoma de México, Mexico City.

Faunce, William A. 1958. "Automation in the Automobile Industry: Some Consequences for In-Plant Social Structure." *American Sociological Review* 23 (4):
401–7.

Federación de Trabajadores del Distrito Federal. 1968. "Proposiciones del Congreso del Trabajo en relación al anteproyecto de la Ley Federal del Trabajo
que presentará la comisión redactora adscrita a la Secretaría del Trabajo y
Previsión Social." Mexico City.

Felix, David. 1982. "Income Distribution Trends in Mexico and the Kuznets
Curves." In *Brazil and Mexico: Patterns in Late Development,* edited by
Sylvia Ann Hewlett and Richard S. Weinert. Philadelphia: Institute for the
Study of Human Issues.

Fernández Christlieb, Paulina, and Octavio Rodríguez Araujo. 1985. *En el sexenio
de Tlatelolco, 1964–1970.* Vol. 13 of *La clase obrera en la historia de México,*
edited by Pablo González Casanova. Mexico City: Siglo Veintiuno Editores.

Ferrocarriles Nacionales de México. 1952. *Cien años de ferrocarriles.* Mexico City.

Ferronales (Mexico City).

Financiero, El (Mexico City).

Fojo de Diego, Ángel. 1973. "Estudio de un conflicto industrial: El caso Auto-
mex." Centro de Estudios Sociológicos, El Colegio de México, Mexico City.
Mimeographed.

Franco G. S., José Fernando. 1987. "El papel del derecho del trabajo y el movimiento obrero en México." Paper presented at the Center for U.S.-Mexican
Studies, University of California, San Diego.

———. 1991. "Labor Law and the Labor Movement in Mexico." In *Unions,
Workers, and the State in Mexico,* edited by Kevin J. Middlebrook. La Jolla:
Center for U.S.-Mexican Studies, University of California, San Diego.

French, John D. 1992. *The Brazilian Workers' ABC: Class Conflict and Alliances
in Modern São Paulo.* Chapel Hill: University of North Carolina Press.

Fuentes Díaz, Vicente. 1951. *El problema ferrocarrilero de México*. Mexico City: N.p.

——. 1954. *Los partidos políticos en México*. 2 vols. Mexico City: N.p.

——. 1959. "Desarrollo y evolución del movimiento obrero a partir de 1929." *Ciencias Políticas y Sociales* 17: 325–48.

Fullan, Michael. 1970. "Industrial Technology and Worker Integration in the Organization." *American Sociological Review* 35 (6): 1028–39.

Furtak, Robert K. 1978. *El partido de la revolución y la estabilidad política en México*. Mexico City: Facultad de Ciencias Políticas y Sociales, Universidad Nacional Autónoma de México.

Gaitán Riveros, María Mercedes. 1984. "El movimiento minero, 1950–1951." In *Las derrotas obreras, 1946–1952*, edited by Víctor Manuel Durand Ponte. Mexico City: Instituto de Investigaciones Sociales, Universidad Nacional Autónoma de México.

Galindo, Magdalena. 1977. "El movimiento obrero en el sexenio echeverrista." *Investigación Económica* 4:97–127.

Gamboa Ojeda, Leticia. 1980. "La CROM en Puebla y el movimiento obrero textil en los años 20." In vol. 2 of *Memorias del encuentro sobre historia del movimiento obrero*, edited by Centro de Investigaciones Históricas del Movimiento Obrero. Puebla: Universidad Autónoma de Puebla.

Garavito Elías, Rosa Albina. 1990. "Así les fue a los trabajadores." In *México en la decada de los ochenta: La modernización en cifras*, edited by Rosa Albina Garavito and Augusto Bolívar. Mexico City: Universidad Autónoma Metropolitana–Azcapotzalco.

Garrido, Luis Javier. 1982. *El partido de la revolución institucionalizada: La formación del nuevo estado en México, 1928–1945*. Mexico City: Siglo Veintiuno Editores.

Gill, Mario. 1971. *Los ferrocarrileros*. Mexico City: Editorial Extemporáneos.

Gómez Tagle, Silvia, and Marcelo Miquet Fleury. 1976. "Integración o democracia sindical: El caso de los electricistas." In *Tres estudios sobre el movimiento obrero en México*, edited by José Luis Reyna, Francisco Zapata, Marcelo Miquet Fleury, and Silvia Gómez Tagle. Mexico City: El Colegio de México.

Gómez Z., Luis. 1979. *Sucesos y remembranzas*. 2 vols. Mexico City: Editorial Secapsa.

González Casanova, Pablo. 1976. *La democracia en México*. 8th ed. Mexico City: Ediciones Era.

——. 1980. *En el primer gobierno constitucional, 1917–1920*. Vol. 6 of *La clase obrera en la historia de México*, edited by Pablo González Casanova. Mexico City: Siglo Veintiuno Editores.

Goodspeed, Stephen S. 1955. "El papel del jefe del ejecutivo en México." *Problemas Agrícolas e Industriales de México* 7 (1): 13–218.

Grayson, George W. 1989. *The Mexican Labor Machine: Power, Politics, and Patronage*. Washington, D.C.: Center for Strategic and International Studies.

Gregory, David. 1986. *The Myth of Market Failure: Employment and the Labor Market in Mexico*. Baltimore: Johns Hopkins University Press.

Gruening, Ernest. 1928. *Mexico and Its Heritage.* New York: Century Company.

Guadarrama, Rocío. 1981. *Los sindicatos y la política en México: La CROM, 1918–1928.* Mexico City: Ediciones Era.

Guerrero Tapia, José. 1987. *Y después de mí, ¿quién?* Mexico City: Editorial Scorpio.

Gutiérrez G., César. 1988. "Grupos sindicales y división interna en la Federación de Trabajadores de Nuevo León (CTM), 1936–1942." In *La CTM en los estados,* edited by Centro de Estudios del Movimiento Obrero y Socialista. Culiacán: Universidad Autónoma de Sinaloa.

Gutiérrez Garza, Esthela, ed. 1989. *Reconversión industrial y lucha sindical.* Mexico City: Editorial Nueva Sociedad.

Haber, Stephen H. 1989. *Industry and Underdevelopment: The Industrialization of Mexico, 1890–1940.* Stanford: Stanford University Press.

Hale, Charles A. 1989. *The Transformation of Liberalism in Late Nineteenth-Century Mexico.* Princeton: Princeton University Press.

Hamilton, Nora. 1982. *The Limits of State Autonomy: Post-Revolutionary Mexico.* Princeton: Princeton University Press.

Hansen, Roger D. 1971. *The Politics of Mexican Development.* Baltimore: Johns Hopkins University Press.

Harrington, Christine B. 1985. *Shadow Justice: The Ideology and Institutionalization of Alternatives to Court.* Westport, Conn.: Greenwood Press.

Hart, John Mason. 1978. *Anarchism and the Mexican Working Class, 1860–1931.* Austin: University of Texas Press.

————. 1987. *Revolutionary Mexico: The Coming and Process of the Mexican Revolution.* Berkeley and Los Angeles: University of California Press.

Haworth, Nigel. 1989. "Political Transition and the Peruvian Labor Movement, 1968–1985." In *Labor Autonomy and the State in Latin America,* edited by Edward C. Epstein. Boston: Unwin Hyman.

Hemingway, John. 1978. *Conflict and Democracy: Studies in Trade Union Government.* Oxford: Clarendon Press.

Hernández, Salvador. 1980. "El magonismo en México: Cananea, Río Blanco y Baja California." In *De la dictadura porfirista a los tiempos libertarios,* by Ciro F. S. Cardoso, Francisco G. Hermosillo, and Salvador Hernández. Vol. 3 of *La clase obrera en la historia de México,* edited by Pablo González Casanova. Mexico City: Siglo Veintiuno Editores.

Hernández, Víctor. 1951. *Andanzas de un ferrocarrilero.* Guadalajara: Cooperativa de Ferrocarrileros Jesús García.

Hernández C., Benjamín. 1979. "Del pacto de sindicatos industriales a la represión: Enero a octubre de 1948." In vol. 2 of *Memoria del segundo coloquio regional de historia obrera,* edited by Centro de Estudios Históricos del Movimiento Obrero Mexicano. Mexico City: Centro de Estudios Históricos del Movimiento Obrero Mexicano.

Hernández Chávez, Alicia. 1979. *La mecánica cardenista.* Vol. 16 of *Historia de la revolución mexicana,* El Colegio de México. Mexico City: El Colegio de México.

Hirschman, Albert O. 1968. "The Political Economy of Import-Substituting Industrialization in Latin America." *Quarterly Journal of Economics* 82 (1): 1–32.

Huitrón, Jacinto. 1974. *Orígenes e historia del movimiento obrero en México.* Mexico City: Editores Mexicanos Unidos.

Humphrey, John. 1982. *Capitalist Control and Workers' Struggle in the Brazilian Auto Industry.* Princeton: Princeton University Press.

Huntington, Samuel P. 1968. *Political Order in Changing Societies.* New Haven: Yale University Press.

———. 1970. "Social and Institutional Dynamics of One-Party Systems." In *Authoritarian Politics in Modern Society: The Dynamics of Established One-Party Systems,* edited by Samuel P. Huntington and Clement H. Moore. New York: Basic Books.

Instituto Nacional de Estadística, Geografía e Informática. 1985. *Estadísticas históricas de México.* 2 vols. Mexico City: Secretaría de Programación y Presupuesto.

Instituto Nacional de Estudios Históricos de la Revolución Mexicana. 1986. *La constitución de la Confederación de Trabajadores de México.* Mexico City: Talleres Gráficos de la Nación.

Jenkins, Rhys. 1987. *Transnational Corporations and the Latin American Automobile Industry.* Pittsburgh: University of Pittsburgh Press.

Jornada, La (Mexico City).

Justicia Social (Mexico City).

Katz, Friedrich. 1981. *The Secret War in Mexico: Europe, the United States, and the Mexican Revolution.* Chicago: University of Chicago Press.

———. 1986. "Mexico: Restored Republic and Porfiriato, 1867–1910." In *The Cambridge History of Latin America,* edited by Leslie Bethell, vol. 5. Cambridge: Cambridge University Press.

Kaufman, Robert R. 1977. "Mexico and Latin American Authoritarianism." In *Authoritarianism in Mexico,* edited by José Luis Reyna and Richard S. Weinert. Philadelphia: Institute for the Study of Human Issues.

———. 1988. *The Politics of Debt in Argentina, Brazil, and Mexico: Economic Stabilization in the 1980s.* Berkeley: Institute of International Studies, University of California, Berkeley.

Keck, Margaret E. 1989. "The New Unionism in the Brazilian Transition." In *Democratizing Brazil: Problems of Transition and Consolidation,* edited by Alfred Stepan. New York: Oxford University Press.

Kenney, Martin, and Richard Florida. 1988. "Beyond Mass Production: Production and the Labor Process in Japan." *Politics and Society* 16 (Mar.): 121–58.

Kerr, Clark, John T. Dunlop, Frederick H. Harbison, and Charles A. Myers. 1960. *Industrialism and Industrial Man: The Problems of Labor and Management in Industrial Growth.* Cambridge: Harvard University Press.

Kerr, Clark, and Abraham Siegel. 1954. "The Interindustry Propensity to Strike—An International Comparison." In *Industrial Conflict,* edited by Arthur Kornhauser, Robert Dubin, and Arthur M. Ross. New York: McGraw-Hill.

King, Timothy. 1970. *Mexico: Industrialization and Trade Policies since 1940.* London: Oxford University Press.

Knight, Alan. 1984. "The Working Class and the Mexican Revolution, c. 1900–1920." *Journal of Latin American Studies* 16 (May): 51–79.

———. 1985. "The Mexican Revolution: Bourgeois? Nationalist? Or Just a 'Great Rebellion'?" *Bulletin of Latin American Research* 4 (2): 1–37.

———. 1986. *The Mexican Revolution.* 2 vols. Cambridge: Cambridge University Press.

———. 1987. *U.S.-Mexican Relations, 1910–1940: An Interpretation.* La Jolla: Center for U.S.-Mexican Studies, University of California, San Diego.

———. 1992. "The Peculiarities of Mexican History: Mexico Compared to Latin America, 1821–1992." *Journal of Latin American Studies* 24 (Quincentenary Supplement): 99–144.

Korzeniewicz, Roberto P. 1993. "Labor Unrest in Argentina, 1930–1943." *Latin American Research Review* 28 (1): 7–40.

Krasner, Stephen D. 1982. "Structural Causes and Regime Consequences: Regimes as Intervening Variables." *International Organization* 36 (2): 185–205.

Kronish, Rich, and Kenneth S. Mericle, eds. 1984. *The Political Economy of the Latin American Motor Vehicle Industry.* Cambridge: MIT Press.

La Botz, Dan. 1992. *Mask of Democracy: Labor Suppression in Mexico Today.* Boston: South End Press.

Lajous Vargas, Alejandra. 1979. *Los orígenes del partido único en México.* Mexico City: Instituto de Investigaciones Históricas, Universidad Nacional Autónoma de México.

Latin American Weekly Report (London).

Leal, Juan Felipe. 1985. "Las estructuras sindicales." In *Organización y sindicalismo.* Vol. 3 of *El obrero mexicano,* edited by Pablo González Casanova, Samuel León González, and Ignacio Marván. Mexico City: Siglo Veintiuno Editores.

Leal, Juan Felipe, and Fernando Talavera. 1977. "Organizaciones sindicales obreras de México, 1948–1970: Enfoque estadístico." *Revista Mexicana de Sociología* 39 (4): 1251–86.

Leal, Juan Felipe, and José Villaseñor. 1988. *En la revolución, 1910–1917.* Vol. 5 of *La clase obrera en la historia de México,* edited by Pablo González Casanova. Mexico City: Siglo Veintiuno Editores.

Leal, Juan Felipe, and José Woldenberg. 1980. *Del estado liberal a los inicios de la dictadura porfirista.* Vol. 2 of *La clase obrera en la historia de México,* edited by Pablo González Casanova. Mexico City: Siglo Veintiuno Editores.

Lear, John Robert. 1993. "Workers, *Vecinos,* and Citizens: The Revolution in Mexico City, 1909–1917." Ph.D. diss., Department of History, University of California, Berkeley.

León González, Samuel. 1986. Introduction to *La constitución de la Confederación de Trabajadores de México,* Instituto Nacional de Estudios Históricos de la Revolución Mexicana. Mexico City: Talleres Gráficos de la Nación.

León González, Samuel, and Ignacio Marván. 1985. *En el cardenismo, 1934–1940.*

Vol. 10 of *La clase obrera en la historia de México,* edited by Pablo González Casanova. Mexico City: Siglo Veintiuno Editores.

Levy, Daniel, and Gabriel Székely. 1987. *Mexico: Paradoxes of Stability and Change.* 2nd ed. Boulder, Colo.: Westview Press.

Lewis, Arthur W. 1954. "Economic Development with Unlimited Supplies of Labour." *Manchester School of Economic and Social Studies* 22 (2): 139–91.

Lieuwin, Edwin. 1968. *Mexican Militarism: The Political Rise and Fall of the Revolutionary Army.* Albuquerque: University of New Mexico Press.

Linz, Juan J. 1964. "An Authoritarian Regime: Spain." In *Cleavages, Ideologies, and Party Systems,* edited by Erik Allard and Yrjö Littunen. Helsinki: Transactions of the Westermarck Society.

———. 1975. "Totalitarian and Authoritarian Regimes." In *Macropolitical Theory.* Vol. 3 of *Handbook of Political Science,* edited by Fred I. Greenstein and Nelson W. Polsby. Reading, Mass.: Addison-Wesley Publishing Company.

Liphart, Arend. 1971. "Comparative Politics and the Comparative Method." *American Political Science Review* 65 (3): 682–93.

Lipset, Seymour Martin, Martin Trow, and James Coleman. 1956. *Union Democracy.* Glencoe, Ill.: Free Press.

Lombardo Toledano, Vicente. [1927] 1974. *La libertad sindical en México (1926).* Reprint, Mexico City: Universidad Obrera de México "Vicente Lombardo Toledano."

López Aparicio, Alfonso. 1952. *El movimiento obrero en México.* Mexico City: Editorial Jus.

López de la Cerda, Coral, and José Othón Quiroz Trejo. 1981. "La huelga de la General Motors, 1980." *Teoría y Política* 2 (6): 91–106.

López Villegas-Manjarrez, Virginia. 1983. *La CTM versus las organizaciones obreras.* Mexico City: Ediciones El Caballito.

Lovera, Sara. 1992. "Las reformas a la Ley Federal del Trabajo." *La Jornada Laboral,* 31 Jan.

Loyola Díaz, Rafael. 1980. *Conflictos laborales en México, 1928–1929.* Mexico City: Instituto de Investigaciones Sociales, Universidad Nacional Autónoma de México.

———. 1991. *El ocaso del radicalismo revolucionario: Ferrocarrileros y petroleros, 1938–1947.* Mexico City: Instituto de Investigaciones Sociales, Universidad Nacional Autónoma de México.

Lustig, Nora. 1992. *Mexico: The Remaking of an Economy.* Washington, D.C.: Brookings Institution.

Malloy, James M. 1977. "Authoritarianism and Corporatism in Latin America: The Modal Pattern." In *Authoritarianism and Corporatism in Latin America,* edited by James M. Malloy. Pittsburgh: University of Pittsburgh Press.

Malpica Uribe, David. 1980. "Las Juntas de Conciliación y Arbitraje en Puebla, 1931–1940." In vol. 2 of *Memorias del encuentro sobre historia del movimiento obrero,* edited by Centro de Investigaciones Históricas del Movimiento Obrero. Puebla: Universidad Autónoma de Puebla.

Mann, Michael. 1988. *States, War, and Capitalism: Studies in Political Sociology.* Oxford: Basil Blackwell.

Manzetti, Luigi, and Marco Dell'Aquila. 1988. "Economic Stabilisation in Argentina: The Austral Plan." *Journal of Latin American Studies* 20 (1): 1–26.

Marks, Gary. 1989. *Unions in Politics: Britain, Germany, and the United States in the Nineteenth and Early Twentieth Centuries.* Princeton: Princeton University Press.

Márquez Fuentes, Manuel, and Octavio Rodríguez Araujo. 1973. *El Partido Comunista Mexicano (en el período de la Internacional Comunista, 1919–1943).* Mexico City: Ediciones El Caballito.

Martin, Roderick. 1968. "Union Democracy: An Explanatory Framework." *Sociology* 2 (2): 205–20.

Martínez Baez, Antonio. 1992. Interview with author. Mexico City, 22 June.

Marván L., Ignacio. 1985. "El proyecto nacional de las organizaciones obreras." In *La política y la cultura.* Vol. 5 of *El obrero mexicano,* edited by Pablo González Casanova, Samuel León González, and Ignacio Marván. Mexico City: Siglo Veintiuno Editores.

McCoy, Jennifer L. 1989. "Labor and the State in a Party-Mediated Democracy: Institutional Change in Venezuela." *Latin American Research Review* 24 (2): 35–67.

McPherson, William Heston. 1940. *Labor Relations in the Automobile Industry.* Washington, D.C.: Brookings Institution.

Medin, Tzvi. 1982. *El minimato presidencial: Historia política del maximato, 1928–1935.* Mexico City: Ediciones Era.

Medina, Luis. 1978. *Del cardenismo al avilacamachismo.* Vol. 18 of *Historia de la revolución mexicana,* El Colegio de México. Mexico City: El Colegio de México.

———. 1979. *Civilismo y modernización del autoritarismo.* Vol. 20 of *Historia de la revolución mexicana,* El Colegio de México. Mexico City: El Colegio de México.

Mejía Prieto, Jorge. 1980. *El poder tras de las gafas: Hacia un análisis del cetemismo y Fidel Velázquez.* Mexico City: Editorial Diana.

Méndez, Luis, and José Othón Quiroz. 1990. "Organización obrera: Nuevos rumbos, ¿nuevas perspectivas?" *El Cotidiano* 36 (July–Aug.): 47–56.

———. 1991. "El FAT: Autogestión obrera y modernidad." *El Cotidiano* 40 (Mar.–Apr.): 37–43.

———. 1993. "Productividad, respuesta obrera y sucesión presidencial." *El Cotidiano* 58 (Oct.–Nov.): 71–78.

Mercado de Valores, El (Nacional Financiera, S.A., Mexico City).

Mericle, Kenneth S. 1977. "Corporatist Control of the Working Class: Authoritarian Brazil since 1964." In *Authoritarianism and Corporatism in Latin America,* edited by James M. Malloy. Pittsburgh: University of Pittsburgh Press.

Mexico Journal (Mexico City).

Meyer, Jean. 1971. "Los obreros en la revolución mexicana: Los 'batallones rojos.' "
    Historia Mexicana 21 (1): 1–37.
———. 1977. *Estado y sociedad con Calles*. Vol. 11 of *Historia de la revolución
    mexicana*, El Colegio de México. Mexico City: El Colegio de México.
———. 1986. "Mexico: Revolution and Reconstruction in the 1920s." In *The Cam-
    bridge History of Latin America*, edited by Leslie Bethell, vol. 5. Cambridge:
    Cambridge University Press.
Meyers, Frederic. 1964. *Ownership of Jobs: A Comparative Study*. Los Angeles:
    Institute of Industrial Relations, University of California, Los Angeles.
———. 1979. *Mexican Industrial Relations from the Perspective of the Labor
    Court*. Los Angeles: Institute of Industrial Relations, University of California,
    Los Angeles.
Middlebrook, Kevin J. 1981. "Political Change and Political Reform in an Authori-
    tarian Regime: The Case of Mexico." Working Paper #103, Latin American
    Program of the Woodrow Wilson International Center for Scholars, Smith-
    sonian Institution, Washington, D.C.
———. 1982. "The Political Economy of Mexican Organized Labor, 1940–1978."
    Ph.D. diss., Department of Government, Harvard University.
———. 1986. "Political Liberalization in an Authoritarian Regime: The Case of
    Mexico." In *Latin America*. Pt. 2, *Transitions from Authoritarian Rule: Pros-
    pects for Democracy*, edited by Guillermo O'Donnell, Philippe C. Schmitter,
    and Laurence Whitehead. Baltimore: Johns Hopkins University Press.
———. 1988. "Dilemmas of Change in Mexican Politics." *World Politics* 41 (1):
    120–41.
———. 1989. "The Sounds of Silence: Organised Labour's Response to Economic
    Crisis in Mexico." *Journal of Latin American Studies* 21 (2): 195–220.
———. 1989. "Union Democratization in the Mexican Automobile Industry: A
    Reappraisal." *Latin American Research Review* 24 (2): 69–93.
———. 1990. "Reestructuración industrial y política sindical en la industria auto-
    motriz mexicana." In *La inserción de México en la cuenca del Pacífico*, edited
    by Alejandro Álvarez Béjar and John Borrego, vol. 2. Mexico City: Facultad
    de Economía, Universidad Nacional Autónoma de México.
———. 1991. "The Politics of Industrial Restructuring: Transnational Firms'
    Search for Flexible Production in the Mexican Automobile Industry." *Com-
    parative Politics* 23 (3): 275–97.
Miller, Richard Ulric. 1974. "American Railroad Unions and the National Railways
    of Mexico: An Exercise in Nineteenth-Century Proletarian Manifest Destiny."
    Labor History 15 (2): 239–60.
Millon, Robert P. 1964. *Lombardo: Biografía intelectual de un marxista mexicano*.
    Mexico City: Universidad Obrera de México "Vicente Lombardo Toledano."
Molina A., Daniel. 1977. "Notas sobre el estado y el movimiento obrero." *Cuader-
    nos Políticos* 12:69–88.
———. 1978. *La caravana del hambre*. Mexico City: Ediciones El Caballito.
Mondragón, Ana Laura. 1993. "Contratos-ley y sindicatos: Huleros y textileros."
    El Cotidiano 56 (July): 18–22.

Montiel, Yolanda. 1987. "Volkswagen: Un triunfo significativo." *La Jornada,* 28 Aug.

————. 1991. *Proceso de trabajo, acción sindical y nuevas tecnologías en Volkswagen de México.* Mexico City: Centro de Investigaciones y Estudios Superiores en Antropología Social.

————. 1992. "¿Una modernización con pies de barro?" *Avances de Investigación* (El Colegio de Puebla) 8, no. S-2 (Dec.): 47–62.

Moreno, Daniel. 1967. *El congreso constituyente de 1916–1917.* Mexico City: Coordinación de Humanidades, Universidad Nacional Autónoma de México.

Moreno Toscano, Alejandra. 1980. "Los trabajadores y el proyecto de la industrialización, 1810–1867." In *De la colonia al imperio,* by Enrique Florescano et al. Vol. 1 of *La clase obrera en la historia de México,* edited by Pablo González Casanova. Mexico City: Siglo Veintiuno Editores.

Mosk, Sanford A. [1950] 1975. *Industrial Revolution in Mexico.* Reprint, New York: Russell & Russell.

Navarrete, Alfredo. 1971. *Alto a la contrarrevolución.* Mexico City: Testimonios de Atlacomulco.

Needleman, Carolyn, and Martin Needleman. 1969. "Who Rules Mexico? A Critique of Some Current Views of the Mexican Political Process." *Journal of Politics* 31 (Nov.): 1011–34.

News (Mexico City).

New York Times.

Nie, Norman H., and Sidney Verba. 1975. "Political Participation." In *Nongovernmental Politics.* Vol. 4 of *Handbook of Political Science,* edited by Fred I. Greenstein and Nelson W. Polsby. Reading, Mass.: Addison-Wesley Publishing Company.

O'Donnell, Guillermo. 1977. "Corporatism and the Question of the State." In *Authoritarianism and Corporatism in Latin America,* edited by James M. Malloy. Pittsburgh: University of Pittsburgh Press.

————. 1986. "Introduction to the Latin American Cases." In *Latin America.* Pt. 2, *Transitions from Authoritarian Rule: Prospects for Democracy,* edited by Guillermo O'Donnell, Philippe C. Schmitter, and Laurence Whitehead. Baltimore: Johns Hopkins University Press.

————. 1988. *Bureaucratic Authoritarianism: Argentina, 1966–1973, in Comparative Perspective.* Berkeley and Los Angeles: University of California Press.

Olvera, Alberto J. 1992. "The Rise and Fall of Union Democracy in Poza Rica, 1932–1940." In *The Mexican Petroleum Industry in the Twentieth Century,* edited by Jonathan C. Brown and Alan Knight. Austin: University of Texas Press.

Ortega Aguirre, Maximino. 1977. "El movimiento ferrocarrilero, 1958–1974." Lic. thesis, Facultad de Ciencias Políticas y Sociales, Universidad Nacional Autónoma de México, Mexico City.

————. 1992. "La CROC y la política salarial." *La Jornada Laboral,* 25 June.

Ortega Arenas, Juan. 1977. Interviews with author. Mexico City, 30 Nov. and 2 Dec.

Ortiz Hernán, Sergio. 1974. *Los ferrocarriles de México: Una visión social y económica*. Mexico City: Secretaría de Comunicaciones y Transportes.

Oszlak, Oscar. 1981. "The Historical Formation of the State in Latin America: Some Theoretical and Methodological Guidelines for Its Study." *Latin American Research Review* 16 (2): 3–32.

Otra Cara de México, La (Mexico City).

Padgett, L. Vincent. 1976. *The Mexican Political System*. 2nd ed. Boston: Houghton Mifflin.

Palacios, Guillermo. 1977. "México en los años treinta." In *América Latina en los años treinta*, edited by Pablo González Casanova. Mexico City: Instituto de Investigaciones Sociales, Universidad Nacional Autónoma de México.

Parkes, Henry Bamford. 1950. *A History of Mexico*. Boston: Houghton Mifflin.

Partido Revolucionario Institucional. 1986. *CTM: Cincuenta años de lucha obrera*. 10 vols. Mexico City: Instituto de Capacitación Política, Partido Revolucionario Institucional.

Payne, Leigh A. 1991. "Working Class Strategies in the Transition to Democracy in Brazil." *Comparative Politics* 23 (2): 221–38.

Pellicer de Brody, Olga, and José Luis Reyna. 1978. *El afianzamiento de la estabilidad política*. Vol. 22 of *Historia de la revolución mexicana*, El Colegio de México. Mexico City: El Colegio de México.

Perlmutter, Amos. 1981. *Modern Authoritarianism: A Comparative Institutional Analysis*. New Haven: Yale University Press.

Pimentel González, Nuri, and Francisco Rueda Castillo. 1991. "Reforma del PRI: Entre la apertura económica y el proteccionismo político." *El Cotidiano* 39 (Jan.–Feb.): 26–31.

Piña, Isaac. 1952. "Las pérdidas de los F.F.C.C.N.N. en el transporte de minerales montan a 450 millones." *Ferronales*, 15 Oct.

Pino de la Rosa, Miguel Ángel. 1977. Interview with author. Mexico City, 26 Oct.

Popular, El (Mexico City).

Portes Gil, Emilio. 1954. *Quince años de política mexicana*. Mexico City: Ediciones Botas.

Portillo Ceballos, Jaime Rogelio. 1986. *La CTM: Orígenes y funciones dentro del sistema político mexicano*. Mexico City: Costa-Amic Editores.

Pozas, María de los Angeles. 1993. Interview with author. Monterrey, 17 June.

———. 1994. *Industrial Restructuring in Mexico: Corporate Adaptation, Technological Innovation, and Changing Patterns of Industrial Relations in Monterrey*. La Jolla: Center for U.S.-Mexican Studies, University of California, San Diego.

Pozzi, Pablo A. 1988. "Argentina, 1976–1982: Labour Leadership and Military Government." *Journal of Latin American Studies* 20 (1): 111–38.

Prewett, Virginia. 1941. *Reportage on Mexico*. New York: E. P. Dutton.

Pries, Ludger. 1992. "Contexto estructural y dinámica de acción en el conflicto de Volkswagen de México (1992): ¿Se logró una victoria pírrica o se cortó un nudo gordiano?" *Avances de Investigación* (El Colegio de Puebla) 8, no. S-2 (Dec.): 3–46.

Proceso (Mexico City).

Przeworski, Adam, and Henry Teune. 1970. *The Logic of Comparative Social Inquiry.* New York: John Wiley & Sons.

Punto Crítico (Mexico City).

Purcell, Susan Kaufman. 1975. *The Mexican Profit-Sharing Decision: Politics in an Authoritarian Regime.* Berkeley and Los Angeles: University of California Press.

Purcell, Susan Kaufman, and John F. H. Purcell. 1980. "State and Society in Mexico: Must a Stable Polity Be Institutionalized?" *World Politics* 32 (2): 194–227.

Quandt, Midge. 1993. *Unbinding the Ties: The Popular Organizations and the FSLN in Nicaragua.* Washington, D.C.: Nicaragua Network Education Fund.

Quintana, Miguel A., Jorge J. Crespo de la Serna, and Rafael Rosado Aragón. 1943. "Estudio sobre los Ferrocarriles Nacionales de México." Study prepared by the Comisión de Estudios Económicos y Sociales, Secretaría del Trabajo y Previsión Social, Mexico City.

Quintero Ramírez, Cirila. 1992. "Reestructuración sindical en las maquiladoras mexicanas, 1970–1990." Ph.D. diss., Centro de Estudios Sociológicos, El Colegio de México.

———. 1993. "Tendencias sindicales en la frontera norte de México." *El Cotidiano* 56 (July): 41–46.

Quiroz, José Othón. 1980. "Proceso de trabajo en la industria automotriz." *Cuadernos Políticos* 26:64–77.

Quiroz, José Othón, and Luis Méndez. 1992. "El conflicto de Volkswagen: Crónica de una muerte inesperada." *El Cotidiano* 51 (Nov.–Dec.): 81–91.

Remolina Roqueñi, Felipe. 1976. *Evolución de las instituciones y del derecho del trabajo en México.* Mexico City: Junta Federal de Conciliación y Arbitraje.

Retinger, J. H. 1926. *Morones of Mexico: A History of the Labour Movement in That Country.* London: Labour Publishing Company.

Reyes del Campillo, Juan. 1990. "El movimiento obrero en la Cámara de Diputados, 1979–1988." *Revista Mexicana de Sociología* 52 (3): 139–60.

Reyna, José Luis, and Raúl Trejo Delarbre. 1981. *De Adolfo Ruiz Cortines a Adolfo López Mateos, 1952–1964.* Vol. 12 of *La clase obrera en la historia de México,* edited by Pablo González Casanova. Mexico City: Siglo Veintiuno Editores.

Reynolds, Clark W. 1970. *The Mexican Economy: Twentieth-Century Structure and Growth.* New Haven: Yale University Press.

Rimlinger, Gaston. 1971. *Welfare Policy and Industrialization in Europe, America, and Russia.* New York: John Wiley & Sons.

Rivera Castro, José. 1983. *En la presidencia de Plutarco Elías Calles, 1924–1928.* Vol. 8 of *La clase obrera en la historia de México,* edited by Pablo González Casanova. Mexico City: Siglo Veintiuno Editores.

Rivera Flores, Antonio. 1984. "Unión General de Obreros y Campesinos de México." In *Las derrotas obreras, 1946–1952,* edited by Víctor Manuel Durand Ponte. Mexico City: Instituto de Investigaciones Sociales, Universidad Nacional Autónoma de México.

Rivera Marín, Guadalupe. 1955. *El mercado de trabajo: Relaciones obrero-patronales*. Mexico City: Fondo de Cultura Economica.

―――. 1963. "Movimiento obrero." In *México: Cincuenta años de revolución*, edited by Nacional Financiera, S.A. Mexico City: Nacional Financiera, S.A.

Rocha Bandala, Juan Francisco, and José Fernando Franco. 1975. *La competencia en materia laboral: Evolución*. Mexico City: Editorial Cárdenas.

Rodea, Marcelo N. 1944. *Historia del movimiento obrero ferrocarrilero*. Mexico City: N.p.

―――. 1988. "La huelga de 1926–1927." In *Cuatro sindicatos nacionales de industria*, edited by Centro de Estudios del Movimiento Obrero y Socialista. Culiacán: Universidad Autónoma de Sinaloa.

Rodríguez Guillén, Raúl, and Juan Mora Heredia. 1993. "El agotamiento del autoritarismo con legitimidad y la sucesión presidencial." *El Cotidiano* 58 (Oct.–Nov.): 22–28.

Romero Miranda, Miguel Ángel, Luis Méndez, and Augusto Bolívar Espinoza. 1993. "Muchos cambios legales que agitan las aguas políticas." *El Cotidiano* 58 (Oct.–Nov.): 60–70.

Romualdi, Serafino. 1967. *Presidents and Peons: Recollections of a Labor Ambassador in Latin America*. New York: Funk & Wagnalls.

Ronfeldt, David, ed. 1984. *The Modern Mexican Military: A Reassessment*. La Jolla: Center for U.S.-Mexican Studies, University of California, San Diego.

Ros, Jaime. 1986. "Mexico's Stabilisation and Adjustment Policies, 1982–1985." *Labour and Society* 11 (Sept.): 335–60.

―――. 1994. "Mexico in the 1990s: A New Economic Miracle? Some Notes on the Economic and Policy Legacy of the 1980s." In *The Politics of Economic Restructuring: State-Society Relations and Regime Change in Mexico*, edited by Maria Lorena Cook, Kevin J. Middlebrook, and Juan Molinar Horcasitas. La Jolla: Center for U.S.-Mexican Studies, University of California, San Diego.

Roxborough, Ian. 1984. *Unions and Politics in Mexico: The Case of the Automobile Industry*. Cambridge: Cambridge University Press.

―――. 1986. "The Mexican Charrazo of 1948: Latin American Labor from World War to Cold War." Working Paper #77, Helen Kellogg Institute for International Studies, University of Notre Dame.

―――. 1992. "Mexico." In *Latin America between the Second World War and the Cold War, 1944–1948*, edited by Leslie Bethell and Ian Roxborough. Cambridge: Cambridge University Press.

Roxborough, Ian, and Ilán Bizberg. 1983. "Union Locals in Mexico: The 'New Unionism' in Steel and Automobiles." *Journal of Latin American Studies* 15 (1): 117–35.

Rubin, Jeffrey W. 1990. "Popular Mobilization and the Myth of State Corporatism." In *Popular Movements and Political Change in Mexico*, edited by Joe Foweraker and Ann L. Craig. Boulder, Colo.: Lynne Rienner Publishers.

Ruble, Blair A. 1981. *Soviet Trade Unions: Their Development in the 1970s*. Cambridge: Cambridge University Press.

Rueschemeyer, Dietrich, Evelyne Huber Stephens, and John D. Stephens. 1992.

Capitalist Development and Democracy. Chicago: University of Chicago Press.

Ruiz, Ramón Eduardo. 1976. *Labor and the Ambivalent Revolutionaries: Mexico, 1911–1923.* Baltimore: Johns Hopkins University Press.

Sabel, Charles F. 1982. *Work and Politics: The Division of Labor in Industry.* Cambridge: Cambridge University Press.

Salazar, Rosendo. 1956. *La CTM: Su historia, su significado.* Mexico City: Ediciones T. C. Modelo.

——. 1956. *Historia de las luchas proletarias de México, 1930–1936.* Mexico City: N.p.

Salinas de Gortari, Carlos. 1991. *Tercer informe de gobierno, 1991.* Mexico City: Presidencia de la República.

——. 1992. *Cuarto informe de gobierno, 1992: Anexo.* Mexico City: Presidencia de la República.

——. 1992. Interview with author. Mexico City, 8 Dec.

——. 1993. *Quinto informe de gobierno, 1993: Anexo.* Mexico City: Presidencia de la República.

Sánchez Díaz, Sergio G. 1990. *El "nuevo" revisionismo en el sindicalismo "de izquierda" en México entre 1982 y 1988.* Mexico City: Centro de Investigaciones y Estudios Superiores en Antropología Social.

Sánchez González, Agustín. 1991. *Fidel: Una historia de poder.* Mexico City: Editorial Planeta Mexicana.

Saragoza, Alex M. 1988. *The Monterrey Elite and the Mexican State, 1880–1940.* Austin: University of Texas Press.

Schmidt, Henry C. 1978. *The Roots of Lo Mexicano: Self and Society in Mexican Thought, 1900–1934.* College Station: Texas A&M University Press.

Schmitter, Philippe C. 1971. *Interest Conflict and Political Change in Brazil.* Stanford: Stanford University Press.

——. 1974. "Still the Century of Corporatism?" In *The New Corporatism: Social-Political Structures in the Iberian World,* edited by Fredrick B. Pike and Thomas Stritch. Notre Dame, Ind.: University of Notre Dame Press.

Scott, Robert E. 1964. *Mexican Government in Transition.* Rev. ed. Urbana: University of Illinois Press.

Secretaría de Comunicaciones y Obras Públicas. *Memoria,* various years. Mexico City.

Secretaría de Comunicaciones y Obras Públicas, Departamento de Ferrocarriles en Explotación. *Estadística de los ferrocarriles y tranvías de concesión federal,* various years. Mexico City.

Secretaría de Comunicaciones y Transportes. *Memoria,* various years. Mexico City.

Secretaría de Gobernación. 1928. *Código Federal del Trabajo de los Estados Unidos Mexicanos (Proyecto).* Mexico City: Talleres Gráficos de la Nación.

Secretaría de Industria y Comercio, Dirección General de Estadística. *Anuario estadístico,* various years. Mexico City.

Secretaría de Industria, Comercio y Trabajo. 1928. *Del trabajo y la previsión social.* Vol. 3 of *La industria, el comercio y el trabajo en México durante la gestión administrativa del Señor Gral. Plutarco Elías Calles.* Mexico City: Tipográfico Galas.

———. 1929. *Proyecto de Código Federal de Trabajo para los Estados Unidos Mexicanos.* Mexico City: Talleres Gráficos de la Nación.

———. 1931. *Ley Federal del Trabajo.* Mexico City: Talleres Gráficos de la Nación.

———. 1931. *Proyecto de Ley Federal del Trabajo.* Mexico City: Talleres Gráficos de la Nación.

Secretaría de Industria, Comercio y Trabajo, Departamento del Trabajo. 1928. *Legislación del trabajo en los Estados Unidos Mexicanos.* Mexico City: Talleres Gráficos de la Nación.

Secretaría de Industria, Comercio y Trabajo, Junta Federal de Conciliación y Arbitraje. 1928. *Reglamento de las juntas federales de conciliación y arbitraje.* Mexico City: Talleres Gráficos de la Nación.

Secretaría de la Economía Nacional, Dirección General de Estadística. *Anuario estadístico,* various years. Mexico City.

Secretaría del Trabajo y Previsión Social. 1957. *Evolución histórica de la Secretaría del Trabajo y Previsión Social.* Mexico City: Talleres Gráficos de la Nación.

———. *Memoria de labores,* various years. Mexico City.

Shabot, Esther. 1982. *Los orígenes del sindicalismo ferrocarrilero.* Mexico City: Ediciones El Caballito.

Shafer, Robert J. 1973. *Mexican Business Organizations: History and Analysis.* Syracuse, N.Y.: Syracuse University Press.

Shaiken, Harley. 1988. Interview with author. Mexico City, 14 Oct.

———. 1993. "Myths about Mexican Workers." Democratic Study Center, DSC Report Series, Washington, D.C.

Shaiken, Harley, with Stephen Herzenberg. 1987. *Automation and Global Production in Mexico, the United States, and Canada.* La Jolla: Center for U.S.-Mexican Studies, University of California, San Diego.

Shaiken, Harley, Stephen Herzenberg, and Sarah Kuhn. 1986. "The Work Process under More Flexible Production." *Industrial Relations* 25 (2): 167–83.

Sheahan, John. 1991. *Conflict and Change in Mexican Economic Strategy: Implications for Mexico and for Latin America.* La Jolla: Center for U.S.-Mexican Studies, University of California, San Diego.

Sindicato de Trabajadores Ferrocarrileros de la República Mexicana. 1946. *Acuerdos tomados por la Sexta Gran Convención Ordinaria.* Mexico City: N.p.

———. 1946. *Estatutos del Sindicato de Trabajadores Ferrocarrileros de la República Mexicana aprobados por la Sexta Convención Ordinaria.* Mexico City: N.p.

———. 1947. *Acuerdos tomados por la Tercera Convención General Extraordinaria.* Mexico City: N.p.

———. 1949. *Estatutos aprobados por la Cuarta Convención General Extraordinaria.* Mexico City: N.p.

Skocpol, Theda. 1979. *States and Social Revolutions: A Comparative Analysis of France, Russia, and China.* Cambridge: Cambridge University Press.

Smith, Peter H. 1979. *Labyrinths of Power: Political Recruitment in Twentieth-Century Mexico*. Princeton: Princeton University Press.

Smith, Robert Freeman. 1972. *The United States and Revolutionary Nationalism in Mexico, 1916–1932*. Chicago: University of Chicago Press.

Solís, Leopoldo. 1977. *La realidad económica mexicana: Retrovisión y perspectivas*. 7th ed. Mexico City: Siglo Veintiuno Editores.

Solís, Vicente. 1992. "La modernización de Teléfonos de México." *El Cotidiano* 46 (Mar.–Apr.): 60–67.

Spalding, Hobart J., Jr. 1977. *Organized Labor in Latin America*. New York: New York University Press.

Stahler-Sholk, Richard. 1987. "Nicaragua." In *Latin American Labor Organizations*, edited by Gerald Michael Greenfield and Sheldon L. Maram. Westport, Conn.: Greenwood Press.

————. 1992. "Labor/Party/State Dynamics in Nicaragua: Union Responses to Austerity under the Sandinista and UNO Governments." Paper presented at the International Congress of the Latin American Studies Association, September, Los Angeles, California.

Stepan, Alfred. 1978. *The State and Society: Peru in Comparative Perspective*. Princeton: Princeton University Press.

Stevens, Evelyn P. 1970. "Legality and Extra-Legality in Mexico." *Journal of Inter-American Studies and World Affairs* 12 (Jan.): 62–75.

————. 1974. *Protest and Response in Mexico*. Cambridge: MIT Press.

Streeck, Wolfgang. 1987. "Industrial Relations and Industrial Change: The Restructuring of the World Automobile Industry in the 1970s and 1980s." *Economic and Industrial Democracy* 8 (4): 437–62.

Talavera Aldana, Luis Fernando. 1976. "Organizaciones sindicales obreras de la rama textil, 1935–1970." *Revista Mexicana de Ciencias Políticas y Sociales* 83: 227–99.

Talavera Aldana, Luis Fernando, and Juan Felipe Leal. 1977. "Organizaciones sindicales obreras de México, 1948–1970: Enfoque estadístico." *Revista Mexicana de Sociología* 39 (4): 1251–86.

Tamayo, Jaime. 1987. *En el interinato de Adolfo de la Huerta y el gobierno de Álvaro Obregón, 1920–1924*. Vol. 7 of *La clase obrera en la historia de México*, edited by Pablo González Casanova. Mexico City: Siglo Veintiuno Editores.

Tello, Carlos. 1979. *La política económica en México, 1970–1976*. Mexico City: Siglo Veintiuno Editores.

Thorp, Rosemary. 1992. "A Reappraisal of the Origins of Import-Substituting Industrialization, 1930–1950." *Journal of Latin American Studies* 24 (Quincentenary Supplement): 181–95.

Tiempo (Mexico City).

Trejo Delarbre, Raúl. 1978. "Cronología de la Tendencia Democrática, 1960–1978." *Siempre*, 4 Oct.

————. 1990. *Crónica del sindicalismo en México, 1976–1988*. Mexico City: Instituto de Investigaciones Sociales, Universidad Nacional Autónoma de México and Siglo Veintiuno Editores.

Trueba Urbina, Alberto. 1950. *Evolución de la huelga*. Mexico City: Ediciones Botas.

Trueba Urbina, Alberto, and Jorge Trueba Barrera. 1988. *Ley Federal del Trabajo*. 58th ed. Mexico City: Editorial Porrúa.

Tsunekawa, Keiichi. 1989. "Dependency and Labor Policy: The Case of the Mexican Automotive Industry." Ph.D. diss., Cornell University.

Turner, Frederick C. 1968. *The Dynamics of Mexican Nationalism*. Chapel Hill: University of North Carolina Press.

Tutino, John. 1986. *From Insurrection to Revolution in Mexico: Social Bases of Agrarian Violence, 1750–1940*. Princeton: Princeton University Press.

———. 1990. "Revolutionary Confrontation, 1913–1917: Regional Factions, Class Conflicts, and the National State." In *Provinces of the Revolution: Essays on Regional Mexican History, 1910–1929*, edited by Thomas Benjamin and Mark Wasserman. Albuquerque: University of New Mexico Press.

Ugalde, Antonio. 1970. *Power and Conflict in a Mexican Community: A Study of Political Integration*. Albuquerque: University of New Mexico Press.

Unificación Ferroviaria (Mexico City).

United Nations Economic Commission for Latin America and Nacional Financiera, S.A. 1971. "La política industrial en el desarrollo de México." Mexico City. Mimeographed.

Universal, El (Mexico City).

Unomásuno (Mexico City).

U.S. Department of State. 1942. "Rehabilitation of Certain Mexican National Railways." Executive Agreement Series 289.

Valdés Ugalde, Francisco. 1994. "From Bank Nationalization to State Reform: Business and the New Mexican Order." In *The Politics of Economic Restructuring: State-Society Relations and Regime Change in Mexico*, edited by Maria Lorena Cook, Kevin J. Middlebrook, and Juan Molinar Horcasitas. La Jolla: Center for U.S.-Mexican Studies, University of California, San Diego.

Valenzuela, J. Samuel. 1989. "Labor Movements in Transitions to Democracy: A Framework for Analysis." *Comparative Politics* 21 (4): 445–72.

Vázquez Rubio, Pilar. 1990. "Por los caminos de la productividad." *El Cotidiano* 38 (Nov.–Dec.): 10–14.

Vázquez Tercero, Héctor. 1975. *Una década de política sobre industria automotriz*. Mexico City: Editorial Tecnos.

Velasco, Carlos. 1986. *Fidel Velázquez*. Mexico City: Plaza y Janes.

Velasco, Miguel Ángel. 1978. Interviews with author. Mexico City, 10 Jan. and 27 Apr.

Veliz, Claudio. 1980. *The Centralist Tradition of Latin America*. Princeton: Princeton University Press.

Ventura Rodríguez, María Teresa. 1988. "La consolidación de la FTP-CTM en Puebla, 1938–1952." In *La CTM en los estados*, edited by Centro de Estudios del Movimiento Obrero y Socialista. Culiacán: Universidad Autónoma de Sinaloa.

Verba, Sidney. 1967. "Some Dilemmas in Comparative Research." *World Politics* 20 (1): 111–27.

Vernon, Raymond. 1963. *The Dilemma of Mexico's Development: The Roles of the Private and Public Sectors.* Cambridge: Harvard University Press.

Villafuerte, Carlos. 1959. *Ferrocarriles.* Mexico City: Fondo de Cultura Económica.

Villarreal, René. 1977. "The Policy of Import-Substituting Industrialization, 1929–1975." In *Authoritarianism in Mexico,* edited by José Luis Reyna and Richard S. Weinert. Philadelphia: Institute for the Study of Human Issues.

Walker, David W. 1981. "Porfirian Labor Politics: Working Class Organizations in Mexico City and Porfirio Díaz, 1876–1902." *The Americas* 37 (3): 257–89.

Waterman, Harvey. 1981. "Reasons and Reason: Collective Political Activity in Comparative and Historical Perspective." *World Politics* 33 (4): 554–89.

Weber, Max. 1978. *Economy and Society: An Outline of Interpretive Sociology.* 2 vols. Edited by Guenther Roth and Claus Wittich. Berkeley and Los Angeles: University of California Press.

Weiner, Myron. 1971. "Political Participation: Crisis of the Political Process." In *Crises and Sequences in Political Development,* edited by Leonard Binder et al. Princeton: Princeton University Press.

Weyl, Nathaniel, and Sylvia Weyl. 1939. *The Reconquest of Mexico: The Years of Lázaro Cárdenas.* New York: Oxford University Press.

Whitehead, Laurence. 1989. "Political Change and Economic Stabilization: The 'Economic Solidarity Pact.'" In *Mexico's Alternative Political Futures,* edited by Wayne A. Cornelius, Judith Gentleman, and Peter H. Smith. La Jolla: Center for U.S.-Mexican Studies, University of California, San Diego.

———. 1991. "Mexico's Economic Prospects: Implications for State-Labor Relations." In *Unions, Workers, and the State in Mexico,* edited by Kevin J. Middlebrook. La Jolla: Center for U.S.-Mexican Studies, University of California, San Diego.

Whiting, Van R., Jr. 1992. *The Political Economy of Foreign Investment in Mexico: Nationalism, Liberalism, and Constraints on Choice.* Baltimore: Johns Hopkins University Press.

Wilkie, James W. 1973. *The Mexican Revolution: Federal Expenditure and Social Change since 1910.* Berkeley and Los Angeles: University of California Press.

Wilkie, James W., and Edna Monzón de Wilkie. 1969. *México visto en el siglo veinte: Entrevistas de historia oral.* Mexico City: Instituto Mexicano de Investigaciones Económicas.

Willatt, Norris. 1974. *The Multinational Unions.* London: Financial Times.

Williams, Philip J. 1994. "Dual Transitions from Authoritarian Rule: Popular and Electoral Democracy in Nicaragua." *Comparative Politics* 26 (2): 169–85.

Womack, John, Jr. 1970. *Zapata and the Mexican Revolution.* New York: Vintage Books.

———. 1986. "The Mexican Revolution, 1910–1920." In *The Cambridge History of Latin America,* edited by Leslie Bethell, vol. 5. Cambridge: Cambridge University Press.

Yañez Reyes, Sergio L. 1984. *Génesis de la burocracia sindical cetemista*. Mexico City: Ediciones El Caballito.

Zaldívar Lelo de Larrea, Arturo F. 1993. "La propuesta priísta de reforma política." *Examen* 51 (Aug.): 8–10.

Zamora, Gerardo. 1990. "La política laboral del estado mexicano, 1982–1988." *Revista Mexicana de Sociología* 52 (3): 111–38.

Zapata, Francisco. 1979. "Las organizaciones sindicales." In *Fuerza del trabajo y movimientos laborales en América Latina*, edited by Rubén Kaztman and José Luis Reyna. Mexico City: El Colegio de México.

———. 1986. *El conflicto sindical en América Latina*. Mexico City: El Colegio de México.

———. 1989. "Labor and Politics: The Mexican Paradox." In *Labor Autonomy and the State in Latin America*. Winchester, Mass.: Unwin Hyman.

Zazueta, César, and Ricardo de la Peña. 1984. *La estructura del Congreso del Trabajo: Estado, trabajo y capital en México*. Mexico City: Fondo de Cultura Económica.

INDEX

Acción Socialista Unificada, 122
Agency for International Development
(United States), 314
Alemán, Miguel: economic policies of, 209,
211–12; and economic restructuring at
FNM, 110, 135–36, 140, 143, 145, 147,
384 n167; and government intervention
in STFRM, 136, 138–40, 381 n147; labor
policies of, 107, 110, 117, 150, 160, 181,
184; and 1947–51 labor crisis, 107–10,
119, 136, 147–49, 160
Alfonsín, Raúl, 265
Algeria, 336 n12
Alianza de Agrupaciones Obreras y Campe-
sinas de la República, 50
Alianza de Ferrocarrileros Mexicanos, 345
n26
Alianza de Obreros y Campesinos de
México, 117–18, 379 n36
Alianza de Tranviarios, 368 n32
All-Union Central Council of Trade Unions
(Soviet Union), 316
Almazán, Juan, 95, 362 n92
American Institute for Free Labor Develop-
ment, 314
American Smelting and Refining Company,
130
Amilpa, Fernando, 62, 115, 119
Anarchism, 17, 74, 75, 80
Anarchosyndicalism, 44, 73–75, 78, 80
Argentina, 265, 311, 418 n44
Armed forces, 24, 361 n86
Article 123, 57, 63; and labor rights, 21, 42,
47, 48, 68, 77, 162, 288
Associational Registry. *See* STPS, union
registration by
Authentic Labor Front. *See* FAT
Authoritarian regimes, subtypes of, 311, 336
n11
Authoritarianism, in Mexico: and bases
of elite control, 29, 207, 290, 324, 341
n81; characteristics of, 3, 29, 291, 299–
302, 304, 324; comparative analysis of,
2–3, 335 n8; and presidential succession,

300–301. *See also* Postrevolutionary
authoritarian regimes
Auto-Mex/Chrysler union, 225, 407 n89;
and CTM, 225, 227, 234, 239, 403 n48;
labor control in, 228, 233, 234, 236, 239;
mobilizational activities by, 250–51;
worker-employer relations at, 240–43,
245–49; worker participation in, 238, 239
Automobile industry: conflict resolution
in, 248–49, 280–83; consequences of
workplace change in, 210, 225, 230–32,
235–36, 253–54; contract flexibility in,
279–80, 285–86; development of, 225,
270–72, 402 n45, 403 n47; employment
in, 230, 231, 271; government regulation
of, 231, 270, 271, 402 n45; and industrial
restructuring, 257, 267, 269, 271–76,
287, 412 n49; labor control in, 226, 232–
33; post-Fordist industrial relations in,
257, 277–79; production process in,
247–48, 280–83; production volumes in,
225, 230, 271–72, 412 n47; promotion
procedures and employment security in,
240–41, 245–47, 280–83; temporary
workers in, 241, 245, 269–70, 282, 407
n89; and transnational firms, 225, 269,
403 n47; union democratization in, 210,
222, 254, 404 n56; wages and fringe
benefits in, 230, 275–76, 404 n56. *See
also* Automobile workers; *and names of
individual automobile firms*
Automobile workers: democratization
among, 222, 223, 226–27, 228–29, 232,
237–52, 254, 269–70; political control
of, 226, 228–29, 233–36, 253, 254, 270,
272, 274–75, 283; and post-Fordist industrial relations, 278–79; presidential labor
policy and democratization among, 228,
229, 254, 404 n51; strikes and work stoppages by, 250–52, 270, 273, 276, 284, 412
n44; wages and fringe benefits for, 230,
237. *See also* Automobile industry; *and
names of individual automobile workers'
unions*

Library of Congress Cataloging-in-Publication Data

Middlebrook, Kevin J.
  The paradox of revolution : labor, the state, and authoritarianism in Mexico /
Kevin J. Middlebrook.
      p.   cm.
  Includes bibliographical references and index.
  ISBN 0-8018-4922-5 (alk. paper). — ISBN 0-8018-5148-3 (pbk. : alk. paper)
    1. Mexico—Politics and government—20th century.   2. Labor movement—
Mexico—History—20th century.   I. Title.
JL1281.M54   1995
320.972—dc20   94-29470